Collective Writings on the Lessac Voice and Body Work: A Festchrift

Marth Munro, Sean Turner, Allan Munro and Kathleen Campbell

With critical reader Deborah Kinghorn

An official LTRI publication

Second print

Published in the USA by the
Lessac Training and Research Institute (LTRI)
60 Seaman Avenue #1D
New York, New York 10034
www.lessacinstitute.org

Copyright © 2019 Lessac Training and Research Institute
All rights reserved. No part of this publication may be reproduced without permission by the LTRI.

Cover design: Michael Mufson

ISBN: 978-0-9996164-4-4 (paperback)

Printed and bound in the United States by Ingram Spark

Original print

© 2009 Marth Munro, Sean Turner, Allan Munro and Kathleen Campbell EDs

ISBN: 978-1-60594-343-5

Printed in the United States of America by Llumina Press

Library of Congress Control Number: 2009909903

Previously published material reprinted with permission from

The American Speech-Language-Hearing Association
The Annals of Otology, Rhinology and Laryngology
The National Inquiry Services Centre (NISC)
The Voice Foundation
The Voice and Speech Trainers Association (VASTA)

To Arthur, in celebration of a lifetime of work.
To all who explore the integration of body, mind and voice holistically.

List of Contributors

These people have either contributed new material towards the book or allowed the editors to request the inclusion of articles previously published elsewhere. In cases where more than one person wrote the previously published article, the person who has an active relationship with the Lessac Training and Research Institute was con-tacted to request permission.

Acker B; Barkmeier J.M; Barrichelo-Lindström, V; Behlau M; Berry D; Burke M.K; Caldwell E; Campbell K; Carr R; Chan R; Coetzee M-H; Cuyler R; Cuyler S; Druker D.G; Dunn K; Glaze L; Hess M; Hoffman H.T; Hurt M; Kinghorn D; Krebs N; Kur B; Laukkanen A-M; Leino T; Lessac A; Lessac M; Marple G.A; Montequin D; Moraitis K; Munro M; Nitisaroj R; Palmer P.M; Park S; Peterson K.L; Raphael B; Robbins C; Samawi H; Scherer R; Terny G; Titze I.R; Tocchetto De Oliveira M.R; Turner S; Verdolini K; Wissing D.

Acknowledgements for the 2009 print

The editors of the book acknowledge with deep gratitude the contributions of the following people.

- Arthur Lessac.
- All the contributors of the material in the book.
- The critical reader Deborah Kinghorn.
- The Lessac Training and Research Institute and the board members.
- The cover designer Michael A. Mufson.
- Anina Heinemann for transcriptions and general assistance.
- Susarah du Plooy for retyping the previously published articles.
- Nicole Li for assistance with the graphs in the Verdolini articles.
- All the editors of the Journals in which the republished articles were published originally. Thank you for allowing us to reprint the articles. Specific reference to the journals can be found below the title of each of these articles.
- The reviewers Nancy Krebs, Deborah Kinghorn, Barry Kur, Karina Lemmer and Daan Wissing who spent long hours writing copious notes.

Without the committed and positive input of the people mentioned above, the book would never have come to fruition.

From Marth Munro as editor-in-chief to the three other editors — Sean Turner, Allan Munro and Kathleen Campbell: You were an excellent team! Your different fields of specialization and willingness to always do more, contributed to the quality of the book. Thanks!

Further acknowledgements for the 2019 reprint

The editors gratefully acknowledge the contributions of:

- Selma Schiller for preparing the book for the second print.
- Michael A. Mufson for the design of the new cover.
- The LRTI for funding the preparation for the printing of the second print.

Notes to Readers

When reading this book, please keep the following in mind:

The Lessac Kinesensic Voice and Body Training is constantly in a process of organic growth. As such, the chosen terminology changes to reflect the holistic character of the work. Due to this, the articles in reprint are immensely valuable in that they provide a reflection of research that has been done with regard to the Lessac work, but some of the terminology used in the articles is no longer in use within the current framing of the Lessac work by the Lessac Training and Research Institute. Terms such as 'method', 'system' and 'approach' were relevant during certain times of the development of the work. The Lessac Training and Research Institute currently prefer to refer to the work as the Lessac work or Lessac training for short and officially as the Lessac Kinesensic Voice and Body Training. In line with this, the Institute prefers the use of words like 'muscle yawn' instead of 'stretch', 'exploration' instead of 'exercise', and so on. The thinking behind this is that the choice of words must truly reflect the organic and holistic character of the work.

In the Oral Histories the voice of each of the interviewees is extremely important. In an attempt to capture the uniqueness of each of these people, the editors allowed stylistic differences as well as formatting differences.

The formatting of the previously printed articles, especially with regard to the use of footnotes and styles of reference, was not changed.

Many of the figures and graphs from the previously published articles had to be scanned from the already printed material. As such the quality is not always what we would have wished for.

The points of view, arguments and personal testimonies shared in the material in the book, are those of the authors and do not necessarily reflect the official stance of the Lessac Training and Research Institute.

Foreword

Marth Munro

Collective Writings on the Lessac Voice and Body Work: A Festchrift was first published in 2009. The purpose of the book was to celebrate Arthur Lessac's 100th birthday. It was indeed to pay tribute, to honor and rejoice in his 'lifetime of work' – work that was shared by him in written and oral format. Part of this tribute was to demonstrate, primarily to him but also to others, how this sharing influenced the personal and professional lives of those exposed to his approach. The further purpose of this *Festschrift* was to provide evidence of research that was already done on Lessac Kinesensics, thereby validating the approach and indicating that Lessac Kinesensics is effectively contributing to various fields such as Vocology, Voice therapy, Performance efficiency and well-being.

The above information is presented in two sections in the book.

In the first part of the book dialogical narratives tracing the development of the work from Lessac's own perspective. Evidence of how the work contributed to the shaping of the lives and careers of various Lessac trainers are collected and presented. This section celebrates, through testimony, anecdote, narrative and other forms the pungent impact the work had on people. In the second part of the *Festschift* scholarly articles previously published as well as two new articles about Lessac Kinesensics are presented.

The *Festschrift* was the first book published about Lessac Kinesensics not written by Arthur Lessac himself. It paved the way for many books and articles to follow. The three books published after the *Festschrift* are:

- *Arthur Lessac's embodied actor training* by Melissa Hurt (2014);
- *Essential Lessac: Honoring the Familiar in Body, Mind, Spirit* by Arthur Lessac and Deborah Kinghorn (2014). Deborah completed and published this gem after Arthur's passing;

- *Play with Purpose: Lessac Kinesensics in Action* edited by Marth Munro, Sean Turner and Allan Munro (2017) which presents some of the development of the work since the *Festschrift*, specifically regarding Performance and Well-being.
- And in 2019, the reprint of *Body Wisdom,* written by Arthur Lessac and with a new foreword by Deborah Kinghorn, which contextualises the development of Lessac Kinesensics.

Ten years after the original publication of the *Festschrift* we are reprinting the book. In pondering why this should be necessary, we realised the following: Firstly, as the original print run is exhausted, it seemed right to make the work available again. Perhaps one of the driving reasons for the reprint is the impact of Lessac Kinesensics as it has spread exponentially across the world, making significant inroads in countries like Brazil, Croatia, South Africa and Australia. As the practice spreads, so the research needs further dissemination. The second reason is that so much of the first part of the book was written (and edited) by people who were seeking authentic ways of reporting on experiences so that these experiences might be shared. These experiences are valuable not only as testimonies, but also as authentic research approaches in themselves. As such, the book provides possible writing models for emulation as the work is deepened, extended and disseminated.

The *Festschrift* remains a living archive of fascinating interactions between a burgeoning, vibrant and potent *bodymind and voice approach* developed by a remarkable man, on the one hand, and the empowered, dedicated and energised trainers, practitioners – explorers in the true sense of the word – on the other, while Arthur Lessac was with us. The reprint makes this book as archive available to the next generation. Being able to look back and trace the roots of the work as it was presented in 2009, is valuable. Observing what development and research have taken place since 2009, is exciting.

It is our hope that the reprint of this book will provide impetus for further research on, and development of, Lessac Kinesensics. Indeed, with a 'childlike curiosity', let us continue to explore.

Contents

Introduction to Dialogical Narratives   1
Sean Turner

  Era One: Arthur Lessac   9
  Sean Turner

  Key Note at 2009 Lessac Institute Conference   50
  Michael Lessac

  Era Two: Teacher Training   88
  Sean Turner

    Sue Ann Park   89

    Richard and Saundra Cuyler   106

    Nancy Krebs   122

    Deborah A. Kinghorn   129

    Barry Kur   138

  Era Three: The future   145
  Sean Turner

    Kathleen Dunn   146

    Crystal Robbins   158

    Gert Terny   173

    Robin Carr   179

    Melissa Hurt   185

Research Perspectives and Applications of the Lessac Work   195
Marth Munro (with Allan Munro)

  Physiological and Therapeutical Perspectives of the Lessac Work   201
  Katherine Verdolini Abbott

Comparison of Aerodynamic and Electroglottographic Parameters in Evaluating Clinically Relevant Voicing Patterns	208
K. Linnea Peterson; Julie M. Barkmeier; Katherine Verdolini-Marston; Henry T. Hoffman	
Preliminary Study of Two Methods of Treatment for Laryngeal Nodules	238
Katherine Verdolini-Marston; Mary Katherine Burke; Arthur Lessac; Leslie Glaze; Elizabeth Caldwell	
Laryngeal Adduction in Resonant Voice	263
Katherine Verdolini; David G. Druker; Phyllis M. Palmer; Hani Samawi	
A Quantitative Output-Cost Ratio in Voice Production	286
David A. Berry; Katherine Verdolini; Douglas W. Montequin; Markus M. Hess; Roger W. Chan, Ingo R. Titze	

Acoustic Perspectives on the Lessac Work — 305

Acoustic Properties: The 'Ring' of Truth — 305

Nancy Krebs

Vocal Tract Adjustments for the Projected Voice	308
B.F. Acker	
Voice Modification of Stage Actors: Acoustic Analyses	320
Bonnie N. Raphael; Ronald C. Scherer	
Lessac's Y-Buzz as a Pedagogical Tool in the Teaching of the Projection of an Actor's Voice	329
Marth Munro; Timo Leino; Daan Wissing	
On the Effects of Lessac Method on Female Voices: Preliminary Observations	342
Marth Munro; Anne-Maria Laukkanen; Timo Leino	

The Contribution of Lessac's Y-buzz from Two Brazilian Voice-therapists' Perspectives *Viviane Barrichelo-Lindström and Mara Behlau*	353
Use of Lessemes in Text-to-Speech Synthesis *Rattima Nitisaroj and Gary A. Marple*	364

Pedagogical Explorations and Other Applications 377
Sean Turner

Unlocking the Voice Inside Rochester Young Offenders: The Impact of Lessac Voice Training Within a Socially Excluded Community *Katerina M. Moraitis*	389
The Ecstatic Birth: Lessac Training and Childbirth Preparation *Crystal Robbins*	408
The Body Energies in the Actor's Performance *Maria Regina Tocchetto de Oliveira*	413
Lessac Energies and Classical Texts *Kathleen Campbell*	428
Lessac Kinesensic Dialect Acquisition: Adapted Excerpts from the Text of STAGE DIALECT STUDIES *Barry Kur*	436
The Lessac Approach as a Pedagogical Answer to Outcomes-Based Education And Training, and Whole-Brain Learning *Marth Munro and Marie-Heleen Coetzee*	448
Testing the Use of Lessac's Tonal NRG as a Voice Building Tool for Female Students at a South African University—A Perceptual Study *Marth Munro and Daan Wissing*	464

An Oral History of Lessac Summer Workshop Intensives 487-491

Citation Map 493

Introduction to Dialogical Narratives

Sean Turner

Doctorate candidate, School of Education, State University New York, Buffalo
Year of Certification as a Lessac Voice, Speech and Body Trainer: 2003

In the spring of 1995, as I was completing my first year of Theatre study at California State University—San Bernardino, I took a voice class from a pseudo-radical teacher named Leonard Meenach.[1] Like many beginning actors, I had no idea what I was doing with my voice and body within performance, but I wanted to learn. And so, after doing a "passion workshop"[2] during which I talked about my dream of using drama within the streets of San Bernardino, Leonard told me that I really needed to study with Arthur Lessac—and literally a few weeks later, after getting to meet one of the most influential teachers of voice and speech in American theatre, I was on a plane to Mary Baldwin College and taking part in my first Lessac Summer Intensive Workshop.

To say the experience was transformative would be a gross under-statement, as the intensive had a *significant* and *therapeutic* effect on me. I had come from a "broken" home, and struggled for many years to come to grips with who I was. I had dropped out of college, enlisted in the Navy, got kicked out of the Navy, attended Junior College, dropped out of Junior College, moved to Hollywood, went back to Junior College, and 10 years after I first enrolled in Junior College,[3] finally had moved on to a regular four year theatre program; I was sleeping on a friend's coach, with barely a cent to my name. But, nonetheless, there I was, this novice-struggling-student-actor, who hadn't even read Arthur's books yet, exploring consonants with a famous mime from Europe, a great physical actor who had studied with Lecoq, as well as other professional actors and performers. It was slightly surreal—but extremely life transforming—as the teachers of the intensive never treated me any different or expected any less from me than any other person who was attending. It was also a

---

[1] Leonard Meenach earned his MFA at the University of Arizona, and studied extensively with Eric Morris and Arthur Lessac. In 1996, he left the U.S. to teach at the Queensland Academy of Arts.
[2] Exercise from Eric Morris (1992) *Irreverent Acting* in which the actor unconsciously talks about what he or she is passionate about.
[3] San Bernardino Valley College.

valuable lesson that I hold true to this day—which is that great teachers can teach and work with anyone, regardless of whether their *talents* are buried or easily accessible.

During this experience, I remember the first time that I was able to feel the full tone of my voice within an exploration, and how that feeling led to a physical discovery of character. I was assigned to a small group, wherein the people in the group were expected to explore different lines from Shakespeare with specific vocal and body NRG and then receive feedback/coaching from Sue Ann Park. Sue Ann, who could be very intimidating in her own right, was not in a particularly pleasant mood that day, which only added to my own general anxiety about being in a group of actors who had a lot more experience of working with Shakespeare. But for some reason, as I started to yawn, a potency NRG began to shape my body and my voice, which immediately created a harmonious connection (synergy) between my body, my voice, and the character, that allowed me to be carefree. It was a sensation I had never quite felt before—almost as if I was a spectator at my own performance watching as my voice began to fill and shape the character, the room, me…which is exactly at the moment when I first felt a tone so rich, so powerful, so vibrant, that every bone in my body resonated with its ring and the words just flowed out of me like I had been speaking this type of language my whole life. I think I was so shocked, that I just sat there frozen, not sure what to do, and then I looked over at Sue Ann Park, calmly smiling and nodding her head, who then proceeded to say in a matter of fact voice: "Good job, boy."

I was so moved by this experience that I returned to my undergraduate program, and immediately went into the Theatre department office and gave notice to my Chair[4] that I was ready to be a Shakespearean actor, ("Sue Ann Park, told me I did a good job") which of course was met with great skepticism and ridicule.[5] Later on, after taking two more summer intensives,[6] I would find out that Arthur had viewed my initial work as therapeutic,[7] but by then it didn't really matter, as I had continued to go on using the work in almost all aspects of my life, including acting, directing, and teaching.

---

[4] Patrick Watkins was chair of the Theatre Department.
[5] I was kidded for my youthful exuberance and belief that I had learned to act Shakespeare in 6 weeks.
[6] Ball State University (1996) and SUNY Fredonia (1999).
[7] Arthur would say that my first workshop was "therapy," and only after taking the second workshop was I truly able to begin to explore the work in a more performance context and application.

During the five years that took place between my first and last workshops, I would sporadically go down to Santa Monica to visit and work with Arthur, sometimes working on my voice—most of the time just sharing and discussing his views on politics, theatre, film and life. As a result of these discussions, I grew to cherish and love this man, who in many ways not only became a father figure to me, but also helped me to see the world from different perspectives—including the potential of applying theatre in an educational context. And while I never became a professional Shakespearean actor, I have always felt that in many ways, I would not be the person I am today without these experiences.

As a result, I have long been curious about further inquiry into the impact of the Lessac work and, in particular, what ways, if any, the work has impacted the lives of other people who have taken part in the Lessac Summer Intensives. The significance of this impact, at least in my opinion, would allow for the Lessac work to be situated within a socio-historical context and foster a larger, more significant dialogue regarding the implications of Lessac training in the future.

As with any research task, there are methodological, theoretical, and epistemological assumptions to work through. In the case of this study, these are even more complex, as Arthur has clearly situated his own way of thinking within his writing and books. Often these assumptions go against the traditional thinking found in educational studies and research and at other times these assumptions represent such out of the box thinking and new ideas that they sound esoteric. This is exemplified by an argument Arthur made to me, while I was taking classes in my doctoral program, in which we were discussing the benefits of researching the Lessac work. While Arthur acknowledged the potential benefits of research, he dissented from the view that only a few should have access to this power, and argued, rather passionately, that the notion of the *researcher* should be embodied through the use of *kinesensic* explorations, wherein all people can use their own physical and vocal explorations to make social, cultural, and political change—and thus do their own research.

For anyone who is not familiar with the Lessac work, this, of course, might come across as somewhat absurd, as the contributions of research are quite well known, and the assumption that inquiry into the Lessac work would not be beneficial to the work itself, is, well, just not logical. But, as with almost any of the assumptions that Arthur has ever made, there is usually a greater truth lying underneath his way of thinking. And in this case, and in order to understand this way of thinking, one only has to interpret his argument as being a call for a shift in the research paradigm, from notions of traditional methodologies, whereby a researcher collects data and then analyzes said data for the purpose of writing, towards a more performative radical ethnographic inquiry, where notions of social, cultural, and political change can be crystallized and discussed by all members of the community. The latter understanding clearly situates his original argument as neither absurd nor esoteric, as many scholars have already started to advocate for this type of thinking, including Denzin (2003:ix), who argues that "we are in the seventh moment of qualitative inquiry, a postexperimental phase, performing culture as we write it."

In order to address some of these types of research complexities, I have attempted to use open-ended questions and dialogical narratives to develop oral histories (or in some cases "her stories") as a means for further inquiry and discussion by all members of the community at large on the impact of the Lessac work. The use of interviews is well supported in educational, critical, and drama research. For example, within the field of literacy studies, Kendall (2008:133) argues that "more than any other method, qualitative interviews are to be used for the exploration of meaning, especially as meaning is constructed by the participants regarding a topic or setting of interest." This is also supported within drama education, by Gallagher (2001), who argues that the semi-structured, open-ended form of interviewing in many cases can become an open discussion wherein a negotiation of meaning takes place. Within the field of critical studies, LeCompte and Preissle (2003) note that the interview process allows for the larger question of the inquiry to be answered through a type of elicitation and personal interaction.

In terms of dialogical narratives, it is important to understand that notions of sharing oral histories have a long tradition going back to many non-Western civilizations. For example, both Rudolfo Anaya and Tomas Rivera have argued that if you want to understand history, you must listen to the stories that have been passed down by the people.[8] This is also exemplified in the work of El Teatro Campesino, a theatrical

---

[8] Rudolfo Anaya is best known for his critically acclaimed novel, *Bless me Ultima* and Tomas Rivera is best known for his short stories, poetry and literary essays, such as the *Harvest* and *Salamanders*. Quote came from Roberto Con Davis, in a graduate seminar class in Chicano Literature during the Spring of 1998 at the University of Oklahoma.

company which used methods of story telling to develop plays as a form of social protest in the late 1960's, and by recent performance artists, such as Anna Deavere Smith and Rhodessa Jones, who have performed interviews, as a means of radical performative ethnography (Denzin 2003).

The Study

Originally this inquiry was based on a select group of Master Lessac teachers discussing five open-ended questions that I sent within an E-mail with an option for people to participate either by writing or talking over the phone. The original intent was to have people respond to the initial questions, and then let the dialogue/narrative between them and myself go from there. The original questions were as follows:

(1) Describe the context in which you were introduced to Lessac training. For example, when did you receive the training, who provided the training, why did you choose this type of training, and how did the training take place?

(2) In what ways have you applied or incorporated the Lessac work within the context of what you do for a living, whether that is as a performer, artist, scholar, healer, teacher, therapist? Please identify what you do, and how, if at all, this process has developed or evolved over time.

(3) Please describe one context or vignette that best represents the way(s) in which you have you applied or incorporated Lessac training within the development of your own voice and body, and how, if at all, this process has been used by you as a means for problem-solving, learning, healing, performance, communication, and/or increasing your own vitality of life.

(4) In what local or global context do you see the future of kinesensics, or kinesensic training taking place within the next 50 years? In particular, what needs or possibilities, if any, do you think the Lessac work will address or shape in the future?

(5) In what ways, if any, do you think that the Lessac training (workshops and intensives) can and should still be developed in the future?

By the time all the initial interviews were completed, it was vividly clear that a poignant and radiant history was being mapped out, and that additional people were needed, which led to a total of 11 Lessac teachers taking part in the interviews.[9] After either responding to the questions in writing or through a recorded interview, which I transcribed, each of the 11 teachers discussed their written narratives, performative speeches, recollections, or responses to questions with me and then used said dialogue to help shape their oral histories.

The format of each oral history varies in the degree to which *our* dialogue is represented in the writing, meaning the participant either responded to direct follow up questions or the dialogue is embedded in the narrative. In terms of the former, the follow up questions I gave to each person are highlighted in bold. In terms of the latter, no questions are included. As some of the dialogue and stories are based on oral transcriptions and other on written responses, there is also a difference in circular and linear types of language used. While I do not attempt to analyze, frame, or make arguments within any of the oral histories, the reader will see and hear my voice at times, and unless otherwise noted, this will be in the form of the questions I posed to the person who is telling the story, usually marked in bold font, or in the footnotes I have provided which give an historical context for some of the references that the person is using in their story, or in brackets.[10]

In addition to the oral histories, I attempt to construct a historical narrative of the life of Arthur Lessac, which was developed from interviews with Arthur Lessac and data found in his personal archives. And Michael Lessac provides a revised version of the 2009 Lessac Institute Conference key note speech,[11] wherein his personal reflection on his father allows the reader a current and perspicacious framework in which to situate Lessac.

The overarching purpose of each of these texts is for the reader to be able to look deeper into the impact, if any, of the Lessac work, and to discuss how that impact, if any, fits within a historical context. As such, these texts are not meant to be read, or

---

[9] Melissa Hurt responded to a different set of questions, which allowed her to situate her research and interviews of Arthur Lessac as well as her own experiences with the Lessac work.

[10] Parentheses were used to note authorial clarifications, while brackets were used to note editorial clarifications made by myself. In cases were there was a blending of voice between myself and the person being interviewed, parentheses were used.

[11] The 2009 Lessac Institute Conference: *Reconnecting with the work* was held in Carlsbad, California January 8 through January 10, 2009.

analyzed, but instead are meant to be listened to, and in some cases performed. They are not fixed accounts of history, but are fluid narratives (of living history) with contradictions, disruptions, pauses, beats, half-notes, and rhythms all intersecting—within both linear and circular forms of language that require response and participation from the community at large.

Framing Lessac History through Dialogical Narratives

After a process of dialogue had taken place with each of the people who agreed to participate in the inquiry, I began to organize and categorize their stories as dialogical narratives representing three eras over the past Century. While the notion of era is typically used to refer to a specific period of time, eras themselves do not have to exist in separate spaces or periods of time, and can also be used to represent a period by its distinctive character, fixed point or events that took place. As such, it is my position that there are distinct characteristics that allow these stories to be experienced through three different lenses.

Within the first era, which I characterize as "Arthur Lessac," significant events/threads/patterns are highlighted within the historical narrative about Arthur Lessac's life, which is further contextualized by Michael Lessac's key note speech given at the 2009 Lessac conference.

Within the second era, which I characterize as "Lessac Training," six Master Lessac Teachers—Sue Ann Park, Dick Cuyler, Saundra Cuyler, Deb Kinghorn, Nancy Krebs, and Barry Kur—respond to the initial five questions I posed, as well as individual follow up questions, highlighting significant events and developments of the Lessac work over the past 40 years. Since these six teachers collectively represent the training provided at every Summer Intensive since 1969, their stories situate the training and Lessac Institute within a historical context by highlighting significant events that took place during this period, including how they were introduced to the work, how they have applied the work, and how the work has impacted their own perspectives of education, theatre, and performance.

Within the third era, which I characterize as "The Future," certified teachers, Kathleen Dunn, Crystal Robbins, Gert Terny, and Robin Carr, as well as researcher and Lessac trainer Melissa Hurt, discuss the impact of the work on their lives within a global context, and offer dialogical narratives that in my opinion represent the voices of those who will continue to teach the work for the next 40 years.

References

Denzin, N. 2003. *Performance Ethnography: Critical Pedagogy and the Politics of Culture.* London: Sage Publications.

Gallagher, K. 2001. *Drama Education in the Lives of Girls: Imagining possibilities.* Toronto: University of Toronto Press.

Kendall, L. 2008. 'The conduct of qualitative interviews: Research questions, methodological issues, and researching online.' In Coiro, J., Knobel, M., Lankshear, C., & Leu, D. *Handbook of Research on New Literacies.* New York: Lawrence Erlbaum Associates.

LeCompte, M. & Preissle, J. 2003. *Ethnography and Qualitative Design in Educational Research.* London: Academic Press.

Era One: Arthur Lessac

Sean Turner

Over the past years, Arthur Lessac has been reluctant to have people write about his life and in particular to discuss his early childhood or to place emphasis on his accomplishments. Although he has granted interviews to various people working on dissertation studies, he has provided only a few details about his life, and has repeatedly advocated for his legacy and for his contribution to society to be illustrated through the development of the Lessac work, sometimes called the Lessac kinesensic voice and body training. While there has been a considerable amount of writing about the Lessac work, there has been very little written about the life of Arthur Lessac.

The following historical narrative marks an attempt to paint a picture of some of the significant events that have taken place in the life of Arthur Lessac, and provide a backdrop that the reader can use to contextualize the oral histories that follow and to participate in a greater dialogue about the impact of Arthur Lessac, his work and possibilities for the future. Although the historical narrative is based on interviews[1] I conducted with Arthur Lessac and data collected from his personal archives,[2] I do not use a theoretical lens to contextualize the data, or pull from traditional research methods. As such, this text supposes that there will be inconsistencies with some of the names, dates, and places, and hopes that the reader will view these inconsistencies as part of a living body of text, which they can use for further inquiry, critical dialogue, or reflection.

The narrative originated with interviews of Arthur Lessac by Melissa Hurt during 2008, which led to her writing a paper discussing significant events in his life.[3] From that paper, a time line was further developed through inquiry at the New York City Library of Performing Arts, searches in online academic databases, and interviews with Lessac teachers.[4] As names, dates, and places started to emerge through this in-

---
[1] Four-hour interview, February 16, 2009. Various interviews conducted during a visit and stay at Arthur's apartment April 8, 9, and 10, 2009.
[2] Collected April 8, 9, and 10, 2009.
[3] Hurt, Melissa. 2009. "The Journey of a Boy who Never Stopped Exploring." Unpublished paper submitted to editors of this book.
[4] These interviews were focused on developing a time line of Lessac Summer Workshops, including a list of teachers at each workshop.

quiry, Arthur Lessac and I started discussing the data, at first through E-mails, and then in person,[5] wherein Arthur began to reflect on his past. In the process, he became excited about remembering some of his own history, which in turn led to him inviting me to stay with him for a few days "in order to really go over things."[6] During this visit, I would take 60 pages of notes based on personal records, newspaper clippings, copies of published papers and reports, books, brochures, pictures, miscellaneous artifacts and reflections Arthur made to me while going through his files.[7] These notes were then used to weave[8] a new time line of events, from which I began to develop a historical narrative of Arthur Lessac.

While this narrative tells a significant story, the narrative itself includes many inconsistencies and disruptions,[9] and should not be viewed as auto-biographical, a critical examination of the evolution and/or teaching of the Lessac work, or inclusive of every major event in his life. In terms of the narrative not being auto-biographical, while it is true that Arthur reflected[10] on almost all of the data used to write the narrative, he did not review what was written or what was contextualized, and never contributed to the writing itself. As such, the narrative is constructed from my own weaving together of the data, and accepts that there will be both inconsistencies and disruptions within its construction. In terms of the narrative not being a critical examination of the work, while it is true that I cite and identify occasional Lessac phrases or notions, this is usually done in relation to a specific context being told within the story, and not for the purpose of critiquing or examining how Lessac should be taught or understood, which are sufficiently addressed by Arthur Lessac within his own writings and books. And finally, in terms of the narrative not being inclusive of all major events, it is significant to note that I have not identified a large percentage of students and teachers of Lessac, and I apologize in advance for any possible misrepresentations I might have made for those I did or did not identify. In addition, it is significant to

---

[5] Notes about history of Arthur Lessac were taken at the 2009 Lessac Conference, in addition to interviews in February and April of 2009.
[6] Invitation included permission to access his personal archives.
[7] We only got through three boxes of personal archives, which accounted for approximately 20% of the total amount of data in his archives.
[8] The notion of weaving is used to represent the integration of social, political, and cultural references, most of which are included in citations provided in the footnotes. Information with citation is either general knowledge or pulled from Wikipedia.
[9] Most inconsistencies are noted in the excessive footnotes provided.
[10] Quotations (without citations) are used to note reflections provided by Arthur during one of the interviews conducted.

note that his narrative is only inclusive of the three drawers of archives that I was able to go through, and that there is a significant number of boxes and files that remain, and which are not part of this narrative.[11]

In addition to the historical narrative, Michael Lessac's key note speech, given at the 2009 Lessac conference, is provided in the form of a *Reflective Ethnography Performance* wherein a crystallization of different social, cultural, and political perspectives of his father is added to the living body of the historical text through the means of performance. Presented in verse form, this speech should be heard (not read), as it examines, narrates, and performs the "memories" of his Dad and the Lessac work.

In my opinion, Michael Lessac helps us contextualize the historical narrative of Arthur Lessac in three important ways. First, Michael sheds light on how his father has diverged from traditional types of thinking found in education, science, and research. Second, Michael critically discusses the impact of his father's work within a larger economic, political, and social landscape. Third, Michael shapes a performative space for a larger discussion about the possibilities of hope that Lessac training might offer, and in particular how "changes in behavior, through organic instruction" can lead to social, cultural, and political transformation.

Reflective Ethnography Performance is not new, as interpretive ethnographers, and performance artists have used their field notes and autoethnographic observations to shape performance narratives over the past 20 years (Bochner & Ellis 1996, 2002; Turner 1986). From a critical perspective, Denzin (2003) argues that we should think of performance autoethnography as a seventh moment of qualitative inquiry, a postexperimental phase, whereby the researcher performs culture as they write it, and the meanings of lived experience become inscribed and visible through performance.

The Early Years (1909-1928)

Arthur Lessac was born in Haifa-Palestine (currently known as Israel) on September 10, 1909[12] and came to the United States with his parents around the age of two.[13]

---

[11] The Arthur Lessac Archives will be eventually stored at the University of New Hampshire.
[12] Arthur was born a week before the Jewish New Year, which falls on a different date each year (on the Christian calendar). According to Arthur, this means that his birthday could have been on the 8th or the 10th of September, although it is listed on his passport as September 10, 1909.

A week after coming into the country, significant issues arose in his parents' marriage, which, according to Arthur, led his parents to "find a Rabbi that would give them a divorce" and Arthur to begin "to live an orphan life." And while the details of this "orphan life" are somewhat vague,[14] at least in terms of his early childhood, it is clear, at least from Arthur's perspective, that he was on the move quite a bit once he arrived in the United States, and that after his parents' divorce, he found himself without "a home with [his] real father and mother."

Despite not having a traditional childhood, Arthur did go to elementary schools[15] and began to develop a "love for humming, exploring and being inquisitive" while growing up. The latter was probably best exemplified by an early experience singing in a choir,[16] wherein Arthur remembers that he "would often help other boys with voice work that was too hard, or was hurting them in some way" even though he had not had any formal voice training up to that point, only what he had learned from "his own inquisitive nature." Whether or not this type of problem-solving was a direct result of having to adjust to being on the move is not clear, although it is significant to note that from Arthur's perspective "no one sat and taught me how to read [at home], or read books [to me] at night," so instead of focusing on the "mind intellect through such things as reading, I was exploring and being inquisitive."

Somewhere around the time that Arthur turned 12 years old (1921), his father decided to move to Argentina, and took Arthur with him.[17] Although his father had relatives in Argentina, the move was probably done out of necessity, as a result of an economic depression that took place in New York City immediately following World War I, and indirectly by the influx of immigrants at the turn of the century, both of which significantly limited the number of economic opportunities available. Regardless of the circumstances, Arthur was excited about the possibilities of going to a new

---

[13] According to Deborah Kinghorn, Arthur first lived in Newark, New Jersey, when he came to the United States (E-mail correspondence, June 7, 2009).
[14] It is not clear if Arthur lived with his mother, who had re-married shortly after the divorce with his father, or with his father, or a combination of both, only that from his perceptions, once his parents divorced, he began to live an orphan life.
[15] Copy of application for employment to California State University, Fullerton (Personal Archives: School History).
[16] Arthur remembers that the synagogue paid for young people to sing in the choir during holidays. This probably took place when he was around 11 or 12 years old.
[17] According to a resume in his personal archives, Arthur's educational studies were interrupted by one year in which he was in Buenos Aires, Argentina: 1921-1922.

country, an excitement that quickly turned to disenchantment when he found that his living circumstances in Argentina included "residing in unsettling neighborhoods, sleeping on other people's cots, and being aware that some people in the house kept guns under their beds for protection." After a year in Argentina, his father sent Arthur back to New York City (1922), where according to Arthur, "[he] had to go through Ellis Island a second time" and was only allowed to enter the country again after his mother "reluctantly agreed to come to Ellis Island and pick me up."

The following year (1922) was a time in his life that Arthur recalls as being "rather unpleasant," but a time in which he was able to move forward with his life, as evidenced by the fact that he had his Bar Mitzvah in Brighton Beach at the age of 13 and was able to get a job at a local grocery store delivering groceries to the houses of nearby customers.[18] Although it is unclear if Arthur stayed near or with his mother in Brighton Beach,[19] all indications are that whatever limited relationship he had with his parents previous to Argentina had been completely severed by 1922. This was exemplified in the following reflection of his childhood: "I was never homeless. I always had a home. One year I stayed in ten different places, just never [with] a father and mother."

During 1922, Arthur began to develop a friendship with one of the people he delivered groceries to, Esther Lessack, who was married to a very prominent accountant named Isadore Victor Lessack. On one of his visits to the Lessac household, Arthur inquired if the Lessacks would be willing to allow a 13 year old to rent a room, which was quite uncommon even for this period of time. Knowing a little about Arthur's background and living situation, Esther Lessack told Arthur "anytime you are ready, just let me know."[20] And thus Arthur went to live with the family,[21] whose last name

---

[18] The legal age to work at that time was 14 years old, although indications are that Arthur was working at 12 or 13.
[19] According to Deborah Kinghorn (E-mail correspondence dated June 7, 2009), Arthur only lived for 3-4 weeks with his mother in Brighton Beach. According to interviews with Arthur, he might have also lived in a near-by bungalow as well during this period of time he returned from South America and lived with the Lessack family.
[20] As remembered by Arthur Lessac in an interview, February 16, 2009.
[21] In follow-up correspondence with Deborah Kinghorn (June 7, 2009), she notes that the Lessacks had a summer home in Brighton Beach and the rest of the year lived in Hoboken, New Jersey. Arthur lived with the Lessacks in Hoboken, New Jersey.

he would eventually take on as his own.[22] Arthur didn't elaborate too much on why he took the name later on in his life,[23] except to say that he wanted to change his name and "these were good people, who had as good as name as any, so I decided to take it."

Arthur had not been living at the Lessack house too long, probably less than a year, when Esther took him on a visit to her sister. While there, Arthur saw a very young child run out of the house with no pants or underwear on, and thinking this was "quite inappropriate" went over and picked the child up and spanked him. Esther's sister was not very happy about this and refused to let the Lessacks come over to her house anymore while Arthur still lived with them. This put Esther in a very difficult position. At the time, her husband had been diagnosed with Parkinson's and Esther was feeling slightly overwhelmed taking care of him, and yet she still did not want to kick Arthur out of the house. So, instead, she reached out to some of her friends and found a place in Pleasantville, NY, that took in boys from broken homes. So somewhere around the age of 14, "maybe 13," Arthur went to stay at the Hebrew Sheltering Guardian Society.

The history[24] of the Hebrew Sheltering Guardian Society (HSGS)[25] is a complex one, but an important one in the history of New York City, as the society (now called JCCA)[26] is one of the oldest community based organizations in the city, and at one time was referred to as "undoubtedly the best equipped Institution for children in the world..."[27] The history of HSGS started with the merger of the Hebrew Benevolent Society and German Hebrew Benevolent Society in 1860; later (in 1879) it became the Hebrew Sheltering Guardian Society. Like many Jewish orphan asylums, the HSGS wished to Americanize its immigrant children through public school and vocational education, and by raising them on the tenets of Reform Judaism versus the Orthodoxy of their parents.

---

[22] Archives at his house and at the New York Performing Arts Library indicate that Arthur first spelled his name with a "k" as in "Lessack" which he later dropped by the middle to late 1940's.

[23] During this period of time, many Jewish immigrants coming to the U.S. took on different names, often because they were easier to pronounce and sounded American.

[24] Information on the history of HSGS was found at http://www.ajhs.org and summarized by me in the following four paragraphs, up to footnote 28.

[25] The records of the Hebrew Sheltering Guardian Society of New York (Orphan Asylum) (HSGS) are kept at the American Jewish Historical Society (see www.ajhs.org).

[26] Jewish Child Care Association, date to 1822—and the Hebrew Benevolent Society, see http://www.jccany.org/site/PageServer?pagename=about_history1.

[27] Dr. Hastings H. Hart, Director of the Russell Sage Foundation, wrote on October 23, 1912 on a visit (http://findingaids.cjh.org/?pID=251734).

Around 1904, Dr. Ludwig Bernstein, a language teacher from De Witt Clinton High School, was appointed superintendent of the HSGS and allowed the children time for healthy and unrestrained play, introduced social and literary clubs, and encouraged freedom of social interaction and self government. He abolished the monitoring system that existed previously, replacing it with self-governing Boys' and Girls' Republics in 1906; the republics governed the society, managed a savings bank, a Co-op store, and the library.

Due to the large influx of immigrants at the turn of the Century, the population at HSGS had risen to almost 700 students, and by 1912 the society had moved to Pleasantville, New York, for the purpose of securing facilities that could better accommodate the growing number of students. Once in Pleasantville, groups of 25-30 students were assigned to twenty-five cottage homes and incorporated a big-brother system, in which older children supervised younger children's daily activities. Each cottage was overseen by a cottage mother, who had received intense five week training before being hired and who assisted with activities that took place in the cottage. The students would also attend an in-house school that combined academic, religious, and vocational education within a very comprehensive curriculum.

Beginning in 1916, the school started experiencing financial setbacks as there was more competition for charitable funds to help overseas Jews, and because of the increased role of the Federation for the Support of Jewish Philanthropic Societies in New York City, which felt that the school really was luxury. As a result, many services were cut, students were annexed to P.S. 62 in Manhattan, and the length of stay was kept at a minimum. By the mid 1920's, the student population had radically changed, and students were often second generation Americans, grown up amidst social, economic, and family issues pertaining to their parents' immigrant hardships. By 1925, there were only 270 children at Pleasantville.[28]

During his stay, which I am estimating to be from somewhere between 1922-1924,[29] Arthur stayed at cottage seven, which was overseen by a woman named Eva Levinson. During his years there,[30] Arthur went to school and took commercial

---

[28] Information on the history of HSGS was found at http://www.ajhs.org.
[29] According to Arthur, he was at HSGS for almost two years.
[30] Under Dr. Bernstein, the school was part of HSGS and included a nine year accelerated curriculum taught by certified teachers. When the school was annexed, Bernstein resigned in protest, and HSGS

classes, which he remembers doing very well in, although he wasn't one of the "do-gooders," and was exposed to a lot of sports, "like football and ping pong," which he recalls as having "a natural feeling for" as well as theatre arts, which "he enjoyed very much." In addition Arthur never felt like he was being punished for being sent to the society, as "everything was like it was on the outside. It was a normal place, except that you were living with a couple hundred people, including both boys and girls" that had similar circumstances as he had.

There were also quite a few significant events at HSGS that Arthur recalls as having an impact on his life. First, Arthur remembers being deemed by the Rabbi "to be good enough" to read the Torah at services held on the Sabbath when the Rabbi was out of town. Since the Torah had "notes [that] represented small melodies wherein each symbol represented a one to four or five note melody," Arthur began to further develop his taste for singing by reading in a song-like quality each week. Second, Arthur remembers being introduced to a "friend" of the Hebrew society, a Mrs. Fingerhood, who had written a new musical, called *Oh, Spinach*. Arthur would later go on to play the main role (while at HSGS) and sing songs during the run of the show, which was significant in its own right, as it was probably the first official theatre performance of Arthur's career,[31] but also significant, in that Mrs. Fingerhood's husband would play a major role in Arthur's life, 15 years later.

And third, Arthur remembers that, after he had demonstrated that he was able to make good marks in school, Rabbi Solomon asked Arthur if he would like to have his bar mitzvah. Arthur replied that he had already had his bar mitzvah, but the Rabbi asked if he would be willing to have a second bar mitzvah, in order to "help the other 10 boys receive theirs." Arthur thought about this unorthodox request, since it was "really against orthodox custom and law to have two bar mitzvah's" but decided "if it would help others then he would do it." And so Arthur received a second bar mitzvah, where he both gave a speech and sang, in order to help lead the way for the other ten boys. The significance of this, at least in my opinion, is that this represents an early glimpse into his leadership potential, as well as his views about society and social con-

---

was taken over by Dr. Leon Goldrich, who significantly cut teachers and staff and emphasized having students either leave by the ages of 14-15, or be branched out to other organizations (http://www.ajhs.org).
[31] Previously, Arthur had auditioned for musical choirs in the synagogue in Yom Kippur and got paid for singing during the holidays.

tracts (doing something for the greater good of society). The latter sentiment still resonates when one considers that the majority of Lessac summer intensives (1968-2004) would not have taken place unless Arthur personally underwrote them and took a personal financial loss. Despite this loss, he never paid his teachers less money, or charged his students more money, or cut any services originally offered, all of which would have significantly affected the quality of instruction and the impact upon the lives of his students. He just simply decided, "If it would help others, then he would do it."

While these experiences appear to suggest that Arthur was able to have a sense of normalcy during his HSGS days, at least in terms of a home, Arthur also remembers encountering some rather unpleasant events during this period of time. One of those "unpleasantaries" [sic] took place when Arthur argued with a person in charge about an issue within the household.[32] While the issue was minor enough that Arthur can't remember what the disagreement was about, the person did not take too kindly to a resident of the society questioning his authority and went to a higher-ranking commissioner to complain about Arthur, as well as to request that something be done about his "insolence." The commissioner, who was "a rather large and athletic guy who liked to play sports," came down to the cottage, pulled Arthur away from the other youth, and he proceeded to punch Arthur in the face with a force so violent that it knocked out his two front teeth. Even though Arthur would have the teeth replaced and worked on later in his life, the violence of the act would cause significant discomfort and some physical issues that affected his singing over the span of his life.

After leaving HSGS, Arthur returned to the Brighton Beach area and attended James Madison High School,[33] from which he graduated in 1928. The school, which is located at 3757 Bedford Ave in Brooklyn, New York, opened in 1925, and according to its first principal, Mr. Clark, "half the students who entered actually graduated."[34] The overarching goals of the school were (a) to develop high standards of scholarship

---

[32] According to Arthur, the society at HSGS was overseen by a ranking commissioner and lesser ranking lieutenants, who enforced rules and behavior codes.
[33] According to a resume and job application found in his archives, Arthur graduated James Madison High School in 1928, but according to E-mail correspondence dated February 22, 2009, Arthur indicated that he graduated Lincoln High School, which according to the school website did not open until 1929.
[34] http://www.jamesmadisonalumni.org/principals.htm

(review problems from all sides before coming to a rational conclusion), (b) teach good citizenship and respect for the rights of others, and (c) practice good sportsmanship in life and games. During this period of time, Arthur took classes in "singing, dancing, and acting" and performed in various theatrical productions at the school. In one of those productions, *The Admirable Crichton*,[35] which was performed for three nights at the Brooklyn Academy of Music (BAM),[36] Arthur played the part of "Ernest-the epigram guy" and remembers the opening night:

> We had been rehearsing all day and into the late afternoon and had had no food, until we all ordered sandwiches. Well, mine came with a tiny schmear of butter on the bread and of course with my taste intolerance I couldn't eat it. I didn't know what to do with it, after all, I didn't want anyone to see me throw it out, but there was no way I could eat it! So, even though it was opening night and I was hungry, I ended up wedging it into the space in an elevator shaft and letting it fall down the shaft. I remember that opening night as one where I felt acting in my stomach. Acting was my food, so to speak.[37]

While there is little documentation about Arthur during this period in his life other than his recollections, it does appear to be significant that Arthur remembers taking classes in the performing arts as well as performing in quite a number of theatre productions. It is also significant to note that although Arthur returned to the Brighton Beach area,[38] Arthur indicated that he had no help with his transition finding a place to live or work while in high school[39] and that there were no arrangements made for him to re-connect with his parents.[40]

---

[35] *The Admirable Crichton* is a comic stage play written in 1902 by J. M. Barrie. In 1903, the play was produced on Broadway by Charles Frohman, and starred William Gillette. A 1918 film adaptation was directed by G. B. Samuelson.

[36] Founded in 1861, Brooklyn Academy of Music (BAM) is a major performing arts venue in Brooklyn, NY, and is currently known as a center for progressive and avant-garde performance (http://en.wikipedia.org/wiki/Brooklyn_Academy_of_Music).

[37] E-mail correspondence, February 22, 2009.

[38] James Madison High School is located about one mile from Brighton Beach, Brooklyn.

[39] It is unclear where Arthur stayed at while going to high school, but it is assumed that he stayed somewhere in the Brighton Beach area or possibly in a nearby Bungalow. After he graduated high school, Arthur moved to Manhattan and stayed and worked at the Young Men's Hebrew Association (YMHA).

[40] Although Arthur did not re-connect with his parents, Arthur did visit Esther Lessack a few more times after he graduated High School, including when his son Michael Lessac was two years old (E-mail Correspondence with Deb Kinghorn, June 7, 2009).

A new start (1928-1935)

At some point after Arthur graduated high school (1928-1931), he began taking classes with Laura Elliot at the East 3rd Street Music School Settlement,[41] which provided classical music classes to immigrants living on the East Side. According to Arthur, he was taught music and singing,[42] and given the opportunity to perform in many concerts at the school. This training, along with the exposure to performing arts that he received during high school appeared to be significant during the next three years, as Arthur would go on to sing professionally and to perform in various theatres, including, but not limited to, (a) performing outside at a theatre in Brooklyn where the famous crooner Russ Columbo[43] was performing, and his job was to sing "Columbo's songs for people while they were in the lobby, waiting in line, and then sell copies of his sheet music," (b) participating and performing in various productions that took place in the Yiddish Theatre district,[44] where he remembers watching Molly Picon[45] perform, and "taking part in a couple of theatres on 2nd Ave," (c) performing in two Maurice Swartz productions,[46] where he remembers "how poor the sets were and how little he got paid," and (d) working in Vaudeville, where he remembers participating in a bit called "McCarthy's Telephone Troubles" in which his "job was to sing something like 'Four Walls Each Morning'—which may not have been the song, but its the

---

[41] Third Street Music School Settlement, the nation's oldest community music school, was founded in 1894 by Emilie Wagner, who believed that music could offer the impoverished immigrants of New York's Lower East Side some respite from their daily struggles (http://www.thirdstreetmusicschool.org).
[42] In one reflection, Arthur notes that before he studied formally, "(He) enjoyed humming and singing, and later on realized that these were perfect relaxer-energizers."
[43] Russ Columbo composed the songs "Prisoner of Love," "You Call It Madness (But I Call It Love)" with Con Conrad, Gladys Du Bois, and Paul Gregory, "Too Beautiful For Words," recorded by the Teddy Joyce Orchestra in 1935, "When You're in Love, My Love," "Let's Pretend There's a Moon," recorded by Fats Waller and Tab Hunter, and "Hello Sister." He is also recognized as one of the original "crooners" (http://en.wikipedia.org/wiki/Russ_Columbo).
[44] The Yiddish Theatre District, located on 2nd Ave between Houston and 14th Street, included the Second Avenue Theater (1911) a 1,986-seat house built especially for David Kessler, the National (1912), a 2,000-seat house built for Thomashefsky, the Yiddish Art Theatre, and the Public, a 1752-seat house (http://www.jewish-theatre.com). Bigger than Life: *The Boundless Genius of Yiddish Theater* (http://www.barrypopik.com/index.php/new_york_city/entry/yiddish_broadway_or_yiddish_rialto_second_avenue_in_manhattan/).
[45] Molly Picon (Hebrew:מאָלי פּיקאָן) (February 28, 1898– April 6, 1992) was an American actress of stage, screen and television, as well as a lyricist. She was first and foremost a star in Yiddish theatre and film, but as Yiddish theatre faded she began to perform in English-language productions (http://en.wikipedia.org/wiki/Molly_Picon).
[46] Maurice Schwartz, producer, director, actor, and occasional playwright, was a powerhouse of a man who, more than anyone else, defined the shape of the artistic Yiddish theater in America during the 1920s and 1930s (http://www.jewish-theatre.com).

song I remember," and (e) working on a small circuit that traveled to Texas, and "ran out of money as soon as we arrived," which forced him to find an alternative route back to New York City.

Arthur's participation in the arts during this period is significant, as he took part in Yiddish Theatre when this movement was noted by many as the great cultural passion of the immigrant Jewish community in the United States,[47] and he took part in Vaudeville at a time in which the growing popularity of radio and records, along with the impact of the great depression,[48] lead to the demise of this great form of entertainment. While Arthur himself had no direct impact on either, it is assumed that these experiences must have had a significant impact on his development as a performer, singer, and actor.

In 1931, Arthur was offered a partial voice scholarship to attend the Eastman School of Music in Rochester, New York. According to Arthur, "Eastman was impressed with the quality of my voice, rather than the power or range of my voice," and despite the costs of re-locating, Arthur decided to accept the offer. This was significant, as the school, under the leadership of Howard Hanson, was at that time recognized as one of the most prestigious music programs in the world. This was exemplified during the period in which Arthur would attend the school (1932-1935), when Hanson's opera *Merry Mount*[49] was premiered in 1934 with a mostly American cast at the Metropolitan Opera in New York and in 1935 when Hanson wrote *Three Songs from Drum Taps*, based on the poem by Walt Whitman.

While at the school, Arthur "undertook a complete set of studies which included piano, music theory, harmony, and dictation." According to Arthur, during this time, [he] was concerned with teaching voice and speech, but also with acting, and felt that Eastman was a "great school to do both." In addition, Arthur was able to continue to play and participate in sports, and remembers that he "was pretty good playing volleyball."

---

[47] http://www.jewish-theatre.com/visitor/article_display.aspx?articleID=1411.

[48] The great depression started with the stock market crash in 1929 and lasted until World War II, almost ten years.

[49] *Merry Mount* is credited as the first American Opera written by an American composer and an American librettist on an American story. It premiered with a mostly American cast at the Metropolitan Opera in New York in 1934 (http://en.wikipedia.org/wiki/Howard_Hanson).

During his second and third years at Eastman (1933-4, 34-5), Arthur participated in several classical operas. His accompanist during his first opera was a top piano student from the school. His accompanist during his second opera was his piano teacher, "the eminent Emanuel Balaban."[50] In addition, and in order to earn money, he organized concerts, "regular full-singing concerts with classical songs, ballads, lieder art songs, and so on." According to Arthur, he reveled in singing ballads like *Danny Deever*,[51] *Der Erlkönig*,[52] "because I could do a lot of acting while singing."

While the school paid him a small amount of money to sing, Arthur had to take out loans to help pay the costs of tuition and relocating to the area. During the next three years, Arthur rented a room from a family who owned/managed a local grocery store and took various singing jobs to earn extra cash. In addition to organizing concerts, he also sang regularly on Friday nights in the synagogue and on Sundays in the Catholic Church. During the summers he would work at various Borscht Belt hotels in the Catskills and often held two jobs at a time, waiter by day, and entertainment director at night, where he also managed talent. As a result, according to Arthur, "he was the first student at Eastman who paid back his loans while still attending the school."

During this period of time, there were numerous and significant events that took place, and which would radically change his life. First, while at Eastman, Arthur was able to study with Professor Bernard Kwartin, who was a famous specialist in methods of voice pedagogy, including experimenting with feeling the correct sound rather than hearing it, which is noted in Kwartin's (1941) book *Fundamentals of Vocal Art:* "Sound wave can be consciously directed to a certain pre-determined spot on the hard palate." In 1945, Arthur would hire Mr. Kwartin as head of voice at the National Academy of Vocal Arts (NAVA), and would use Kwartin's ideas as well as those of "relying on feeling" used by opera star Lilli Lehmann (1902) in her book *How to Sing*, as a "point of departure" for further exploration of the development of the human voice.[53]

---

[50] Emanuel Balaban taught music at Eastman, Columbia, Julliard, and served as conductor for various recordings of classical music and concerts throughout the world.
[51] "Danny Deever" is an 1890 poem by Rudyard Kipling, one of the first of the Barrack-Room Ballads (http://en.wikipedia.org/wiki/Danny_Deever).
[52] "Der Erlkönig" (often called just Erlkönig) is a poem by Johann Wolfgang von Goethe. It depicts the death of a child assailed by a supernatural being, the Erlking or "Erlkönig" (suggesting the literal translation "alder king", but see below). It was originally composed by Goethe as part of a 1782 ballad opera entitled *Die Fischerin* (http://en.wikipedia.org/wiki/Der_Erlk%C3%B6nig).
[53] In a report provided to the Lessac Institute (1967) by Arthur Little, Inc., it is noted that idea of "relying on feeling" was not originated by Arthur, but derived in part from early work completed by Lilli

Second, during his third year at Eastman, Arthur was having difficulties with his "upper register," and repeatedly complained to the Dutch Maestro Adelin Fermin,[54] asking for help. After numerous requests and complaints from Arthur, Fermin, who was known for working with singers at the Metropolitan Opera at the time, finally relented, and agreed to work with Arthur. After meeting with Arthur and listening to him sing, he gave Arthur the following advice: "Arthur, one morning you are going to wake up and it will be there," which signified the end of the teaching session and the extent of the help he was prepared to give Arthur.

While on the surface, the event might appear to be somewhat inconsequential, it was significant on two levels: First, the experience, or the inability of his Master voice teacher to "teach" him, made Arthur question the extent by which the school had anything left to offer him, and second, as he would eventually discover his own upper register while singing in a hotel later that year, he began to realize that he was able to teach himself, both of which helped influence his decision to not return to the school after his third year.

Third, before his final opera concert at the school, Arthur developed a severe cold, which had become significantly worse by the day of the concert, and had affected both his voice and sense of hearing. According to Arthur, he "couldn't cancel the concert as tickets had been sold and money passed." In order to address this problem, he adapted the music from a strong aria to an easier Italian aria on the day of the concert, and using his ability to act, "was able to sing the song without knowing what it would sound like" and without "any impression of suffering." This would appear to be significant in that it marks an early event in his life in which Arthur was able to connect body behavior (acting) to the use of the human voice and for the purpose of solving a "vocal problem."

Fourth, as a result of working at hotels in the Catskill mountains, Arthur was able to participate in a significant historical era that pre-dates the national popularity of the

---

Lehmann and Bernard Kwartin, which focused primarily on how to teach people to sing. The report notes that Arthur used this earlier work as a point of departure in his own research and exploration of the development of the human voice.

[54] Adelin Fermin (1867-1941) was a member of the voice faculty during the earliest years of the Eastman School. Before coming to Eastman in 1921, Mr. Fermin—known to many as "Daddy Fermin"—taught at the Hague and at the Sweelwicks School in his native Holland (http://www.esm.rochester.edu/places/portraits/fermin.php).

Catskills resort in the 1940's and 1950's and is illustrated by the large amount of Borscht Belt hotels, bungalow colonies, and summer camps in Sullivan and Ulster counties frequented by Jewish New Yorkers during this time period.[55] According to Arthur, he remembers "waiting on tables, singing operas, and being in charge of entertainment" and that often famous people, like Danny Kaye,[56] would come up and do their bits or shows in order to work out bugs."[57]

Fifth, while working at the Shawanga Lodge, Arthur was in charge of entertainment, including hiring and managing labor at the hotel, which led him to develop a relationship with Elmer Rosenberg,[58] who had previously been a union activist "industrious in the fire cooperative, the first vice president of the International Ladies Garment Workers Union (ILGWU),[59] and one of the ten people first elected to the New York State Assembly by the Socialist Party of America in 1917."[60] According to Arthur, Rosenberg was [at that time] in charge of organizing labor at a majority of the hotels in the area, and as their relationship began to develop, he might have influenced Arthur's views towards social contracts, labor, and the Socialist Party of America. Although Arthur would not become a member of a Workers Union during this period, and never was directly connected to any communist party, it is significant to note that his relationship with Rosenberg marked the beginning of a friendly and long standing association with labor and moderate socialistic ideas.

---

[55] One of the hotels that Arthur remembers working at, "Shawanga Lodge," was an example of what was at first a "Christian hotel", which was sold to Jews, and became famous for being a Borshet Belt Bugalow (www.temple.edu/tempress/chapters_1100/1353_ch1.pdf). The hotel was just recently sold, indicating that it was probably very successful during its hey day, as other famous resorts, such as the Concord, Grossingers, and Kutcher's continued to run well in the 1990's, but most of the smaller independently owned places went out of business by 1970.

[56] Danny Kaye left school at the age of 13 to work in the so-called Borscht Belt of Jewish resorts in the Catskill Mountains. It was there he learned the basics of show biz. From there he went through a series of jobs in and out of the business. In 1939, he made his Broadway debut in *Straw Hat Revue*, but it was the stage production of the musical *Lady in the Dark* in 1940 that brought him acclaim and notice from agents (http://www.imdb.com/name/nm0001414/bio).

[57] Arthur also remembers that Imogene Coca and Zero Mostel frequented the Borscht hotels he was at. According to Wikipedia, both of these careers started around 1937, which might indicate that Arthur continued to work in this region past his Eastman years, and into the late 1930's.

[58] Rosenberg was also a cousin of his wife (Birdie).

[59] The International Ladies' Garment Workers' Union was once one of the largest labor unions in the United States, one of the first U.S. unions to have a primarily female membership, and a key player in the labor history of the 1920s and 1930s. Its history includes internal power struggles between leftist "red" union leadership and moderate socialists (http://en.wikipedia.org/wiki/International_Ladies%27_Garment_Workers%27_Union).

[60] Lavender & Steinberg. 1995. *Jewish Farmers of the Catskills*.

Sixth, during the summer of 1935, as it was his habit to send the money he earned while working at the Borscht hotels back to Rochester, he went up to a "quiet and petite" young girl, who was the daughter of the owners of the hotel,[61] and asked, "if she could mail this large amount of money back home for him." The young girl just nodded her head as Arthur talked, and didn't say a word, but Arthur trusted that she would do what he asked. Later that evening, at a social dance, Arthur saw the same quiet girl, who now "was wearing heels and a strikingly pretty dress," and being rather surprised at her beauty, which he hadn't noticed before, asked her to dance. Which they did. And, as they danced, Arthur thought, "this is the most amazing dancer I have ever met." The significance of this is demonstrated by the fact that within a month of that dance, Arthur Lessac and Bertha B. Braverman (Birdie) were married and on their way back to New York City to start a new life.

Finding success (1935-1949)

Upon returning to New York, Arthur and Birdie rented an apartment in the part of town "where a lot of artists and writers lived, but not the Village." From 1935-1937, Arthur would take various acting and teaching jobs, and more than likely continued to manage entertainment.[62] According to a bio found in his personal archives (dated around 1939), the jobs he took during this period included Director of Voice and Dramatics with the Workmen's Circle Schools[63] and the Pen and Hammer Club in New York. In addition he continued to perform concerts, including in New York and Buenos Aires, Argentina.[64]

Around 1937 Arthur found out that there was a Labor Stage Theatre that was hiring members from both unions in the Men's Garment district and the Women's Garment District, so that these members "could either study or work," and help produce a musical about the garment workers. As the Labor Stage Theatre began to start hiring and bringing in dance, acting, and speech people, Arthur and a friend snuck in and attempted to audition. Arthur recalls that "I was not on a teaching line, I was one

---

[61] Mr. and Mrs. Braverman owned the hotel that Arthur was working at during the summer of 1935.

[62] I make this assumption based on the fact that Birdie's family (Bravermans) still owned a hotel in the Catskills, there is little documentation of what he did for money during these two years (and this was still during the depression era), and that Arthur makes references to seeing Imogene Coca and Zero Mostel frequent the Borscht hotels he was at, which probably didn't take place until around 1937.

[63] The Workmen's Circle's unique Jewish supplementary schools (in Yiddish, shules) teach positive Jewish cultural identity and Yiddish language skills (www.circle.org/featured-events.html).

[64] It is unclear, if he made contact with his father while in Argentina, or if his father still lived there.

of the other boys. [We] snuck in as trade workers and got the job. We were given acting roles."

The only problem was that neither Arthur nor his friend, who came with him, were union members, and a minor ruckus quickly ensued when the head of the Labor Stage Theatre, Luis Schaffer, found out. At first, Arthur was kicked out of the company, but then the husband of his old friend Mrs. Fingerhood, who was currently working within the union, intervened and "tapped Luis Schaffer on the shoulder, and said: You can use him," and pointed to Arthur. And thus Schaffer hired him as a member of the teaching staff for the *Pins and Needles* production.[65]

After the original show, *Pins and Needles*,[66] became a success, a second and third company were hired to do additional shows. Arthur got to work with all three companies simultaneously, and earned $150.00 a week ($50.00 per show), which was significant in itself, as the great depression would last until almost the end of World War II. The legend is that Arthur used to take the $150.00 back to the apartment where Birdie and he stayed at and he just would throw up all the bills in the air and let them fall on the ground, and then say "let it stay there until you need some money, and then pick up what you need." He would continue with Labor Stage Theatre for a number of years, (1937-1941) doing various shows.[67]

One of the shows that Arthur directed was reviewed by the New York Times (January 5, 1940) which noted that "the Local 91 of the International Ladies Garment Workers Union (ILGWU) sponsored a show directed by Arthur Lessac at the Windsor. "Half of the show consisted of topical sketches and the other half of the operetta enti-

---

[65] Although Arthur did not ever become a union member of the workers union, resumes in his personal archives indicated that he was part of the teaching staff, which at first included special voice work, and then later directing for Labor Stage Theatre (1937-38), Amalgamated Clothing Worker's Union, Cultural Program (1938-1939), and the Ladies Garment Workers Union Cultural Program (1940-41).
[66] According to a program found in his archives, *Pins and Needles* was originally staged by Charles Friedman, directed (in later productions) by Robert Gordon, produced by Labor Stage Theatre, performed by the IGLWU players and included original music by Harold Rome. Arthur Lessack was noted on the program for "special vocal work." According to John Bush Jones (*Our Musicals, Ourselves: A Social History of the American Musical Theatre*, 2004, p. 116), *Pins and Needles* "was a show topically tied to its time" and ran for 1,108 performances.
[67] It is unclear what role, if any, Elmer Rosenberg, who was the first president of the ILGWU, might have also had in helping Arthur earn a position at Labor Stage Theatre.

tled *A Day in the life of a Shopworker,* with music by George Kleinsinger[68] and libretto by Alfred Hayes."[69] The latter Arthur would go on to direct again alongside Jack Gilford's[70] *We are the People* (1941). About that production, Morton Wishengrad, Educational Director of the ILGWU, would later write "the performance of the players was absolutely sterling. The diction was excellent and the staging was imaginative and clever."[71]

While working with Labor Stage Theatre, Arthur took part in an important period of time in labor history and became associated with unions like the ILGWU[72] that developed social and cultural activities for their members that went beyond just the issue of workers rights, and which were shaped by strong views towards the cultural and social development of its members. This is supported in a *Pins and Needles* program (1939) in which it is noted that "all the actors, dancers and singers who appear in [this show] come from: A vast cultural and recreational program with classes in Dramatics, Mandolin Playing, Choral Singing, Athletics, and the Modern Dance, all of which were held at the Arts Center of the International, 106 West 39th Street." Although he never became a member of any of the unions associated with Labor Stage Theatre, it is significant to note that Arthur was clearly associated with one of the largest and most powerful unions during this period of time.

In addition, while serving as part of the teaching staff, Arthur began a professional relationship with Doris Humphrey, who was "in charge of dancing" on various shows and cultural programs that were produced by Labor Stage Theatre and would go on to work in later years alongside Arthur in the musical *Sing Out Sweet Land,* with Alfred

---

[68] George Kleinsinger was an American composer from San Bernardino, California, best known for his collaboration with Paul Tripp on the 1940s children's song "Tubby the Tuba." He also authored the Broadway musical, *Shinbone Alley* (http://en.wikipedia.org/wiki/George_Kleinsinger).

[69] New York Times Article entitled "Broadway to Lose Two More Shows" (January 5, 1940).

[70] There was some confusion if this is Jack Guildford or Jack Gilford. Jack Gilford was an Academy Award- and Tony Award-nominated, and Daytime Emmy Award-winning American actor on Broadway, films and television. He had a unique blend of the earlier style of the Yiddish theater, Vaudeville and Burlesque and started the tradition of monology such as later comedians Lenny Bruce and Woody Allen used and developed a series of musical revues in 1940-41 entitled *We are the People*. (http://en.wikipedia.org/wiki/Jack_Gilford).

[71] Quote as well as program found in personal archives.

[72] ILGWU also developed co-ops for its members to live in the Bronx and which were designed to enhance the culture development of a shared community through "social contracts" (*We Shall Remain: American Experience. A Trail of Tears.* 9:00 p.m. Channel 13, WNET, New York, March 27, 2009).

Drake[73] and Burl Ives.[74] In later years, Ms. Humphrey would become known as a key figure in the modern dance movement, in particular for her work which extensively explored the nuances of the human body's responses to gravity, how the flow of breath affected her movement, and how the human body could shape her response to fall and recovery. She would also serve as a faculty member of the Bennington School of Dance and Julliard, as well as director at the Humphrey-Weidman Company and Jose Limon Dance Company and would posthumously be recognized as a great contributor to dance in the modern era.[75] Although it is difficult to make an assumption about shared views, if any (between Lessac and Humphrey), it is significant to note that Lessac worked for quite a few years with a key figure in the modern dance movement, whose work regarding breath and body might be consistent with those espoused by Arthur Lessac in later years.

During the years Arthur was directing and teaching at Labor Stage Theatre (1937-1941), he was also on the faculty of the New Theatre School (1938-39),[76] was head of the voice and speech department at the YMHA (1939-1941),[77] completed his Bachelor of Science in Voice-Speech clinical therapy at New York University (1941), organized "continuous entertainment at Shack Lessac for artists on the front to win the war,"[78] and taught a summer program at the Bard College (1941). He also remembers something about[79] a troupe called the Revuers, which performed at the Village Vanguard, a

---

[73] Born Alfred Capurro in New York City, Drake is best known for his leading roles in the original Broadway productions of such American musicals as *Oklahoma!, Kiss Me, Kate*, and *Kean*, and for the roles of Marshall Blackstone in the original production of *Babes in Arms* (in which he sang the title song) and Hajj in *Kismet* for which he received the Tony Award. He was also a prolific Shakespearean, notably starring as Benedick in *Much Ado About Nothing* opposite Katharine Hepburn (http://en.wikipedia.org/wiki/Alfred_Drake).

[74] Burl Icle Ivanhoe Ives (June 14, 1909 – April 14, 1995) was an American actor, writer and folk music singer. He was known for roles in movies such as *East of Eden* (1955); *Cat on a Hot Tin Roof* (1958); and *The Big Country* (1958), for which he won an Academy Award for Best Supporting Actor, and television productions, such as the Rankin-Bass animated television special, *Rudolph the Red-Nosed Reindeer* (1964). He also recorded numerous albums, including the country music hits, "A Little Bitty Tear," "Call Me Mr. In-Between," and "Funny Way of Laughing" (http://en.wikipedia.org/wiki/burl_Ives).

[75] The Doris Humphrey Collection of archives is at the New York City Library of Performing Arts.

[76] Located at 132 west 43 St.

[77] Young Men's Hebrew Association-92nd Branch. Under direction of Dr. William Kolodney, taught classes in speech to foreigners, accent elimination, and singing (http://www.92y.org/content/unterberg_ctr_mission_history.asp).

[78] Postcard found in archives included drawing of Shack under Manhattan Bridge.

[79] It is not clear to what degree, if any, that Arthur was connected to the troupe. It appears from my notes that he might have been a frequent visitor to the club, where they performed, or participated in

club in Greenwich Village. Among the members of the company were Adolph Green; Betty Comden;[80] a young comedian named Judy Tuvim, who later changed her name to Judy Holliday; Green's good friend, a young musician named Leonard Bernstein, who frequently accompanied them on the piano; and Al Hammer. And finally, but most important to him, Arthur and Birdie had their first child, Michael Lessac, in 1940.

During this period, Arthur also began to teach more privately,[81] including working with professional singers, actors, and dancers in a private studio. One of his students was a famous dancer (Maria Ley-Piscator[82]) who was married to the great German director, Erwin Piscator,[83] and had a very thick German accent. As a result of working with Ley-Piscator, Arthur remembers beginning to explore the notion that "neutrals in American speech" represented a majority of vowel presentation, and that by having Maria "burp out the vowels, she was able to quickly speak American." Because Ley-Piscator was able to speak American so quickly, he started to form a personal relationship with her husband, who would go on to hire Arthur to work with his actors on voice when he produced shows in New York, as well as recommend Arthur to other theatre groups.

One of those recommendations took place around 1939, when Piscator recommended Arthur to work with German speaking actors[84] on the Broadway show *From Vienna*. Herbert Berghof[85] was re-producing the show with the help of Mrs. George S.

---

some way, although it is important to note that he never identified himself as a member. The time period for the Revuers was around 1938, and before any of its members became famous.

[80] Adolph Green was an American lyricist and playwright who, with long-time collaborator Betty Comden, penned the screenplays and songs for some of the most beloved movie musicals, particularly as part of Arthur Freed's production unit at MGM, during the genre's heyday (http://en.wikipedia.org/wiki/Adolph_Green).

[81] A brochure dated 1945 notes that Arthur's studio was located at 355 86th Street.

[82] Born on August 1, 1898 in Vienna, Austria-Hungary (now Austria), Maria Ley sought to create a theatrical career for herself as a dancer in Paris and Berlin. Later, she turned to choreography and helped in several stage productions with Max Reinhardt, including *A Midsummer Night's Dream* (http://en.wikipedia.org/wiki/Maria_Ley_Piscator).

[83] Erwin Friedrich Maximilian Piscator (17 December, 1893 in Greifenstein-Ulm – 30 March, 1966 in Starnberg) was a famous German left-wing theatre director and producer who, with Bertolt Brecht, was the foremost exponent of epic theatre. Along with his wife (Maria), they founded the Dramatic Workshop at the New School for Social Research. Their students included Harry Belafonte, Marlon Brando and Tony Randall (http://en.wikipedia.org/wiki/Erwin_Piscator).

[84] Viennese Theatre Group.

[85] Austrian-American theatre performer, director, and writer, who was a student of Max Reinhardt and was married to Uta Hagen.

Kaufman[86] at the Music Box, and had taken part in the original production directed by Max Reinhardt in Berlin and Vienna. The show depicted, in a "Machiavellian sense of humor" the effect of Nazism upon Jews living in Vienna. Arthur's job was to get the German-speaking actors to talk without an accent in only six weeks.[87] No small feat considering that the actors reportedly didn't speak English. According to Arthur, "he had to feel his way to making discoveries, which led to a certain type of problem solving that would eventually lay the foundation for [his] books."[88] Needless to say, the show was a success, and Arthur started to earn both national and international acclaim for his work with the actors. Legendary theatre critic Brooks Atkinson gave Arthur high praise for his work,[89] as did Abel, *Variety*, and *the Wall Street Journal*. The *Hollywood Reporter* noted that "Arthur Lessac would be a good bet for any studio with a foreign star on it." And the *Herald Tribune* declared that "Lessac has had to be more than Professor Higgins to a dozen Pygmalions." After the success of *From Vienna*, another production was developed entitled *Reunion in New York* and ran with equal success at the Little Theatre (1940), where one critic noted that "the Germans spoke better English than Americans."[90]

As a result of the growing achievements and noted success from both shows, Arthur became a hot commodity as a voice teacher in the 1940's, as actors, dancers, and singers were knocking at his door to study with him, and he began to offer beginning, intermediate, and advanced classes in speech for the foreign born, including correction, accent elimination, and dialect correction. Some of his students included a piquant Maria Palmer, who wanted to portray a young Norwegian widow in John Steinbeck's *The Moon is Down*, but had only a few months to learn to speak English without an accent[91] and Franz Werfel, the famous poet, novelist, and playwright, who wrote *Song of Bernadette* and *The Forty Days of Musa Dagh,* and who noted after

---

[86] According to article in New York Times (March 10, 1940) entitled *From Vienna and to a Reunion in New York,* Victor Gruenberg invited Mrs. George Kaufman to watch the actors who played in Berlin and Vienna under Max Reinhardt perform in an empty theater. According to the article "Kaufman was so impressed with their work that she arranged an imposing committee to sponsor their ambition to reunite as an entity in New York."
[87] *New York Times* (March 10, 1940).
[88] Melissa Hurt noted that Arthur had indicated that he was able to "discover that sustaining consonants can bring about accent elimination" through his explorations and work with actors in both shows.
[89] *New York Times*, 2 July 1939.
[90] Quotes are taken from either copies of articles of brochures found in personal archives.
[91] Was part of a back stage article entitled "A Refugee Learns the Hard Way" found in his personal archives.

working with Arthur in preparation of a national tour (1942): "Not only was my English clearly understood and liked by the audiences, but I also received much praise....I must say that I never could find anyone who [sic] your uncanny gift of permanently eliminating mistakes in such a precise, effective, and artistic manner." As a result of the success of many of his students, the New York Times would refer to Arthur as "a remarkable teacher."[92]

In addition to his private studio work, Arthur was also invited to lead voice workshops around the world,[93] and in the summer of 1941, Arthur became a member of the performing and teaching faculty of Bard College Summer Theatre and School, where he performed lead roles in *Everyman* by Hofmannsthal,[94] and *The Wild Duck* by Ibsen, and organized a three week workshop with 15 members of the cast (*Reunion in New York*) which Eleanor Roosevelt came to watch.

According to a resume found his archives, Arthur also directed, acted, and produced shows in stock theatre and radio during this period, including adapting and directing *A Life in the Day of a Secretary*, a musical by George Kleinsinger (1944) and directing the verse chorus in the Theatre Guild's *Sing out, Sweet Land,*[95] with Burl Ives and Alfred Drake (1944). He would also publish articles in the *New York Times* (1942) and the *New York Post* (1947).[96] But most importantly, in 1944, Arthur and Birdie would give birth to their second child, Fredi Lessac.

Around 1944, Arthur and Margrit Wyler attempted to open The Experimental Dramatic School, which was geared for actors to work "on mastery of craft, experience, and inspiration," at 151 West 86th Street. The original plan for the school included classes in directing, voice, acting, body technique, and play production, including 10 productions in its first year, and was "in the interest of furthering the

---

[92] Quotations are taken from brochures in personal archives.
[93] Arthur remembers being invited to do a workshop in Germany, where he and Birdie were put in precarious position once they discovered that their living quarters were owned by a member of the Nazi party.
[94] Hugo von Hofmannsthal (February 1, 1874–July 15, 1929) was an Austrian novelist, librettist, poet, dramatist, narrator, and essayist. In 1912, he adapted the 15th century English morality play *Everyman* as *Jedermann* (http://en.wikipedia.org/wiki/Hugo_von_Hofmannsthal).
[95] Dance directors included C. Weidman and Doris Humphrey. Production was first produced at Bushnell Memorial and than later at the International Theatre (Playbills found in personal archives).
[96] *New York Times*. 1942. "On Language as Spoken from the Stage"; *New York Post*. 1947. "What Dreadful Voices You Women Have."

cultural and educational activities of Trade Unions and other community organizations."[97]

Although the school never opened, it appears that Arthur was able to expand on some of these ideas, when, later in 1944, he was able to open the National Academy of Vocal Arts (NAVA)[98] at 6 5th Ave. The Academy offered classes in singing, radio technique, special speech and voice study for actors, public speaking, and accent reduction, as well as specific educational programs in performance, from pre-school to junior division; elementary, intermediate, and advanced levels; all of which incorporated performing, coaching, orchestra, dance, music, acting, and individual instruction. According to the September 19, 1946 issue of the *Greenwich Village Sketch*, NAVA did not view singing, speaking, and acting as separate entities maintaining a mutually exclusive and static relationship, but rather "as vital interdependent factors that must be coordinated into a single dynamic art form."[99]

Instead of marketing just to "Trade Unions and other community organizations," NAVA attempted to reach a wider audience, including veterans returning from the war,[100] children and adolescents in New York city, the corporate/business world, those speaking English as a second language, and people looking to work in radio, television, and theatre. This type of diverse audience was exemplified in a panel discussion held in the Provincetown Theatre on August 26, 1946, which was attended by hundreds of veterans looking for jobs, and who expressed interest in voice training for stage, radio, public speaking or sales work. Speakers included James Harvey, NBC, John Payne, ASCAP, Bob Schnizer, National Theatre Conference and Equity, and Arthur Lessac, Director of National Academy of Vocal Arts.[101]

Unlike other vocal and performing arts programs who only accepted those who had "tremendous potential" or "talent" and then devoted the whole of their training to

---

[97] Quote taken from program for school found in personal archives.
[98] NAVA ceased to exist when the building it resided in (at 6 5th Ave) was torn down.
[99] Brochure found in Lessac archives. The argument is based on the writings of Arthur in which he called for a new type of dramatic training that went beyond teaching these entities separately, which implied that programs were at the time teaching as such.
[100] Arthur had been in charge of speech and phonetics for the Friends of the American Service Committee and NAVA was an accredited program granted the G.I. Bill of Rights.
[101] Lessac advocated for a meeting on a veteran's theatre to be called, and for a veteran's theatre to be established that could train and provide jobs for permanent stock companies in cities of more than 500,000. *Greenwich Village Sketch*, September 19, 1946.

one entity, such as opera (Academy of Vocal Arts in Philadelphia) or acting (Yale School of Drama), the National Academy of Vocal Arts viewed that all people had tremendous potential, a belief that was supported in NAVA's primary advertising slogan, "Don't envy a good voice, have one."[102]

In addition, NAVA marked the first time that Arthur was able to hire teachers of voice, dance, music, and drama. Although it is unclear to what degree Arthur was able to work with his faculty beyond exploring his notion of integrating singing, acting, and speaking as one art form,[103] it is significant to note that he had hired teachers with impeccable credentials, including Bernard Kwartin, who was listed as head of the voice department; Katherine Rosantonaki, who was listed as director of children's workshops; Paul Wilhousky, who was listed as musical director; Florence Fallow, Jan Linderman, Dorothy Thompson and Blanche Bernard, who were listed as teaching voice, and might have also taught phonetics, diction, and oral interpretation;[104] Milton Feher, Anne Widman, Margit U. Schendel, who taught dance; Robert Stewart, Theodore Thurston, and Joanne Manners, who taught drama; Mitchel Chetel, Mortimer Cass, and James R. Anthony, who taught music; Blanche Bernard, James R. Anthony, Jean Renolt, and W. Thomas Jones, who taught piano; Chistos Vrionides, who taught instruments; and Irving Halevy, who served as the Academy's administrator.[105]

It also appeared that people from around the world took classes at NAVA, including John Reich, who had previously worked with Max Reinhardt in Germany, and would go on to become Director of The Goodman School of Drama at the Art Institute of Chicago; Don Wilson, a prominent business man and lawyer; high school students who been awarded scholarships to attend the prestigious academy;[106] veterans from

---

[102] New York City Library of Performing Arts/Archives. *New York Times* clippings.

[103] In an original paper titled "The Boy Who Never Stopped Exploring," Melissa Hurt (Mar. 03, 2000), notes that "Lessac further developed the feeling process of voice and movement studies with his twenty-one teachers (at NAVA), who trained with him to teach his work." Although this argument is supported by E-mail correspondence between Hurt and Lessac, dated Dec, 2008, it is important to note that there is no record in his personal archives that any of the teachers who worked at NAVA taught with him in later years, or were recognized as teaching what would later become known as the "Lessac" work.

[104] Listed in program dated 1947. Personal Archives.

[105] The names listed here are from a program/concert dated 1948 and it is unclear if these faculty taught for all five years. An earlier document (found in the New York Library of Performing Arts) indicated that, in addition to these people, Vivian Chiesa and Hedy Su were pianists and Ivan Petrott, and Donald Dame were judges at event for students to earn scholarships to NAVA (New York Times, 1948).

[106] National Academy of Vocal Arts, New York City Library of Performing Arts, Archives.

the war; and people who just wanted to have a good voice. In addition, the Academy would produce professional theatrical productions, concerts, and shows.[107]

Sometime around the year 1949, the building at 6 5th Ave had to be torn down,[108] which not only marked the end of NAVA, but also signified the beginning of a new era in Arthur's life. The depression had long ended, primarily as a result of World War II, and the country was developing a new sense of nationalism, and as a literate and homogenized society, which was shaped, in part, by images produced in mass media (television and print), which represented an American ideal, and by the federal government's attempts to secure its place as a dominant world power, wherein social, economic, and political ideals of the left, were viewed as radically un-American.

While Arthur himself had never been a member of the Garment District Unions or associated with any "leftist" group,[109] whom the government (in post World War II) would later identify as being "red," he was noted to be a friend of labor, and had, at least in terms of his association with various cultural and educational programs, strong ideals that were not always consistent with the ideals of many who would come into power during the McCarthy Era. This inconsistency was exemplified in later years, as Arthur would argue that group culture, identity and image should be understood through the individual wherein the "destruction [of any culture] becomes impossible if a sense of real integrity is instilled within him."[110] This was a view which appeared to be opposed to those (of that time) who advocated for stronger Nationalistic ideals, and the marginalization of diversity and pluralistic identity within American society, and more consistent with McLuhan (1964) who wrote that: "For the man in a literate and homogenized society ceases to be sensitive to the diverse and discontinuous life of

---

[107] A program from Arthur' personal archives indicates that NAVA produced a concert at Steinway Concert Hall (January, 1947). In July (17) 1948, the *New York Times* reported that OnStage, the little theatre group, was planning on producing seven presentations in as many weeks at NAVA. In February (11) 1949, the *New York Times* reported that Actors' Creative theatre (Stanley Philips and Rodney Hale) presented *Dark Morning* by Thelma Royton and Alice Thomson.

[108] Arthur noted on April 09, 2009, that NAVA ceased to exist because the building was torn down, and on December 14, 2008 (in E-mail correspondence to Melissa Hurt) that NAVA ceased to exist because the building lease was not renewed by himself and Halevy.

[109] Although there were some leaders within the ILGWU who were later accused of being "red," Arthur was never a member of the union, and there is no documentation that Arthur was anything more than a teacher in a social/cultural program designed for union members.

[110] Karen Rubin. 1971. "Being and Becoming: Method of teaching acting, every behavioral gesture emanates from Self." Copy of paper in personal archives.

forms. He acquires the illusion of the third dimension and the private point of view, as part of his Narcissus fixation, and is quite shut off from Blake's awareness or that of the Psalmist, that we become what we behold."[111]

Arthur's strong views regarding the "integrity of the individual" were also exemplified while he was director of NAVA, as Arthur went against standard hiring practices of the time, and hired African-American teachers. According to Arthur, as a result of these hiring practices, another of his teachers, who "might have been a racist," reported him to the House Un-American Activities Committee, where he had to answer questions about his hiring practices and associations with unions. Although Arthur was never blacklisted, or received any judgment from the committee, this experience probably influenced his views about being an American,[112] as exemplified almost 60 years later, in his response to Eli Kazan[113] being given an honorary Oscar, which was recorded in an article in the *Washington Post*:[114]

> Arthur Lessac, an 89-year-old retired teacher—his frail hands shaking with age—said he was infuriated by the decision to honor Kazan. "It's very simple," he said. "Great artists are not necessarily fine people. I believe what he did was evil, even though he's a great artist. As an artist he was a leader, as a person he wasn't.

A new perspective on voice training (1950-1961)

After NAVA closed, Arthur continued to perform, direct, and produce in theatre, radio,[115] and television. He specially recalled co-authoring, co-producing and directing

---

[111] McLuhan, M.1964. Understanding Media: The Extension of Man. New York: McGraw Hill.

[112] Arthur expressed to me, during visits to his apartment in the 1990's, that he thought Paul Robeson, the actor, singer, and activist, represented what an ideal American should be. This is probably significant as Mr. Robeson was denied (for many years) the right to leave the country to perform as a result of his political and social views.

[113] Elia Kazan, director of such acclaimed films as A Streetcar Named Desire, On the Waterfront and Gentleman's Agreement was given an honorary Oscar in 1999, which ignited an unexpected storm of controversy that cast a shadow over the glamorous ceremonies. The award angered those who believe the director betrayed others when he testified before the House Un-American Activities Committee in 1952, naming eight colleagues who were former communists (Waxman, S. March 22, 1999).

[114] Waxman, Sharon. March 22, 1999.

[115] Multiple bios for Arthur Lessac, found in his personal archives, indicate that Arthur "worked in stock theatre, radio, television, and film" throughout his career. Although there is not a complete record of the shows and productions he was involved in, it is assumed that he either performed, produced, and/or directed shows during each of the decades represented within a 65-year period of time (from the mid 1920's until the late 1980's).

a television musical fantasy at WATV called *Chizzlecrimp in the Land of Anything* (1951), singing weekly alongside Burl Ives at the Church of St Mary the Virgin,[116] and doing various voice-over work, such as reading the commercial notes (1954) for an episode of the *Guiding Light*.

During this period of time, Arthur also continued to research singing and speech, as well as body movement, and completed graduate work in speech education, speech pathology, physiology, anatomy, neurology, and psychoanalytical training.[117] In 1953, Arthur would earn a Masters Degree in voice-speech clinical therapy from New York University (NYU), and would be accepted into a doctoral program at NYU, where he studied under John F. Daly,[118,119] which included doing "work in anatomy and neurology at Bellevue Hospital".[120] In 1957, he would complete a clinical internship at St. Vincent's Hospital. In 1958, he would earn and receive a clinical certificate in Voice and Speech from the American Speech and Hearing Association (ASHA). From 1959-1960, he would complete psychoanalytical training in New York City (NYPIPA[121]). And in 1961, he would study Tai Chi Ch'uan with Sophia Delza.[122]

After completing all his required coursework for his doctorate, Arthur submitted a proposal for his dissertation study, which was based on his studies into clinical areas[123] and used notions of "feeling and sensing," rather than an "intellectualized" perspective of problem solving.[124] As it was standard practice during this time to have

---

[116] Lasted for a six-month period, probably in the mid 1950's.
[117] Report presented by Arthur Little, Inc. (1967) for the Lessac Institute. Personal Archives.
[118] Dr. Daly was an eminent Otolaryngologist-Head and Neck Surgeon, who served as acting Chairman of the Department of Otolaryngology from 1946-47 and as Professor and Chairman from 1947 to 1980. During his leadership, the Department grew both in number of faculty and national prominence (http://ent.med.nyu.edu/education/lectureships).
[119] Also remembers studying with a Dr. Lee, while working on his doctorate at NYU.
[120] Quote comes from bio in personal archives.
[121] I was not able to determine what the acronym NYPIPA, which what was listed as previous education on a job application for California State University of Fullerton (1987), stands for. The New York Psychoanalytic Institute and Society was founded in 1911, and has offered training and education opportunities for research over that period. Other associations include American Psychoanalytic Association (APsaA), Institute for Psychoanalytic Studies (IPS), Institute for Psychoanalytic Training and Research (IPTAR), and New York Freudian Society (NYFS).
[122] Sophia Delza Glassgold was a modern dancer and teacher and an expert in the ancient Chinese exercise form called tai chi (*New York Times* Obituary, July 7, 1996).
[123] A complete set of data and notes from his clinical studies (at NYU) are preserved in his personal archives.
[124] In his reflections about his doctoral work, Arthur would differentiate his work from others by noting this work is based on a process of "feeling and sensing" within the whole body versus a more "intellec-

one's research be largely based on the previous research and/or work of others,[125] Arthur received a considerable amount of resistance from his dissertation committee. According to Arthur, he "was not creating something new. It was already in the body," a view which might be best represented in the following anecdote Arthur has told over the years: "I once worked with a psychologist's patient who had lost his voice for no apparent physical reason: It was hysterical aphonia.[126] I thought heck with the speech. I need to get him to either laugh or cry or both."

Rather than compromise what he had proposed, Arthur decided to leave before completing his dissertation. Although Arthur would use part of his research for the basis of his book *The Use and Training of the Human Voice* (1960), his battle with his doctoral committee represented the beginning of an ongoing tension between himself and academia that (arguably) still exists to this day. Part of this tension is rooted in an epistemological difference Arthur had with his committee over the assumption that one could make discoveries/findings through "feeling and sensing" (which would be based on the belief that the whole body can be involved in the problem solving process) and not just through intellectual and rational thought (which in contrast, would be based on the belief that thinking or analysis of data derives solely from the brain). But part of this tension is also rooted in Arthur's personal beliefs about what the role of research is, and who its intended audience should be. From Arthur perspective, the discoveries he made through "feeling and sensing" should not be solely contextualized through an academic discourse, wherein the findings would be intellectualized and responded to by only a few of the elite, but should be passed along to a wider audience, for the purpose of that audience, using the same process of "feeling and sensing," making their own discoveries, through which they not only transform themselves but others as well.

---

tualized" process of thinking that emphasized just the brain. In particular, Arthur was against situating his notion of "feeling and sensing" through this type of thinking process.

[125] In *McLuhan: Pro and Con* (1968), Raymond Rosenthal argues that one of the problems Academia had with Marshal McLuhan's (1963) controversial book *Understanding Media: The Extensions of Man*, was that 90% of what McLuhan said was new, and that it was generally accepted that 90% of your work (in academia) would be based on other research, with only about 10% being new.

[126] Hysterical aphonia is one of the so-called conversion disorders under somatoform disorders according to the DSM-IV. It refers to loss of ability to speak and utter sound due to psychological as opposed to physiological or anatomical disturbance
(http://www.bluepoppy.com/cfwebstorefb/index.cfm?fuseaction=feature.display&feature_id=268).

While completing his graduate and clinical studies, Arthur would continue to teach in many different contexts. He taught at the Stella Adler School of Theatre for one year (1951), was in charge of all voice and speech training, therapy, and coaching at the Jewish Theological Seminary of America,[127] was a lecturer (Psychology and Religion) at The Adult Institute of Jewish Studies of The Whitestone Hebrew Center (1955), offered a two day research/experimental workshop for staff, students, and patients of the National Institute of Deaf,[128] in which he remembers "using the physical process as a substitute for the ear for 10 congenitally deaf students," and was a voice and speech consultant for the Army/Air Force Exchange Service (1959-1960).

In addition, he would continue to expand and market individual classes at his private studio, which after NAVA closed was "somewhere on the East Side," but eventually moved to 160 73rd Street,[129] where he would stay for approximately 17 years.[130] During the early 1950's, the studios operated under the name of the Voice Craft Center, and marketed Lessac teaching methods as "a new craft approach to voice training" and a "scientific and logical approach to voice and speech".[131] By 1953, and throughout the rest of the decade, Lessac would use the names Lessac Institute of Voice and Speech, Institute of Voice and Speech, and Lessac Institute of Vocal Arts,[132] and adapted its marketing approach to reach out to people who were interested in (a) developing "a pleasant speaking voice in everyday business and social life," (b) "how to acquire a proper voice personality," and (c) "all phases of voice and speech work, from training operatic singers, popular singers, and actors, to people who require speech correction and voice improvement."

---

[127] While at the Theological Seminary, Arthur edited a book by Markowitz, Sidney. 1954. *What do you know about Jewish religion, history, ethics, and culture?*

[128] Given at the Rochester Institute of Technology estimated to be somewhere in the mid 1950's. Reference comes from bio listed in report provided to Lessac Institute (1967), which was found in his personal archives. Arthur remembers going there before he was hired at SUNY Binghamton and after NAVA.

[129] A 1953 program for voice classes lists an address of 160 72nd Street.

[130] Both Sue Ann and Arthur mention that there were multiple studios around the time the first voice book was published in 1960, but it is unclear if the multiple studios were in the same building or at different locations. Since no other address was found in the personal archives, it is assumed that the studios were on different floors of the same building.

[131] As part of his scientific study, Arthur would conduct a six part diagnostic test designed to help provide individual speech, voice and communicating personality profiles, which included "Audio and video recordings of incoming students, which would then be analyzed and evaluated; findings checked against initial interviews" (1961).

[132] Noted by various programs and advertisements found in personal archives.

By 1961, Lessac had expanded his list of course offerings to include voice building, public speaking, speech correction, accent elimination, diction and phonetics, microphone technique, effective selling, parliamentary procedures, conference speaking and presentation, singing, repertoire coaching, choral speech, acting and directing, dialect training, dramatic characterization, conducting glee clubs, mixed choruses, voice rehabilitation, speech therapy, and clinical therapeutic techniques for stuttering, cleft palate, habitual and hysterical aphonia, aphasia, radical articulatory disorders, teaching the deaf and the hard of hearing, and other voice anomalies.

Students during this period of time included Irene Dailey,[133] Bud Greenspan,[134] Nina Foch,[135] and Lee Cass,[136] and Arthur's teaching methods continued to be praised and respected throughout the country. The Elad Theatre School was based on his work,[137] his teaching methods were featured in articles in the Sunday *Mirror Magazine*[138] as well as in the *World-Telegram* and *Saturday Magazine*,[139] and in1956, he published another article in the *New York Times* entitled "New Ways of Correcting Stuttering."

As a result of his national acclaim, the subsequent "pushing of Don Wilson,"[140] and requests by his students to have a written exposition that they could refer back to,

---

[133] An American actress, perhaps best known for her work on Broadway and on daytime television, Dailey taught acting classes at the Herbert Berghof Studio in New York City and later (1961) opened her own school, the School of the Actors Company (http://en.wikipedia.org/wiki/Irene_Dailey).

[134] Bud Greenspan is an eight-time Emmy Award-winning film director, writer, and producer, mostly known for his sports documentaries (http://en.wikipedia.org/wiki/Bud_Greenspan).

[135] Nina Foch was an Academy Award-nominated Dutch-born American actress and leading lady in many 1940's and 1950's films (http://en.wikipedia.org/wiki/Nina_Foch). Although the specific dates that she studied with Arthur are not clear; she was one of the case studies used for his first voice book, indicating that she studied with him prior to the book being published.

[136] When NBC experimented with televised opera in the early 1950's, Lee Cass was a regular in its casts. He sang at the New York City Opera, the Cleveland Opera, the Civic Light Opera of Pittsburgh and the Santa Fe Opera Festival. He would go on to appear in several Broadway productions and teach voice at Carnegie Mellon University (http://www.nytimes.com/1995/05/06/obituaries/lee-cass-bass-baritone-70.html).

[137] Program for Elad Theatre School found in Arthur's archives, with a picture of Michael Lessac on the cover, notes that "school was based on the teaching methods of Arthur Lessac." According to Arthur, he and a partner ran the school at a time when ballroom dancing was big—the *Dale* style in particular. "I spelled Dale backwards and got Elad and called the school the Elad School For Children."

[138] *Accents: Voices Built Rehabilitated*. Forrest Duke (Personal Archives).

[139] *"Diction does cut a figure."* George Keaney (New York City Library of Performing Arts Archives). Personal archives also identifies an article with same actresses entitled "How to Cut, Cultivate Foreign Accents," but it is unclear what source is (possibly *Sunday News*).

[140] Don Wilson, a lawyer and business consultant, was a managing partner at Arthur D. Little, the management consulting firm, in the late 1960s when he wrote the plan for what later became Lexis-Nexis, an early computerized system for retrieving information.

Arthur began putting together notes from his teaching, his dissertation proposal, and clinical studies in order to write a book. At first, most of the publishers to whom he submitted his proposal refused to accept the book, because as Arthur remembers it, the publishers thought the book was "not technical enough for professional work and not simple enough for a popular book." But despite the negative response, Arthur decided if nobody would publish his work, he would just do it himself, which led to many nights in which he would sit at his desk in his apartment, arranging his notes while "Birdie typed them on an old type writer, page by page, which we would take one at a time to the printer to be copied." Over time, the word got out that Arthur Lessac was putting together a book,[141] which, along with the help of Arthur Seelen of the Drama Book Shop, led to 600 copies of *The Use and Training of the Human Voice* being sold in the early 1960's.[142]

Situating Lessac (1962-1969)

As his book began to grow in popularity[143] in the 1960's, the name Lessac would become increasingly situated within and across multiple business, performance, and educational contexts. In terms of business, Arthur would train management at companies such as Transworld Airlines, Revlon, Remington Road, Texaco, Lehman Bros, Credit Bureau of Greater New York, American Christian Committee For Refugees, Delahanty Institute, Shell Chemical, Johns-Manville, Dasol Corporation, Burlington Mills, Presolite Manufacturing, First Investors, Corp, and Vick Chemical,[144] wherein one of the goals was to teach people how to relax. As a result of the success of his work with many of these companies, he was asked by the American Management Association to write *Your Personal Management—You Can Learn To Relax,*[145] which focused on the paradox of "feeling" and "observing" elements of posture and breathing, and included the phrase: "A Yawn in Time."

---

[141] Copies of the first editions of the book have been preserved by Arthur Lessac in his personal archives.

[142] Arthur says the book "came to the attention of Seelen", but it is unclear when that actually took place. The Drama Book Store would eventually publish the book, but at first responded that "they didn't know what to do with such a book." A report by the Lessac Institute (1967) notes Seelen's early involvement in the first book.

[143] A revised edition would be published in 1967, with a new introduction by Irene Dailey.

[144] Part of survey/report published for the Lessac Institute by Arthur Little, Inc (1967). It was unclear if this training included the 1950's as well as the 1960's.

[145] Published by the American Management Association. December, 1962.

In 1965, Arthur formed the Lessac Institute for Applied Research in the Communicating Arts and Skills, Incorporated.[146] According to a survey/report[147] commissioned by the Institute in 1967, the initial goals of the Institute included: (a) to have a studio for advanced work on the Lessac approach, (b) to organize master teachers and a select group of actors already trained to experiment in advanced work and assist in revision of the Voice book, (c) to produce interactive videos for educational and public use, (d) and to fund further research in health and creativity.

One of the first tasks of the newly formed Institute was to produce a "Summer Workshop in the Lessac System of Voice and Speech," which took place from July 26, 1965 through September 3, 1965 and included Arthur Lessac, Sue Ann Park, James S. Kennedy, Dick Pyatt, Bobby Troka, and Michael Lessac. By 1969, the Summer Workshop had expanded to six weeks, and had been given in New York City during 1967 and at Ohio University and SUNY at Binghamton in 1969.

In terms of performance, Arthur would work with actors studying at Irene Dailey's newly formed School of the Actor's Company, the Paul Mann Workshop, and The Goodman School of Drama at the Art Institute of Chicago, and in 1962, he was invited by Elia Kazan[148] and Robert Whitehead to train the original Lincoln Center Repertory Theatre Company along with Robert Lewis and Anna Sokolow; the company included young actors such as Frank Langella, Michael Douglas, Faye Dunaway, and Martin Sheen. In 1966, Arthur leased Theatre Four, at 424 W 55 St,[149] to book theatrical productions and for the purpose of developing a repertory company[150] and, as was his

---

[146] Pursuant to section 10 of the Membership Corporation Law of the State of New York. Initial bylaws for corporation were signed by Arthur Lessac, Michael Lessac, David Goldstein, Morton Ginsberg, and Martin Sheen.

[147] In 1967, the Institute commissioned Arthur Little, Inc. to develop a report that would include the history and present status of the Lessac system of voice training, state Lessac's posits in the field of voice and speech, explore what importance the Lessac system could have, and identify the possibilities for a workable financial framework. The report is preserved in his personal archives.

[148] The relationship between Lessac and Kazan appears to be both complicated and ambiguous, as represented by Lessac's strong objection to his being given an honorary Oscar in 1999. Although Lessac was on the faculty with Kazan at the Lincoln Center and had previously trained some actors who ended up also working with Kazan, it is unclear what their working relationship, if any, entailed.

[149] The *New York Times* article (August 11, 1966) written by Sam Zolotow states that "Theatre Four has been leased to L.G.B. Productions, headed by Arthur Lessac and Val Bisoglio. They intend to book other productions at the 299 seat house, participate as co-producers and develop a repertory company."

[150] While little is known about the efforts to create a repertory company, the theatre itself still exists today, currently named the Julia Miles Theatre, and reportedly has a plaque of Arthur in the lobby (As reported by Cory Hinkle, Assistant to Julia Miles, 2002).

nature, continued to explore other performance techniques and approaches, including the Alexander Technique at the Alexander School (1962) and Grotowski's body training program at La Mama Theatre (1969).

In 1967, Arthur would revise *The Use and Training of the Human Voice: A Practical Approach to Speech and Voice Dynamics*[151] with a new introduction by Irene Dailey. The new edition received positive reviews, such as by Jack Clay, who wrote that "Arthur Lessac is today in the vanguard of stage voice training, continually testing and qualifying his ideas,"[152] and by John Reich who noted that Lessac "fits smoothly into the American interpretation of Stanislavksy."[153] According to Arthur Little, Inc, (1967) the significance of the book was that it offered a revolutionary new perspective and framework for voice training, which began from a singer's and actor's point of voice, discarded the traditional notion of relying on the ear, assumed that voice training laid the foundation for speech training, and was based on the scientific analysis of the mechanisms involved in producing the human voice. This is supported in the following quotation:

> For over 50 years, since Garcia's pioneering efforts, few basic changes have been made in the way people have been taught to speak until now. The contrast is astonishing. It is as striking as the difference between the horseless carriage, with all its bumps and blowouts, and today's streamlined, pleasure-giving automobile. This book takes one from the horseless carriage age of speech instruction, to a new, scientific and logical approach to voice training. It is a step-by-step process of training your voice to speak and sing better.[154]

In terms of an educational context, Arthur would continue to offer classes at his private studios on 72nd Street, as well as teach to diverse populations around the world. In 1963, he was invited by Kenneth Marshall[155] to teach at the Harlem Youth Opportuni-

---

[151] Published by Drama Book Stores.
[152] Clay, Jack. 1968. "Speech for the performer: Arthur Lessac's Revolution." In *Educational Theatre Journal*.
[153] Quotation printed on brochure for Lessac Summer Workshop found at New York City Library of Performing Arts.
[154] Quotation was found in personal archives, single space typed paper, with no source cited, except "Lessac" at the top.
[155] Personal letter written by Kenneth Marshal, Program Planning Director, HARYOU and addressed to Arthur Lessac, 160 72nd Street, New York. Within context of letter, Marshall requests Arthur's services for the primary purpose of improving the "speech deficiencies of Harlem's youth."

ties Unlimited (HARYOU)[156] Theatre Program, where he also collaborated with James Kennedy, of Brooklyn College and director Bill Robinson[157] for about a year. In the mid 1960's, he was invited on three different occasions to teach in Puerto Rico, including at the Teatro Escolar in Puerto Rico, the University of San Juan (1964), where he gave a workshop in Spanish, and at the University of Puerto Rico, Rio Piedras (1965).

In addition, Arthur would begin publishing his work in educational journals and trade magazines, and, along with Sue Ann Park,[158] would present aspects of the Lessac training at conferences held around the country. In 1963, Sue Ann Park introduced the core principals of Lessac training at the American Education Theatre Association Conference (AETA), which was followed up by Arthur writing a paper entitled "Lessac System for the Use and Training of the Human Voice," which he presented at a joint conference of the Speech Association of America (SAA) and the American Education Theatre Association (AETA).[159] In 1965, Arthur wrote a paper[160] entitled "Speech: Vocal and Verbal Life as an Intrinsically Felt Energy,"[161] which he presented at the AETA national conference. In 1966, Sue Ann Park sat on a panel discussion with Kristin Linklater, Robert Parks (sitting in for Edith Skinner), Dorothy Mennen, and Robert Chapline, that examined speech training in the United States.[162] In 1967, Arthur wrote a paper entitled "A Single Approach and a Euphonic Standard in Voice and Speech Training" at the request of Emerson College, where he presented his findings in the same year, and argued that the ear is "not a selectively sensitive instrument" as exemplified in the following excerpt from the paper:

---

[156] Harlem Youth Opportunities Unlimited, more commonly called HARYOU, was a social activism organization founded by Dr. Kenneth Clark in 1962 and directed by Cyril DeGrasse Tyson. The group worked to increase opportunities in education and employment for young African-Americans in Harlem (http://en.wikipedia.org/wiki/Harlem_Youth_Opportunities_Unlimited).

[157] According to proposals (written by Robinson and Kennedy) found in his personal archives, one of the focuses of HARYOU theatre program was on the "Artist to disrupt," while another was on an in-service grant for training youth with leadership potential.

[158] Sue Ann Park is a Master Lessac Teacher and is currently Director of Training for the Lessac Institute.

[159] December 27, 28, 29, 30. LaSalle Hotel, Chicago Illinois. 28th Annual Convention. Program in archives.

[160] Lessac, A. 1965. "Vocal and verbal life as an intrinsically felt Energy." Part of panel discussion entitled: Speech for the actor: An eclectic colloquy. Personal Archives.

[161] Part of panel discussion titled: "Speech for the actor: An Eclectic Colloquy."

[162] While everyone on the panel agreed that voice and speech cannot be separated in their training nor in their concepts, it appeared that Sue Ann was very vocal about the differences between the various types of voice training being discussed (paper found in Arthur's archives).

It is most important to note here that during the stages of training, the ear is not a selectively sensitive instrument, as we often assume it to be. For example, I once suggested that [sic] accent student say "back" instead of "beck." When I pointed out [the difference], he [still] continued to say "beck" [and] would answer, "oh no, I didn't say "beck," I said "Beck." We then recorded the phrase and as he listened he would still insist, "But I didn't say 'beck', I said 'Beck.'" In other words he was able to hear his mistake on the tape and still could not correct it in his speech.

In 1969, Arthur would publish articles in *Players Magazine* ("Voice for Actors") and in the *Quarterly Journal of Speech* ("A New Definition of Dramatic Training"), and wrote a paper entitled, "The Use and Care of the Adolescent Voice,"[163] which he presented at the 1969 AETA conference.[164]

It was around this time, that Robert (Bobby) Lewis, who had served on the faculty at the Lincoln Center Repertory Company, had been offering a "special class for actors" in New York, and one of the people who took the class, Dr. Alfred Brooks, asked Bobby if he knew of anyone who had his own way of thinking—"Someone who wanted to do things different, a kind of fresh breeze," and Bobby, with a smile, said, "I only know of one person." Thus it wasn't long before the Chancellor of the State University of New York, at the urging of Al Brooks, offered Arthur an immediate tenured, full-professor position at SUNY at Binghamton, where he was given a mandate to organize the acting program.

At the time he was offered the position, the Lessac work had been taught exclusively at The Goodman School of Drama at the Art Institute of Chicago, Sonia Moore Studios, School of the Actor's Company, Southern Methodist University, Columbia College in Chicago, The Fine Arts Workshop, Hunter College, Brooklyn College, Ohio University, Dallas Theatre Center, Meshiva University, The Mummers School (Oklahoma City), Long Island University, Purdue University, The School Theatre

---

[163] Lessac, A. 1969. "The Use and Care of the Adolescent Voice."
[164] The paper appeared to be revised a number of times (copies in personal archives) and might have been presented in 1970 as well. It is also might be of significance to note that, based on data in his archives, Bobby Troka found the Lessac training to be very effective with pre-teens and teens, and that Lessac might have been part of this work, including exploring ways in which the training lay a foundation for reading readiness in young children.

Program at the University of the Commonwealth of Puerto Rico, and the Catholic University in Belgium. "Teachers of the Lessac Method" included Irene Dailey, Beverly Shimmen, Allan Bellknap, Dick Pyatt, Bobby Troka, Anita Lande, Marlene Holbert Marlowe, Dr. Russ Gillis, Dr. Robert Hobbs, Dr. James S. Kennedy, Sue Ann Park, Dorothy Mennen, Jack Clay, Jack Jones, Fay Von Saal, Sister Therese, and Raye Birke.[165]

Expanding the Work: (1970-1982)

During Arthur's tenure at SUNY Binghamton, his work would expand within and across many contexts. At SUNY Binghamton, Arthur was able to bring Sue Ann Park, Libby Roman, and Dick Cuyler into the theatre department, which allowed for the Lessac training to be an integral part of the acting program, as exemplified by a Lessac certification program being implemented for graduate students (1976-1977), and by the use of Lessac training in productions directed by Dick Cuyler and Sue Ann Park. The latter of these is supported in an article in a Binghamton paper[166] in which it is noted that in the production *Crime on Goat Island*,[167] Sue Ann Park was the "first to incorporate use of the popular Lessac method in her directing for a full production."

According to Arthur, during this period of time he was also able to explore the use of body energy states, body movement, and body esthetics as part of heuristic creative problem solving, which led to him to write *Body Wisdom: The Use and Training of the Human Body* (1978, 1981). The book included introductions by Dr. Alfred Brooks and Dr. Walter Lowen, as well as collaboration with Dr. Michael Lessac,[168] who noted that the book attempted to "take eastern wisdoms and put them into western understanding of man."[169] The book was given positive reviews by both the *Educational Review Journal* and *Theatre Quarterly*, which called the book "a remarkable resource."[170]

---

[165] As recorded on original handwritten note in personal archives.
[166] "Pipe Dream: State University of New York at Binghamton." Tuesday April 11, 1972.
[167] Written by Ugo Betti.
[168] Michael Lessac started his career in theatre after having received a Ph.D. in developmental and perceptual psychology and completing research fellowships (1965-1971) at Columbia University and the University of Minnesota. In addition, he was given a two year Ford Foundation Grant to work at the National Theatres of England, Italy, France, Poland, Romania, Yugoslavia and the Soviet Union, and founded the Colonnades Theatre Lab in 1974 (http://en.wikipedia.org/wiki/Michael_Lessac).
[169] Paper written by Michael Lessac, in personal archives.
[170] As referenced on back of cover. Lessac, A. 1981. *Body wisdom: The Use and Training of the Human Body*.

In addition, Arthur would begin to explore ways in which the Lessac training could be integrated into other academic areas and research. Along with Bill Melnitz,[171] he would begin to integrate Lessac training within courses offered in the music department, including an introductory music course that Arthur developed in which he remembers that he taught students to "start on any pitch. *One, three, five, three, one, three, one, five, three.*[172] And by feeling, I would get [them to be aware of] a note in both chords. *One, three, five.* [Which led to them being aware of a] whole progression in chords, including minor, and dominant seventh chords, purely by feeling the tones."

In 1971, he would contribute to Gary Truce's research on the effect of Lessac training on long distance running.[173] In 1973, he contributed to Norma Berkely's study, which examined if the "Lessac method of voice and speech" could be successfully taught to large groups of general-studies students.[174] In 1974, Arthur was identified as a Distinguished Teaching Professor[175] and began doing research at the School of Advanced Technology (1974-1975), in collaboration with Dr. Walter Lowen, and explored the relationship of physical intelligence to voice and body dynamics primarily dealing with sensation. In 1975, he advised Steven Day on his thesis project, "An experiment in applying the Lessac principals in human voice and body training to remedial reading."

While he was a professor at SUNY at Binghamton, the Lessac Institute was expanded,[176] in part through the developing business partnership between Arthur Lessac and Don Wilson, as well as the efforts of Michael Lessac to analyze the work in relationship to current developments in psychology.[177] In 1973, plans for a task force[178] were initiated,

---

[171] Visiting Professor from U.C.L.A.
[172] Italics represent Arthur singing the word/numbers in italics.
[173] Part of dissertation completed by Gary Truce, who at the time was a track/field coach.
[174] Berkely, Norma. 1973. "The crowded Lessac-60-1: A speech program to beat the odds." Research completed in Baltimore, in conjunction with department of Development Education (not SUNY).
[175] Awarded by the State University of New York at Binghamton.
[176] Papers within personal archives identify Arthur Lessac, Donald Wilson, Alfred Brooks, Michael Lessac, David Morgan, Richard and Mary Williams as being part of a "Sensics Company," which appears to be either an extension or offshoot of the "Lessac Institute."
[177] Throughout the late 1960's and early 1970's, videos and transcriptions of activities at the Summer Workshops were recorded, which Michael used to analyze and identify trends as being part of a Human System Knowledge. The data, which includes thousands of pages of text, is in Arthur's personal archives.
[178] Included Michael Lessac, David Morgan, Allan Belknap, Dick Pyatt (Circle in the Square Theatre), Ruth Metzger, Lilly Landerer (United Nations), Patrick Thaddeus (Columbia University), Robert Arnold (Pan American Airlines), Brian Appel, John E. Preshlack, James Lewis, Irene Dailey, and Beverly Shimmen.

with the intended purpose of developing new markets, including the self-realization area, communications, athletics, and text-to-speech technology[179] based on Lessac's sensory feedback vocal training.[180] According to a report given by Don Wilson, the "revolutionary potential of the system" was based on learning by sensation instead of rote:

> Lessac apparently intuitively anticipated what is now called "servo-feedback" the powerful new electronic [sic] system perfected in the 50's and 60's upon which nearly every sophisticated machine now depends. Pre-Lessac, one trained one's voice by instructor or book. As everyone knows when he hears his own recorded voice for the first time, this imitative approach won't produce something that sounds to you like it sounds to others. Also the same is true of other functions, driving a golf ball, for example. When you try to imitate Arnold Palmer, you really don't know what you look like because you are inside of you but outside of Arnold Palmer—two very different viewpoints. Arthur Lessac discovered the key—instead of "Do as I do," he said, "this is how, it should feel to you. Do it so it feels right, and it will be right."

In addition, the Lessac Institute hired Dr. Charles McGaw[181] to provide an outside report and evaluation of Lessac training at various campuses around the country.[182] Dr. McGaw, who had been part of a National Endowment of the Arts study regarding the training of voice teachers in the United States, noted that although some on the panel "preferred the Warren-Linklater approach, it seems likely that the Lessac's personal enterprises will provide America's teachers of voice" in the future. McGaw's report was further supported by reports[183] provided by Sue Ann Park, Robert Hobbs, Steve Mackenroth, Randy Moore, and Norma Levin Moore regarding training at different programs as well as the summer workshops being given[184] wherein it was noted that "participants, al-

---

[179] Beginning in 1974, patents (based on the Lessac system) would be filed with the U.S Government, including speech training method with color instruction, speech training method with alternative proper pronunciation database, text to speech, and speech recognition method.

[180] Don Wilson would later develop Lessac Technologies, and spent the later part of his life "focused on text-to-speech technology based on Mr. Lessac's approach to voice training" (*New York Times*, November 25, 2006).

[181] Dr. Charles McGaw was Dean of The Goodman School of Drama at the Art Institute of Chicago and wrote the book *Acting is Believing,* wherein McGaw notes Arthur Lessac as an "influential approach to acting training" (1992: 56-7). After his death, Larry D. Clark re-wrote the book in 1992.

[182] At the time, the Institute reported that 72 institutions were using Lessac training.

[183] Sue Ann Park. 1972. "A short description of what is happening at the workshops." Personal archives.

[184] Thirteen Summer Workshops were given between 1970 and 1983.

most all of them experienced and professional, ranged from age, in the sixties to just out of their teens, and all of them had to learn through teaching and had to start with themselves" and that students were able to "readily pick up the concepts of free, body directed, organic movement" and "were doing beautifully with the vocal work."

During this time period, Arthur would continue to present at national conferences, such as at the AETA convention (1971) where he posited that voice, speech, and acting are integrated elements of an organic whole and that this integration was created through the discovery of the "feeling" of the physical processes, and awareness of what is happening inside the body,[185] and would be largely recognized as a notable name in American theatre.[186] This is exemplified by aspects of his work being discussed in *Theatre Quarterly*,[187] *Theatre News*,[188] *The Drama Review*,[189] and *Theatre Speech and Voice Newsletter*.[190]

In the early 1980's, Arthur retired from SUNY Binghamton[191] and began working on new ways to further explore and develop his work, including researching vocal nodes and how Lessac training might serve as an alternative to surgery,[192] when his beloved wife, Birdie, became ill and passed away rather unexpectedly.[193] It was a devastating loss to Arthur and, in a letter to Donna Aronson[194] dated June 17, 1983, Arthur noted that due to his wife's death, he was packing up his belongings to stay with his son Michael[195] in Los Angeles for a six-week period to see if the area would be a suitable place to live. The move marked the end of a 75-year period of history during which Arthur had been an integral part of New York culture and the arts.

---

[185] Lessac, A. 1971. "The Actor Explores – Vocal life on the Stage." August 18. Chicago AETA convention.
[186] As noted by White, J. (1976) in his book *Notable Names in the American Theatre*.
[187] *Theatre Quarterly*. 1979: Vol. IX, No. 33.
[188] David Stern. May 1979. "Understanding voice quality by understanding voice function." In *Theatre News*.
[189] Jack Clay. March 1972. "Self-Use in Actor Training." In *The Drama Review*.
[190] *Theatre Speech and Voice Newsletter*, Dorothy Mennen, Winter, 1974.
[191] Due to mandatory retirement laws enacted (at the time) by the State of New York.
[192] Corrigan, Lessac, Keaton, Allan. 1983. "Nodes; The Salutary Effects of Good Tone; the Alternative to Surgery." Tuesday August 9, 1983. Paper accepted to be presented at American Theatre Association.
[193] Arthur did not teach at the Summer Workshop and cancelled his presentation at the American Theatre conference that was scheduled later that summer.
[194] Department of Theatre and Speech, University of California, Los Angeles (UCLA).
[195] Michael Lessac had moved to Los Angeles and would direct in television (*Taxi, Newhart, Grace Under Fire, Everyone Loves Raymond*) and film (*House of Cards*).

Ol' Man River Keeps Rollin' Along: (1984-2009)

Like the song, made famous by Paul Robeson, Arthur would just keep on rollin' along over the next 25 years. After moving to Southern California and getting a large and spacious apartment with an ocean view, Arthur would continue to explore new possibilities for his work and research.

As an actor and director, he would act in various television, film, and theatre productions, including in an episode of *Cheers*, in Blake Edwards' *Mickey and Maude*, and as Kilgore Trout in *God Bless You Mr. Rosewater* at the Matrix Theatre. In 1984, he was invited to be an actor at the school of the Sundance Institute Playwright's Conference, where he acted and served as a "resource specialist" for the three summers (1984-6).

As a researcher and writer, he would publish articles in numerous journals, magazines, and books, including *Southern Theatre* (1991), *Movement Theatre Quarterly* (1991), *Journal of Voice* (1995), *Vocal Visions: A View of Voice* (1997), *Speech and Voice Disorders* (1998), and *Voice and Speech* (2000). In addition, he would complete further research on his training methods, including the impact of Lessac training on age, illness, and pregnancy. In 1996, he would revise his book *The Use and Training of the Human Voice: A Bio-Dynamic Approach to Vocal Life*, which includes a new introduction by Frank Langella. And around 2004, along with Master Lessac Teacher Deborah Kinghorn, he began to write a new book on three additional energies and their impact on health and humaneness.[196]

As a master teacher and distinguished professor, Arthur would go on to teach and lead workshops in many different contexts, including serving as Master Teacher at 12 Lessac Summer Workshops (1984-2000), being invited as a distinguished visiting professor at the University of Virginia and California State University at Fullerton, and teaching master classes at training programs, theatres, and Universities throughout the world, including the United States, Canada, South Africa, Yugoslavia, Germany, and Belgium.

In addition, during this period of time, he would also be invited by Blasé Bonpane to be part of a delegation of noted scholars, artists, and teachers that traveled to Nica-

---

[196] Book is being co-written by Arthur Lessac and Deborah Kinghorn.

ragua to examine social and humanitarian conditions (late 1980's), and in later years would take part in different delegations that traveled to Russia, China, and South Africa. In 1991, he would receive the Southeastern Theatre Conference's Distinguished Career Award. In 1998, he would be recognized for his Career Achievement as Outstanding Teacher by the Association for Theatre in Higher Education. And in 2002, he would receive the New England Theatre Conference Excellence in Theatre Education Educator of the Year Award.

In 1998, a group of Lessac certified teachers met at Swarthmore College to discuss the future of the Lessac Institute, which led to a new process for certification being discussed, including a board of mentors and master teachers being created to oversee certification and training at official workshops. In 2004, a board of directors was elected to run the Institute,[197] for the purpose of promoting the Lessac work, sharing ideas and research, and ensuring that the teaching of the Lessac work will continue to grow during the next 100 years. In January, 2009, Arthur Lessac gave a workshop on the "Kinesensic Singer" at the 4th annual Lessac Conference, which included a Key Note speech by his son, Michael Lessac, and is currently planning on providing a keynote speech at the Voice and Speech Trainers Association (VASTA) conference, which will be held in the summer of 2009, in New York City.

As his 100th birthday approaches, Ol' Man River keeps rollin' along.

---

[197] Arthur Lessac continues to actively serve as part of the committee of Lessac Master Teachers, and along with Sue Ann Park, holds a position as a lifetime director of the board of the Lessac Institute.

Key Note at 2009 Lessac Institute Conference

Michael Lessac
Marriott Hotel. Carlsbad, California. January 10, 2009.

Michael Lessac has directed at the National Theatre of Yugoslavia, the Guthrie Theatre in Minnesota, the Denver Theatre Centre, the Arena Stage, the Kennedy Centre in Washington D.C., and the Public Theatre in New York City. He wrote and directed the feature film House of Cards, *starring Tommy Lee Jones and Kathleen Turner, and has directed over 200 television shows and sixteen pilots including* Taxi, Newhart, Grace Under Fire, The Drew Carey Show, The Naked Truth, Just Shoot Me, Everyone Loves Raymond, George and Leo, Titus, *and* Lucky *among others. Dr. Lessac is also a singer/songwriter and has recorded an album for Columbia Records called:* Sleep Faster, We Need The Pillow. *He holds a doctorate in developmental psychology, and has taught both theatre and psychology at numerous universities in the USA.*

In 2001, Dr. Lessac took a leave of absence from his Los Angeles TV and Film career to return to the Colonnades Theatre Laboratory he had founded 25 years before in New York City where he had produced and directed over thirty productions and over a ten year period had maintained and trained a company of eighteen actors, three playwrights and four composers. Wanting to create a way of telling the story of the South African Truth and Reconciliation Commission, Dr. Lessac conceived of the notion of doing so through the eyes of the interpreters who had translated the proceedings into the 11 official languages of the country; he developed, wrote, and directed the Truth in Translation Project, *which seeks to create a non-threatening platform, through theatre music, and film, for provoking dialogue.*[1]

On the way down
On the train,
I made some notes
And then started to sequence them
But it soon became clear
It didn't matter

---

[1] Bio taken from *Truth in Translation* webpage.

What order
I put them in.
This always happens to me.
It reminded me a bit of the work you are all involved with.
Which is to say,
Everything relates to everything,
And comes full course upon itself,
No matter where you start
And no matter where you end.
As you know, Dad is going to be 100 years old…
The Chinese would say he is in his 100th year right now.
So I have to tell this joke:
I don't know if any of you have ever heard of the great Lubitski?
OK.
There were these two explorers
That got lost in the wilderness…
Somewhere.
And they were trouping around
With no water
And no food.
And In the distance
They saw these lights
Which as they walked towards
Brought them upon this large tent
With lights.
It looked like a circus.
And right at the top of one of the tents,
There was a large sign
Announcing…
A show staring the great Lubitski.
So they figured they would go in.
"Maybe we will get something to eat."
So they went inside
And they watched a few acts.

Wherein,
All of sudden,
The lights came down.
And out on the stage,
As the lights started to come back up,
They see a small platform
With three small blocks of wood,
Each having an acorn resting on top.
When out comes this man,
Glistening,
Oiled,
Muscled.
VERY well endowed.
Which was obvious,
Because he was stark naked!
And he comes out
Grabs a hold of…
That which was well endowed
And takes it up
And smashes each acorn
Smashing it to bits…
And the place goes wild.
The place goes wild!
And these people are absolutely astonished.

30 years later,
Maybe 40 years later,
The same explorers
Were lost in another place
Wondering around
When they come upon a tent again.
And there they see the same lights
And a sign.
Which said "the Great Lubitski."

And they said,
"It can't be", "It can't be."
Well they go inside,
And indeed,
After a few acts,
The lights come down
And out comes…
NOW,
Forty years later…
Of indeterminate,
But considerable age
The same man
Except on the blocks of wood
Are coconuts and not acorns.
Again,
The great Lubitski
Grabs his fame
And smashes each coconut.
Well these people were absolutely astonished.
Astonished…
So they said
"We have to go back stage."
Back stage,
They come up to the great Lubitski,
And tell him
"You are unbelievable,
We saw you forty years ago,
And here you are,
We don't know how old you are,
But here you are,
You are still doing it,
But we don't understand
Why are they coconuts instead of acorns?"
And the great Lubitski says,

"Well you know, when you get older,
You kind of lose your eyesight."

So that takes care of Dad's body…

Now let's look at the mind.
I grew up around it
And what is clear
Is that it is an unbounded curiosity.
Not hindered by a traditional education.
And I think that is key.
Not hindered by tradition.
As I grew up
And as I went into college,
I became a scientist first,
Before I went into the Theatre,
Dad was always trying to figure out various ways,
To make the Lessac system very scientific.
"Scientific. Scientific…"
He would always say….
And I kept on saying
You know science isn't really what it is cracked up to be…
It is only going to answer certain questions
And not the questions you are asking.
So to ask for that,
Is something like having joy
And asking for money to support it.
You don't need it.

The first thing that I remember….
Was the voice.
What about the voice?
Well,
Somehow or other

Dad decided
That Caruso[2]
And a baby
Had the same voice production.
Well now,
That is a pretty simple idea,
Is it not?
It's just a perception.
It's not genius yet.
It is just a perception.
But think of it…
You all know the depths
Of that very, very
Simple conception.
That somehow
Or other,
This means
That the very best
Was to be found within a two-year-old child.
A lot of things come out of that.

What else do I remember?
He used to say,
Because I hated mosquitoes,
If there was a mosquito
And I was outside,
And I hated them.
I just despised them,
He would say
OK…imagine

---

[2] Enrico Caruso (born Errico Caruso; February 25, 1873 – August 2, 1921) was an Italian tenor. Caruso was also one of the most significant and renowned singers in any genre in both the 19th and 20th Centuries, and one of the most important pioneers of recorded music (http://en.wikipedia.org/wiki/Enrico_Caruso).

There was a fly coming down your cheek,
See if you can imagine it is a bead of sweat.
What happens if you change
The way you think you are perceiving?
I will get to this later,
A little more,
But remember what we think about fear.
Remember what peoples' mentality have changed through fear.
Just think about it.
What is the difference?
If you think there is a fly on your cheek
Or if you think there is a bead of your own sweat on your cheek.
What does fear do?
And keep this in mind too:
(In case I get to it later).
Just keep it in mind the William James question
"Do people run because they are afraid?
Or;
Are they afraid because they run?"
A pretty profound statement.
Then there was always the story,
You all know, the beck and back story
Right?

A man says beck when he means back.
"I'm going beck home"
Don't say beck, say BACK
His teacher says
He says
"I didn't say beck,
I said beck!"
What's happening here?
The ear is entering into the denial of the personality.
Well isn't that interesting

At that time,

What Dad discovered

Cut through

The entire science

Of the understanding of hearing.

The understanding of consciousness.

Because again,

What is the ear?

The ear adapts to something

And told you in a split second

That you're doing one thing,

When you were doing something opposite.

I ask you to put into your minds

"What does this have to do with the concept of denial"?

In a world

Where people will kill people

Because they are in denial

About who they are

And what they should be about…

And so (this) tiny little piece of

Psycho

Biological

Wisdom

Applies to the larger universe

That is responsible for us

Killing people around the world right now

While we eat our breakfast

Without getting sick.

Stretch and strength.

That always impressed me as well.

It is so visible.

Now I understand it is no longer politically correct to say, "stretch."

You are suppose to say, "yawn."[3]

It doesn't matter.

I'll tell you why it doesn't matter....

Because what everybody here is about is process.

Dad will take a word apart

Change the syllables

And

Put it back together

Why?

Because somehow, for him,

The word wasn't good enough in the first place

To interpret and instruct the body.

As you know,

Obviously,

It is in the books,[4]

That this brings us to

That familiar event[5]

That is supposed to incorporate

The Organic instruction to the body

What does that really mean?

Aren't we talking about interpretation?

Obviously you can see

Where I am going...

No....

Seeing through each other's eyes

I suppose I should tell you.

This story I have been telling...

---

[3] In "Potency, or Muscle-Yawn", the sustained extension of potency is a power-potential reach, (wherein) a flexible, muscular strength is supported through a powerful, yawn-stretching body (Lessac 1981:34).

[4] *The Use and Training of the Human Voice*, 3rd Edition, (Lessac 1997) and *Body Wisdom: The Use and Training and Training of the Human Body* (Lessac 1978).

[5] In Lessac Training, body training includes selecting a familiar situation in which the student knows, from experience, and wherein their body behaves naturally and instinctively well (Lessac 1978:22).

With a group of South African Actors
And a magnificent South African Composer
About the truth commission[6]
Is told through the eyes of the translators
—they'd rather be called interpreters—
Who interpreted
For Victim
And
For Perpetrator
So these are people
Who sat between both
And had to
Negotiate real tensions
…that were created from real conflict,
…atrocities
Negotiate people's souls and humors
….not just their words.
"If I am going to translate for you
When you are the perpetrator
And you are the victim
I have to flow both of you through me
Or else I can't translate…
…let alone interpret!!
Well, what about a command
You want to make to the body?
This also requires translation,
Interpretation from mind to body.
Isn't that another fundamental part of the system?[7]

---

[6] *Truth and Translation* (2007), conceived and directed by Michael Lessac, was created in workshop between him, writer Paavo Tom Tammi, actors from the South African Theatre, produced by the Colonnades Theatre Lab (NYC) and Market Theatre (SA) and is based on actual testimonies given during South Africa's Truth and Reconciliation Commission that started in 1996 (http://en.wikipedia.org/wiki/Truth_in_Translation).

Same thing, isn't it...
Interpreting for ourselves
as
For others.

Think about what is happening around the world.
Because we can not see
The world through each other's eyes
We fail to see ourselves at all.
Because I cannot see my enemy.
Because I cannot see myself
Through my enemy's eyes.
I feel uniquely entitled.
Because I am a victim
Because if I am still a victim,
There must be somebody out there
That I am 'entitled' to kill.
I am entitled to remain a victim.
In South Africa,
What happened is
They had a truth commission,
And they discussed the nature of forgiveness
—Which is important, if not yet
...really understood.

But in the word forgiveness
If we really ever figured out what
It actually means
What it says about us
We would find
That this has something to do

---

[7] The Lessac Kinesensic Voice and Body Training (as it is now referred to) includes the epistemological, theoretical, and pedagogical assumptions used during officially sanctioned teaching of the work, such as, but not limited to, the assumption that the body can self-teach itself throughout organic instruction.

With this kind of odd ball way of thinking
That Dad always has had
I have it too….
In a different context
Based in Theatre
And so I see relationships between
What is very specific,
And what is very magical.
What is very scientific?
And very elusive?
Put them together and they become
Very healing.
(*pause*)
And so I'd like you to consider how
It could so easily be
Completely
blown
Into
Other fields
That nobody has even considered;
With so many new possibilities,
How about
—as Desmond Tutu truly believes—
that
Forgiveness
is a "familiar event"

Victim hood and cherished wounds
How many of you have students that come in
And really get pissed off at you because you are changing their voice?
And their voice is horrendous,
And you are trying to help them,
But they're pissed off at you.
That voice is a cherished wound.
Whether it is because a woman grows up with a tiny little voice,
Because that's the way she thought (she had to be) to be pretty,

Or whether it is because somebody else is scared,
Or whatever it is—
Nobody knows the psychology of this
Nobody can pretend to know the psychology of this—
But the point is,
That this is really a cherished wound.

If you will,
And I know there will be some disagreement here
I put this right next to the cherished wounds
Of the Jews.
The right wing Jews in Israel,
Right now
Whose Cherished wounds are such
That it entitles them to be
Able
To kill.

Same thing happened in South Africa.
The same thing happened in the former Yugoslavia.
The same thing happened in Rwanda.
The same things happening in Zimbabwe.
And the same thing happened in this country
For the last 8 years.
So, again,
Denial.
Where did that denial come from?
It is now complex,
But it is still comes from the perceptual truth that
Is in all of us.
On one level the denial of the ear
That says,
I am not going back home.
I am going beck home.
I didn't say beck,
I said beck.

The ear on one hand
And the mind and body follows.
And this is truly perceptual.
It's not political.
The ear said to you,
"You are right.
You are always right.
No matter what you do,
You are right."
My voice is nice
Because I can hear
My voice only
—and I like my voice only—
You are telling me
It's not nice—
That's like telling me
I'm not pretty—
I know I am not pretty
But I know my voice,
Because I can hear it
Without a mirror.
I am terrified of hearing my voice
Through other people's ears…
And we are all terrified
Of seeing the world
Through other people's eyes.

Perception vs. Behavior
When you're talking about habitual awareness,[8]
Fact is you are talking about perception
For example,
If we were to talk about
Humor

---

[8] The "Habitual Awareness Principal" assumes that there is an ongoing, internal sending and receiving system that processes the cues and signals from the performance of any act (Lessac 1978:6).

(Which Dad does in his new book)[9]
He talks about laughter
The experience,
The kinesthetic feel of laughter.
For me,
My point should probably be
"What's funny?"
Before you laugh,
What's funny?
I got to know
What I am laughing at
 I can't do laughter,
Unless I know what's funny.
So, again, it's that same
Sense of
Can I change my sense of perception?
I do an exercise with actors
In every ensemble.
It helps (me) put together an ensemble.
What I'll do is 2 things.
I'll take people and I will sit them in front of each other,
And let them look at each other's face
Now, I can look at your face and I can make,
As a make up artist
Or as a person
Your face look like anything I decide
I want it to
Look like.
I wanted my actors to be able to do the unthinkable?
If I had to kill somebody on stage
As a actor
I wanted them to look, as they had to look to justify
My wanting to kill them.

---

[9] Arthur Lessac and Deborah Kinghorn are currently co-writing a new book on three additional energies and their impact on health and humaneness.

I need to create that threat perceptually.
I didn't want them to have to generate all the inner stuff
And just kill whatever actor comes in front of them.
I want them to feel justified.
So what I asked them to do was to begin to take this face
And shift it.
How would I make up your face to make you play Iago?[10]
Where is the evil?
Where is the Jealousy?
If I wanted to make you look like a six year old,
What do I have to do to see your face in my mind look like a six year old?
This change of perception actually happens.
And these actors can begin to see things
Where they actually see a new different person
In each other's face.
And I will take them across
From baby…
To 80 years old.
From the worst person in the world…
To the most beautiful person in the world.
Try it some day.
Somebody comes up to you,
Some old bitch,
Or some crotchety old guy comes up to you in a store,
Or that person in the store treats you like a piece of shit,
Take a look at their face
And try and to see what they look like when they were six years old.
But really try.
Don't say
I'm going to do an acting exercise.
It's not an acting exercise,

---

[10] Iago is an antagonist to Shakespeare's Othello.

It's a perceptual exercise.
It's a powerful thing,
And my feeling is
That you can change people's opinion about perceptions
Before you can change their opinions.
You have to change their perceptions
Before you change their emotions.
Again, it seems to me
That this is very much like the work you are doing.

So, it is a question of denial or ignorance
In every country,
When atrocities occur
Everybody will say:
"I didn't know!"
I didn't know??
That is bullshit!
They didn't want to know
That's it
Clear
Absolutely
That's what it is
They didn't want to know!
Because the information was out there.
You don't see
It's just there
Denial for yourself
Denial for your voice
Denial about what you sound like
Denial about who you are
(*Pause*)
It's all the same.
What is it about the stretch?
Or the yawn?

The stretch because
That is what Dad always use to do
When he was showing off
When He could push 300…
200…
300-pound men off with ease[11]
The push wouldn't do it.
Why?
Let me just put it into my context
It is there because the concept of push
Has resistance to it
Therefore
If you decide everything is going to go wrong
You might start creating
The behavior in yourself.
That will justify
This honest prediction.
Now I'm not talking about "betting" psychology
Because "Betting" psychology says,
"I am going to lose
Cause it feels so good to win"
But I'm talking about that other side of it
When you feel something in yourself
"I don't have a voice."
"I'm not very big."
"I'm not very important."
"So my voice is very very…(*in whisper voice*)"
There is a denial in there
And you are taking advantage of yourself
And so when people come to you
And you train them

---

[11] Arthur Lessac, who weighed at best a little under 135 lbs, would demonstrate the power of the "yawn" in his workshops by lifting (sustaining in mid air) significantly larger men, who often weighed around 300 lbs or more, and were asked to place their whole body on top of him, while he lay on the floor.

And you train them through kinesthesia
You overcome it
Because
There is distraction…
Distraction is a form of perception that keeps you alive.

Which brings me to the familiar event
What is all that about?
That familiar event?
Again, I don't know what the Lessac political correctness
Is about that right now,
I've been with Dad
When he first started talking about it:
You smell a flower
I mean, that is practically the logo of this group
You smell a flower,
And you want to learn from that
HOW TO BREATHE
So he takes this one image
And puts it together
Into a physical shape;
But at the same time,
What you are thinking about,
If you are doing it right;
You are really trying to smell something.
You are trying to smell the flower.
If you are doing it wrong,
You are imitating it,
And its not going to happen anyhow.
The olfactory sense is distraction
Just as "stretch"
Is a distraction
From
"Oh, I can't lift this

How can I possibly lift this?
Look at my size, look at this
I can't possibly lift this
Oh, I can stretch it
Well, ok, I'll try that
I'll try it."
(Pause)
Because it doesn't seem to be impossible
(Pause)
This goes all the way into the whole
Psychology and philosophy of education
Because,
If you can keep your self
Distracted long enough,
You can get a lot done.
I always say to my actors
If you can stay off balance
You're going to be interesting,
But as soon as you absolutely know
What the hell you are doing,
You're a bloody bore;
And I have to figure out a way
To throw you off balance again.
…
Directing is that very subtle thing:
How do you throw somebody off balance?
So they become themselves,
Because the very way they don't become themselves
Is because they think through
What they should be,
And once they think through
What they should be,
They get boring.
Well, again,

That is why Dad has attacked
The intellectual side of everything
Saying that people think that real thinking
Is when
People make opinions through the intellect.
The fact is
They only make pretend opinions
Out of the intellect.
They don't make real opinions out of the intellect,
They make real opinions out of perception….
"You look wrong."
"I'm going to have you out of here."
"Your black, uh uh,
It probably comes off."
You can't imagine what goes on….
We had Africans coming to Southern Serbia
They had never seen a black person before
You have never seen peoples so startled in their life
In their life!!!
Again, perception….

Habits
Habitual awareness, habits
We don't want habits
We don't want unthinking habits
We don't want un-rare habits
We know that in terms of behavior
You don't play tennis by habit
We don't do anything by habit
Have we thought of behavioral habit?
Have we thought of emotional habit?
Thought of perceptual habit?
If every time I see something strange
It causes fear in me,

What is that all about?
If you have the curiosity,
Maybe you would like to consider this as
A palpable energy
(Pause)
When we search for truth,
What are we searching for?
When we search for forgiveness,
What are we searching for?
Are we perceptually curious enough to
Do that job?
There was this man in South Africa
Albie Sachs,
A man who lived through an Apartheid car bomb.
Lost an arm and an eye and almost died.
We talked to him one night when we were researching
Truth in Translation:
What's the truth?
"Here we have a truth commission
And we are giving amnesty to people, if they tell the whole truth
Because we want the truth
The truth is more important to us
Then killing the person who did what they did to my son"
The truth is more important.
Once you get into that
You tend to get into forgiveness
(Sighs)
Desmond Tutu
If I was to pin him on this,
And we talked a lot,[12]
But if I were pin him on this,
Desmond Tutu would say:

---

[12] Michael Lessac interviewed, over a two-year period, various political civic, and religious, leaders of South Africa as research for the pre-production and development of his play, *Truth in Translation*.

"To him, forgiveness is where he rests"

For him, "forgiveness comes first"

Then we'll try and figure it out."

(Pause)

That's a hard one to take

Isn't it?

It's impossible!

But it's not.

Maybe we have to redefine the word.

Maybe its just another one of those words that just needs to be

Twisted, Turned, Changed….

Interpreted, told in story, to be

Understood.

Maybe I forgive because I don't want to be a victim anymore

Maybe I have to forgive me because the pain within me is so great

I just have to remove the pain.

(Pause)

I talked to an Irishman in Belfast[13]

Who forgave the people who killed his son.

We talked for a long while

And he said

"I gotta tell you something:

I did forgive.

I forgave because of what Tutu said

My priest said

Rabbi said

I forgave for all the right reasons

And I felt good,

But,

Every time I would walk on the beach

---

[13] While on international tour of the play *Truth in Translation*, Michael Lessac and company participate in interactive workshops to bring people from diverse backgrounds and histories together. To date, his company has performed and completed workshops with culturally diverse populations in Bosnia, Croatia, Serbia, Zimbabwe, Northern Ireland, Scotland, Sweden, and the United States (http://www.truthintranslation.org).

And hear a child's laughter
I hated myself
What right
Did I have to forgive
The killer of my son?"
His son,
Who is his ancestor now.
These are all
Part of a process.
It's not about being right or wrong
It's about process
Just as Albie Sachs asked:
"What is the truth that the truth commission is going after?"
What is the truth about the human body
That you are going after?
And what is the truth about acting
That I am going after?
What is the truth about humor
That cuts through
…so much ego
…and denial
…and entitlement
…and bad acting?
What is that truth
About forgiveness?
Why do we hate academic papers?
Why do we hate academics?
Because they write these academic truths
About non-academic events.

That's why
Albie Sachs called Truth Commission truth,
"Dialogic truth,"
Truth that floats when all stories have been told
When everyone has told their story:

"It's not legal truth
It's not objective truth
It's not subjective truth"
It's the truth that floats
Coming out of stories
That had to be told.
If you follow science
In the last 20 years
You realize that the physics
That is alive in the world right now
No longer has the same structure
Of truth
That people thought science had
20, 30, 40 years ago.
It's beginning to blend with things
That were once the most unscientific things in the world
When early science carried ego behind its ear
There's a book out there that I recommend that everyone read:
The brain that changes itself[14]
For the last 50 years,
Research has been out there showing that
The brain is capable of change beyond our dreams.
If you are blind…
I can put a camera on your shoulder;
Put a piece of metal on your back,
Have that camera translate the visual image
Into a touch image on your back…
And you will be able to do this
(Gestures…grabs for a glass and catches it)
Are you seeing?
I don't know.
(Pause)

---

[14] Doldge, Norman. 1997. *The Brain that Changes Itself: Stories of Personal Triumph from the Frontiers of Brain Science.* New York: Penguin Books.

Do you know The Stanley Milgram Experiment?[15]

Again, I am trying to go

From pure perception to

What you could be teaching

In terms of the body and the voice

And how this translates into the world of horror

And

Evil that we find ourselves in right now

And how people are able to accept evil

On a level that would be inconceivable

If you were human

Just inconceivable to do that!

What this says is

The brain can re-map itself

For good or for evil

At any time in (its own) development

It is not a thing that only happens between the age of 1 and 7[16]

The brain is capable of re-mapping itself

You can change the way people perceive

I can put a pair of glasses on you

Turn the world upside down

And first,

You are going to trip over everything

But then you won't…

I can change the world from right to left

To get this far you'll reach like this *(Gestures in wrong direction)*

Then an hour later, you'll reach like this *(Gestures in right direction)*

If I take the glasses off,

You'll reach like that again

What is all that about?

---

[15] Controversy surrounded Stanley Milgram for much of his professional life as a result of a series of experiments on obedience to authority, which he conducted at Yale University in 1961-1962 (http://www.stanleymilgram.com/milgram.php).

[16] Cognitive psychology and education theorists argue that significant socio-emotional development is formed during years 1-7, as supported by the research of Sigmund Freud and Eric Erikson.

Let me shift you again,
There was an experiment done by Solomon Ashe[17]
Where you walk into this room
There are 30 people in the room
You are the only subject
There are 3 lines on the wall
One this big *(Gestures)*
One this big *(Gestures)*
And one this big *(Gestures)*
And they say,
Which line is the biggest?
And all 30 people say
This one *(points to a smaller line)*
And the person
Goes crazy
And finally says
"You may be right
Hold on
You may by right,
Yep,
I think you are right
I agree"
There were close to 60% of the subjects that did that
OK
Smash cut to
A room
A person comes into this room
I have a white coat on
I come over to you
And I say

---

[17] Experiments led by Solomon Asch asked groups of students to participate in a "vision test." In reality, all but one of the participants were confederates of the experimenter, and the study was really about how the remaining student would react to the confederates' behavior (http://en.wikipedia.org/wiki/Asch_conformity_experiments).

"I want you to sit over there

And in that booth over there is a man

Who has got to answer questions,

And every time he gets a question wrong

I want you to push that button

And that will shock him.

Every time you shock him

That shock's going to go up

And there's the meter

Over there

It is a little shock

You felt that

You stuck your hand under there

That's not too bad

That's ok

It's only going to hurt somebody

If you are a 100 years old"

Not dad,

But somebody else

Here, on the wall, the speaker was dead silent—dead silence

Same percentage of people

Who acquiesced and said that this short line on the wall was big

Shocked these people to "death"!

Then had to be talked down

Almost had a nervous break down.

So you ask yourself

How do you get one-half of Rwanda

Macheting the heads off

Of the other half of Rwanda[18]

How do you get

---

[18] The Rwandan Genocide was the 1994 mass killing of hundreds of thousands of Rwanda's Tutsis by Hutu militia. Over the course of approximately 100 days, from the assassination of Juvénal Habyarimana on 6 April up until mid July, at least 500,000 people were killed. Most estimates indicate a death toll between 800,000 and 1,000,000 (http://en.wikipedia.org/wiki/Rwandan_Genocide).

One half of Germany

Putting 6 million people[19]…

How do you get

Israel claiming that there was no genocide with the Armenians[20]

Why?

(Pause)

Because somehow or other

It was important to them to hold on to their holocaust

Identity had become victim hood

Former Yugoslavs have it

The Serbs have it

Croatians have it

And we Americans have it,

(Pause)

We saw all of this….

There is a saying in South Africa:
"UBUNTU"

It means

"I am because you are."

Very simple

A basic microcosm of coming full circle.

A basic …..

Dad and I took divergent paths in what we did in our lives

I took a group of actors in South Africa

To the rest of the world

---

[19] Approximately six million European Jews were killed during World War II, as part of a program of deliberate extermination planned and executed by the National Socialist German Workers' Party (Nazi) regime in Germany led by Adolph Hitler (http://en.wikipedia.org/wiki/The_Holocaust).

[20] Israel's state policy of Armenian Genocide denial, and its fevered efforts to coerce American politicians to back off bringing HR 106 to a U.S. Senate vote, prompted many of Israel's Armenian citizens—roughly 5,000 Christians and 20,000 Jews—to take to the streets in protest (http://www.bloggernews.net/111338).

And these actors
Portrayed translators
Who were translating for the truth commission
And they went from country to country…
Performing for people who were either still killing each other,
Killed each other very recently,
Or were going to kill each other tomorrow
People who still think they hate each other
They hate the religions
They hate the nationalities
Some are even changing their historic common language
As a form of ethnic cleansing
To be different
They were going back to apartheid
We took our show to these people
And we thought some places would like us,
But some people were going to hate us.
Yugoslavia is going to hate us
Flint Michigan was going to hate us.
But they didn't
They saw themselves in the show
As we had exposed ourselves within the show
They often were angry at what we were trying to say
The stage was adding humor to atrocity, music to pain and was creating absurdity out of killing and it was chaos
And was making people crazy,
And we were not portraying killers
Or victims of extreme atrocity
But the ones who interpreted for killers and victims.
We portrayed people who could not turn away
On that stage were
7 tribes
3 white tribes
4, sometimes 5 black tribes

'colored' tribes'
All arguing with each other
In collaboration
But they are up there
They got a reason to be up there.
(Pause)
Why did these audiences from
All over the world
Talk to us?
Because we are nobody…
We are not authorities
We're not people
Who run countries
We're not psychologists
I am, but I hid it,
You know,
We were not "important"
We were a platform where…
If they don't want to talk to us about something important right now,
They'll say
"Why did you have to make a joke?"
"Why do you make a joke,
When we are talking about people being killed?
Or tortured?"
"Why did you play beautiful music,
With those most horror ridden lyrics?"
Hugh Masekela[21]
Wrote the most beautiful music in the world
And took the testimony from the tortured
…from the victims

---

[21] Hugh Masekela is a world renowned jazz composer and musician, and arguably South Africa's most distinguished musician, who has recorded such hits as "Up, Up and Away," "Grazin' in the Grass," and "Bring Him Back Hom*e,"* which became an anthem for the movement to free Nelson Mandela in 1987 (http://www.truthintranslation.org/index.php/v2/masekela/).

And he made songs out of it
And they were gorgeous,
But now you are having 2 things happening at once
It doesn't make sense
Because it is not objective, it is not subjective, it is not legal….
But it floats

Full circle
…Well, I think when you try and change somebody's voice
And they think they are somebody…
I mean, how many of you have had
Any experience where you may have deepened the voice
Of a very pretty, cute girl?
You may well get resistance,
But to understand that that resistance
Is not truly emotional,
It's perceptual.
Well, it's that same ear
That said,
"Beck, Back"
That same ear is saying,
"Pretty,"
He wants to make me butch
Right,
That's what you need to get into—
Is to see,
Once again,
Through the other people's eyes
Just like you as teachers,
See each other,
I have to see actors
Through their eyes.
(Pause)

So, what else am I talking about?
The re-mapping of the brain thing
Actually, that is what you are doing.
And now there is science to back you.
The science is hard
Science
It's got to do with electrodes,
Microelectrodes in the brain:
Well, I can see the brain shift
By a different use of these two fingers *(gestures)*
If one finger is cut off,
And I bind the stump to the other finger,
This finger will start reading the brain
Like one finger.
Touch this side,
It will feel to them
Like the side of both
Of one finger,
Autism was considered
Irreversible
"Can not be cured…."
I once said to a psychologist
"Well, what if somebody has autism
And then they don't have autism?"
And then that psychologist said to me,
He was the biggest person in the field,
He said,
"Then it wasn't autism"
It was defined by not being able to be cured.
What does that mean?
That means
That you are defined by an academic.
Think of the cultural things we were talking about,
"You are defined"
"You are a victim"

"You are defined"
"I kill anything that is not a victim"
"I kill anything that is going to come after me"
What about that perception?
Can I see the six year old in that monster that is coming after me?

(*Pause*)
I am just going to touch on a few things
That I really wanted to say
That maybe someday we can all talk about:
Again, can forgiveness become an organic instruction?
Can it become a familiar event?
Is reconciliation that impossible?
A man said to me,
A very wealthy,
Seemingly silly man,
Who I grew to respect tremendously
Said to me
"Oh, forgiveness
You know what that is?"
He was a very rich man
"You know what that is?
It is a deal,
It is a deal,
I forgive you,
You forgive me.
That's a deal
We both got to walk away with something good
Or else its not going to last."
That strange mentality
In a man who we would
—under normal circumstances—
Dismiss
Because he is the least artistic person
He is a businessman,

He makes money
And that is what he does.
But somehow or other,
This man
Had a sensitivity
Within his own money making,
Which, I think just indicates
What happened in South Africa;
That it is possible
For men,
Whose family
Has killed another group of people for 400 years
To begin to say:
"Wait a minute
This mother,
She is the only one here
Who looks at me.
She looks like my mother
She is the only one here
Who has been nice to me.
And we have killed her whole family
And she was there to decide
If she was going to forgive him or not."

So,

Small instances
Of miraculous humanity
Happened
Within something like this
And those small incidents
Are parts of a process,
Because somebody told these stories,

Not because somebody is a better person
Than another person
Or more talented than another person,
Because people told their stories
To each other.
Desmond Tutu said to me,
He really changed me,
Because I talked to him
As the sensitive wise ass Jew
From the streets of New York;
That got the shit kicked out of him
Just about every day he walked the streets,
"Forgiveness wasn't in my mentality,
How can I hurt them?"
That was what I wanted.
So I could be strong enough
I could be proud enough to say
"They didn't get me this time
I got them."
And Tutu listened to me
And said to me,
"You don't understand something,
You look at me
With my purple robes
And you say
I want you to consider forgiveness
Because I believe all people are basically good.
That's not the case at all
I am asking you to consider forgiveness
Because all people are capable of the worst possible atrocities
And the worst horrors in the world
Including you and me
That's why you have to consider forgiveness."

Because God does not make trash.
…there is a little perceptual hook here
That could be turned
There is some hope
And that hope comes out of process
Not out of opinion.

To interpret,
Again, I think the same thing happens in the work here
To interpret well, you have to **drop your mask**
Somebody, once asked me,[22]
"What do I want them to walk away with?"
I want them to walk away with this following notion
If you drop your mask
You will not die.
That's all
If you drop that frame,
That denial
That you got,
Even of yourself,
You will not disappear.
"Got to be strong"
"We don't"
"Yes you do"
You don't have to really be strong
The way you think you have to be strong
"I got to shoot.
Somebody betrays me
I got to shoot them,
Or else I am a wimp."
(Sighs) Yea,
If you really want to think that way

---

[22] After watching the play *Truth in Translation*.

But a perceptual change
Can change it.
Lots of things can help the change
An actor's sense of humor
…an actor for me is not an actor without
A sense of humor.
Oh well…
I don't even know what I was going to end up with,
Except, I will tell you this
I wish for all of you
That when you are a 100
That in one way or another
That you can smash coconuts.

Era Two: Teacher Training

Sean Turner

The following oral histories were based on interviews with Master Lessac Teachers Sue Ann Park, Richard Cuyler, Saundra Cuyler, Nancy Krebs, Deborah Kinghorn, and Barry Kur.

Barry Kur, Nancy Krebs, and Deborah Kinghorn responded to the initial five open questions (identified in the previous introduction) through written responses and were provided additional follow up questions specific to their answers. Portions of earlier interviews with Deborah Kinghorn (*Lessac Newsletter* October 2005) and Sue Ann Park (*Lessac Newsletter* January 2009) were inserted within both interviews. Sue Ann Park as well as Richard and Saundra Cuyler were interviewed at the 2009 Lessac Institute Conference held January 8-11 in Carlsbad, California and followed up with revisions and edits to their original transcriptions.

Sue Ann Park

Sue Ann Park was the recipient of the American Theatre Higher Education Association (ATHE) Career Achievement Award for Academic Theatre in 2006; at that time she was described as "a dedicated and talented performer, teacher, mentor, and advocate for theatre training and the arts for over fifty years."[1] Professor Park holds an M.F.A. in acting from the Yale School of Drama and studied at the Shakespeare Institute at Stratford-Upon-Avon in the United Kingdom in her early career. Professor Park was Supervisor of Voice and Speech at The Goodman School of Drama at the Art Institute of Chicago. After a number of years of summers of study with Arthur Lessac, she became the first Lessac Master Teacher, and in 1971 joined Arthur at the State University of New York at Binghamton, where she taught until she retired as Professor Emeritus in 1988. Still active today, Professor Park is a member of the Board of the Lessac Institute, where she is Senior Master Teacher, Director of Training, and continues to train Master Teachers and oversee the faculty of the Lessac summer intensives. In 1996, she contributed a chapter to the book Vocal Visions, and she is currently developing the official Lessac Teacher Training Manual.

Describe the context in which you were introduced to Lessac training.

During 1961, I was a Voice teacher at The Goodman School of Drama[2] at the Art Institute of Chicago (The Goodman) when its director Dr. John Reich[3] handed me a copy of *The Use and Training of the Human Voice*[4] and said: "This voice text was written by a friend of mine. See what you think of it."

---

[1] Excerpts taken from introduction given to Sue Ann Park at 2006 ATHE award presentation of the *Career Achievement Award for Academic Theatre*.

[2] The Goodman School of Drama at the Art Institute of Chicago was founded in 1925 in Chicago, Illinois, and became part of DePaul University in 1978 and was renamed The Theatre School at DePaul University in 1982 (http://en.wikipedia.org/wiki/Goodman_School_of_Drama).

[3] At the end of the 1950s, the Goodman School of Drama was losing money and watching its audience base erode. Upon Dr. Maurice Gnesin's death in 1957, the Art Institute conducted a national search to replace him and hired Dr. John Reich as the new head of the Art Institute's Department of Drama. Reich was given wide-ranging power to rebuild the School and set as a long-term goal the return of a professional repertory company (http://www.goodmantheatre.org/About/History/Index.aspx).

[4] The 1st edition of *The Use and Training of the Human Voice* (1960) was privately published by Arthur Lessac.

I had just been assigned to teach three sections of first-year acting students in the Fall, which was a significant assignment to be given, as our second and third year students had a heavy performance schedule and in my judgment many of their voices were worse, some even damaged, at the end of three year's traditional voice work (which included mostly ear-training, IPA, rote drill, imitation, etc).

Upon reading the text, I found that I was completely open to Lessac's unique Kine-sensic training. That was understandable, since I really had little to compare it to. Although I had a BS degree from Syracuse University in Speech and Drama (1941) and an MFA in Acting from The Yale School of Drama (1952), I had not had comprehensive voice, speech or body training at either school,[5] (which was since remedied, of course).

Upon exploring Arthur's text, I was gripped by the training's reliance on internal sensations (muscular, vibratory or tactile) instead of ear training, to produce, identify, and evaluate the quality of every sound. It also provided voice training for both speech and singing by treating both as music. Three benefits stood out immediately for me: First, I was fascinated to find how pleasurable and easy articulation and diction became when the whole body was recognized as a musical Instrument.

Can you elaborate on this a little further? What do you mean by the whole body being recognized as a musical instrument?

In the Lessac work, we recognize the *human voice* as a solo instrument accompanied by the symphonic consonant orchestra. Every consonant instrument has its own qualities of melody, rhythms, and sustained tonal colors. Thus *playing* the consonants guarantees intelligibility, meaning, and variety and contrast without our having to be careful in using them. This musical metaphor doesn't include trying to imitate the actual sound of an *N* violin, or a *TH* clarinet, or a *D* kettle drum, nor is it an external image intended to change the speech and behavior, when voice coaching: "Do that line as if you are doing a waltz."

---

[5] Sue Ann notes that at Yale (1949-1952), "we had only four weeks of International Phonetics in our third year acting class."

The musical metaphor resonated for me, almost immediately, probably as a result of Connie Welsh's[6] suggestion that "The *N, M,* and *NG* are a golden chain of resonance on which the other jewels of other sounds are strung." I had loved feeling the energy in the humming vibration of those three consonants but had never realized that the same energy and music were available in six other consonants—*V, Z, ZH, L, TH.* That was a strong, tantalizing hook into the work for me. A brief example:

"If 'twere done when tis done, then 'twere well it were done quickly".

Secondly, I thought I understood Lessac's concept that the Structural Vocal NRG could produce desirable English vowels, whether familiar or uncomfortably unfamiliar, with ease, good voice quality, and no force. The fact that Structural Vocal NRG also eliminates the harsh quality of the American "rhotic" or pre-consonantal "R," and synergistically makes both Consonant NRG and Tonal Vocal NRG work better in providing effortless projection, also resonated with me. In their turn, each vocal NRG makes the other two work even better. Each has its own special synergistic benefits.

Finally, and most important to me, it seemed as if the Lessac text provided training that was aesthetic, democratic, non-elitist, non-regional, non-imitative, and based on the healthful use of the voice without effort or conscious use of breath. From the very beginning, I thought it possible that these attributes might well eliminate the students' resistance, fear, and the feeling that one's own personal speech, and therefore one's own self, was "not good enough." I knew I was not the only one who had been traumatized at being told to change some of my Pennsylvania R's and eliminate others entirely.

That summer [1961], I used what I then understood of the Lessac text for some of my private students and had encouraging success with the work. As a result, I mailed Arthur a nine page, embarrassingly presumptuous response including many questions.[7]

Was this then when you began to work with Arthur Lessac?
Well, in August [1961], I told Dr. Reich I wanted to adopt Lessac's Kinesensic work for The Goodman's first year voice training. He agreed and made it possible for

---

[6] Taught at Yale University.
[7] Arthur had put a request for comments within the first edition of his text (1960).

me to have one interview with Arthur in New York City.[8] There Arthur tested my voice and answered my questions for six hours. Finally, at one o'clock in the morning, Arthur said he thought I could go ahead with learning and teaching the work from his text. The best advice he ever gave during that interview was: "If you will do the sensory work with integrity, the work will continually teach you how to expand its use and how to teach it more effectively."

Starting in September [of 1961] and for the next ten years, I gradually experienced how the training provided such a continual discovery. As Supervisor of Voice and Speech, I had the luxury of teaching three sections of first year actors, for six hours a week, for two semesters. From then on I never came across a vocal problem that Lessac training couldn't solve or that Arthur couldn't teach me[9] how to solve with the Lessac work. And after almost fifty years of teaching it, for my personal use, as a professional actor, and director, vocal coach and sometime therapist, Lessac training is still endlessly interesting and surprising.

I remember that you used to tell the story (at the Intensives) of how you received a lot of your training with the work over the phone. Was this around the time that this type of training started? If so, can you elaborate a little more on what this type of training entailed?

Yes, Arthur didn't leave me floundering that first year. He sent me instructions via letters, phone, and a even a few times on demonstration tapes,[10] very reluctantly, for fear that by listening to them I might continue to rely on ear-training and not get to the heart of the sensory/ kinesensic work.

During this time, long distance calls were very expensive. Many people would set kitchen timers when they called their college children. The Goodman allowed me only one long-distance call a month, at 11pm Chicago time, midnight for Arthur in NYC. I

---

[8] In August 1961, Sue Ann went to visit Arthur at his 72nd Street Studios.
[9] Sue Ann also noted in a follow up E-mail that she would continue to go to NYC to study with Arthur during the 1960's, including sometimes together with Jack Jones, who she noted was a fine actor from the Mummer's Theatre in Oklahoma City and eventually would be hired at The Goodman, where he remained after she left for SUNY. "Some years later he was murdered in the parking lot behind the Dallas Theater Center."
[10] Sue Ann reports that there were demonstration tapes of the Calls.

had all my questions written down to save time. He would answer a month's worth of questions as well as work on my voice. He also came to Chicago in the Spring [1962] and taught all my classes so that I could observe him.

In those early years, all my students knew I was new to the training. I learned that it was safe for me to answer a question with: "I don't know; I'll work on it and get back to you" or "I'll ask Arthur when I phone him." The student actors enjoyed their classes and improved. After two years we began getting praise, instead of pans, in the reviews of our Children's productions; and after three years, we started to receive more praise for our Main Stage productions.

As you reflect on this period of learning, teaching, and discovery, what are some of the more significant events that took place during this time?
First, around 1963, before Arthur was chosen to teach Voice for the new Lincoln Center Acting Company, Robert Whitehead, Bobby Lewis, and Elia Kazan were going around the country visiting many Theatre schools looking for a Voice teacher. After I did the first demonstration of the Lessac training for them with my students, they had Arthur come to The Goodman and further demonstrate his work with our students. That, in part, contributed to his being chosen as voice trainer for the Lincoln Center Acting Company, a group that included Faye Dunaway and Martin Sheen.

Second, during the first three years, I began to have revelatory moments within my classes that confirmed Arthur's assurance to me that if I worked well with the work, the work would teach me. For example, I remember one time when I was using optimal Structural NRG myself while instructing my students of that Vocal NRG in sentences, I said to the class: "Now all of you explore that sentence." Suddenly, as I raised my pitch for emphasis and gave optimal mouth/buccal space to the vowel in *ALL*, I felt for the first time how the *ping* or *ring*[11] in our Call Tonal NRG is used for emphasis in conversational speech. While this was just one example, over the years, I have had many similar moments where the work has taught me the wide-ranging uses

---

[11] The subjective sensory experience of the F3-F5 formant cluster that is characteristic of the actor's formant (also sometimes referred to as the speaker's formant) and singer's formant is sometimes referred to as a "ping" or a "ring". See, for example, "Acoustical Perspectives on the Lessac Work" elsewhere in this book.

of kinesensics and confirmed Arthur's earlier assurance to me *that if I worked well with the work, the work would teach me.*

Third, before I moved to SUNY Binghamton, I taught one of our first year Acting Classes. We would rehearse Classic plays, rotating the actors so that each got to play some scenes in a leading role and some scenes in supporting roles. Dean Charles McGaw[12] wanted to face our first year actors with the demands that would be made on them in the future. After four weeks, the plays were performed for our faculty. It turned out to be great motivator for students in the Voice classes.

It was during these acting classes that I began to understand how Vocal Exploration could be an incredible innovation for directing and I eventually found that with experienced actors, we could use their Lessac Vocal NRGs for text explorations as the basis for play rehearsal. For example, when directing my final play, *The Prodigal,*[13] the actors memorized ten pages daily, then explored each French Scene[14] three times using each Vocal NRG in sequence. This gave actors many different interpretations and behaviors to use while rehearsing. The results were so unusual and exciting that Arthur came to Chicago to see first the performance of my using his work within the rehearsal process.

Fourth, Dorothy Mennen[15] attended my panel presentation of the training at an old ATA convention in Chicago [1964], and we met to talk about the Lessac work. Later, after Dorothy completed two six-week Summer Intensives, she founded the first Voice Project in the ATA, and after it dissolved, formed the Voice Speech Trainers' Association (VASTA). Lessac Trainers are fortunate and very grateful that her support of the Lessac work has been strong and steadfast all through the years.

---

[12] Dr. Charles McGaw was Dean of the Goodman School of Drama at the Art Institute of Chicago and wrote the book *Acting is Believing*. After his death, Larry D. Clark re-wrote the book in 1992.

[13] *The Prodigal,* by Jack Richardson was produced at The Goodman Theatre. Sue Ann also notes that she would go on to use the Lessac work while directing 7 other plays at SUNY at Binghamton including *The Lady's not for Burning* by Christopher Fry, *Crime on Goat Island* by Uto Betti, *Under Milkwood*, by Dylan Thomas, and *Good Woman of Setzuan* by Bertolt Brecht.

[14] Sue Ann notes that she is using the term French Scene to mean the variable amount of time that one set of actors is on stage. "When a new person enters or someone leaves, a new French scene starts. Moileré's plays are divided that way. When I was younger, rehearsals were sometimes scheduled that way."

[15] Dorothy Runk Mennen created the voice curriculum at Purdue University where she taught until 1985. She organized the Voice and Speech Project for the American Theatre Association in 1968, and in 1986 helped to found the Voice and Speech Teachers Association (VASTA) (http://www.vasta.org/resources/vegac/mennengrant.html).

Fifth, in 1967, as Arthur published the 2nd Edition of the Voice Book, I had found we needed two new consonant instruments, the *DL* and the *TL* (as in ladle and little) and suggested calling them Woodblock Clicks. We also needed the addition of the Neutral vowels and Neutral diphthongs, as in: put, pit, pet, putt and poor, pier, pear, pour.

In what ways have you applied or incorporated Lessac work into what you do for a living?

On first being interviewed for a position at The Goodman, Dr. Reich commented that I was a "generalist" in training and experience; that I needed to be "specialist." By handing me Arthur's voice book, he turned me into a Lessac specialist. Teaching the Training has been my main work for forty-five years. Occasionally, as a vocal coach for actors who have not had Lessac Training, I have used the IPA. Otherwise, I found that Lessac work would solve every problem I encountered.

As a director at SUNY at Binghamton, I was always able to cast acting majors who had all or some amount of the basic Lessac Voice and/or Body training so they would have guided experience of the work in rehearsal and performance. This was a liberating experience for the actors and for me, as we would often do days of Voice and Body explorations on each memorized scene without my giving any comments or instructions, aside from reminding them to stay with the particular combination of NRG's they were using at the time. Although I didn't comment or give instructions during these explorations, I would take notes on which NRG's were evoking fresh voice and body characterizations, relationships and even blocking.

I have directed eight productions using this process, including for some doing the explorations in dialects, while in others doing the explorations to have actors develop more than one character. As a result, I have found that explorations are also an efficient way to learn lines without getting into *set* line readings before you have explored the whole play.

My favorite was my production of *Under Milk Wood*,[16] where we had 11 days of explorations, enabling twelve actors to develop six different characters each. In some instances we even did explorations in costume with valuable results.

---

[16] *Under Milk Wood* is a play for radio by Dylan Thomas, later adapted for the stage. A film version, *Under Milk Wood* directed by Andrew Sinclair, was released in 1972 (http://en.wikipedia.org/wiki/Under_Milk_Wood).

I remember one night while I was working on the seaman's bar scene,[17] elsewhere on set, the girls, on their own, were creating dressing tables by draping their scarves over their high stools and primping in imaginary mirrors. They were preparing a scene for the next cue:

> *"...and in their rooms the young girls were*
> *in their rooms, preparing for the...Dance of life"*

The next moment another young girl, seducing the dreaming "no-good-boyo" in his boat, had made her shawl into a negligee, then turned around again and quickly turned front again with her shawl turned into a Geisha's Kimono!

I, too, have always used the combined Voice and Body Text Explorations as an actor, and in order to find a fresh voice and character for well-known roles and performances. My training with the Lessac work started at the Goodman, where I taught twenty-two hours a week for ten years and I learned many things about the work from teaching and working with Arthur. However, I didn't really know about subtext specific explorations[18] until I got to SUNY Binghamton. There I was finally able to understand how by breaking personal speech patterns they connect actors to their inner emotional and physical experiencing system, and the subtext life of the character.

What do you mean by the word "pattern," and can you elaborate more on how "patterns" are perceived within Lessac training?

Well, Arthur often refers to undesirable "habit-patterns" as any that is repeated over and over again and makes a pattern in the same way as forming a habit-pattern makes a pattern that we repeat involuntarily. If we are behaving in a patterned way completely and involuntarily we feel secure and in control; however, it also means we have foregone an aware control over our actions and find it hard, frightening, or impossible to change. To "create" is to make or bring into existence something new, whether it is in our personal or professional lives.

---

[17] "…The set went up in steps with high bar stools on each of the platforms...that each represented a house."
[18] Specific Explorations work by taking the time on each NRG-identified, stressed word, to feel its quality—its identifying sensation…muscular, vibratory or tactile, beyond what feels habitually comfortable and until one is experiencing its most refined musical quality. You experience an entirely new behavior.

My own view is that some people are performers and are very successful artists while using the same patterned behavior over and over, while great actors are people who are able to portray characters that are radically different from their own recognizable modes of behavior. For example, Olivier[19] is said to have romped in a crazy fashion all over the rehearsal hall on the first few days of a new production to break out of his former characters' behavior. He also said that an actor's mannerisms are the collection of body actions the actor has accumulated over many roles in order to make himself feel comfortable.

As an actor, the combined Voice and Body Text Explorations have been the basis for my finding a fresh voice and character, and in particular for well known roles and performances. When I am rehearsing a role, each day I do a different combination of vocal and body NRGs so that I don't go to rehearsal with set interpretations. Playing Lady Bracknell, I used them to get Dame Edith Evans's[20] recording of *The Importance of Being Ernest*[21] out of my head. I could have imitated her but I didn't want to. I wanted to find my own voice for the role. By doing specific Vocal Explorations I was able to do that even though it wasn't as stunning a performance as Dame Edith Evans. For those of us working in theatre, the infinite number of kinesensic body and vocal explorations that are available allows for the fullest preparation of a role. As such, one is always ready to respond to whatever the play, the moment, a fellow actor or the director may require, free of our personal habit-patterns and mannerisms.[22]

The objective is never to imitate something done before; if some particular, previously-experienced moment needs to be experienced again in performance, one knows that by doing the specific "leading" NRG that evoked it before, it will happen again as the moment comes up; or if a fellow actor is more intense one night than the previous, one is also flexibly prepared to participate in the moment as needed.

---

[19] Sir Lawrence Olivier was an actor many considered to be the greatest in the English-speaking world during the twentieth century (http://en.wikipedia.org/wiki/Laurence_Olivier).

[20] Dame Edith Mary Evans was an actress who had a long and distinguished career on the British stage. Later in her career, she appeared in a number of films, for which she received three Academy Award nominations, plus a BAFTA and a Golden Globe award. She was particularly effective at portraying haughty aristocratic ladies, as in two of her most famous roles: Lady Bracknell in *The Importance of Being Earnest* (both on stage and in the 1952 film), and Miss Western in the 1963 film of *Tom Jones*.

[21] The *Importance of Being Ernest*, written by Oscar Wilde (http://en.wikipedia.org/wiki/Edith_Evans).

[22] Sue Ann Park writes about this extensively in her article "Voice as a Source of Creativity: For Acting Training, Rehearsal, and Performance." In *Vocal Visions* (1997) edited by Barbara Acker and Marion Hampton.

Of course, at times, this can be of great difficulty, as there are certain lines within literature that seem to me to always be spoken in the same patterned way:

- *The Lord is my shepherd, I shall not want...*
- *Four score and seven years ago our fathers*
  brought forth on this continent...
- *Halloo your name to the reverberate hills*
  And make the babbling gossips of the air
  Cry out 'Olivia'...

But, if these lines are just explored with each of the voice and body NRGs and their dialects, there are scores of fresh interpretations, many that would make good or better sense of the lines without violating the poetry.

Another example of how Lessac training can help an actor break free of patterns can be evidenced when exploring iambic pentameter. With the vocal and body NRGs each iamb doesn't have to be the same length in order to observe the meter. The playable consonants alone turn the iambics into jazz; an unstressed syllable can be lengthened and the flow of vocal NRGs can still give the stressed syllables their due. With consonant NRG leading, innate changes of tempo are discovered as in:

> *The breath of worldly men cannot depose*
> *The deputy elected by the Lord.*

That second line has a built-in quicker tempo unlike the first since it has no sustainable/playable consonants. It has made me feel like shaking my finger at someone. Since there are no playable Strings or Woodwinds, the tempo moves quickly to the end.

I love the fact that each English word is different from every other word in tonal quality and rhythms. Of course they have to be spoken intelligibly but they don't have to be spoken the way one has been taught at some time. Before I knew Arthur's work, Dr. McGaw would often jibe at me in rehearsal "Sue Ann, there's more than one way to read a line!"

As you became situated as a "Master Lessac Teacher", what became your objectives for voice and speech training?

First, my objectives for basic voice and speech training have always been for the students to discover and develop their own range of vocal dynamics for their professional and personal use in their first two semesters. They should have developed voluntary control over their voices because they have an internal sensory identification for every use of their voice and have experienced behaviorally how their voices tap into their emotional and physical store of life experiences, evoking fresh pattern-free behavior in real time.

I wanted the acting students to be able to trust the training as they moved into second year classes and begin performing for the public. I believe that actors in both Conservatories and Degree granting Universities deserve to be sufficiently trained so that they do not need and have to depend on voice coaches. They should know how to use their voices healthfully.

I got closest to fulfilling those objectives at SUNY at Binghamton because we finally had the Body training working with the Vocal training. After a few years, Libby Roman[23] and I taught the work two hours a day, four days a week, while Richard Cuyler[24] taught the body work four hours a week.

In what ways, if at all, has your teaching changed over the years?

While I was at SUNY at Binghamton, students would often tell me in their second year that they "*...used to be afraid of me,*" because I was "*tough.*" I finally realized their fear was probably triggered by the fact that for much of my life I was an angry woman. I have a strong voice, so that even when I wasn't in any way angry at a student, my anger showed through. One colleague told me I even sounded angry when I was giving compliments. A student, who heard the restrained anger in my voice, said, "*Don't be*

---

[23] Lisbeth "Libby" Jane Roman, passed away in Kansas City, Mo., on May 3, 2006. She earned a PhD. in theatre from the University of Illinois, taught in the theatre department at the State University of New York at Binghamton, acted in the Colonnades Theatre Lab and the Ensemble Studio Theatre in New York City, and was one of the first Master Lessac teachers. In 1982 she became associate professor at the University of Missouri, where she worked until retiring in 1996.

[24] Dick Cuyler was invited to be part of the faculty at SUNY at Binghamton in 1973 and taught there for almost 20 years, during which time he would earn Master Teacher certification.

impatient with me." Another Workshop student said I was *"a cross between a drill sergeant and a nurturing mother,"* which I took to mean I was making some improvement.

In the 2001 Intensive, a student who was so unresponsive the first week that I thought he might be slightly delayed, told me that from childhood he had always been laughed at because he had a tiny and very high-pitched voice. I told him no one on the faculty would laugh at him or embarrass him in any way. We didn't. He believed me and bloomed. Since then, the very first thing we say to a beginning students is that no one is going to laugh at them, ridicule, shame, or berate them. We also tell them immediately that they are not here to please us; we are here to see that they have pleasure in working on their voices. As a result, even older participants who have had lots of training and professional experience suddenly relax and they stop resisting. We also tell participants at the Intensives other things in order to diffuse their resistance and fear, which is important, as I believe everyone fears voice and speech training because they think it is intended to change the way they learned to talk and that makes them feel they are *"not good enough."*

Since that learning experience, Deb Kinghorn, Nancy Krebs[25] and I have started to re-examine how we teach, including sharing our own observations of Arthur teaching and what we had learned from teaching kinesensics in classes of 18 to 25 or 30 people. While I could always refuse to take more than 18 in a class, since that was as many as I could work with individually during a two-hour twenty-minute class, I realize that many voice teachers do not have the luxury. In the larger class settings, it takes experience, skill and planning to see that each student can really identify a new sensory-guided vocal action well enough to work on it alone between classes.

As you reflect on how voice and speech training is situated today, how do you see the teaching of voice and speech being situated for both professional actors and those who do not end up spending their life in the Theatre?

I know from teaching kinesensics (for over 45 years) that Arthur speaks truthfully in saying everyone can have a good voice if there has been no birth defects, disease, or accident damage. Not every acting student will work in the professional theatre. Ac-

---

[25] Deb Kinghorn and Nancy Krebs are both past presidents of the Lessac Institute and current Master Lessac Teachers currently serving on the faculty of the Lessac Summer Intensives.

knowledging that, I was always comforted, knowing the Lessac training could benefit their personal and professional lives, their emotional and physical health, and their participation in the arts or sports.

Regretfully, I am appalled at the present state of Voice training in our University Theatre Departments and Conservatories. I regard it as essentially criminal or fraudulent to teach either Voice or Body as they are now being scheduled and taught in many schools. I believe students should have only one vocal training philosophy in their first year, whether it's Lessac Voice and Body, or Linklater and Colianni, Fitzmaurice and Housek, etc. I truly believe that the variety of additional kinds of Voice and Speech Training should be postponed to the second or third years (of training). Otherwise, students only have time to learn about training instead of actually being trained.

Voice Training is as physical a discipline as any sport. It is outrageous to teach IPA for only three hours, one day a week, or voice as well as singing on two consecutives days. Voice is as physical a kind of training as dance or sports. Students need class every day or every other day so that they not only have time to develop the work they have already been introduced to but return in the next day or two, to be checked and then move ahead again.

I think it unforgivable that Department Chairpersons hire adjunct voice teachers to teach actors Voice only once a week or twice a week on two consecutive days. I think it is fraudulent to hire two different Voice trainers (teaching two different types of Voice training to three sections of first year students so that two sections have the same training and the third a completely different kind of training.) This suggests that some departments' Chairpersons don't have a good understanding of the difference between types of voice training or what the objective of voice training is within an acting program.

Have the Intensives stayed the same over the years?

No, but I believe they have changed for the better. A big change was our finding successful ways to shorten the length of the Intensives, first to five weeks, and then to four weeks, and still teach all the basic training. In the more affluent 1960's, many University Theatre Departments could fund our participants and our population was 35 or thereabout. Since then the number has varied greatly but Intensives have never been as large as those in the '60's. Fortunately that has meant every participant gets more individual attention.

After I retired as Director, Nancy Krebs and Deb Kinghorn, as co-directors, successfully continued to further improve the Intensives. A two-week Teacher Training Program, coordinated with the Intensive, was developed by Nancy Krebs and Barry Kur,[26] including the development of the written and oral exams, now required as part of Certification Training. Kinghorn, Krebs, and Kur each mentor teacher trainees throughout the year and all three Master Teachers have a close rapport with their enthusiastic trainees by E-mail, telephone, and DVD's.

Please describe one context or vignette that best represents the way(s) that you continue to apply Lessac training within the development of your own voice and body, and how, if at all, this process has been used by you as a means for problem-solving, learning, healing, performance, communication, and/or increasing your own vitality of life?

At dinner, this past November, I left my friends at the table for a few minutes, when I returned I tried to speak, but my speech was completely garbled and the right side of my face was paralyzed. I realized at once that I had had a stroke and insisted on going to the ER.

Later, unable to sleep in the ICU, I slowly and sinuously played structural NRGs *Woo-Woe-War-Wah-Wow* many times every hour during the night. By morning, the facial paralysis was all gone except for a droopy right eyelid and slow reaction on the right rim of my tongue and lips. These made the *W* flute difficult and affected the *L* saxophone, *R* trombone, and surprisingly, the *N* viola as well. I found I could speak clearly, but only one word at a time with no connected speech.

I realized that the stroke was in my left side of my brain where much of speech is controlled and I remembered that stutterers don't stutter when they sing, research telling us that much of singing is controlled by the right side of the brain. So, I wondered if that would work for me. I sang *America the Beautiful* all the way through and could link with complete ease and intelligibility. Then I spoke the words easily, enjoying the

---

[26] Current President of the Lessac Institute, Barry Kur earned his first teaching certificate in 1977 with Arthur and Sue Ann at SUNY-Binghamton and his Master Lessac Certification in 2009.

music of the consonants and carrying over the music into the vowels and speech intonation. A-ha! I thought. If I try to pronounce the words carefully, it's hard work and achieved word by word. But, when I sing, music solves the problems.

I continue to sing and to discover. I found that when playing drumbeats and creating blends with *R* trombone and *L* saxophone that I access the feel of those instruments easily and musically. I taste extravagant explorations and quicken the tempo. I use the body NRGs with physical therapy, my hands bicycling with wheels and I sing *76 Trombones* with a crisp, clean marching step beat: Singing, connecting words and feeling buoyancy.

What else are you interested in pursuing in terms of the work itself?
I'm interested in completing a Lessac Teacher's Manual because I finally realized that learning to develop voice and body with Kinesensics is essentially teaching oneself through sensation in the parts of the body over which one has voluntary control because the body action can be felt. As Arthur says, it is working "self-to-self" and learning through feeling rather than through thinking. Nancy, Deb and I have worked for the past eight years on teaching the way Arthur does and incorporating what each of us has learned about classroom teaching. Arthur doesn't rely on traditional teaching practices: Inspiration, ear-training, imitation, external imagery, or rote drill.

When you start to teach the work, it becomes working *self to other*. However it is teaching that cannot rely on usual kinds of assistance. It is counter-productive to give negative instructions. I have never heard Arthur say "Don't" or use language that contains any hint of the possibility of failure, such as: "Do it again," Try it again," or "What if you did…?", "Do it again and do the *D* Drumbeat you missed."

In 40 years, I remember only two instances where his comments might be considered negative: Once he asked a student: "How dare you do a Call that isn't singing?" and another time he said: "[student's name], you are resisting change in the work." He'll say instead "Do (or explore) another version and play that *N* Violin on another string. Do another version and feel how that final *D* drumbeat feels in contrast to the *N* Violin:" Always giving positive organic instruction takes a radical change in your vocabulary and attention when you are teaching.

In what ways do you see the Lessac work expanding during the next 50 years or going beyond theatre training?

During the years that I was teaching the Lessac work at The Goodman School of Drama at the Art Institute of Chicago, I was preoccupied with learning the work, learning to teach the work, and finding all it could do for the theatre world. Then I began to realize that more and more often my students were telling me things about what the work was doing or had done for them in many different areas of their lives: Students who had facial paralysis and injurious dental work talked about the healing nature of the work. Others talked about waking up without pain for the first time in their lives. Betty E. used structural NRG to regain activity in her paralyzed facial muscles due to poor dental work. An actor, when told he needed surgery to remove nodes on his vocal folds, treated them for three weeks with just the Y-buzz he had learned in class, and as a result ended up not having surgery, as did two other students with nodes.

Other students told me about how the work improved their self-image. From tonal NRG, a young student Casanova said his Y-buzz quality voice was seductively successful. From structural NRG, two young women completing my classes were delighted to show me before and after photos showing they both had finally acquired visible upper lips in class and no longer felt self-conscious about the way they looked. [This was significant because] one of their Mothers had told [her daughter] that "it was indecent to move your upper lip when you talk." At NBC-TV, I treated their weatherman for his undesirable, immobile upper lip acquired from playing the trombone.

Over the past 45 years, we have continued to receive many anecdotal reports, including those from certified Lessac teachers. Young people, in particular, respond enthusiastically to the body training, perhaps because so many live such hectic lives—the tension relief from their own body's natural *relaxer-energizers* allows them to experience feeling good in a very short period of time.

In addition, there have been two Lessac teaching professors and a Master Lessac Teacher who have suffered comas with paralysis, all for different reasons, and been given poor recovery prognosis. Libby Roman, Tim G, and Matt M. found that by adding Lessac body work to their rehab physical training, they were able to disprove their discouraging prognosis. Arthur's own therapeutic work has also included treating the deaf, laryngectomy patients, and those suffering from psychological trauma to their voices, (as well as) teaching accent-elimination and the ESL populations.

Finally, there is Arthur himself, who, as he turns 100, continues to report that he knows his work "has kept him growing younger while growing older" as he approaches the age of 100.

I now have come to believe that kinesensics has therapeutic gifts for humans that reach far beyond the theatre world—to infinite unexplored applications for healing physical, emotional, and psychological wounds. Lessac-trained people know in their bodies what the work has done for them. Our efforts now need to expand into the areas where the truth of Arthur's genius needs further controlled research to validate kinesensics remarkable benefits for all humans.

Richard Cuyler

Richard Cuyler *(Dick) is a Master Lessac trainer and one of the original faculty members of the Lessac summer intensive. He taught acting, directing, mime, circus acts, and the Lessac work at the State University of New York at Binghamton for over 20 years and before that for 11 years at Skidmore College, where he was Chair of the Drama Department. Mr. Cuyler holds graduate degrees in direction, voice, and speech, and studied acting with Uta Hagen, Gene Frankel, and Robert Lewis, and movement with Tony Montanaro (Mime), Fred Garbo, Sacha Paviata (Tumbling), Bob Berky, John Towsen (Clown), Michael Moschen (Juggling), and David Leong (Unarmed Combat). Mr. Cuyler currently teaches juggling at Flat Rock Playhouse's YouTheatre and The Chautauqua Institution and is a member of Actor's Equity, AFRA, and the International Jugglers Association.*

Sandra Cuyler

Saundra Cuyler *is a certified Lessac trainer and holds an M.A. in Directing and an M.F.A. in Acting. She taught for 20 years at The University of Maryland and State University of New York at Binghamton in their undergraduate and MFA programs. A national winner of the Irene Ryan Acting Award presented at the Kennedy Center, Ms. Cuyler has acted in over sixty productions, directed twenty, and vocal coached forty-five. Her last two years in Binghamton, she was the Artistic Director of the Cider Mill Playhouse. In 1998, she and her husband, Dick, "retired" to Etowah, N.C., 25 minutes south of Asheville. Caring for her mother and aunt, who live a block from her, Ms. Cuyler still has quite a busy schedule and is actively involved with the drama ministry at her church where she teaches seniors in an interdenominational, neighborhood Bible study, and directs and acts at Grace Center, Hendersonville Little Theater, and Flat Rock Playhouse. She also teaches privately, specializing in acting for actors and singers, stage dialects, polishing business presentations, and television announcing skills. Ms. Cuyler is a commercial voiceover talent with ProComm Studios and Sun Spots Productions and is a member of AFTRA and AEA.*

(To Dick) Describe the context in which you were introduced to Lessac training.

Dick

I went to Oberlin College[1] where there was no drama or theatre department, but a very fine teacher and director of the Oberlin Dramatic Association, who taught in the English department and directed all the plays. I got interested in theatre really through him. I'm very glad, because I got introduced to a very broad spectrum of literature, not only English literature, but also American, Spanish, French, Russian, and German literature. All translated in English, by the way, except for the French. These studies provided me with a rich and diverse background from which I found that I loved Shakespeare; and although I didn't quite know how to act Shakespeare (at the time), I was already kind of in that mix, where I found that I wanted to go further. So, after I got out of the Army,[2] I got a fellowship at Bennington College,[3] all girls in the 1950s, with only eight guys, and I got my Masters there, and decided that I wanted to be an actor and go to New York, which I did. I spent five and a half years in New York City. Sometimes getting work, most of the time not. During that time, I had no idea that I wanted to teach, which ironically is what I ended up doing.

In 1961, I was hired to teach classes at Skidmore College[4] in voice and speech, public speaking, and oral interpretation, and used a rather old and well used text by Avery, Dorsey and Sickels.[5] Although I originally thought the job was going to be temporary, after about four years, I decided I might want to see if there were any other voice books out there which might serve me and my students better in teaching these voice classes, which is how I came across Arthur's[6] book on a shelf at The Drama Bookshop. I remember that Arthur's book looked so different, and that I was kind of afraid to even try it...so I took the safe way out and continued with Avery, Dorsey and

---

[1] Oberlin College is a Liberal Arts College in Ohio, which presents a rich and balanced curriculum in the humanities, social sciences, and natural sciences (http://new.oberlin.edu).
[2] Dick served in Army during the Korean War from 1952-54.
[3] Bennington College is located in Vermont, and uses a teacher-practioner model of teaching, whereby students direct the course of their own education (http://www.bennington.edu/go/about-bennington).
[4] Skidmore College is a private Liberal Arts college in Saratoga Springs, New York.
[5] Avery, Elizabeth, Jane Dorsey, and Vera A. Sickels. 1928. *First Principles of Speech Training.* New York: Appleton-Century-Crofts, Inc.
[6] The 1st edition of *The Use and Training of the Human Voice* (1960) was privately published by Lessac in a printing of 600 for the use of his students. Demand grew with four additional printings in the next six years, with extensive revisions in 1964 and 1965. Nearly 4000 copies of the 1st edition were sold.

Sickels. But it still kind of ate at the back of my mind, so around 1969, seeing that another edition[7] had come out, I bought the book.

In 1970, I saw an ad for two Lessac Voice workshops, one at SUNY Binghamton and the other at SMU in Dallas. I was accepted at both, but chose to stay a little closer to home, so during the summer of 1970, I began a five and a half week workshop at SUNY Binghamton and the teachers were Arthur, Sue Ann and Michael.[8] Along with the voice we did some very interesting meditative work with Michael. Back at Skidmore, I felt that I knew enough to make the jump and teach the work, but I quickly found out how little I knew about tone and structure. It was really the consonants and their music that made more sense to me and I think that's what I hooked on to. So, the next summer, I decided I'd better go to San Antonio [Trinity University].[9] There I learned to *call* on Call words (you know, like "hello" and "unearth") from Jack Jones[10] in an outdoor swimming pool. At the same time, Arthur was beginning to explore the ramifications of the bodywork more and more. All this had a significant effect on my teaching, and during the next semester back at Skidmore, I found that I was not only teaching better, but that I was also introducing the body work in my own voice classes.

The next year [summer of '72], Arthur and Sue Ann held an eight week workshop at SUNY Binghamton and because Steve Mackenroth and Randy Moore[11] had to be somewhere else for the last two weeks, Arthur called me and said: "Come on down. Come help us teach the last couple of weeks." So I learned quite a bit about explorations at that time—both voice and body. Then in '73, I was offered a position at SUNY Binghamton. Arthur spoke for me and Al Brooks[12] listened. And (this is when) the wheels started to turn, and I took the position. I was originally hired as a director,

---

[7] The 2nd edition (greatly expanded and completely rewritten) was published in 1967 by Drama Book Publishers.
[8] Arthur Lessac, Sue Ann Park, and Michael Lessac.
[9] More than 35 four-, six- to eight-week intensive workshops for theater professionals, trainers, teachers, students and researchers have been offered since 1960.
[10] Jack Jones taught previously at the Goodman School of Theatre and was on faculty at the Lessac Workshop held at Trinity University in 1971.
[11] Steve Mackenroth, Randy Moore, Sue Ann Park, Libby Roman, and Arthur Lessac were instructors during the 8-week summer intensive held at SUNY Binghamton in 1972.
[12] Dr. Alfred Brooks was Chair of the Theatre Department at SUNY Binghamton.

and the first play I directed was *Uncle Vanya*, in which I worked with both graduate and undergraduate students using the voice and developing body work. Since the graduate students at Binghamton had already had quite a bit of experience with the work, we all took the plunge and it turned out pretty successfully.

Then in '74, I began to work more closely with Arthur. Early in the morning we'd meet around five o'clock at the gym and would work two to three hours, three times a week. And this is about the time when Al Brooks, said: "Arthur you've got to write a book about the body." So Arthur started writing the book *Body Wisdom*[13] about the same time. I began to teach during the summers at the intensives, along with Arthur, Sue Ann and Libby Roman, all of who were also currently teaching at SUNY Binghamton.

All of this had a major influence in my development as a teacher, especially in terms of really beginning to teach something that I had learned through feeling, rather than books, as well as being able to make sense of the work in my own life, through working and teaching directly with them. I continued to teach with Arthur and Sue until they retired[14] and probably taught in 16 summer workshops over that span of time, ending in 1991.

Can you elaborate a little more about these "workshops"?

Dick

The workshops, or as they're now called, the intensives were just that: *Intense*. They were usually ran six weeks in length (at least during the time I was teaching), five days a week, and about eight hours a day, wherein a group of students (usually about sixteen to twenty-four) and teachers (usually about four or five) would go through everything that was in the voice book. It was a challenging time, because we (the teachers) would often gather three to four days before the students arrived for the workshop[15] and Arthur would say: "Well…Sue Ann what did we start with last year." And Sue Ann would say: "Consonant NRG." And so Arthur would say something

---

[13] Lessac, Arthur. 1978, 1981. *Body Wisdom: The Use and Training of the Human Body*. New York: Drama Book Specialists.
[14] Arthur Lessac retired from SUNY at Binghamton in 1981 and Sue Ann Park in 1985.
[15] For many years, teachers who taught at the intensive met a few days before the intensive to receive training from Arthur and Sue Ann and to go over the order of curriculum.

like: "Well I think we ought to start with Structure this year"…because the whole point was to demonstrate that you could start anywhere, with any of the vocal NRGs and then find a safe way into a second and a third, etc. We also found that around the fourth week, a small group of people would begin to say, "It's too much..." you know, "...my head's exploding," or "I can't do this," and "I really want to leave, but I guess I'll stick it out," which, once we helped them through that crisis, or see that they could make it, it all came together by the time we got to doing full explorations.

Why was there a need to have these workshops if all of you (Sue Ann, Libby, Arthur, and you) were already teaching at Binghamton?

Dick

I think there were two larger issues going on. First, there was a need to get the word out about the work itself. Binghamton was really a very small population, and even though we had a good strong theatre department, with fifteen or sixteen on staff (at least in the early years. Eventually that number would dwindle considerably by the time I retired), we wanted the workshops to get the word out about the training. This also was significant because, in the 'sixties, Kristin Linklater[16] had gotten a Rockefeller grant, which allowed her to work with ten to twelve people over a two year period, without having to charge much money, which in turn allowed her a spring-board for marketing her own approach to voice.

Second, there was an expanding need during the 1970's for people to be trained organically so that they could teach voice and speech with lasting results in the burgeoning BFA and MFA programs. Many theatre departments' spokespersons were still saying, "We're not making any progress here, our students still sound just like they did their first year here."

In fact, many of the people who attended the workshops were teachers who were as frustrated, as a lot of us had been, with: *How do you teach voice and speech?* For me, I liked teaching, but I never had had any previous training other than one voice

---

[16] Kristin Linklater (born April 23, 1936) is a prominent vocal coach, dialect coach, acting teacher, actor and director. She is currently Head of Acting in the Theatre Arts Division of Columbia University (http://en.wikipedia.org/wiki/Kristin_Linklater).

and speech course at Teacher's College,[17] and yet, there I was, a relatively new hire at Skidmore, expected to teach voice and speech to budding young actresses.

(To Saundra) And what about the context in which you were introduced to Lessac training? Was it similar to Dick's?

Saundra

Well, the way I came to the work is not a way that I would recommend to others, but I was really highly motivated. I had been married. I had been divorced. After I left New York, I moved back to my hometown of Cullman, Alabama and taught oral interpretation, acting, and remedial English in grades 10-12, in addition to directing and producing two plays a year. Although I was treated with great respect, 80% of the people I worked with had never SEEN a live play outside of a Christmas pageant at church! Then—after three years—I thought, " high school teaching is the hardest work I've ever done. I can't do this anymore!" So I went back to college and got a Masters. THEN *I thought, "THIS is really fun…,"* so I got an MFA.[18] Through a number of coincidences, I got a job at the University of Maryland to teach voice and movement for the acting classes in the department of theatre. How great, but it was already May! That left me with less than 3 months to *learn* to teach what I had been *hired* to teach. I had never had a speech course, or *any* voice work of *any kind*!!!

Dick

…And of course you said: "Yes, I will do it."

Saundra

Sure yeah. And they had also hired me to vocal coach the theatre productions and… creative dramatics and then the next semester, Acting Shakespeare. So I thought: "I have to do something really quick. This is the scariest place I've ever been." And I've been in some scary places! Well, there was, on the wall at the University of Florida, a poster for a Lessac workshop. And it advertised better voice, movement, you know. So I thought "that's it." And I called a phone number on the poster and I was off to Duluth, Minnesota. The Intensive teachers were Arthur, Sue Ann, Libby Roman and Dick Cuyler. And the first day in the class they said: "Why are you here?" And I

---

[17] Teachers College is part of Columbia University in New York City.
[18] Saundra Cuyler earned an MFA degree at University of Florida in May 1980.

said: "I don't know. I just don't know, but I really, really have to be here." And...that was it.

(Pause)

What a mess I was....

That was the summer of 1980, and then...I went to the University of Maryland and did okay teaching. Although I believed in the Lessac work, I was really uncomfortable during that first teaching year and constantly discussed the work with Dick. We had become close friends at the Duluth workshop and we kept in touch and he coached me through that year of teaching, because one six-week workshop just doesn't prepare you to teach!

Dick

And at that time I think, most people thought, "I have to learn this right away so I can teach it."

Saundra

...Which was just the most awful way to go into it because it greatly magnifies the performance pressure as you are experiencing your *first* exposure to the work.

Dick

Absolutely.

Saundra

So then... in '81 I went back to Duluth and there was a summer acting troupe at the University, and I'm not sure why, but I was assigned to teach that acting group as well as sit in on the Lessac classes[19] so...I was learning and I was teaching at the same time. But I had a little bit of experience from the year at Maryland and the association with Dick to build on. And then the next year, '82, which I think was the third year at Duluth, Arthur was not at the workshop, and I became part of that, of that *fab four*, you know, that "austere teaching team" (Dick, Libby, Sue Ann, and myself). I can tell you that my knees were shaking—to be standing with those fabulous teachers!!

---

[19] Classes during the summer workshop were taught by Sue Ann Park, Dick Cuyler, and Libby Roman.

And how long did you end up teaching at the intensives?

Saundra

Let's see, Dick and I married in '83, and we spent two summers in '87 and '88 in Denver.[20]

Dick

Boulder.

Saundra

Boulder, Colorado. Then we went on sabbatical in Europe. Then I taught in the 1990 and 1991 intensives in Pella, IA. You know, while each six-week session was different, they were still all the same. What I mean is, the first time that some one comes to train in the Lessac work, they have no idea, NO idea what is in store. Each person comes into an intensive with their own agenda, but by the end of the training sessions—every person changes!

And during all of it, I watched Sue Ann and Libby,[21] who was a wonderful teacher. I mean, you know, Sue Ann is premiere but she was, well, really scary at first but...

Dick

Yeah she is...

Saundra

but, by then we were friends, and she was...

Dick

She was like a sergeant.

---

[20] Dick and Saundra Cuyler were on the faculty during the Summer Intensives held at University of Minnesota, Duluth (1982 and 1984) and University of Colorado at Boulder (1987 and 1988) and Central College, Iowa (1990 and 1991).

[21] Lisbeth "Libby" Jane Roman, passed away in Kansas City, Mo., on May 3, 2006. She earned a PhD. in theatre from the University of Illinois, and taught in the theatre department at the State University of New York at Binghamton and acted in the Colonnades Theatre Lab and the Ensemble Studio Theatre in New York City. In 1982 she became associate professor at the University of Missouri, where she worked until retiring in 1996.

Saundra

She was terrifying because she was so…powerful…! I loved her and I feared her at the same time. I've never known another person like her. Not ever. Never!

So that 1991 intensive in Pella was the last one for me, as far as teaching in the workshops. It was ALL really quite a major life experience, because I saw first hand that experimenting with the Lessac work…any student changes. If they're even a little bit open minded—any student changes. And that was extremely fulfilling work to be a part of. Gee,…I'm feeling teary-eyes as I remember the 1980's and the rich heritage that I was bathed in. To have these wonderful teachers that now are old. Only they *weren't* old then! They were *doing their thing* and they were moving with ease and everybody was *creating* together and finding new ways to make the work more clear! And it was just…I don't know…you were close to the *beginning* and it was so *revolutionary* and exciting…!!!

Dick

Well, Arthur keeps using the term "Bauhaus"…You know, we "Bauhaused."[22]

Saundra

Yeah you know, and this unique approach to voice and body still is being created and codified, as Arthur made the point today. But it has a lot more form now, that's set down, that's written. And so many *more* people now! I mean, it's *international* now,[23] and just huge compared to what it was back then.

In what ways have you applied or incorporate Lessac within…what you do?

Saundra

It helped an awful lot with my acting, because all my degrees had been in performance, so I had a lot of stage time, but my voice was not all that good. It (my voice not being good) was more an attitude towards life, I think, than a problem with my

---

[22] Arthur has had a "bauhausing" session at each of the Lessac Institute conferences (since 2006), where he and the members just sit and talk, problem-solve, and explore.

[23] Presently there are multiple certified Lessac teachers working outside the U.S: Kat Moraitis teaches at the Central School of Speech and Drama in London; Marth Munro and Yvette Hardie teach, direct, and perform in South Africa; Gert Terny who founded the European Lessac Center in Belgium, leads voice workshops throughout Europe; William Noone taught extensively in China; and Sookhee Kim teaches in Korea (and has translated the Voice book in Korean).

voice (itself). And the attitude was one of—it's got to be right or don't do it at all. So…until I figured out how to make it "right," I literally wasn't willing to do it. To understand this, you have to understand the context of where I grew up, in Alabama, and where I was taught that women should be subservient but strong, kind of a Steel Magnolia[24] type of thing—it's a world of men and they are the power and *you just be quiet*. If you can't say something really smart *you just be quiet*. So I was, in a way, very receding and got around that by being a Southern belle type: "Oh you just got to help me, cause you're so big and strong and I just don't know how." So I had quite a Southern accent that, in real life, I had tremendous difficulty controlling. On stage it wasn't quite so bad, because I'd step into somebody else's shoes. But it was really fear of dealing with people that made me hide behind that defense of false weakness. It's not uncommon for women to hide their ability, but it took me a while to realize that my vocal inability was a reflection of cultural conditioning. As I finally began to find vocal strength in tone and potency, my self-esteem began to change. I started to see that with structure and consonants, my Alabama accent was neutralized. Buoyancy gave me poise and potency helped me recognize an emotional depth. My attitude toward people and being able to communicate became more confident. So that was a huge thing for me. I wasn't *dumb*; I had just *pretended* to be!!!

And then there was the breathing. I didn't breathe at all when I came to this work, not at all. I was not a singer, and I wasn't aware that I needed to breathe diaphragmatically when I was acting. Naturally, I suffered from voice loss when the vocal demands of a character were great. So learning to breathe optimally—well, that's been a tremendous thing health wise for me also. You know, he [Arthur] talks about releasing the toxins and stuff like that…and I actually went into therapy after my exposure to Arthur's work…cause I knew something about me was…odd. I sensed that something about my whole system was toxic! I was emotionally very limited and I started to see that, when I realized that I couldn't do a darn thing without gauging *the result*. I was not open AT ALL to exploration. I had lost my childlike curiosity. It was too dangerous. I could not afford it. Physically, I was also

---

[24] *Steel Magnolias*, by Robert Harling, is a 1987 off-Broadway play, made into a movie in 1989. Based on the author's experience with the death of his sister, *Steel Magnolias* is a comedy-drama about the bond among a group of Southern women in northwest Louisiana (http://en.wikipedia.org/wiki/Steel_Magnolias).

starting to get a shoulder hump from a hyper-extended neck position. So the C-curve with buoyancy postural work helped that tremendously. I was stalking like an Indian in the forest, rolling on my leg wheels up and down football bleachers, floating with my groceries up three sets of stairs, opening doors with potency while maintaining a C-curve, and feeling great! After a couple of years in the work, I was not only standing up but I was also breathing!

As I've said, I was also a nervous, nervous wreck when I first turned up in Duluth in 1980.

In the early 70's, I had lived in Manhattan. I had acted…I had seen too much, I had done too much. *Drunk too much.* I was just really damaged…by my divorce and by my part in causing my divorce. So emotionally, I was just really in a picnic basket! I mean…in 1980 at that first intensive, every time I heard a sharp noise I screamed. That might have been the result of living in New York, I guess…where I had been robbed and assaulted. It was physically a very bad experience. So you know, in the wake of all of this, I came to Arthur's work. And I was just a nervous wreck. And then of course, you try to do something 'right' and it's not, and you just start to beat up on yourself. Actually that's how we met (to Dick) I left the class crying, crying, crying...

Dick

Yeah she was in another teacher's class and I came out to have a drink of water and she was *boohooing* there at the water fountain…

Saundra

You know this was pretty much at the beginning of my first intensive, because I remember feeling stupid when I couldn't see the principle behind the structure work and *reproduce it,* you know?

Dick

You said: "I can't do this, I can't do this." And this was just our first week into the thing.

Saundra

Oh yeah, couple of days, and I'm giving up. And you said: "Just go back in class." That was the attitude all the teachers at that intensive had. "Its okay, just chill out, just give it another try." This was an attitude I was not familiar with. I was familiar with: "Next!" Because of my life experience in my twenties and early thirties, I had a hardness in my worldview that the teachers in this workshop didn't seem to have.

Even though I was afraid of Sue Ann, as was everybody else, she was not *hard*. As stern as I first thought she was, I discovered she has a way of "loving on"[25] everybody in her *own* way, and when you recognize this you go: "This is so unusual. This whole group of people is unusual. This work is really unusual. I want to be more like them!" By the time I came to my first workshop, the failure of my marriage, disappointment with life, and disappointment with myself was causing me to emotionally go under. I really don't know what I would have done if I hadn't found something that could give me help, really could make me open to going through some therapy to find out why I was afraid of everything. I was...*I was afraid of everything!* I had prayed for mentors—and I got them in Sue Ann and Arthur. I can still see Arthur holding out his arms to me and calling "Helloooooo", so that I wanted to ANSWER him. To reengage in play. To start over. To hope again. So that's another thing the work gave me...a chance to be who I truly was—the playful, curious child beneath the anxious, insecure adult. In the Lessac workshops: *You can come from where you came from and you are welcomed as you are and you are treated with respect.*

Dick

(Overlapping) I was in deep analysis while I was still an actor in New York. After I got up to Skidmore, I began to have a lot of stomach problems, and I was really worried because I was hired for only one semester. We had sub-let our apartment in New York to a couple of Columbia students and fully intended to return there.[26] I was there trying out *teaching* and what happened was, the woman who was on sabbatical decided to extend her leave for another six months. So I was hired again for another semester. And then the woman who was the acting chairman up and left and I was hired for another year. Long story short, I ended up as chairman of the department my last four years at Skidmore. That first semester, my stomach had gotten much better because I went back to my old analyst to get my head screwed on right every Friday. I had also received an "observership" at the

---

[25] Slang phrase: the act of showing someone love.
[26] Dick was previously married, with three children, and then divorced. He met Saundra in 1980.

Actor's Studio,[27] so I was able to combine the two things. I was pretty much a Stanislavsky teacher and figured that all my emotions were all I needed. Well, I spent two years going back and forth from Saratoga Springs to New York. It was great. I mean, I learned a lot from the observer-ship and I also got my head back in order fairly quickly. Like within a couple of months this whole thing, you know, had diminished. So I had been in analysis (during the late fifties and more therapy until the mid-sixties) and I was ready to go into some deeper teaching and it was very interesting that in 1970, after I came back from a sabbatical in England, where I went to different theatre schools and saw some really intense work, I thought 'this is the path I need to take, but I don't want to teach acting the English way, because the English way was really not as organic, or not really organic. It was still, you know, really the poetry of it all, etc, etc. So I mean really, when I came into that first Lessac workshop…although I had stopped therapy, it was hugely therapeutic. The whole experience of suddenly realizing that there was a voice in there that had been bottled up for so long affected me both physically and emotionally, and it was a very good place for me to be.

Was this about the same time, you started exploring juggling?

Dick

This same year was a critical year in my life. In 1970 the chairperson [at Skidmore] had come back…she was an actress and she had an agent in New York, who told her about this mime who had studied with Marceau[28] and with Decroux[29] in Paris, a fellow named Tony Montanaro.[30] She said, "You have to see his performance. The college really might like that". He came up and blew everybody away because, as you know, when Marceau first arrived in 1956, everybody was "blown away." They'd

---

[27] The *Actors Studio* is a membership organization for professional actors, theatre directors and playwrights founded October 5, 1947 by Elia Kazan, Cheryl Crawford, and Robert Lewis (http://en.wikipedia.org/wiki/Actors_Studio).

[28] Marcel Marceau (22 March 1923–22 September 2007) was a French mime artist and actor (http://en.wikipedia.org/wiki/Marcel_Marceau).

[29] Étienne Decroux (19 July 1898 in Paris, France–12 March 1991 in Billancourt, Somme, Picardie) studied at Jacques Copeau's Ecole du Vieux-Colombier, where he saw the beginnings of what was to become his life's obsession—Corporeal Mime. During his long career as a film and theatre actor, he created many pieces, using the human body as the primary means of expression (http://en.wikipedia.org/wiki/Etienne_Decroux).

[30] Tony Montanaro (1927-2002) was one of the great mime artists of the 20th century. After seeing Marcel Marceau's historic 1956 performance at New York's Phoenix Theatre, Montanaro flew to Paris to study under Marceau and Marceau's teacher, Etienne Decroux (http://www.filmsbyhuey.com/montanaromovie.html).

never seen anything like it. And at that time, Tony was one of only two Americans who had studied with both Decroux and Marceau. We were on a "four-one-four program" at the time, so January was open, and we invited Tony to do a workshop for us. I was immediately hooked. But it wasn't until January of 1976 and I was at SUNY Binghamton that I was able to go to Maine, where Tony had established a mime company (The Celebration Mime Company), to study mime in a barn for three weeks during an incredibly cold and snowy winter. So suddenly I had parallel courses (With both Tony and Arthur) and I asked: "How does mime inform Arthur's work and how does Arthur's work inform mime?" And during this time, what was happening to me physically was very good. I was becoming, you know, very...much more flexible from both aspects—the body NRGs that were being developed and explored in my work with Arthur and then the mime with Tony. So that's part of my training. I had never really had this kind of focus before: first with Arthur, continuing with Arthur, then with Tony and continuing with him. And it just so happened that in subsequent workshops that I took with Tony, there were some jugglers. And while I liked mime an awful lot, I thought, "I like real objects better." So I began to make the shift into juggling, about 1977.

And within that journey, of connecting Lessac and juggling...did you stay connected to your previous acting training?

Dick

I began to see how it all fit together. The thing that was great about it was...about Arthur's work...and about Sue Ann's, was that you didn't have to go into affective memory. You could start a tonal exploration and the next few seconds you'd be crying and you didn't have to ask, "where is this coming from"? It was just there; it was real. And I thought, " wow, what a connection that is. I want to teach that."

Saundra

And the physical health that has come from...(to Dick) you had mentioned growing under two masters...It's incredible, you know, Dick's internist says: "I want to be you when I grow up."

Dick

Oh, my doctor, he's seen me work on the street, you know. I still street perform, you know, in Hendersonville.

Saundra

That's why we moved there, because Dick could continue to work until he COULDN'T work anymore. And he's still working, you know!!

Dick

And not just my doctor but other people say: "You're so flexible". I say: "Well it's my training and it's juggling and, you know, it's body NRG.

Do you see a bridge to the next 50 years with these 'young certified' people taking the work forward?

Dick

I see more streamlining of the work and more specific development, especially with the process and support for certification. With Barry Kur...don't forget, Barry is now a master teacher.[31] Really has been for years. Saundra and I were *grandfathered* in, let's face it, Libby as well...

Saundra

There was no procedure for certifying anybody. There was not even a name for it.[32]

Dick

It's just...We talked with them (Sue Ann, Arthur, and Libby) in the workshops. And we just kept learning from that.

Saundra

Sue Ann kept saying: "Arthur you've got to make other people teachers, you've got to figure out how to do that." And he was willing, but it was uncharted territory.

Dick

Yeah, it took a while.

---

[31] Barry Kur earned Master teacher certification in 2009.
[32] An official and rigorous process for certification in Lessac training, including both oral and written exams, was developed in 1999 and continues to be overseen by the board of Lessac Master teachers.

Saundra

And now—to see the stuff that everyone did this morning.... I've finally met Crystal[33] and she's more than I ever imagined. I've read her articles (in the newsletter), about teaching young children the work, but her workshop this morning was extraordinary.

Dick

Yeah, to see it in action.

Saundra

And if you can teach the children...if you can teach *the children*, then they can grow up in the fun and the musicality. It's bound to affect their lives. It HAS to. That's what we are ALL saying, "gee, this affected my life." That's the nature of the Lessac work. And currently, I just see...just all different kinds of capable, respectful, talented people contributing and I'm thrilled. And I cry and I smile at the same time, because my heart is very...I'm really happy that there are people, not only to carry on but to take it to new levels, to take it to...

Dick

Arthur's vision is continuing and growing. It's more of a worldview now, it really is.

Saundra

And that was the conversation in our lunch group today—we each brought our broken bodies in...and the way we viewed life's challenges was changed. And now, the purpose of this Lessac Institute group seems to be so much larger than just change in yourself, it's about empowering and opening the way you view the world.

---

[33] Crystal Robbins writes a column in the newsletter on what she calls "kindersensics," which talks about incorporating kinesensic training for young children. At the 2009 conference, she led all the adults through a kindersensics workshop.

Nancy Krebs

Nancy Krebs was the first individual to be named a Master Teacher in both the Voice and Body Training by the Lessac Institute in 2002. She was introduced to this training while in graduate school at the Dallas Theater Center, and has used it extensively in both her own professional acting and singing career, as well as her teaching and coaching career. Ms. Krebs is much sought after as a dialect/vocal coach for professional theatre productions, and teaches the Lessac training to students on the high school level at the famed Baltimore School for the Arts. She has served on the theatre faculty there as the senior voice instructor since 1981. Her own studio: "The Voiceworks," focuses not only on individuals who wish to improve their speaking and singing voices, but also on clients who seek training in voice-over technique, accent reduction, and presentation skills. She teaches the Lessac work solely as her approach—because this training offers a unique way of learning by integrating voice, speech and movement to deepen communication, unlock potential and heighten creativity. Ms. Krebs has been on the faculty of the Lessac Summer Intensives since 1995 and is currently co-director, and also co-teaches the Teacher Training workshop with fellow Master Teacher, Barry Kur. She leads introductory workshops in the training in the Mid-Atlantic region on a regular basis. Nancy also has a very active music career, a singer-songwriter with seven CDs of original music released and receiving air play throughout the U.S. and abroad. She is a member of AEA, AFTRA, SAG and VASTA.

Describe the context in which you were introduced to Lessac training.

I was first introduced to this wonderful training at the Dallas Theater Center in 1972. Voice training was not my first priority, though when I discovered this work, it became a major focus. I had entered the DTC graduate program with an emphasis on the acting process, but soon discovered how the Lessac work gave me skills that I could use, not only as an actor—but also as a singer. I was taught by Randy Moore and Norma Levin, and the course was part of the Graduate Acting Program under the direction of Paul Baker.[1] Eventually, after graduate school, when I became a professional actor/singer, I was able to use this work exclusively to keep my voice healthy, strong and flexible both professionally and personally.

---

[1] Paul Baker was noted by Sue Ann and others as an early champion of the Lessac work.

Can you describe the contexts of your first meetings with Arthur Lessac, as well as Sue Ann Park, and the effects if any, that it had on your subsequent use of the work, and/or your own training?

My first meeting with Arthur Lessac is actually an interesting story—and serendipitous to me. I have taught at the Baltimore School for the Arts since 1981. The gentleman who directed the school from its inception to the mid-1990's was David Simon. I knew David as a musician, painter and extraordinarily talented individual. What I didn't know is that he was the original illustrator of Arthur's first version of his book, *The Use and Training of the Human Voice.* In 1991, David saw me leaving the school one afternoon, and remarked in his strong New York City accent, "Oh, I see you have Arthur Lessac's book." I explained that I taught his work here, and did he know Arthur? He told me to look under the *acknowledgments*; and there in the first paragraph—was the name David Simon. Well, one thing led to another, and David made it possible for Arthur to come and teach a few days of Master Classes for our theatre students. It was a dream come true for me. I had never met Arthur before, and never thought that I would. But when I met him for the first time at the airport, it was as if I'd known him all my life. I felt as if I was meeting my artistic *grandfather.* At the time, he was 81 years old, and obviously practiced what he preached. He was young in so many ways. His voice had such tone and distinction. His posture was that of a much younger man. His teaching and interaction with my students was inventive and exciting, as I expected it would be. Taking my cue from that marvelous experience, I decided to further my studies of the training at that next summer's Intensive, and continued refining my knowledge during that time. At the 1992 Summer Intensive at Pomona College, I met Senior Master Teacher Sue Ann Park. She had been teaching side-by-side with Arthur for many years, and I was bowled over by her amazing command of the work. I loved how clear her instructions were, how organized she was, and how she seemed to eat, sleep and breathe this training. Both she and Arthur became mentors to me, and friends for life. In 1993, I became certified. I was invited to join the faculty of the Summer Intensive in 1995, and through extensive further training, earned Master Teacher status in 2002.

In what ways have you applied or incorporated Lessac, within the context of what you do for a living?

First of all, it became the foundation for my own professional career as a singer and actor. Upon leaving graduate school, I entered the field of professional acting: in regional theatre, dinner theatre, voice-over and on-camera TV, film and radio work. Later, I became interested in teaching voice, and was hired by the director of the theatre department of the Baltimore School for the Arts to function as the voice instructor. I have continued teaching there since 1981. In 1994, I started my own voice studio, *The Voiceworks*, and the studio work has grown over these many years to include dialect and vocal coaching for theatres as well as building a clientele of individuals wishing to improve their speaking voices for a variety of reasons. I also have used this work to develop and maintain my own personal speaking/singing voice, and have launched yet another career as a singer-songwriter of Christian meditational music. I have released several CDs, which are enjoying air play throughout the world.

What events led, or helped shaped, you to become a Master teacher in the Lessac work, and develop the Lessac teacher training workshop?
Master Teacher:

There is a history involved in that quest. When I began teaching at the Summer Intensive in 1995, I had been certified since 1993, teaching the work since 1981, and introduced to it in 1972. So, I had a long association with the training. While teaching that summer, Kathleen Dunn (also on the faculty) and I often discussed the work, and the certification process specifically and asked Arthur and Sue Ann at one of our faculty meetings, if they would share with us their certification process and what qualifications they felt were necessary so we could pass on this information. This question and the subsequent information we gleaned led me to ponder the future of the Lessac training in general: how its integrity could be preserved; how guidelines based on Arthur and Sue Ann's qualifications for certification could be fully realized for future generations of practitioners, among other questions.

This led me to spearhead the first organized meeting of Lessac practitioners and interested associates now known as the Swarthmore Meeting in 1998, assisted by Fred Nelson. At this weekend-long series of meetings, an Organizational Board and a Mentor Board were established to begin finding solutions to the many questions about preservation and promulgation of the Lessac body of work. From that meeting, eventually the institute became incorporated through subsequent gatherings, under the leadership of Deb Kinghorn.

During the many years that I had been a faculty member of the Summer Intensive, teaching with Arthur and Sue Ann, learning from them how to be a better teacher of this work, it dawned on me that someday we wouldn't have them to look to for guidance, at least not in the flesh. Who would preserve the integrity of the pedagogy? Arthur and Sue Ann were *Master Teachers* of course, but who else was there to keep the body of training intact for the future? That is when I asked them if I might pursue the training necessary for the Master Teacher status. Ideally, I should have waited for them to invite me. But I audaciously yet with great trepidation suggested that I would be more than willing to undertake the rigors of this training in order to help carry this work into the 21st century—if they felt that I would be a good candidate. Arthur and Sue Ann took up the challenge of training me personally. In 2002, I achieved this status, thanks to their expert guidance and their desire to see the work move forward.

Teacher Training:

The Teacher Training workshop came into being as a means of assisting those who wish to teach this work more effectively, as well as a tool for assessing and training candidates for certification. When an individual attends a Summer Intensive, or is introduced to this training in a workshop or classroom setting, the focus is always on learning how to teach oneself. The Intensive curriculum is designed to be a self-teaching modality in the principles and applications of kinesensic training, which is sensory-based. The focus is not on learning how to teach *others* how to do this work. However, those who attend this workshop often *do* want to teach the work eventually. They see and experience the benefits and want to share those benefits with their students. So the Lessac Institute needed to create a training forum in which the self-to-self experience becomes *self-to-other*. In brain-storming sessions during Institute board meetings in 2003-2004, we began developing the idea of a Teacher Training workshop, and in 2005, the first such workshop was presented at DePauw University in Greencastle, Indiana, team-taught by myself and certified trainer, now Master Teacher, Barry Kur. Since that inaugural workshop, further development and refinement has taken place in order to improve the experience for those who wish to expand their knowledge of the teaching principles unique to this kind of training. We hope to continue to enlarge upon what we currently have in place in order to best serve our teaching community.

Please describe one context or vignette that best represents the way(s) in which you have you applied or incorporated Lessac training within the development of your own voice and body, and how, if at all, this process has been used by you as a means for problem-solving, learning, healing, performance, communication, and/or increasing your own vitality of life?

One of the most graphic examples of how this training affected my professional life took place after I left the Dallas Theater Center, and became a professional actor working in an arena-style setting (in the round). This was my first professional job, and I was working for—and acting with a very large, bigger-than-life actor/manager, who had a huge voice and presence onstage. I was only a petite 5'2" and he was 6'5" and massive. I couldn't even stand next to him without feeling completely dwarfed by his stature, physically and vocally. I was losing my voice trying to top him, or at least keep my volume at his level. All of a sudden I remembered my tonal NRG and how to tap into it, and create more sound without strain. Everything became instantly easier, and through the Y-buzz, +Y-buzz like focus and using more structure to Call instead of scream, I was able to maintain a comfortable performance-level voice at all times, both in rehearsal and during the actual show. Never again did I feel the need to push, and always took a step back physically rather than force myself to stand close to him and crane my neck in order to look him in the face (unless blocked to do so for effect!).

My second scenario came from a time when I was working in a touring company where I was one of two actors playing multiple roles—on a daily basis—in many different types of school theatres and gymno-class-a-cafeterias. I got a cold, and didn't have enough time to recover fully, because I had to keep working, (or the company would have had financial problems), so I got a good case of laryngitis—which eventually developed into vocal nodules through overuse, misuse and no down-time. I was completely in a panic, since the only way this company could survive was for us to work every day for another couple of weeks. Of course, I immediately went to a highly respected performers' otolaryngologist, who recommended complete vocal rest for six weeks—and offered no therapy at all! I called Arthur, and he immediately gave me his advice over the phone: to begin gently Y-buzzing only for myself. Keep my voice in the Y-buzz range for the last 2 weeks of the contract; which would mean sacrificing some of the range I was used to using. Then, after the run was completed, continue to sustain easy Y-buzz humming, changing pitches just a little bit throughout each day, and speak only quietly.

So, after the contract ended, I continued to rest, speak only in my quietest voice—but with the addition of easy humming with the Y-buzz periodically throughout each day; and in 3 weeks, my voice was completely healed. The nodules had vanished through the gentle vibration of the Y-buzz! Needless to say, my otolaryngologist was amazed. But Arthur wasn't—he knew the power and the therapeutic benefits of the Y-buzz. And after this experience, so did I. I love sharing this story with my students, because I want them to understand that vocal problems can beset even the most experienced actors, but that they now have the tools to often minimize those issues and even heal themselves through the training that they have received.

In what local or global context do you see the future of kinesensics, or kinesensic training taking place within the next 50 years? In particular, what needs or possibilities, if any, do you think this type of training or work will address or shape in the future?

My hope is that this work can continue to spread and that it will have an impact in the arenas of wellness (especially in the area of the treatment of such disorders as clinical depression and anxiety), speech pathology, singing, and physical fitness. It should not only be considered specifically actor training any more—but 'life' training. For instance, in my own personal studio, clients come for accent reduction or modification, and are not necessarily performers, but are presenters. They want to be understood by their audiences, yet still retain their indigenous accents. I have worked with congressmen from D.C. who want stronger, more articulate voices in order that they may be able to present their platforms or programs more effectively. Lawyers seek out my studio in order to learn how to use their voices in the court room, members of the clergy come to discover how they can more easily move the hearts and minds of congregations through the power of the spoken word. And the list goes on. When people recognize that they need assistance with regard to vocal issues, this training can help them uncover and discover the voice that lies within.

We are very familiar with the phrase *the eyes are the window to the soul*. Well, I feel that if this is true, then *the voice must be the door to the soul*. After all, the voice carries our thoughts, desires, ambitions, emotions, persuasions etc. to our immediate world and to the world at large. Possessing an effective, communicating body/voice enables us to more easily interact as we move through our daily lives. So, this training can indeed be training for life.

In what ways, if any, do you think that the Lessac work/approach can and should still be developed in the future?

First of all, the work would best be served by continuing to offer comprehensive training, not only for those who want this work for their own personal development, but also for those interested in teaching this work. It's imperative that our certified trainers know this work inside-and-out, not only for their own self-use, but also in order to share it within their spheres of influence. Secondly, we need to develop centers for workshops that are geared toward the needs of those interested in the field of self-improvement with regard to health and wellness, as well as vocal strengthening and empowerment. We also should continue to grow in our clinical research, and develop and encourage the writing of books and articles that support the efficacy of this body of work.

Deborah A. Kinghorn

Deborah A. Kinghorn (Deb) is a 25-year veteran teacher who still gets butterflies in her stomach on the first day of classes. She has taught Acting I, Advanced Acting, Movement and Vocal Production, The Actor's Voice through Text, Dialects, Period and Style, and Audition Technique. She holds degrees from SUNY at Fredonia (BA, Theatre) and Trinity University through the Dallas Theatre Center (MFA, Theatre, with emphasis in Acting). She has also done a year of intensive study in Acting, Voice and Movement at the Manchester Polytechnic School of Theatre in Manchester, England. She is a Master Teacher of Lessac Kinesensic Training. She is a member of the Voice and Speech Trainer's Association (VASTA). She currently serves on the Board of Directors of the Lessac Training and Research Institute, where she was recently honored with the first annual Leadership award, and regularly teaches at the Lessac Summer Intensive Workshop. She has been the Voice, Dialects and Text coach for over 100 shows in many theatres, including the Alley Theatre in Houston, Texas, the Dallas Theater Center, the Houston Shakespeare Festival, and Stages Theatre, also in Houston. As a director, she has chosen from a wide variety of styles of plays, including Shakespeare in Hollywood, Much Ado About Nothing, Lend Me a Tenor, Tartuffe, Macbeth, Kindertransport, The Memory of Water, The Bear, The Proposal, The Last Night of Ballyhoo, Urban Voices (an original musical), My Left Breast, A Murder is Announced, *and* The Servant of Two Masters. *Her favorite acting roles include Cecily in* The Importance of Being Ernest, *Curley's Wife in* Of Mice and Men, *Hannah Mae Bindler in* A Coupla White Chicks Sitting Around Talking, *Desdemona in* Othello, *Lorraine in* Shoulders, *and the many characters she portrayed in the comedy* Greater Tuna. *She received the University of Houston Teaching Excellence Award in 1995. Deb presently serves as Chair of the Department of Theatre and Dance at the University of New Hampshire. Her current research involves the kinesensic training and its applications to the subtle energies of the mind and soul. She loves to sing. She and her husband, Jeff are often seen making fools of themselves over their two mini-dachshunds, General Bonaparte and Mocha.*

Describe the context in which you were introduced to Lessac training.

I first encountered the Lessac training in 1973, in my undergraduate school (SUNY at Fredonia) during my theatre education. My professors, Jack and LeeAnne

Cogdill, had attended a summer workshop and came back teaching our voice and diction class in this new way. (Prior to that, we had been learning Skinner technique.) I liked the work very much, because it was simple to grasp and did not involve endless repetition. Following undergraduate school, I attended graduate school at the Dallas Theatre Center (1976-1980) where I studied with Randy and Norma Moore, who also taught the Lessac work. By my journeyman year (third year), I was given an opportunity to assist both of them with their teaching of the work. In 1980, I was fortunate enough to work with Jack Jones for the brief time he taught at the Theatre Center. Once I got my first job in academe, I realized I was not as fully prepared to teach the work as I had thought. I applied for and received funding to attend the 1984 Lessac Summer Workshop held in Duluth, Minnesota. There is where I met Arthur, Sue Ann (Park), Dick (Cuyler) and Libby (Roman). It was a six-week workshop, where I encountered the Body NRGs for the first time, and I was hooked. That next year (1985), Arthur asked me to teach with him at a training workshop for ACTF Irene Ryan winners. Teaching alongside him was a revelation and the hours spent discussing the work during the off-times cemented my desire to teach this work.

What do you mean by that last statement? Can you elaborate a little more about your relationship with Arthur, since 1985, and about what types of revelations, if any, evolved over time?

I was able to watch Arthur teach during that time, and I was amazed at how quickly he could get results from people, and how they always loved the results and were eager to learn more. Now, it's not just the immediate gratification factor, which kept them learning. It was the fact that he took away all the obstacles that so many of us had heard were true of voice work: it would take a long time, you had to work really hard at it, you had to give up your own personality and sound different from yourself, some people would succeed, some wouldn't, etc. Arthur proved, in the first ten minutes, that ANYONE could do this work, and that you could experience growth immediately; moreover, that ANYONE could feel their true voice and feel the resulting power and centering and balance that comes when we feel free in our expression, and finally, he made it so much fun! It was all play, and that's what made it so freeing. Were the students working? Of course! But they did not think of it as work, so they learned twice as fast, and they learned, as we now know from research, with their whole brain, and their whole being. This was revelatory to me, and I wanted to teach the same way. That took a longer time to develop, but I believe I have come to a place in my life where my teaching of this work embodies those principles I saw in action when he taught.

What was revelatory about the discussions we had was the scope of his vision for the work. In the beginning, I was simply overwhelmed by all the things that he saw were possible. Moreover, I did not think I could attempt those things (like "world peace"!), because, after all, I was just trying to teach voice and movement, right? But the more I talked with him, the more I began to see connections everywhere. And it was only when I began teaching the Intensives, and began working with him on a consistent basis, that I saw that his vision was not beyond reach, because every time we taught an Intensive, people responded—with joy, with love, with laughter, with openness. People bonded. People cared about each other. People learned how to solve problems together. And then it began happening in the one-weekers as well. So it couldn't just be the amount of time spent together—it had to be in the work itself. That's really when I committed myself to a life-long exploration and continuation of this work.

What were the most difficult parts of the work to learn?
This varies, of course, for everyone. For me, it was learning to feel, not to listen. We are so bombarded each day with visual stimulation, and are so accustomed to listening to ourselves, or being fed visual and aural at the same time, that to accomplish a true sense of the feeling process can take a long time. It did for me. Since the rest of the work is built on this premise, I think it affected everything. It did NOT stop me from learning. It was simply, as Arthur puts it, a habit that I had to diffuse. I have been very successful with my own students in blocking out some of the outer environment and helping them to turn inwards towards the feeling process by use of blindfolds.

Which parts of how the work was taught were most beneficial to your learning?
I was most influenced by experiencing through sensation, rather than relying on outside imagery. It was a revelation to me that I did not have to flounder around as I used my voice, but that I could, very simply, feel and reproduce a sensation, which would result in good tone, or in better articulation, or relaxed jaw, or whatever it was I

might be searching for. This idea that everything I needed was present in my own body, if only I could find the organic instruction for it, galvanized my whole approach to voice work, and my whole idea of voice training. I liked knowing that I was in control of all of it—I did not have to rely on someone else's imagery to help me, nor did I have to suffer (as I had often done in the past) as I tried to figure out what the teacher meant by the given image. Their idea of that image and mine might be completely different, and lead to completely different endings, sometimes disastrous. A clear example would be the instruction to hit the final consonants. I learned to articulate this way, making sure every one of those things was hit; and HOW! The amount of pressure and force being used was detrimental to both vocal health and to clarity, surprisingly enough. The overuse of the facial muscles, which resulted from this direction, caused thinning of my tone, strain in my jaw, and a general sense that this was too much work. And it WAS!! I discovered, once I began the Lessac training, that NO force was ever used. In playing a consonant, one connects to both the musicality of the sound itself, and to the artistry that any musician employs in playing an instrument. No artist forces, pushes, squeezes, etc. I discovered that articulation was easy, efficient, and fun. It was very simple, then, to incorporate that into my everyday life, because it felt good, and I enjoyed doing it. But to reiterate, my initial problems came from an outside image: HIT the consonants. The solution came from within—feel the musicality of the consonant (humming or tapping). Another detrimental thing I have been told (by non-Lessac instructors) was to "open wider," or "relax your jaw." Both these instructions, while not imagery, put my body into conflict. The more I "opened wider," the more tension I felt, and the more I would close down. I would leave lessons with an aching jaw, in tears, because I was certain that I would never be able to do what my instructor wanted. How could I open any further? And no matter how far I opened my mouth, I did not seem to be getting the tone he was asking for. What could be wrong? I didn't know, until I began studying the Lessac work, and I discovered the power of the yawn. Here, finally, was a way to experience the fullest opening of the oral cavity WITHOUT strain. I never felt like I was pulling on the jaw; in fact, I stopped thinking about the jaw altogether! The tones that came out were amazing—rich, full, vibrant—I sometimes was amazed that they were coming from me! This, all because the yawn is a natural body relaxer (and energizer)—so of course, the jaw relaxes—but without me telling it to do so. I can't TELL my jaw to relax. I can only do what the body normally does to inspire relaxation in the body—I can yawn, or shake, or float, or dance. You can hum or laugh or smile—these all produce relaxation in the body. But my point is that these sensations are universal, and can be felt/experienced by anyone. To link these to learning how to speak or sing was revolutionary in its time, and I think is still widely under appreciated.

Another part of how the work is taught which has influenced me is the philosophical choice of eschewing practice and drill in favor of exploration and experimentation. I remember, before I studied the Lessac work, sitting with a textbook by a well-known voice teacher, saying endless word lists over and over for a particular sound. I was not at all connected to myself, or learning much from the process, because I was bored. I don't know if I actually improved the sound, because I didn't know what I was working for, except that somehow, by repeating it over and over, it would get better or it would become a part of my daily speech.

Lessac's work is experiential, meaning you must be fully present in the process to learn. I think most voice/movement approaches would say that is what they aspire to as well—but aspiring to and finding the vocabulary to make it happen are two separate things. I found such terms as exploring and experimenting (vs. practice, or drill, or exercise) opened up a new world to me—one in which there wasn't a defined right or wrong but one in which there were vast uncharted territories. This was stimulating, and invited me to go further and further, rather than thinking there was a specific *right* way of doing something, and therefore, an end. Therefore, I could fully explore the playing of the violin (n) for its musicality and feeling, and what kinds of response it engendered in me, without there being a set stopping point. I would stop when I had reached, for that day, a sense of completion and fulfilment. The beauty of this, of course, is that, while exploring, I was also improving tone, structure, form. This is true for all aspects of vocal and physical production. Again, it is wonderfully freeing and inspiring—it makes you curious, you want to know more.

Finally, a huge influence on me has been the understanding of the inner vs. the outer environment. We spend so much time in the outer environment that we tend to ignore or muffle the stirrings of our inner environment. Yet, for an artist, (and I think for anybody) this is the source of creativity. We often think of this as the "voice inside," or a "sixth sense," or "gut feeling." Yet this is only the tip of the iceberg, so to speak. Our inner environment is as vast and complex as the outer environment, perhaps more so. By learning to tune into feeling, by taking time to shut out the outer environment, filled with its noise, distractions, and poisons, we can discover the beauty and power of our inner selves, and at the same time, repair the damage which comes from constant interaction with the outer environment. Some would call this meditation, and I do not disagree that it is partly that. But this meditation, for us, can be reflective OR quite active, as when one is exploring a piece of text. In fact, there is no true stillness, although one can give an appearance, outwardly, of such. However, within the body, systems are constantly in motion, in action—heart pumping, blood flowing, lungs expanding and contracting, muscles fluttering, etc. It is what Arthur calls "gentle inner turbulence." Tuning in to this inner turbulence is in itself a meditation, which is both calming and energizing. I think all of this has been important to my learning because I have always felt the existence of the inner environment, and tried to find my way to it through yoga (and I was successful to a degree—physically, but not vocally). Lessac opened up this vastness to me through his use of the term "energy." I had always known that we are composed of energy; indeed, that all things are energy, but I had never heard anyone delineate various energy qualities the way he did. It immediately caught my attention, because I felt that understanding energy was the way to understand much more than science—I felt that energy is what linked all of us, in the end, to each other, and to the earth, and to the cosmos. Anything that promoted that idea and could lead me further on the path of discovery was something I wanted to be a part of. So consequently, what began as a way of improving my voice became, for me, a way of viewing life, an entire philosophy, which I continue to explore and experiment with today. I am not, nor will I ever be, at the end of my exploration. I find that challenging, inspiring, and exciting. It is what keeps me going.

In what ways have you applied or incorporated Lessac, within the context of what you do for a living, whether that is as a performer, artist, scholar, healer, teacher, therapist, etc?

I have always been involved with theatre, and the jobs I have taken have fallen into the realm of acting, voice, movement, and dialect training (Beyond my own history as an actor and a director). In the beginning, I confined the work to my voice classes, and continued to teach my acting classes as if they were a separate entity. I just didn't know, at that time, how to put them together. And in fact, my training had always separated the two, so I thought it was quite natural. However, over and over again my students would tell me that the voice class was the best acting class they had ever had. And that set me to thinking. What was I doing in the voice class that was better acting training than in the acting class? As it turns out, it was quite simple. In the acting class, I was following the way I had been taught—Stanislavsky-based objective, obstacle, intentions, etc. I taught how to break the scene down into beats, and I made people learn about verbs. Well, all of that is good, but unless you had already felt the acting process fully, as I had in the profession, it easily became intellectual and separate from the body. In my voice classes, the students began from the feeling process and were awakened to their own creativity. They were making all the same choices I had them make in acting class, but it was coming from a different place—their hearts, not their minds. After this discovery, I did what I could to unite the two, but it took me a long time to do so. Once I began directing (around 1995) this process speeded up. The one thing that has evolved continually for me is my deeper and deeper understanding of the feeling process. What I came away with from my six-week workshop and what I know now about it is a night and day difference. Perhaps the greatest change to my teaching has been my attention to health and wellness as the basis for all of the work, both voice/movement and acting. Now not a day goes by when I do not utilize this work. I teach acting classes via the feeling process, I teach voice and movement the same way, I teach dialects using this training, and I myself use it every day in my communication with others. I use it to find relief from arthritis and bursitis, to keep myself strong, and to become more in tune with my body and my inner environment, and learn what I can from what my body is teaching me.

How valuable is the Lessac Training to your performance skills?

The pre-rehearsal process of exploration frees me from making decisions too early about my character. It is often true that actors come into rehearsals with line readings that are so set; it is nearly impossible to change them. The Lessac exploration work gives me wide latitude in discovering the character, and helps me find deeper understanding of her. It often takes me to unexpected places, which I sometimes feel, when alone, couldn't possibly apply in the real production, but when in rehearsal, those are the exact feelings that pour forth and lead to deeper, truer understanding and playing the character. These beautiful moments almost always end up in the real production! This work keeps me from becoming set, so that I am always open to what my partner is doing, and responding in the moment to it. All in all, it is simply freeing. The training of the voice and body have, of course, sustained me in ways too numerous to mention. A few of these would be: sustainable vocal and physical health, even under the stressful conditions of rehearsal and performance; fullest, easiest expressiveness of voice and body (an instrument which responds without effort); the ability to portray characters who have negative traits (hunching, tight-jawed, physical deformity, or even harder, psychological darkness and anger—bigotry or prejudice) without damaging my own instrument with that negativity—in other words, as Arthur so often says, "learning how to do the incorrect thing correctly."

Please describe one context or vignette that best represents the way(s) in which you have you applied or incorporated Lessac training within the development of your own voice and body, and how, if at all, this process has been used by you as a means for problem-solving, learning, healing, performance, communication, and/or increasing your own vitality of life.

As I mentioned (previously), I suffer from arthritis and bursitis (hips, knees, ankles), which has worsened over the past few years. I also have constant lower back pain, stemming from several unrelated accidents in my younger years. I work with the body and vocal NRGs, the C-curve, and the full breath to counteract the negative effects of those traumas on my body. Muscle-yawning has been particularly effective in keeping me flexible, and working out with small ball and expanded sphere, especially with the atom-to-atom movement, has protected my back and reduced the pain to that which is manageable. Since I am reluctant to take pills, I have been very thankful to have this way of working which seems to be just as effective as pills, if not more so! The vocal work that I do is just as important as the body work—because the vibrations of singing, humming, and calling create an inner massage for the body which is soothing and invigorating at the same time. I lead a very active life, and am probably like many people—over-committed because I care about so many things. Sometimes the stress is a lot, but I find that smelling the flower, humming, singing, muscle yawning, Y-buzzing, Calling, laughing out loud—well, all of these help disperse the stress. I believe they have helped me get through some very busy times without getting sick.

In what local or global context do you see the future of kinesensics, or kinesensic training taking place within the next 50 years? In particular, what needs or pos-

sibilities, if any, do you think this type of training or work will address or shape in the future?

I will answer these together, because I think they are inseparable. Lessac training is open-ended, in that it cannot stop growing. But it cannot stay within the realm of theater alone. Yet that is still where we attract our biggest audience. In the future, I can see this training used in primary education, teaching kids the musicality of their own voices. I can see it in all kinds of athletic and workout endeavors, creating a healthier workout and a safer experience. I can see it having an effect on the "pill" industry—after all, if you can make yourself feel good, what do you need pills for? But I can also see it as a way of teaching people how to communicate better with one another. This is where it has the potential to have the greatest impact. Our society, and our world, is struggling with lack of communication, regardless of all the modern conveniences, which help us "stay in touch." And though on the surface it seems we have come a long way from racial/gender/religious stereotyping and prejudice, we have a long, long way to go, and this work can HELP, by giving people a way of truly feeling themselves as whole and connected to everything else in the universe, through the power of energy. This is not a pipe dream. We see this happen every single summer in the Intensive, and we see it happen even in the one-week experiences. It isn't a matter of time. It is a matter of message—getting the message out there—that in this work, there is a way for ANYONE to help himself or herself feel better, look better, sound better, and enjoy their life more. It is not too much to think that our work can address public enemy number one: fear. In fact, we address fear at every step of the way in the Intensive—fear of meeting new people, fear of looking different, fear of not doing it right, fear of failure—all the fears that, left alone, create problems for everyone, as behavior spins out of control. On a large scale, this is what happens in the world. But in our work, we help the student find the hard and harsh places within, and soften them. We help them find the way to laughter, openness, and ease in communication. That is a worthy goal, which goes beyond the theater. Will it result in world peace? Hardly my place to say. But I think the elevation of the human spirit to a higher plane of experience is a worthwhile endeavor.

Barry Kur

Barry Kur is a Master Lessac Teacher and has been a voice, speech, dialect and text coach for over 100 productions in university and regional professional theatres throughout the United States. Mr. Kur is currently the Associate Director of the School of Theatre, Penn State University, where is voice/speech specialist for all actor training programs. He is the recipient of Penn State's George W. Atherton Award for Teaching Excellence. He is currently President and the Director of Certification of the Lessac Training and Research Institute. In addition, he has been on the faculty of Ohio University, the South Carolina Governor's School of the Arts and Humanities, and is the past-president of the Voice and Speech Trainers Association (VASTA). During the spring of 2001, he was an invited guest teacher of four theatre-training programs in South Africa. He is the author of "Stage Dialect Studies: A Continuation of The Lessac Approach to Actor Voice and Speech Training" and teaches summer workshops of the Lessac Institute.

Describe the context in which you were introduced to Lessac training? For example, when did you receive training, who provided the training, why did you choose this approach, and how did the training take place?

As a Masters degree candidate at State University of New York—Binghamton, 1974-76, I enrolled in elective courses in voice/speech work with Professor Sue Ann Park. During that time, I became aware that Arthur Lessac, Sue Ann Park, Richard Cuyler and Libby Roman were all on the faculty in the Department of Theatre. Arthur and this team of master teachers of the Lessac work initiated a yearlong certification program in 1976. In 1977, after my two semesters of work with Sue Ann, I was accepted into the second and, unfortunately, the final yearlong certification program. This program included six students, lasting two full semesters, and met Monday through Friday. Each day included body work for three hours, two hours of voice work each day, buddy work and private lessons throughout the week, singing lessons, and some of us were involved with the Department of Theater productions.

In my initial experience with the work, I was introduced to an area of actor training missing from my undergraduate work. I simply took to the work because I seemed to readily grasp it. In addition, as a former theatre and secondary education major, I was attracted to the progression of events that were so seriously constructed by Sue Ann as part of the teaching process. I found a clear process to expand my creative sensibilities and I found an *artful* way of teaching.

As a certification candidate, I was immersed in the work. I discovered how it related to my entire physical life and how it gave me confidence and the potential for almost anything I cared to explore (sports, singing, tai chi, classical acting, healing needs, etc.). I was a keen observer of my instructors and continued to sense how it was being taught as well as what I was gaining personally. At the close of the year, I was given a recommendation to begin a teaching career at Ohio University's MFA Actor Training Program. I got the job replacing the retiring Lessac trained teacher, Ginny Hahn.

In what ways have you applied or incorporated Lessac, within the context of what you do for a living, whether that is as a performer, artist, scholar, healer, teacher, therapist, etc.? Please identify what you do, and how, if all, this process developed or evolved over time.

Since 1977, I have taught in Professional Actor Training programs as the primary voice/speech specialist. I began my career at Ohio University's MFA Actor Training program and in 1982 I was hired by the Penn State University School of Theatre to teach in all of its actor training programs (BA, BFA Musical Theatre, MFA Acting). For 22 years, I was the sole voice/speech specialist, who taught and coached all of the students. I have been there for 26 years and I now work with a colleague with whom I share the teaching and coaching duties. I am a tenured full professor and also serve as Associate Director of the School of Theatre.

All of my voice/speech classes are strictly Lessac based. The amount of time spent with the work varies for each training program. However, all of my students experience the basic progression of events leading to awareness and application of the vocal NRGs (infused with the body NRG work).[1] In addition, I have developed a process of acquiring Stage Dialects through the Lessac work and am the author of *Stage Dialect Studies:*

---

[1] "Once experienced kine-sensically, these different energy (NRG) states can be categorized, recognized for the synergistic inter-relationships, and perceived as unique/familiar events" (Lessac 1978, 1982:32).

A Continuation of the Lessac Approach to Actor Voice/Speech Training.[2] All of the students have an opportunity to work with dialects in my advanced-level classes.

For twenty-two years, I also taught the Lessac work to talented and gifted high school theatre artists in a five-week intensive training program at the South Carolina Governor's School for the Arts and Humanities.

Over the last six years, I have been a member of the teaching team of the Lessac Institute's summer workshops: The Summer Intensive Workshop, The Teacher Training Workshop or the One Week Introductory Workshop.[3]

Can you elaborate about or discuss your evolution into working with those who want to *teach the work*?

Each training program presents variables that present interesting challenges in the teaching of the Lessac work; the time structure of events, the students' life experiences, their desire to adapt vocal/body behavior, and the issue of whether they are enrolled in the course as an elective or a degree requirement are some of those variables.

I enjoy the challenge of adapting the selection or order of training events for a given group or even a private tutorial. As I often profess to new teachers as a teacher-training mentor, "teach what you know and recognize that what you know is a rich toolbox of resources." This becomes extremely important when asked to work with an individual who may need special attention on a challenge that some may consider rehabilitation as well as actor training. I often need to empathetically sense what the individual is experiencing. Sue Ann Park often mentions that when I was a beginning student in her classes, I would intensely focus on her and my classmates as they explored a challenge. She would see me nodding affirmatively as her suggested solution was the same as mine would be. I spent much time learning by empathetically experiencing what I thought my classmates were feeling or doing. This was so much of the yin-yang of the certification program—teaching self and teaching others.

---

[2] Kur, Barry. 2006. *Stage Dialect Studies: A Continuation of the Lessac Approach to Actor Voice and Speech Training.* Self-Publication (see www.lessacinstitute.com to order).

[3] The Summer Intensive Workshop and Teacher Training Workshop currently take place at DePauw University. The one-week introductory workshop, which also takes place during the summer, is currently held at The University of Mary Washington (www.lesacinstitute.com).

One other issue of evolution that continues to develop is the training of those who wish to teach the Lessac work. Nancy Krebs and I have modeled our summer workshops after the development by Sue Ann Park of the teaching process. To traverse from self-to-self discovery toward self-to other instruction is an ever-evolving element of the Lessac work.

Could you elaborate further on what you previously called "a process of acquiring Stage Dialects through the Lessac work," and the significance, if any, you have observed or reflected on, when connecting the Lessac work to the training of Stage Dialects within an acting training program?

The development of my dialect textbook began simply because of my Ohio University job description, which included teaching stage dialects. Initially, I utilized Jerry Blunt's *Stage Dialects,*[4] but supplemented the text with handouts with the Lessac tono-sensory phonetic transcriptions. I was learning the dialects at the same time as my students but with a knowledge of physical, as opposed to auditory, adaptations through my Lessac training. Eventually, I was able to codify the physical awareness of facial postures, tone quality sensations, pitch and fluency elements of each dialect and their effect upon phonemes, which evolved into a kinesensic training of dialect acquisition.

I find that dialect study became an extension of the basic work rather than just a special skill on the bottom of one's resume. It's a study in vocal agility and gives the actor a remarkable new conduit of expression beyond his/her close- to-self vocal behavior. In fact there are some actors who reveal more inner life, awarded a kind of permission of emotional life, in the behavior of an accent than in their familiar vocal behavior.

In what ways was the experience of teaching "talented and gifted high school artists" similar or different to your experience as a primary voice/speech specialist at a major University?

The South Carolina Governor's School Drama program was structured as a pre-professional conservatory actor-training program. The students were selected, through interviews and auditions, according to acting talent and a willing attitude to immerse in the training. However, they were sixteen-year-old boys and girls with the common

---

[4] Blunt, Jerry. 1994. *Stage Dialects.* New York: Dramatic Publishers.

social pressures and concerns of all adolescents and they were all South Carolina residents. My task was to introduce the value of voice/speech training, develop an awareness of creative exploration through voice/speech craft, and introduce the ability to adapt their vocal behavior suitable for the professional theatre, which included working in plays where a Southern dialect would not be acceptable. The Lessac work provided a non-threatening process of discovery and learning because the students became aware of their speech and voice behavior as physical sensations and not auditory judgment of good or bad from me.

In addition to the application of the Lessac work into dialect studies, I continue to find more and more *bridging* elements to the musical voice and musical theatre. It may appear obvious to those who are aware of the *musical metaphor* inherent in the basic work but as a performer and teacher, this element of evolution is always exciting to experience by newcomers and/or veteran performing artists. As a newcomer to traditional singing lessons late in life, my awareness of making vocal music with the Lessac work was a familiar event and provided great confidence in those singing lessons. As I teach musical theatre students at Penn State, I find that these students cross the bridge from vocal musician to actor-singer through their awareness of the Lessac consonant orchestra. The lyrics become more valuable through consonant awareness and because the consonants are musical instruments, what was once technical *diction* becomes an extension of the musical lyric.

Please describe one context or vignette that best represents the way(s) in which you have you applied or incorporated Lessac training within the development of your own voice and body, and how, if at all, this process has been used by you as a means for problem-solving, learning, healing, performance, communication, and/or increasing your own vitality of life?

The context in which I have applied the work is a holistic one. The Lessac work possesses a challenging strength in that from the work you have the body knowledge for so many life events. Lately, I've been referring to my *inner monologue* when referring to how I apply the concepts of the work to my vocal/physical life. The inner monologue is how I instruct or re-instruct myself in a challenging physical activity, in working on a performance, in healing an ailment, or when encountering an unfamiliar event. (I often ask my students when recalling a vocal event in class, "What was your inner monologue, how did you instruct yourself to recall that event or to improve the quality of that event?")

Now in my mid fifties, I feel relatively healthy and remain physically active. However, when exercise walking or weight training, I often remind myself about body symmetry, application of a body NRG, *contiguous continuity*, etc. Even after 30-plus years of teaching, I still assure myself that I will have a confident presence in the classroom by tuning up and modeling well the vocal NRGs. My 50th birthday was a very celebratory time for me, not because of a party or gift, but because of vitality in my life—a vitality partly due to my awareness of self through the work.

In what ways, if any, do you think that the Lessac work/approach can and should still be developed in the future?

A few years ago I was introduced to book by Daniel H. Pink, entitled *A Whole New Mind*[5]. In the introduction, Pink states:

> The last few decades have belonged to a certain kind of person with a certain kind of mind—computer programmers who could crank code, lawyers who could craft contracts, MBA's who could crunch numbers. But the keys to the kingdom are changing hands. The future belongs to a very different kind of person with a very different kind of mind—creators and empathizers, pattern recognizers, and meaning makers. These people—artists, inventors, designers, storytellers, caregivers, consolers, big picture thinkers—will now reap society's richest rewards and share its greatest toys.
>
> …We are moving from an economy and a society built on logical, linear, computer like capabilities of the Information Age to an economy and society built on the inventive, empathic, big-picture capabilities of what's rising in its place, the Conceptual Age.

I could go on sharing Pink's words about the future but instead I invite those reading this reflection to read his book and draw upon many of the same kinesensic connections to his ideas. I recall in my early Lessac body and voice work how much I

---

[5] Pink, Daniel. 2005. *A Whole New Mind*. New York: Penguin Books.

could feel as if I was (sense the inner life of) a dancer, singer, or great orator as I explored the various training events. With the body (including vocal) wisdom in my personal toolbox, I have confidence to solve problems, confront challenges, and empathize with others' sensations. I am aware of the difference between those actions/conditions that may anesthetize my senses and those that keep my expressive conduits open to impulse, imagination, honesty, and discovery. Kinesenic learning is about seeing the big picture—a gestalt.

I believe the scope of application of the Lessac work is endless.

Era Three: The Future

Sean Turner

The following oral histories include dialogues with Kathleen Dunn, who was one of the first people Arthur began training when he moved to the West Coast in 1983; Crystal Robbins, who became Arthur's personal secretary in 1998; Gert Terny, who developed the European Lessac Center in 2006; and Robin Carr, who earned a Lessac teaching certification in 2008 and, along with Daisy Nystul[6], became one of the first to be able to intern during the summer intensives. Each of these histories highlights new possibilities for the Lessac work in the future, as well as situates a new era of Lessac trainers.

In addition, I have included a dialogue with Melissa Hurt, who is currently going through the Lessac certification process and is working on her dissertation, which is focused on kinesensic theory (the perceptual feeling process) and how this articulates and accommodates an embodied acting practice. The significance of this dialogue is that it allows Hurt to develop her story around her research and interviews with Arthur Lessac, which took place during 2008, as well as her dissertation and current experiences going through the Lessac teaching certification process.

---

[6] Daisy Nystul (née Bristow) was certified in 2008 (www.lessacinstitute.com).

Kathleen Dunn

Kathleen Dunn is a Lessac certified Voice and Body Instructor who has taught and worked extensively with professional actors, teachers, voice therapists, and ESL clients throughout the country, as well as teaching acting, speech and dialects at the University of Southern California, Los Angeles and Santa Monica College. Kathleen has been a professional TV/film/stage actress for over twenty years. Her recent credits include leading roles in the films Cold Intelligence *with Michael Denney,* Joy Riders *with Martin Landau,* Tilly *(which won the Boston Film Festival 2004), and* Fish, *which was a Project Greenlight finalist in 2004, as well as television roles in* ER, Sons and Daughters, *and* Bold and Beautiful. *Kathleen has won four drama awards in the Los Angeles area for her stage work.*

Kathleen Dunn is recognized within the Hollywood TV/film industry for "uniting voice, body and imagination" in her accent and dialect coaching. Her recent acting clients have been: Ken Watanabe in Shanghai, *Chow Yan Fat in* Dragon Ball Evolution, *Kate Towne in* Blu, *Koyuki Katou and Gianna Jun in* Blood: The Last Vampire, *Jun-Dung Kun in* Laundry Warrior, *Chris Hemsworth in* Star Trek 2009, *Jessica Pare in* Life, *Gina Bellman in* Leverage, *and both Katee Sackhoff and Damon Herriman in* Lost and Found, *and Max Martini from* The Unit.

Describe the context in which you were introduced to Lessac training. For example, when did you receive training, who provided the training, why did you choose this approach, and how did the training take place?

I first came across Lessac Training in my undergraduate theatre program at Western Michigan. I was introduced to Arthur's book via Russell Grandstaff, a compassionate director and devoted supporter of actor training. The theatre program required the students to pick up the book, *The Use and Training of the Human Voice.*[1] Mr. Grandstaff provided the beginnings of my training and would encourage us to feel "easy up" with our posture, and forward tone. During the summer months, I would return to the farm where I grew up in Indiana. Here, I had many open spaces to explore the voice work in Arthur's book. I would take the book into our barn and do the

---

[1] Lessac, Arthur. 1967.

explorations and experiments. I don't know why I needed to do this, but I continued with this type of self-exploration. During my time at Western Michigan, I began to incorporate the work in my extensive summer stock experiences as well as other acting experiences in theatre and film. By the time I had graduated Western Michigan University, I had been offered two choices: I had been accepted to the American Academy of Dramatic Arts and Music in New York OR I could pursue an internship to get my master's degree in theatre performance at Cal-State Fullerton.[2] It was a difficult decision, but knowing that I wanted to pursue a career both in TV/film acting and teaching, I decided to move to California and study for my masters in actor training. It was during my first year at Cal-State Fullerton that Mr. Arthur Lessac came into our classroom and became my teacher[3] and life-long mentor. I have read about serendipity—following your heart and the underlying *voice* that tells you to do things before you know why—and I think that best describes how I was introduced to the work: I was *feeling my way*, something that Arthur has always encouraged us to do. After working with Arthur at Cal-State, I spent four more summers focusing on getting certified, during which I continued to work with him as well as the other master teachers, including Sue Ann Parks, Libby Roman and Richard and Saundra Cuyler.

I remember the first time the work had penetrated my bones; I was working on Linda Rotunda from *Savage in Limbo*.[4] There was the phrase: "ugly girls," which I was vocally skimming over. After having the introduction to consonant energy, Arthur had asked me, "explore feeling the *g* drumbeat in that phrase and see what it gives you."…All of a sudden, the connection to the *g* drumbeat music gave me pain of being rejected by Tony and his need to date ugly girls…and images of what those ugly girls looked like. To discover those images internally in my own body, stuck with me and thus the discovery of the voice/body connection became my life-long passion in performing, in training the beginner to advanced actor, and finally in my professional coaching of actors of TV/film/and theatre in the areas of dialect acquisition and accent modification. And most recently, the joy I find in coaching the English as Second Language (ESL) client.

---

[2] The Theatre Arts and Dance Department. California State University at Fullerton currently offers Master of Fine Arts degrees in acting, directing, scene design and technical production, and secondary teaching (http://www.fullerton.edu).
[3] Arthur Lessac served as a distinguishing visiting professor at California State University, Fullerton during the late 1980's, where he taught voice and movement workshops.
[4] *Savage in Limbo*, written by John Patrick Shanley.

In what ways have you applied or incorporated Lessac, within the context of what you do for a living, whether that is as a performer, artist, scholar, healer, teacher, or therapist? Please identify what you do, and how, if at all, this process (I.e. the application or incorporation of Lessac within your work) has developed or evolved over time.

In my work as a professional accent coach and dialect coach for TV and Motion Pictures, I have worked with studios such as 20th Century Fox, Paramount Studios, Universal Studios, NBC, and the Weinstein Company, as well as business clients such as Crystal Cruises, Conexant, and Leet Corp.

Using the training I have received through the Lessac Institute has allowed me to become my own problem-solver. Most recently, I have worked as an Accent & Dialect Coach in: German, Russian, Polish, Boston, Tennessee, Texan, New York Bronx, Middle Eastern, Irish, Romanian, RP British English, Cockney, and prepared actors in Geordie accents for Elton John's Broadway musical, *Billy Elliot*.[5]

Warm-Ups

The first job I had in working with accent modification and dialect acquisition was with actors from Australia and England. Most came to me because they were having difficulty in embodying the American accent. Many were taught that the non-regional American accent was throaty and monotone. One of my first professional experiences with this was coaching a young Australian actor Khan Chittenden in the film *Introducing the Dwights* (2007). Mr. Chittenden wanted me to help him brush up on his American accent. I introduced to him the sensation that a non-regional American speech is not a throaty sound rumbling in the throat, but a healthy flexible voice with forward tone. A general American speech has some wonderful open vowels that bring warmth and expression to the voice. During a warm-up that I created for him, he discovered that his voice was freer and more expressive without vocal strain.

Use Of Consonant Energy

My next client was Ken Watanabe who had acted in films such as *The Last Samuari* (2003) and *Memoirs of a Geisha* (2005). I worked as Mr. Watanabe's Dia-

---

[5] Based on the critically acclaimed feature film, *Billy Elliot* was brought to Broadway by the movie's original creative team—director Stephen Daldry, choreographer Peter Darling and writer Lee Hall—along with music legend Elton John (http://www2.billyelliotbroadway.com).

logue Coach for the films *Cirque du Freak* (2009) and the period film *Shanghai* (2009). In *Shanghai*, Mr. Watanabe was to portray a Japanese Colonel in WWII. Although Mr. Watanabe was to create a Colonel who had Japanese roots, through our research of his character, we concluded that Mr. Watanabe needed to sound clear as a commanding officer with a slight British RP accent. We took weeks to develop his clarity with the English language, that is to say, lessoning of his native Japanese accent. During one of our sessions, I decided to begin with feeling the British middle *T's* as drumbeats. I begin tapping out a *T* drumbeat rhythm on the table, and soon we were playing with words; I showed him the pictures of consonants as instruments and he said: "oh, music; I play the trumpet!" We then began to feel the *N*, *TH*, and *L's* as sustainable music, and as a result, clarity became fun to experience. Since British RP is very fluid and connected, it was very important to connect the "little words" together, so we incorporated the idea of fluidity using the concept of prepare and link utilized in Lessac Training. Speaking English as a Second Language Speaker clearly and with a British RP Dialect was not the only challenge. Mr. Watanabe's character also had to speak Chinese Mandarin in several of his scenes as well.

I then hired a Mandarin language teacher and together we learned his lines in Mandarin. *Shanghai* was shooting in London, UK and Mr. Watanabe made arrangements for me to be on-set with him as his scenes were filmed. Mr. Watanabe needed to remain flexible in shooting as his scenes were both in Chinese Mandarin as well as British RP English. Due to the pre-production work with Mr. Watanabe and his exceptional talent, he was able to perform convincingly in Mandarin as well as British RP, with praises from the director Mikael Hafstrom.[6]

In my experiences of coaching accents and dialects, I need to encourage more body/ voice integration so the dialect doesn't sound artificial. Mr. Watanabe has that exceptional talent to embody his character and make it organic.

Accent Reduction
In the area of accent reduction coaching and ESL client coaching, I approach this process not as *elimination* or *modification*, but exploring and gaining new *consonant music* or

---

[6] Directed films *1408* (2007); *Derailed* (2005).

consonant sensations. Since my time is limited, sometimes just meeting acting clients for the first time before an ADR session,[7] I have to avoid musical terms, since I don't know how they would respond to the idea of music. However, my regular acting and ESL clients love to hum and sing the consonant orchestra as well as explore various scripts and texts with their newfound vocal energies. Again, keeping a gentle awareness of embodying by breathing and not tensing, exploring vocal dynamics to increase emotional phrasing, and using the various body energies for various modes of communication and expression.

Prepare & Link, Use of a Familiar Event

On the film *Dragonball Evolution*[8] my assignment was as ADR Dialogue Coach for Chinese actor, Chow Yun Fat.[9] Mr. Chow Yun Fat has a great ability for producing the English consonants individually, however the speed and tempo with which his character spoke on screen was a bit of a tongue twister for any native speaker in English. In order to address this problem, I utilized the "prepare and link" concept from the Lessac work.[10] I was taking a chance with this actor, since I had never worked with him previously, and didn't know what he would think about linking and flowing. I sensed that this was the next level to proceed with him in his English speaking. The ADR session went smoothly, and they asked him to do the prologue and trailer for the movie. Again, we had only a few hours to sight read and explore the phrasing and tempo, and he was very open to exploring the text in different ways. Through the use of feeling the consonants in a flowing connected manner, he improved his command of English in a new and subtle manner.

Another challenge was that the director[11] wanted to have more of an American sounding short "a" as in "can't." We could produce a beautiful British broad "ah," but the short "a" was inconsistent until we discovered that he was familiar with Jean

---

[7] The process of automated dialogue replacement, or ADR for short, includes re-recording lines an actor spoke during filming that must be replaced to improve audio quality or reflect dialogue changes (http://en.wikipedia.org/wiki/Dubbing_(filmmaking)).

[8] 2009, Twentieth Century Fox. Filmed on set in Los Angeles, California.

[9] *Crouching Tiger, Hidden Dragon* (2003); *Anna and the King* (1999); *Shanghai* (2009).

[10] Refers to marking-up the text according to a phonetic markup system identified in Arthur Lessac's *The Use And Training Of The Human Voice* (1997). In comparison to the I.P.A. system, which does not deal at all with the operational linking together of sounds within words, phrases and larger units of speech, the Lessac linking together different sounds where different emphasis can vary meaning.

[11] James Wong.

Hagen's portrayal of the "whiny actress" in *Singing in the Rain*.[12] She has this line, "I can't stand it…" So, having him feel the "a" in such an extravagant, playful manner, allowed him to have a sense of this in his American dialogue. Whatever triggers a playfulness and a natural organic response is what Arthur terms as a familiar event for an actor. I never thought a whiny "I can't stand it…" could be a positive familiar event, but I am definitely open to new ways of problem solving.

In one of the final moments, where it is very physical, he has to call out a line with a lot of *R* and *L* consonants. We were hung up on the pronunciation of the words, rather than just Calling out in a heightened manner, so we began to call the lines back and forth, which freed his voice, and brought a balanced clarity. Mr. Chow Yun Fat was another talented actor whose training included precision yet being open to trying new things. His talent, combined with the curiosity of exploring and gift of improvising made it a pleasurable and memorable coaching experience.

Academic Training Applications

Beyond my professional work, I am a professor of voice, speech and dialect studies at the University of Southern California, Los Angeles (USC) and Santa Monica College. At both universities, I am helping actors discover the connection between the body and the voice, and to make discoveries of how this connection comes into communion with organic behavior when exploring text and dialect performances. I have been teaching this work for 18 years and I start *new* every time. I walk into the class with a *plan* but the work may take us in a slightly different manner. However the body and vocal energies are always there to keep us on track; it's just that the body and vocal energies allow for new discoveries for meaning and behavior. I find that various acting exercises are more fully embodied when the students have experienced the vocal and body energies. Transitions between monologues for auditions become a wonderful experiment in body transformation. When the actor is required to put two contrasting pieces together, we begin by exploring through the various vocal and body energies. Through the sensations of these energies, the student begins to create two human situations and personalities, and therefore two 'contrasting pieces' that many acting programs require of the student.

---

[12] Jean Hagen played Lina Lamont in the 1952 movie *Singing in the Rain*, directed by Stanley Donen and Gene Kelly (http://www.imdb.com/name/nm0353405/bio).

Can you provide an example that illustrates the way either you have integrated the work within acting for Film and Television, or a way in which you teach your students to integrate the work during filming?

This reminds me of an earlier experience where I used "the Call" during the filming of the movie *Titanic*, directed by James Cameron.[13] What he wanted to hear piercing the cold, lonely night were voices that were losing life. During my audition, I was informed that Mr. Cameron himself was going to hand select the actors for this part of the story. He wanted to see who got it. Who felt the pain? Who lived the action? Who understood "the calling for your life!" I was chosen for one of the unfortunate passengers aboard The Titanic. I was flown to Mexico to work with Mr. Cameron for several weeks filming this part of the tragedy: people crying and Calling out to the lifeboats as they froze to death in the icy waters. It was the most unforgettable experience. Mr. Cameron was a wonderful director, very meticulous and literally in love with every moment of the story. We spent time as a cast creating a back-story, who I was and why I would be on the Titanic. Another actor and I decided to be the honeymoon couple whose lives ended in tragedy. By the twelfth hour of shooting, as you might imagine, some voices were tiring. What was amazing to me was that Mr. Cameron never said, "yell" for the lifeboats, or "shout out" for the lifeboats. No, he instructed us to "call" for the lifeboats. We were to use the urgency of the situation: the sinking ship, the frozen waters, the destruction, the death, the fear, and the sadness. Twelve-hour days and two weeks later, we were exhausted and done. Some months later, his production company called me in to do some looping for the death and freezing scenes. Upon returning to the studio, Mr. Cameron said to me, with a twinkle in his eye, "Okay, Kathleen, do that thing you do so well." As a teacher, I find that the Call experience is a great way to help a young theatre artist develop healthy dynamic volume.

I preach to my young actors the importance of voice and body work in relation to the creative process. When I played the lead role of Sarah in the movie *Tilly*,[14] I was

---

[13] The Lessac work eliminates any basic difference between singing and speaking by utilizing three vocal energy states (tonal, consonants, and structural). "The Call goes beyond the Y-buzz and the +Y-buzz in tonal NRG and is designed to expand and develop range, pitch, volume production and quality of practically the entire speaking voice...." (Lessac 1997:137). The Call emphasizes the sensory awareness of bone conduction as well as a yawn-like forward orientation of the facial muscles and leads to 'a characteristic vibratory ringing sensation...that expands the technical and emotional ranges of the voice (Ibid).

[14] *Tilly* won the Boston Film Festival in 2004.

able to practice what I preach. After finishing the film, a two-week shoot, one week in Costa Rica and another in Colorado Springs, I returned to my teaching filled with excitement and inspiration. Months later, I received a call from the production company asking me to come back to Colorado Springs. Apparently, we needed to loop not just a scene or two, but the entire story, due to technical difficulties on the set. This challenge provided me with a unique opportunity to draw on my voice and bodywork, and my imagination. For me, the work started long before I boarded the plane.

What I needed was time to *re-tap into the story*. To start, I would lie down or sit comfortable in a chair. Once my mind was relaxed and free, I began using my imagination to actually see the environment: the grounds, the beauty, the people, the home, its furnishings. I began to hear the sounds: the running creek, the laughter of the children, the footsteps. I could actually smell the air: its thickness, its dampness. The deeper I went into my imagination, the more intense my breathing became. It seemed to match my experience. First faster, then slower, more shallow, then deeper. I continued on with every scene. I began asking myself questions of the story always allowing my imagination to be free. With each breath I responded: no words were spoken...just breathing: full, free creative breathing. Next, I started recalling my words by heart. Aware of how mere patterned repetition of words can kill vitality and can destroy the spirit of the role, sometimes I would explore the words with the image and sometimes tasting the sounds within the words. By doing this, I was creatively re-discovering the words through sounds and vibrations within my body, not listening to myself on the outside, but more like seeing what sounds within the words would give my imagination an organic response and an organic picture.

The following are some key situations that I found particularly challenging to recreating during the looping sessions. However challenging, through utilizing the use of body, voice and imagination, this obstacle is not without solution. The first take was a scene at the cemetery where I am being drawn to a woman mourning at a gravesite. It was as if I was drawn to her by some mystical energy, something out my control. I needed to recall how my body felt: light, cloudlike, and buoyant. In his books, Arthur stresses awareness of the various languages of the body: "buoyancy": a sense of lightness, of float; "radiancy": a sense of body humor, a spark, and excitement evidenced by a person who seemingly has a twinkle in their eye; and "potency": a sense of power, of a yawning expansion of the body. After spending time working with and developing these energies, in forms of dance, voice work, acting, and daily living, the body was able to physically recall that sensation of a 'mystical moment.' It could be as simple as breathing. I breathed buoyantly. I filled my entire body with lightness. With the first take, it seemed like I was just acting from the neck up. I felt it and so did the director. On the first take, I was working too hard to recreate the moment. I felt my body tighten and I knew from my training that this was not a recipe for success. In take two, I allowed myself to breathe the pain into my body and release the technical *pushing*. The emotion poured out of me and into my voice. Take two was a go.

If your breathing is *produced*, as I stress to my students, then the sound will also be *produced*. To breathe is to inspire oneself. If you plunge into a speaking moment with a stiff body, expect stiff results. Breathing needs to match the circumstances of the story, whether it's a quick radiant breath of being startled, a breath of buoyancy in order to recover a sense of calm or a powerful breath in order to fortify your position and to stand your ground.

Another challenge was during the final situation, I had to break down and beg for forgiveness. I had to get to this place and get there fast. Again, I began tapping into story. My short, quick radiant breath energy quickened my heart and body and I could sense how my consonants are filled with longing. Knowing how expressive consonants can be and how one can paint a rainbow of emotion through them helped me to create the feelings that were now required of me. The challenge was to not just *hit* the consonants but to make them full of behavior.

There were also intense moments of openness that occurred during the heart to heart talks with my daughter, Tilly. Knowing how to tap into the *openness* of vowels to create feeling, or what Lessac (1996) terms "structural NRG,"[15] allowed me to connect to my heart and to my imagination. This in turn, helped to allow for an intimate and vulnerable *heart to heart* with my daughter.

---

[15] NRG is a trademark phrase coined by Arthur indicating energy and is used to "identify the dynamics of the body NRG states and qualities…" (Lessac 1997:20). It is indicated elsewhere in the Lessac work that it also reflects the notion of Neural-Regenerative-Growth.

So many times when I hear students trying to feel and explore the structural shapes of vowels and consonants, I detect a tendency to be technical and careful. I remind them of the importance to allow their body energy to support them, as Arthur has always stressed that the body reflects the voice and the voice reflects the body.

I can attest without question or reservation to the importance of voice and body work in Hollywood. I have found that working in television and in film requires more skill to fill out subtle moments, like the fine dots within a pointillistic painting.[16] Compare this to theatre, a larger environment, where one can include broad brush-strokes, if you will, like that of a Picasso. In theatre, we are challenged to deliver the experience with more tonal quality, fuller body and more vocal expressiveness. However, we are still challenged to fully use our body energies to bring a 500-seat house to tears by a single sigh, or a simple look or reaction. I believe that when you unite voice, body and imagination, you will have created the most fascinating canvass in the world from which to work.

Please describe one context or vignette that best represents the way(s) in which you have applied or incorporated Lessac training within the development of your own voice and body, and how, if at all, this process has been used by you as a means for problem-solving, learning, healing, performance, communication, and/or increasing your own vitality of life?

Coaching in various venues can add stress to the body, so as I travel from place to place, I continue to hum and sing in the car. I am constantly challenged by the lack of time and pressure to "demonstrate" as I coach. My body and voice must be in a creative responsive state. If I am sounding technical or careful, so will the actor. Knowing that actors are fearful of sounding artificial, the Lessac training encourages the feeling of inner sensations of tone, clarity and vowel pronunciation rather than *producing the correct sound* or *perfect R*. I must be able to do this organically in order for the actor to trust me. I find this process of working allows the actor to relax and to become curious about the inner sensations of speech rather than *listening* or *judging*. When there are clarity issues, or vocal issues, I have to be able to demonstrate not only to them, but also be able to embody these demonstrations myself. I must then train the actor to feel and recall these new sensations himself. As for the use of my voice, I am con-

---

[16] Pointillism is a style of painting in which small distinct points of primary colors create the impression of a wide selection of secondary and intermediate colors (http://en.wikipedia.org/wiki/Pointillism).

stantly using a calming tone to talk to actors, producers and directors. If I am breathing calmly, others will also respond more calmly. I never hesitate to address the client's breath or body state in order for the sound to live more organically and truthfully. As for the use of breathing for myself, I tap into my lower back breathing many times on the set! Remembering to smile also helps calm the nerves of a frantic producer.

In my personal life, I have had the experience of sharing the care-taking of my elderly father, who was ninety-five when he passed, I found that the exercises the physical therapists gave him became very forced and mechanical. So I would encourage him to *float* his arm up, and *yawn* and reach for those imaginary apples. His balance was a big concern for him and the fear of falling had become a major factor in walking. So feeling his feet as 'rims and rockers' gave him a sense of balance. The physical therapists taught him how to roll if he should fall. We had a mat, and he would slowly go down on his side and roll through his back. He had great pain in his legs at this time; however he had great upper body strength and could use the yawning push up to get himself to his side and onto a chair. I feel kinesensic training is vital to keep the elderly vital. He also had a walker and would slump when he walked, so this also gave him greater mobility with his feet. Physical Therapy for the Elderly and exercise classes utilizing the quality body energies give them something to feel and be creative with, so they are free of "exercise" and it becomes a beautiful movement. I will never forget going home and spending New Years Eve on his 94th year. His favorite musical was *Singing in the Rain*. Despite his pain, he would smile and laugh and move his legs to all the dances. When it was time for him to go to bed, I remember watching him dance with his walker as he was singing down the hall…. As my siblings and I cared for him, he taught us about compassion, patience, and the small joys in life and about "SINGING IN THE RAIN…" to take all pain away. Singing and dancing (represent types of) the natural relaxer energizers that Arthur has developed in his training process. My father did them because they made him naturally feel better.

In what local or global context do you see the future of kinesensics, or kinesensic training taking place within the next fifty years? In particular, what needs or possibilities, if any, do you think this type of training or work will address or shape in the future?

As environmental issues and the interest in health increase, kinesensics would be the next logical center to open within a yoga studio, a spa, and anywhere that promotes health and well-being. Kinesensic training process has already aided many therapists: physical therapists, speech therapists, and mental health professions in regaining clients' physical and vocal well-being. Many psychology centers actually look for speech therapists that also specialize in a process that enhances voice and body confidence of their clients.

It is a vital force in the ESL world. I currently work with an institute that prepares their clients for the TOEFL.[17] Their institute helps non-native speakers become more comfortable with speaking of English, as they become dentists, nurses, and pharmacists. I work with this institute to help ESL clients embody clarity, musicality, variety, voice dynamics, and effective and expressive communication. The ESL client begins to laugh, sing, and hum…and to discover their voices which helps develop their confidence. I believe that many institutes that serve the ESL learner would be greatly enhanced through kinesensic training.

In what ways, if any, do you think that the Lessac work/approach can and should still be developed in the future?

This may seem very practical, but I believe we have strong possibilities with our certified members, as we continue to develop in the areas of performance, psychology, speech therapy, physical therapy, business communications, and the over-all health and well being of the individual. I believe that it could be very compatible with yoga centers, spas, community centers, performing arts centers, and rehabilitation centers; anyplace where well-being is the mission of that particular community. Thank you, Arthur.

---

[17] The world's most common requirement for university and college admissions, ETS TOEFL (Test of English as a Foreign Language) is an English proficiency test (www.ets.org/toefl/).

Crystal Robbins

Crystal Robbins *has been teaching Voice for the Stage at Santa Monica College since 2000. She is a working actress in film, television and theatre and enjoys voice coaching and directing; but her primary job is that of mom to her two young kids. Luckily, raising them with Lessac training has proven to be a bountiful addition to her professional and creative life! She was certified as a Lessac Voice, Speech, and Body Trainer in 2003.*

Describe the context in which you were introduced to Lessac training? For example, when did you receive training, who provided the training, why did you choose this approach, and how did the training take place?

My first introduction to Arthur's work was while in England in 1992. Much against the advice of my agent in Los Angeles, I left in the middle of making films and doing national tours to pursue a life-long dream of exploring Shakespeare in England. I studied with The British-American Drama Academy at Oxford and Mary Corrigan,[1] a noted Linklater[2] teacher, was the voice instructor. She introduced us to Linklater, Laban[3] and Lessac and spoke highly of Arthur and his work. I found out later that she had done her master's thesis on Arthur's work. At the time, I really didn't pay much attention to the differences between teachers and ways of doing things. I was an actress, with no consideration for teaching or directing, not even an inkling. I loved Shakespeare. I had a history of getting cast in roles that required big voices and then in promptly losing my voice the nearer we got to opening. I had some vocal skills and knowledge, but not a connection to my voice in my body and not in my body's use and carryover to vocal work and certainly not a vocal process in place that deepened character development and emotional life.

After I returned from England and my post-school travels, I quickly became even more disenchanted with film life. I continued to audition, but my focus changed to

---

[1] In 1993, Mary Corrigan called Arthur Lessac "a pioneer in voice production for this country" as cited in the Folger Shakespeare Institute's *Bibliography: Shakespeare and Performance* (1993).
[2] Kristen Linklater is a noted voice teacher and author of the books *Freeing the Natural Voice* (1976; 2006) and *Freeing Shakespeare's Voice* (1992).
[3] Devised by Rudolf Laban, Laban draws on his theories of Body, Effort, Space and Shape to describe, interpret, document and create human movement (http://en.wikipedia.org/wiki/Laban_Movement_Analysis).

traveling. I'd gotten the itch and couldn't quite stop. For the next four years I regularly returned to England to see friends, see the season's new plays and travel throughout the United Kingdom (U.K.). In 1996 Jim[4] and I married and then spent roughly three years traveling around the world together with a backpack and a tent. It wasn't all consecutive. We would travel a month, come home and work for a month and then leave again for somewhere else. A job at United Airlines gave us free air travel and we took advantage of that for as long as we could. 250,000 miles later, I came back to a reality of auditions and playing high school seniors at age 29 and it felt very unrewarding and downright pointless. I loved acting and knew somehow that I was gifted in it, but it didn't marry into my new world of exploration and discovery. I was happiest when traveling. It seemed that when I was truly wandering and in the midst of finding something new, testing my own boundaries of acceptance, trust, my place in the world, and my mark on the world that I felt completely at ease and relaxed. I liked to say in those days that my best self was the "me when I was on foreign soil." I seemed to see life through a more real lens than when I was home. The other times that I really *filled the well* were the odd, occasional jobs that involved Shakespeare or working in the theatre. In Los Angeles (L.A.) those are few and far between. So we kept traveling. And if I could be traveling AND working in the theatre, all the better. That happened in 1997. First I was asked to direct a Shakespeare production for a theatre in Louisville and I created a matinee program that brought in school children to see the show. Then, I got asked to work at New York Theatre Workshop in an original production, written by friends who said the role was written with me in mind. It was a wonderfully collaborative experience, easy to be held in the collective wisdom of a group of people who knew me well and who trusted my own body of work to ask a lot more out of me than the typical L.A. casting director. My father died right before opening night and I made the quick trip back to my hometown for the funeral and then flew back for the show. Certain that he always mandated the show would go on. Being amongst my oldest friends performing a quality role was the best restorative I could've had.

---

[4] Crystal's husband Jim Czerwinski is currently a fifth-grade teacher in the Burbank Unified School District.

After the show was over I was immersed in a long, slow anxiety-ridden process involving my father's estate. I won't get into it here, suffice it to say it wasn't easy or pretty and as executor of the estate it required my complete attention. I was worn-out, physically exhausted, mentally strained, emotionally raw and creatively tired. As a result, I had little interest in getting out and seeing people. I had too much work to do and too many demands on my time and I couldn't travel or perform while performing those duties. The real me, *the me* at my best was somewhere, but most likely hidden in piles of paperwork. It was into this climate that I met Arthur.

My voice teacher from college, Anita Jyo Lenhart, currently a Certified Trainer, though not at the time, was in town working with Arthur. She'd gotten a six-week grant to work with him and was studying with him at his Santa Monica office. She'd asked me to dinner with them once, I'd ended up bowing out of it. I may have been sick, I may have just been tired, I don't remember. I do remember being amazed that Arthur was still with us. I vaguely remembered hearing about him from Mary Corrigan. I didn't remember anything about the work.

Jyo (as I always called her) called and asked me again to join them. They'd gotten tickets to a show at the Ahmanson[5] with Ian McKellen and wanted to know if I could join them. I did want to see her while she was out here and I wanted to meet Arthur, but I felt a bit intimidated to meet such a figure in theatre training and history. I offered to pick up dinner for a picnic and then to drive us all downtown to the Ahmanson.

I remember hugging Jyo when I got to Arthur's place and meeting Arthur for the first time. I looked into his eyes, the exact color and life in them as my father, and taking a deep breath, knowing it was somehow going to be easier than I thought. And it was. We chatted the whole way on the crowded 10 freeway across town. No car pool lane, just messy Friday traffic at 5 p.m. in L.A. No wonder it is so hard to see people regularly in this town. It took us over an hour to get to the theatre. We pulled out the many to-go containers that I'd brought from Angeli Caffe on Melrose. Salad, panini, pizza, sparkling water, chicken, cake. The three of us never stopped talking, laughing

---

[5] Ahmanson Theatre is part of the Center Theatre Group in downtown Los Angeles.

and sharing. Arthur talked about playing King Lear. I talked about playing Cordelia.[6] Jyo laughed and said that I'd be good for him to have around. Or maybe that he'd be good for me to have around. We laughed and sang as the sun began to sink and the night grew colder, even on a L.A. summer.

We watched the show. Our seats were not all together and Arthur graciously sat further back with me and gave Jo the seat closer up. We drove home, still talking and Jo kept kicking around the idea of me working with Arthur. I was not interested in taking on more employment and it seemed like he needed someone more adept than I was on the computer. I was currently working part-time with the chef owner at Angeli Caffe as her personal assistant, who I'd known for six years at that point. I liked her and the job was flexible and allowed me to audition and travel and write, as I was beginning to put some of our travels down into stories and articles. By the time I dropped them back off in Santa Monica, Arthur asked me to consider working for him. I told him I didn't think I was the right person. I said it a few times. I was on my way to a travel-writing workshop north of San Francisco for a week. Arthur said to come see him when I got back. I did. I remember sitting on his couch and him explaining what he needed and that what we didn't know, we would learn together. This appealed to me. I was still not committing to it and then he said he'd give me lessons every week as well. How could I resist? I started the next week.

For months I went through his files and paperwork organizing. There were mountains of paperwork that needed filing. Twice a week during that first three months we worked together for an hour or more. I felt vibration on my hard palate in a palpable way that never again left me. I began to work with letting that sensation guide me. I began to taste music. I began to move away from understanding the work as metaphor and move towards understanding it as music. I discovered the freedom and release of smelling the flower and in feeling the breath move around the back and up the spine. I didn't understand all the physical work and its connections to my vocal work when we explored on the floor, but I trusted that he did and that I would eventually. I knew I liked the physical work and that I had fun and felt good. I liked feeling like a dancer again. I liked feeling like a singer again. Even when walking and talking. At month

---

[6] Cordelia is the daughter of King Lear in the William Shakespeare play *King Lear*.

three of my intense sessions with Arthur, Jim and I found out that I was pregnant and so my workouts with Arthur took on the added dimension of exploring sound and movement with my pregnant self. Here was a place of wandering with real newness and experimental learning that I could relate to. Here was a new journey to savor.

We did all the body work, all the rolls, the sit-ups and push-ups, me adjusting and finding and discovering where I needed to adapt and Arthur getting a kick out of enveloping the child in such good feelings. I've written about this process some in my article "The Ecstatic Birth,"[7] which was about creating a natural birthing process with my understanding of Arthur's work. I think it was about five or six months into the pregnancy when I was first explaining something I'd noted about the work and Arthur simply and quietly stated that I would be a good teacher. I fervently disagreed, said I had no leanings in that way, no interest whatsoever. He just smiled.

Maeve was born in July, and I continued for another year to work for him and study in one-hour private sessions. Finally, two years after I'd first met him and probably 200 hours of working with him privately, I was able to attend my first workshop. I attended the five-week Mercersburg Workshop 2000 with a nearly one-year old, nursing daughter, husband and a variety of relatives and friends helping out with the babysitting. Workshop teachers that year were Arthur, Sue Ann Park, Nancy Krebs and Kathleen Dunn.

Kathy Dunn was currently teaching at Santa Monica College (SMC), but had been offered some teaching work at The University of Southern California (USC). In order for her to accept that job she needed coverage for one of her classes at SMC. Somehow, I was lucky enough to be asked to teach that class. I had only just started my first workshop. I had not been interviewed or submitted a resume. I hadn't taught college before; I had only done ad hoc acting coaching and a little directing. I didn't have a master's degree. I had only theatre and film experience. And yet, they called to tell me to expect to show up for orientation and that I had a full class already. I started teaching that fall, slightly terrified but with all the adrenaline of stepping off a plane in Hong Kong without a place to stay. I began training for certification and was assigned mentors (Kathy and Arthur) and used my classroom as an experimental training ground for myself and

---

[7] Robbins, Crystal. 2000. "The Ecstatic Birth." In *Voice and Speech Trainers Association Newsletter*, Fall 2000, Vol. 14, no. 3: 8-14.

for the students. I had great advantage to have Kathy's consistent input and Arthur's oversight as well. What a wonderful immersion experience to exit the Intensive and immediately begin teaching, consistently using and growing with the work. I attended my second workshop in 2002, now a four-week, with the addition of Kate Ingram in the workshop faculty and was certified in May of 2003. If you had told me that I would love teaching, that I would be on this path, I wouldn't have believed you.

I don't feel that I chose this work. It has consistently chosen me. And like the boy I ran into accidentally, crying on his shoulder, who now is my husband; and like the friend who was assigned to be my roommate in a London hostel and who became a sister of my heart; and like the old man from Corfu who ended up seeing through me on an Athens bench; and like the wild white horse that greeted me on hillside north of Dublin, some things just happen because they are supposed to.

And what impact, if any, has knowing the differences between Linklater, Laban, and Lessac, had on your ability to perform, explore Shakespeare, and work in film...Do you integrate the other approaches into your performance, teaching, and directing?

I don't integrate the other systems because I don't remember them and I certainly never embodied what they were about, so I would not presume to teach something that I don't feel like I truly know. In other words, I was not connected to them in my body in a visceral, palpable way in order to draw upon them later. I'm sure I used them at the time I was introduced, I'm sure I could be coached with their terminology, but I didn't properly understand physically how to use them. I had wonderful teachers who I respected and admired. Who can really say why and how something 'sticks'? Was I not as open before? Was I at a different place as an artist?

Do you feel the Lessac Work compliments or contradicts any other approaches to voice and body?

I use the Lessac work as a performer because it is the only thing I've personally used that works for my voice, that stays with me, that I call upon and get result, immediately, every time. As a teacher and director, I love allowing the artist to make their own discoveries and this work yields that. I love that the emotional life of the character opens up in an exciting new ways when an artist is guided by this work. I love that the voice development is simultaneously character building. I love the gentleness that is inherent in the instruction of the material. I think it fosters the right kind of inner sensing to achieving results.

I'm sure there can be found relationships between approaches, but I feel I don't know enough about them to be the person for that research. For me, the immersion into the Lessac work is what made the difference, the completely salutary, healthful acquisition of the body work, the building step-by-step on things that I could already do well just resonated with me in a new way. And because it was a slow, feeling process of acquisition, it stuck. What I am newly discovering is that the *Viewpoints*[8] work in particular resonates beautifully with Arthur's work. I find that the similarity of getting it into the body is the key link. In fact, I use *Viewpoints* to map out the dynamics that we so often refer to in the book (slow vs. fast, focused vs. dilute, voiced vs. unvoiced, etc.)

In what additional ways have you applied or incorporated Lessac, within the context of what you do for a living? Please identify what you do, and how, if at all, you have incorporated the Lessac work.

I am a mom and a teacher. My children were born into a world of Y-buzz,[9] smell the flower and small ball rolls. I teach Lessac work because I don't recognize it as some sort of technique that is exclusionary but rather as a way of being that I know in my bones literally. It is so foreign to me now to NOT be in full use of the vocal and body NRGs[10] that I have trouble remembering how to NOT use them when I give examples. Arthur always threatened me that there would be a time when I wouldn't think about it, it would just be within me and it is true! My body seeks out quality tone, the feel of instruments, the rhythm of music, the diversity of shape. I don't consciously use it, it just uses me. That happened over time. I remember being in what I'm quite sure was postpartum depression and recognizing that I wasn't in a body NRG. I consciously chose to use the body NRGs and smelling the flower to be in a state of buoyancy to test Arthur's theory that one couldn't embody poisons when in buoyancy. Now when I start to feel that overtired, worn-out feeling, I allow the body to choose an NRG for me. The instinctual qualities of

---

[8] Bogart, Anne. 1995. *Viewpoints.* New Hampshire: Smith and Krause

[9] Lessac, Arthur. 1997. *The Use and Training of the Human Voice.* Mayfield Publishing: Mountain View, California.

[10] NRG is acronym for energy states, as identified in both the body and voice books of Arthur Lessac (1978; 1997).

this work have become so ingrained that I don't actively seek the work. My body does it for me, but I allow it to. It is this fact alone that convinces me that the body work is absolutely essential. An ingredient that cannot be stressed enough. I believe we can access any part of the Arthur's work through body work alone. That every element of the body NRGs directly impacts and affects the voice. I believe you can teach the body NRGs alone and see dramatic vocal improvement. This was the theory behind why Laurie Mufson[11] and I believed so fervently in the validity of a one-week workshop.[12] It is true, one cannot teach all the work in one week, but one can get enough body work and the fundamentals of the voice work explored enough to see change. We believe that the one-week workshops bear fruit for that reason. It is the same experimentation that I've done with children's voices. I've taken the work into pre-school-elementary classrooms, usually with only a 10-15 minute *unit* to work with. I've used the work with preschool and older theatre dramatics sessions and introduced the body work to see changes in their little voices. Teachers have reported back to me that there are higher than normal improvements in reading, phonics and class presentation projects after the kids have played with the work over the course of a term. My work with the young has always influenced my college classes. The more that I bring in the spirit of how children learn, the more I feel I'm in line with the true nature of this work. No theories or big words or concepts. Pare down. Move the body, ask questions.

In terms of your vision for a one-week workshop, and your argument that "the fundamentals of the voice work (can be explored) enough to see a change," can you elaborate on what you mean by "change"? Wouldn't there be "change" in anyone who took a voice workshop or performing arts classes over a one-week period?

By change in terms of our work, I mean an understanding of the musicality of the consonant orchestra *that you can feel and that can stay with you*, an understanding of tone *that you can feel and that can stay with you*, an understanding of vowel shape/structure *that you can feel and that can stay with you* and that you can be empowered with relationship to the work to begin to work with it right away. I think it is

---

[11] Laurie Mufson is a Lessac Certified Trainer and has served on the board of the Lessac Training and Research Institute since 2004. In 2008, she was elected to be the incoming president for the Institute (2010-2012).
[12] In 1994, Laurie Mufson and Crystal Robbins created the one-week workshop entitled *Lessac for You*. It was the first one-week workshop sanctioned by the Lessac Institute and was originally geared for teachers of the adolescent actor.

the body work that achieves this. The body work gets it into the marrow bone and helps to do all that wonderful cross-referencing/synapse/whole body learning so that it actually does the teaching for you.

So, yes, absolutely anyone can take one-week workshops of any kind of voice training and pick up tools. I did it. But for whatever reason, it didn't take with me. (*I didn't feel it in my body and it didn't stay with me.*) It was separate from me, a skill, a tool. Oh, I had the notes, the books, good experiences. But I did not have a way of moving through life with a system in place that was integral to me. Now I do. I'm not trying to infer that this work is the only way. Just that it was the only way for me.

We have become so deadened to sensation of any kind. We're so protective as a people nowadays. Lessac kinesensics gets people to feel again. There are different portals and access into feeling and that has been what is fascinating to me about working with children. There is a great deal of research out there on different learning modalities and I'm not the researcher to elucidate on all of that. I do know that I cannot be prescriptive about the path it takes to feeling. I must continually be the guide for the exploration that can be scary, but is always freeing. That is something that has carried over for me in the classroom. There isn't one way of learning and some ages are more open than others. Kinesensics is about learning through feel and kids FEEL the presence of what their imaginations offer them. They FEEL the power of the lion, the flit of the butterfly wings, the melt of the ice cream cone in their bodies. I think that regardless of what one is teaching one can do it in the spirit of this work. Quality over quantity, but that doesn't mean that quantity is incapable of quality. A thousand birds lifting off the ground and moving on the wind together is quality and quantity.

What do you mean when you say, "your work with the young has influenced your college classes"…Can you elaborate on this influence a little further?

Working with the young requires that I be flexible with terminology, that I use the words that are part of the kids' vernacular, that I encourage them to "use their words" (like all parents say to wee ones) for what they are experiencing. I have taken that philosophy into the college setting. Is it more important that a student gets the feeling process or that they define it the way Arthur does? I think it is more important they get the process. Also, I experiment a lot with the little kids. The games, different ways of introducing voice/body work have kept me on my toes and necessitated a real exploratory mode for me. I carry over those games and make adaptations constantly in my classroom. When my five year old discovered that he could flick the tab on a can and feel vibration in the can the same way his body vibrated when he sang, I brought a can into my college class! I must be the explorer, too! There are very different modalities at work between kids and young adults. There have been protections put into place with adults; they are more cynical and less in touch with simple reaction. For example, if you ask a room of five year olds to reach their hands up and tickle the air, they burst into laughter and start giggling, as if they are being tickled on their bodies. It is then easy to get them to talk about what they are feeling inside even though nothing is physically tickling their actual bodies. They can connect to an inner environmental *happening* if you will. Adults will put their hands up and tickle the air, but do not laugh until they are given permission to laugh or grin or giggle. Why? That fascinated me. So the work with kids is informing me on the differences between the adult actor and the child's imagination and I'm not sure of all my conclusions at this point, but I find it thrilling to be in the journey.

It sounds as if you are talking about teaching pedagogy, and in particular how the Lessac Work itself has the potential to transform the young...is there a difference in teaching pedagogy when you work with so many age groups?

Mostly I'm talking about my understanding of the nature of learning and how we help others access the nature of the work. Just as Arthur has his leitmotif[13] and tells us we can access the work from any starting place, I think we can also use the work with different learning styles within each person. It is so easy to say, "be a kid," "find your inner child," etc, etc. But that's not what I'm referring to. If we as Lessac trainers are focusing on an *inner environmental awareness* kind of learning and there is a child or teenager or adult who does not learn that way, we can still get them there. We should always be about the problem solving, we should always be open to finding the way that works for that one need, that one creative answer that will perhaps only work with that one person. I'm finding there are differences in how to approach the work with

---

[13] A leitmotif is a recurring musical theme, associated with a particular person, place, or idea. The word has also been used by extension to mean any sort of recurring theme, whether in music, literature, or the life of a fictional character or a real person (http://en.wikipedia.org/wiki/Leitmotif).

kids and adults. We say kinesensics is an inside-out type of system. From the beginning, feeling processes are about identifying the feeling inside the body: vibration, music, tone, theatrical space, pleasure, breath—all involve the perception of how the body is reacting inside the body and those good harmonious, pleasurable feelings yield more healthful experiences that we build upon. With children, their very make-up is that of being an explorer of life outside the body, and yet their little imaginations are so real and present they are also richly discovering the wealth of their inner life. They are acquiring the outside world and introducing it into their own little worlds. They have many fewer familiar events to draw upon; they are finding their familiar events in life. They are making memories that will be familiar events for their futures. Perhaps what I do with children would be better called pre-kinesensics, rather than kindersensics,[14] because it is really a slightly different approach. What I find interesting is that rather quickly they come to their own understanding of what is happening inside vs. outside…like the tickling. And then they do have a framework for an inner environment vs. outer environment context.

Please describe one context or vignette that best represents the way(s) in which you have you applied or incorporated Lessac training within the development of your own voice and body, and how, if at all, this process has been used by you as a means for problem-solving, learning, healing, performance, communication, and/or increasing your own vitality of life?

Only recently I was diagnosed with asthma. It came at the end of a rather troublesome period of a strange onset of lack of breath. I found that I was using the work to consciously create more breath. When I felt like I couldn't take a deep breath I curled in a ball and breathed low in the back, allowing the reserve to completely fill. This process would immediately relax me and coax more quality breaths in and would work for a while. Many times I fell asleep curled in my little ball. At the time, I didn't know anything about asthma. I just thought I had stress. Small child, first job teaching, cooking healthy meals and intent on creating the 'family meal time' each night in addition to working with Arthur twice a week was a full life on not much sleep. My small ball breathing helped for several months and then the familiar occurrence of getting less

---

[14] Since 2004, Crystal has written a column for the Lessac newsletter entitled "Kindersensics," which focuses on applications of the Lessac work for younger children.

breath invaded. I could no longer fill the reserve as easily or as full. My intake of air grew less and less. I noticed a wheeze when I took my morning run. I made an appointment to see the kindly lung specialist who had helped me so much after the birth of my daughter. His office was at the top of a hill and I walked it, kid in tow. By the time I got there I was in a full-blown asthma attack. He immediately gave me a breathing treatment (albuterol) to open the airways and we then proceeded to do all the necessary testing. The doctor, by now familiar with how the Lessac work had helped me after Maeve's birth when fluid was filling with my lungs, was amazed that I'd gone so long without seeking medical help. He shook his head in amazement that the work had helped me for as long as it had and that I had used my body so creatively to eke out breath. He also knew that I was a firm believer in as much natural medicine as possible. He said, "You have done a great job in solving this for as long as possible. Right now the airways are inflamed both inside and outside and you need some meds in order to open that up. We will get it under control and find a way to reduce the meds or get you off entirely." Over the course of the next few years I went from needing daily meds to just having emergency meds available for the rare attack. We were able to diagnose triggers to my asthma, newly discovered allergies, and make changes to my environment that helped as well.

I tell this in detail because I do not know what would've happened either in this case, or in the case of my childbirth experience with Maeve if I had not been aware of what my body was doing or if I had not had tools for how to calm my body, feel breath in my back and creatively use that knowledge. The body truly is a font of wisdom, should we choose to acknowledge it. This, too, has been instrumental in how I approach the work in total. I spend a great deal of time in my college classes on bodywork. Probably half of the time is body work. I find it is the way I best explain any detail of the work.

In what local or global context do you see the future of kinesensics, or kinesensic training taking place within the next 50 years? In particular, what needs or possibilities, if any, do you think this type of training or work will address or shape in the future?

Locally for me means the multi-cultural community of Los Angeles, immigrant, English Language Learners. There is HUGE future and development for the work this area because the reality is one that is growing in every part of the country, not just the ports of entry. We need development, syllabi that specifically address these needs and training programs that go into that community of teachers. The question that needs to be asked is this: Do we need to train these teachers to be Lessac teachers or can we teach enough fundamentals so that these teachers can take it into their classrooms and get real results?

Both locally and globally, we have a completely untapped market for taking this work into the preschool and kindergarten classrooms. If we could pull together a cohesive, coherent adaptation of how we perceive phonics, a step-by-step process complete with a prototype of the accompanying materials we could test it more thoroughly and get financial backing for making kits for teachers. We could institute teacher in-service programs for those early grade levels that would not only help the teaching of letters and sounds, but also facilitate easier acquisition of the language for new language learners. I've found teachers to be very responsive, but I've only introduced it in a few classrooms on a volunteer basis. I've also learned a lot by watching what the teachers are using in its place and this is what I've tried to refine or to re-phrase with a more authentic feeling process. Some elements that are definitely working are in using the whole body to feeling the shape of the sound, visual/physical cues that work together, a sense of play and discovery, physical examples of instruments that can be integrated in craft-building units, tie-ins to music units that give a frame of reference for orchestral music.

I am a big believer in the world peace aspect to this work. But our job first is to find ways to actually teach it so that it can delightfully grow and allow that reality take shape. It is a great idea that resonates with truth. But we need to get the work out there.

In what ways, if any, do you think that the Lessac work can and should still be developed in the future?

Within the context of what I was just talking about, I think we could develop a package of materials, which would include a CD of handouts, materials/posters, step-by-step instructions and samples. This could be a package available for sale at teacher in-service meetings or conferences.

On a smaller scale within our institute, and for our immediate use, I'd like to see more sharing of syllabi, perhaps offer sample syllabi to new teachers and offer a CD with handouts/tests/grading criteria that new teachers can use or develop further on their own. It would be as simple as getting all current teachers to submit their current materials and putting them all on one disk and making copies of it. I know of no reason to not share and learn from one another about the most practical of things.

I've recently consulted with a marketing person who mentioned the idea of creating online lessons. There is a market for it and there is money to be made and if we are not offering the work in this context someone else will. It is possible with technology these days to create a series of lessons, post it on a website and have consumers download and *own* their copy of these lessons to proceed at their own pace. Perhaps every two or three lessons some interactive online exchange could happen to check on the individual's self-teaching. This would earn money for whoever created it and perhaps the website could take a small cut for advertising, hosting the link. It is the modern equivalent of how Arthur wrote the voice book. He said he thought up an individual and progressed through exactly how he would teach that individual every step of the way. No, this type of training would not qualify towards certification, but it does get the content of our work out there and it can help people in this context. People who like it, feel improvement, WILL respond by delving into live workshops. We have to think of this type of client as potential workshop attendees. Do people deserve to hear about our work? Absolutely! Do they deserve to try to experiment with it on their own? Of course. If we interest people, if we help people where they are, they will come more readily to us.

I would love to see the vision of a Lessac Theatre Company come to fruition.

I think we should pull together archives of the work, including old photos, video and fresh new video of Arthur. I think we need to start compiling displays of these sorts of things to connect our newer members to more of our history. This can take the form of copying from Arthur's archives, enlarging, mounting and displaying at conferences; creating an *archive box* that can go from meetings to Intensives to conferences for people to peruse (this would house copies naturally) to creating DVDs of all the pictures, documents that could be made available.

For the immediate future, I see a need for us to have more of a social media presence: Facebook, Myspace pages, etc.[15] with more advertising on Google and other

---

[15] Web 2.0 applications for social networking.

search engines. We are not reaching the numbers we should and we need to open our doors to allow easier access to us. The listserv, while modern at its inception, is now outdated and not user-friendly. I'd advocate a more up-to-date manner of achieving the same purpose.

Thanks for asking me to do this and to get some of these thoughts on the page. It has truly been a joy to be involved in this work and in Arthur's life. I say it often but it is so true, how lucky am I to sit across from him every week….

Gert Terny

Gert Terny is a certified Lessac teacher and is currently a director and voice, movement, presentation and communication coach at VoiceFactory and the European Lessac Centre, located in the Antwerp area of Belgium. He has also started teaching the Lessac work at the International Institute of Performing Arts in Paris and London. He has directed and acted in various professional theatres throughout Europe, and has served as a vocal coach at the educational department of the Royal Opera House, in Brussels and Flemish Radio and Television. In addition to teaching and directing, Gert continues to collaborate with colleagues from all over the world on various research and performance based projects and is currently interested in working with colleagues in South Africa on further exploration of connections and similarities within Dutch and African cultures. For more information about Gert or the European Lessac Center, go to www.voicefactory.be or info@voicefactory.be.

Describe the context in which you were introduced to Lessac training?

The first time Arthur Lessac and his work were mentioned to me was when I was taking a voice workshop at Patsy Rodenburg's[1] *Voice and Speech Centre* in London. Majella Hurley, one of the teachers over there, told me that Arthur's work might be something for me. I had already gone to drama school and university, and took singing lessons in Belgium,[2] and although people would always tell me that I had a good voice, problems began to arise after a time. To me it seemed that either my voice would function on a particular day or it would not, which began to seem very hazardous to me, as if there was nothing I could really do about it. It was as if the notion of *Voice* was something completely outside of me. At first, my eyes were opened to this by the people at the Voice and Speech Centre, and then I read both Sue Ann Park and Arthur's articles in *Vocal Vision*.[3] This happened after I was playing in a theatre production where I had no clue of what the director wanted me to do. During one of the final rehearsals, I decided not to think about any of the instructions the director had given me, but to concentrate

---

[1] Patsy Rodenburg is the author of number books on voice including *The Actor Speaks: Voice and the Performer*, which includes a forward by Judy Dench, and is director of the Voice and Speech Centre in London.
[2] Gert is originally from Belgium.
[3] Marion Hampton and Barbara Acker (eds). 1997. *The Vocal Vision: View of Voice.* New York: Applause Books.

on the words, the sounds. Suddenly it seemed as if I entered a complete new world. The world of the character, where—at least for a while—not one director, nor the public, could upset or scare me. A world in which strong and clear emotions and situations could evolve, without me losing control of what was happening. Neither me, nor the director nor my fellow actors knew what had happened. It took place instantly and suddenly. But after reading Sue Ann's article I knew there was a strong link between what had happened that day and what Sue Ann had written about the Lessac work: Using the sounds, the energies, the inner harmonic sensing that evolves from all that…. That day I decided I wanted to meet those people and work with them, which led me to going to the 2002 Lessac Intensive, where I was introduced to the work by Arthur himself, Sue Ann Park, Nancy Krebs, and Kate Ingram. Later I also worked and learned from Deborah Kinghorn who was in my mentoring team when I pursued certification. [Each had] completely different personalities with different teaching approaches, but who were not just preaching, but demonstrating and living what this work was about including: Being true to yourself. Making the fullest possible use of your human potential, vocally, physically, sensorially, and emotionally. Becoming aware of your inner and outer environment. Listening to what is happening inside and around you and what the text and the author are giving you. Discovering what is meant by vocal life and body wisdom and understanding that this is not just another *technique*, but the essence of who and what we are—creative human beings who need to be playful, curious, childlike in order to function in a healthy way. To transmit this message, all the teachers, whatever their personality or teaching style might have been, were using very clear, logical and organic instructions. Suddenly my voice and the acting process were no longer notions that existed outside of me, but something I could really, physically feel and trace every single inch of the creative process.

In what ways have you applied or incorporated Lessac, within the context of what you do for a living, whether that is as a performer, artist, scholar, healer, teacher, therapist, etc?

I don't want to be *religious* about all this, because none of the Lessac teachers behave like gurus. But as Frank Langella[4] said: "Arthur's work is certainly a piece of heaven and once you incorporated it, it will never leave you". For me, the work became

---

[4] Frank Langella wrote the introduction to the Lessac's *The Use and Training of the Human Voice* (1997).

not only a wonderful acting and directing tool, but also a huge part of who I am and the way I stand in life. I found out that this work is not pushing actors in one direction or the other. It just makes them aware of the wonderful instrument they all are and how to use it in order to create the performance they want to. I was lucky enough to be able to study, teach, direct and act in countries with completely different theatre and acting traditions including the Flemish and Dutch avant-garde theatre, a more *cerebral* French theatre, as well as theatre in England and the States. All of which gave me an expansive context to use this work to train and coach people and help people discover how to use the work themselves to open up their voice, sense of rhythm and dance, their fantasy, and strengthen their confidence. This included teaching professional and community theatre actors as well as coaching classical, opera, jazz, pop, musical, and rock singers, chansonniers, and groups of 100 and more choral society singers.

I also used this work to train presenters for the VRT [the Flemish National Radio and Television], TMF [The Music Factory, a European TV-channel] and MTV [Music Television]. They considered this one of the best trainings they ever got as it helped them to adapt to the style of the specific station and program they were working for, while remaining true to themselves and really becoming aware of the communication with their viewers and listeners.

I also used this work to train teachers and welfare workers. Within this context, people discovered how they could *protect* themselves against negative feelings sometimes coming from the people they had to work with, without losing empathy, and while being able to use whatever energy or emotion they wanted to, to have the necessary impact on their audience. I also was able to use Lessac voice and body work for *therapeutic* reasons, including working with people who had extreme authority and communication problems. For example, I worked with a lady who exhibited severe vocal problems, in part, as a result of being in a car crash, which made her lose 30% of her lung capacity, and after suffering from a malignant tumor on the thyroid gland. By the time I met her, she had spent the past 15 years going to otolaryngologists, movement and relaxation therapists, rebirthing classes, yoga, speech therapists, including those who used techniques such as Pahn and Koblenzer speech therapy, etc, all in order to treat her vocal problems. And yet, despite the validity of many of these methods she had made little progress. She still suffered greatly with her voice. But after only five sessions working with the Lessac work, she was able to make incredible progress and, even more important, as she mentioned herself, for the first time in years, she enjoyed speaking again and was no longer afraid to go shopping, speak up for herself, attend meetings etc.

In addition, I have been able to introduce the Lessac work in various post-graduate programs throughout Belgium and the Netherlands, including for speech therapists and otolaryngologists, for members of the Law faculty of the Antwerp University and for interpreters being trained at the university in conference interpreting at the European Parliament and other European government institutions

Please describe one context or vignette that best represents the way(s) in which you have you applied or incorporated Lessac training within the development of your own voice and body, and how, if at all, this process has been used by you as a means for problem-solving, learning, healing, performance, communication, and/or increasing your own vitality of life.

The Lessac training became a part of who I am and the way I interact with my environment, not only people, but also with animals and all living elements in nature. As a result, it increased my awareness for one of the most basic and fundamental principles in life—*Respect*—and gave me the courage to use this principal in my interactions with others as well as myself. Within this context, the Lessac training not only made me a better listener, speaker and mover, it also taught me to deal with stress and anxiety in a better and thus healthier way. It increased my empathy, improved my energy-management, stimulated my curiosity and helped shape me into being the teacher, coach and director I am now. As a result, whenever I teach, the message I am trying to convey isn't just on the *intellectual* content but on the medium in which the content is transferred, including emphasizing that message through the organic part of my being, wherein the understanding of the message is on the physical (that of the *Aha-Erlebnis*[5]) and as well an intellectual level. And I guess this is what helps me, not only

---

[5] Aha-Erlebnis is the German term to which Jacques Lacan (*The Mirror Stage,* 1949*)* alludes as representing the ah-ha experience. It is also used by researchers, such as Wolfgang Köhler who observed that learners experience a moment in which the elements of their task or problem "come together"—in Kohler's terms, emerge as a gestalt—for them in ways that significantly advance their understanding and problem-solving success (http://www.english.hawaii.edu/criticallink/lacan/terms/ahha.html).

to understand the people I'm working with, but also to teach in a *natural*, rather *instinctive* way.

In what local or global context do you see the future of kinesensics, or kinesensic training taking place within the next 50 years? In particular, what needs or possibilities, if any, do you think this type of training or work will address or shape in the future?

Almost all the people I worked with, whether actors, singers, politicians, teachers or therapy clients agree that this work should be part of everyone's basic education—that it should be one of the first things we learn at school and that which we pass onto our children. In a society where real human-to-human communication is more and more replaced by chat sessions and sms-messages,[6] where abbreviations not only become a means for faster communication, but in some cases become all that's left of the communication process, where we drop so many vowels and consonants that we no longer know the original words, and where we'll live with so many people on small surfaces and disconnected spaces, this kind of voice and body work will become a necessity. Because in order to survive and maintain a certain quality of life we will need physical and spatial awareness, wherein we use space to increase our awareness of our inner and outer movements, and as a result, rediscover the sound, rhythm and the fundamental, deeper meaning of words in order to be able to feel and communicate the things that really matter in life. It is also, in my view, the kind of voice, body, language and communication work that will become a very important tool to save us from George Orwell's 1984,[7] as the ability to recognize and utilize nuances in vocabulary, verbal and non-verbal communication will become even more essential for real understanding and sharing of thoughts and emotions. If people lack these skills in a future global society, it will influence their capacity to think, reflect and react, their

---

[6] There are two primary types of messaging within recent software development, those which focus on direct one on one communication, such as text messaging, instant online messaging, and those that focus on social networks, where web formats, such as facebook, allow people to post wikis, write blogs, and upload visual images within their network. For some scholars such as Kress (*Literacy in the New Media Age,* 2003) and Lemke ("Travels in Hypermodality." *Visual Communication* 1, 2002: 299-325) this type of technology has allowed for a hybridity of language, wherein notions of time and space are part reshaped within the communication process, and the written language is reshaped through visual mediums.

[7] *1984* is a classic dystopian novel by English author George Orwell. Published in 1949, it is set in the eponymous year and focuses on a repressive, totalitarian regime (http://en.wikipedia.org/wiki/Nineteen_Eighty-Four).

mental and—eventually—physical health. Their lack of communication skills will empower others, and give them all the opportunities to manipulate and abuse the *communication-impaired.* Thus, this kind of communication training is a guarantee and a necessity for a fair and respectful society.

In what ways, if any, do you think that the Lessac work/approach can and should still be developed in the future?

Any development of the work should happen in an organic and not in an intellectual way. Development should take place by training true practitioners who have the fullest possible understanding of the work and who are able to take it to all levels of society, not only into the theatre, but also into aspects of education and the work force, including teacher training programs, educational programs as well as research (that focus on language, learning, and psychology), sports programs (kinesthesiology), medicine, and human resources, including both labor and management.

Unfortunately, our actual society is ruled by definitions, intellectual theories, statistics and people who promote them. More often than not, governmental decisions are based on *empirical* evidence[8] and not on how people really function on *gut-feel*. In order to develop our work and give it the place that it rightly deserves in society, we will need to find the people who are completely immersed in the Lessac work, but also manage the tools (scientific research, statistics) and language needed to translate what we, practitioners, know, feel and live, into the language of decision makers and financers….

---

[8] There is much debate in research communities about the paradigms and epistemological underpinnings of empirical studies, including notions of objectivity and statistical significance, and who benefits in society from its implications, and who is negatively affected by it implications.

Robin Carr

Robin Carr is an Associate Professor of Voice and Acting in the Department of Theatre and Dance at the University of Southern Mississippi (USM). Since she has been at Southern Miss, Robin has directed Songs for a New World, Voice of the Prairie, Little Shop of Horrors, Cabaret, And the World Goes Round, *and* Picasso at the Lapin Agile. *Ms. Carr also directed* Coyote on a Fence *for the Kennedy Center/American College Theatre Festival (KC/ACTF) and has served on the regional selection committee for KC/ACTF. Ms. Carr has been the dialect coach for various USM productions such as* Waiting for the Parade, Candida, The Country Wife, *and the University of New Orleans' production of* Our Country's Good. *Robin has taught at the University of Connecticut, Old Dominion University, and at the Berkshire Theatre Festival. A member of Actor's Equity, Robin has performed such roles as Fefu in* Fefu and Her Friends, *Mrs. Lovett in* Sweeney Todd, *and Ouisa Kittredge in* Six Degrees of Separation. *She holds an MFA in Acting from the University of Connecticut and a Shakespeare Acting Certificate from the Royal Academy of Dramatic Arts. Robin is a Certified Lessac Trainer.*

Ms. Carr is vice president of the Voice and Speech Committee for the Southeastern Theatre Festival and is a member of the International Centre for Voice (ICV), The Lessac Training and Research Institute, and Voice and Speech Trainers Association (VASTA). She is also the co-director of Midsummer Musical Theatre Experience, a musical theatre youth camp held on the campus of USM. Robin is the 2008 USM recipient of the Innovation Award for Creative Activities.

My Lessac Journey...

I would first like to open with one word: wow. This describes my time with Arthur Lessac's work in so many ways. From my first introduction to Arthur to the first time my facial posture was engaged; my jaw became unlocked, my voice did not hurt and I found myself.

I feel privileged to be able to write this narrative in knowing so many of those who read this have experienced Arthur's work far longer than I have. In many ways I am only in the first stage of my journey. However, I hope I can speak for the newly trained and certified student in saying this system is ageless. No matter how long or short you have lived in it, the work always will reveal layers upon layers of the person who is experiencing it.

I was introduced to the Lessac training in a very unconventional way, according to some,[1] in a very large group with lots of Lessac Instructors at the University of Florida in Gainsville. It was the 2005 Lessac Summer Intensive. It was unusual because Lessac is usually experienced in small groups to allow plenty of time for the learning process. This group was composed of about twenty-two students and five instructors (including Arthur himself).

Let me back track a bit. I was hired at the University of Southern Mississippi as a voice and acting teacher in the fall of 2002. I had a good ear and strong music background from playing piano and violin. I had taught acting and voice for two years prior. However, I had little to no idea what I was doing. I had also lived through many vocal obstacles: strain, nodes, hoarseness, etc. I relied on a myriad of vocal *techniques* and bag o' tricks to get me through in life, stage and instructing. To teach, I would piece together a voice class from the combination of what I could remember from my own graduate education and handouts from teachers, but had no real process. I was lost and needed help. So one day I received a brochure from the Lessac Institute about their summer intensive. I brought it home and discussed it with my husband. We knew it was the right decision for me to attend but had no idea how much it would impact our lives. I will always be forever grateful for my husband's never ending love and support through this entire process.

I then came to the University of Florida, unpacked my bags in a tiny apartment shared by three other women and attended the first meeting. Let me say this—I am not quite sure why my husband (Matt) and I knew this was the training I needed, but we knew. When I walked into the first meeting, I then understood. The answers were revealed to me in my instructors: Arthur Lessac, Sue Ann Park, Deborah Kinghorn (who would later become my mentor), Diane Gaary, and Yanci Bukovec. When I heard Arthur speak and he told us we were Stradivarius violins with such radiancy, I was

---

[1] Sue Ann Park has advocated for a cap on the number of students who can be taught during one intensive. From 1995-2005, this number was, on average, between of 10-14 students.

intrigued. When I saw Deb Kinghorn do forward facial posture with buoyancy, I wanted to know more. When I heard Sue Ann potently state that she was not here to convince us about the training, she knew it worked—I was sold.

I think the biggest discovery for me in the work was SLOWING DOWN. By nature, I am a *project-done* kind of person. I like planning, organizing and finishing something as quickly and precisely as possible. I think back when I played the fool in *King Lear* in graduate school. I had a close friend come and see me. He commented on how he loved my character but attention to the words was lost. I was not aware of what he meant at that point. I was saying the words and my sense of rhythm and meter was apparent. However, when I began to physically and vocally feel, taste and breathe a piece of text through Lessac's "atom-to-atom" approach,[2] it all started to make sense. I remember at my first intensive finally taking my time with the small ball (it was so difficult for me!), feeling the sense of rhythm change in my body, and allowing myself to experience life. Nothing was rushed. I could breathe, observe, and communicate with absolute freedom!

In the following years of my training, I have come to understand how the Lessac work becomes you and how you become the work. As an actress, I incorporate the tasting of words, making music and breaking habitual tendencies. As a director, I lovvvvvvve the body NRGs for character relationships and the use of rhythm and movement for scene work. I really use Lessac concepts in *every* class I teach. The concepts of exploring and contiguous continuity now are the basis of my teaching.

This work has not only affected my teaching and creative work, but it has also opened a new window for my artistic research. In the spring of 2008, I won an Innovation for Creative Activities award at the University of Southern Mississippi for Integrating Tadashi Suzuki's Actor Training with the Lessac work. I had studied Suzuki Japanese movement for three years with Eric Hill at the University of Connecticut and studied an additional year with Leon Ingulsrud at Old Dominion University. The combination of the Lessac work and Tadashi Suzuki's movement is a

---

[2] Atom-to-atom discovery refers to the *Principal of Contiguous Continuity*, which means not moving from one spot (atom) on the body until you successfully experience the feel of its most proximally adjacent (closest touching) spot (Lessac 1978).

breakthrough concept. I do not know of anyone exploring this integration. In the past, Suzuki experts and Lessac trainers have not met eye to eye. There has been a huge gap between the two stemming from a preconceived notion that one method has very little to do with the other.

I made the connection between the body and the voice through Tadashi Suzuki's Japanese movement and Arthur Lessac's voice and body training. I integrated these two methodologies through the creative activities of performance, directing and vocal coaching. I have also presented workshops at the Southeastern Theatre Conference (SETC) titled: "Lessac with a Twist of Suzuki." These workshops were geared for performers interested in maintaining a healthy vocal life along with exploring Tadashi Suzuki's Japanese training for actors.

I am still open to finding other ways to use the Lessac work. I co-produce a children's musical theatre camp in the summer for ages 9-14 at the University of Southern Mississippi. I want to incorporate the training into their warm-ups and character development. I am also talking with a friend who is interested to bring vocal training to anesthesiology studies.

I believe the Lessac work is always exploring the possibility of an optimal world where we can freely and openly communicate with others—a world where healing can take place and acceptance is found. At the core of it all, the Lessac work seeks to find what is truly human in all of us. I would like to end this narrative with the introduction I wrote on my final examination for certification,[3] I believe it sums up my experience with the Lessac work:

This certification to me represents over three years of exploring Kinesensic training. Since the summer of 2005, my journey brought me to the University of Florida and DePauw University. I have experienced three Summer intensives; two as a student and one as an intern. In addition, I enrolled in the teaching training course and have attended the Lessac Conference since its inaugural meeting. What I have gleamed from these experiences I can never fully explain. It has changed my life so completely

---

[3] Lessac final written examination, submitted by Robin Carr to board of Master Lessac teachers (2008).

and it is still evolving. The one thing that always stays constant is when I am teaching this work, I feel as if I could dance at any moment. This written examination based on collaboration between my personal experiences and point of view; my gifted mentor, Deb Kinghorn; other inspirational Lessac trainers including Sue Ann Park, Nancy Krebs, Barry Kur, Kathleen Dunn and Diane Gaary; The books: *The Use and Training of the Human Voice* and *Body Wisdom;* and finally, Arthur Lessac himself, the inventor. *Arthur—you gave me a gift and never asked for anything in return. Thank you for inviting me into this circle.*

Can you elaborate a little more on what you mean when you say: "In the following years of my training, I have come to understand how the Lessac work becomes you and how you become the work"?

I always feel the *training* when I am teaching. When I am introducing a concept, I am always relishing my words and found…its fun! This training has made me so carefree and fearless about language. It opens the "It's OK if I fail" door to creativity. I have found the more I explore with the work, it starts to become something else entirely. It's never a *technique*. I think the clearest example I can use is going on a diet vs. eating right. Vocal and physical techniques always feel like going on a diet to me. With Arthur's work it always makes you feel good like eating right, so you want to keep on doing it!

You and Daisy Nystul were the first two people who have been given the opportunity to be "interns" at the intensive. Can you explain what this internship was, and how, if at all, you think it impacted your process towards certification?

I will try to be concise, but it is so challenging to express to anyone how much the internship impacted me. The Internship was a wonderful opportunity to learn from master teachers Nancy Krebs and Deborah Kinghorn. Daisy and I would have administrative duties that we divided up and we also had teaching opportunities that grew in length over the course of the intensive. I will have to say I don't think I could have done the Internship without Daisy. She is and will always be my Lessac buddy for life. While we were teaching, we would be taping our sessions for Sue Ann Park and Arthur to view.

After the Internship was over I can confidently say my knowledge of the work doubled. I have lived, loved, cried, floated, yawned, and shaken my way into Arthur's training. The reason why the Internship was so vital to my training was the day-to-day feedback from the master teachers. Their critique and encouragement made our teaching improve at a rapid pace. Teaching Lessac is a different thing all together than experiencing it yourself. The Teacher Training introduced this and the Internship solidified it.

In what ways do you believe that you have made a bridge between two methodologies (Suzuki and Lessac) that as you said, "in the past, didn't see eye to eye"? Please explain what you mean, and any breakthroughs you have had.

Great question! When I was exploring the Suzuki method in school, I loved how strong it made me feel—very potent. However, I began to get vocal nodes from pushing my voice into a very low register to match the power I felt in my body. I love the Suzuki actor training and felt bad when any voice colleagues would turn their nose up when I mentioned how much it influenced my acting process. In other words, I wanted to keep parts of what I loved, but needed something else.

I then learned the Lessac work and I started to figure out that some of the concepts could be used with Suzuki and it made Suzuki even better! Instead of pushing my voice into a lower register, I needed tone. Instead of holding my breath and tensing my upper body, I would smell the flower. I feel like I can speak two languages and communicate with anyone who has apprehensions about Suzuki in the voice world and assist Suzuki actor's with Lessac's vocal therapy.

Melissa Hurt

Melissa Hurt is a doctoral candidate in Theatre Arts at the University of Oregon. Her dissertation appraises Lessac's kinesensic theory as an embodied acting practice using Merleau-Ponty's ideas of embodiment. She earned the Betty Foster McCue Scholarship for Human Performance and Development in 2008 for her dissertation research. Melissa became a practitioner of Lessac's voice and body work in 2008. Melissa also holds an MFA in Theatre Pedagogy-Directing from Virginia Commonwealth University. She has publications in Theatre Symposium, the Northwest Theatre Review and the Voice and Speech Review. She has presented papers and workshops at the Annual Conference of the Australasian Society for Continental Philosophy, American Theatre and Drama Society ATHE pre-conference, International Federation for Theatre Research, the KC/ACTF Conferences for Regions I, IV, and VII, and Theatre Alliance.

How has the Lessac work and training impacted you personally? In particular, can you reflect on how you were introduced to the work, and what training you have had, and your own perceptions of its impact?

Although I pursued this work for professional reasons, the impact has infiltrated my entire life! But, first I will share how I came across the work. I first experienced Arthur Lessac's voice and body work when he visited Virginia Commonwealth University in 2003 for a short introductory workshop during the pursuit of my MFA in Theatre Pedagogy. I remember the anticipation that had been aroused in me by my colleagues familiar with his work (they had built him up as a demigod) and then entering the studio to meet a small-framed 94-year-old man. I thought, "This tiny man is responsible for whatever gives my friends such a rush of pedagogical frenzy?" I soon realized his talents. I felt the smooth resonance of what he called the "N violin" and the freedom from tension with the body's natural buoyancy. When the workshop ended, I appreciated the experience, but did not think I would use what Lessac brought.

Two years later I began my PhD and one of my first classes was acting theory. I read acting practices and theories as far back as Plato and spanning the greats such as David Garrick, Ellen Terry, and Sarah Bernhardt. These legends spoke of the importance of the voice, the agility of the body, and how these elements are the performer's utmost tools. I felt something was missing in my professional training. I had taken voice and speech in college and a few dance classes, but they were always separate from each other. My acting classes focused solely on psychological and imaginative investigations of character. I had never experienced how voice, body and imagination come together and mutually enhance each other. I yearned for an intensive training experience so I could taste a kernel of what would echo in my acting theory texts. I remembered Lessac's visit, did a quick search for him online, and stumbled upon the Lessac Training and Research Institute webpage advertising applications for the 2006 Summer Intensive. I read about his work and could not believe I could experience voice *and* body training in one workshop! I applied, was accepted and the doorway to a new path of my life began in late June.

Deb Kinghorn and Kathy Dunn led the four-week intensive with enthusiasm, fervorr and seemingly unending energy. I took in what they offered and immediately tried translating the information to how I would teach it. I asked Deb a question in an early class so I could attempt to teach what she explained when I returned home. She simply said, "Why don't you let yourself be a student and just experience the work?" I felt immediate release from an assumed responsibility. I was allowed to simply *be*. I attended each session with an open mind and allowed the work to wash over (and through) me. Although exhilarating in that I was finally getting the training I felt I lacked, I had no epiphanies about the work as some of my dorm mates, who studied in an intensive the previous year, had. However, my final session of the intensive with Kathy changed everything. We were working on structural vowels in Shakespearean passages and I made a connection between what I learned was my body's wisdom and the emotional subtext of the passage. I felt a "hook" into a character without any intellectual process—a departure from my previous acting training. I felt enthralled, yet also disappointed that the intensive was ending! I knew I needed to attend the next year's intensive, savor the work again, explore my subtextual connection and determine if there would be any others.

The 2007 Intensive was a real privilege since it was not only lead by two Master Trainers, Deb Kinghorn and Nancy Krebs, but Arthur was joining us for one week while Nancy taught the Teacher Training Workshop. I experienced the work anew. Whereas I experienced everything of Lessac's work for the first time the previous year, that year I knew what all of the items were and could now revel in and explore the subtleties of each. I absorbed the work as a sponge takes in water. I had a new passion for the work and felt the nuances of my voice and body in creative expression. I explored Shakespearean passages with intensity and commitment that I previously shied away from. My voice felt amazing and enriched, my body flowed like a dancer in the body work sessions, and I felt like everything I needed in my training as an actor was complete. Moreover, I felt like an integral component of my life had arrived: I needed to continue with this work, share it with others, follow the steps to certification and place this work more in the center of my teaching interests.

On a more personal level, this work has completely changed how I regard well-being. The perceptual feeling process transcends feeling voice and body rhythms and resonance for expression. It also impacts how I regard my diet. Often I would notice that after eating or drinking something, I either felt really jumpy or tired. I simply would not feel right. I began investigating nutrition and health, became vegan in January 2008 and moved into about 80% raw food in August 2008. Now I feel good all the time and think Lessac's work has inspired me to extend the feeling process to all avenues of my life. Arthur's livelihood at 99 years old has inspired me to reach the same level of well-being into my 90s and beyond!

(From my perspective) it is significant to note that you were one of the first people,[1] at least in the recent era, who have been given permission to record Arthur reflecting about his life and personal accomplishments, and write about the historical and cultural significance of what he has accomplished (outside of the work itself). What events led up to your being given this access, and in particular, what is your perspective on the significance, if any, of being granted this access?

I did not realize until you mentioned it that I was one of the first people granted such access. I am not sure how Arthur came to trust that I could write about his work. It is certainly not because I am a famous biographer or oral historian! I can only guess that it may be because of several things. First, Arthur's first personal conversation with me was regarding a dissertation idea. I spoke with him and Deb Kinghorn in 2006 about writing my dissertation on exploring subtext through this work. Perhaps hearing me talk about his

---

[1] Within his personal archives, there is evidence that he participated in additional interviews with Heather Jewell (E-mail correspondence 11/07/02) and an unknown author (E-mail correspondence 6/09/03). Additional interviews were conducted by Ruth McKenney (1986) and by Little (1967).

work and its uses outside of voice and body convinced him that I really enjoy thinking about the possibilities for his work. Second, I talked to Deb extensively several times about dissertation ideas and questioned research methods. So, I suppose a lot of it may be from Deb convincing Arthur about my character—that I am not out to exploit him or the work, that I have a genuine passion and curiosity about it, that I am a kind person! Last, I changed my dissertation idea several times and pursued writing a professional biography of Arthur. I spoke about it with Deb and explained the significance of Arthur's work in American theatre throughout the 20th century to today. I have always loved 20th century American theatre history and felt Arthur was such an interesting figure since he has witnessed so much! Additionally, after looking at the different editions of his voice books, I wanted to know what happened professionally that prompted the evolution of kinesensics and, thus, influenced the changes in each edition.

I asked Arthur if I could write about him, I think at the 2007 intensive when he filled in for Nancy Krebs for one week. He and Deb talked about it and I was granted permission as long as he read what I wrote and approved it. I felt this was completely fair and I felt honored to be trusted by him. We had our first phone interview on September 20, 2007 and the first thing he said was for me to not be nervous since we were "just chatting." He was so easy to talk to and he told me several stories about teaching the work over the years. We spoke for about an hour and a half! I was surprised he gave me so much of his time. He closed the conversation inviting me to call again if any other questions came up. Well, I called him again on March 7, 2008 to see if I could clarify some events in his career. Again, he told me fascinating stories about his career. That is something I truly love about him—he does not give a one-sentence answer, but really investigates the question and finds stories to explain how or why something happened. We spoke for about two hours and, as Arthur calls himself, "ol' man river" rolled along the whole time. I feel honored to have a friendship with Arthur and his willingness to work with me is something I will cherish always.

How has your research agenda, as a doctoral student, been shaped or impacted by the your experience with the Lessac work and your inquiry into the Lessac history, and what, if any, is the significance of your current research?

Well, I am no longer doing a professional biography on Arthur's career and the development of his work (my department did not approve that prospectus). Instead,

I am writing about kinesensic theory (the perceptual feeling process) and how this articulates and accommodates an embodied acting practice. Since I am writing about the perceptual feeling process I find myself continually *checking in* with my perceptions as I write about this work! For example, when I write about "intrinsic active meditation" I find myself stopping to waft and wave in my chair to then write about the myriad of sensations happening in one instance. I am a practitioner-researcher in my dissertation and I find that theory and practice mutually enhance each other. While I have been working on my dissertation, I have also been researching and writing a historical context for Arthur's life. This has been a wonderful experience. I find a real storytelling component to Arthur's career and when my head gets exhausted with theory, I shift gears and write about an incident in Arthur's teaching that revealed something significant about kinesensics. In return, writing about the history has helped me to clarify better my ideas about kinesensic theory since I have an understanding of how Arthur may have come up with an idea for, say, the familiar event principle. As for significance with my current research, I hope people will find something they can hold onto and extend to a new way to think about Lessac's work, embodiment, or acting in general. I am using Merleau-Ponty's phenomenology to describe embodiment as it relates to the acting process, in particular learning a new technique. I look at how the actor builds a foundation in her practice by feeling the effects of meditation and tuning into the gestalt of perception. I look at how the actor learns a technique through the perceptual layers of the body. I look at how the actor relates to external space and discovers her internal living space for movement and expression. I look at how the body and mind function in concert and how the actor can use this relationship to determine subtextual meanings. I think it is pretty exciting! I hope someone can read my dissertation and find my use of Merleau-Ponty significant as a way to think about acting. I hope people gain a deeper understanding of Lessac's work and finally regard it as not just a voice and body technique, but also an embodied acting approach. As for my work with Arthur's history, I hope someone may read it and find the significance in his career for herself! It is not my place to tell the reader what is significant in his life, but I think the reader can clearly see how many amazingly influential people he has worked with in American theatre and see the threads that his work has laid down in many different arenas, from ESL to therapy to acting!

What events or stories, as told by Arthur Lessac to you, do you perceive he thinks are most historically and culturally significant?

I can only answer this by recalling two stories that he took the most time to tell me ensuring that I did not miss the significance of each. The first story that comes to mind is a story Arthur tells of teaching a group of at-risk youths that I feel illustrates how community-building and increasing self-image results from his voice and body work. In 1963 in New York City, Arthur was asked by an officer of The Harlem Youth Project, Called Haryou, to teach fourteen young boys aged between 13-19 years old and work with them twice a week (E-mail correspondence, 14 Dec 2008). Arthur remembers how the project functioned and his involvement with it:

> The officer considered this group of young men to have leadership ability and prospects, even with little education....The beginning of this group was part of a proposal to simply gather in, from the streets, as many young people as possible to find out if they had any special interest in anything at all (art, culture, learning, camera work, painting, etc.) and each [group] was given a space, equipment, material and the benefit of recognized experts in those given fields. The work they exhibited at the end of six months was so wonderful as to be unbelievable. In a strange way, my experience with them had a similar quality and experience for me (E-mail correspondence, 14 Dec 2008).

Arthur taught them his vocal work with consonants, tone and vowels. At one point, he thought he had reached a plateau in his teaching and decided to have them teach each other something while utilizing their new approach to language and movement. The students immediately felt discouraged by the assignment. Lessac asked them how many performed basic tasks around the house or had younger siblings that they helped. The students acknowledged that they each had at least one thing they did as a part of their routine they could show the others. Arthur then observed something significant when they began their teaching demonstrations:

> The most significant thing happened, and it's hard to believe, these were young people who could hardly put three words together, you know?...They began to teach and their voices changed, especially when they suddenly realized that everybody was interested and actually learning and they became poets. And they

become teachers and, sure your own language and that sort of thing, but you look at them and you suddenly realize this is an absolutely unbelievable experience! Of course, it helped them a great deal, so that then they weren't frightened with anything I asked them to do (Telephone interview, 10 Sept 2007).

As each displayed his task and got others involved in how to execute it, Arthur noticed the students' voices change throughout their presentations. Once a student realized others were interested in and learning from him, he then used language and his means of expression in much more lyrical ways. Arthur knew he was witnessing a breakthrough—the young men were flourishing before his eyes. Their vocal abilities improved dramatically and their spirits and senses of self grew as well.

Arthur then worked with them on exploring the K drumbeat in his consonant energy work. He asked the youths to play with the word "characteristic." The students repeated: "charaKter*i*stiK," "charaKter*i*stiK." Suddenly they discovered a rhythm inherent in the word and they became more engaged in their exploration. They then felt buoyancy in their bodies as they danced in their chairs while singing their beat: *"charaKterIStiK," "charaKterIStiK."* Arthur announced the lesson was over and the students danced out of their chairs, formed a line and, in a manner reminiscent of an Ancient Greek dance, said *"charaKterIStiK"* and then took a step in unison. *"CharaKterIStiK,"* they chanted and then took a step. They repeated this out the door and down the street on their ways home. Arthur's observation affirmed that, when students enjoy the feeling process, their expressive abilities improve with their self-value as communicative and sensitive members of society.

The second story that comes to mind is his work at the Jewish Theological Seminary of America in 1951. Arthur was in charge of teaching the students seeking ordination how to deliver sermons with optimal speech, voice and enthusiasm. Instead of simply reading the sermons from the weekly scrolls, Arthur taught them how to connect with the text and then move the audience through their vocal delivery. These lessons inspired the students to not imitate an admired rabbi and orator in their school, but to find the passion within themselves and communicate it through their individual relationship with the text. Through his teachings of the feeling process and connecting text and spirit, students discovered their individuality in expressing their sermons.

Upon learning Arthur's feeling process while enriching tone and articulation, Seminary students took an examination with him that determined their completion of the studies. Arthur says, "They couldn't get ordained unless I passed them" (Telephone interview, 9 March 2008).

One of Arthur's favorite stories occurred on the last day of a semester. As he was putting away his books he noticed all of the students present after class. They were discussing something and looking at him. One of the students approached him and said, "None of us slept a blink last night. We were up arguing all night and we would like you to know that we took a vote and we unanimously believe you to be the most religious of us all" (Telephone interview, 9 March 2008). Arthur understood the depth of this compliment. He knew that "religious" in this context meant the man most honest and "loving." The journey Arthur took his students upon for them to come to such a conclusion illuminates why they would think so highly of their teacher from the first day of class. Arthur told these students that they needed not to simply read the words in a service, but to understand the text intellectually and emotionally. He taught them how to connect with language through a perceptual attunement to the articulations and resonances of the spoken word, find the love in communication, and express the emotion beneath the text to their listeners. He told them that even if a person does not understand the Hebrew or English languages (both of which were used in the sermons), she would still feel the meaning beneath the text due to the rabbi's connection to it. As a result of their voice studies, Arthur claims, "When they left my class they felt like a human being who felt, how should I say, more organically religious" as the depth of the love of religion grew and intensified (Telephone interview, 9 March 2008).

Arthur's pedagogy was different from the seminary's previous voice and speech teachers (or even typical voice and speech teachers of his day).[2] He did not simply teach elocution and pronunciation and insist students learn these techniques by rote. Rather he encouraged students to love their language, honor the message in the text and commune with all of the meanings beneath. While students explored language through the feeling process, they enriched their tonal qualities and developed their pronunciation and enunciation in ways unique and optimal for each student. Arthur

---

[2] A side note from Melissa: "This may still be the case since the Lessac work was, and continues to be, unique because of his focus on the feeling process to learn optimal voice and movement."

never urged a standard of voice, but inspired and helped students find the optimal uses of their own voices and bodies to aid in creative and heart-felt expression. Arthur's time with them lasted until 1971.

I think both of these stories are significant because they illustrate how his voice work extends beyond enriching the voice or becoming more articulate, although those things certainly happen! These stories show how one connects to language through this work and how that, in return, elevates the expressive spirit. This then enriches a sense of self, community and, in the case of the rabbis, connection to their religion.

From the data you have collected regarding either the historical context of Arthur's life or the development of the Lessac work, or both, discuss one or two emerging themes that you have found, and their significance within either theatre pedagogy, history, performance, or education.

The biggest theme that stands out is that one already possesses everything she needs to have a dynamic speaking voice and expressive body. Arthur's ideas of the "familiar event principle" and "organic instruction" are pedagogically very liberating in the sense that the student does not need to rely on an external source to ensure she "gets it." Instead, she uses what her body instinctively gives her and entrusts her body's inherent knowledge. Arthur has employed these principles throughout his career, whether he knew it or not, for what he calls accent elimination, speech therapy, connecting how one develops articulation and vocal tone (which had always been taught separately), and his idea that learning is circular—it never ends since the body is different everyday! I love that I can always tune into my Y-buzz to develop my voice and that I do not need a teacher to tell me if I am doing it correctly. I can feel the yawn space in my lifted soft palate, my forward facial posture, floating up through the crown of the head, and the vocal resonance on the upper gum ridge. I have everything I need to be self-sufficient!

From the data you have collected, specific to the history as told to you by Arthur Lessac, what do you perceive as being the major implications of the Lessac work and training for the future?

The biggest implication of the Lessac work and training for the future I think comes down to health and wellness of the individual and how that grows in gestalt to a community. That is actually one of the first things Arthur told me in our first interview—that his work is about health and wellness. It is not just about voice and movement. As I discovered with my nutritional choices, when one tunes into the perceptual feeling process, she gets a better sense of how her body feels overall. If someone feels bad somehow—either physically exhausted or emotionally down—she can use a body energy (NRG) to diffuse tension and take control of her inner environment again. I think this can also extend to performance. If an actor has to be onstage for an extended amount of time, the body NRGs are a great way to keep up one's stamina! I see so many theatre students drinking tons of coffee and soda for caffeine fixes, eating pizza and other chemically charged foods and then attempting to perform. They end up burning out! How great would it be if students moved from one body NRG to the next before rehearsal and performances to keep themselves alert and, thus, stayed away from these nutritionally and energetically draining things! I suspect Arthur would agree with me on that sentiment!

But, getting back to how health and wellness impacts the individual and then society. If people feel good and are relaxed (which they will be if they continually diffuse negative energy through a voice and/or body NRG), it will impact how they relate to people. This kind of relaxed, positive energy is contagious and slowly flows out until, before you know it, everyone feels peaceful. Not to say people are anesthetized from their lives. On the contrary, they are better equipped to *feel* their lives and respond with their full selves! Thus, the future of Lessac training will, I think, continue along these lines. We will continue to teach in acting studios, guide others through therapeutic applications of the work, and help with physical ailments. But, I also foresee this work extending to community centers, like YMCA's for example, so anyone can experience the work and benefit from kinesensics. How great would it be to look on a wellness calendar at the local YMCA and see yoga, Pilates and Lessac!

Research Perspectives and Applications of the Lessac Work

Marth Munro (with Allan Munro)
Year of Certification as a Lessac Voice, Speech and Body Trainer: 1990

The previous section framed Lessac Kinesensic training as an intensely personal experience. It provided wonderful examples of how the Lessac work fosters growth in the personal and professional spheres. This rings true for so many participants of the Lessac workshops!

Many moons ago in the Southern tip of Africa, a 26-year-old actress/singer struggled to find the relationship between her singing and speaking voice. She struggled to find congruency between her body, voice and emotions. A sense of uneasiness and despair surrounded her, as she desperately wanted to be centered in herself, as human, as performer.... As it was meant to be, her husband overheard two colleagues in the theatre department talking about a workshop in a far-a-way land...in America. And this was where it all began....

I was that young actress/singer. I eventually attended three Lessac workshops[1]—we even once had to sell our car to find money to attend. Just before the last workshop, we unexpectedly became parents, but we made the sacrifice and I left a Daddy and a newborn behind in order to seek, to find....

Living in a country so far away from what was then perceived as the Lessac hub created obstacles in its own right. I had to plan phone conversations with the erudite Lessac team with great care, as time differences and financial constraints limited the direct contact potential (in those early days e-mail was on the distant horizon). And how does one check a Y-buzz or radiancy in written form? What was then initially perceived as a frustration became for me the biggest gift. The potentially limited contact forced me towards what I still perceive as the essence of the work: kinesensics

---

[1] Boulder (1988), Fullerton (1989) and Pella (1990).

that encapsulates organic instruction through sensory awareness. I still had to find a way to determine whether what I was doing was optimal, whether the recall of my familiar event was truly organic and not habitual. This led me to heuristic research and further. In my Masters I investigated teaching theatre voice from a primarily Lessac perspective. My doctoral degree pivoted around the acoustic properties of the tonal NRG in the Lessac work, specifically focusing on the effect thereof on the multi-lingual female student body at a tertiary institution. Some other projects are reflected upon elsewhere in this section.

In reading about other research around the Lessac kinesensic training, it became evident that most scholars engaging in research in the Lessac work all had a positive experience of the work first—as such, most research around the Lessac work contains a heuristic element. Heuristic research is research where the researcher is actively immersed in the material being researched, where the researcher has experienced the material subjectively and then tries to collate tacit or cognitive knowledge about the material. Artists may refer to this as the move from rehearsal to performance. Researchers refer to this as moving from the experiential to the model.

Most research follows choices in two sets of categories. In one set the researcher works from a usually chaotic set of data, experiences, phenomena and observations and the researcher pursues a pattern of predictability in the work—a structure. This is known as inductive reasoning, as the researcher builds a model, a way of explaining those seemingly random occurrences that ring true. The model gives form to new knowledge, knowledge that is transferable, repeatable and testable. So much of the writings that have been generated in the previous section resonate with this new knowledge building coming from experiences that are formulated into a model of understanding. Alternatively, the researcher works from a theory (or model) or sets of theories (or models) to use them to test the phenomena or process that is being represented, and whether the claims that it makes are valid. Deductive thinking tests the unknown by using the known as a map, a compass. However, as we all know, the map is not the territory; the map of theory can never replace the territory of the experience. However, at least we know, from some of the deductive research outputs that are presented here, drawing on the models and theories of other disciplines as well, that one can now make conclusions beyond the subjective claims of truth, and that system of validation is good.

Furthermore, there is a second set of concerns about research that is useful to the task at hand. Basically the purposes of research can be encapsulated in the demands to *explore*, to *describe* and to *explain*. All Lessac aficionados know that the Lessac work is about exploring—the peek into the unknown, the tiptoeing into what seems to be uncharted territories, "to boldly go…"; "wandering/wondering through wilderness" as Arthur puts it. In this sense the Lessac work *is* about research, and the knowledge gained is not captured in books, in essays or in articles, but in performance, in better communication, in making contact, in making art, in healing. If it were only experienced, if it were not presented in performance, how else would it be presented but in the written form, and for that to happen, these types of researchers need to reach out to systems of description—ways of capturing what is happening in the Lessac work in words. Arthur himself does this in his books—what is the consonant orchestra other than a way of capturing in an organic and creative way the demands of the ephemeral? Thus the second demand of research is met—the demand to describe that which is discovered in the explorations. Is it enough to claim that the Lessac kinesensic training works? Surely we need to explore the reasons why it works—explain the dynamics in ways that move beyond the accusations of the idiosyncratic to touch the chords of the universe? And some of the articles in this section do that—they use the theories and models of nature to explain why the Lessac kinesensic training works.

A research orientation does not limit the type of research and the methods can be both qualitative (where the experiences of the participants form an intense and central part of the research, and the capturing of those experiences, in what qualitative researchers call "thick descriptions," teases out the heart of the work) and quantitative (where the approach is empirical, measured, and searches for the predictable). The multi-layeredness/ multi dimensionality/ holistic nature of the Lessac kinesensic training allows for the research method to be determined by the problem statement, hypothesis or investigative question. Research approaches focusing on the Lessac work can thus either be, for example, action research, applied research, or even clinical trials. It can draw on autoethnographic approaches, on medical as well as statistical interrogations. It can be collaborative or individual. It can interrogate itself, or its application in other fields. It is wonderful to observe that the research reflected upon in the submissions in this section, is representative of various approaches of research. The Lessac work is, in itself, so encompassing and multi-leveled that it begs for multiple research approaches to be accessed to determine the effectiveness and outcomes of the work. And even with such research attempts to quantify and qualify the outcomes of the work, the essence of the work may still elude scholarly research approaches due to its holistic nature. Research strategies and means of measurements often still have to be developed or defined to determine the influence that the work has on various walks of life. Does that then mean that we as researchers with an investment in the Lessac kinesensic training should not do research on the work? No! We need to use accepted research methods to prove what is, within the currently acceptable research paradigm, provable. It is our duty to validate the Lessac kinesensic training though explorations, descriptions and explanations. A flower (no matter how often it is smelled!) will die, despite its seeming perfection, if it is not fed and nurtured through time, and space, across countries and cultures, for young and old, in different places and applications.

Thus it is also our responsibility to seek proof for that which we know is true about the influence of the training in our private and professional lives. As an example of this, allow me to offer the following: The subjective experiences of the multi-faceted organic complexity of the holistic voice/body/mind/ interrelatedness of the Lessac work urged a colleague[2] and myself to determine the effect of the Y-buzz on brain waves[3] in a pilot study. The aim was to determine objectively the "healing properties of" and "conscious access to creativity through" the use of the Y-buzz. The effect the Y-buzz had on the brain waves of the participants was compared to existing literature regarding brain wave relationships and the meaning thereof.[4] Comparing the outcomes of the unique personal brainwave profiles of each of our participants to the scholarly literature that exists in neuroscience regarding the brainwaves and how the brainwave activity reflects upon specific states or attributes of human function, the pilot study indicates that the execution of the Y-buzz may allow one to make the following reasonably stable predictions:

- The Y-buzz may enhance relaxation, intuition, body/mind integration;
- It may promote well-being;
- The Y-buzz may create a bridge between the subconscious and conscious;

---

[2] Mariana Pretorius.
[3] Delta, Theta, Alpha, Beta and Gamma.
[4] The outcomes of the initial pilot study were shared with the Lessac community in a paper presented at the Lessac Conference in State College, 2007.

- It may lead to mental resourcefulness, self-control and abstract thinking;
- It may prepare an individual towards a state of optimal learning and problem solving;
- It may allow a person to enter a state where creativity can be accessed and where the person is alert enough to act on it.

Too good to be true? Maybe. But is it not what so many Lessac practitioners experience often when they use the Y-buzz and other tonal NRG explorations as part of their survival kit? Do we have to do a lot more research on this? Of course. We need to increase the number of participants in the test group. We need to use means of triangulation—for example journaling. We may even engage with means of measurements that are not widely accepted within the scientific community, such as Kirlian photography.[5] What we may not do is stop and say: Science does not yet serve the Lessac work to it's fullest and therefore we will refrain from motivating why Lessac kinesensic training is a valuable asset in both our professional and private lives.

Through various methods of research, we potentially have a way of bridging the gap between those who have been privileged to know the work and those who do not, and we have a way (another way, beyond testimony) to argue the case, to make the connections, to speak the other's language, to recruit, to extend the work, to grow. This is what the following three sub-divisions share as a goal.

The sub-divisions in this section are entitled:

- Physiological and Therapeutic Perspectives of the Lessac work;
- Acoustical Perspectives on the Lessac work;
- Pedagogical Explorations and Other Applications.

These three sub-sections all contain new material as well as previously published material, which demonstrate various research outcomes that share the importance of

---

[5] *Kirlian photography* is also known as *electrophotography* or *corona discharge photography*. Subjectively I can report that after 2 minutes of Y-buzz, I could detect a slight difference in the energy fields around my fingers when a master student of mine and I "played around" with pre- and post-testing by taking Kirlian pictures of my fingers!

the Lessac work with the greater community. Each of the sub-divisions has a lovely introduction that links the initially heuristic need for seeking and sharing with the research reported on.

Physiological and Therapeutical Perspectives of the Lessac Work

Katherine Verdolini Abbott
Professor, Communication Science and Disorders, University of Pittsburgh
Professor, Department of Otolaryngology, University of Pittsburgh
Member, McGowan Institute for Regenerative Healing, University of Pittsburgh
Member, Center for the Neural Basis of Cognition, Carnegie-Mellon University
and University of Pittsburgh
Year of Certification as a Lessac Voice, Speech and Body Trainer: 2003

My first encounter with Lessac's work came sometime in the mid 1980s. I was a classically trained vocalist with manifest inclinations towards musical theatre, jazz, folk, and rock music. Years earlier, I had been occupationally injured with the dreaded vocal fold "nodules." Finding no one who could cure me at the time, I had ventured into the land of speech-language pathology. My primary intent thereupon was to heal myself and subsequently, to heal the remainder of the singing universe. As a budding clinician, the approach that I used dutifully replicated the going paradigm at the time in singing pedagogy circles, readily heard behind and in front of most studio doors. That approach adhered to the conviction that the ideal speaking voice for vocal health involves some sort of head registration bordering on reinforced falsetto. I was convinced. Based on what I knew, the approach made biomechanical sense. Especially falsetto generally involves some degree of separation between the vocal folds throughout the so-called phonatory "duty cycle," and in the extreme, vocal fold contact may not occur at all. It seemed intuitive that by limiting vocal fold contact, the tissue would be afforded sufficient rest to recover from phonotraumatic injury (injury caused by phonation). Also the likelihood of future "phonotraumatic injury" (injury from phonation) should be limited.

My patients, particular my singer patients, generally had quite good success with this approach in the short term. Their various vocal phonotraumatic maladies associated with nodules, polyps, etc., often improved in very brief time. Patients went on their way as satisfied customers. The problem arose when my laryngologist colleague at the time—Dr. Robert Bastian then of Jewish Hospital in St. Louis—and I started seeing patients for their 1-yr follow-up. We were seeing more recurrences and more aggravations of vocal fold lesions that we would have liked (and of course, we would have liked to have seen none at all). We also noted that patients' vocal fold configurations had often migrated from the time of first discharge from treatment to later follow-up. At the time of discharge, we often observed something of a straight glottis from front to back of the vocal folds, corresponding to what they produced in head or reinforced falsetto voice. At follow-up, we were often seeing more extreme separation towards the back of the folds but compression at the midpoint—roughly where phonotraumatic lesions form. In fact, this very same configuration, generally dubbed "posterior glottal chink (or gap)," had been suggested to predispose individuals to the very same nodules we were aiming to treat (e.g. Morrison, Rammage, Belisle, Pullan, & Nichol 1983).

The explanation we gave ourselves was that apparently, during treatment, we had somehow elicited a straight-line glottis in our patients for their achievement of head/reinforced falsetto voice, which has an element of "breathy" or "fluty" quality, if you will. However, for unknown reasons during the period following discharge, many patients seemed to migrate towards a posterior glottal gap to achieve a similar element of "breath," thereby potentially endangering the health of their vocal folds.

It was at about that point that I attended a 30-min workshop by Bonnie Raphael at the annual Voice Foundation Symposium (approximately mid 1980s?). In those 30 min, Bonnie—in her characteristic fashion—managed to expose us to the rudiments of Lessac's "consonant orchestra" with amazing alacrity and efficiency. I felt the effect right away in my own voice. This was something different. I felt a vocal "balance" I had not felt before. In my previous experience with head voice speech, I had indeed felt "light" in speaking. But retrospectively, I also felt somewhat disembodied. With the consonant orchestra, I felt as though my vocal feet were deeply implanted in the sand of the earth's "terra firma" while at the same time my head still floated in vocal ether above. I quickly observed clinically that this vocal experience, which I ultimately came to call "resonant voice" in my own work (Verdolini-Marston, Burke, Lessac, Glaze, & Caldwell 1995), tended to be generated with *straight* vocal folds without much of a gap between the folds at all. We will come to the point of this observation shortly.

I immediately started implementing the strategy in my training of voice students and patients. Voilà. Anecdotally, patients not only seemed to improve quickly; their rate of recurrence of pathology also seemed to plummet. Stated differently, not only did they seem to get better quickly. They also seemed to *stay* better for a long time. I don't know if it was partly due to my work, the Zeitgeist, or a bit of both, but the resonant voice approach to voice therapy soon became all the rage for many conditions in the US and later South America and Asia (Europe is slowly catching on).

In the meantime, I had gone on to acquire a PhD. My research centered on many issues, several of them pertinent to Lessac work. The subsequent years brought something of a flurry of studies pursuing this "resonant voice" phenomenon. Some of the foundational papers are published in this section of our *Festschrift*. First, we established that resonant voice—which I defined as easy voice involving perceptible anterior oral vibrations (Verdolini-Marston et al. 1995)—indeed involved vocal folds that were barely touching or barely separated at the vocal processes, both in vocalists with and without vocal fold pathology (Peterson, Verdolini-Marston, Barkmeier, & Hoffman 1994; Verdolini, Druker, Palmer, & Samawi 1998). Second, in a small clinical study we conducted with Arthur Lessac, Kate Burke, Leslie Glaze, and Elizabeth Caldwell, we found that the training of resonant voice produced at least as good clinical results for patients with nodules or polyps in terms of laryngeal appearance, voice quality, and phonatory ease as the more traditional, conservative "quiet breathy" approach, in the short term (2 wk post-therapy follow-up; Verdolini-Marston et al. 1995). Based on clinical experience, I would anticipate that the resonant voice approach would have shown superior results in the longer term, but that suggestion is speculative because we did not obtain long-term data in that study. As important, subjects' reported *use* of "resonant voice" outside the clinic was vastly greater than for reports of use of "quiet-breathy voice," for those who had been therapized with it. This result is not surprising; resonant voice is clearly *functional* (it can be readily heard over a distance and in background noise), whereas quiet-breathy voice is *not*. Thus, surely not only biomechanical but also compliance factors would underlie the good long-term benefits for resonant voice training that we were seeing clinically.

However, the most exciting development among the papers included in this *Festschrift* involved a look at resonant voice from the perspective of a term coined by our collaborator, Ingo Titze: "vocal economy" (Berry, Verdolini, Montequin, Hess, Chan, & Titze 2001). Vocal economy (E_V) is defined as the ratio of voice output intensity to vocal fold impact intensity. In general, a high ratio is a good thing, because it reflects the greatest possible voice output intensity (and clarity) *for* the least amount of impact between the vocal folds, and thus the least likelihood of injury. Stated differently, a large E_V ratio indicates voice is relatively strong and clear while the risk of injury is generally fairly small. It turns out that the vocal fold configurations that optimize E_V are in the range of those corresponding to our beloved Lessac-inspired "resonant voice" (Peterson et al. 1994; Verdolini et al. 1998).

Since that work was conducted, we have completed several other studies that have been published or are in final phases of write-up at the time of this writing. First, we completed a study on 40 adults with phonotrauma who all received resonant voice training. Subjects were divided into different groups, in which not the target but the approach to training was varied. Half of subjects received training using Lessac's "consonant orchestra" metaphors (imagery condition), and the other half was simply instructed to attend deeply to the oral vibratory sensations and ease associated with resonant voice (perceptual condition). Within each of these groups, half of subjects received "variable practice" with resonant voice, that is, practice of resonant voice in numerous phonetic, environmental, and emotional contexts. The other half of subjects received less variable practice, that is practice of resonant voice using "m" (only) as the main practice sound, and further practice with resonant voice in conversation without ambient or emotional variations. Final statistical analyses of the data are pending. However, the raw data showed that the best results—at least in terms of voice-related quality of life—were obtained for the perceptual processing/variable practice condition. Regrettably, consonant orchestra training fared poorly, as did less variable practice. This result was obtained despite the fact that subject questionnaires indicated subjects who received consonant orchestra and limited variability practice *liked* their training and thought it helped their voices. Other very large studies that I have conducted in motor learning more generally have produced similar results: instructions promoting perceptual processing appeared to lead to better learning than instructions involving even the best-conceived metaphors (Verdolini-Marston & Balota 1994).

Results notwithstanding, I will say I am still fond of "consonant orchestra" metaphors, even extremely so. I just reserve its use in voice therapy training for special cases—although I use it more broadly in regular speech training, to be sure. The theoretical issues are broad and deep. Unfortunately, we do not have space to elaborate here but I look forward to further discussions with Arthur and other Lessac devotees on this matter. In the meantime, I have developed an approach to voice therapy for a wide range of conditions based on the *voice quality* that "consonant orchestra" so brilliantly elicits—and that I call resonant voice—incorporating these findings. Specifically, this program, called "Lessac-Madsen Resonant Voice Therapy" to honor both Arthur Lessac and Mark Madsen, another voice trainer I deeply admire, emphasizes both perceptual processes and variable practice in the training of resonant voice (Verdolini Abbott 2008a; 2008b).

Other work we have conducted in the interim is very exciting to us, most of it as yet unpublished but hopefully soon forthcoming. Some of that work shows that resonant voice exercises, derived from Lessac's consonant orchestra (and by extension Tonal NRG), appear to promote healing following vocal fold injury more than voice rest, at least for subjects we tested. These results have been shown not only in human subjects but also in "virtual subjects" that my former doctoral student, Nicole Li, created with computer simulation (Li, Verdolini, Clermont, Mi, Rubenstein, Hebda, & Vodovotz 2008). Speculatively, the reason for this result can be culled from findings from other tissue domains showing that certain forms of tissue mobilization, in particular those involving tissue stretching, reduce inflammation due to changes in cell signaling caused by tissue deformation. Lessac-derived resonant voice is an ideal candidate for this wound healing mechanism because it involves large-amplitude vocal fold oscillations (and therefore tissue stretching) while at the same time limiting vocal fold impact and thus further injury to the tissue (Berry et al. 2001).

Finally, our most recent speculations have centered on immunomodulatory effects of resonant voice by way of an additional mechanism beyond cells in local tissue. That is, based on published literature in other domains, we speculate that resonant voice (and possibly some other forms of phonation) may stimulate a "relaxation response" that downregulates vocal fold inflammation (for introductory discussion of the relaxation response, see for example Benson 1982; 1989; 1997). Such effects should be qualitatively similar to those for meditation. If we are right, we will have come full circle. Lessac's work will be shown to have value for tissue protection and healing not only due to local biological mechanisms, but also higher-order neurological or even "spiritual" mechanisms, if you will. Such a finding would only seem an appropriate reflection on the individual who has infused such *spirit* into his lifelong work. Arthur's spirit is one that has infected so many. His spirit is revealed in the indomitable twinkle of his eye, it fuels his voice, and it has fuels ours.

To you, Arthur: Namaste.

References

Benson, H. 1982. 'The relaxation response: history, physiological basis and clinical usefulness.' In *Acta Med Scand Suppl., 660,* 231-237.

Benson, H. 1989. 'Hypnosis and the relaxation response.' In *Gastroenterology, 96(6),* 1609-1611.

Benson, H. 1997. 'The relaxation response: therapeutic effect.' In *Science, 278(5344),* 1694-1695.

Berry, D.A., Verdolini, K., Montequin, D.W., Hess, M.M., Chan, R.W., & Titze, I.R. 2001. 'A quantitative output-cost ratio in voice production.' In *Journal of Speech, Language and Hearing Research, 44(1),* 29-37.

Li, N.Y., Verdolini, K., Clermont, G., Mi, Q., Rubinstein, E.N., Hebda, P.A.,& Vodovotz, Y. 2008. 'A patient-specific in silico model of inflammation and healing tested in acute vocal fold injury.' In *PLoS ONE, 30;3(7),* e2789.

Morrison, M.D., Rammage, L.A., Belisle, G.M, Pullan, C.B., & Nichol, H. 1983. 'Muscular tension dysphonia.' In *J Otolaryngol, 12 (5),* 302-306.

Peterson, K.L., Verdolini-Marston, K., Barkmeier, J.M., & Hoffman, H.T. 1994. 'Comparison or aerodynamic parameters in evaluating clinically relevant voicing patterns.' In *Annals of Otology, Rhinology, and Laryngology, 103(5 Pt 1),* 335-346.

Verdolini, K., Druker, D.G., Palmer, P.M., & Samawi, H. 1998. 'Laryngeal adduction in resonant voice.' In *Journal of Voice, 12(3),* 315-327.

Verdolini Abbott, K. 2008a. *Lessac-Madsen Resonant Voice Therapy: Clinician Manual.* San Diego: Plural Publishing, Inc.

Verdolini Abbott, K. 2008b. *Lessac-Madsen Resonant Voice Therapy: Patient Manual.* San Diego: Plural Publishing, Inc.

Verdolini-Marston, K., & Balota, D.A. 1994. 'Role of elaborative and perceptual integrative processes in perceptual-motor performance.' In *Journal of Experimental Psychology: Learning, Memory and Cognition, 20(3),* 739-749.

Verdolini-Marston, K., Burke, M.K., Lessac, A., Glaze, L., & Caldwell, E. 1995. 'Preliminary study of two methods of treatment for laryngeal nodules.' In *Journal of Voice, 9(1), 74-85.*

Comparison of Aerodynamic and Electroglottographic Parameters in Evaluating Clinically Relevant Voicing Patterns

This peer-reviewed article was originally published in the *Annals of Otology, Rhinology and Laryngology*. 103:1994, pp. 335-346. Permission to reprint has been graciously granted by the *Annals of Otology, Rhinology and Laryngology*.

K. Linnea Peterson, MD – *Los Angeles, California*
Julie M. Barkmeier, MA – *Iowa City, Iowa*
Katherine Verdolini-Marston, PhD – *Iowa City, Iowa*
Henry T. Hoffman, MD, MS – *Iowa City, Iowa*

The purpose of the present study was to identify one or more aerodynamic or electroglottographic measures that distinguish among voicing patterns that are clinically relevant for nodule pathogenesis and regression: a presumably pathogenic pattern (pressed voice), a neutral pattern (normal voice), and two presumably therapeutic patterns (resonant voice and breathy voice). Trained subjects with normal voices produced several tokens of each voice type on sustained vowels /a/, /i/, and /u/. For each token, maximum flow declination rate, alternating current flow, and minimum flow were obtained from inverse-filtered airflow signals, and closed quotient and closing time were obtained from electroglottographic signals. The results indicate that for /a/ and /i/ (but not for /u/), the closed quotient provides a sensitive tool for distinguishing the voice types in physiologically interpretable directions. Further, post-hoc analyses confirmed a direct relationship between the closed quotient and videoscopic ratings of laryngeal adduction, which previous work links to nodule pathogenesis and regression.

KEY WORDS: aerodynamic measures, electroglottography, vocal nodule, voice.

Vocal fold nodules are benign, space-occupying lesions that develop at the midpoint of the membranous portion of the vocal folds. Nodules appear to be caused by intraglottal trauma,[1-4] although a direct link not has been unequivocally established. The causal pattern that has been most convincingly argued involves two successive hypotheses. First, chronic adductory hyperfunction during phonation produces high vocal fold contact stress (force of collision per unit area of tissue contact) during phonation, and second, high vocal fold contact stress causes local trauma and, over time, chronic lesions.[5] Jiang[6] provided evidence simultaneously consistent with both hypotheses in an experiment using excised canine hemilarynx preparations. In his study, increased arytenoids approximation during induced phonation resulted in increased contact stresses along the excised vocal folds, and in general the greatest contact stresses occurred at the midpoint of the membranous folds.

Not surprisingly, behavioral therapy for nodule reduction generally focuses on voicing patterns assumed to minimize focal trauma, by limiting intraglottal contact stress. Examples include "breathy" voice and "resonant" voice[7-9] (also Verdolini-Marston et al, unpublished observations). "Breathy" voice is associated with the auditory perception of breathiness, or audible air escape during phonation. "Resonant" voice is associated with the proprioceptive perception of oral vibratory sensation on or near the alveolar ridge and other facial plates, and in healthy voices, the auditory impression of a "ringing" voice. Preliminary analyses from an ongoing study indicate that in fact the training of both breathy and resonant voice types may provide some benefit in the behavioral management of nodules (Verdolini-Marston et al, unpublished observations). The results from such studies may be clinically useful. However, the direct investigation of the physiologic mechanisms that regulate nodule formation and regression is currently limited by the lack of quantitative measurement tools for in vivo situations. The purpose of the present study was to address this limitation by identifying one or more quantitative measures that may effectively distinguish among four critical voice production types in clinically and physiologically interpretable directions: pressed voice (a voice type presumed to be pathogenic), normal voice (a neutral voice type), and resonant and breathy voice (presumably therapeutic voice types). The results could be applied to future physiologic studies investigating these voicing patterns and their contribution to the pathogenic process. The results may also provide some information about physiologic factors in nodule pathogenesis and regression.

The measures that were selected for investigation included a series of aerodynamic and electroglottographic (EGG) measures, previously described by other authors,[5,10-17] that may reflect vocal fold contact stress, or force per unit area of vocal fold contact.

The aerodynamic measures were derived from inverse-filtered airflow signals, and included maximum flow declination rate (MFDR), alternating current (AC) flow, and minimum flow. The EGG measures were closed quotient and closing time.

The MFDR indicate the maximum rate of vocal fold deceleration during closing. According to some authors, this measure may reflect the force of vocal fold contact during phonation.[5] The AC flow indicates the amount of modulated air during phonation. This measure varies inversely with MFDR,[18] and thus might corroborate the findings for MFDR or even prove to be a more sensitive measure. Minimum airflow, which reflects the amount of unmodulated airflow through the glottis during phonation, may inversely indicate vocal fold contact area, or the denominator in the contact stress parameter (Verdolini-Marston, unpublished observations). Regarding the EGG measures, closed quotient (proportion of the glottal cycle during which the folds are together) may indicate the relative degree of medial compression or arytenoids "pressing," and therefore variations in contact stress. In fact, according to at least one report, increases in the closed quotient correspond to increases in laryngeal adduction or "pressing"[19] and presumably, following Jiang's evidence, also increases in intraglottal contact stress.[6] The EGG closing time might reflect vocal fold collisional forces, assuming constant frequencies and amplitudes.

An effective measure was defined a priori as a measure that statistically distinguishes between the voice types in clinically and physiologically interpretable directions. That is, a conceptual plot was envisioned for each dependent variable (aerodynamic and EGG) over three critical spaces: a pathogenic space (pressed voice), a neutral space (normal voice), and a therapeutic space (resonant and breathy voice). An effective measure would satisfy the following criteria: 1) when plotted against these voicing patterns, over the boundary from the pathogenic to the neutral space, the curve would reflect a statistically significant discontinuity that is physiologically interpretable with respect to pathogenesis, and 2) from the neutral to the therapeutic space, the curve would reflect either no change, continued discontinuity in the same direction as from the pathogenic to the neutral space, or a reversed discontinuity the value of which does not equal or exceed the value indicated in the pathogenic space, regardless of which therapeutic voice type is considered.

As a final introductory comment, it should be noted that the voice types used in this investigation were assumed to represent pathogenic, neutral, and therapeutic production modes on the basis of clinical impressions and also previous data[6] (also Verdolini-Marston et al, unpublished observations). However, no attempt was made to actually cause lesions, nor to reverse them, in the present study. Such manipulations will be left to other studies.

Methods

Subjects

Seven adults with extensive voice training (6 singers and 1 actor) participated as volunteers in the study. Trained voice users were selected because of their presumed ability to volitionally vary voice production patterns. Subject included 4 men and 3 women, ranging in age from 21–40 years (average age 28.2 years). Only nonsmokers without current illness were included. The average length of previous voice training was 9.4 years, with a range of 5 to 15 years. All subjects were engaged in regular voice performance requiring loud voice output in large halls, and on questioning, all confirmed familiarity with 'resonant voice' (1 of the voicing patterns evaluated in this study.) All subjects had a negative history of voice disorders, despite their demanding performance schedules, except for 1 subject (subject 7), who had incipient ulcers 6 months prior to his participation in the study. This subject was asymptomatic at the time of his participation and exhibited no evidence of dysphonia as assessed by the examiners. Thus, his results were retained and are included with those for other subjects. Subjects were unaware of the specific purpose of the study.

Equipment

The equipment used to collect aerodynamic and EGG measures is shown in Fig.1. A Rothenberg circumferentially vented face mask connected to the input of a Glottal Enterprises amplifier (MS100-A2) was used to collect airflow signals. The main output of the amplifier was routed through an attenuator (Hewlett Packard 350D) and then in parallel to 1) a voltmeter (Hewlett Packard 3466A Digital Multimeter) for on-line calibration of airflow signals, 2) a model PC-108M Sony Digital Audio Tape (DAT) recorder for permanent data storage, and 3) a Gateway 2000 386 computer for direct data collection by means of Hypersignal software. The EGG signals were collected with a Synchro Voice Electroglottograph, connected to the DAT recorder for long-term storage of signals. Acoustic signals were also collected, by means of a Sony Electret Condenser Microphone (ECM-44B) powered by a Symetrix SX202 Dual Mic preamplifier. As for airflow and EGG signals, the acoustic signal was conducted to the

DAT recorder for storage and possible later analysis. The three outputs from the DAT (airflow, EGG, and acoustic signals) were connected to a DATA 6000 oscilloscope for monitoring of active signals. Aerodynamic and EGG waveforms were analyzed with CSpeech (Version 3.1) software after digitizing the signals into Hypersignal. A Casio keyboard was used both to extract an average conversational pitch prior to experimental trials and, later, to provide a constant target pitch for these trials.

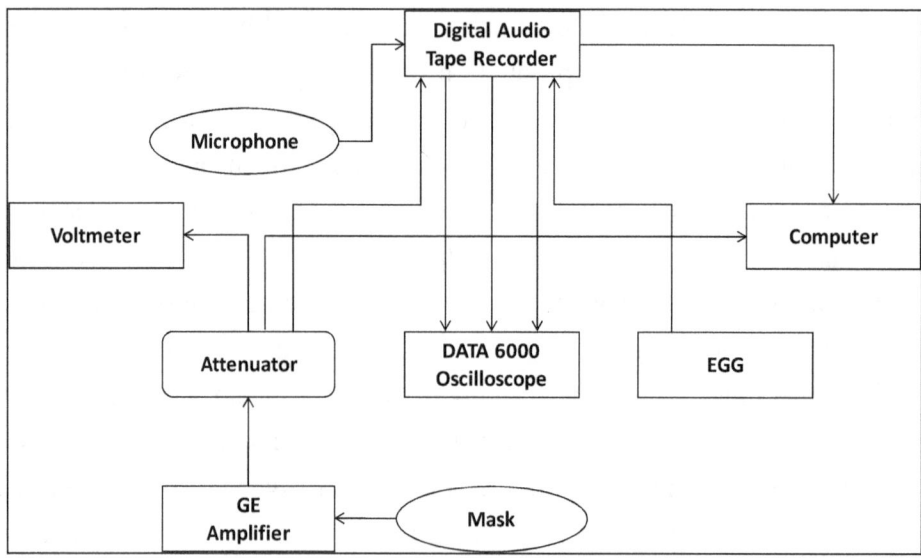

Figure 1. Equipment setup.

Videostroboscopic images were obtained with a 90^0 R. Wolf 4450.47 rigid telescopic endoscope in conjunction with a Karl Storz 9000 mini solid state CCD video camera and a Bruel & Kjaer rhino-larynx stroboscope light source, type 4914.

Equipment and Software Management for Data Collection, and Explanation of Aerodynamic, EGG and Videostroboscopic Measures.

During data collection, aerodynamic signals were simultaneously digitized into the computer and stored on a DAT tape. The EGG and acoustic signals were stored on the DAT tape and digitized at a later time. Both airflow and EGG input channels to the DAT were set to a sampling frequency of 10 kHz, and the acoustic input signals was set at a sampling frequency of 20 kHz. The voltages of all three input channels to the DAT were monitored for signal saturation throughout the experiment. The voltmeter, set on a ± 20-V scale and receiving input from the airflow system, was also monitored constantly and re-zeroed as necessary to correct for drift in the airflow signal. Zero-input voltages were noted on the voltmeter for each phonation token during data collection.

For airflow analyses, the data were digitized in Hypersignal at 10 kHz; then each airflow signal was imported to CSpeech. All subsequent manipulations of the airflow signal were done with this software program.

The initial portion of the signal, which represented zero flow input, was first measured to obtain a baseline offset reading. For AC and minimum flow, three 20-millisecond sections from the midportion of each signal were chosen randomly for analysis, and each of the segments was analyzed in the same way. The selected segment was inverse-filtered by first differentiating it, followed by linear prediction correlation analysis, integration, and a final linear prediction correlation analysis. The middle peak from the resulting sample display was selected, and the peak value for this wave was measured to indicate peak flow in liters per second after subtracting the baseline offset value. The trough of the same cycle was measured to reflect minimum flow, also in liters per second, again correcting for any nonzero offset (Fig. 2). The AC flow was later calculated by subtracting the minimum flow value from the peak flow value. After peak and minimum flow values were obtained, the waveform was differentiated again and the minimum point on the resulting middle wave was measured to reflect MFDR in liters per second squared.

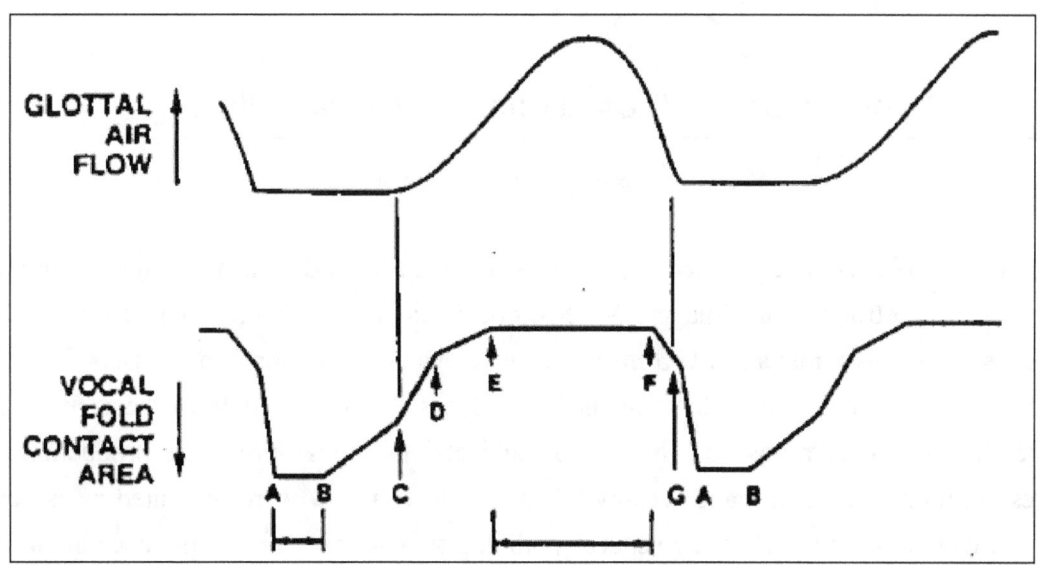

Figure 2. Airflow signal measurements.

Following data collection, the EGG signals were also recorded into Hypersignal at 10 kHz and then imported into CSpeech. Again, for each token imported, three 35-millisecond segments were selected randomly from the midportion of each signal for independent analyses, and each was analyzed in the following way. The waveforms were oriented so that the open portion of the glottal cycle was represented at the top of the wave. A middle waveform in the display was selected for measurement of closed quotient, open quotient, and closing time, as indicated in Fig. 3. The measurements of the closed and open quotients were taken at 65 % of the amplitude of the waveform as described by Rothenberg and Mahshie.[15] The EGG data were discarded for 2 subjects (subjects 5 and 6) because of un-interpretable signals. The EGG study was not performed on 1 subject (subject 2).

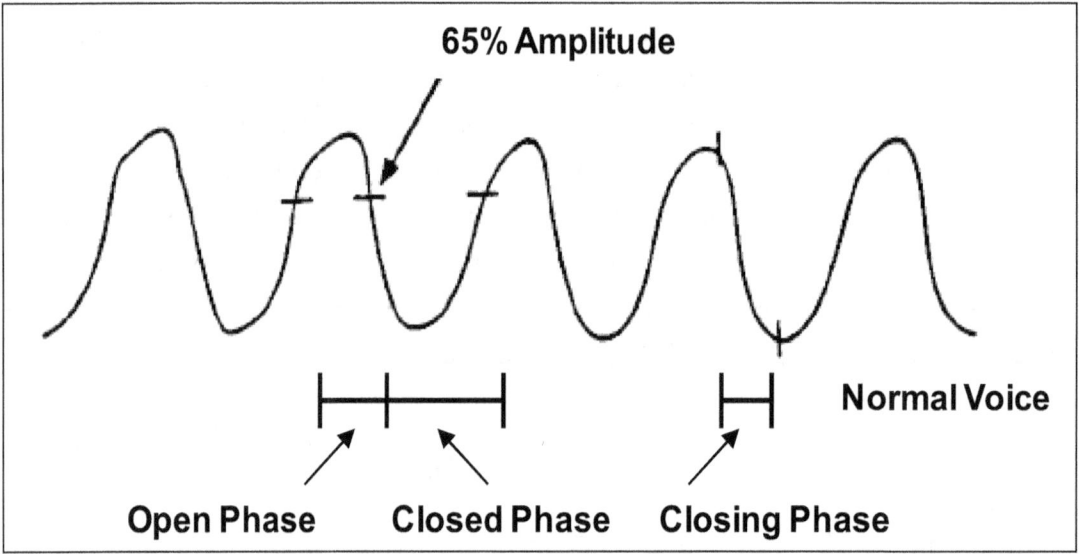

Figure 3. Electroglottographic measurements.

Videostroboscopic equipment was managed in the standard clinical fashion for collection of videostroboscopic images. Videostroboscopic images were analyzed after the results for aerodynamic and EGG measures were evaluated, to confirm or disconfirm the hypotheses about the physiology of the voice types that emerged from these findings. Specifically, videostroboscopic images of subjects' larynges during the production of pressed, normal, resonant, and breathy tokens of the vowel /i/ were presented in random order, without sound track, to two speech pathologists with extensive experience in videoscopic evaluation, and to two attending laryngologists at our university. The viewer-judges rated the degree of perceived laryngeal adduction for each voice type on an ordinal scale from -5 (extreme hypoadduction) to +5 (extreme hyperadduction). All judges were uninformed about the intended voice types for each segment at the time of viewing.

Procedures

Subjects were tested individually. Experimenters maintained consistent roles throughout the data collection. For each subject, the approximate average fundamental frequency was first obtained during a rote speech task (counting). That is, the subject counted out loud from 1 to 5, and his or her pitch on the sustained vowel in the word "three" was matched to a keyboard pitch and subsequently confirmed (in frequency) by CSpeech. The pitch identified in this way was used for all subsequent vowel productions for that subject. Next, the subject was given a demonstration of the four voice types that would be required for critical trials: pressed, resonant, normal, and breathy voice. (The model for breathy voice was relatively quiet). For this study, and on the basis of reports of previous authors[6] (also Verdolini-Marston et al, unpublished observation), pressed voice was assumed to be a pathogenic voice type, and resonant and breathy voices were considered therapeutic voice types, and will be discussed as such for the remainder of the paper. After receiving models of the four voice types from the examiner, the subject practiced the voice types on the vowel /o/, on the designated pitch provided vocally and with a portable keyboard. This procedure was repeated until both the subject and the experimenter were satisfied that the target voice types could be consistently produced. For most subjects, only one practice trial was required for each voice type. During practice trials, the subject was also trained to place the airflow mask firmly over the nose and mouth 1 second after data collection was initiated (the first second of data collection provided a zero-input signal to be used for calibration during subsequent analyses), to hold the mask firmly in place for 4 seconds, and then to sustain the target production at the designated pitch for 4 seconds. The EGG collar and the audio microphone were in place throughout. The subject was then provided with a list of tokens for the experimental trials. The list indicated a random ordering of three different vowels (/i/, /a/, and /u/) and, within each vowel, a random ordering of 4 voice types (pressed, normal, resonant, and breathy), including three tokens of each voice type. Thus, each subject produced a total of 36 voice tokens (three vowels times 12 tokens per vowel) as trained. The orders of vowel and voice type were varied across subjects. All subjects were encouraged to repeat any token that they judged to be a poor exemplar of the target voice type. (Only three tokens were repeated in the entire experiment). As a validity check, two blinded and independent experimenters indicated on separate scoring sheets the voice type perceived for each trial. Later analyses indicated a 79% agreement across trials. That is, on approximately 79% of trials, both of the judges perceived the voice type that the subject in fact intended to produce. All tokens produced were included in the analyses.

The vowels produced in this way provided simultaneous airflow and EGG and acoustic signals for analysis in this study. Following these productions, videostroboscopic images were obtained of the four voice types. That is, subject produced at least one token of each of the four voice types during the vowel /i/, under videostroboscopic examination. Videostroboscopic tokens were also judged for voice type by two independent, blinded raters. Analyses of these tokens resulted in 93% agreement across trials (i.e. on 93% of trials, both judges perceived the voice type that the subject intended to produce). Tokens in question were noted immediately and the subject was asked to repeat the trial. No token required more than one repetition. Only valid tokens were included in subsequent analyses.

Analyses and Design

For aerodynamic measures, the primary analyses of interest involved the vowel /a/ because of this vowel's suitability for inverse filtering, related to a high-frequency first formant. Aerodynamic analyses for the vowels /i/ and /u/ were also carried out, because airflow signals for these vowels were collected simultaneously with EGG signals.

Although the aerodynamic analyses for /i/ and /u/ were of limited conceptual interest because of their low-frequency first formant encroaching on the fundamental frequency, especially in female voices, the results of analyses for these vowels are nonetheless reported. For EGG analyses, all vowels were of conceptual interest. Videostroboscopic analyses involved only the vowel /i/, as this was the only vowel that was assessed endoscopically.

Because of the focus on different vowels depending on the particular measure, and also because initial statistical analyses indicated interactions between vowel and voice type, for both aerodynamic and EGG measures the analyses reported here involve the results for the three vowels assessed independently, with an emphasis on those particularly relevant for the measure in question. For all measures, statistical analyses involved paired comparisons among all four voice types, with a total of six comparisons (pressed versus normal, pressed versus resonant, pressed versus breathy, normal versus resonant, normal versus breathy, and resonant versus breathy). For aerodynamic and EGG measures, the analyses involve a randomized block design with one within-subject fixed factor, voice type (x4). For videostroboscopic measures, analyses also included the random factor of judge (x4).

To reiterate, the criteria for identifying an effective measure used the plot of the measure over voice type. From the pathogenic to the neutral space, the curve would reflect a statistically significant discontinuity that was physiologically interpretable with respect to pathogenesis. Over the boundary from the neutral space to the therapeutic space, the curve would reflect no change, continued discontinuity in the same direction as from the pathogenic to the neutral space, or a reversed discontinuity the value of which did not equal or exceed the value indicated in the pathogenic space, regardless of which therapeutic voice type was considered. It turns out that to satisfy these criteria, the paired comparisons that had to indicate significant differences (in physiologically interpretable directions) were comparisons between pressed voice and all other voice types (pressed versus normal, pressed versus resonant, and pressed versus breathy). The remaining paired comparisons might or might not differ.

TABLE 1: AVERAGE MAXIMUM FLOW DECLINATION RATE FOR FOUR VOICE TYPES

Vowel	Group	Voice Type				Significant Paired Comparisons					
		Pressed	Normal	Resonant	Breathy	Pressed/ Normal	Pressed/ Resonant	Pressed/ Breathy	Normal/ Resonant	Normal/ Breathy	Resonant/ Breathy
/a/	N = 4	-303.28	-232.34	-303.39	-262.62	*			*		
	N = 7	-301.70	-227.89	-293.11	-198.54	*		*	*		*
/i/	N = 4	-168.45	-157.48	-205.40	-174.30		*		*		
	N = 7	-207.29	-172.30	-238.31	-162.89	*	*	*	*		*
/u/	N = 4	-202.23	-172.16	-237.62	-175.86				*		*
	N = 7	-214.29	-186.05	-241.83	-159.21	*	*	*	*	*	*

Data are in liters per second squared
*p < .05

TABLE 2: AVERAGE ALTERNATING CURRENT FLOW FOR FOUR VOICE TYPES

Vowel	Group	Voice Type				Significant Paired Comparisons					
		Pressed	Normal	Resonant	Breathy	Pressed/ Normal	Pressed/ Resonant	Pressed/ Breathy	Normal/ Resonant	Normal/ Breathy	Resonant/ Breathy
/a/	N = 4	0.196	0.199	0.223	0.233			*		*	
	N = 7	0.192	0.198	0.216	0.244		*	*		*	
/i/	N = 4	0.173	0.176	0.232	0.220		*	*	*	*	
	N = 7	0.198	0.196	0.246	0.231		*	*	*	*	
/u/	N = 4	0.206	0.213	0.257	0.193		*		*		*
	N = 7	0.209	0.214	0.247	0.210		*		*		*

Data are in liters per second
*p < .05

Results

As already noted, airflow and videostroboscopic data were obtained for all 7 subjects, but interpretable EGG signals were obtained only for 4 subjects. The results for both data sets (N = 4 and N = 7) are indicated as appropriate in the Tables and Figures, and are discussed in the text. Tables 1-5 and Fig 4-9 displays the average values obtained across subjects.

TABLE 3: AVERAGE MINIMUM FLOW FOR FOUR VOICE TYPES

Vowel	Group	Voice Type				Significant Paired Comparisons					
		Pressed	Normal	Resonant	Breathy	Pressed/ Normal	Pressed/ Resonant	Pressed/ Breathy	Normal/ Resonant	Normal/ Breathy	Resonant/ Breathy
/a/	N = 4	-0.03	-0.02	-0.03	0.09			*		*	*
	N = 7	-0.03	-0.02	-0.04	0.07			*		*	*
/i/	N = 4	-0.04	-0.04	-0.06	0.06			*		*	*
	N = 7	-0.05	-0.04	-0.07	0.06			*	*	*	*
/u/	N = 4	-0.06	-0.04	-0.07	0.04	*		*	*	*	*
	N = 7	-0.06	-0.05	-0.06	0.05			*	*	*	*

Data are in liters per second
*p < .05

Individual results for the closed quotient of the EGG signal are indicated in Table 6, because analyses indicated that these values were of particular interest. The significance level was set at p < .05 for all statistical tests.

MFDR

Average values for MFDR as a function of voice type are shown in Table 1 and in Fig 4. The general trend was the highest values were obtained for pressed and for resonant voice, and lower values were obtained for normal and for breathy voice. If MFDR reflects the potential for intraglottal trauma, the relatively high value obtained for one presumably therapeutic voice type (resonant voice) is counterintuitive. Statistical analysis confirmed that MFDR failed to differentiate among the voice types according to the pre-established criteria. For the vowel /a/, the primary reason was a failure to reliably distinguish between the pathogenic voice type (pressed voice) and one therapeutic voice type (resonant voice) for sample sizes of both $N = 4$ and $N = 7$, and further, between the pathogenic voice type (pressed voice) and the second therapeutic voice type (breathy voice) for the sample of $N = 4$. Also, for the vowels /i/ and /u/, which were actually not of conceptual interest for this or other airflow measures, for both $N = 4$ and $N = 7$, several of the paired comparisons between pressed voice and other types did not indicate significant differences, or revealed differences in the wrong direction: the three significant distinctions that were obtained between pressed voice and resonant voice (of four possible distinctions) indicated greater MFDRs (and presumably collisional forces) for a therapeutic voice type (resonant voice) than for the pathogenic voice type (pressed voice).

AC Flow

Table 2 and Fig 5 show the average values for AC flow. The general trends was that relatively high AC flow values were obtained for resonant and for breathy voice, and relatively lower values were obtained for normal and for pressed voice. If AC flow reflects the potential for tissue injury, this result is also counterintuitive. Statistical tests further confirmed that this measure did not effectively distinguish the voice types according to pre-established criteria. Across all vowels, for both $N = 4$ and $N = 7$, none of the paired comparisons between pressed and normal voices were reliable. Further, the significant comparisons that were obtained between pressed and resonant voices, and between pressed and breathy voices across vowels, were in the wrong direction, compared to what was anticipated: as already noted by inspection of the data. AC flows were higher for the therapeutic as compared to the pathogenic voice types.

Because of the covariation of AC flow with MFDR reported by previous authors,[18] the relation between these measures was evaluated for our data. We calculated Pearson

r values between AC flow and MFDR, using individual data and collapsing across vowels and voice types. For both sample sizes, the correlations were negate and reliably different from chance: $r = -.75$, $p = .0001$ for $N = 4$, and $r = -.71$, $p = .001$ for $N = 7$. Thus, our data generally reflect the same inverse relation between MFDR and AC flow described by the previous authors.[18]

TABLE 4: AVERAGE CLOSED QUOTIENT IN PROPORTION OF TOTAL CYCLE FOR FOUR VOICE TYPES

Vowel	Group	Voice Type				Significant Paired Comparisons					
		Pressed	Normal	Resonant	Breathy	Pressed/ Normal	Pressed/ Resonant	Pressed/ Breathy	Normal/ Resonant	Normal/ Breathy	Resonant/ Breathy
/a/	N = 4	0.61	0.54	0.54	0.48	*	*	*		*	*
/i/	N = 4	0.64	0.57	0.55	0.47	*	*	*		*	*
/u/	N = 4	0.59	0.56	0.58	0.44			*		*	*

*p < .05

TABLE 5: AVERAGE RATINGS OF LARYNGEAL ADDUCTION FOR FOUR VOICE TYPES, BASED ON VIDEOSCOPIC VIEWS

Vowel	Group	Voice Type				Significant Paired Comparisons					
		Pressed	Normal	Resonant	Breathy	Pressed/ Normal	Pressed/ Resonant	Pressed/ Breathy	Normal/ Resonant	Normal/ Breathy	Resonant/ Breathy
/i/	N = 4	2.38	0.19	0.47	-1.66	*	*	*		*	*
	N = 7	2.55	-0.18	0.02	-1.21	*	*	*			

-5 ---- Extreme hypoadduction, 0 ---- neutral, +5 ---- extreme hyperadduction
*p < .05

Minimum Flow

For minimum flow, the results were no more encouraging than for the other two aerodynamic measures. The average results for this measure are shown in Table 3 and Fig. 6. Minimum flow was generally low for pressed, normal, and resonant voice types, and was considerably higher for breathy voice. For the vowel /a/, the only comparison between pressed voice and the other types that indicated a statistically significant difference was the comparison between pressed voice and breathy voice (N = 4 and N = 7). Similar results were seen for the other vowels, with the addition of a statistically significant difference between pressed voice and normal voice for /u/ (N = 4). Thus, minimum flow was discarded as a useful investigatory tool, in particular because it failed to consistently distinguish between the pathogenic voice type and one therapeutic voice type (resonant voice).

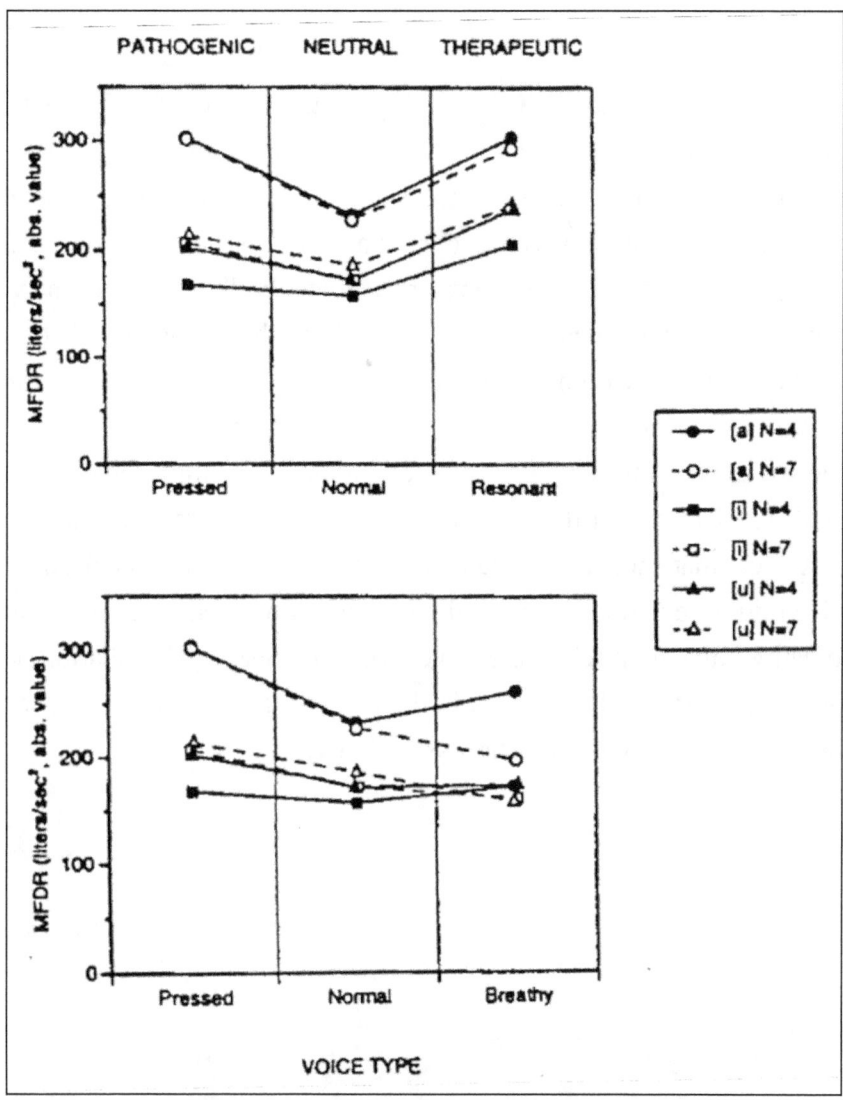

Figure 4. Average maximum flow declination rate (MFDR), in liters per second squared (absolute value), as function of voice type, for vowels /a/, /i/, and /u/ (N = 4 and N = 7).

Note that with the exception of breathy voice, average minimum flows were negative. We feel quite confident that this finding does not reflect calibration errors, not only because we monitored for signal drift during data collection, but also because for each token produced, a zero-input flow value was obtained and subtracted from all subsequent values for minimum flow. Our interpretation is that negative minimum flows in this study reflect incompletely filtered vocal tract resonance phenomena, or perhaps laryngeal depression during vocal fold closure. In any event, negative minimum flows do not reflect a backflow of air across the glottis during phonation.

Closed Quotient

The average values for the (EGG) closed quotient are shown in Table 4 and in Fig 7. Across all vowels, the highest closed quotients were obtained for pressed voice, intermediate values were obtained for normal and for resonant voice, and the lowest values were obtained for breathy voice. For /a/ and /i/, both of which were of interest, statistical analyses indicated that this measure acceptably distinguished the voice types according to the pre-established criteria. For both of these vowels, all of the paired comparisons between pressed voice and the other voice types indicated significant differences. Further, the differences were in a direction that was physiologically interpretable with respect to the pathogenic continuum. Assuming that, as indicated in previous studies, increases in the closed quotient reflect increasing laryngeal adduction,[19] and further, that increasing adduction leads to increased local contact stress,[6] pressed voice might be associated with the greatest contact stresses and normal, resonant, and breathy voice with relatively lower contact stresses. The relation between the closed quotient and laryngeal adduction in the present study was investigated with follow-up videostroboscopic analyses, discussed shortly.

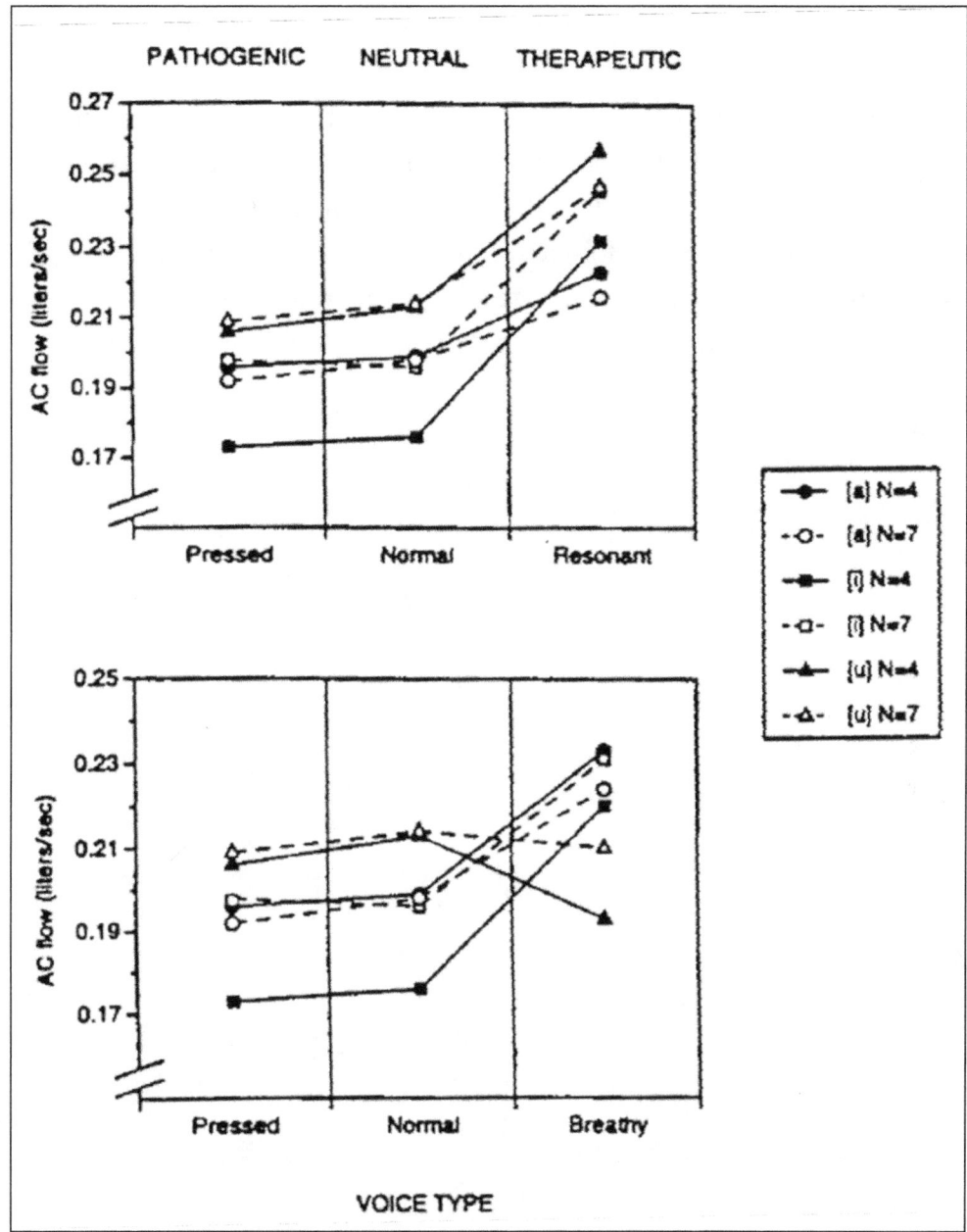

Figure 5. Average AC flow, in liters per second, as function of voice type, for vowels /a/, /i/, and /u/ (N = 4 and N = 7).

For the vowel /u/, the closed quotient was unacceptable as a useful measure to distinguish the voice types. For this vowel, the closed quotient failed to consistently distinguish between pressed voice and all other voice types. Specifically, the comparisons between pressed and normal voices, did not indicate significant differences.

Because the average values for the closed quotient effectively differentiated the voice types for /a/ and /i/, individual data were inspected for these vowels and are displayed in Table 6. For /a/, for 3 of the 4 subjects for whom EGG data were available, the closed quotient was greatest for the pathogenic voice type (pressed voice). For /i/, for 2 of 4 subjects the quotient was the greatest for this voice type. For both /a/ and /i/, subject 3 was an exception to the trend noted (in addition to subject 7 for /i/).

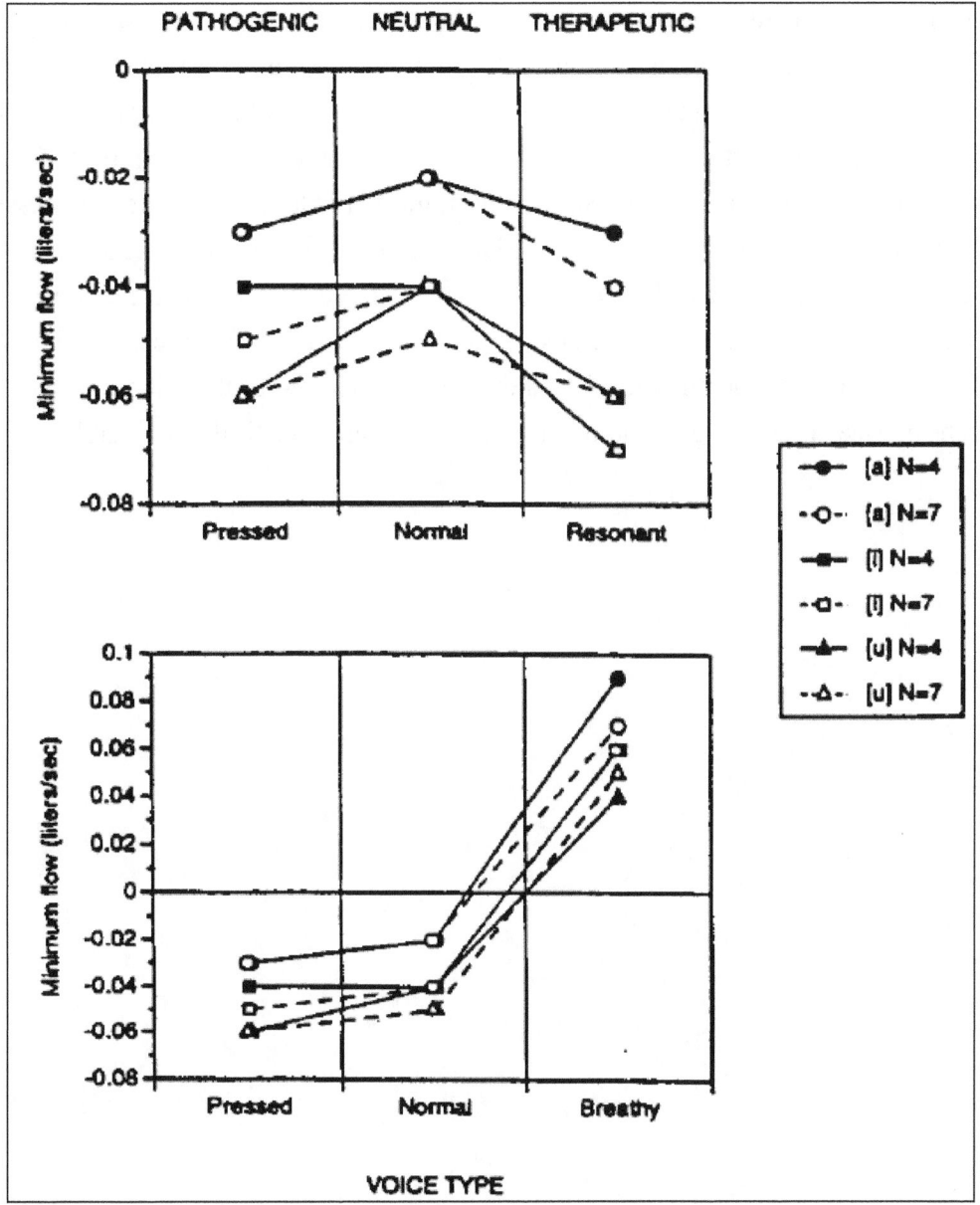

Figure 6. Average minimum flow, in liters per second, as function of voice type, for vowels /a/, /i/, and /u/ (N = 4 and n = 7).

Closing Time

The notion that the EGG closing time might reflect the force of vocal fold closure was based on the assumption of a constant frequency and amplitude of vocal fold vibration across voice types. Although frequencies were kept constant within subjects by the experimental protocol. AC flow data indicated that the assumption of a constant amplitude was not met. Therefore, closing time was discarded as a useful investigatory tool. (Note that an attempt was made to normalize closing time data by amplitude. For this manipulation, AC flow, which reflects vocal fold amplitude, was divided by closing time, for each subject and for each token produced. The resulting variable approximately represented average vocal deceleration during closing. This variable is a poor one, because AC flow was used as the numerator and EGG closing time as the denominator in the term. However, the results indicated the greatest average deceleration for breathy voice, and considerable lower deceleration for the other voice types. Most of the critical paired comparisons between pressed voice and other voice types were statistically unreliable).

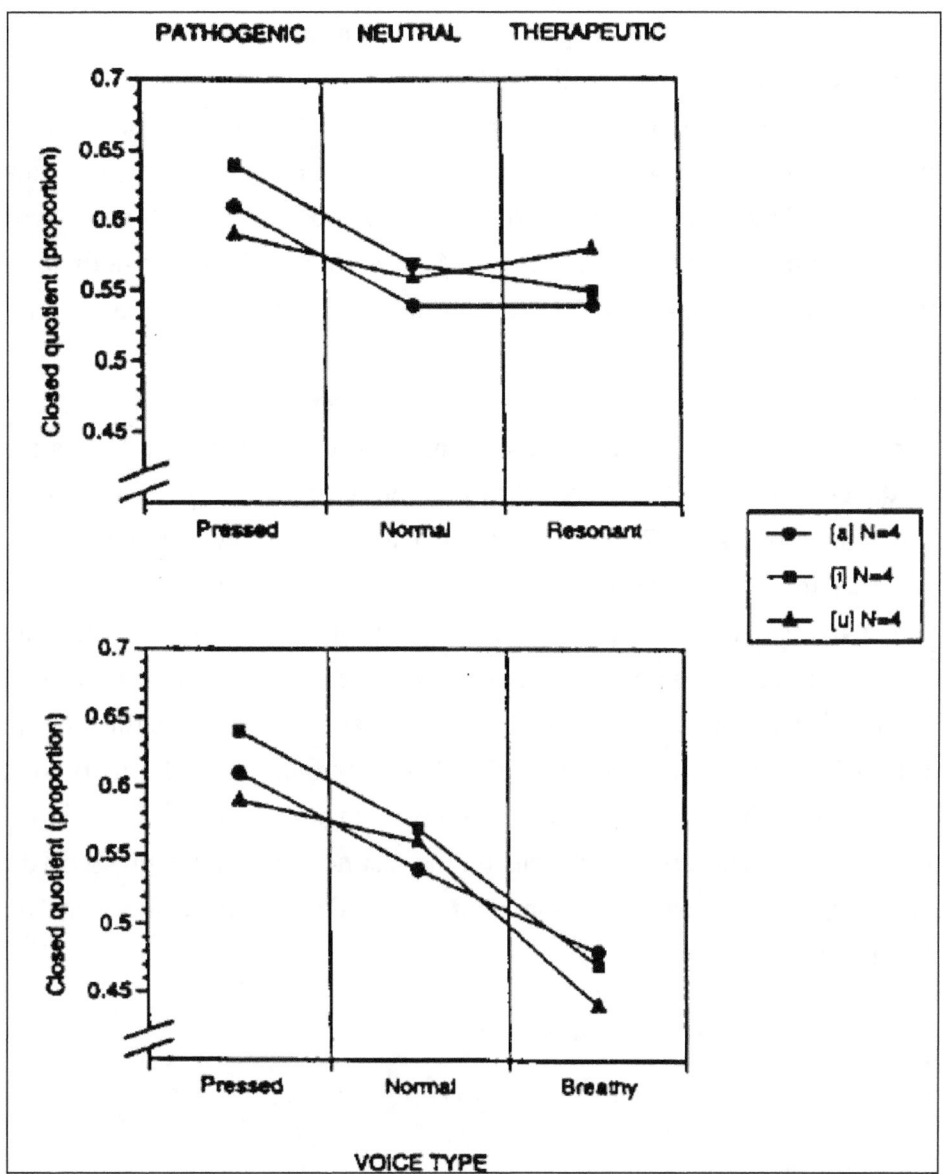

Figure 7. Average closed quotient, in proportion of total cycle, as function of voice type, for vowels /a/, /i/, and /u/ (N = 4 and N = 7).

Videostroboscopic Evaluation and Comparison of Visual Ratings With Closed and Open Quotients

Videostroboscopic evaluation of the larynx were conducted as a follow-up to the results for the EGG closed quotient to determine if, as reported by previous authors,[19] the closed quotient might reflect laryngeal adduction level. Before comparing the closed quotient to the videostroboscopic ratings, the consistency of laryngeal ratings across judges was assessed, and differences in laryngeal ratings were also evaluated as a function of voice type. Two independent, two-way analyses of variance (ANOVAs) were conducted (for N = 4 and N = 7), with voice type (N = 4) as a within-subject factor and judge (N = 4) as a random factor. In both ANOVAs, the effect of judge was unreliable. Thus, the judges appeared consistent in their ratings of laryngeal adduction.

The results for the laryngeal ratings themselves are indicated in Tables 5 and in Fig. 8. Adduction ratings clearly varied as a function of voice type, in the anticipated direction. When both 4 and 7 subjects were considered, the highest adduction ratings were obtained for pressed voice, consistent with the impression of hyperadduction; intermediate ratings close to neutral were obtained for normal and for resonant voice; and the lowest ratings were obtained for breathy voice, consistent with hypoadduction. Paired comparisons confirmed that for both N = 4 and N = 7, the ratings for pressed voice differed significantly from those for all other voice types. Further, for N = 4 (but, oddly, not for N = 7), normal and breathy ratings also differed, as did resonant and breathy ratings. Thus, with the focus on the distinction between pressed voice and other voice types, laryngeal adduction ratings provided critical distinctions between the voicing patterns.

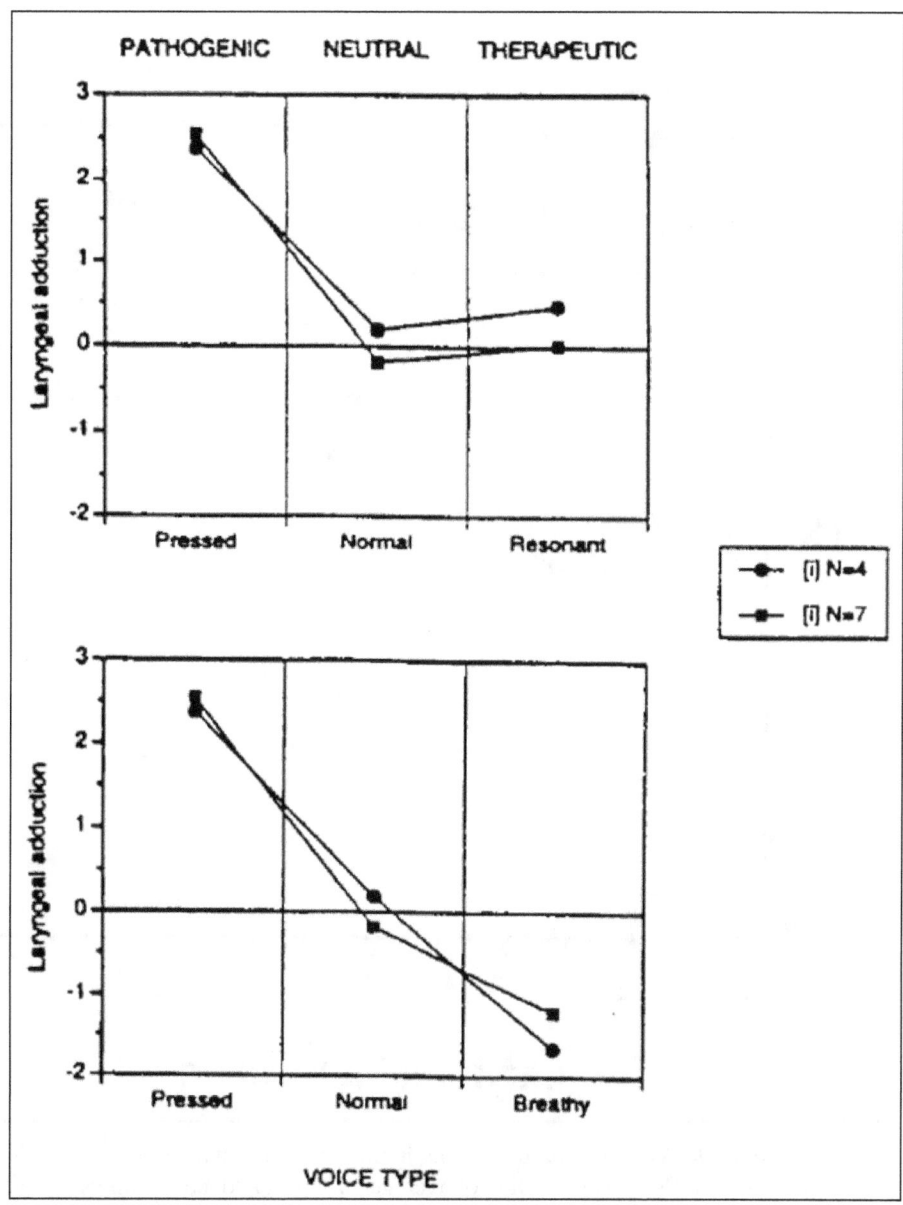

Figure 8. Average laryngeal adduction ratings (-5 = extreme hypoadduction, +5 = extreme hyperadduction) as function of voice type, for vowel /i/ (N = 4 and N = 7)

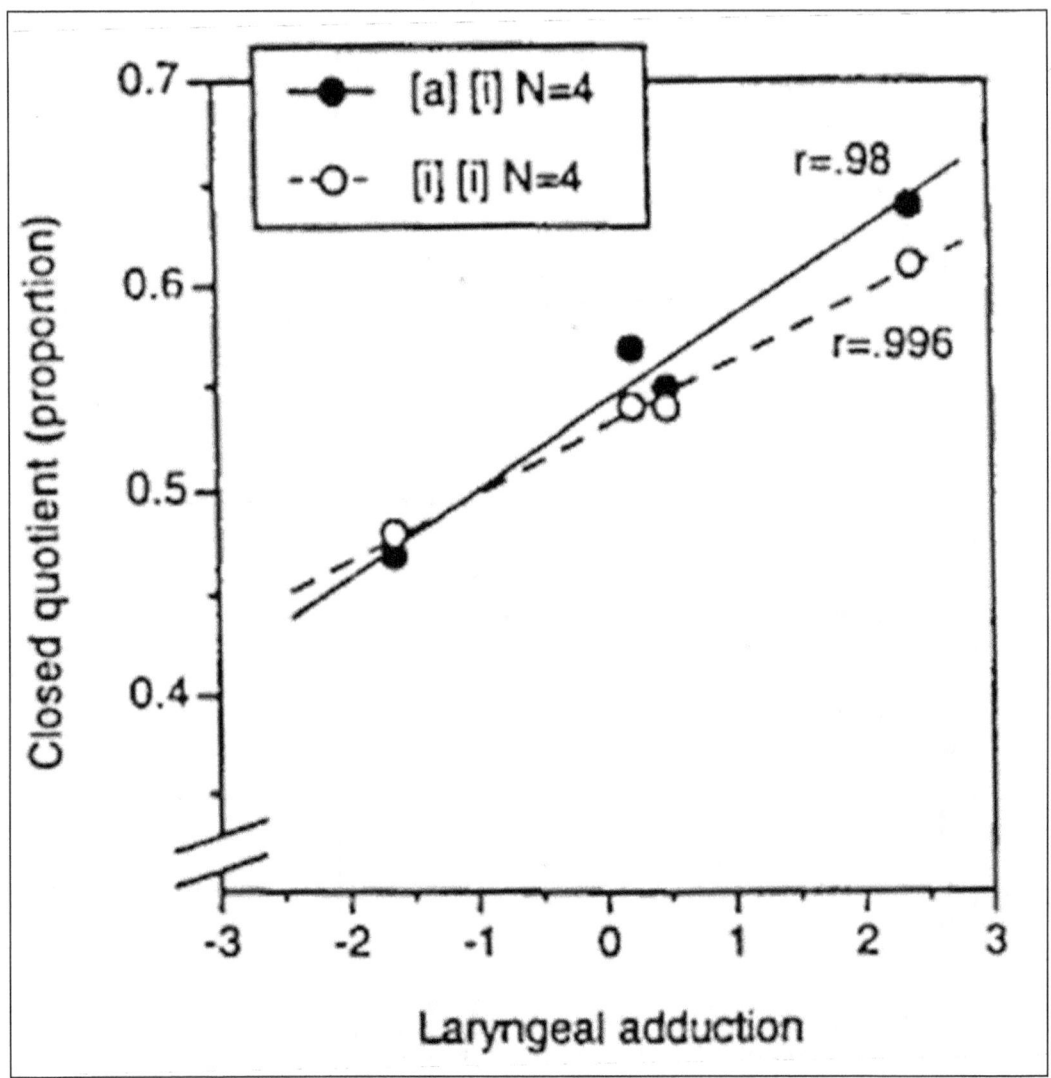

Figure 9. Average closed quotient, in proportion of total cycle, for //i/ and /u/ (N = 4) as function of average laryngeal adduction ratings for /i/ (N = 4; -5 = extreme hypoadduction; +5 = extreme hyperadduction).

TABLE 6: INDIVIDUAL DATA FOR CLOSED QUOTIENT IN PROPORTION OF TOTAL CYCLE, FOR FOUR VOICE TYPES (n = 4)

Vowel	Subject	Voice Type			
		Pressed	Normal	Resonant	Breathy
/a/	1	0.61	0.56	0.53	0.49
	3	0.54	0.61	0.58	*
	4	0.61	0.46	0.49	0.50
	7	0.61	0.54	0.57	0.46
/i/	1	0.61	0.54	0.53	0.51
	3	0.67	0.67	0.62	0.46
	4	0.70	0.49	0.46	0.45
	7	0.58	0.58	0.59	0.45

* Missing data

To specifically assess the relation between the closed quotient and laryngeal adduction ratings, correlations were calculated between these measures for the 4 subjects for whom both EGG and videostroboscopic measures were available. First, correlations were calculated from average data for both the closed quotient and the laryngeal ratings. These results are shown in Fig. 9. When the average closed quotient for /i/ is compared to the average adduction rating (also for /i/, which was the only vowel assessed endoscopically), increases in the closed quotient correspond to increases in adduction ratings (Pearson $r = .98$, $p < .01$). A similar pattern was noted for the comparison between the closed quotient for /a/ and the adduction ratings for /i/ (Pearson $r = 0996$, $p < .01$). (Relations between the EGG closed quotient for /u/ and laryngeal adduction ratings were not assessed, because the results for /u/ closed quotients were unreliable). Stated differently, for the vowels assessed there was a remarkable linear relation between the average closed quotient and the average adduction rating, both decreasing across the continuum from the pathogenic to the therapeutic voice types. Correlations using individual data also indicated significant relations: when individual closed quotients for /i/ are compared to individual adduction ratings for /i/, Pearson $r = .59$ (p, .02); and when individual closed quotients for /a/ are compared to individual adduction ratings for /i/, Pearson $r = .70$ ($p < .01$).

Discussion

On the basis of the results from the present study, for the vowels /a/ and /i/, one physiologic measure was identified that may effectively distinguish voice types that appear relevant for nodule formation and regression: the EGG closed quotient. A series of aerodynamic measures, including MFDR, AC flow, and minimum flow, as well as another EGG measure, closing time, failed to acceptably differentiate between canonical tokens of pathogenic, neutral, and therapeutic voice types for any of the vowels, as did the EGG closed quotient for the vowel /u/.

In greater detail, average EGG closed quotients for /a/ and /i/ were reliably greatest for a voicing pattern that may be pathogenic, i.e., pressed voice. Closed quotients were intermediate for a neutral voicing pattern (normal voice) and for another voicing pattern that may be therapeutic (resonant voice), and were the smallest for another possibly therapeutic voicing pattern (breathy voice). High closed quotients were seen for pressed voice, not only for the subject group as a whole, but also for most individual subjects.

Evidence from other authors suggests a link between the EGG closed quotient and laryngeal adduction.[19] Confirmation of this relationship was sought in the present study by comparing closed quotients for /i/, which was assessed videostroboscopically, to laryngeal adduction ratings for the same vowel, and also by comparing closed quotients for /a/ (which was not assessed videostroboscopically) to laryngeal adduction ratings based on the vowel /i/. The results of these comparisons agree with those reported by the previous authors, indicating linear relations between the closed quotient and laryngeal adduction ratings, both when group data and when individual data were considered. The link to nodule pathogenesis and regression was provided by Jiang,[6] whose data suggest an increased likelihood of trauma with increasing adduction.

Thus the main points that emerge from this study are 1) that clinically important voicing patterns may be effectively distinguished by the closed quotient from the EGG signal, for sustained vowels /a/ and /i/ (but not /u/), and 2) that a critical dimension in the pathogenic-therapeutic voice use continuum may be laryngeal adduction level.

At a general level, our results are consistent with a framework proposed by Hillman et al.[5] According to this framework, laryngeal adduction is a critical dimension for pathogenesis. However, our results do not agree with one of these authors' specific conclusions. In the study by Hillman et al, subjects with nodules and polyps generally produced higher MFDRs than normal, whereas voice-disordered subjects without lesions produced normal MFDRs. The conclusion was that MFDR may predict the potential for pathogenesis, by reflecting force of vocal fold collision. In our study, MFDRs for the pathogenic voicing pattern were not reliably different from those for one putative therapeutic pattern (resonant voice) for the vowel of particular interest (/a/); and for the other vowels (/i/ and /u/). MFDRs were reliably greater for the same therapeutic voicing pattern as compared to the pathogenic pattern. The difference in the results across studies is likely attributable to a difference in voice tasks, and also to subject differences. In the study by Hillman et al, voice-disordered subjects produced their own spontaneous (and possibly pathogenic) voicing pattern at soft, medium, and loud levels. Intentional variations in voice across a pathogenic-therapeutic continuum were not included. In our study, vocally healthy subjects produced not only spontaneous ('normal") patterns, but also patterns assumed to be pathogenic and therapeutic. In our study, the inclusion of "resonant voice" in particular was critical, because it produced results indicating that MFDR may not distinguish well between pathogenic and nonpathogenic voicing patterns.

Although our results for MFDR indicate this difference with respect to one previous study, we did replicate a report by other authors of a reliable covariance between MFDR and AC flow. Specifically, as reported by Sundberg et al,[18] our data suggest a significant inverse relation between MFDR and AC flow. However, as already noted, in our study neither of these measures provided much insight into mechanisms regulating nodule pathogenesis and regression. The data for AC flow are particularly interesting in this regard. Although most of the paired comparisons between the presumably pathogenic and therapeutic voice types indicated significant differences, the data were skewed in a direction that is difficult to interpret within the pathogenic-therapeutic framework. The AC flows were smallest for the pathogenic voice, and were greatest for the therapeutic voice types. If AC flow is a direct reflection of vocal fold collisional force, this result is difficult to interpret. Why should AC flows be greatest for a therapeutic voice type, and least for a pathogenic voice type? We do not have any answer to this question, and it is an intriguing one. However, our findings agree with a general approach to voice training and therapy suggested by Gauffin and Sundberg,[20] which emphasizes "flow mode," or an overall high utilization of glottal flows during phonation. Our findings also indicate that high-amplitude vocal fold vibrations may be associated with therapeutic voicing patterns, in some cases, as opposed to low-amplitude vibrations, as often assumed.

Returning to the main finding from our study, and that is the sensitivity of the EGG closed quotient for distinguishing clinically relevant voicing patterns, it is important to point out the limitations of our results and the remaining questions. First, before accepting the EGG closed quotient as a useful physiologic investigatory tool, the present results should be confirmed in follow-up studies with both normal and pathologic subjects. The EGG signals are sometimes poorly obtained. Thus, the resulting measures may be available only in a restricted proportion of cases. In fact, in our study, valid signals were obtained only for 4 of 6 subjects for whom EGG was attempted. Factors that may contribute to poor signals include thyroid cartilage angle, relative fat and soft tissue in the neck, electrode slippage, and the presence of laryngeal disease resulting in poor long-term signal conduction across the larynx. Particularly, the possibility of poor EGG signals for pathologic subjects indicates the need for follow-up studies with this population, for whom evaluations seem particularly relevant.

Second, from the present study it is not clear why the EGG closed quotient distinguished between the voicing patterns for /a/ and /i/, but not /u/. The finding of vowel differences for these measures should be confirmed or disconfirmed with follow-up studies, and if confirmed, the finding should be explained. However, if the present results are replicated, it should be kept in mind that the closed quotient may be meaningful for physiologic investigations only for a restricted set of vowels.

Third, although the present results are consistent with the hypothesis that laryngeal adduction level is an important parameter for nodule development and reversal, as suggested by previous authors (for example, Hillman et al[5]), in the present study the reasoning is based on inference only. In our study, subjects produced voice types presumed to be pathogenic or therapeutic, but there was no independent verification of this assumption. Longitudinal causal studies are needed for confirmation or disconfirmation of the relationships between pressed voice, normal voice, resonant voice, and breathy voice and pathogenesis. The main contribution of the present study is the finding that perhaps the identified EGG measure (closed quotient) could be used as an investigatory tool in future studies of this type.

In conclusion, the results from this study indicate that the closed quotient from EGG signals for the vowels /a/ and /i/ may be useful for future physiologic investigations of clinically relevant voicing patterns. The results also indicate that this quotient varies with intralaryngeal adduction level and, by extension, contact stress. However, follow-up studies are needed to confirm the present results over a larger subject sample including normal and pathologic subjects, and to investigate the possible relation between the closed quotient and intraglottal contact stress. Assuming that the present findings are replicated, longitudinal studies are also needed to determine if, in fact, nodule development and regression can be predicated by the closed quotient.

Acknowledgment: The first and second authors contributed equally to the project. Ingo Titze is thanked for his comments on an earlier version of this paper, Jon Lemke and Kice Brown for assistance with statistical management, Mark Peters and Kay Klein for assistance with graphics, and Julie Lemke and Phyllis Palmer for technical support.

References

1. Epstein SS, Winston P, Friedmann I, Ormerod FC. 'The vocal cord polyp.' *J Laryngol Otol*, 1957;71:673-88.

2. Gillman T. 'Treatise on collagen.' In Gould BS, ed. *Biology of collagen*. Vol 2. New York, NY: Academic Press, 1968:334.

3. Sonninen A., Damste PH, Jol J, Fokkens J. 'On vocal strain.' *Folia Phoniatr (basel)*, 1972;24:321-36.

4. Kleinsasser O. 'Pathogenesis of vocal cord polyps.' *Ann Otol Rhinol Laryngol*, 1982;1:378-81.

5. Hillman RE, Holmberg EB, Perkell JS, Walsh M, Vaughn C. 'Objective assessment of vocal fold hyperfunction: an experimental framework and initial results.' *J Speech Hear Res*, 1989;32:373-92.

6. Jiang J. *A methodological study of hemilaryngeal phonation and the measurement of vocal fold intraglottal pressure and impact stress* [Dissertation]. Iowa City, Iowa: The University of Iowa, 1991.

7. Boone DR. *The voice and voice therapy*. Englewood Cliffs, NJ: Prentice-Hall, 1977.

8. Colton RH, Casper JK. *Understanding voice problems: a physiological perspective for diagnosis and treatment.* Baltimore, Md: Williams & Wilkins, 1990.

9. Cooper M. *Modern techniques of vocal rehabilitation*. Springfield, III: Charles C Thomas, 1973.

10. Fog Pederson M. 'Electroglottography compared with synchronized stroboscopy in normal persons." *Folia Phoniatr* (Basel), 1977;29:191-9.

11. Childers DG, Krishnamurthy AK. 'A critical review of electroglottography.' *CRC Crit Rev Biomed Eng,* 1985:12:131-61.

12. Childers DG, Hicks DM, Moore GP, Alsaka YA. 'A model for vocal fold vibratory motion, contact area, and the electroglottogram.' *J Acoust Soc Am*, 1986;80:1309-20.

13. Scherer RC, Druker DG, Titze IR. 'Electroglottography and direct measurement of vocal fold contact area.' In: Fujimura O, ed. *Vocal physiology: voice production, mechanisms and functions.* New York, NY: Raven Press, 1988:279-91.

14. Scherer RC, Gould WJ, Titze IR, Meyers AD, Sataloff RT. 'Preliminary evaluation of selected acoustic and glottographic measures for clinical phonatory function analysis.' *J Voice*, 1988;2:230-44.

15. Rothenberg M, Mahshie JJ. 'Monitoring vocal fold abduction through vocal fold contact area' *J Speech Hear Res*, 1988;31:338-51.

16. Holmberg EB, Hillman RE, Perkell JS. 'Glottal airflow and transglottal air pressure measurements for male and female speakers in soft, normal, and loud voice.' *J Acoust Soc Am*, 1988;84:511-29.

17. Colton RH, Conture EG. 'Problems and pitfalls of electroglottography.' *J Voice*, 1990;4:10-24.

18. Sundberg J, Scherer R, Titze IR. 'Phonatory control in male singing. A study of the effect of subglottal pressure, fundamental frequency, and mode of phonation on the voice source.' *J Voice*, 1993;7:15-29.

19. Scherer R, Vail V. 'Measures of laryngeal adduction.' *J Acoust Soc Am*, 1988:84 (suppl 1).

20. Gauffin J, Sundberg J. 'Spectral correlates of glottal voice source waveform characteristics.' *J Speech Hear Res* 1989;32:556-65.

From the Department of Otolaryngology – Head and Neck Surgery (Peterson, Barkmeier, Hoffman), the National Center for Voice and Speech (all authors), and the Department of Speech Pathology and Audiology (Verdolini-Marston, Barkmeier), The University of Iowa, Iowa City, Iowa. Dr Peterson is currently at the Department of Otolaryngology-Head and Neck Surgery, University of California, Los Angeles, School of Medicine, Los Angeles, California. This work was supported in part by grant P60 DC 00976 from the National Institutes of Health/National Institute on Deafness and Other Communication Disorders.

Presented at the meeting of the American Laryngological Association, Palm Desert, California, April 11-12, 1992.

Preliminary Study of Two Methods of Treatment for Laryngeal Nodules

This peer-reviewed article was originally published in the Journal of Voice. 1995. Vol. 9, No. 1, pp 74-85. Permission to reprint has been graciously granted by the Voice Foundation.

*†*Katherine Verdolini-Marston, ‡*Mary Katherine Burke,*
§*Arthur Lessac,* "*Leslie Glaze, and* **Elizabeth Caldwell*

*Department of Speech Pathology and Audiology, The University of Iowa; †National Center for Voice and Speech, Iowa City, Iowa; ‡Old Globe Theatre, San Diego; §Lessac Institute, Santa Monica, California; and "Midwest Voice and Speech Institute, Saint Paul, Minnesota, U.S.A.

Summary: To date, a limited number of formal studies have assessed the efficacy of voice therapy for laryngeal nodules. The present study represents a preliminary stage of inquiry in a series of planned studies on this topic. Thirteen women with nodules participated as paid subjects. Some subjects received "confidential voice therapy," some received "resonant voice therapy," and some received no therapy (control condition) over a period of ~2 weeks. Pre- and post-therapy measures of phonatory effort, auditory-perceptual status of voice, and laryngeal appearance provided evidence of a benefit from therapy. Baseline measures were then repeated 2 weeks after therapy was terminated. The final results indicated that, for auditory-perceptual and phonatory effort measures, the likelihood of benefiting from therapy directly covaried with *compliance* scores (reflecting the reported extraclinical utilization of the therapy technique), but not with therapy type (confidential vs. resonant voice therapy). At this level, the results point to the importance of assessing not only therapy type but also compliance in future, larger studies. A series of other positive and negative factors in the present research design were identified based on the results. These should be considered in future studies.

Voice therapy is generally viewed as an important aspect of treatment for laryngeal nodules, either alone or in conjunction with microsurgery. Some empirical support for this view has been reported over the past several years (1,2,3). Large-scale, controlled studies are still needed. One of the impediments to such studies is that a series of challenges confront the researcher interested in the efficacy of voice therapy. Therapy is difficult to describe in detail a priori, it may be delivered inconsistently across subjects, it may be susceptible to therapist effects, and treatment benefits may be generally difficult to detect due to large inter-subject variability in the response to treatment, related to a series of factors including differences in initial severity levels and in extraclinical behaviors (4). Preliminary studies are needed to address some of these challenges before larger studies are undertaken.

The purpose of this study was thus to conduct a preliminary investigation on the effectiveness of voice therapy for nodules, considering some of these challenges, in preparation for later, larger studies. The first-level question was whether there was any evidence of a benefit from therapy, as compared with results for a control group. The second-level issue was evaluate the role of therapy type (confidential voice vs. resonant voice therapy) and of compliance (the extraclinical utilization of the voicing technique taught in therapy) in predicting the likelihood of benefit from therapy. If compliance factors turned out to be relevant, post hoc information would be used to assess which factors may affect compliance. An experimental paradigm was used that attempted to address some of the research challenges noted.

General Description of Therapy Types

Confidential voice therapy is often utilized by speech/language pathologists for the treatment of nodules. According to Colton and Casper (5), focus of this type of therapy is the elicitation of a minimal intensity, low effort, and somewhat breathy phonation mode, as if speaking confidentially at close range. Videoscopic examinations show that at least breathy phonation is associated with a persistent glottal gap during phonation, at variable locations along the anteroposterior dimension of the folds (6). Confidential voice therapy is considered particularly useful during initial stages of treatment, for maximum early reduction of lesions and of dysphonia.

Resonant voice therapy is perhaps more regularly encountered in performance domains such as theatre and classical music. As described by various authors (7,8), resonant voice involves vibratory sensations on the alveolar ridge and other facial plates during phonation. These sensations apparently arise, in part, from a relative acoustic "tuning" of the supraglottic cavities to the glottal source spectrum (9). Voice output is not necessarily quiet with this approach. Our videoscopic observations and those from other clinics (for example, Rammage, personal communication) indicate that resonant voice is generally produced with relatively complete anteroposterior vocal fold closure during phonation. The likely reason is that more or less complete (and rapid) vocal fold closure is a prerequisite for the production of a sufficient harmonic series, for availability to supraglottic enhancement (10,11).

Model of Therapy Benefits And Predictions

As noted, in addition to the general question of whether therapy for nodules produces any benefit, an important focus in this initial study considered the role of therapy type and of compliance in predicting the likelihood of a benefit from therapy. This question is related to the proposal that, to be effective, any voice therapy method should be sound from at least three perspectives: physiological, learning, and compliance. That is, the method must emphasize a physiology that has the potential for reversing pathogenic voicing patterns. The method must also be "learnable." And finally, the method must be one that subjects are likely to utilize out- side the clinical situation. How can the two methods under investigation be considered, from these three perspectives?

Regarding the physiological perspective, the results from recent studies (12,13) have provided information about both "breathy voice" (similar to confidential voice, in the present study) and "resonant voice." In those studies, both of the voicing modalities were produced with a generally abducted laryngeal posturing, as compared with "pressed voice" (a presumed pathogenic voicing mode). Breathy voice resulted in a frank abductory posture, and resonant voice resulted in a slightly abducted or barely adducted posture. "Pressed voice" resulted in a clearly hyper-adducted laryngeal posturing. Thus, lesion reduction may be favored with both confidential and resonant voice therapy approaches, as compared with pressed voice (which for many patients may represent a pathogenic factor), because of a direct relation between vocal fold adduction level and intraglottal impact pressure (14), and further, between intraglottal impact pressure and pathogenesis (14). Because of the relatively greater abduction associated with confidential as compared with resonant voice, the confidential voice therapy method may be physiologically superior in its potential for lesion reversal.

From the learning perspective, there is no obvious a priori reason why either the confidential voice or the resonant voice therapy approach should be more effective than the other. A learning model that honors skill acquisition principles, such as the relevance of attention to perceptual information (15,16), consistent repetitions (17), and knowledge of results (see Schmidt (18), for review), could be used with either approach, as could a learning model that violates the same principles. The effectiveness of either type of therapy would be anticipated to vary with the learning model, to some degree.

From a compliance perspective, there are also no clear-cut predictions. Health-care studies indicate that compliance with therapeutic regimens may depend on a series of factors, including "self efficacy," or the patient's perception of his or her ability to carry out the prescribed behavior (19, 20). In the context of voice therapy, self-efficacy would involve the patient's perception of his or her technical ability to produce the type of voicing trained. From this viewpoint, confidential voice therapy could result in greater compliance than resonant voice therapy, because of the informal impression that most patients are able to produce confidential voice to the conversational level with little training, as compared with resonant voice, which tends to require more training. However, another consideration may offset this possible advantage for confidential voice therapy. By definition, confidential voice involves quiet phonation. Thus, patients may fail to utilize this type of voicing in situations requiring more normal loudness levels. In contrast, patients may more readily utilize the resonant voice technique even in situations requiring louder phonation, because this production mode allows for relatively loud output.

In summary, from a physiological perspective, confidential voice therapy may be expected to result in greater reductions in laryngeal nodules and in dysphonia than resonant voice therapy, although both may have the potential for producing benefits. From the learning and compliance perspectives, less confident predictions can be made. The experiment reported here focuses on the role of physiological factors (therapy type) and of compliance factors (extra clinical utilization of the therapy technique) in determining relatively longer-term benefits with therapy. Specifically, first the outcomes of confidential and resonant voice therapy are assessed as compared with the outcome for a control group, following a 2-week intensive therapy period. Then, likelihood of a relatively longer-term benefit with therapy is assessed as a function of therapy type and compliance measures. If the results indicate a role of compliance, a further post hoc question considers which factors may in turn affect compliance. The experimental design attempts to address some of the challenges in voice therapy efficacy research noted at the beginning of this article, namely, the description of therapy and the consistency of therapy administration across subjects, a control for therapist effects, and a control for intersubject variability in severity level and in extraclinical behaviors, all of which may affect the outcome of therapy.

Methods

Subjects

The original subject group consisted of 18 women who were recruited from college sororities to participate in the study for pay. Sororities were considered optimal recruiting environments because of the perceived high density of voice disorders among this population at our university. Although all 18 subjects did participate in the protocol, only 13 yielded a complete set of utilizable data.[1]

These are the subjects described in this report. The average age of this subject set was 20 years, with a range of 18-22 years. Subsequent to their recruitment and shortly before initiation of the protocol, a diagnosis of laryngeal nodules was confirmed for each subject by an otolaryngologist. The average time since onset of symptoms was 4.5 years, with a range of 0.33 (4 months) to 14 years. Therefore, nodules were considered chronic for all subjects. None of the subjects had received previous voice therapy, and at the outset of the experiment all denied previous voice training of any type.

By self-report, none of the subjects had ever smoked regularly, although five smoked sporadically, socially (subjects MS, JO, KG, LP, and JR). For these subjects, the number of pack years, or packs per day times number of years smoked, ranged from 0.04 to 1.14 years. With the exception of one subject, all denied active illnesses,

---

[1] One subject developed the flu and could not come in for the final measurement session. Three subjects' videoscopic views of the larynx were altered during dubbing procedures, or were un- available, and one subject's audio tapes were unavailable. No subject was excluded on the basis of the results obtained. The data for excluded subjects were carefully examined, and it was determined that, as best we can estimate, the pattern of results reported in this study was not qualitatively affected by their elimination.

ongoing medical conditions, or regular medications. The exception was subject MR, who took 0.125 mg of Synthroid daily for control of hypothyroidism. Hearing screening indicated pure tone thresholds of 20 dB or lower in the better ear, for 11 of the 13 subjects. For the remaining two subjects, thresholds were not obtained, but there was no indication of hearing loss for these subjects.

Therapists

As an attempt to control for therapist effects, two therapists each provided both confidential voice therapy and resonant voice therapy to different subjects. Both therapists were nationally certified in speech/language pathology, with membership in the American Speech-Language-Hearing Association. One was a doctoral level speech/language pathologist (LG) with about 5 years of experience in voice therapy. She had previous experience with the confidential voice therapy approach, and expressed confidence in its effectiveness for the treatment of nodules. Before her participation, she had no experience with the resonant voice method. However, she considered that it might also be effective. The other therapist (AL) had practiced as a voice trainer and therapist for about 60 years, and had developed the resonant voice approach used in the protocol (the Lessac approach). Not surprisingly, he believed that resonant voice therapy was effective in the treatment of nodules. Before his participation in the study, he had no experience with the confidential voice therapy approach, and he was frankly skeptical about its therapeutic potential.

Cross-training of therapists and description of therapies provided

For 2 days immediately preceding the initiation of therapy, the two therapists engaged in cross-training for confidential voice and resonant voice therapy, for a total of ~7 h. Therapist training was intended to enhance the consistency with which therapy would be administered during the experiment. On the first day of cross-training, the therapists worked with each other and with another experimenter for 3-4 h. The next day, five patients (who were not involved in the data set reported here) were brought in for the therapists to work with, with reciprocal feedback, for another 3-4 h.

The confidential voice therapy method was modeled after descriptions by Colton and Casper (5). For this type of therapy, the focus was (a) the production of a minimal effort, minimal loudness, and slightly breathy phonation mode, as if speaking confidentially at short range, without perceptible perilaryngeal "squeezing," and (b) general body relaxation, obtained for example by shaking out the jaw and shoulders and by breathing easily. The resonant voice therapy method was modeled after descriptions by Lessac (8). For this type of therapy, the focus was (a) the production of concentrated vibratory sensations on the anterior palate during phonation, using an "inverted megaphone" facial posture (slightly expanded pharynx and a slight forward stretch in facial muscles, with labial protrusion), and (b) upper body relaxation, using manual manipulations to reverse any obvious head, neck, or shoulder tensions, and to obtain good head and neck alignment.

In addition to these distinguishing characteristics, common aspects across the two therapy types were also emphasized. Therapists were instructed to display an overall attitude of confidence in both methods, and to characterize both methods to subjects as well-established and successful clinical approaches that are quite easy to implement. Also for both methods, therapy was to start with work on sounds in isolation (typically vowels for the confidential voice approach, and both consonants and vowels for the resonant voice approach). Then therapy was to proceed by stages to the conversational level and real-life applications outside the therapy room, based on the clinicians' impression that earlier levels in the therapy hierarchy had been satisfactorily mastered. Finally, for both methods, exercises were to be as interesting as possible, numerous repetitions of target behaviors were to be included, and frequent positive feedback about subjects' performance was to be provided.

All therapy sessions were videotaped for possible later reference, and an experimenter observed most sessions on-line, as well. Informally, these observations indicated that the therapies were largely delivered as trained. In particular, although there may have been different biases about the effectiveness of the methods across the two therapists, observations of therapy sessions did not reveal any obvious evidence of such biases.

Procedures and design

When the therapists had completed cross-training, subjects initiated their participation in the protocol. They first received general (logistic) information about the protocol. Then they were instructed to observe general, extraclinical voice hygiene practices, as an attempt to control for some extraclinical behaviors which might affect the outcome of treatment. That is, subjects were instructed to limit alcohol and caffeine intake, smoking, and "heavy voice use" (for example, yelling). They were provided daily logs to indicate their adherence to these directives. After they received these instructions, subjects underwent a series of voice and laryngeal examination procedures described shortly. All test procedures were conducted by an experimenter who was uninformed about which therapy treatment subjects were about to receive. (For logistic reasons related to the therapists' availability, it was necessary to run control subjects in the protocol sometime after therapy subjects had completed their participation. Thus, the experimenter was aware of control subjects' status as controls.)

Subjects who would receive therapy were then assigned to a therapy group. In the original subject set, six subjects were assigned to the confidential voice therapy group (three subjects were assigned to LG and three were assigned to AL), and six subjects were assigned to the resonant voice therapy group (again, three subjects were assigned to LG and three were assigned to AL). The assignments were made on the basis of severity ratings made before the initiation of the protocol, from videoscopic views of the larynx with audio, such that each therapy/therapist cell in the experiment would be comprised of subjects with the same approximate degree of hoarseness and nodule severity. (Control subjects were also subsequently selected so that the severity distribution would be about equivalent for this group, as compared with the two therapy groups.) This assignment procedure was used as an attempt to control for possible differences in severity levels across the groups, which might obscure treatment effects. However, as already noted, the data for some of the subjects were subsequently excluded from analysis because of missing data: Five subjects were retained for the confidential therapy group, of which two received therapy from LG and three from AL, and three subjects were retained for the resonant therapy group, of which two received therapy from LG and one from AL. (Five subjects were retained for the control group). The result was a data set that regrettably reflected different initial severity distributions across the groups.

For therapy subjects, therapy was then initiated the same day or the following day. (Control subjects were simply asked to follow general voice hygiene measures, as instructed, and to return for follow-up measurements 12 days later.) Therapy subjects received a total of nine therapy sessions across an ~12-day period. For each subject, eight of the sessions were 1-h individual sessions, and one was a 1-h group session together with all other subjects in the same therapy condition (confidential or resonant voice).

The rationale for administering therapy over an ~2-week period was related to the preliminary nature of the present study. Usually, voice therapy is administered over a longer time span, with one or two sessions per week. For the present, initial inquiry, we elected to support a briefer, more intensive protocol. We anticipated that reliable changes in voice and in the larynx could be obtained within the 2-week period, based on the findings from another efficacy study that we conducted recently on hydration treatments (21).

Following the final therapy session, i.e., about 12 days following therapy initiation, therapy subjects underwent the same voice and laryngeal testing procedures as previously. They also filled out questionnaires that assessed their perceptions about therapy. Control subjects received posttests of the voice and of the larynx (but did not fill out questionnaires) at the same time interval. Therapy subjects then returned 2 weeks later for a final measurement session, so that their relatively longer-term status could be assessed. Control subjects did not return for a later follow-up.

A final note is that voices and larynges tended to vary with day of the week in our subject population. Status tended to be relatively worse following weekends, and relatively better following the work week. To control for this factor, and to maximize the likelihood of detecting changes in this initial experiment, we administered all pretreatment measures earlier in the week (mostly on Sunday or Monday), and all post-treatment measures later in the week (mostly on Friday). As noted, gains would be maximized by this approach. However, they would be maximized equivalently across groups. Thus, any group differences could be attributable to the independent variables of interest.

Measures and equipment

The primary pre- and postmeasures of the voice and of the larynx consisted of (a) phonatory effort ratings, (b) auditory-perceptual ratings of voice, and (c) visual-perceptual ratings of the larynx. Acoustic measures of voice (jitter, shimmer, and signal-to-noise ratio) and aerodynamic measures (phonation threshold pressure) were also made, as supportive measures. However, these measures are not reported here because their inclusion would increase the number of subjects that would have to be excluded because of missing or un-interpretable data.[2] Other critical measures in the experiment, reported here, were (d) estimates of adherence to instructions about general voice hygiene practices (for all subjects), (e) measures of subjects' perceptions about therapy methods (for therapy subjects), and (f) estimates of ongoing compliance following therapy termination, i.e., of the relative continued utilization of the therapy technique after therapy was discontinued (for therapy subjects).

Measures of phonatory effort were based on a procedure, originally described by Colton and Brown (22) and Wright and Colton (23), that we modified for this and other experimental and clinical procedures. For these measures, subjects were required to rate the perceived effort of phonation, in general, on a magnitude estimation scale on which "100" indicated "a comfortable amount of effort during phonation," "200" indicated "twice as much effort as comfortable" (i.e., "very effortful"), and "50" indicated "half as much effort as comfortable" (i.e., "very easy").

Auditory-perceptual ratings of the voices were based on tape recordings made during the reading of a standard passage, "A Man and his Boat." Recordings were made in a quiet room, using an AKG C 460 B condenser microphone powered by a Symetrix SX202 Dual Mic preamplifier. Signals were routed to a Realistic STA-785 digital synthesized Am/Fm stereo receiver/amplifier and a Panasonic digital audio tape (DAT) deck SV-3500. During recordings, the microphone-to-mouth distance was ~7", and recording levels were monitored for an approximately constant value on the VU meter of the DAT recorder. After the experiment was completed, three recordings from each subject were played successively to four listener-judges (speech pathologists) independently, in free-field, over Realistic Minimus 7 speakers. For subjects who received therapy, the recordings included one segment made just before the initiation of therapy, one made following therapy, about 12 days later, and one made ~2 weeks following the termination of therapy.

---

[2] Interpretable acoustic and aerodynamic data were not obtained for one control subject, for the baseline measurement session, and interpretable acoustic data were not obtained for another control subject, for the 2-week measurement session. As best we can estimate, the overall pattern of results was not qualitatively affected by the omission of acoustic and aerodynamic data. Specific information is available from the first author on request.

For control subjects who did not receive therapy, the recordings included one segment from before participation, one segment from 12 days later, and then a repeat of one of the other two segments. (A repeat was included for control subjects so that three segments would be presented, consistent with the number presented for therapy subjects. The presentation of only two segments might have provided a "clue" about control subjects' status as somehow different.) Across subjects, the order of presentation of the three segments was counterbalanced to control for order effects. All of the listener-judges reported normal hearing; they were uninvolved in any other phase of the experiment, and they were unfamiliar with the subjects and subjects' specific conditions (pre- vs. post-, and confidential vs. resonant voice vs. control condition). The judges independently rated each taped segment on an ordinal scale, where 1 = "healthy voice," 2 = "mildly impaired voice," 3 = moderate," 4 = "moderate-severely impaired voice," and 5 = "severely impaired voice."

Visual-perceptual measures of the larynx were based on views of the larynx obtained with an R. Wolf 4450.47 90° rigid videoscope, connected to a Karl Storz 9000 Mini Solid State CCD video camera and a Brüel and Kjaer Rhino-Larynx Stroboscope light source, Type 4914. Views were monitored on a NEC autocolor PM-1971A color television monitor at the time of collection. After all data were collected, videoscopic segments were played back using a SONY CVM Trinitron video monitor. Four independent judges (two speech pathologists with experience in videoscopic evaluation of the larynx and two otolaryngology residents at our institutions) were presented with three ~5-s video segments for each subject, in succession. For subjects who received therapy, the recordings included one segment made just before the initiation of therapy, one made following the termination of therapy, ~ 12 days later, and one made about 2 weeks after termination of therapy. For control subjects who did not receive therapy, the recordings included one segment from before participation, one segment from 12 days later, and also a repeat of one of the other two segments. (Again, a repeat was included to avoid a distinction in the number of segments presented, as compared with the number presented for therapy subjects.) The order of segments was counterbalanced across subjects. All 5-s segments were selected as "the best 5-s view of the larynx" from longer, taped segments, by a research assistant who was not involved in any other aspect of the experiment, and without regard to treatment condition. Also, none of the judges who rated the segments were involved with any other phase of the experiment; they were unfamiliar with the subjects and they were uninformed about subjects' treatment conditions upon viewing. Each judge independently rated each video segment on a 5-point ordinal scale, where 1 = "healthy vocal folds," 2 = "mild nodules/polyps or related," 3 = "moderate," 4 = "moderately severe," and 5 = "severe nodules/polyps or related." The term "related" was intended to refer to characteristics that may accompany nodules, e.g., erythema.

For all subjects, daily logs indicated subjects' adherence to the instructions about general voice hygiene practices during the initial 2-week period of the protocol. For therapy subjects, measures of subjects' perceptions about therapy were obtained using a questionnaire that was administered upon therapy termination. The questionnaire included a set of 12 questions that we thought might be in some way interesting in the subsequent interpretation of the results. At the time they were formulated, the questions were motivated more by practical than by rigorous theoretical considerations. The questions are indicated in Appendix A. Subjects responded to all questions with ordinal ratings from "1" (maximum negative response) to "5" (maximum positive response).

Finally, for therapy subjects, estimates of ongoing compliance (continued utilization of therapy techniques following therapy discontinuation) were made on the basis of responses to an open-ended question: "To what extent have you continued to use [the therapy technique] since therapy was terminated"? Subjects' responses were literally transcribed by one of the experimenters. For scoring purposes, the transcriptions were later dichotomized by a clinician who was uninvolved in any other aspect of the protocol. A score of "0" indicated a report of early discontinuation of the therapy method following therapy termination, and a score of "1" indicated a report of at least some continued use of the method. Dichotomized compliance scores were used because they were considered to provide the appropriate level of differentiation in this preliminary study.

Results
Adherence to general voice hygiene instructions

Table 1 indicates that on most parameters, subjects in all groups appeared to follow instructions on general voice hygiene practices to about the same degree, at least according to the daily logs that they filled out. Subjects in all groups drank an average of about one alcoholic beverage per day (although for all subjects, drinking tended to cluster on weekends, without drinking during the week). Subjects drank about one or one and a half cups of a caffeinated beverage per day, and they did not smoke or smoked an average of less than a third of a cigarette per day. The primary discrepancy across the groups appeared to come from amount of "heavy voice use." Subjects in the confidential voice therapy group appeared to restrict heavy voice use the most (-0.10 h/day, on average), subjects in the resonant voice group were intermediate (-0.30 h/day), and subjects in the control group appeared to engage in heavy voice use the most (-0.70 h/day). The relatively high value for the control group was not necessarily attributable to the lack of participation in therapy for all subjects: excluding subject AH, who reported an average of 2.62 h of heavy voice use per day, the average "heavy voice use" for the control group was -0.20 h/day (less than for the resonant voice therapy group).

TABLE 1. SUBJECTS' LOGS ON COMPLIANCE WITH GENERAL VOICE HYGIENE PRACTICES OVER FIRST 2-WEEK PERIOD OF PROTOCOL

Group/Subject	Alcohol	Caffeine	Smoking	Heavy Voice Use
Confidential				
MS(13)	1.31	0.15	0.92	-
BB(12)	1.67	2.08	-	0.25
JO(11)	1.09	1.18	0.64	-
MR(12)	-	1.75	-	0.08
SN(09)	1.11	2.56	-	0.33
Average	1.04	1.54	0.31	0.13
Resonance				
CS (07)	1.00	0.29	-	0.57
SC(07)	-	0.07	-	0.29
SD(12)	1.25	2.08	-	0.14
Average	0.75	0.81	0.00	0.33
Control				
WK(13)	2.27	0.77	-	0.28
AH (13)	-	1.00	-	2.62
KG(12)	1.25	4.33	1.33	0.23
LP(13)	0.54	0.92	-	0.08
JR(12)	0.58	0.42	-	0.25
Average	0.93	1.49	0.27	0.69

" Alcohol (average drinks/day), caffeine (average cups/day), smoking (average cigarettes/day), and heavy voice use (average hours/day). Number of days that subjects filled out logs indicated in parentheses.

Overall effect of therapy

The first question was whether therapy produced any benefit, as compared with the control condition. There was some evidence that it did. The raw data are displayed in Tables 2-4. Because initial severity distributions were unequal across the groups, the data were evaluated non-parametrically. For each subject, a " + " score was used to indicate a numeric improvement in the phonatory effort measure, in the auditory-perceptual rating of voice, and in the visual-perceptual rating of the larynx, from baseline to the 2-week follow-up. Tables 2-4 show these " + " values, as well as the proportion of therapy and control subjects who improved on each measure. The same proportions are indicated graphically in Fig I.

TABLE 2. EFFORT MEASURES•

Group/Subject	Baseline	Two-week measures	Four-week measures
Confidential			
MS	100	100	100
BB	100	50 +	75 +
JO	140	80 +	45 +
MR	110	100 +	100 +
SN	125	120 +	163
Average	115	90 (P = 0.80)	97 (P =0.60)
Resonance			
CS	125	90 +	75 +
SC	200	125 +	115 +
SD	100	100	100
Average	142	105 (P = 0.67)	97 (P = 0.67)
Combined Therapy group averages		96 (P = 0.75)	97 (P = 0.63)
Control			
WK	100	200	
AH	100	200	
KG	125	150	
LP	150	100 +	
JR	100	100	
Average	115	150 (P = 0.20)	

•*Plus sign indicates improvement relative to baseline; P refers to proportion improved.*

Figure 1 shows that on all measures (effort, auditory-perceptual, and visual), a greater proportion of therapy subjects improved over the initial 2- week period, as compared with control subjects. Further inspection of Tables 2-4 shows that 3 of 8 subjects in the therapy groups improved on all three measures, as compared with 0-5 control subjects. Statistical analyses indicated that these results exceeded chance levels for the combined therapy groups ($z = 2.14$, $p = 0.016$), but not for the control group ($z = .85$, $p = 0.198$). At this level, the results provided evidence of a specific benefit from therapy, beyond benefits that may be obtained by simply observing general voice "conservation" practices (avoidance of alcohol, caffeine, smoke, and heavy voice use).

Returning to the raw data for a moment, it is noteworthy that control subjects appeared to deteriorate markedly in phonatory effort over the initial 2-week period. This finding points to the possibility that, sometimes, symptoms of laryngeal nodules may be degenerative without treatment.

TABLE 3. AUDITORY-PERCEPTUAL RATING•

Group/Subject	Baseline	Two-week measures	Four-week measures
Confidential			
MS	2.28	2.93	100
BB	3.03	2.63 +	75 +
JO	3.00	3.75	45 +
MR	2.08	1.63 +	100 +
SN	2.48	2.95	163
Average	2.57	2.78 (P = 0.40)	97 (P =0.60)
Resonance			
CS	2.20	2.13 +	75 +
SC	4.50	3.05 +	115 +
SD	2.48	2.20 +	100
Average	3.06	2.46 (P = 1.00)	97 (P = 0.67)
Combined Therapy group averages Control	2.76	2.66 (P = 0.63)	97 (P = 0.63)
WK	3.20	2.50 +	
AH	2.05	2.88	
KG	3.33	3.33	
LP	1.20	1.60	
JR	1.27	1.50	
Average	2.21	2.36 (P = 0.20)	

•Plus indicate improvement relative to baseline; P refers to proportion improved.

Effect of therapy type versus compliance

The second question of interest considered the role of therapy type and of compliance (extraclinical utilization of the therapy technique following therapy discontinuation) in predicting the likelihood of relatively longer-term improvements with therapy. The relevant raw data are again displayed in Tables 2-4, and also in Table 5.

TABLE 4. VISUAL-PERCEPTUAL MEASURES•

Group/Subject	Baseline	Two-week measures	Four-week measures
Confidential			
MS	1.63	1.43 +	1.88
BB	2.50	2.18 +	2.43 +
JO	2.23	2.13 +	1.88 +
MR	1.75	1.25 +	1.88
SN	1.50	1.50	2.08
Average	1.92	1.70 (P = 0.80)	2.03 (P = 0.40)
Resonance			
CS	2.25	3.58	2.78
SC	3.63	2.45 +	2.25 +
SD	3.00	2.50 +	2.63 +
Average	2.96	2.84 (P = 0.67)	2.55 (P = 0.67)
Combined Therapy group averages	2.31	2.13 (P = 0.75)	2.23 (P = 0.50)
Control			
WK	2.38	2.33 +	
AH	2.00	2.13	
KG	4.13	4.13	
LP	2.93	2.88 +	
JR	2.33	1.63 +	
Average	2.75	2.62 (P = 0.60)	

•Plus indicate improvement relative to baseline; P refers to proportion improved.

Statistical analyses involved three sets of association tests, one set for phonatory effort measures, one for auditory-perceptual measures, and one for visual-perceptual measures. Each set separately assessed the degree of association between therapy type and the likelihood of an improvement from baseline to 4-week testing for the measure of interest, and between compliance scores and the likelihood of an improvement for the same measures.

For all three measures, there was no identifiable relation between the type of therapy that was administered and the likelihood of benefiting from therapy (x^2 [I] = 0.850 for effort and also for auditory-perceptual measures, and x^2 [I] = 0.533, p = 0.465 for visual-perceptual measures). In contrast, there was evidence of a relation between *compliance* scores and the likelihood of a benefit from therapy, for phonatory effort and auditory-perceptual measures.

Subjects who reported at least some continued use of the therapy technique following therapy termination were more likely to improve in effort and auditory-perceptual measures relative to baseline, as compared with subjects who did not (x^2 [I] = 4,444, p 0.035 for both measures[3]).

In fact, for seven of eight subjects, the compliance score (0,1) corresponded to the improvement score (0.1) for both of these measures. A similar trend was noted for the visual-perceptual measure, but a relation to compliance scores was not confirmed statistically (x^2 [I] = 2.667, p = 0.102; Fisher exact p = 0.429, two-tailed*)*.

Based on these results, compliance scores appeared to partially predict the likelihood of longer-term improvements in phonatory effort and in auditory-perceptual ratings with therapy, but therapy type did not. A relation between compliance scores and visual-perceptual measures of the larynx was not supported statistically.

Factors that may have affected compliance

Table 6 shows individual subjects' responses to questions about therapy, when therapy was terminated. As noted in this table, subjects' responses tended to be skewed in a positive direction, as is often the case for questionnaire data of this type. Table 6 also displays the correlations between subjects' responses about therapy and compliance scores, already indicated in Table 5. At numeric level, the strongest corre-

---

[3] Because each of the cells in the analysis was comprised of four observations, as compared with the five observations usually preferred for x^2 tests, Fisher exact tests were conducted as a follow-up. These tests confirmed marginal significance for both effort and auditory-perceptual measures, p = 0.107, for two-tailed test.

lations were obtained for the questions about how interesting therapy was, and about how technically able subjects thought they were in producing the voice type trained (r = 0.58 and 0.52, respectively). However, even these correlations failed to strongly confirm reliable relations (p = 0.13 and 0.19). Skewed questionnaire data undoubtedly contributed to relatively small correlational values.

Discussion

The findings of the present study are preliminary and are primarily useful for planning future, larger studies. At 2-week follow-up testing, there was some evidence of a specific benefit from therapy, beyond effects attributable to general voice hygiene practices, when pre- and post-experiment measures for therapy subjects were compared with those for control subjects. Beyond these results, an important finding in this study is that compliance factors appear to affect the outcome of therapy, and thus should be considered in future studies. Compliance measures (reported extraclinical utilization of the therapy technique following therapy termination) correctly predicted the relative benefit from therapy from therapy for seven of eight subjects for phonatory effort and for auditory-perceptual measures at 4-week testing.

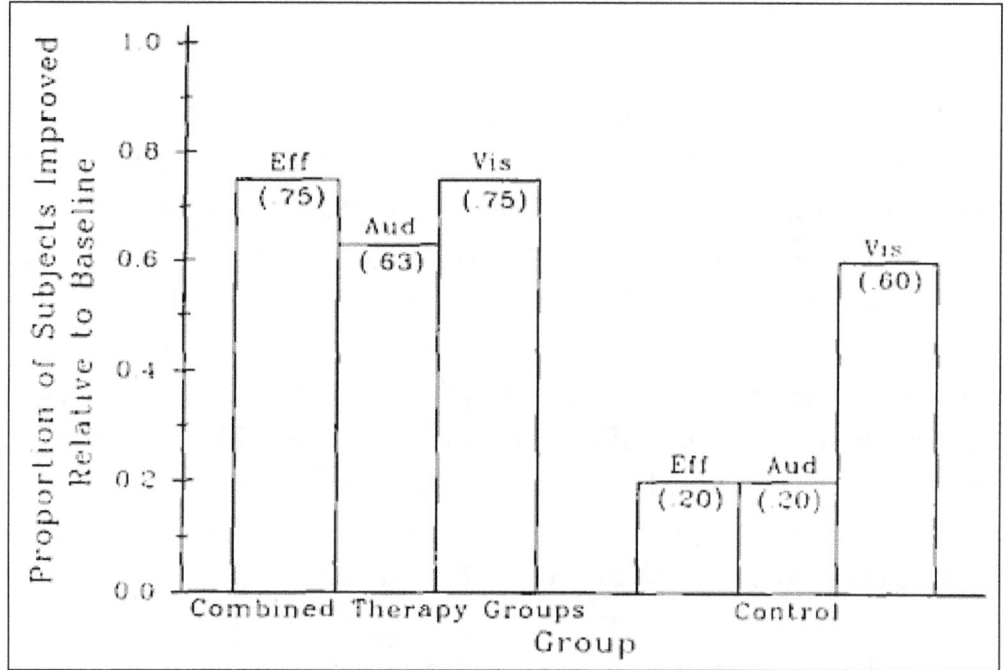

Figure 1. Proportion of therapy and control subjects improved on effort measures, auditory-perceptual ratings of voice, and visual-perceptual ratings of the larynx, from baseline to 2-week follow-up.

TABLE 5. SUBJECTS' SCORES FOR CONTINUED UTILIZATION OF TECHNIQUE FOLLOWING THERAPY TERMINATION•

Group/Subject	Score
Confidential	
MS	0
BB	1
JO	1
MR	1
SN	0
Resonance	
CS	1
SC	1
SD	1

- • 0 = *early reported discontinuation*: 1 = *reported continued*

(A similar trend was not confirmed statistically for visual-perceptual measures of the larynx). In contrast, there was little evidence that either confidential voice therapy or resonant voice therapy produced a greater likelihood of a benefit for any measure. Stated differently, both types of therapy examined had about the same likelihood of producing improvements, provided that subjects actually applied the therapy method outside of the clinic.

Further considering the findings for compliance, a secondary, post hoc question considered which factors may affect compliance, as estimated by subjects' reports. The only factors that appeared even weakly relevant were (a) subjects' perceptions about how interesting therapy was, and (b) subjects' perceptions about their technical ability to actually produce the type of voicing that was trained.

The trend for this second factor is consistent with the suggestion that "self-efficacy" may affect compliance with health-care regimens in general (20). However, the relations of both factors to compliance scores were relatively small ones, not confirmed statistically in the present study.

Having summarized the results in this way, a series of considerations emerged that should be useful in planning future studies. First, it is obvious that therapy needs to be administered to a larger subject number, over a longer time period, to evaluate therapy effects more fairly. The use of actual clinical patients (as opposed to recruited subjects for pay) may also affect the results [see Nisbett and Wilson (24) for a discussion of payment and its effects on attitudes and behaviors].

Second, future larger studies should evaluate the magnitude of therapy effects (using continuous variables) and not only their likelihood (using dichotomous variables) as in this study. Magnitudes were not considered the appropriate level of analysis for the present study, but would be in future large studies.

Third, our attempt to establish an equal distribution of severities across the experimental groups was a good one. The failure of this attempt (due to subject drop-out and data losses) forced the use of low-power, nonparametric statistics in evaluating the data. Future studies should ensure equal intergroup severity distributions which, not incidentally, should be more easily obtained with large subject numbers.

Fourth, if compliance is a focus in future studies, finer-grained scaling methods should be used and an attempt might be made to verify subject-reported compliance levels. If questionnaires are used to evaluate factors possibly affecting compliance, the problem of questionnaire data-skewing should be considered.

Fifth, a series of other experimental design factors were considered positive and should be retained in future studies. These factors included some of those mentioned in the introduction; an a priori description of therapy, pre-experimental training of therapists, the use of more than one therapist to control for therapist effects, the attempt to control for subject severity levels across experimental groups, and the attempt to control for extraclinical behaviors (smoking, yelling, alcohol, caffeine) that might affect the outcome of treatment. In fact, the impact of these general voice hygiene practices might also be specifically evaluated.

TABLE 6. SUBJECTS' RESPONSES TO QUESTIONNAIRE REGARDING PERCEPTIONS ABOUT THERAPY●

Group/Subject	Overall improvement	Like therapy	Voice Easier	Voice Clearer	Accept Voice Type	Can be yourself	Therapy fun	Therapy interesting	Able to use technique	Willing to use technique	Predicted future use	Recommended therapy to a friend
Confidential												
MS	5	4	5	4	4	4	4	4	3	4	4	4
BB	4	4	4	3	4	3	5	5	3	3	3	5
JO	5	5	4	4	4	5	4	5	5	5	4	5
M	3	5	4	4	3	2	4	4	3	3	4	4
R	3	4	3	4	3	3	3	4	3	4	3	5
SN												
Average	4.0	4.4	4.0	3.8	3.6	3.4	4.0	4.4	3.4	3.8	3.6	4.6
Resonance												
CS	4	4	4	4	4	3	3	4	4	3	3	4
SC	4	4	4.5	4	3	4	3	5	4	4	3	5
SD	4	5	5	4	4	4	5	5	4	5	5	5
Average	4.0	4.3	4.5	4.0	3.7	3.7	3.7	4.7	4.0	4.0	3.7	4.7
r	0.00	0.45	0.22	-	0.15	0.00	0.28	0.58	0.52	-	0.10	0.15
p	1.00	0.27	0.60	0.22 0.60	0.72	1.00	0.51	0.13	0.19	0.09 0.83	0.81	0.72

●Plus indicate improvement relative to baseline; P refers to proportion improved.

A final comment is that in this experiment, we compared confidential and resonant voice therapy as if they were *alternative* approaches to the behavioral treatment of laryngeal nodules. In actual clinical practice, some clinicians consider the approaches complementary, with confidential voice used in early therapy stages under the assumption that it promotes a rapid reduction in lesions, and resonant therapy (or similar therapy types) used in later stages, to enhance voice output while protecting from further injury. A related point is that in the "real" clinical world, therapy type is dictated not only by diagnostic category, but also by the characteristics of the patient in question and by the clinician's preferences and skills in one technique or another. Future studies could consider these issues and investigate them systematically.

Appendix

Questionnaire for therapy subjects regarding their perceptions of therapy

Circle number of your choice

1.	How much do you think that your recent voice therapy *improved* your voice, overall?				
	1 Not at all	2 Very little	3 Somewhat	4 Quite a bit	5 A lot
2.	How much did you *like* the therapy approach that was used?				
	1 Not at all	2 Very little	3 Somewhat	4 Quite a bit	5 A lot
3.	To what extent did therapy make your voice *easier*?				
	1 Not at all	2 Very little	3 Somewhat	4 Quite a bit	5 A lot
4.	To what extent did therapy make your voice *clearer*?				
	1 Not at all	2 Very little	3 Somewhat	4 Quite a bit	5 A lot
5.	To what extent do you *accept* the type of voice use that was trained in therapy?				
	1 Not at all	2 Very little	3 Somewhat	4 Quite a bit	5 A lot
6.	To what extent do you feel you can be *yourself*, using your voice the way you learned to use it in voice therapy?				
	1 Not at all	2 Very little	3 Somewhat	4 Quite a bit	5 A lot
7.	How much *fun* was voice therapy for you?				
	1 Not at all	2 Very little	3 Somewhat	4 Quite a bit	5 A lot
8.	How *interesting* was therapy for you?				
	1 Not at all	2 Very little	3 Somewhat	4 Quite a bit	5 A lot
9.	To what extent are you *technically* able to use the technique trained in therapy, in "real life" situations?				
	1 Not at all	2 Very little	3 Somewhat	4 Quite a bit	5 A lot
10.	To what extent are you *willing* to use the technique trained in therapy in "real life: situations?				

	1	2	3	4	5
	Not at all	Very little	Somewhat	Quite a bit	A lot
11.	To what extent do you think you will use the technique trained in therapy in "real life" situations in the future?				
	1	2	3	4	5
	Not at all	Very little	Somewhat	Quite a bit	A lot
12.	To what degree would you recommend this type of therapy to a friend who is having voice problems?				
	1	2	3	4	5
	Not at all	Very little	Somewhat	Quite a bit	A lot

Acknowledgment: This work was partially supported by University of Iowa Junior Faculty Seed Grant G98 to authors KVM and MKB, and by Grant No. P60 DC 00976 from the National Institute on Deafness and Other Communication Disorders. The authors also acknowledge Sharon Lindsey, Kay Klein, Mark Peters, and Robin Michel for technical support, and Kevin Spratt and Hani Samawi for statistical consultations.

References

1. Kotby MN, El-Sady SR, Basiouny SE, Abou-Rass YA, Hegazi MA. 'Efficacy of the accent method of voice therapy.' *J Voice* 1991;5:316-20.

2. Lancer M, Syder D, Jones AS, Le Boutillier A. 'The outcome of different management patterns for vocal cord nodules.' *J Laryngol Otol* 1988;102:423-7.

3. Murry T, Woodson GE. 'A comparison of three methods for the management of vocal fold nodules.' *J Voice* 1992;6:271-6.

4. Verdolini K. 'Voice therapy and its effectiveness: overview of newsletter and special challenges in formal research.' *American Speech-Language-Hearing Special Interest Divisions Newsletter: Voice and Voice disorders.* 1993;3:1-4.

5. Colton RH, Casper JK. *Understanding voice problems: a physiological perspective for diagnosis and treatment.* Baltimore: Williams & Wilkins, 1990.

6. Casper JK, Colton RH, Woo P, Brewer D. *Investigation of selected voice therapy techniques.* An amalgamation of two papers presented at the 18th and 19th Symposia: Care of the Professional Voice, Philadelphia, PA, 1989-90.

7. Cooper M. *Modern techniques of vocal rehabilitation.* Springfield, IL: Charles C. Thomas, 1973.

8. Lessac A. *The use and training of the human voice: a practical approach to speech and voice dynamics.* New York: Drama Book Publishers, 1967.

9. Raphael BN, Scherer RC. 'Voice modifications of stage actors: acoustic analyses.' *J Voice* 1987;1:83-7.

10. Gauffin J, Sundberg J. 'Spectral correlates of glottal voice source waveform characteristics.' *J Speech Hear Res* 1989; 32:556-65.

11. Titze IR, Sundberg J. 'Vocal intensity in speakers and singers.' *J Acoust Soc Am* 1992;92:2936-46.

12. Peterson KL, Verdolini-Marston K, Barkmeier J, Hoffman H. 'Comparison of aerodynamic and electroglottographic parameters in evaluating clinically relevant voicing patterns.' *Ann Otol Rhinol Otolaryngol* 1994 (in press).

13. Verdolini K, Druker DG, Palmer PM, Samawi H. 'Physiological study of "resonant voice."' *J Speech Hear Res 1994*; in press.

14. Jiang JJ, Titze IR. 'Measurement of vocal fold intraglottal pressure and impact stress.' *J Voice* 1994;8:145-56.

15. Nissen M J, Bullemer P. 'Attentional requirements of learning: evidence from performance measures.' *Cogn Psychol* 1987;19:1-32.

16. Verdolini-Marston K, Balota DA. 'The role of elaborative and perceptual integrative processes in perceptual-motor performance.' *J Exp Psychol Learn Mere Cogn* 1994;20: 739-49.

17. Schneider W, Fisk AD. 'Concurrent automatic and controlled visual search: Can processing occur without resource cost?' *J Exp Psychol Learn Mem Cogn* 1982;8:261-78.

18. Schmidt RA. *Motor control and learning: a behavioral emphasis.* Champaign, IL: Human Kinetics Publishers, 1988.

19. Bandura A. 'Self-efficacy: toward a unifying theory of behavioral change.' *Psychol Rev* 1977;84:191-215.

20. Poll IB, De Nour AK. 'Locus of control and adjustment to chronic haemodialysis.' *Psychol Med* 1980;10:153-7.

21. Verdolini-Marston K, Sandage M, Titze IR. 'Effect of hydration treatments on laryngeal nodules and polyps and related voice measures.' *J Voice* 1994;8:30-47.

22. Colton RH, Brown WS. *Some relationships between vocal effort and intra-oral air pressure.* Paper presented at the 84th meeting of the Acoustical Society of America, Miami, FL, November, 1972.

23. Wright HN, Colton RH. *Some parameters of autophonic level.* Paper presented at the American Speech and Hearing Association Convention, November, 1972.

24. Nisbett RE, Wilson TD. 'Telling more than we can know: verbal reports on mental processes.' *Psychol Rev* 1977;84:231-59.
    Accepted November 9, 1993

Address correspondence and reprint requests to Dr. Katherine Verdolini-Marston, SHC 121-D, The University of Iowa, Iowa City, IA 52242, U.S.A.

An earlier version of this work was presented at the Twenty-First Symposium: Care of the Professional Voice, Philadelphia, June 1992.

Laryngeal Adduction in Resonant Voice

This peer-reviewed article was originally published in the Journal of Voice. 1998. Vol. 12, No. 3, pp 315-327. Permission to reprint has been graciously granted by the Voice Foundation.

*Katherine Verdolini, †‡David G. Druker,
†Phyllis M. Palmer, and **Hani Samawi

*Division of Otology and Laryngology. Harvard Medical School;
*Voice and Speech Laboratory, Massachusetts Eye and Ear Infirmary;
*Communications Sciences and Disorders, MGH Institute of Health Professions;
*Voice/Speech/Swallowing Division, Beth Israel Deaconess Medical Center and Brigham and Women's Hospital, Boston, Massachusetts;
†Department of Speech Pathology and Audiology;
**Department of Preventive Medicine and Environmental Health, Biostatistics Division, The University of Iowa;
† National Center for Voice and Speech, Iowa City, Iowa;
††Office of Information Resources, University of Utah Hospitals and Clinics, Salt Lake City, Utah, U.S.A.

Summary: The primary question in this study was whether subjects with nodules and subjects with healthy larynges would produce "resonant voice" with a similar laryngeal configuration. A second question regarded whether the electroglottographic closed quotient (EGG CQ) could be used to noninvasively distinguish resonant from other voice types. Twelve adult singers and actors served as subjects, including 6 persons with healthy larynges and 6 persons with nodules. Performers were used as an attempt to maximize token validity and stability. Subjects produced repeated tokens of resonant, pressed, normal, and breathy voice during sustained vowels. Laryngeal adduction was directly estimated using blinded, ordinal, visual-perceptual ratings based on videoscopic views of the larynx. EGG CQs were further calculated based on separate trials. The perceptual ratings indicated that subjects in both groups produced resonant voice with a barely adducted or barely abducted laryngeal configuration that was distinct from configurations for pressed and breathy (but not normal) voice. Previous literature suggests that this configuration may be relevant in many cases of voice therapy (1). Average CQs distinguished resonant from pressed voice, but inconsistently distinguished resonant from breathy voice. Further CQs were reliably different across healthy subjects and subjects with nodules. Thus, the utility of this measure to noninvasively estimate resonant voice may be limited, particularly without ongoing subject-specific calibration procedures.

Key Words: Resonant voice—Laryngeal adduction—Voice therapy Electroglottography—Closed quotient.

Previous computational work has indicated that a barely abducted, or a barely adducted, laryngeal configuration may be favorable in the treatment of voice disorders arising from a range of etiologies (1). Specifically, barely abducted vocal folds have been proposed to produce maximum "vocal economy" (Ev-max) defined as the maximized ratio between voice output (dB) and intraglottal impact stress (kPa) under constant subglottic pressure and frequency conditions. Ev-max may be conceptually relevant for many cases of voice therapy because it theoretically represents an optimum tradeoff between voice output (maximized) and intraglottal impact stress (minimized), which is a desirable objective for many patients. According to the model, the objective in therapy for hyper-adducted conditions, such as nodules, would be to train the barely ab/adducted laryngeal configuration by decreasing adduction. For conditions involving hypo-adduction, including paralysis and bowing, the objective would be to train a similar configuration by increasing adduction. Thus, the same physiological goal might be used in therapy for different patient populations.

Speculations about Ev-max are based on a combination of simulated and excised larynx data (1,2). The model has not yet been tested in human subjects because the technology for reliably measuring intra-glottal impact stress in humans is still under development (3). Awaiting that technology, we propose that the Ev model may be a reasonable one to use as a framework in some voice therapy studies for three reasons. First, other global, quantitative, theoretically and empirically based models of voice therapy are not available. Reference to an incompletely verified model provides a better rational framework for therapy investigations than no model at all. Second, by pursuing simulated and canine data, internal validity is enhanced due to a level of experimental control not possible in awake humans. Third, at least some studies conducted within the model's framework should provide evidence regarding the model's viability, thus constraining further theoretical developments.

Given these considerations, it would seem helpful to identify voicing patterns that may involve a barely abducted or barely adducted laryngeal configuration, and then to study the effect of their training in controlled clinical trials. Two voice types possibly involving this target configuration, "flow phonation" and "resonant voice," have been previously described in the literature. Flow phonation has been formally defined as "that type of phonation that has the highest possible glottogram amplitude that can be combined with a complete glottal closure" (4, p. 559). Inspection of inverse-filtered waveforms for flow phonation in fact reveals a slightly positive minimum flow offset, implying barely abducted vocal folds (4, p. 558).

A second voicing pattern that may involve a barely ab/adducted laryngeal configuration is "resonant voice." This general type of phonation mode has been used in theatre and singing pedagogy for generations (5) and more recently has also been used in speech pathology (6). In the present context, resonant voice is defined as a voicing pattern involving oral vibratory sensations, particularly on the alveolar ridge and adjacent facial plates, in the context of what subjects perceive as "easy" phonation. One previous study indicated that vocally healthy, trained subjects produced resonant voice with barely abducted, or barely adducted, vocal folds, and thus a configuration within the range of those producing Ev-max (7). A preliminary efficacy study indicated some evidence of a therapeutic benefit from resonant voice for patients with nodules, presumably because adduction, and thus intraglottal impact, was reduced compared with a previous pathogenic voice pattern, while voice output intensity remained adequate for functional purposes (6).

The purpose of the present study is to further pursue the "resonant voice" phenomenon as a possible example of a voice type involving barely ab/adducted vocal folds. Specifically, two questions were asked. The first and primary question was if subjects with nodules produce resonant voice with a barely abducted (or barely adducted) laryngeal configuration at conversational pitches, as do vocally normal subjects. Laryngeal adduction was estimated using visual perceptual ratings from videoscopic views of the larynx.

The second question was whether resonant voice could be noninvasively identified using the EGG CQ. Assuming that resonant voice would indeed be produced with the barely abducted or barely adducted laryngeal configuration of interest as in a previous study (7), the identification of a noninvasive tool to detect it might be clinically useful. For both questions, pressed, normal, and breathy voice types were used as comparative voicing modes.

Methods

Subjects

Twelve adult, vocally trained singers or actors participated in the experiment as volunteers. Trained subjects were used in this study because we anticipated that they would require relatively little training to produce valid samples of the voice types to be evaluated, and that they would produce the voice types with minimal variability as compared with untrained subjects.

Subject characteristics are shown in Table 1. Subjects were divided into two groups. Six subjects, 3 males and 3 females, were vocally healthy. They denied any history of a voice disorder, their voices were judged as normal by a professor of clinical voice on the day of the experiments, and videoscopic examinations during the protocol (described later) further confirmed normal laryngeal status for these subjects. These subjects were current or former graduate students in Voice in the Department of Music at our university (N = 5 and N = 1, respectively). The average age in this subject group was 27 years (range = 22-30 yr).

The remaining six subjects, also including 3 males and 3 females, were recruited from the voice caseload in our clinic among patients with laryngeal nodules. These subjects had completed at least a portion of voice therapy, and were also trained singers (N = 5) or actors (N = 1). They complained of persisting or recurring hoarseness despite improvements made in therapy, they demonstrated some degree of hoarseness on the day of participation, and videoscopic examinations during the experiment confirmed the persistence of nodules. The average age in this subject group was 29 years (range = 20-39). Although gender and age characteristics were similar across the two groups, subjects were not specifically matched in a pairwise fashion.

In addition to age and gender, Table 1 also displays years of prior voice training, duration of prior voice therapy, and for subjects with nodules, the number of therapy sessions received and change in auditory- perceptual status of voice following therapy, based on clinical records. For this change score, a 5-point scale was used to indicate severe (5), moderately severe (4), moderate (3), and mild dysphonia (2), and normal voice (1). A unit change of "1" would indicate an improvement from any one of these scaler values to the next, less severe grade of dysphonia (for example, improvement from moderately severe to moderate).

TABLE 1. SUBJECT CHARACTERISTICS INCLUDING AGE, GENDER, YEARS OF PRIOR VOICE TRAINING, DURATION OF PRIOR VOICE THERAPY AND NUMBER OF THERAPY SESSIONS, AND UNIT CHANGE IN VOICE WITH THERAPY*

Subject	Age	Gender	Training (yr)	Therapy (mo)	# Sessions	Voice change
01 = Healthy	30	M	12	NA	NA	NA
02 = Healthy	29	F	15	NA	NA	NA
03 = Healthy	22	F	9	NA	NA	NA
04 = Healthy	23	M	6	NA	NA	NA
05 = Healthy	28	F	13	NA	NA	NA
06 = Healthy	28	M	12	NA	NA	NA
07 = Nodules	30	F	6	2.00	5	2 (S - M)
08 = Nodules	25	M	7	8.00	22	1 (Mi-N)
09 = Nodules	20	M	8	5.00	7	0 (Mi-Mi)
10 = Nodules	20	F	4	7.00	.23	3 (MS-N)
1 1 = Nodules	39	M	6	0.75	3	2 (MS-M)
12 = Nodules	38	F	8	2.00	5	2 (S - M)

†5 = S = Severe; 4 = MS = Moderately Severe; 3 = M = Moderate; 2 = Mi = Mild; 1 = N = Normal

Measures of Laryngeal Adduction

The primary, direct measure of laryngeal adduction involved an ordinal rating of adduction based on videoscopic views of the larynx during vowel production. Specifically, expert judges who were uninformed about subjects' experimental conditions and about the experimental hypotheses were shown 5-sec segments of videotaped segments of the larynx during vowel productions using pressed, resonant, normal, and breathy voice. Segments were presented without the audio channel, and multiple views were offered if the judges required them. Judges were instructed to rate each segment on an ordinal, visual-analogue scale on which - 5 indicated "extreme hypoadduction" and +5 indicated "extreme hyperadduction." Intermediate, noninteger values were allowed and encouraged. A rating of zero was to indicate a "neutral" adduction rating, or barely adducted vocal folds. Judges were told to use their own internal criteria for the ratings. Although changes in anteroposterior and supraglottic activity may accompany vocal fold changes, judges' attention was directed to the vocal folds' medial dimension. No other instructions were provided, nor were examples of the various ratings provided in this study. The segments were presented to judges blocked by subject, in randomized order within subjects. After all the segments had been presented the first time, they were presented again using new random orders within and across subjects.

Perceptual, ordinal measures of laryngeal adduction were used in this study for a combination of reasons. First, interval and ratio measures using metric (mm) scales are not yet available in live humans. Percent scores of relative intralaryngeal distances (e.g., intervocal process distance divided by length of the membranous vocal folds) were inappropriate, because these measures are made at discrete moments in time, whereas time-integrated measures were sought in the present study. Also, the precision of such relative measures is unknown and may be no different from the precision obtained with ordinal measures. Ultimately, the ordinal measures provided the integrated assessments of laryngeal adduction that were pertinent to the study questions.

Assuming that direct, perceptual measures of adduction would identify resonant voice as associated with barely ab/adducted vocal folds, a secondary, noninvasive estimate of adduction was also assessed for its potential to identify resonant voice, and the target laryngeal configuration, in clinical situations. This was the EGG CQ. The EGG signal reflects the amount of translaryngeal current passage between bilateral surface electrodes, typically during phonatory tasks. This signal is thought to be a good estimate of changes in vocal fold contact area during phonation (8,9). The CQ, derived from the EGG signal, reflects the proportion of vocal fold closed versus vocal fold open time during the glottal cycle. The CQ is anticipated to increase as glottal adduction increases, because of greater glottal resistance to subglottic pressure and thus, longer closed phases. Previous empirical studies confirm this prediction by showing a covariance of the CQ with direct, visually based measures of adduction (7,10). In the present study, the question was whether the EGG CQ would be sensitive enough to distinguish resonant voice from other voice types.

Equipment

Videoscopic images of subjects' larynges were obtained using a 90° R. Wolf 4450.47 rigid telescopic endoscope, a Karl Storz 9000 Mini Solid State CCD Video Camera, and a Bruel and Kjäer Rhino-Larynx Stroboscope light source. Type 4914. Images were later played back to judges on a large screen color television monitor, Sony Ideo Projection System KP-5000, using a Sony U-matic videocassette recorder.

A SynchroVoice Electroglottograph was used to collect EGG signals. Simultaneous audio signals were collected with an AKG C 460 B condenser microphone powered by a Symetrix SX202 Dual Mic preamplifier. Aerodynamic signals were also collected at the same time as EGG and audio signals for analysis purposes that are not further described here. All signals were recorded on a PC-108M SONY Digital Audio Tape (DAT) recorder with DC frequency response capabilities, and stored for later analysis. Signals were also monitored online using a Data 6000 digital oscilloscope. Following data collection, a Hewlett Packard 350D attenuator was used to attenuate files that were clipped during initial digitizing, but were not clipped during data collection.

Because subjects would produce constant pitches during EGG data collection, a Casio keyboard was used to provide pitches for critical experimental trials. A Wittner Taktall Piccolo metronome was used to indicate seconds elapsed for the experimental trials, which involved constant durations across all conditions.

EGG Analysis Software

After data collection was completed, EGG signals were digitized at 12.5 kHz with a 16-bit resolution Ariel DSP 32-c coprocessor board for analogue-to-digital conversion, using Hypersignal software (1989) installed in a Gateway 386 computer. As noted, the EGG signal is thought to be a good estimate of changes in vocal fold contact area during closure (8,9). By setting an appropriate criterion level, a single cycle of EGG signal can be divided into open and closed phases. The CQ is then calculated as "glottal closed phase divided by period" (9, p. 343). A locally written computer program calculated the closed quotient for each cycle (pitch period) of the EGG signal (Fig. 1). This procedure is similar to the one described by Rothenberg and Mahshie using the 35% criterion they suggest, but more complex due to the consideration of possible signal drift as discussed below.

Each utterance was analyzed as follows. The investigators first examined the signal from each utterance in its entirety using a waveform editor and identified the portion of the waveform with stable phonation. In most cases this was almost the entire duration of voicing, or 4 sec for each utterance. In such cases the program was able to analyze all cycles, which included about 300-600 successive cycles depending on the fundamental frequency (f_0). However, some utterances were contaminated by noise. In some cases, no stable phonation could be identified for analysis, or the computer program was otherwise unable to perform analyses (N = 25/144 utterances for the vowel /i/, but no cases for the vowel /a/). In other, rare cases, only a relatively small number (as few as 30) of cycles could be analyzed for a given utterance. It should be noted, however, that with one exception, for all subjects at least one token was partially or fully available for analysis for each of the four voice types produced and described later. The exception was Subject 12, for whom no token of resonant voice was analyzable for /i/.

Once the window of stable phonation was identified for analysis, the initial period of one EGG cycle was measured using cursors provided by the waveform editor. Starting and ending times of acceptable phonation and an estimate of the pitch period were entered into the program. The program then found the maximum and minimum signal levels for each cycle, and calculated the signal level at vocal fold closure on the nth cycle $s_c(n)$ as

$$S_c(n) = \min(n) + 0.35\,(\max(n) - \min(n))$$

where min(n) and max(n) are the minimum and maximum EGG signal levels during the nth cycle. Signal level at vocal fold opening $s_o(n)$ was similarly calculated as

$$s_o(n) = \min(n+1) + 0.35\,(\max(n) - \min(n+1))$$

where min(n + 1) is the minimum EGG signal level of the subsequent cycle. Cycles were assumed to begin and end with vocal fold closure. It is necessary to separately calculate the closing and opening signal levels by using the closest maximum and minimum, to compensate for low frequency components in the EGG signal. Rothenberg and Mahshie (9) discuss the causes of these components, including artifacts from movement of electrodes and the structure of the neck. Low frequency components, which appear as "DC shift" of the average signal level, were present in all the signals collected in this study. It is possible to attenuate these components by high-pass filtering the signal with a linear phase filter; the technique used here produces similar results (9).

Using $s_c(n)$ and $s_o(n)$, the program located the closing and opening times for each cycle and calculated the closed quotient as

$$CQ = \frac{\text{closed duration}}{\text{total period}} = \frac{t_o(n) - t_c(n)}{t_c(n+1) - t_c(n)}$$

Where $t_c(n)$ and $t_o(n)$ are the closing and opening times for the nth cycle, respectively. As the program proceeds through the signal it readjusts the pitch period estimate using the opening and closing times of the preceding cycle. Because subjects were instructed to maintain constant pitch during each utterance, these adjustments were small. All times were interpolated for greater accuracy. The program wrote the average closed quotient for all analyzed cycles as its output.

During data analysis, it was noted that 13 of the digitized EGG files for /i/ were clipped. However, the corresponding utterances were unclipped in their original format on the DAT tape, and were redigitized using 20 dB attenuation. This manipulation did not affect CQ estimates, which are time-based estimates that do not depend on absolute signal magnitudes.

Procedures

Data were collected in a quiet room. Subjects were seated throughout the experiment. EGG data were collected first, followed by laryngeal videoscopy. First, each subject's typical conversational f_0 was estimated because all EGG trials would be completed at the conversational pitch. These pitches were examined because they are usually the most relevant for the greatest proportion of voice therapy tasks. Constant pitches within subjects were further necessary because laryngeal configuration is known to vary with f_0 changes (see for example, Hollien, 1974), and we did not want the interpretation of EEG date to be confounded by f_0–related factors.

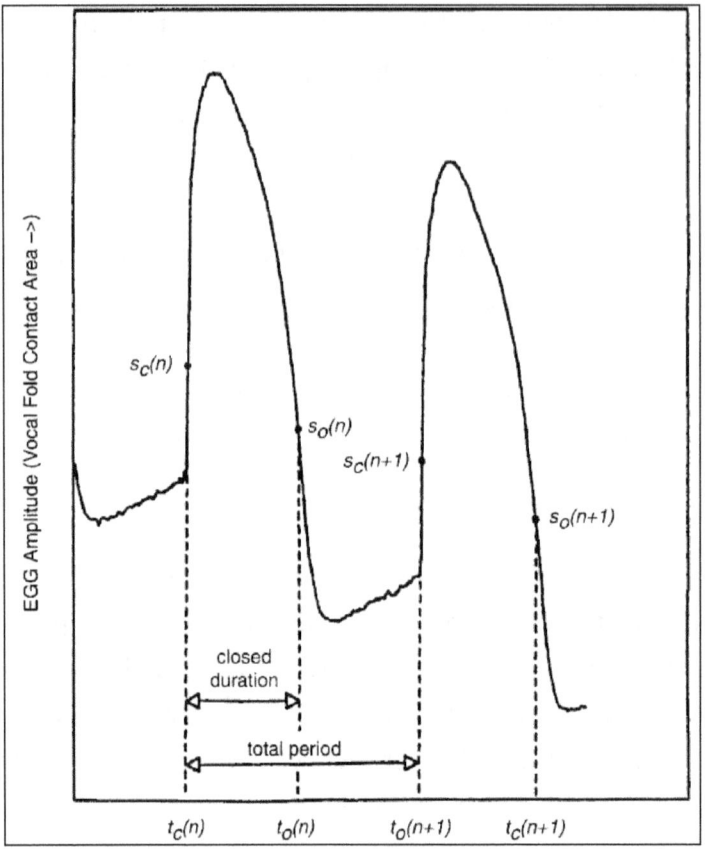

Figure 1. This figure depicts two cycles of EGG oriented with vocal fold contact area (maximum closure) up. Closing and opening events for each cycle determined by 35% criterion levels are indicated by dots and labeled by $s_o(n)$, $s_o(n)$, $s_o(n+1)$ and $s_o(n+1)$. Corresponding closing and opening times are marked on the abscissa with $t_o(n)$, $t_o(n)$, $t_o(n+1)$ and $t_o(n+1)$, respectively. The mean voltage level of the waveform descends over time due to low frequency components in the signal, but criterion levels are calculated separately for each glottal closure and opening. This yields good estimates of closed duration and total period.1974), and we did not want the interpretation of EGG data to be confounded by f_0-related factors.

To determine each subject's typical conversational pitch, the subject was asked to count out loud from 1 to 5 in a normal conversational voice, sustaining the vowel in the word "three". The f_0 for that vowel was determined from an oscilloscopic display, and the corresponding pitch was used for all subsequent EGG trials for that subject.

After the subject's conversational pitch had been determined, the subject received training for the experimental procedures. The training period was designed to be brief, to minimize fatigue before the experimental protocol. For that reason, a single vowel was chosen for training. This vowel was different from the ones used in later data collection (/i/, (a) and (u)), to avoid a differential training effect for one of those vowels. Specifically, for training, subjects were instructed to produce the vowel /o/ continuously, at the identified conversational pitch provided with a keyboard, for 4 seconds following a "Ready... now ... begin ... " statement. A metronome set at 60 beats per minute indicated the number of seconds elapsed. The subject practiced producing /o/ in this fashion using pressed, normal, resonant, and breathy voice, following demonstrations by the experimenter. Training trials were repeated until both the subject and the experimenter were satisfied that the target voice types were consistently produced. Because of the subjects' prior voice training and status as singers or actors, no more than a few training trials were required for each voice type, for any subject. Although the subjects' skilled status likely affected the speed with which they could be prepared for the experimental protocol, based on our experience the qualities of the voice types were similar to those produced by non-singer, non-actor subjects who have received sufficient prior training in the voice types in voice therapy or elsewhere.

Specific verbal descriptions of the voice types were somewhat challenging, and they were demonstrated rather than verbally described to each subject. Pressed voice was demonstrated as a high effort phonation mode, as if pushing with a relatively closed airway. Normal voice corresponded to a conversational voicing mode. Resonant voice was modeled as a low effort phonation mode with a "ringing" or "focused" voice quality, accompanied by oral vibratory sensations. Breathy voice was also demonstrated as a low effort phonation mode, relatively quiet, with audible air escapage during phonation.

Following training (about 10 min), subjects produced the actual experimental tokens by sustaining the vowels /a/, /i/, and /u/ in blocked fashion, with vowel order counterbalanced across subjects. Within each vowel, subjects produced 3 tokens each of pressed, normal, resonant, and breathy voice, with the order of the 12 tokens (4 voice types X 3 tokens) randomly ordered within each subject. The order of vowel by voice-type trials was indicated on a sheet of paper individually supplied to each subject. Subjects were instructed to repeat any trial that they considered an invalid example of the target voice type, and the experimenter also requested repeated tokens for trials that she considered poor exemplars. Including 3 vowels by 4 voice types by 3 repetitions, each subject produced a total of 36 tokens considered valid by the subject and the experimenter.

A speech-language pathology doctoral student with an emphasis in clinical voice science and who was uninformed about the order of the voice types provided a further, independent estimate of the tokens' validity by indicating which voice type she perceived for each token. This judge was also allowed to request repeats of any token. However, she did not reveal her judgments nor request verification regarding voice type during data collection, because she was informed about the number of intended tokens for each voice type within vowel (three). Verification procedures would have allowed her to progressively narrow down the possible voice types remaining within each vowel and thus compromise her uninformed status. Subsequent analyses revealed that there was agreement between this listener's perceptions and the subject's intended voice type on 89% of trials for /a/, with 72% and 76% agreement rates for /i/ and /u/ respectively. The agreement level may have been affected by a degradation in the acoustic signal due to the placement of a face mask used for the collection of aerodynamic data not described here. The degradation effect was apparently stronger for this judge than for the primary experimenter, who also verified trials; because the judge was seated about 5 ft from the subject, whereas the experimenter was seated within about 1 ft. All tokens were retained for statistical analyses; the reason is that assuming a generally valid data set, the exclusion of not fully corroborated trials would introduce a bias in favor of the experimental hypothesis, in this case a difference in CQs as a function of voice type.

Microphone signals were also recorded during EGG trials. These signals were used to provide a "chatter channel" during later data analysis to aid in identifying tokens to be analyzed. However, no acoustic analyses were performed for the tokens because of the acoustic degradation across the face mask, which has been already noted.

Following this first part of the experiment, which lasted no more than about 20 min including training and data collection, videoscopic images of subjects' larynges were obtained using a rigid endoscope during sustained /i/, produced with pressed, normal, resonant, and breathy voice in randomized order across subjects. EGG and videoscopic data were not obtained in tandem because the positioning of the face mask during EGG trials prohibited simultaneous rigid endoscopy. The vowel /i/ was used for videoscopy because this vowel facilitates a full view of the larynx during phonation.

For videoscopic trials, subjects used a consistent, comfortable conversational pitch that allowed for adequate views of the larynx. This pitch was the same used for EGG trials or within a maximum of three whole tones above or below that pitch. Slight differences between pitches for video versus EGG trials were required in some cases to obtain an adequate laryngeal view. These differences did not pose a problem for the experimental design because the point was not to directly compare video and EGG measures, but was to obtain different estimates of laryngeal adduction for the voice types examined within the conversational pitch range: a direct measure for investigatory purposes and an indirect one for potential clinical application.

Videotaping continued for each voice type produced until the examiner considered than an adequate view of the larynx had been obtained for each token, and the subject and the examiner both considered that a valid exemplar of the voice type had been produced. Again, a listener who was uninformed about the intended order of voice types (either a postdoctoral otolaryngology fellow or a speech-language pathology professor of voice disorders) further indicated on a sheet of paper the voice type that she perceived for each trial. For these trials, there was 100% agreement between the intended and perceived voice type, across the subject, the experimenter, and the listener-judge. Thus, without a face mask in place as for EGG trials, the voice types were clearly and consistently distinguished by subjects and listeners.

After the experiment was completed, four independent judges (two otolaryngologists and two speech pathologists, all with extensive experience in videoscopic imaging of the larynx) evaluated videotaped segments for each token produced under videoscopic examination. For each token, a 5-sec segment was selected as the "best view of the larynx" by a research assistant specialized in voice disorders who was uninformed about the order of the voice types and was further naive to the experimental hypotheses. The selected segments were presented in random order to the judges, without audio and with tokens blocked by subject. After all tokens had been presented once to the judges in this way, the tokens were presented again without audio in a different random order. Judges were instructed to rate each segment on a visual-analogue scale described in a previous section to indicate amount of perceived adduction. Multiple viewings were allowed, if the judges required them.

Although rigid endoscopy can affect laryngeal configuration, this possible source of distortion is probably not extremely relevant for the present investigation. First, as noted, videoscopic examinations continued until a valid exemplar of each voice type had been produced. Presumably, such exemplars required representative laryngeal physiologies for the voice types, and adduction ratings were based on these final samples. Further, the potential problem of different camera angles affecting perceived adduction was a self-limiting one within this experimental situation. If reliable differences in abduction rating were detected as a function of voice type, then effects of this type were smaller than those occurring for changes in voice type.

Statistical Analyses

Statistical analyses focused on the results for the vowel /i/, which was consistent across videoscopic and EGG tasks. For EGG, the results for /a/ were also analyzed and reported for all subjects because of the relatively good agreement rates between subjects and examiners for this vowel (89%; agreement for /i/ was only 72%). Because /u/ productions were neither recapitulated under videoendoscopy, nor were agreement scores particularly compelling (76%), the results for this vowel were inspected and reported for two randomly selected subjects.

Results

Laryngeal Adduction Ratings

Average adduction ratings are shown in Table 2, which shows that the largest ratings were obtained for pressed voice, with those ratings indicating a relative hyperadduction. Lower ratings consistent with a barely adducted or barely abducted vocal fold configuration were obtained for resonant and normal voice types. The lowest ratings, indicating laryngeal hypoadduction, were obtained for breathy voice.

Statistical analyses first involved a Cochran-Mantel-Haenszel Test of Association (11, pp. 873-874) to determine the degree of agreement between judges for the ratings. The Row Means Scores Difference from this test indicated that judges scores were associated ($p < .04$), showing good agreement. Therefore, scores from all judges could be included together in subsequent analyses. A Multivariate Analysis of Variance (MANOVA) treating each judge's score as a separate outcome, with group (healthy larynx versus nodules) as a between-subjects factor and voice type (pressed, resonant, normal, and breathy) as a within-subjects factor, was conducted to assess a possible group times voice type interaction in the results. This analysis failed to reveal any interaction ($F_{(3,184)} = 0.28$, $p < .85$), and thus a subsequent Repeated Measures Analysis of Variance (ANOVA) with group and voice type was conducted without the interaction in the equation to avoid overfitting the model. In this analysis, the main effect of group was unreliable[1] $F_{(1,187)} = .63$, $p < .44$), but the main effect of voice type was reliable ($F_{(3,187)} = 29.67$, $p < .0001$). Thus, subjects with nodules and subjects with healthy larynges showed similar effects.

TABLE 2. AVERAGE LARYNGEAL ADDUCTION RATINGS AS A FUNCTION OF VOICE TYPE, FROM VIDEOSCOPIC VIEWS, ON /I/[*]

Voice type group	Pressed	Resonant	Normal	Breathy	Average
Healthy	1.23 (1.45)	0.04 (1.04)	-0.36 (0.85)	-1.33 (1.97)	-0.10
Nodules	1.31 (1.43)	-.40 (1.36)	-0.46 (1.64)	-1.52 (1.36)	-0.27
Average	1.27	-0.18	-0.41	-1.43	-0.19

[*] +5 = extreme hyperadduction; 0 = barely adducted; -5 = extreme hypoadduction. Standard deviations indicated in parentheses.

Post-hoc comparisons with all subjects pooled indicated that the adduction ratings for all voice types reliably differed from each other ($p < .05$), except normal and resonant voice, for which ratings were equivalent.

---

[1] In this article, the term "statistically reliable" is used in place of the more common term "statistically significant." The reason is related to a point made in an editorial in Journal of Experimental Psychology (12). Reliability refers to the likelihood of replicating the results relative to the null hypothesis, given the amount of variability present in the data, whereas significance implies a conceptual importance that may or may not be present with reliable data.

TABLE 3. AVERAGE EGG CLOSED QUOTIENTS (CQ$_S$) AS A FUNCTION OF VOICE TYPE, ON /I/*

Voice type group	Pressed	Resonant	Normal	Breathy	Average
Healthy	1.23 (1.45)	0.04 (1.04)	-0.36 (0.85)	-1.33 (1.97)	-0.10
Nodules	1.31 (1.43)	-.40 (1.36)	-0.46 (1.64)	-1.52 (1.36)	-0.27
Average	1.27	-0.18	-0.41	-1.43	-0.19

*Standard deviations indicated in parentheses.

EGG Closed Quotient

Average CQs for /i/ are shown in Table 3. This table shows that for both subject groups, subjects produced the greatest CQs for pressed voice, with smaller CQs for resonant and normal voice, and the smallest CQs for breathy voice. On average, CQs for subjects with nodules were lower than CQs for laryngeally healthy subjects. This result is attributable to poorer translaryngeal electrical conductivity in subjects with nodules due to persisting glottal spaces surrounding lesions during phonation. A MANOVA treating each subject as a separate outcome, and with group (healthy larynx vs. nodules) as a between-subjects factor and voice type (pressed, resonant, normal, and breathy) as a within-subjects factor, was conducted to assess the interaction of group and voice type. An interaction was not confirmed by this analysis (Wilks' Lambda $F_{(9.58^2)}$ = 3.58, p < .19). Thus, a subsequent Repeated Measures ANOVA was performed with only group and voice type in the model. In this test, reliable main effects were obtained for both group ($F_{(1,114)}$ = 20.72, p < .0001) and voice type ($F_{(3,114)}$ = 12.75, p < .0001). Thus, although CQs were confirmed as generally smaller for subjects with nodules, the same pattern of CQs was obtained for both subject groups across the voice types. Post hoc Tukey paired comparisons confirmed reliable differences between the CQs for pressed versus all other voice types (p < .05). However, none of the other comparisons indicated reliable differences for /i/.

---

[2] This test uses adjusted degrees of freedom in order to evaluate the results against the F-distribution.

A similar pattern of results was obtained for /a/. The average findings for this vowel are shown in Table 4. Again, the greatest CQs were produced for pressed voice, smaller CQs were produced for resonant and normal voice, and the smallest CQs were produced for breathy voice. As for /i/, an initial MANOVA failed to indicate any group X voice interaction (Wilks' Lambda $F_{(9.9263)} = 0.66$, $p < .75$), and the subsequent Repeated Measures ANOVA again confirmed a reliable main effect of both group ($F_{(1.139)} = 22.64$, $p < .0001$) and voice type ($F_{(3.139)} = 10.43$, $p < .0001$). As for /i/, post-hoc Tukey paired comparisons indicated reliable differences between CQs for pressed and all other voice types, but also a distinction between breathy and resonant voice. EGG results for /u/ were inspected for two randomly selected subjects, one with a healthy larynx and one with nodules. The pattern of results was entirely consistent with those reported for /i/ and /a/ (data not shown).

Discussion

Question 1

TABLE 4. AVERAGE EGG CLOSED QUOTIENTS (CQs) AS A FUNCTION OF VOICE TYPE, FOR /A/ [*]

Voice type group	Pressed	Resonant	Normal	Breathy	Average
Healthy	0.578 (0.063)	0.547 (0.065)	0.531 (0.075)	0.453 (0.095)	0.527
Nodules	0.529 (0.054)	0.467 (0.073)	0.464 (0.046)	0.435 (0.066)	0.474
Average	0.554	0.507	0.498	0.444	0.501

[*] Standard deviations indicated in parentheses.

The primary question in this study was whether resonant voice would be produced with a similar laryngeal configuration by subjects with nodules and subjects with healthy larynges. Specifically, the question was whether resonant voice would be produced with a barely abducted or barely adducted laryngeal configuration in both groups. The data indicated that performer subjects with nodules, as well as performer subjects with healthy larynges, produced resonant voice with the anticipated barely abducted or barely adducted laryngeal posturing during rigid videoendoscopy. For both subject groups, this posture was reliably distinguished from hyperadducted ones used in pressed voice, and from hypoadducted ones used in breathy voice. Adduction for resonant voice was no different from adduction for normal voice (see [10] for similar results for pressed, normal, and breathy voice in healthy singers).

Before discussing the results, there are two important caveats. First, as noted, the present findings were obtained during rigid endoscopy. It is possible that the endoscopic procedure affected laryngeal configurations. This possibility should be explored further. In the meantime, we can say that the results obtained were based on valid tokens of the voice types examined. Thus, the configurations described in this study are certainly included in the range of configurations that may be used for the voice types.

A second caveat is that the findings were obtained in trained voice users. The generalizability of the results to other populations is not known and should be explored in further studies. In the meantime, two observations suggest that the findings might extend to other populations. First, in a previous study evaluating pressed, normal, and breathy voice types, direct adduction measures showed a similar pattern of results as reported here (10). Although those findings were also based on singers, the findings correlated well with abduction quotients (Qas; half of the prephonatory distance between the vocal folds divided by vocal fold vibrational amplitudes) for non-singer/actor subjects producing the same voice types. Thus, there is some evidence that adduction-based measures for pressed, normal, and breathy voice may be similar for singer/actor and non-singer/actor subjects. Second, and related to the first point, our clinical experience suggests that also resonant voice is usually produced with similar laryngeal configurations by singers/actors and by others, given training in this voice type. Thus, although generalization of the present results to non-singer/actor groups cannot be assumed, there are some reasons to think that the results might be generalizable.

Returning to the main points of interest, the potential clinical relevance of the present findings was indicated in the Introduction. The barely abducted, or barely adducted, laryngeal configuration used by both healthy subjects and subjects in this study to produce resonant voice may be clinically pertinent. The reason is that these configurations may subsume those used to produce maximum "vocal economy" Ev-max, under constant subglottic pressure and frequency conditions. Theoretically, Ev-max involves an optimal tradeoff between voice output intensity (maximized) and intraglottal impact stress (minimized), which, computationally, should be produced with barely abducted vocal folds (1). The barely adducted laryngeal configuration used for resonant voice appears to include the range needed for maximum vocal economy. Ev-max may be a therapeutic objective for many voice patients. For virtually all patients, output intensity needs to be strong enough for functional purposes. At the same time, intraglottal impact stress should be limited because of its probable causal relation to laryngeal trauma (13). The maximum ratio of output-to-impact stress or Ev-max represents an optimal relation between these parameters. Patients with hyperadducted disorders including nodules might be trained to reduce adduction towards the configuration producing Ev-max by using resonant voice, with potential therapeutic benefit. The notion that Ev-max, and resonant voice, may be therapeutic found some support in preliminary data indicating a benefit from resonant voice training in patients with nodules (6). On the other hand, patients with hypoadducted disorders, including bowing and paralysis, might benefit from increased adduction towards Ev-max by attempting to produce resonant voice. No data are yet available regarding the potential therapeutic benefits of this approach for glottic insufficiencies. However, our clinical experiences indicate that this may be a reasonable idea to pursue with formal studies.

The barely ab/adducted laryngeal configuration used for resonant voice may have further benefits, beyond the potential for producing Ev-max. Within this range of glottic configurations, the subglottic pressures required for vocal fold oscillation are smaller than for any other configurations, assuming constant f_0 and constant tissue viscosity conditions. This prediction is based on prior computational as well as empirical work indicating a direct reliance of phonation threshold pressure on glottal width (4,14).

Two important questions remain. First, since resonant and normal voice appear to be produced with a similar laryngeal configuration, barely abducted or barely adducted, what is the potential therapeutic utility of training resonant voice? Why not simply train normal voice? Second, if the amount of adduction is similar for resonant and for normal voice, what is the difference between these voice types? The answers to these questions are interrelated. The potential therapeutic value of resonant over normal voice partly depends on how "normal voice" is produced. For many subjects, particularly clinically hyper-adducted or hypo-adducted subjects, normal voice may not be produced with a barely ab/adducted laryngeal configuration without prior training. Clinical subjects in our study did use this configuration, perhaps as the result of training. For others, the institution of resonant voice might be therapeutic as compared with hyper- or hypo-adducted presenting conditions. Regarding the difference between resonant and normal voice, it is likely that resonant voice is often produced with subtle supraglottic adjustments not examined in this study to enhance the glottal spectrum and thus increase oral vibratory sensations. Such adjustments are in fact frequently a part of resonant voice training (5), and can boost oral output by a maximum of about 6 dB with no change in subglottic pressure or glottal resistance (15). Thus, resonant voice training might accomplish output advantages not present in normal voice without additional glottal loading.

Question 2

A second question was whether the EGG CQ might be used to noninvasively distinguish resonant voice, and thus a barely abducted or barely adducted laryngeal configuration. The answer to this question was not entirely straightforward. For both /i/ and /a/, average CQs were reliably smaller for resonant as compared with pressed voice. However, average CQs for resonant voice were not reliably different from those for breathy voice for /i/, although they were for /a/. Thus, the CQ appeared somewhat less sensitive than direct adduction measures for distinguishing resonant voice, and thus for identifying a barely abducted or barely adducted laryngeal configuration.

There is further concern that CQs were quantitatively different for healthy subjects as compared with subjects with nodules. For subjects with nodules, CQs were reliably smaller. This result is likely due to increased resistance to electrical current passage across air spaces surrounding lesions. The implication is that a specific range of CQs cannot be identified for resonant voice across all subjects. The range for every subject should be individually calibrated. Such a procedure is conceptually possible. However, it would be clinically cumbersome. It would be particularly cumbersome because recalibration would be literally required for every training session: As laryngeal conditions change across time, for example with decreased or increased nodule size, the CQs corresponding to resonant voice would be expected to change. At this point, such procedures do not seem practical for most clinical situations.

Summary

In summary, in the present study, singer and actor subjects with and without nodules consistently produced resonant voice with a barely abducted or barely adducted laryngeal configuration. This configuration may subsume a configuration with therapeutic value for patients with both hyper- as well as hypo-adducted conditions. The generalizability of the results should be assessed relative to non-singer/actor populations. The EGG CQ reliably distinguished resonant from pressed voice, but did not consistently distinguish resonant from other voice types evaluated (normal and breathy). Because of this finding, and because of distinct differences in CQs across healthy subjects and subjects with nodules, the results do not strongly support the use of the CQ as a noninvasive indicator of resonant voice or laryngeal configuration in most clinical situations unless ongoing within-subjects calibration procedures are used.

Acknowledgments: The study was supported by Grant No. P60 DC00976 and from the National Institute on Deafness K08 DC00139 and Other Communication Disorders. The authors acknowledge Dr. Linnea Peterson for her assistance with the experiment and Dr. Kenneth Moll for his comments on an earlier version of the paper.

References

1. Verdolini K, Titze IR. 'The application of laboratory formulas to clinical voice management.' Am J Speech-Lang Pathol 199;4:62-9.

2. Berry DA, Verdolini K, Chan RW, Titze IR. 'Indications of an optimum glottal width in vocal production.' J Speech Lang Hear Res (in review).

3. Hess MM, Verdolini K, Bierhals W. Mansmann U, Gross M. 'Endolaryngeal contact pressures.' J Voice 1998;12:50-67.

4. Gauffin J, Sundberg J. 'Spectral correlates of glottal voice source waveform characteristics.' Speech Hear Res 1989;32:556-650.

5. Lessac A. The use and training of the human voice: a practical approach to speech and voice dynamics. Mountain View, Calif: Mayfield Publishing; 1967.

6. Verdolini-Marston K. Burke MD, Lessac A, Glaze L, Caldwell E. 'A preliminary study on two methods of treatment for laryngeal nodules.' J Voice 1995;9:74-85.

7. Peterson KL, Verdolini-Marston K, Barkmeier JM, Hoffman HT. 'Comparison of aerodynamic and electroglouographic parameters in evaluating clinically relevant voicing patterns.' Ann Otol Rhino! Laryngol 1994;103:335-46.

8. Childers DO, Hicks DM, Moore GP, Alaska YA. 'A model for vocal fold vibratory motion, contact area, and the electroglottogram.' J Acoust Soc Am 1986;80:1309-20.

9. Rothenberg M, Mahshie JJ. 'Monitoring vocal fold abduction through vocal fold contact area.' J Speech Hear Res 1988;31:338-51.

10. Scherer R, Vail V. 'Measures of laryngeal adduction.' J Acoust Soc Am 1988;84 : (Suppl. 1):581(A).

11. SAS Institute Inc. SAS/STAT: Users guide. Version 6 4th ed. Cary, NC: SAS Institute, Inc. 1989;1:873-4.

12. Editorial. Exp Psych:General 1990;119:3-4.

13. Jiang JJ, Titze IR. 'Measurement of vocal fold intraglottal pressure and impact stress.' J Voice 1994:8:145-56.

14. Titze IR. 'The physics of small-amplitude oscillation of the vocal fold.' J Acoust Soc Am 1988;83:15361-52.

15. Titze IR. Principles of voice production. Englewood Cliffs, NJ: Prentice Hall, 1994.

Accepted for publication March 10, 1996.

Address correspondence and reprint request to Katherine Verdolini, Ph.D., CSD, MGH IHP, 101 Merrimac Street, Boston, MA 02114 U.S.A.

An earlier version of this work was presented at the 22nd Annual Symposium: Care of the Professional Voice, June 7-12, 1993: Philadelphia, Pennsylvania

A Quantitative Output-Cost Ratio in Voice Production

This peer-reviewed article was originally published in the Journal of Speech, Language and Hearing Research, Feb. 2001. Vol. 44, pp.29-37. Permission to reprint has been graciously granted by the American Speech-Language-Hearing Association (ASHA).

David A. Berry—The University of Iowa. Iowa City, IA
Katherine Verdolini—Harvard Medical School, Boston, MA
Douglas W. Montequin—The University of Iowa, Iowa City, IA
Markus M. Hess—University of Hamburg, Hamburg, Germany
Roger W. Chan, Ingo R. Titze—The University of Iowa, Iowa City, IA

A quantitative output-cost ratio (OCR) is proposed for objective use in voice production and is defined as the ratio of the acoustic output intensity to the collision intensity of the vocal folds. Measurement of the OCR is demonstrated in a laboratory experiment using 5 excised larynges and a transducer designed for use on human subjects. Data were gathered at constant fundamental frequency (150 Hz). Subglottal pressure was varied from 1.0 to 1.6 kPa, and glottal width at the vocal processes was varied from a pressed condition to a 2-mm gap. The OCR was plotted as a function of glottal width. With no vocal tract, the excised larynx experiments yielded broad maxima in the OCR curves, across all subglottal pressure conditions, at about 0.6 mm. Computer simulations indicate that sharper maxima may occur when the influence of the vocal tract is taken into account. The potential clinical utility of the OCR is discussed for treatment of a wide range of voice disorders, including those involving both hyper- and hypoadduction.

KEY WORDS: vocal folds, impact stress, intraglottal stress transducers, vocal efficiency, vocal economy

---

The general concept of an output-cost ratio (OCR) has been considered important in voice physiology for decades. As an example, glottal efficiency (Schutte, 1981) has been defined as the ratio of radiated oral acoustic output power to aerodynamic input power, the latter being mean subglottal pressure times mean flow during phonation

(Bouhuys, Mead, Proctor, D., & Stevens, 1968; Schutte 1981; van den Berg, 1956). As another example, the ratio of AC to DC flow through the glottis during phonation has also been labeled a type of vocal efficiency (Isshiki, 1981; see also Hillman, Holmberg, Perkell, Walsh, & Vaughn, 1989).

However, such measures of aerodynamic efficiency sometimes favor an effortful, pressed production, while ignoring the expense to vocal fold tissues. Clinically, it is reasonable to consider a different type of output-cost relation in phonation, where cost is considered to be the potential insult to the tissue. Within this framework, the OCR would be the amount of acoustic output obtained during phonation divided by the amount of mechanical stress inflicted upon the vocal folds. There is evidence to suggest that impact stress is an important causal factor for vocal nodules (Jiang & Titze, 1994; Titze, 1994; Titze, 1994a), lesions that are common among those who speak loudly or at high pitches (see for example, FitzHugh, Smith, & Chiong, 1958; Nagata et al., 1983). Pathological profiles of nodular tissue include obliteration of microvilli and surface desquamation of epithelial cells (Gray, Titze, & Lusk, 1987), a reduction in basal membrane adherence to the lamina propria, abnormal fibronectin accumulation, and appearance of collagen type IV within the lamina propria (Gray, 1991; Gray, Hirano & Sato, 1993; Gray, Pignatari, & Harding, 1994). Thus impact stress should be a good indicator of potential trauma.

These considerations provided the basis for a previous report that proposed the concept of "laryngeal efficiency" as an approach to output-cost relations in voice production (Verdolini & Titze, 1995). The prediction in this earlier study was that maximum economy would be obtained with barely abducted folds. This prediction was based on (a) acoustic power calculations of an inverse-filtered glottal waveform (Titze, 1994b, Chapter 9), which shows a broad maximum around an open quotient slightly greater than 0.5, and (b) impact stress data obtained from a canine hemilarynx investigation, with results averaged over nine larynges (Jiang & Titze, 1994). Although the general optimization of an OCR was demonstrated by gleaning data from several previous studies, further quantitative experimental follow-up was needed to position it for use in the clinic. Specifically, the measure (a) needed to be performed with a transducer that could be used on human subjects and (b) needed to be explored within the context of a single, cohesive investigation.

In this report, we begin to address these issues by pursuing the concept of an OCR from both a physical and mathematical perspective. Specifically, OCR is measured on excised canine larynges, utilizing a transducer that could be used with human subjects. The specific questions to be addressed were: Do data from the excised larynx experiments confirm the presence of maxima in the OCR function, and if so, for which specific glottal widths? The results should be useful for clinical estimates of glottal configurations that maximize voice output, while at the same time providing relative protection to the tissue from phonotrauma.

Definition of the Output-Cost Ratio

In this paper, the OCR is defined as the ratio of acoustic output *intensity* to the impact *intensity* of the folds (i.e., the rate at which energy per unit area is absorbed by laryngeal tissues due to collision). In a previous study (Verdolini & Titze, 1995), the ratio of acoustic output *power* to impact *stress* was investigated. Although the output-cost idea is similar in either case, most traditional efficiency and economy ratios have been defined as dimensionless quantities. Intuitively, it is appealing to compare similar physical quantities (intensity and intensity, rather than power and stress). Furthermore, when *deviations* are expected to vary across orders of magnitudes, as in this study, it is important to have a dimensionless quantity so that ratios can be reported in a common logarithmic scale as dB. When so expressed, the OCR can be computed as the subtraction of the two intensity curves.

A physical argument will now be given to demonstrate that impact stress squared, rather than stress by itself, is most directly related to impact intensity. First of all, observe that the general definition for the stored energy E in a small volume V of tissue may be expressed by the following integral:

$$E = \tfrac{1}{2} \int_V \sigma \, \varepsilon \, dV \tag{1}$$

where σ is the tissue stress and ε is the tissue strain (deformation). If we assume a linearly viscoelastic material for vocal fold tissues, then a constitutive equation will be of the form (Chan & Titze, 1999; Fung, 1993):

$$\sigma = \mu\varepsilon + \eta\dot{\varepsilon} \tag{2}$$

where μ is an elastic shear modules, η is a viscosity, and ε is the strain rate. For sinusoidal time variation, the strain can be written as:

$$\varepsilon = \varepsilon_0 e^{I\omega t} \qquad (3)$$

which results in the following equation:

$$\sigma = (\mu + i\omega y\eta)\varepsilon_0 e^{I\omega t} \qquad (4)$$

Note that ε can now be written as $\sigma/(\mu + I\omega y\eta)$ and that the impact energy is proportional to σ^2.

Acoustic intensity is measured with a sound level meter, which senses the acoustic sound pressure level P_A and references it to some nominal value of pressure P_0 (normally 20 μPa). This measure is valid because sound intensity is known to be proportional to the square of the sound pressure level, just as impact intensity was shown to be proportional to impact stress. Thus, the output-cost ratio becomes:

$$OCR = 20 \log_{10}\left[\frac{P_A}{P_0}\right] - 20 \log_{10}\left[\frac{\sigma_p}{\sigma_0}\right] \qquad (5)$$

where σ_p is the impact stress and σ_0 is some nominal value of stress. With this definition, OCR can be computed as the SPL (sound pressure level) minus ISL (impact stress level).

Method

This experiment was performed with a stress transducer, which has been used successfully to measure glottal impact stress on human subjects, as will be documented in a future report. In addition, this experiment complements a previous investigation by Jiang and Titze (1994) that utilized a transducer appropriate for a hemilarynx methodology, but not for the clinic. Indeed, one of the purposes of the present investigation was to help bridge the gap between laboratory hemilarynx experiments and experiments performed on human subjects.

Five excised canine larynges were provided by a cardiac research laboratory at the University of Iowa. Canine weights ranged between 20 and 28 kg. Animals were sacrificed for use in cardiac research, and the larynges were made available to us about an hour post-mortem.

The experimental set-up was developed previously (Durham, Scherer, Druker, & Titze, 1987). In addition, specifics pertinent to this study were described in detail in a recent report (Verdolini, Chan, Titze, Hess, & Bierhals, 1998). In brief, the larynx was mounted on a laboratory bench. A three-pronged device, coupled to a micrometer, was used to manipulate the arytenoids and thereby the intervocal process width. Another micrometer attached at the thyroid notch was used to establish vocal fold length. During phonation trials, predetermined intervocal process widths were held constant with wooden shims, the thickness of which had been confirmed with a digital caliper (Mitutoyo Digimatic).

Phonation was induced by delivering humidified, warmed air to the larynx, using an air compressor and a Concha Therm III heater-humidifier (Respiratory Care, Inc.). Subglottal pressures were measured with an open-ended manometer (Dwyer No. 1211). The vocal folds were moistened with saline (0.9%) intermittently throughout the experiment.

Trials were conducted with several intervocal process widths, including -1.0, -0.5, 0.0, 0.27, 0.5, 1.0, 1.5, 1.75, and 2.0 mm. Negative widths did not imply tissues overlap, but rather a squeezing together of the tissue relative to the 0 mm widths. Such negative widths were employed to simulate a "pressed" vocal fold configuration. Acoustic intensity and impact stress were measured for all glottal widths. Within each widths condition, subglottal pressures of 1.0, 1.2, 1.4, and 1.6 kPa were delivered to induce phonation. The target f_0 for most trials was 150 ±5 Hz.

Output intensity measures were obtained in dB using a Brüel and Kjaer 2230 sound level meter at a constant distance of 15 cm and 45 degrees azimuth. The C scale weighting was used to eliminate low-frequency room noise and artifacts below about 50 Hz. Fundamental frequency was measured using a Shure (SM48) dynamic microphone with a dual-beam oscilloscope.

During each phonation trial, impact stress measures were made at the midpoint of the membranous vocal folds. This location was identified with a digital caliper prior to data collection.

For each trial, impact stress was measured with a modified piezoelectric catheter transducer, which used a lateral window for stimulation (see Figure 1a). By itself, the transducer had a catheter diameter of 2.0 mm. which was deemed too large for intraglottal insertion. To adapt the transducer for human subjects and to effectively "thin" out the intraglottal tip, an elliptical silicone bulb was attached to the end of the catheter. The silicone bulb was liquid filled to induce traveling waves from the point of contact (the bulb) to the transducer window. To help stabilize the bulb, a palladium wire (0.2 mm diameter) was arched making a single-wire frame. Measurements and a visual representation of the transducer modification are presented in Figures 1b and 1c. As shown, the dimensions for intraglottal insertion of the modified transducer tip were 1.8 mm in the medial-lateral direction and 3.5 mm in the anterior-posterior direction. The transducer's frequency response ranged from DC to 5 kHz, and the dynamic range was 0-250 psi. Calibration was conducted using a sphygmomanometer (Nissei D-256038) and a Fluke digital multimeter. We evaluated responses between 0 – 40 mm Hg (0-5.32 kPa), and confirmed linearity within this range.

Prior to each trial, the sensor was placed and stabilized at the midpoint of the membranous vocal folds, as noted, by a three-dimensional manipulation micrometer so that the bottom 2-3 mm of the transducer tip was inserted between the folds. This positioning was chosen because further embedding would have precluded visual verification of constant sensor depth, and less embedding would have risked sensor extrusion during vocal fold oscillation.

Acoustic and impact stress signals were monitored online with a Tektronix 2212 60-MH_z digital storage oscilloscope. Output intensities were directly noted from the sound level meter during each trial and saved for later analyses. Impact stress signals were digitized at 10 kHz flowing anti-aliasing filtering and captured with a Sony PC-108M eight-channel, instrumentation cassette, digital audio tape (DAT) recorder.

Data Processing and Analysis

Signals were digitized at 10 kHz with a 12-bit CODAS/WINDAQ A/D conversion board and CODAS software. For each phonation trial, stable segments of 20 or more cycles were visually identified, which corresponded to stable phonation as auditorily perceived. Peak-to-peak values in the Ac stress signal were computed, and an average value was obtained for the segment. Sample impact stress waveforms are shown in Figure 2 for subglottal pressures of 1.0, 1.2, 1.4, and 1.6 kPa. For subglottal pressures greater than or equal to 2.0 kPa, the impact stress waveforms were similar to the "typical" impact stress waveform shown in Jiang and Titze (1994). For each trial, the OCR was calculated using the formula presented in Equation 5.

Figure 1. A schematic of the modified piezoelectric transducer used to measure impact stress.

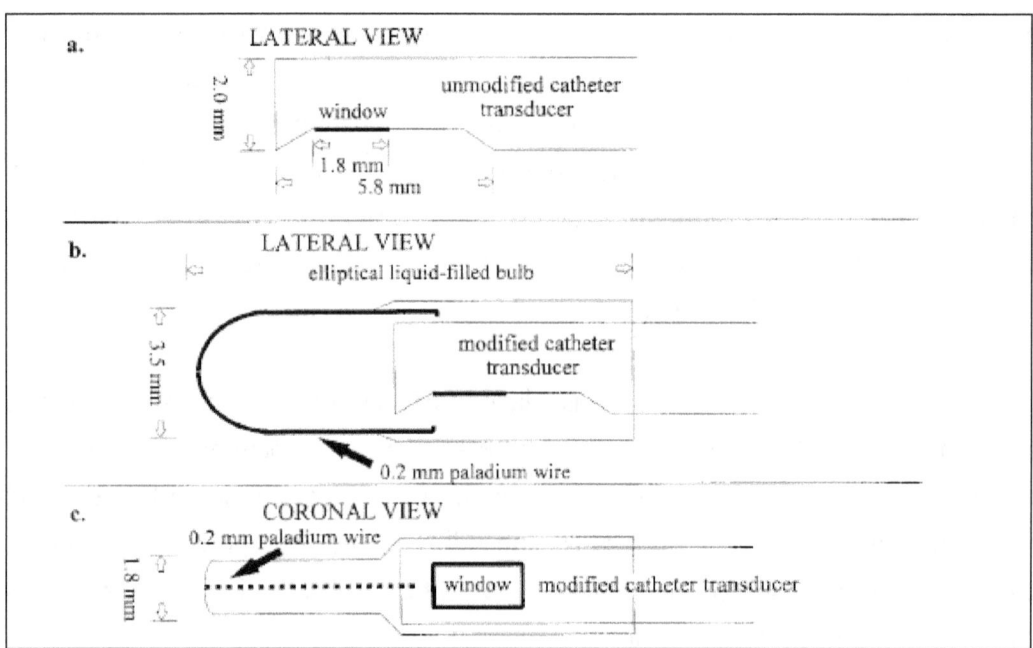

Results

Glottal Output Intensity

The average acoustic data across the five larynges are shown in Figure 3 as a function of glottal width for four distinct subglottal pressure conditions. For all conditions, maximum acoustic intensity was produced with the vocal folds separated by 0.0 – 0.27 mm at the vocal processes. Assuming the data to be linear functions of subglottal pressure, and either linear or quadratic functions of glottal width, best-fit solutions to the data are shown in Figures 3a and 3b, respectively. The R^2 values for solutions in Figure 3a and 3b were 0.86 and 0.90. Cubic functions of glottal width were also considered. Although they captured the acoustic intensity peak between 0.0 and 0.27 mm quite well, they also predicted that acoustic intensity would start to increase again for glottal widths above 1.75 mm. Consequently, the solutions were deemed to be non-physiological.

Vocal Fold Impact Stress

Average impact stress data across the five larynges are shown in Figure 4 for four distinct subglottal pressure conditions. Assuming the data to be linear functions of subglottal pressure and cubic functions of glottal width, best-fit curves are plotted. Cubic functions of glottal width are suggested by the data, as well us logically. The data show an increase in impact intensity as the glottal width approaches zero. They also show a decrease in impact stress for glottal widths above 1.5 mm. In the mid-range (glottal width of 0.5 – 1.5 mm), the impact stress remains relatively constant. A cubic function of glottal widths was needed to describe such curves. The R^2 value for the solutions shown in Figure 4 was 0.89. Solid lines are shown for solutions within the range of data collected, and dashed lines for extrapolated regions. Data values collected at non-positive glottal widths were not plotted and were not used for curve fitting, for reasons to be described in the Discussion section. For comparison, the Jiang and Titze (1994) impact stress data gathered from previous hemilarynx experiments were plotted and fit to a straight line, as shown in Figure 4.

Output-Cost Ratio

Figure 5 shows the OCR function plotted as a function of glottal width. To derive this function, impact intensity curves (referenced to an impact pressure of 1 kPa) were subtracted from acoustic intensity curves. Across all subglottal pressure conditions, the curves revealed maxima in the OCR function for intervocal process widths of approximately 0.6 mm.

Discussion

Acoustic Intensity

In Figure 3, the acoustic intensity data were essentially flat as a function of glottal widths. However, at high and low extremes in glottal width, the acoustic intensity data did tend to decrease. If interpreted as a linear function of glottal widths, the present data have a slope of -0.51 dB/mm, which is essentially flat, as shown in Figure 3a.

This interpretation is consistent with results obtained in a former excised larynx study (Titze, 1988). Although the former study did not investigate the OCR, acoustic intensity was studied as a function of glottal widths, averaged over nine excised larynges. In both studies, peaks/valleys were noted in acoustic intensity data with a peak/valley difference of approximately 3 dB. In the prior study, all nonlinear variations were interpreted as random fluctuations. In the present investigation, the data were still predominantly flat. However, it did appear that at least some of the nonlinear variations in the curves were systematic. In particular, as already noted, the acoustic intensity data did tend to decrease at both high and low extremes in glottal width, with a peak in the region of 0.0 – 0.27 mm. The behavior was best captured by a quadratic function, as shown in Figure 3b.

Figure 2. Sample impact stress waveforms generated from the pressure transducer used in the excised larynx experiment for a variety of subglottal pressure conditions.

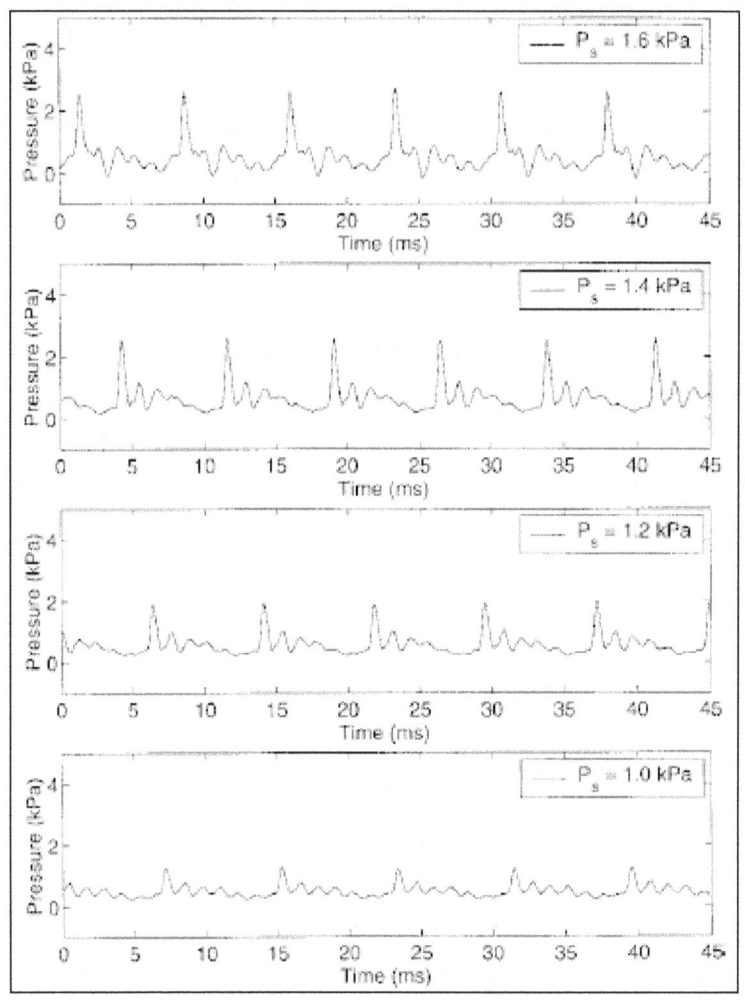

Figure 3. Glottal output power (dB SPL) as a function of glottal width (mm) for subglottal pressures of 1.0, 1.2, 1.4, and 1.6 kPa. Based on an excised larynx study, using a fundamental frequency of approximately 150 Hz. Best-fit solutions are computed as both (a) linear and (b) quadratic functions of glottal width.

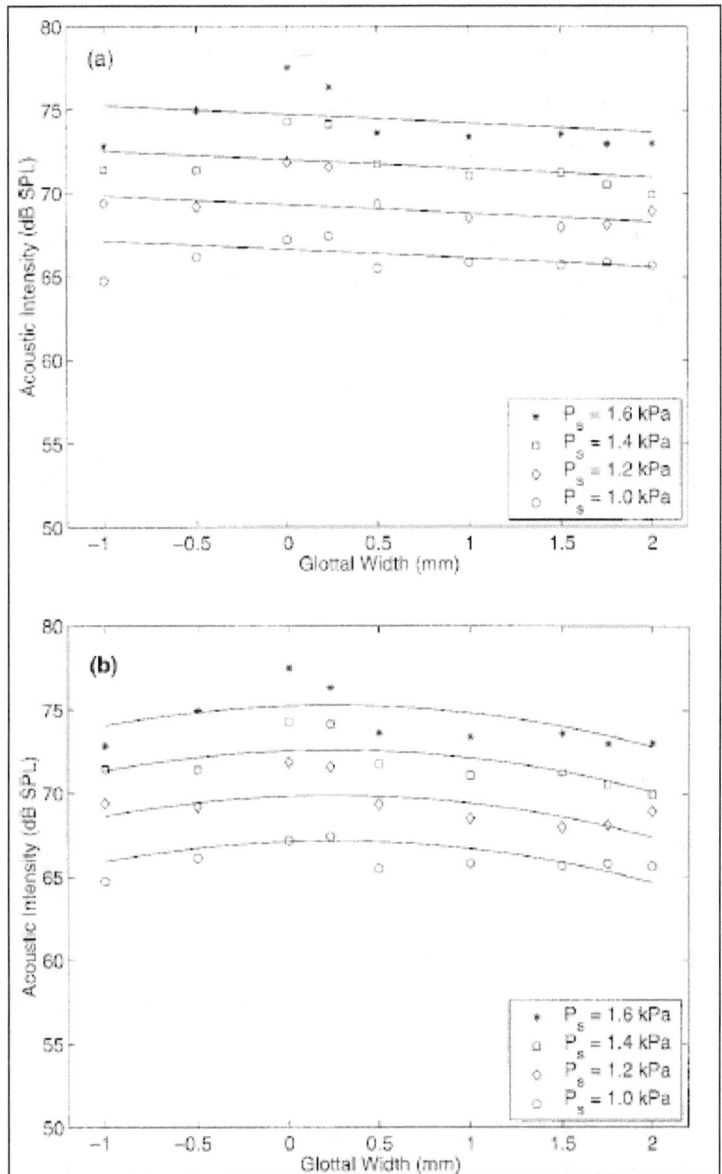

Another important question is whether the acoustic intensity data from excised canine experiments could be used to estimate human data, which include the influence of the vocal tract. Because high frequencies radiate better than low frequencies, and because larger glottal widths would generally result in less high frequency content in the acoustic waves, the radiation characteristics of the vocal tract would probably tend to favor smaller glottal widths. Indeed, this is what is suggested by our computer models of vocal fold vibration (Titze, 1984), as shown in figure 6 for three different vowel configurations. Admittedly, the effect is not as pronounced for /u/, probably because the /u/ spectrum has less high-frequency energy initially, and thus less high-frequency energy to lose as glottal closure becomes more abrupt. For the other two vowel configurations, acoustic energy did decrease substantially with increasing glottal width.

Figure 4. Vocal fold impact stress (kPa) as a function of glottal width (mm) for subglottal pressures of 1.0, 1.2, 1.4, and 1.6 kPa. Based on an excised canine larynx study, using a fundamental frequency of approximately 150 Hz.

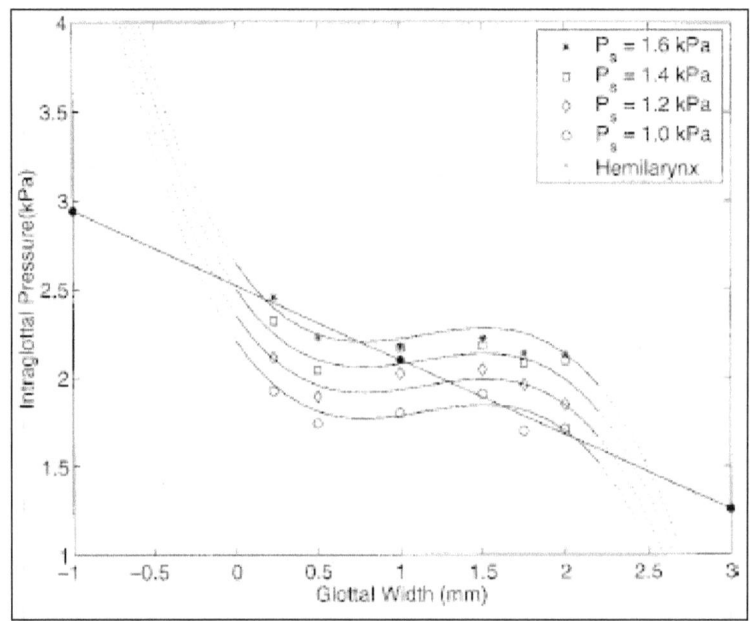

Impact Stress

The data in Figure 4 are also in general agreement with a previous study of impact stress in hemilarynges (Jiang & Titze, 1994). Both investigations reveal a general decrease in impact stress as a function of glottal width. However, it should be noted that a full comparison with the Jiang and Titze study was not possible for several reasons. First of all, the impact stresses from the former study were not reported in kPa, but in normalized, dimensionless units. This was done because of the "large variation of…peak stress(es)…across larynges" (Jiang & Titze, 1994, p. 138). Thus, a comparison of the two data sets is only possible if both undergo a similar normalization. By normalizing the Jiang and Titze data to the present study (e.g., by setting them to be approximately equal at a glottal width of 1mm), generally similar variations are observed in the two data sets. In particular, both data sets indicate that impact stress tends to decrease with increasing glottal widths.

Figure 5. OCR (relative dB) as a function of glottal width (mm), for subglottal pressures of 1.0, 1.2, 1.4, and 1.6 kPa. Based on an excised canine larynx study, using a fundamental frequency of approximately 150 Hz.

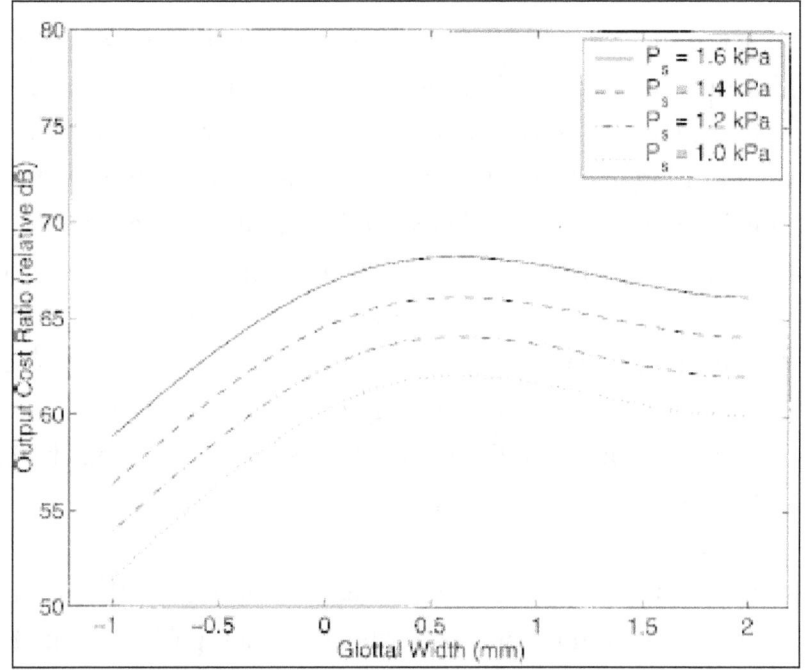

Despite global similarities, some specific differences do exist between the two data sets. For example, Jiang and Titze's (1994) data indicated a linear decrease in vocal fold impact stress with increasing glottal width, in comparison to our data which indicated a more sharp increase in impact stress as the glottal width approached zero. In fact, our data indicated that impact stress was better expressed as a cubic, not a linear, function of glottal width.

This difference was probably attributable to the density in data sampling across the two studies. Jang and Titze (1994) measured impact stress at three distinct glottal widths only (-1 mm, 1 mm, 3 mm), in comparison to our samplings at -1.0, -0.5, 0.0, 0.27, 0.5, 1.0, 1.75, and 2.0 mm. With sparse data sampling, the functional dependence of impact stress on glottal width could not be adequately determined from the Jiang and Titze investigation. However, the data from the present study suggested that a linear dependence of impact stress on glottal width was not adequate. Admittedly, the data were relatively flat between glottal widths of 0.5 and 1.5 mm glottal width. However, the impact stress clearly increased for glottal widths less than 0.5 mm, and decreased for glottal widths greater than about 1.5 mm. For this reason, a cubic dependence of impact stress on glottal width was deemed to be most appropriate.

In another sense, our study presented a limitation with respect to the Jiang and Titze (1994) investigation. Although measurement of impact stresses at negative glottal widths (pressed folds) was possible in the hemilarynx study, it was *not* possible in this study of the full larynx. Undoubtedly, this phenomenon stemmed from the most important methodological, difference between the hemilarynx and full larynx: the effective thickness of the pressure transducer. In the hemilarynx experiment, a single vocal fold vibrated against a glass plate. Because the pressure transducer was embedded in the glass plate and made flush with the face of the plate, it had an effective thickness of zero (i.e., it did not take up any glottal area). In contrast, the transducer in the full larynx had a minimum medio-lateral thickness of approximately 0.2 mm (i.e., the thickness of the palladium wire, as shown in Figure 1).

The finite thickness of the stress transducer *did* influence the resulting impact stress. In particular, this artifact became critical for non-positive glottal widths. At such glottal widths, impact stresses were often underestimated, probably because the silicone bulb was not able to properly re-inflate. Consequently, such impact stresses were discarded in the *present study*. Of course, in a *full* larynx set-up, *all* transducers would encounter problems resulting from their effective thickness. Consequently, this is a problem that cannot totally be avoided as we attempt to extend the measurement of intraglottal stress to clinical situations. However, if non-positive glottal widths could be avoided, the most significant artifact could be eliminated. In fact, because negative glottal widths would be difficult to quantify on human subjects (using endoscopy), this region would be somewhat circumvented naturally.

Figure 6. Oral acoustic intensity for (a) [a], (b) [i], and (c) [u], in dB SPL, as a function of glottal width (mm), for subglottal pressures of 1.0 (dotted lines), 1.2 (dashed-dotted lines), 1.4 (dashed lines), and 1.6 kPa (solid lines). Based on computer simulation with vocal tract, using a fundamental frequency of 150 Hz.

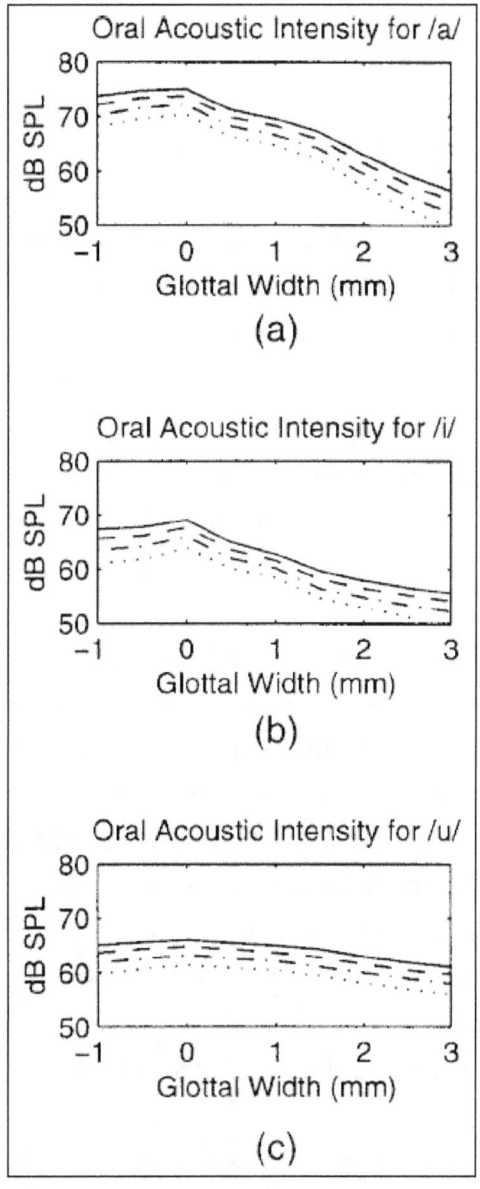

Output-Cost Ratio

As already noted, maxima were present in the OCR curves, across all subglottal pressure conditions, for glottal widths of approximately 0.6 mm. A primary point to consider with respect to extrapolations to humans is that acoustic intensity—which contributes to the numerator of the OCR—appears to be influenced by the addition of the vocal tract. Specifically, our simulation data indicate that the vocal tract should increase the prominence of the acoustic maxima. Thus, mathematically, the prominence of the OCR maxima would also increase.

Conclusions

A quantitative output-cost ratio (OCR) was introduced as a dimensionless, objective measure in voice production (acoustic output intensity divided by impact intensity). The use of this measure was illustrated in an excised larynx experiment. The experiment was performed on five excised canine larynges using a transducer that also could be utilized on human subjects. Comparison of impact stress measurements on a full larynx with previous stress measurements on a hemilarynx revealed artifacts which necessarily must be introduced in the full larynx experiment due to the finite thickness of the stress transducer. This is an artifact that must also be taken in account on human subjects, particularly for all non-positive glottal widths.

Broad OCR maxima were present in the data from the excised larynx experiments at a glottal width of approximately 0.6 mm. When the influence of the vocal tract is taken into account, sharper maxima may appear, as suggested by our computer simulations. The experiment was consistent with prior predictions that the OCR can be optimized as a function of glottal width (Verdolini & Titze, 1995): If confirmed for human subjects, the OCR could have great clinical significance. Indeed, it may be relevant not only for patients with phonatory trauma from hyperadduction, but also for patients with hypoadducted conditions such as paralysis. The barely abducted laryngeal configuration could be seen as a general target relevant for both sets of patients, as suggested in previous work (Verdolini & Titze, 1995).

Currently there are important limitations that prevent generalization of the present data to human subjects. Although excised larynx canine studies allow for greater experimental controls than possible for human subjects, the excised preparation presents some relevant differences with respect to humans. One of the most important differences is lack of innervations to the larynx. Another limitation to generalization is that, in addition to the subglottal pressure and vowel dependency of acoustic output intensity and OCR data, OCR is also frequency dependant. Some of our preliminary computations did indicate differences in the morphology of output and OCR curves when different fundamental frequencies were used (data not shown). Although the glottal widths corresponding to OCR maxima were not substantially different from those described in the present report, the full range of fundamental frequencies should be explored.

For measurement of impact stress of human subjects, several issues arise concerning placement of the stress transducer. For example, elevation of the larynx during phonation or vocal fold surface irregularities could change the transducer location, non-systematically adjusting the stress levels measured by the transducer. Also, application of local anesthesia would be necessary to help the patient tolerate transducer placement. However, the effect of anesthesia could alter the vibratory patterns of the folds, as well as mask pain sensation, possibly introducing additional phonotrauma. Many of these issues have been addressed in previous studies of endolaryngeal sensor placement (Hess, Verdolini, Bierhals, Mansmann, & Gross, 1998).

One of the purposes of the present experiment was to move the impact stress measurements in the direction of the clinic. Significantly, some data in the literature on humans are already in general agreement with the present findings. A voice type described as "resonant voice" appears to be produced with glottal configuration similar to those used to generate OCR maxima in the present study: mostly adducted or barely abducted folds (Peterson, Verdolini-Marston, Barkmeier, & Hoffman, 1994; Verdolini, Druker, Palmer & Samawi, 1998). Of note, a similar glottal configuration has been described as the "flow mode" by Gauffin and Sundberg (1989).

In summary, the data from the present investigation yielded quantitative evidence of maxima in the OCR function. These data converged with results from previous investigations. Because a transducer appropriate for human subjects was utilized in this study, these results should help bridge the gap between previous laboratory experiments and current investigations just beginning to be performed on human subjects. In view of these considerations, OCR is proposed as a quantitative output-cost ratio that may be pursued with potential clinical relevance.

Acknowledgment: This study was supported by grant numbers R29 DC03072, 1 K08 DC00139, and P60 DC00976 and from the National Institute of Deafness and Other Communication Disorders. The design for the transducers used in this experiment was produced by the late Tom McMahon of Harvard. The sensor tip was manufactured by Heinz Roesler and refined by Wolfgang Bierhals, both of the ENT Clinic of The Benjamin Franklin Medical Center, Free University of Berlin, Berlin, Germany.

References

Bouhuys, A, Mead, J., Proctor, D., & Stevens, K (1968). 'Pressure flow events during singing.' *Annals of the New York Academy of Science*, 155, 165-176;

Chan, R. W., & Titze, I. R. (1999). 'Viscoelastic shear properties of Human vocal fold mucosa: Measurement methodology and empirical results.' *Journal of the Acoustical Society of America*, *106*, 2008-2021.

Durham, P. L., Scherer, R, C., Druker, D. G., & Titze, I.R. (1987). 'Development of excised larynx procedures for studying mechanisms of phonation.' *Technical Report. VABL-I.* Voice Acoustics and Biomechanics Laboratory, Department of Speech Pathology, and Audiology, University of Iowa, Iowa City, IA.

FitzHugh, G.S., Smith, D. E., & Chiong, A. T. (1958). 'Pathology of three hundred clinically benign lesions of the vocal cords.' *Laryngoscope*, 68, 855 – 857.

Fung, Y, C. (1993). *Biomechanics, Mechanical properties of living tissues* (2nd ed., pp. 23-65, 242-320). New York: Springer.

Gauffin, J., & Sundberg, J. (1989). 'Spectral correlates of glottal voice Source waveform characteristics.' *Journal of Speech and Hearing Research*, 32, 556-565.

Gray, S. (1991). 'Basement membrane zone injury in vocal nodules.' In J. Gauffin & B. Hammarberg (Eds.), *Vocal fold physiology conference* (pp. 21-28), San Diego: Singular.

Gray, S. D., Hirano, M., & Sato, K. (1988). 'Molecular and cellular structure of vocal fold tissue.' In I. R. Titze (Ed.), *Vocal fold physiology; Frontiers in basic science* (pp. 1-**33),** San Diego: Singular.

Gray, S. D., Pignatari, S. N., & Harding, P. (1994). 'Morphologic ultrastructure of anchoring fibers in normal vocal fold basement membrane zone.' *Journal of Voice*, 8, 48-52.

Gray. S. D., Titze, I.R., & Lusk, R.P. (1987). 'Electron microscopy of hyperphonated canine vocal cords.' *Journal of Voice*, 1, 109-115.

Hess, M., Verdolini, K., Bierhals, W., Mansmann, U., & Gross, M. (1998). 'Endolaryngeal contact pressures.' *Journal of Voice*, 12, 50-67.

Hillman, R. E., Holmberg, E. R., Perkell, J. S., Wallsh, M. & Vaughn, C. (1989). 'Objective assessment of vocal hyperfunction; An experimental framework and initial results.' *Journal of Speech and Hearing Research*, 32, 373-392.

Isshiki, N. (1981). 'Vocal efficiency index.' In K. N. Stevens, & M. Hirano (Eds.), *Vocal fold physiology* (pp. 193-207), Tokyo: University of Tokyo Press.

Jiang, J. J., & Titze, I. R., (1994). 'Measurement of vocal fold intraglottal stress and impact stress.' *Journal of Voice*, 8, 132-144.

Nagata, K. Kurita, S., Yasumoto, S., Maeda, T., Kawasaki, H., & Hirano, M (1983). 'Vocal fold polyps and nodules: A 10 year review of 1156 patients.' *Aurus Nasus, Larynx* (Suppl. 10), S27-S35.

Peterson, K. L., Verdolini-Matston, K., Barkmeier, J. M., & Hoffmann, H. T. (1994). Annals *of Otology, Rhinology, and Otolaryngology*, 103, 335-346.

Schutte, H.K. (1981). 'A clinical method for estimating laryngeal. airway resistance during vowel production.' *Journal of Speech and Hearing Disorders*, 46,138-146.

Titze, I. R. (1984). 'Parameterization of glottal area, glottal flow, and vocal fold contact area.' *Journal of the Acoustical Society of America*, 75, 570-580.

Titze, I. R. (1988). 'Regulation of vocal power and efficiency .by subglottal pressure and glottal width.' In O. Fujimura (Ed.), *Vocal fold physiology: Voice production mechanisms and functions.* (pp. 227-238), New York: Raven Press.

Titze, I. R. (1994a). 'Mechanical stress in phonation.' *Journal of Voice*, 8, 99-105.

Titze, I.R. (194b). *Principles of voice production.* Englewood Cliffs, N. J.: Prentice Hall.

Van den Berg, J. W. (1956). 'Direct and indirect determination of the mean subglottic pressure.' *Folia Phonaiatrica*, 8, 1-24.

Verdolini, K., Chan. R. W., Titze, L. R. Hess, M. M., & Bierhals, W. (1998). 'Correspondence of electroglotto-graphic closed quotient, to vocal fold impact stress in excised canine larynges.' *Journal of Voice*, 12, 415-423.

Verdolini, K., Druker, D. G., D.G., Palmer, P.M., & Samawi, H. (1998). 'Laryngeal adduction in resonant voice.' *Journal of Voice*, 12, 315-327,

Verdolini, K., & Titze, I.R. (1985). 'The application of laboratory formulas to clinical voice management.' *American Journal of Speech-Language Pathology*, 4(2), 62-69.

Received February 27, 2000
Accepted May 10, 2000
DOI: 10.1044/1092-4388(2001/003)

Contact author: David A. Berry, PhD, Division of Head and Neck Surgery, UCLA School of Medicine, 31-24 Rehab. Center, Los Angeles, CA 90095-1794

Acoustic Perspectives on the Lessac Work

Acoustic Properties: The 'Ring' of Truth

Nancy Krebs

Senior Voice Instructor, Baltimore School of the Arts
Lessac Master Teacher: 2002
Year of Certification as a Lessac Voice, Speech and Body Trainer: 1993

I remember when I first entered the world of acting—as a thirteen-year-old fledgling performer. The direction that I seemed to hear most given to all the other student actors around me was 'project, I can't hear you!' This admonition was not usually aimed at me—but I wondered why some voices carried and others did not make it across the footlights (proverbial or actual). I had been blessed with natural vocal amplitude, which was either the product of an irrepressible exuberance onstage, or of being the oldest of seven children growing up in an often-cacophonous household.

However, I recognized that my volume often came at a cost. A price was paid because I wasn't sure just how I was creating full sound onstage, and so was not capable of achieving vocal consistency. A second price tag came with frequent sore throats or a strained voice when trying to sing above what I perceived was my normal range. As time went on, *bel canto* singing lessons took care of some of my issues, but even so, one thing remained certain—when it felt right—I could easily reach an audience and fill a theatre without strain.

It was really only when I discovered Arthur's work in Graduate school at the Dallas Theater Center that I began to glimpse the connection between power in the voice and ease of creating that power. The word 'projection' is rarely used in Lessac pedagogy anymore. It implies an outward direction with some measure of effort; and all of kinesensic training is designed to educate the student/actor/client to feel the voice coursing within the bones of the face and head—*moving upward* not o*utward* with a minimum of effort. As Arthur and Sue Ann Park, our senior master teacher, have always instructed: any amount of effort is too much effort!

However, the result for the audience is the same. The more intensely we (the producers of the voice) feel the vibrations that 'ring' within the bones, tuning into that inner feel—the natural outcome to those listening will be a more focused, resonant, full, rich, mature sound. As Arthur is always wont to say: "fill the theatre of your head with tone, and you will fill the theatre that you are in with sound."

Another added benefit is that when we use our recognition as to how the voice wants to function when free of adverse conditioning (i.e. straining to fill a room) by consistently being guided by the sensation of vibration moving into the bones of the face and head our voices always feel free of tension, naturally strong, resilient, and energy-filled.

Anyone who has been trained in kinesensics can share similar experiences with regard to our own voices and with those we've trained. We've all felt the strength, the power, the range and the healthy placement given to us by tonal Energy (NRG)—the concentration of vibration that enables us to possess power without pain, strength without strain. But our experiences usually have been purely anecdotal. We 'know' that tonal NRG *works* and *how* it works through our collective years of witness to those results, both for ourselves and for others—but can science support our intrinsic, gut-felt knowledge?

So, in this section, various articles are shared, written for the express purpose of giving scientific basis for some of the claims of the vocal NRGs. The first five contributions are reporting on individual studies that deal with acoustics, or the science of sound. Acoustics is a complex field of study on its own, but primarily it is a science that provides us with an objective way to measure what we hear and sense when listening to (carried by air conduction) and producing sound (ideally carried by an experience of bone conduction and guided by the sensory process). To describe this further, all vocal sounds emanated by the human voice are made up of complex sound waves, each with a different *frequency* and *amplitude*. Frequency is the number of complete vibrations per second that a sound wave creates: the higher the frequency of a sound, the higher the perceived pitch of the sound; and the lower the frequency, the lower the perceived sound in pitch. Amplitude is related to sound pressure and determines the volume of the sound. It is measured in decibels (dB). The specific relationship between the various frequencies (each with an own amplitude) of the complex sound wave determines the "carrying power" of a voice. This relationship provides a unique vocal quality, which can be objectively evaluated and subjectively appreciated.

The five contributions concerning acoustic properties posit scientifically based studies that support what those of us who self-use and teach this training have experienced anecdotally. They contain controlled experiments of how tonal and structural NRGs enable actors to create performances with all the vocal power, brilliance and warmth desired without the usual strain that Dionysian vocal exploits often incur. The subjects of these articles range from:

- dissecting how the Call assists the 'carrying power' of the voice
- how the Y-buzz creates a tonal current upon which the voice is carried
- how the structural NRG 'yawn' dynamic contributes to the 'ring' of the free and open production of concentrated strength of tone.

The sixth contribution in this section contains a position paper that takes us in a different scientific direction, although it still falls within the wider field of acoustics. It shares an exciting new development in the creation of synthesized voice, and demonstrates how Lessac kinesensic training and tono-sensory symbols are now being used to create a revolutionary, natural-sounding synthesized voice for text-to-speech (TTS) applications. I have a particular interest in this research and development, for I have been a member of the team for the company involved, by supplying training, mark-up assistance for rules creation, and voice modeling for the database. It's a brave new world!

These contributions all pique our interest, and are tantalizing, for they admit that more study needs to be done. However, it is exciting to read that more and more research is being conducted that hopefully will prove without a shadow of a doubt, what we've known in the marrow of our bones all along.

Vocal Tract Adjustments for the Projected Voice

This peer-reviewed article was originally published in the Journal of Voice. *Vol. 1, No. 1. 1987, pp. 77-82 © Raven Press, New York. Permission to reprint was graciously granted by The Voice Foundation.*

B.F. Acker
Department of Theatre, Miami University, Oxford, Ohio, U.S.A.

One of the basic demands made of the actor's voice is that of audibility. The actor should be able to project without sacrificing the intonation range needed for emotional expressiveness. Some teachers of theatre voice, in their search for ways to train projection effectively, believe that the shape of the vocal tract influences the relative loudness of a phonation. The assumption is that a vocal production made with a relatively large oral cavity and an "open throat" will be perceived as a louder sound than a vocal production made with the same subjective degree of effort, but with a small oral cavity and a "closed throat."

A closed throat vocal production, especially as noted in neophyte acting students, is associated with a raised jaw and tongue and what is presumed to be a constricted throat, as though the voice were being squeezed. An open throat vocal production is characterized by a low jaw and tongue position and a pitch-dependent size of mouth opening. The noted theatre voice teacher, Arthur Lessac (1), describes the open throat production as "a full-bodied, mature, warm tone…with brilliant ringing, penetrating, stentorian qualities." Perceptually, the unconstricted tone is considered to be characterized by a brighter more penetrating quality than a constricted production. The open throat production has been termed "ring" and its counterpart termed "constricted" as a pedagogical convenience to distinguish the perceptual differences the instructor believes obtain to the two vocal tract shapes and therefore hopes to encourage. For the purposes of this study, these terms are merely provisional descriptive labels for two different vocal tract shapes used for the projected voice.

Evidence indicates that the vocal tract shape influences the loudness of the sound for the speaker. Tanaka and Gould (2) suggest that the singer can change the shape of the vocal tract to align a harmonic near the center of the resonance frequency. This is a strategy of tuning the resonator to increase the sound pressure level (SPL) of a vowel; in such a case, the vocal tract creates a resonance effect increasing the loudness of a vowel. Isshiki (3), commenting on the influence of the size of mouth opening, maintains that the great range of intensity variation of 30 dB from conversational effort level shouting is only possible when the mouth opening is free to change. With a constant size mouth opening, the vocal intensity variation is within a much narrower range of ~ 15dB.

The speaker may have some control over the dimensions of the pharynx. Perkins (4) describes an "open" vocal production as a subjective sensation of an expanded throat as in the initiation of a yawn, in contrast to vocal constriction which is the subjective sensation of a tight or squeezed throat experienced as the initiation of a swallow. Beckett (5), in a study of the relation of subjective degree of constriction and pitch perturbation, found that subjects could reliably produce a high, medium, and low degree of vocal constriction; although whether the constriction was apparently under the speaker's control. The question is whether a resonance effect is associated with the vocal tract adjustment for sustained vowels for the actor's projected voice, and specifically, if the open throat, or ring phonation, is associated with a louder sound, and more intense phonation, as compared with the subjectively constricted phonation. Therefore, this study examined the perceptual, acoustic, and physiological features of the ring and constricted vocal production in a listening test with spectrographic evaluation, a graphic level recorder, and conventional radiography. Of two vocal productions, ring and constricted, made with the same subjective effort level, the following questions were asked: Will there be any difference in the judged loudness of the two kinds of vocal productions? Will there be any difference in the spectra or relative amplitude of the two kinds of vocal productions? Will there be any difference in the shape of the vocal tract as seen in lateral x-rays? Specifically, the x-rays are examined to determine the size of the mouth opening, the height of the soft palate, the height of the hyoid bone, the height of the vocal fold level, and the point of maximum constriction introduced by the tongue in the pharynx.

Procedures

The subject for this study was a 39-year-old woman, who had been trained by Lessac in his method of vocal projection, and who has taught theatre voice for 12 years.

The subject could produce reliable samples of /o/ with a subjective sensation of a closed throat, or constricted vocal production.

For the purposes of this study, a ring phonation is defined as the vocal tract adjustment for a projected voice described by Lessac (1). The term ring is used to describe a loud production of vowels using a lowered jaw position, lips rounded and protruded, a pitch-dependent size of lip opening, the tongue tip advanced so that it touches the back of the lower front teeth, the tongue dorsum lowered, the soft palate raised as in the initiation of a yawn, and the subjective sensation of an open throat. Furthermore, the speaker should feel strong sensation of vibrations in the oral cavity (1). A constricted vocal production, for the purposes of this study, is defined as a loud vocal production, using a raised jaw, no lip protrusion, a small lip opening, retracted tongue tip, raised tongue dorsum, lowered soft palate, and the subjective sensation of a squeezed or constricted throat. The speaker should feel little vibration in the mouth.

The stimuli for the perceptual and radiological studies were sustained phonations of the vowel /o/ in ring and constricted modes. This vowel was chosen because it is the most important vowel in the Lessac training of the projected voice. Intensity was not controlled because the two vowel productions would, presumably, be characterized by different sound pressure levels (6). The subject used a comfortable, self-selected *midrange pitch (2).*

Listening test
The perceptual study was a forced-choice listening test. The speaker produced 20 randomized samples of ring and constricted phonations for the 10 pairs of ring/constricted phonations on the listening tape. The vocal productions were made in a sound-treated booth, using a Nagra tape recorder, and a Shure model 545 D (Unidyne, dynamic omni-directional) microphone. The microphone-to-mouth distance was 30 cm.

Ten people who had graduate level training in either theatre or speech science and who reported normal hearing volunteered to serve as judges. Their ages ranged from 24 to 54 years (mean 34 years).

The judges were instructed that they would hear a speaker produce pairs of sustained phonations of the vowel /o/. They were asked to disregard vocal quality and to attend only to the loudness of the sounds. They were further instructed to select the /o/ in each pair that was louder. The judges were seated in a sound-treated booth, and listened to the tape played on a Nagra tape recorder through a Beltone earphone. The volume playback was set at the same level for all judges.

In the results of the listening test, 80% of the judges selected the ring vocal productions as the louder sound in all pairs. One judge selected the ring in 90% of the samples and another judge selected the ring in 70% of the samples.

When asked to describe the basis for their choices, the judges cited perceptual cues, which included: (a) a ringing in the ear and an accompanying sensation of strong vibration; (b) a sound that was not tight and stifled; and (c) a louder, clearer sound that was not choked.

Spectral analysis

The samples from the listening tape and those made during the radiological study were analyzed with the Interactive laboratory System software for speech analysis at The Recording and Research Center in Denver. Files of 1-s duration were created that appeared to reflect fairly steady phonation. The output from an Otari MX5050 tape recorder went to a Digital Sound Corporation (DSC) 240 amplifier, and the signal was then sent to DSC 200 analog-to-digital converter and then into the VAX 11/750 computer. The recordings were digitized at 40,000 samples/s, to insure an adequate number of samples per cycle for a relatively high pitch. The A/D converter is a 16-bit converter with a relatively high signal-to-noise ratio.

The spectra were processed with the Interactive Laboratory System software for speech analysis, using frequency limits of 0-8 kHz, and the FDI command. For each of the files, ~20 cycles of phonation were sampled. Hamming window conditioning was applied to each of the samples prior to obtaining the spectra.

Twelve ring and constricted productions were calculated to have a fundamental frequency of 272 Hz; because pitch in these cases could be discounted as a factor significantly affecting loudness, these six pairs were selected for examination. Because the wide spacing of harmonics in the female voice makes it difficult to determine the formants, only the relative amplitude of the spectra can be compared (7). The spectra for the six ring and the six constricted productions are shown in Fig. 1A and B.

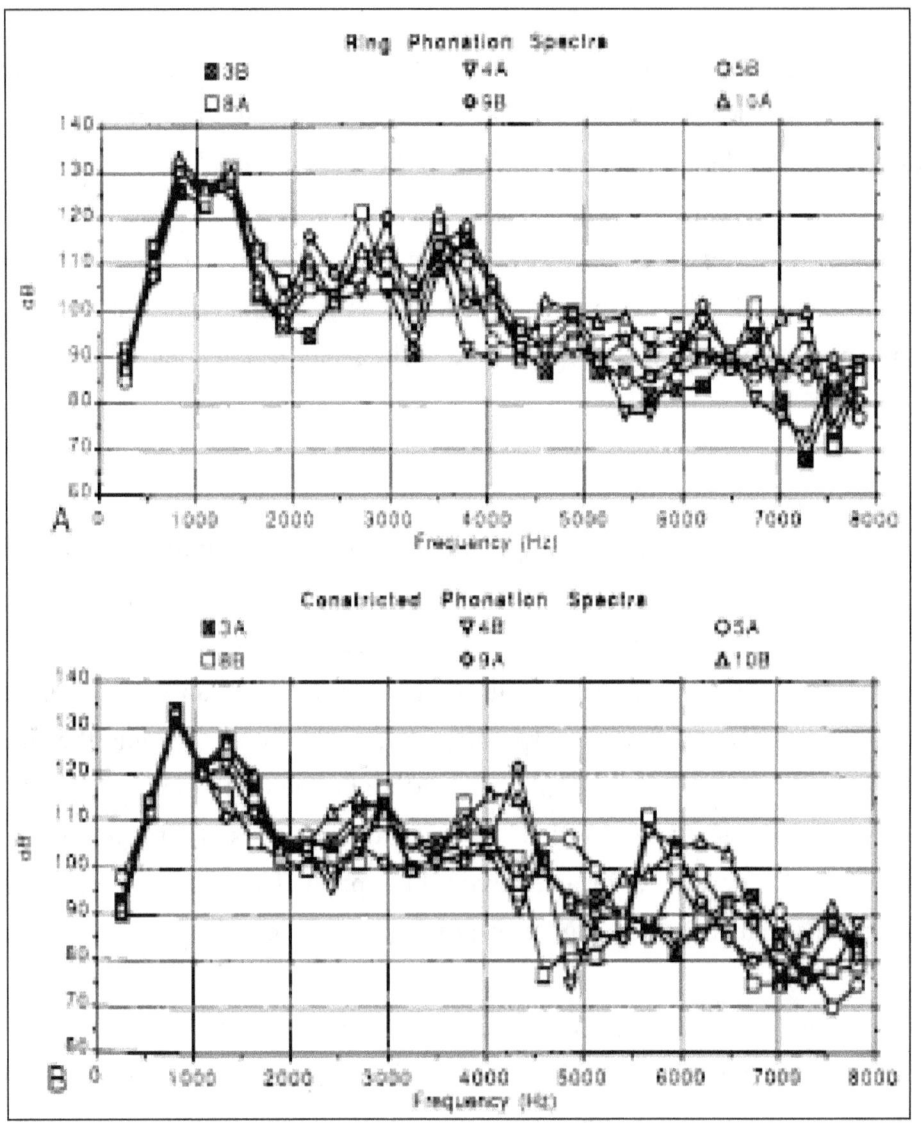

Figure 1. A: Spectra of six ring vocal production. B: Spectra of six constricted vocal productions.

The spectral envelope of the ring shows a decrease in amplitude after the fifth partial, and that of the constricted shows a decrease after the third. The mean spectra of the six rings and six constricted were calculated and are shown in Fig. 2. The first six partials are stable, replicable in both conditions and, for both conditions; the first three partials are nearly identical. For partials > 1.5 kHz, the spectral envelope varied far more unpredictably, as indicated by the vertical lines measuring the confidence intervals for each spectral peak.

Both ring and constricted conditions had a similar pattern of overall amplitude levels. The only spectral differences between ring and constricted that appeared were the higher amplitudes in the ring between 1.3 kHz and 2 kHz and at ~ 3.6 kHz.

Level recorder

To determine the relative sound pressure levels in the ring and constricted conditions, the listening tape was played through a Brüel and Kjaer type 2305 level recorder. The paper speed was 0.3 mm/s, the drive shaft speed was 12 rpm, and the writing speed was 125 mm/s. When the mean peak values of sound pressure level were compared for the two productions, the ring was 6.7 dB higher that the constricted mode. The ring productions ranged from 4.5 dB to 12 dB higher than the constricted vocal productions.

Because the phonations were not controlled for pitch, we decided to compare the relative amplitude differences for those vowels on the listening tape that were calculated in the spectra to have approximately the same pitch. For those phonations of similar pitch, the mean SPL difference between ring and constricted vocal productions was 3.8 dB, so that the judges were selecting a vowel sound of higher amplitude when they selected the ring productions.

Radiography

The x-rays were taken with a Vector model 1050 unit. The film-to-focal spot distance was 6 feet and the film-to-subject distance was ~4 inches. The generator settings were 64 kVp with mAs of 12. Two midsaggital views of the vocal tract were made while the subject produced samples of sustained /o/ in ring and constricted conditions. The subject was standing, and no headhold was used. The phonations were simultaneously recorded on a Nagra tape recorder using a Shure microphone held 30 cm.

The lines of reference for the measures were based on the protocol described by Bush (8). The three anatomical reference lines for the measures were: (a) a palatal line drawn parallel to the palate, (b) a mandibular line drawn from the midmental region to the angle of the jaw, and (c) a cervical line from the posterior point of the transverse process of the second cervical vertebra to the posterior portion of the body of the fifth cervical vertebra.

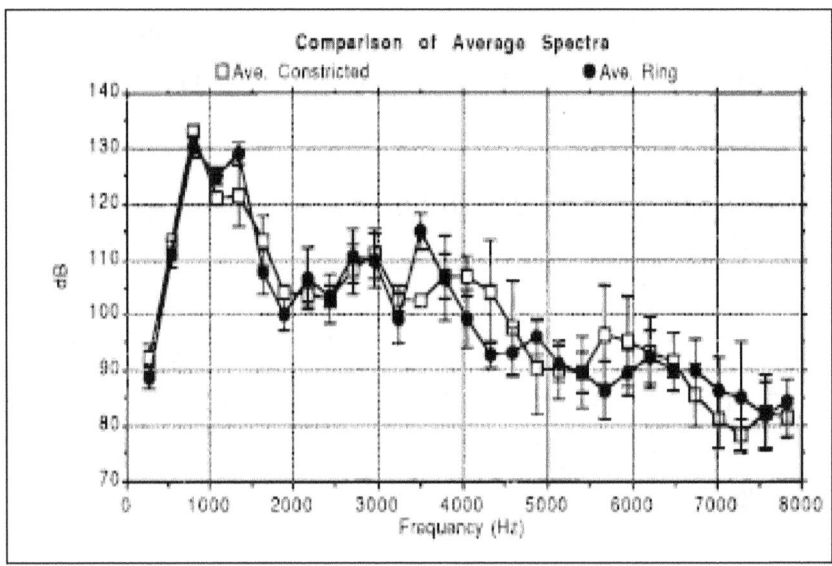

Figure 2. Mean spectra for ring and constricted with error bars.

The mouth opening was measured by determining the distance between the borders of the superior and inferior incisors. The height of the soft palate was measured by determining the highest portion of the soft palate above the line of the palatal plane. The height of the hyoid was measured along a line drawn perpendicular to the line through the mandibular plane to the superior portion of the body of the hyoid. The height of the vocal folds was measured by drawing perpendicular lines from the cervical and mandibular planes to the vocal fold level and then determined along the line from the mandibular plane. The distance of the hyoid from the level of the vocal folds was measured along the same line drawn perpendicular to the mandibular plane. The point of greatest pharyngeal constriction was measured between the pharyngeal wall or soft palate and the tongue at the point at which they were judged to be closest.

In the ring vocal production in Fig. 3A, the mouth opening was 37 mm wide as compared with the constricted vocal production in Fig. 3B, in which the mouth was open only 1 mm. The soft palate was 11 mm above the palatal plane for the ring and 8 mm for the constricted, a difference of 3 mm. The hyoid was higher for the ring, 14.6 mm, as compared with 31.2 mm in the constricted condition. The level of the vocal folds was lower in the constricted condition, measuring 44.4 mm from the mandibular plane, as compared with 34.7 mm in the ring. The distance separating the vocal folds and the hyoid bone was less in the constricted by 4.9 mm; it was 13.3 mm in the constricted and 18.1 mm in the ring. At its highest point in the ring condition, the tongue was 6.2 mm from the soft palate; in the constricted condition, it was 2.7 mm from the pharyngeal wall.

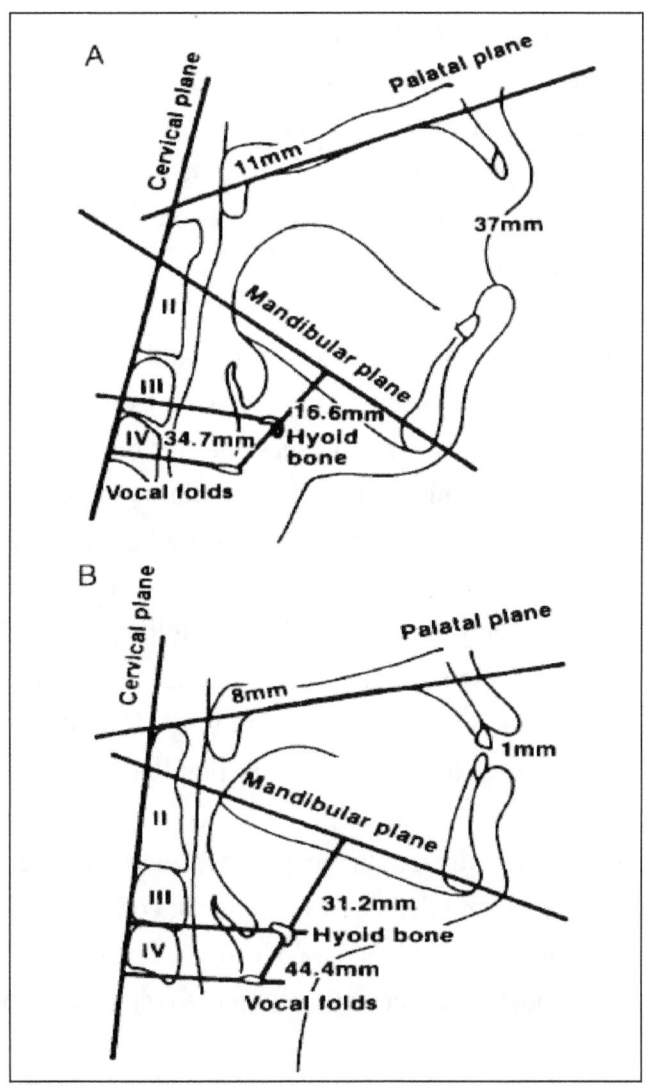

Figure. 3. A: Lateral view of ring phonation showing measurement reference lines. B: Lateral view of constricted phonation showing measurement reference lines.

In the ring condition, the larynx was higher and the tongue dorsum introduced less of a pharyngeal constriction than in the constricted phonation. There was considerable difference in jaw height and some difference in laryngeal carriage and tongue shape and consequent distance between the tongue and the wall of the pharynx.

Discussion

The judges in the listening test selected the ring phonations as louder than constricted ones, which was consistent with graphic level recorder measures, which showed the ring phonations to be of greater amplitude. Of the six pairs of ring/constricted sounds that were close enough in pitch to be able to discount a difference in pitch as a factor influencing the judgment of loudness, the mean difference in SPL was 3.8 dB, which was a moderate increase in loudness in the ring condition. Two of the judges reported physical discomfort during several of the ring phonations, which suggests that the perceptual difference was stronger than the actual difference between loudness levels in a few cases.

The spectra of the two phonations were similar, and only an increase in spectral energy of ~1.3, ~2, and ~3.6 kHz distinguished the ring from the constricted. Because these partials are in the range of maximum sensitivity for the ear, it may be possible to detect an increase of energy in this region. The similarity in spectral envelopes suggests that no appreciable difference in loudness existed between the two productions, since an increase in intensity could be expected to be accompanied by a systematic increase in high frequency energy and in total bandwidths (9, 10). Whether the slight shifts in spectral energy represents higher energy concentrated in lower frequencies, and therefore a louder sound, or if a slight change in spectral slope has sharpened the sound and is related to a change in quality is a question that should be investigated.

Radiographic measures showed that the major differences in these two conditions are oral cavity size, tongue height and degree of pharyngeal, constriction, and level of vocal folds. In ring, oral cavity size is greatly increased, (36 mm larger); this larger mouth opening perhaps increases the radiation efficiency, as Isshiki (3) suggests is possible.

The lower mandible in ring influenced the tongue shape and the distance from the back of the tongue to the pharyngeal wall. A low jaw position moves the tongue away from the pharyngeal wall, so that it no longer constricts the throat; at the same time, it creates the large mouth opening (11). The vocal tract is a more open tube in the ring. There is some evidence that lowering a jaw as much as 23 mm causes the tongue to assume an extreme shape to preserve the phonemic identity of the vowel, which in turn causes an increase in the activity of the antagonist jaw muscles (11). In the ring condition, if the same kind of antagonism exists between the tongue and jaw muscles, the presumably more active suprahyoids may raise the larynx.

In the constricted vocal production, the raised jaw and the high tongue carriage brought the back of the tongue close to the pharyngeal wall. The tongue is mechanically linked to the larynx, by the hyoid bone; therefore, as the tongue shape changes, it can alter the height of the larynx by altering the position of the hyoid. In the constricted condition, the genioglossus may contract to raise the tongue dorsum, pushing down the tongue base and hyoid, so that the carriage of the larynx is low (11, 12).

Summary

These preliminary findings are for one subject only and therefore do not allow any inferences to be made for general differences between the ring and constricted vocal tract configurations. In this one case, the training goal of an open throat was confirmed by radiography, and the associated sound production was judged louder in a listening test.

Whether any perceived difference in loudness is due to the vocal tract shape cannot be determined until the acoustic analysis is made and correlated to the physiological features. Then it may be possible to determine if an effect on resonance, such as tuning, can account for the difference in loudness or if the difference is due to the source function.

Acknowledgment: I gratefully acknowledge The Recording and Research Center of the Denver Center of the Performing Arts and Dr. Ronald C. Scherer for providing the spectral data. I wish to thank Dr. Raymond Daniloff for his help and for generously allowing the use of the facilities at the Speech laboratory at Louisiana State University for this work.

References

1. Lessac A. *The use and training of the human voice*, 2nd ed. New York: Drama Book Specialists, 1967.

2. Tanaka S, Gould W. 'Relationships between vocal intensity and noninvasively obtained aerodynamic parameters in normal subjects.' *J Acoust Soc Am* 1983;73:1316–21.

3. Isshiki N. 'Regulatory mechanism of voice intensity variation.' *J Speech Hearing Res* 1964;7:17-30.

4. Perkins WH. *Speech pathology: an applied behavioral science*. St. Louis: C. V. Mosby, 1971.

5. Beckett RL. 'Pitch perturbation as a function of subjective vocal constriction.' *Folia Phoniatr* 1969;21:416-25.

6. Colton RH. Estill JE. 'Elements of voice quality: perceptual, acoustic and physiologic aspects." In Lass N, ed. *Speech and language: advances in basic research and practice*. Vol. 5: New York: Academic Press, 1981:312–404.

7. Bloothooft G, Plomp R. 'Spectral analysis of sung vowels. II. The effect of fundamental frequency on vowel spectra.' *J Acoust Soc Am* 1985;77:1580–8.

8. Bunch MA. 'A cephalometric study of structures of the head and neck during sustained phonation of covered and open qualities.' *Folia Phonatr* 1976;28:321–8.

9. Brandt JF, Ruder KF, Shipp T. 'Vocal loudness and effort in continuous speech.' *J Acoust Soc Am* 1969;46:1543–8.

10. Glave RD, Rietveld ACM. 'Is the effort dependence of speech loudness explicable on the basis of acoustical cues?' *J Acoust Soc Am* 1975;58:875–9.

11. Lindblom BEF, Sundberg J. 'Acoustical consequences of lip, tongue, jaw, and larynx movements.' *J Acoust Soc Am* 1971; 50: 1166–70.

12. Perkell JS, Nelson WL. 'Articulatory targets and speech motor control: a study of vowel production.' In: Grillner S, Persson A, Lindblom B, Lubker J, eds. *Speech motor control*. New York: Pergamon Press, 1982:187 – 204.

Address correspondence and reprint requests to Dr. B.F. Acker, Department of Theatre, 131 Center of Performing Arts, Miami University, Oxford, OH 45056, U.S.

Voice Modification of Stage Actors: Acoustic Analyses

This peer-reviewed article was originally published in the *Journal of Voice. Vol. 1, No. 1. 1987, pp 83-87© Raven Press, New York. Permission to reprint was graciously granted by The Voice Foundation.*

*Bonnie N. Raphael and *Ronald C. Scherer*

*American Repertory Theatre, Loeb Drama Center, Cambridge, Massachusetts; and
The Denver Center for the Performing Arts, Denver, Colorado, U.S.A

Many stage actors have voices that seem to "ring," a voice quality that enables them to project effectively over crowd noise, scenery shifting, sounds of battle, background music, and other acoustic competition. Does this vocal quality have any acoustic similarities to the "ring" in the opera singer's voice? Several studies (1-5) have investigated the acoustic components in trained opera singer's voices that enable them to be heard clearly over a full orchestra. No similar investigations appear to have dealt specifically with the acoustic characteristics of trained stage actors' vocal production.

A pilot study was conducted in which acoustic analyses were made of actors' voices. Spectral comparisons were made between two types of voice production: the "call" technique as taught by Lessac (6) and a mode of phonation more like conversational speech. Any differences found between stage actors' normal conversational voice and their vocal production for stage might be helpful in the teaching of voice production to stage actors more effectively.

Lessac is a well-known teacher of voice, speech, and movement for actors. His technique of voice and speech training is best described in his text, *The Use and Training of the Human Voice (6),* a text presently being used in a number of actor training programs in this country.

"Call" is one of the techniques which the Lessac system uses to develop an easier, stronger, and more flexible stage voice. According to Lessac (6, pp. 110, 111, 114):

[G]ood call is never a strident scream or...merely a loud shout. The call is an exhilarating, resilient, resonant tone, ...a singing and completely nonthroaty sensation...that] can be achieved only by coordinating vibratory sensation...with the properly coordinated facial posture...the call is the bridge in tonal production between the conversational speaking voice and the singing voice;...the heightened vocal quality necessary for highly emotional speech....The call is always primarily governed by a specific vibratory sensation—a fully concentrated tonal feeling—designed to expand the technical and emotional ranges of the voice where the subtler qualities of vowel articulation are secondary.

Lessac's "call" technique appears to attempt to combine in a specific way the laryngeal tone and the voluntary shaping of the vocal tract, especially in regard to the amount of space between the teeth, the degree of stretch in the cheek muscles, and at the size and shape of the lip opening to enhance vocal resonance and projection. The prescribed physical sensation is quite similar to that of a relaxed half yawn, and the targeted vibratory sensation occurs on the front part of the hard palate and extends up into the front top quarter of the skull.

The decision to use Lessac's call was made not because it is the only way or even necessarily the best way in which to train actors' voices, but rather because call appears to have a rather specific, replicable tonal quality, can be taught, and has had obvious usefulness for projection onstage.

Subjects And Methods

Two men and two women actors were used in this study, each of whom had at least some training in the call technique. Three of the subjects had been trained by Lessac himself at one or more of his national summer workshops, and the fourth had studied his technique with a teacher who had been Lessac's pupil. One of the women was a trained singer as well. Each subject was asked to find a pitch at which he or she could produce a clear, comfortable call on the word "hello" while preserving the identity of the sound /oʊ/. The pitches used were G below middle C (196 Hz) for one of the men, B below middle C (247 Hz) for the other, and D above middle C (311 Hz) for the women.

Each subject was asked to say hello five times in succession in each of two different modes: speech and call. Speech mode was described as the way in which the subject might say hello to an acquaintance in a conversational situation, with two differences: (a) The loudness level should require the same degree of effort that the subject would be using for call; and (b) the subject would be sustaining the first part of the diphthong /ou/ on a predetermined pitch.

For call mode, each subject was asked to maintain the same pitch, the same degree of effort, and the same microphone distance as for speech, while achieving optimum vocal production through whatever adjustments were necessary to produce the "call" sensation as taught by Lessac.*

As each subject switched from speech mode to call mode, the experimenters perceived some variety of phonemic identity among tokens. This variation is not unexpected from subjects trained in the Lessac technique. In discussing how to form vowels at a specific pitch, Lessac states (6, p. 118):

Remember that the call is no respecter of specific vowel sounds…Do not let quality, texture, timbre or tonal focus change. Accommodate the different vowels by means of mental compensation and where necessary, some tongue adjustment, rather than by a change in structural form or lip opening.

The subject seemed to be "finding call" at a given pitch through internal kinesthetic and vibratory cues rather than by listening to the exact vowel that they were forming when they produced a call. All four subjects were targeting their production on the /ou/ sound throughout the experiment, however.

Microphone signals were recorded during the production of five tokens for both vocal modes. Recordings were made directly into a VAX 11/750 computer through an analog-to-digital system with a 16-bit converter at a sampling frequency of 20 kHz. Recordings lasting 2 s were made during prolonged phonations in each vocal mode. Gain was adjusted for each token to maximize the recording amplitude. Acoustic spectra for the microphone signals were obtained by using and Interactive Laboratory System (Signal Technology, Inc., Galeta, CA) software command, FDI. Spectral level in decibels for each partial was determined by visual inspection. All determinations of decibel level were made by one of the experimenters, and reliability checks were provided by the other.

For each spectrum, all partials were equally adjusted to make the decibel value for the first partial equal to zero. For each subject, the arithmetic mean for each partial across the five tokens was then calculated for both call and speech modes. The adjusted acoustic spectra provided information about the relative intensities of the different partials that comprised the vocal signal.

Next, speech and call spectra were compared without artificially maximizing differences at any particular location in the spectra. We believed that manipulation of the spectra that would emphasize the specific location would be equivalent to a possible bias in the eventual results. Thus, the procedure for spectral comparison began with an "overlap" of the average speech and call spectra for each subject.

To overlap the mean spectra, first the average spectral difference was obtained between the two modes across the partials. The average difference was then subtracted form each individual mean partials for each subject that were significantly different between the call and speech modes (at the 0.10 level).

Results

Data analyses revealed that the two vocal modes do differ significantly from one another with regard to certain partials in each subject's spectra. Figure I shows mean spectra for both speech and call modes. The data for the women are discussed first because both subjects were phonating at the same pitch.

For the women (Fig. 1A and B), the partials that differed significantly in decibel level were nearly identical and differed in the same direction when the subjects switched from speech mode to call mode. For both women, the second partial was relatively higher, the third partial was relatively lower, the seventh and eighth partials were relatively higher, and the tenth partial was relatively lower. It appears that for both women, the first formant (F1) was being tuned more sharply in call mode than in speech mode. No significant change occurred for the females in the second formant (F2), but there was a midfrequency enhancement in call mode at ~2,000 – 2,500 Hz, the area between F2 and F3, and there was a significant drop in energy right beyond F3 (at ~3,000 Hz).

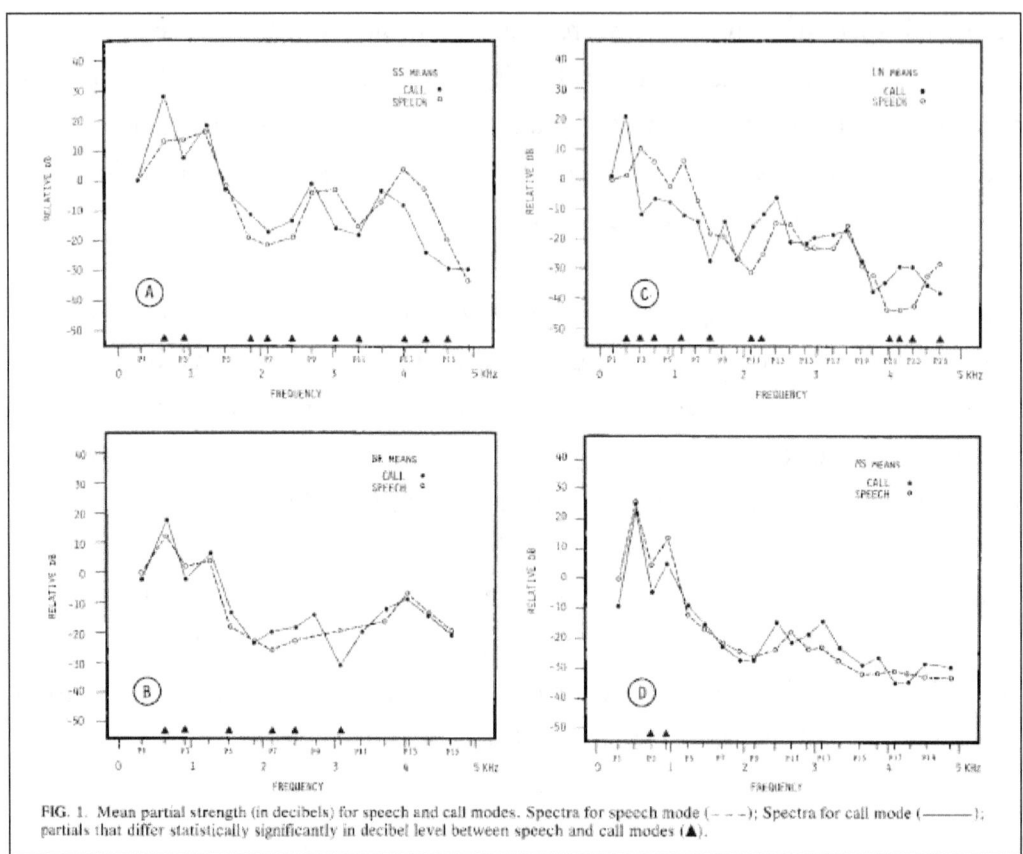

FIG. 1. Mean partial strength (in decibels) for speech and call modes. Spectra for speech mode (- - -); Spectra for call mode (———); partials that differ statistically significantly in decibel level between speech and call modes (▲).

For both men (Fig. 1C and D), F1 also appeared to be tuned more sharply in call mode than in speech mode, and there also appeared to be a relative decrease in F2 in call mode. In addition, subject L.N. showed energy enhancement (to the left of F3 and in F3 itself) when he was phonating in call mode. All four subjects appeared to have an enhancement of the lower end of the spectrum and (except for subject M.S.) of the middle frequency range as well. There was an apparent sharpening of F1 for all and, for at least three of the four, there was also some increase in acoustic energy between 2,000 and 2,500 Hz (on the left skirt of F3).

Perceptually, the vowel identity for the two modes was judged by the experimenters to be similar for subjects B.R. and M.S. and somewhat dissimilar for subjects L.N. and S.S. These perceptual evaluations may relate to the unchanging formant frequencies for subjects B.R. and M.S. and to downward formant shifts for subject L.N. and a strong boost of F1 energy for subject S.S.

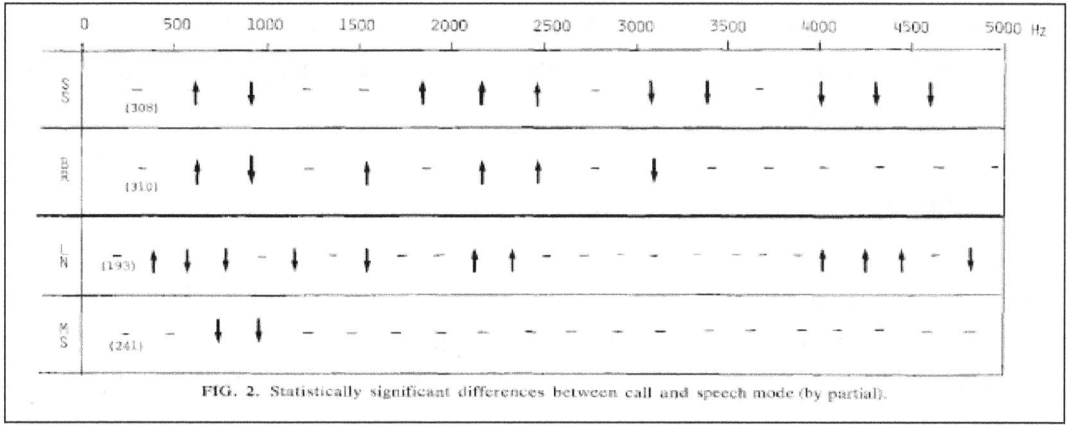

FIG. 2. Statistically significant differences between call and speech mode (by partial).

Figure 2 summarizes the changes in the decibel levels of the partials for all four subjects when switching from speech mode to call mode. Two general tendencies were evident: (a) energy in the range between 700 and 1,000 Hz was relatively lower for all four subjects, more or less in the area of F2, and served to sharpen the prominence of F1; and (b) energy in the range between 2,150 and 2,350 Hz was relatively higher for three of the four subjects (this is just on the low side of F3).

Discussion

Although the present experiment did not include a study of the actual physical changes that the subjects effected in order to produce call mode, in the acquisition of the Lessac call technique the actor is instructed to maintain about two fingertips' worth of space between the top and bottom front teeth for all called vowels except those in the lowest pitches of the range, to adjust lip opening (which is forwardly stretched) to accommodate each different pitch rather than each different vowel, to keep the throat wide "open" and relaxed in feeling.

These instructions may be related to the primary acoustical finding, which appears to be an enhancement of the first formant, more prominent in the call mode than in the speech mode to the point of affecting the targeted sound phonemically.

This enhancement might be accomplished by moving the first formant center frequency closer to the subjects' second partial (an octave above the fundamental frequency). Lowering of the center frequency of the first formant might be dependent on moving the vocal tract constriction more anteriorly and protruding the lips more or lowering the larynx (3,8). Lowering the jaw could help to tune the first formant sensitively in the presence of lip protrusion or larynx lowering, since jaw lowering tends to raise the center frequency of the first formant (3). Although stretching the vocal tract walls might conceivably sharpen formants due to increased stiffness (1,2), this effect needs further study for actors' performance.

One possible weakness in this study is that speech and call tokens for each subject were not matched perceptually to insure that the phonemic identity of the sound being studied was exactly the same for both vocal modes. Both visual and auditory data seem to indicate that two of the subjects (S.S. and L.N.) show greater formants movement difference between the two modes than do the other two subjects, perhaps because they change the vowel more in switching modes. Use of call mode appears to enhance F1, however, even if the vowel being produced is not identical.

The primary finding of enhancement of the first formant for the call technique is dissimilar (in frequency location) to the enhancement of the region near the third formant in male (Western) operatic singing. The secondary effect of enhancement of the third formant skirt in call, however, would be similar in effect to the singer's F3 enhancement.

Pedagogical Note

This study relates the acoustic results of a pedagogical technique for vocal enhancement for stage acting to specific acoustic differences from conversational speech. What application do these finds and interpretations have to vocal pedagogy? On the basis of this study (and electroglottographic data that will be reported in the future), the call mode appears to involve some modifications that are probably related to both the larynx and the vocal tract. If, in training actors for the stage, a teacher were to agree that some value is to be obtained from sharpening the first formant and enhancing acoustic energy in the middle of the frequency range because this seems to give the voice a characteristic ring or "brilliance" desirable for onstage work, that teacher might wish to consider the following vocal tract adjustments suggested by (6); (a) half-yawn sensation in the production of projected voice; (b) two fingertips' worth of space between the upper and lower teeth at the corner of the mouth for the production of a number of the vowels at mid and higher pitches; (c) forward stretch of the cheek muscles feeding into the upper lip in the production of many vowels; and (d) feeling internal vibration on the front of the roof of the mouth and in the skull rather than listening for the right sound.

A number of these concepts are advocated not only by Lessac but by a number of other important voice and speech teachers as well (9 – 12) and others.

*At this point in an oral presentation of this article, a Voice Foundation Symposium audience heard a cassette tape recording of each of four subjects sustaining the /ou/ sound first in speech and then in call mode. Each subject attempted to hold both pitch and degree of effort constant throughout

Acknowledgment: We acknowledge with gratitude the significant contributions made by the following individuals to the completion of this study and the preparation of this article: Julie Artigliere, Kim Greenzweig, Lynn Nichols, Virginia Riedesel, Susan Sweeney, Ingo R. Titze, and Vern Vail.

References

1. Bartholomew, WT. 'A physical definition of "good voice quality" in the male voice.' *J Acoustical Soc Am* 1934;6:25-33.

2. Rzhevkin, SM. 'Certain results of the analysis of a singer's voice.' *Sov Physics Acoust* 1956;2: 215-20.

3. Sundberg, J. 'Formant structure and articulation of spoken and sung vowels.' *Folia Phoniatr* 1970;22:28-48.

4. Sundberg, J. 'An articulatory interpretation of the '"singing formant"'. *Speech Trans Lab Q Prog Status Rep* 1972;45-53.

5. Rothenberg, M. 'Acoustic interaction between the glottal source and the vocal tract.' In: Stevens KN, Hirano M, eds. *Vocal fold physiology*. Tokyo: University of Tokyo Press, 1981: 305-28.

6. Lessac, A. *The use and training of the human voice*, 2nd ed. New York: Drama Book Specialists, 1967.

7. Glass, GV, Hopkins KD. *Statistical methods in education and psychology*, 2nd ed. Englewood Cliffs, NJ: Prentice-Hall, 1984:381.

8. Minifie, FD. 'Speech acoustics.' In: Minifie FD, Hixon TJ, Williams F, eds. *Normal aspects of speech, hearing and language.* New Jersey: Prentice-Hall, 1973:235-284.

9. Anderson, V. *Training the speaking voice*, 3rd ed. New York: Oxford University Press, 1977.

10. Linklater, K. *Freeing the natural voice.* New York: DBS, 1976.

11. Machlin, E. *Speech for the stage.* New York: Theatre Arts Books, 1966.

12. Turner, JC. *Voice and speech in the theatre*, 3rd ed. (revised by Morrison M). London: Pitman, 1977.

Address correspondence and reprint requests to Dr. Ronald C. Scherer, The Denver Center for the Performing Arts, 1245 Champa, Denver, CO 80204, U.S.A

Lessac's Y-Buzz as a Pedagogical Tool in the Teaching of the Projection of an Actor's Voice

This peer-reviewed article was originally published in the South African Journal of Linguistics. Suppl. 34, Dec.1996, pp 25-36. Permission to reprint has been graciously granted by NISC.

Marth Munro, Department of Drama and Opera,
Pretoria Technikon, Pretoria, Republic of South Africa.
Timo Leino, Institute of Speech Communication
and Voice Research, University of Tampere, Finland.
Daan Wissing●, Research Unit for Phonetics and Phonology,
and Department of Afrikaans and Dutch, Potchefstroom University for CHE,
Private Bag X6001. Potchefstroom. 2520, Republic of South Africa.

This article is a preliminary study on the effects, of Arthur Lessac's y-buzz as a tool in teaching projection of an actor's voice. The y-buzz is described as part of the Lessac System. Leino's formulation of the actor's formant is presented. Following this, LTAS analyses of the y-buzz and a prose extract from Lessac himself are done. LTAS analyses of a trained and an untrained male voice doing the y-buzz and speaking a prose extract are demonstrated. These analyses are compared to the LTAS analyses and results collated by Leino. The spectra analysed for the two male voices trained through the Lessac System may be an effective teaching tool in voice projection for actors. The need arises for a more in-depth study in this field.

Contextualization and Problem

The basic premise of theatre work is that the actor, as the "carrier" of the words and subtext of the character, will move and act in a space defined as an aesthetic space, in relation to a second group of people known as the audience. From this premise the actor is vocally and physically confronted with the tasks of using his voice and body as tools to embody the text and the subtext of the character, of doing so in the aesthetic space, and in such a way that the audience can perceive the text and subtext with the minimum of "interference."

Consequently certain demands are placed on the actor's voice: on the one hand the actor needs to be audible at all times (without shouting), and thus the actor needs to be able to project the voice effectively. On the other hand, the actor dare not sacrifice the intonation range needed for emotional expressiveness for this projection (Acker 1987:77; Linklater 1976: 2&3), as this is inevitably tied into the aesthetic experience. Furthermore, the actor needs to be vocally fit, i.e. needs to have a vocal apparatus that is capable of sustained vocalization.[1]

The upshot of these demands underlines the need for effective voice training, and the field of voice training for the actor has become a specialized field of its own. As convincingly argued by Martin (1991) and VASTA Newsletters (1987-1996), the three voice/vocal development systems for actors which are currently dominating the field are the work of Cicely Berry (1973), Kristin Linklater (1976), and Arthur Lessac (1967).

These systems are being used (either singularly or in combination) all over the Western theatre world. To a large extent the valuable work that these practitioners have developed, has been built on extended and extensive practical experience, and it is only recently that their work has begun to be tested scientifically. This had led directly to scientific research on voice development for actors. In this regard the work of Leino with his investigation of the **actor's formant** is breaking new ground. It is necessary, however, to focus on the above-mentioned systems which are already being used, and scientifically determine heir contribution to vocal development.

This article will focus on an aspect of the work of Arthur Lessac. The Lessac voice system is based on Lessac's concepts of **tonal action** (1967:18), **structural action** (1967:17) and **consonant action** (1967:20). The article will focus on the tonal action and specifically on the **y-buzz** which is the cornerstone of this tonal action (1967:81-85). There is already some existing research on one other aspect of the **tonal action**—Acker (1987) and Raphael and Scherer (1987) have done research on the **call** in tonal action. However there has so far (to our knowledge) been no scientific research done on the contribution of the y-buzz to the projection of the stage voice.

Thesis
This article will investigate whether Arthur Lessac's y-buzz correlates with the idea of Leino's actor's formant or the concept of the **singer's formant** (Sundberg,

1988) as a demonstration of vocal projection. Consequently, the y-buzz, as part of the Lessac complete concept of tonal action, may thus be an effective pedagogical tool in the teaching of the production of the actor's aesthetically projected voice.

This article will first draw on the scientific work done in a related field, namely the projection of the singer's voice, and will focus primarily on the phenomenon that allows the singer's voice to project, known as the singer's formant. In correlation with this singer's formant, Leino (1993), and Leino and Kärkkäinen (1995:496) presented data on a comparable but clearly distinguishable phenomenon in the speaking voice, i.e. the **actor's formant** between 3-4 kHz. An overview of Leino's work will be considered briefly.

Following this a critical overview of the tonal action as it functions in the Lessac system will be provided, and the y-buzz specifically will be outlined and discussed.

According to Miller (1986:55&56), the spectral envelop of the voice contains two groups of frequencies, each with its own basic function. On the one hand, the group containing the frequencies of F0 to F2 is responsible for the pitch (F0) and the vowel characterization of the sound (F1, F2). On the other hand, F3 to F5 are responsible for the quality of the sound. Sundberg (1988:15) claims that the closer or more compact the F3 to F5 in frequency (that is to say, the gap between each formant and the next is diminished) so that they form a formant cluster, the greater the potential for projection. In male operatic singing a formant clustering between 2-3 kHz is used to improve voice projection and this phenomenon is called the signer's formant. In male speech of good quality, instead, a formant clustering between 3-4 kHz is seen and Leino (1993) has named this the **actor's formant** since it is specially often seen in male actor's voices.

In an experiment Leino (1993:206-210) asked a group of professionals in the fields of theatre or speech therapy to evaluate a group of text reading samples. According to the points given it was possible to place the samples in categories of *good, fairly good, rather poor* and *poor*. These samples were then subjected to longterm average spectrum (LTAS) analysis. Leino found that voices judged to be *good* are often characterized by a strong peak around 3.5 kHz and the spectral slope is relatively gradual; the voices judged to be *poor,* in turn, usually lack this peak and the spectral slope is steeper (Leino, 1993:209). In a study by Leino and Kärkkäinen (1995) these characteristics of a good speaking voice were set as a goal in a special eight-month training period for student actors. Real-time spectrum analysis was used as an aid during the training sessions. According to the results these characteristics were reached and the voices were also evaluated to be better in quality after training.

Lessac's Y-Buzz

Lessac (1967:20) claims that the voice's projection capabilities can be improved by the tonal action:

> Tonal action develops the full pitch, range, power and projection for the voice and improves quality eliminating nasality, muffled tones, throatiness, and breathiness. With good tonal action, no breath and only the mildest warmth is ever felt on the lips at any level of voice production—the most conversational or the most projected. Tonal action feels good; it stimulates and relaxes the speaker because it functions properly only when all parts of the vocal process are in proper balance. Thus physical tension is relieved while beautifully rich and dynamic tones are produced.

> Through the system of tonal action the student will thus learn to produce this voice optimally so that, most likely, an actor's formant would be established through training—although terminology such as actor's formant does not exist in the Lessac System.

The y-buzz is part of Lessac's tonal action. In this tonal action the student has to sense the vibrations of the voiced tones (and all vowels are voiced). Lessac focuses here strongly on bone conduction instead of air resonance to act as a sensorial guidance for producing an optimal tone (1967:13, 19). His argument is that the voice user can never arrive at a "truthful" (that is to say, externally objective) feedback of his own voice through using the air resonance and, consequently, by "simply listening." The voice will always sound different if the voice producer listens to the voice coming from the inside, than what it will sound like to other people (1967:15). The sensory awareness of the sound-wave through bone conduction is much more reliable in voice production. One has to comment here on the fact that voice researchers like McKinney

(1982:125), Sundberg (1988:16) and Miller (1986:57&60) admit to the fact that there is such a sensation, but, according to them, whether the voice user is aware of the sensation or not will not necessarily influence the sound.

Lessac uses the tuning fork as an aid to create a recognizable event with the sound waves (1967:14). He sets the tuning fork into vibration and then puts the back end of the tuning fork against the upper teeth of the student. The student will now experience the sensation of the sound (through sensory awareness) and experience or feel that sound through bone conduction. This sensation of the sound-waves is similar to that which the voice producer feels when what the Lessac system labels "an optimal tone" is made. This approach is used to give the voice producer a guideline, or a recoverable event that can be used as sensorial matrix, that will be there for him to access in any given situation. In other words, the sensory awareness approach provides the voice producer with a "familiar event." The second step is to match the sensory awareness with the physical action of shaping the air resonator.

The Lessac System addresses the shape of the air resonator in the "structural action"[2] and, although this shape is not the primary focus in the tonal action, it must always be integrated in the tonal action for optimal voice usage (1967:82). Although Lessac doesn't put it in these terms, the System uses the idea that low sounds are resonated in long, relatively wide resonates with a small aperture of the mouth, while high sounds are resonated in short, relatively narrow resonators with a wide aperture of the mouth. Consequently the Structural Action concentrates on actively releasing and lengthening the facial muscles to shape the resonator, while the orbicularis oris must stay soft and pliable at all times. Lessac calls this the inverted megaphone shape and stresses the fact that this must always be in action. "Nothing should be tight or taut; there should be only the dual feeling of relaxed energy and energetic relaxation" (1967:18).

Lessac selected the English "y" sound for this exploration/exercise for the following reasons. Firstly the English "y" is a vowel-like as well as a consonant-like sound. Secondly it is a non-nasal sound—unlike the [n m ŋ] which are sounds that are traditionally used by many other voice systems to "place" the voice (1967:81). Thirdly it is also a sound that correlates well with the [i] vowel (the system uses the words "yes" and "easy" to find the sensation). The [i] vowel has already the formant pattern (clustering of F3-F5), which is the goal for good projection (see Miller: 1986:71&72). This is because the sound is a front vowel, requiring a long resonator with a small aperture. Because of this the [i] or the English "y" or the Lessac System's y-buzz sound will be optimally projected in the low range of the voice. Lessac states that the y-buzz operates in the lower third of the vocal range (1967:81).

A typical y-buzz is an "y/ee"-like sound, being made in the lower third of the vocal range, the cheek and lip muscles lengthened forward, the orbicularis oris being soft and pliable. A buzz or vibration will be felt on the front section of the hard palate.

In the next section we will report some preliminary results of a study of Arthur Lessac's voice production, as well as of a comparison between a male person, trained by the Lessac method, and an untrained male subject.

The Empirical Study

In the introduction, the phenomenon of the actor's formant has been highlighted. Research findings have characterized good actor's voices in terms of this construct. To summarize: in LTAS analyses, a good actor's voice shows a prominent peak between 3 and 4 kHz. (the actor's formant), whereas the poor voices do not (Leino and Kärkkäinen) (1995:496). According to Sundberg, the singer's formant occurs between 2 and 3 kHz. (Sundberg, 1974). In addition to this, Leino also found that the slope of the LTAS is more gradual for good voices and much steeper for poor voices (Leino, 1993:209, see also Leino and Kärkkäinen, 1995). Assuming the effectiveness of the Lessac method of voice training, it might be expected that the above-mentioned, or similar actor's formant will be present in such trainees' voices as well. In the following, preliminary survey, we shall report the findings of an LTAS analysis of the voice of Lessac himself when performing a y-buzz, as well as when "speaking" a sentence in projection mode. In addition to this, we also present LTAS analyses of the y-buzzes and a short paragraph in projection mode of two male persons, one trained by the Lessac method, and the other a totally untrained male.

Methods and Materials

The recordings were made in two different locations, one in the USA (Ball State University, Muncie, Indiana) and the rest locally in Potchefstroom. Different types of equipment were involved on the two occasions. This, however, does not have any negative influence for the present study, where only intra-comparisons are made. Distance between mouth and microphone were in both cases kept constant to 40 cm, and we tried to control the volume level of the recordings. It is known that loudness has an influence on the spectrum: an increase of, say, 5 dB in the overall sound level does not simply give a 5 dB gain at every frequency rage in the spectrum, but instead affects each frequency range differently. The higher frequencies gain more than the lower ones; consequently, the spectrum slope will also become more gradual. This will be controlled closely in future research.

While it seems desirable to use longish speech samples, especially in the case of prose reading (up to 60 sec.), some researchers have used as little as 2 sec. (Raphael & Scherer, 1987:84 in their study of Lessac's "call"). In the case of the y-buzz, our analyzed speech samples were about 8 sec., and 20 sec. in the case of the prose.

Kay Elemetrics' Computerized Speech Laboratory was used for calculation of the long-term average spectra (LTAS). A 512 point narrow band FFT analysis was used; frequency span was 10 kHz, and a Hanning weighting window was used. The output was not smoother in the case of the prose samples, but the y-buzz LTAS's were smoothed (low). The latter was necessary due to the fact that the 8 sec. recording gave an extremely rough graphic presentation. Frequency range was kept between 0 kHz and 4,5 kHz (cf. X-axis of the graph). The amplitude scales (Y-axis, Decibels) were varied according to the specific recordings to give an optimum presentation of the graphics (see Fig. 1 – Fig. 4).

Analysis of Arthur Lessac's voice

Figure 1 presents LTAS of Lessac's own production of the y-buzz. It was recorded during a visit of the first author to the USA. As is clear from Fig. 1, there are four prominent peaks of energy present, namely at 2,2 kHz, 2,6 kHz, 3,2 kHz, and 3,6 kHz. (cf. annotations in the figure). The overall very gradual slope is salient. Most interesting is the very strong peak at 3,6 kHz. Both slopes and peaks referred to are characteristic of a good male speaking voice, and, as taught by the Lessac method, for good projection (cf. the introduction).

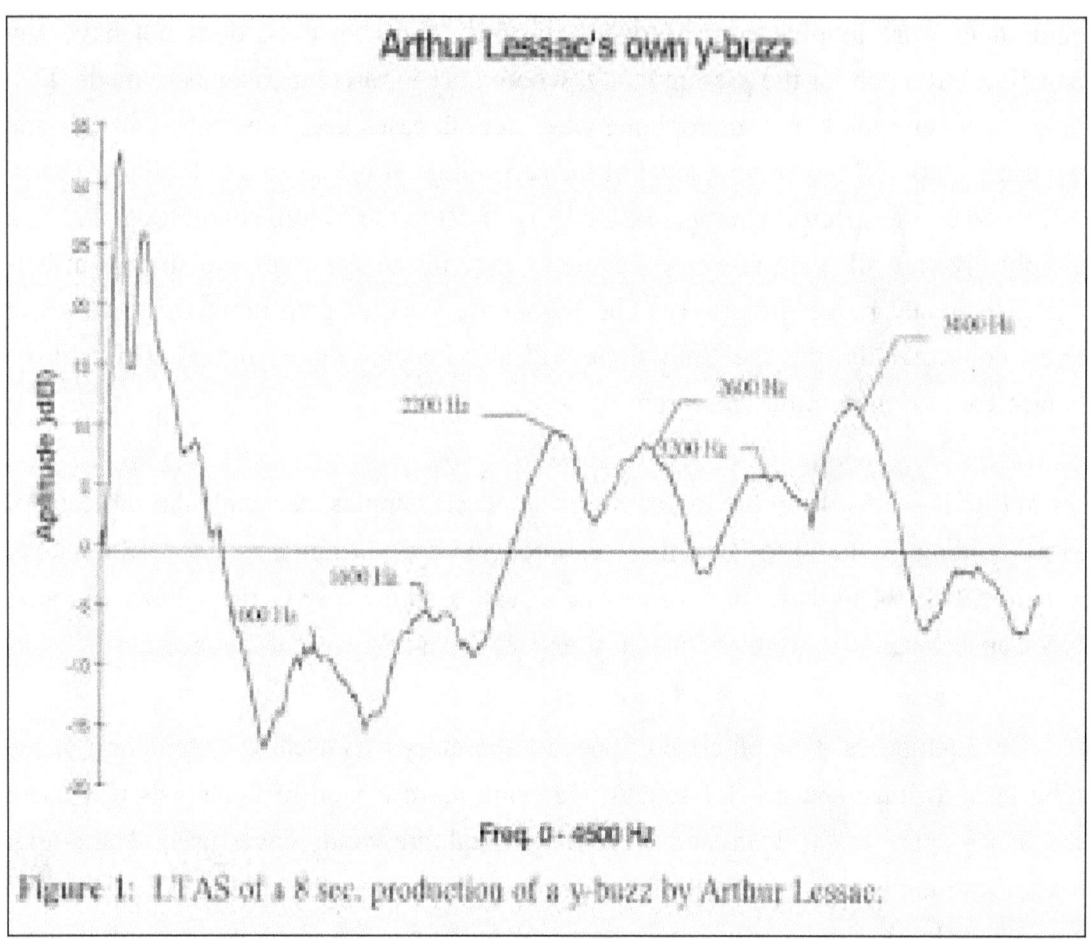

Figure 1: LTAS of a 8 sec. production of a y-buzz by Arthur Lessac.

A sentence ("The evening breeze seems to seep between the leaves"), spoken by Lessac, of comparable length was analysed. The [s]'s (voiceless fricatives) were segmented out before analysis. As there were practically no differences between the LTAS's of his y-buzz and this sentence, a comparison of the y-buzz (cf. Fig. 1) and the sentence (Fig. 2) will suffice. The close resemblance between the y-buzz and sentence leads to the conclusion that the same projector qualities of the y-buzz can be attributable to Lessac's "acting" voice, or, at least, of this specific sentence. It must be added that Lessac's way of speaking this sentence is very prolonged and rather "unnatural" for speaking mode. This is clear, i.a., from the fact that the duration of the sentence of nine words was nearly nine seconds. Also, the sentence contains a great deal of "ee" vowels, which, of course closely resembles the vowel of the y-buzz.

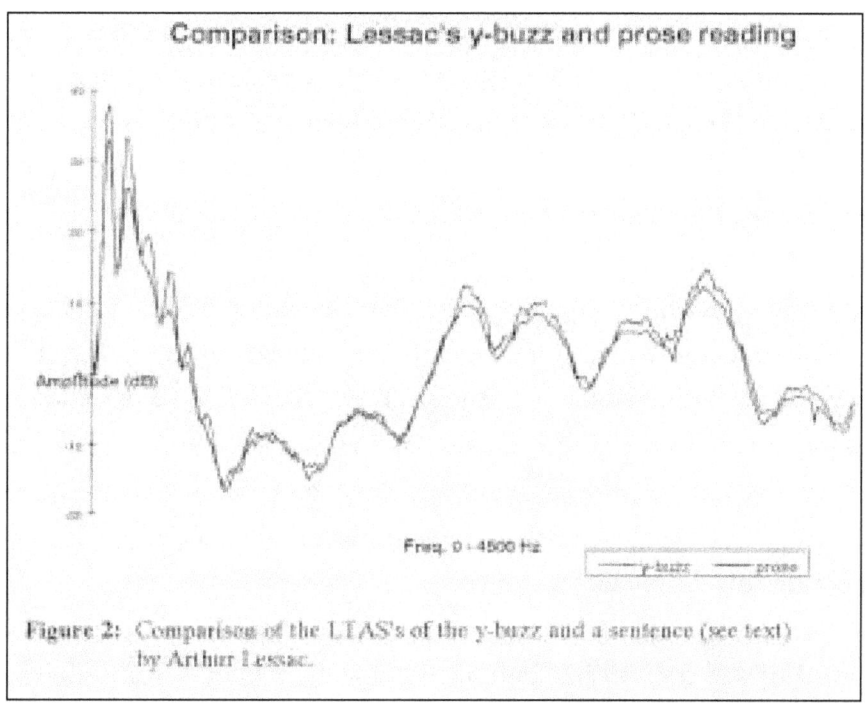

Figure 2: Comparison of the LTAS's of the y-buzz and a sentence (see text) by Arthur Lessac.

The trained and untrained subjects

Figure 3 is a graphical comparison of LTAS's of the trained vs. untrained male y-buzzes.

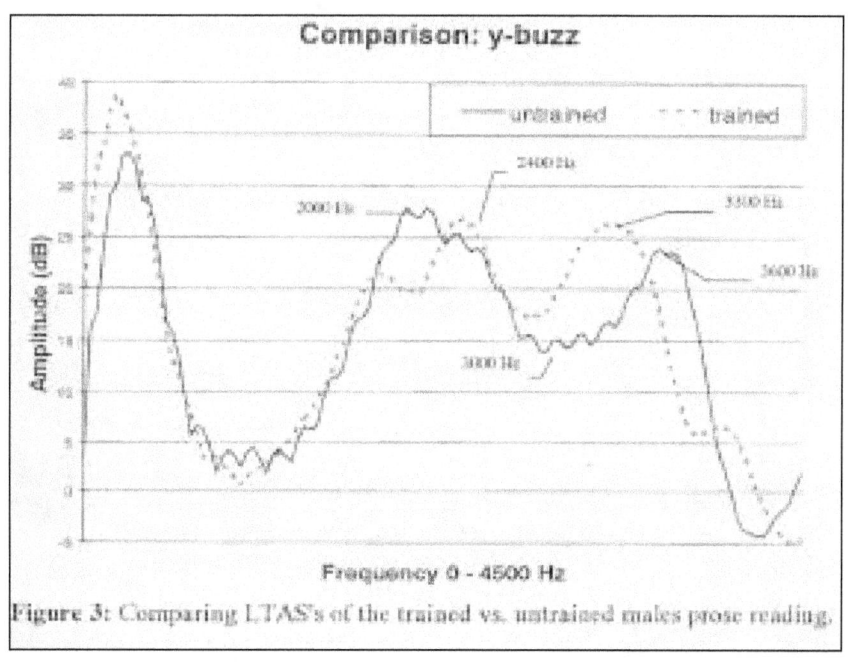

Figure 3: Comparing LTAS's of the trained vs. untrained males prose reading.

No clear difference between the y-buzz of the trained and untrained subjects can be seen. If anything, a slightly more gradual slope is present between the two prominent peaks in the region of 2 kHz and 3,6 kHz in the case of the trained male's y-buzz. Furthermore, his peaks are located a little closer to each other. But in a whole, one has to conclude that the differences are insignificant.

Turning to the prose reading analyses of the trained and untrained males, quite a different picture emerges: firstly, the slope of the trained subject is significantly less steep than is the case with the untrained subject, and secondly, the presence in the case of the two prominent peaks at 2,6 kHz and 3,4 khz is very salient. This is comparable, through not quite as well defined as was the case with Lessac's sentence. In the case of the trained subject, the sentences were spoken much more naturally, which could perhaps account for this difference.

The prose of the trained and untrained subjects exhibited a much wider vowel spread than the prose that was used in the Lessac sentence.

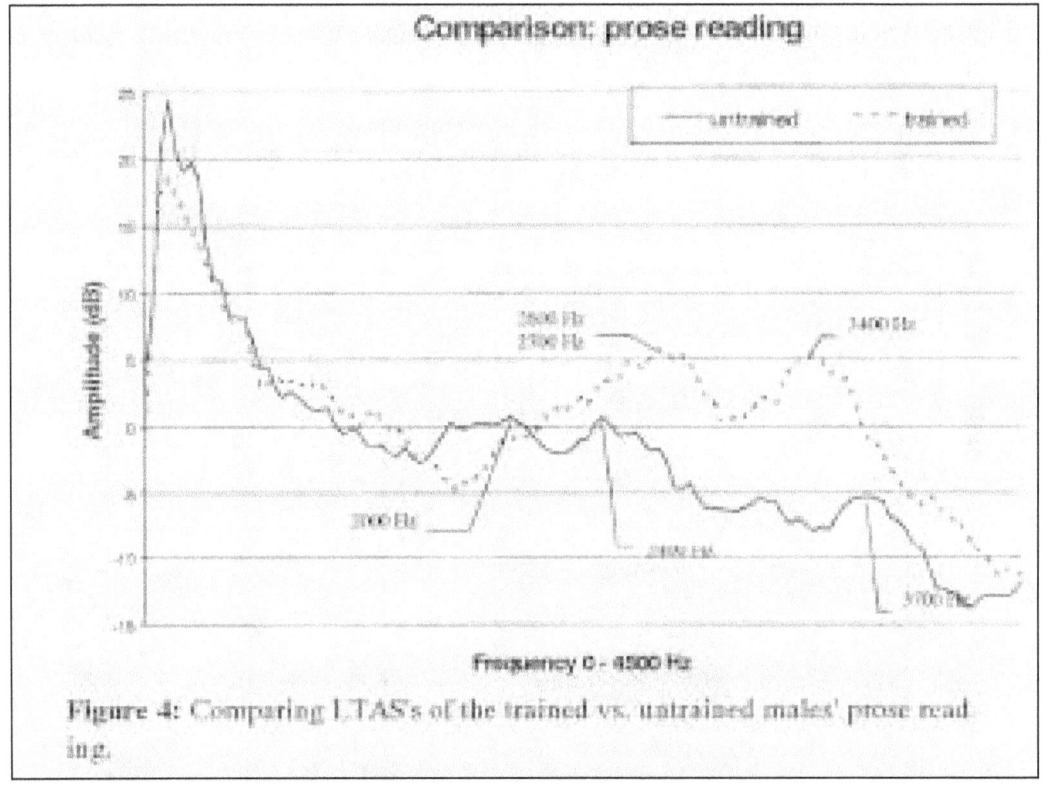

Figure 4: Comparing LTAS's of the trained vs. untrained males' prose reading.

The results as presented in Fig. 4 compared to the results of the study of Leino and Kärkkäinen (1995, cf. Fig.5) are quite similar. Both are in a prose reading mode, and in both cases the less steep slopes and prominent peaks are striking. This suggests a similar effectiveness of the Lessac method.

Conclusion

This pilot study suggests that Lessac's System could potentially be effectively used to provide the actor with a vocal apparatus that will be capable of projection, where the projected voice does not sacrifice intonation. However, as was said very clearly before, one has to be very cautious before coming to any final and resolute conclusions on the basis of this preliminary survey. But it seems clear that we do have enough grounds to warrant a fully-fledged follow-up longitudinal study, in which we will, i.e., investigate the effect that the Lessac System of training has on the voices of both Western and African subjects. The latter are of special interest to us. It seems to be possible that African voices possess a special quality, and it will be interesting to see whether the definition of an actor's formant will be applicable to African voices as well.

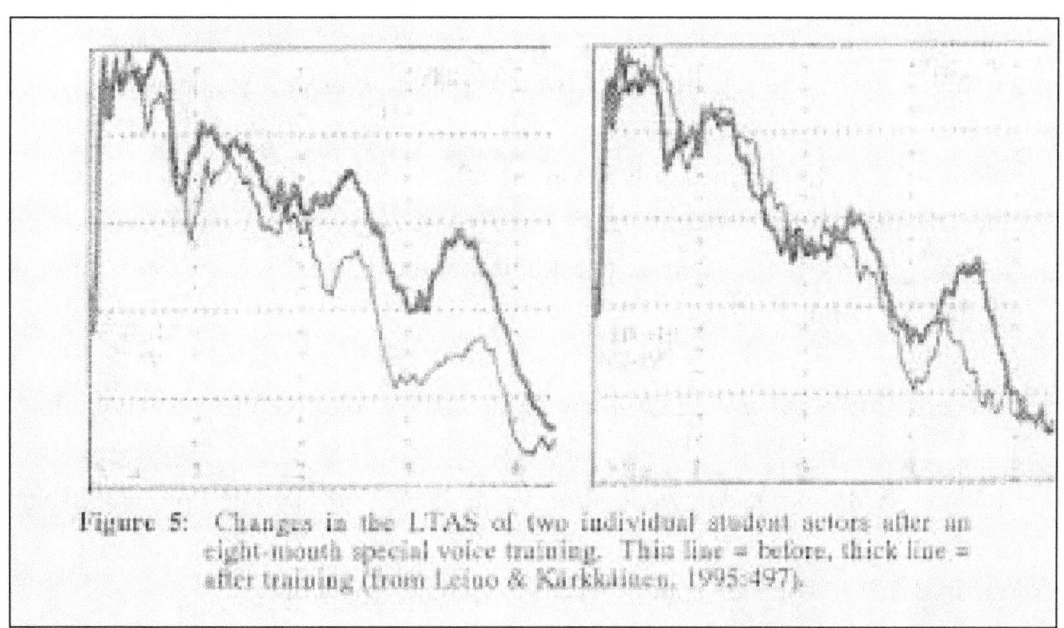

Figure 5: Changes in the LTAS of two individual student actors after an eight-month special voice training. Thin line = before, thick line = after training (from Leino & Kärkkäinen, 1995:497).

Endnotes

[1] Actors are regularly asked to rehearse for 8 hours a day on one project, and then to carry an entire performance of another project that same evening.

[2] The Lessac System's three primary Actions are the Structural, the Tonal and the Consonant Actions. The Structural Action is concerned with "muscular sensations and kinesthetic memory" (in other words the shaping of the air resonator) (Lessac, 1967: 17). The Tonal Action is concerned with the sensations of vocal vibrations (that is, the sensory awareness of bone conduction) (Lessac, 1967: 18), and the Consonant Action is concerned with the way the words to be communicated are structured (Lessac, 1967: 20-21).

Bibliography

1. Acker, B. 1987. 'Vocal Tract Adjustments for the Projected Voice.' In *Journal of Voice*, Vol. 1. No. 1: 77-82.

2. Berry, C. 1973. *Voice and the Actor*. London: Harrap.

3. Leino, T. 1993. 'Long-term average spectrum study on speaking voice quality in male actors.' In *Proceedings of the Stockholm Music Acoustics Conference*, Jul. 28-Aug. 1, 1993. (Ed.: A. Friberg, J Iwarsson, E. Jansson & J Sundberg).

4. Leino, T., & P. Kärkkäinen, 1995. 'On the effect of vocal training on the speaking voice quality of male student actors.' In *Proceedings of the XIIIth International Congress of Phonetic Sciences*. Stockholm, Sweden, 13-19 Aug. 1995. (Eds. K. Elenius & P. Branderud).

5. Lessac, A. 1967. *The use and training of the human voice*. California: Mayfield.

6. Linklater, K. 1976. *Freeing the natural voice*. New York: Drama Book Publishers.

7. Martin, J. 1991. *Voice in modern theatre*. London: Routledge.

8. McKinney, J. 1982. *The diagnosis and correction of vocal faults*. Nashville, Tennessee: Broadman Press.

9. Miller, R. 1986. *The structure of singing, system and art in vocal technique.* New York: Schirmer Books.

10. Raphael, B & Scherer, R. 1987. 'Voice modification of stage actors: Acoustic Analyses.' In *Journal of Voice* Vol. 1, No. 1:83-87).

11. Sundberg, J. 1987. *The science of the singing voice.* Dekalb: Northern Illinois Univ. Press.

12. Sundberg, J. 1987. 'Vocal tract resonance in singing.' In *The NATS Journal* March/April 1988:11-31.

- Also associated with the Centre for Language Practice of the Potchefstroom University for CHE.

On The Effects of Lessac Method on Female Voices: Preliminary Observations.

This study was presented as a poster at PEVOC,[1] Stockholm, 2001 and is re-presented here with permission of the authors.

Marth Munro *, Anne-Maria Laukkanen **, Timo Leino **
* Drama Department, University of Pretoria, South Africa;
** Institute of Speech Communication and Voice Research, University of Tampere, Finland.

Abstract

This study tested the effects of a six-week intensive workshop taught by Arthur Lessac and 3 of his certified teachers using the Lessac system in USA. Vocal exercises and phrases were recorded from 7 American female participants before and after training. Exercises included (1) y-buzz (a prolonged [y] sound almost resembling [j], (2) +y-buzz (a neutral vowel followed by y-buzz as in Hey) and (3) call ([ou] as in Hello, produced rather closed and frontal and with a strong protrusion of the lips).

Long-term-average spectra (LTAS) were made. In most cases, after training, a lowering of formant frequencies, especially that of F1, was noticed and the level of F1 and the level of the energy concentration at 2-5 kHz increased (compared to F0) both in the vocal exercises and in the phrases.

These changes suggest improved energy transfer from the vocal tract implying improved carrying power of the voice.

Introduction

Arthur Lessac's approach to theatre voice is well known in the United States and further afield (see e.g. Lessac, 1997; Hanson, 1997). Despite being widely used, the

---

[1] Pan European Voice Conference.

acoustic effects of the approach have not been extensively studied. The approach is a holistic one and comprises several parts.

This study concentrated on certain vocal exercises that represent the central concepts in the Lessac Approach. These exercises follow the principle of "reverse megaphone," i.e. the vocal tract is shaped so that the back of the mouth cavity is wider than the front part. Closed vowels [y, o, u] are used with a strong orientation towards protrusion of the lips without fixing the lips in a held position. Lessac calls this the "forward facial posture" (Lessac, 1997:50-51) and stresses the movability and adaptability of this orientation.

1. Aim

To investigate the effects of the Tonal NRG of the Lessac Approach (three primary explorations[2] as well as English phrases and Call words), within an intensive workshop situation, on the acoustic quality of the American female actor's voices.

1.1. Sub-aim

To compare and interpret the graphic presentations of the LTAS of the pre-training and post-training recordings, by means of a visual comparison.

2. Participants

Seven American female actors, between the ages of 21 and 45, who attended an intensive six-week workshop, taught by Arthur Lessac himself and three of the certified Lessac teachers. None of the participants had any reported voice or hearing problems.

3. Ethical considerations

These women all voluntarily agreed to participate in this research knowing that the voice samples will be referred to anonymously and that their identities will be protected.

---

[2] Y-buzz, +Y-buzz and Calls. Once recorded these explorations as well as the English phrases and Call words will be referred to as modes.

4. Training period

A six-week intensive Lessac Workshop.

5. Training process

During the workshop all the different aspects[3] of the Lessac Approach were covered. A typical workshop programme includes daily body work, big group sessions where new concepts are introduced and practiced, small group sessions, as well as one-on-one sessions, buddy sessions and time for self-study and practical explorations.

6. Data collection

The three main vocal explorations, and the English phrases were recorded from the participants before and after training.

6.1. Recordings

Recordings were done in an isolation booth (studio in College at Fredonia, New York State University, USA).

A DAT recorder was used.

An Audio Technica 4050 microphone (cardioid, flat response, no bass roll-off, no pad) was used.

The mouth-to-microphone distance was 40 cm.

A Sound Level Meter (CAT 42-3019) was used to control voice intensity. The aim was to keep the sound level between 65 -70 dB.

6.2. Tasks expected from participants

Initially the participants were asked to do an "uh-uh" sound. This was used to determine the pitch given for the Y-buzz sound. The pitch decided on was then given to each participant[4] when asked to do the Y-buzz for both recordings.

---

[3] During this specific workshop Structural NRG was introduced first followed by Consonant NRG and Tonal NRG. During the body sessions optimal body integration and breathing was introduced from the perspective of the Lessac Approach.
[4] A specific note was played on a keyboard.

Instruction given for samples[5] 1-3: "Please do the (different sounds inserted—named and demonstrated) as long and as loud as is comfortably possible while staying in the parameters 65-70dB on the SPL meter."

Instruction given for sample 4: "Please read the following (either English sentences and call words or first language texts) in a comfortable volume for performers in speaking voice."

Different sounds named and/or demonstrated:

1. Y-buzz on certain pitch as determined. The pitch that suited the voice (as decided on for each participant) was given on the keyboard.
2. +Y-buzz
3. Calls
4. Additionally, the following English phrases and Call words were recorded:

   "Leave me alone, I don't need grief!"
   "It may rain today."
   "He complained all day about the pain."
   "H'lo, dover, potato, watermelon"

These phrases and words are used to help the trainees to transfer the principles of the exercises to speech.

7. Data analysis and processing

Long Term Average Spectra (LTAS) were made with a Signal Analyzer (Hewlett-Packard 3561A) at the University of Tampere, Finland.

Visual inspection and interpretations of the graphic representations of the LTAS were done.

---

[5] Throughout this study the word "modes" will be used when referring to the different kind of utterances recorded. Mode 1 is the Y-buzz, Mode 2 the +Y-buzz, Mode 3 the Calls and Mode 4 the English phrases and Call words.

8. Results and discussion

LTAS for the three main Tonal NRG explorations and the phrases recorded before and after training can be seen in the Figures 1 for Y-buzz, 2 for +Y-buzz, 3 for Calls and 4 for English phrases and Call words.

The most consistent changes found after training were:

- An increase in the dB level difference between F1 and F0 in all three the sound samples of the explorations/exercises and in the phrases after training. The increase in F1-F0 dB level difference suggests better formant tuning of F1 to a harmonic, mainly to the second one. This seemed to be achieved by either changing F0 or the frequency of F1. These results support the findings reported by Raphael and Scherer (1987). Better tuning of F1 is likely to improve the energy transfer from the vocal tract.
- A relative strengthening of the spectral peaks at the range of 2-4 kHz compared to the strongest spectral component (FI) in the Y-buzz sound samples. This suggests a further improvement in the projecting capacity of the voice, since the threshold of hearing is lowest in the range 2-5 kHz.

What follow are randomly chosen figures to present the LTAS profile visually of the different modes. Figure 1 provides an example of the pre- and post- recordings of the Y-buzz of one participant. In Figure 2 an example of the pre- and post training recordings of the +Y-buzz of one participant is presented. In Figure 3 an example of the pre- and post- recordings of the Call of one participant can be observed. Figure 4 provides an example of the pre- and post- recordings of the English Phrases and Call words of one participant. These different visual profiles indicate clearly the increase in F1-F0 dB level difference, as well as the relative strengthening of the spectral peaks at the range of 2-4 kHz.

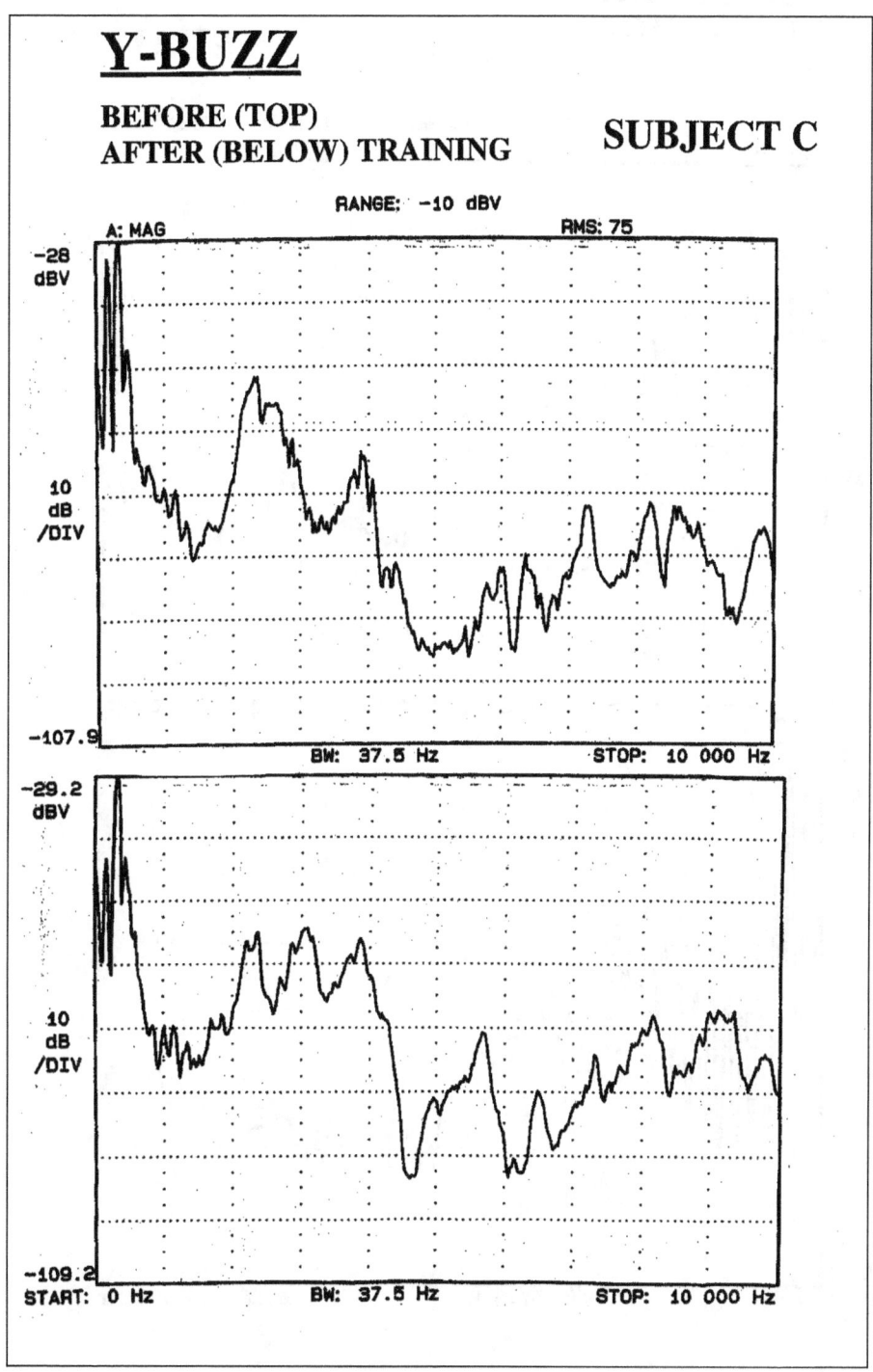

Figure 1: An example of the pre- and post-recordings of the Y-buzz of one participant.

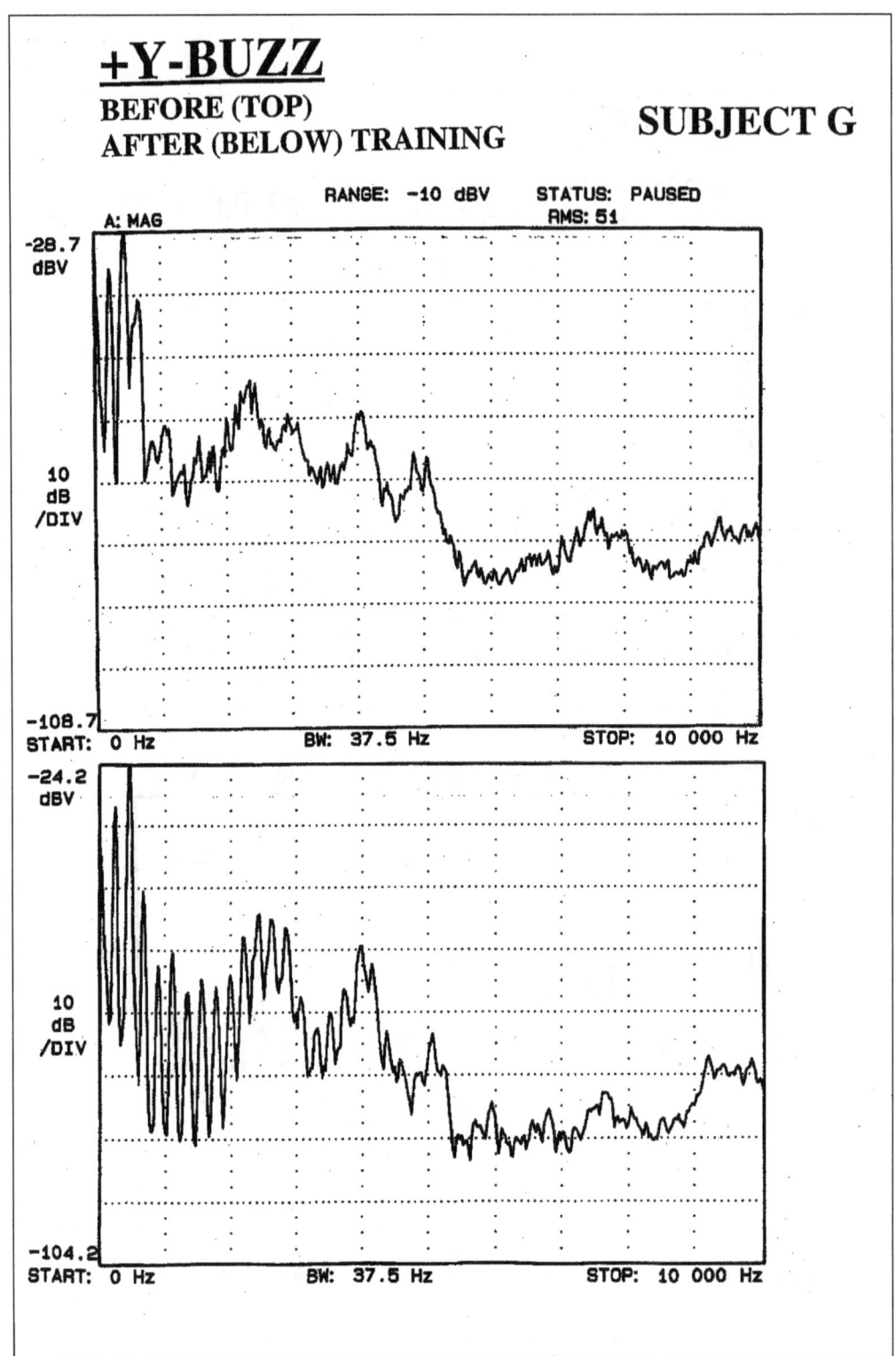

Figure 2: An example of the pre- and post-recordings of the +Y-buzz of one participant.

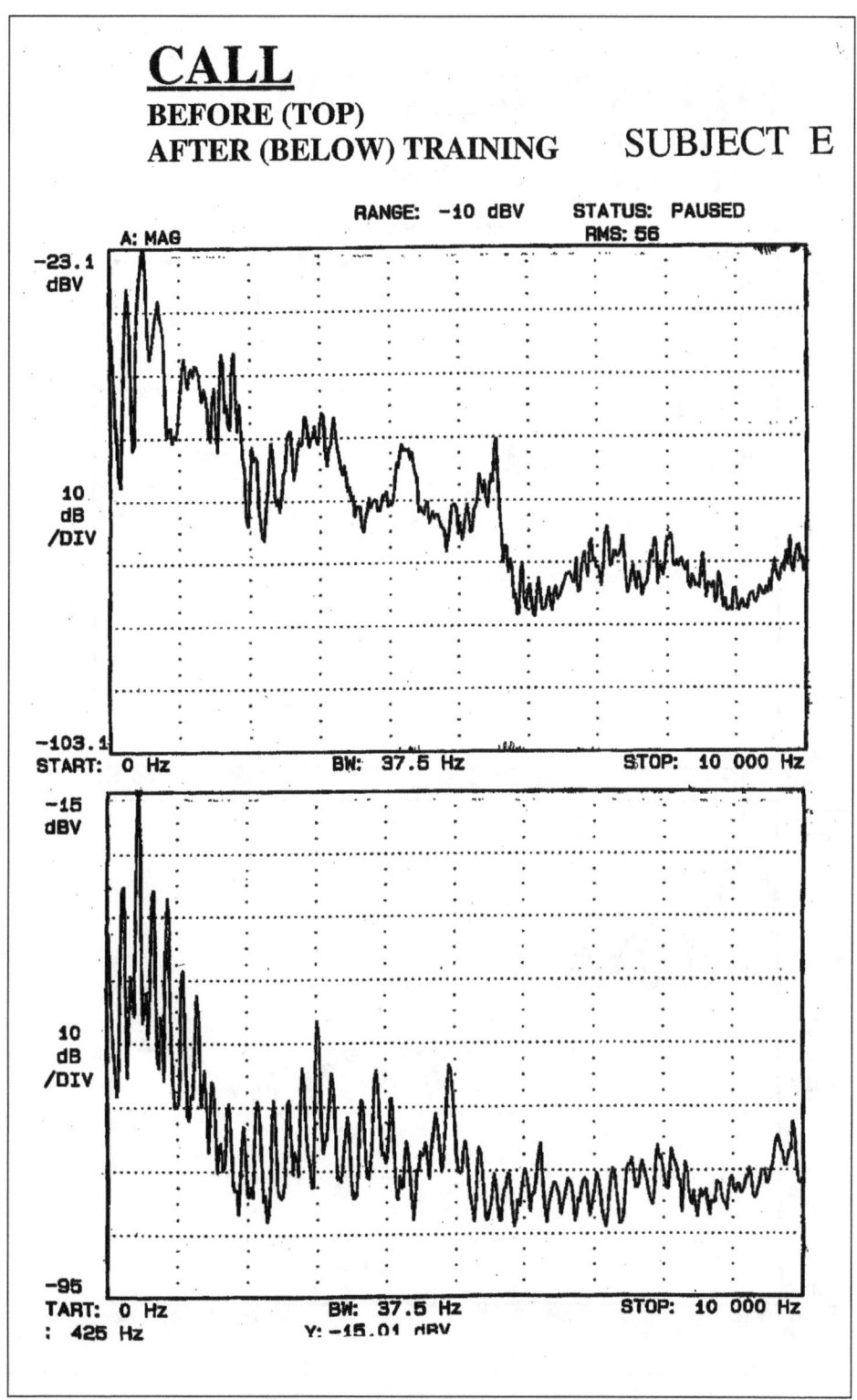

Figure 3: An example of the pre- and post-recordings of the Call of one participant.

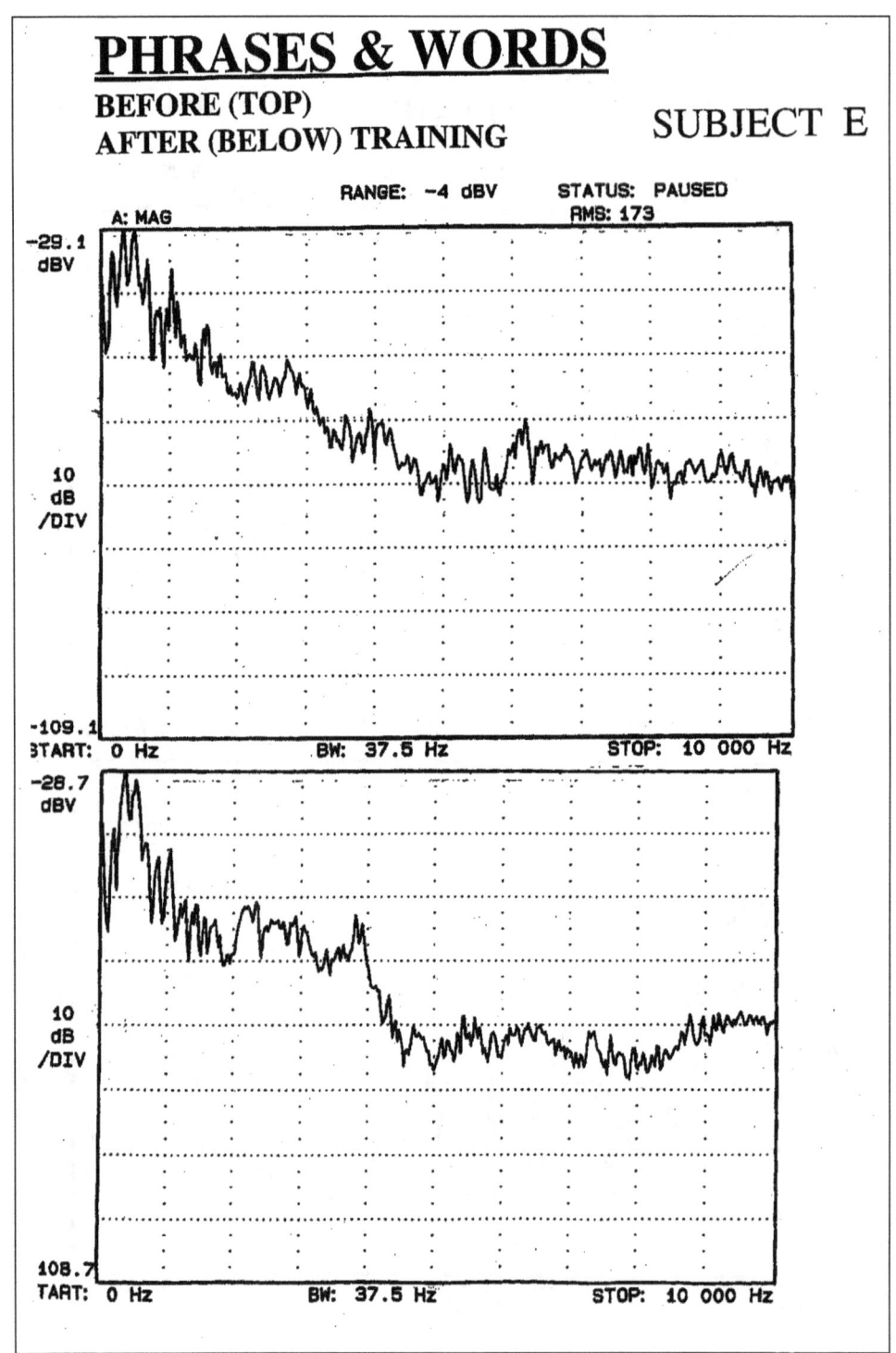

Figure 4: An example of the pre- and post-recordings of the English phrases and Call words of one participant.

In conclusion one has to take into account that phonation on closed vowels and with protruded lips increases the input impedance of the vocal tract. This may have beneficial effects on voice source and vocal fold vibration (Rothenberg, 1981 and 1988; Laukkanen, 1995). Results obtained by Verdolini et al. (1995; 1998) suggest that the "resonant voice" approach makes it possible to achieve sufficient carrying power in the voice economically, i.e. with less vocal effort and with less impact stress during voice production.

Front closed speech sounds (e.g. [i, y, j]) with a fairly high F2 provide strong vibratory sensations in the mouth and facial structures and may thus help the student to control the voice source to obtain a rich harmonic structure. There is, however, a danger that when applying the "reverse megaphone" principle too rigidly and without the guidance of a skilful teacher, the voice timbre may become too dark and articulation may be muffled. This danger can be avoided by focusing on the holistic nature of the Lessac approach.

References

Hanson, AM (1997). 'An Analysis of the Physiological Assumptions in Vocal Instructional Systems for Actors.' Unpublished Ph.D. dissertation. University of Kansas.

Laukkanen, A-M (1995). *On speaking voice exercises*. Published Ph.D. dissertation. University of Tampere, Finland.

Lessac, A (1997). *The Use and Training of the Human Voice. A bio-dynamic approach to vocal life. 3rd ed.* Mayfield Publishing Company: California.

Raphael, BN & Scherer, RC (1987). 'Voice modifications of stage actors: Acoustic analyses.' *Journal of Voice,* 1(1), 83-87.

Rothenberg, M (1981). 'An interactive model for the voice source.' *Speech Transmission Laboratory - fJl.lartp.rlv Prnflrp..\,,\, and Statu,~ Revort.* 4.

Verdolini-Marston, K; Burke, K.M; Lessac, A; Glaze L & Caldwell, E (1995). 'Preliminary Study of Two Methods of Treatment for Laryngeal Nodules.' *Journal of Voice,* 9(1), 74-85.

Verdolini, K; Druker, D.G; Palmer, P.M & Samawi, H (1998). 'Laryngeal Adduction in Resonant Voice.' *Journal of Voice,* 12(3)315-327.

The Contribution of Lessac's Y-Buzz from Two Brazilian Voice-therapists' Perspectives

Viviane Barrichelo-Lindström and Mara Behlau
Centro de Estudos da Voz, São Paulo, Brazil

Introduction

A resonant voice is described in the literature as a voicing pattern easy to produce, resonant and vibrant in the facial tissues, not restricted to low intensity, and helpful in voice therapy (Titze 2001; Verdolini-Marston et al. 1998). For these reasons, a better understanding of its physiological, acoustic and auditory-perceptual nature has been necessary, as it is for all strategies or exercises used in clinical and voice training. Several options for exercises using nasal sounds are available in the Brazilian literature, like sustaining /m/, /n/ and /N/, or in a context of short and long-duration syllables and sentences with words containing nasal sounds, all of them involving necessary sensations and adjustments to reach resonance. However, they imply driving the sound vibrations to the mask with some nasality and many individuals are afraid of developing a more nasal vocal quality (which is not necessarily true). Referred to as a resonant voice production, the Y-buzz proposed by Lessac seemed to be a perfect sound to study to increase our range of possibilities (Lessac 1997). Until the studies mentioned here, the Lessac work hadn't been introduced to the voice-therapists in Brazil. First of all, the Y-buzz does not imply nasality and it is developed through kinesthetic training. Moreover, since it is something new for our language reference, we believe that the benefits of new adjustments are greater, although different from the sounds the individuals are used to produce.

Brazilian Studies

Four major studies were fully developed with native Brazilian speakers. All of them bring the contribution of the Y-buzz to the clinical and training fields. The first two involved auditory-perceptive and acoustic analyzes of the sustained Y-buzz and Portuguese /i/ (like in sing) vowels. The third one focused on the impact of the Y-buzz training on connected speech and the fourth was a qualitative project involving the subjects' self-evaluations after training.

Study 1

We first developed a short study aiming to verify whether the resonant voice based on Lessac's Y-buzz could be perceived by listeners as resonant and different from a habitual Portuguese vowel /i/ and to investigate whether it would acoustically represent a better vocal production (Barrichelo & Behlau 2007). Nine newly graduated actors without voice complaints were trained to produce the Y-buzz. They received a session of Lessac's Y-buzz training from the primary investigator. Before training, they were asked to sustain the vowel /i/ at comfortable frequency and habitual loudness. After training, they were requested to sustain the Y-buzz they had learned also in a comfortable frequency and habitual loudness. Three speech-language pathologists (SLP) trained in voice developed an auditory-perceptive analysis process to judge the more resonant sample of the pair. The voice samples were acoustically compared through the Hoarseness Diagram and acoustic measures using the VoxMetria Software (CTS, version 2.0s, Brazil).

The auditory-perceptive analysis carried out in this study clearly indicated that it is possible to recognize the resonant voice based on the Y-buzz when compared with habitual normal voices in most subjects. The Y-buzz trials were identified as resonant voice in 74% of the time. A single training session was not enough to produce an optimal and perfect resonant voice sample, but all subjects tried to produce what they had learned and felt. Some of them were more successful than others, which explains why not all judges were able to correctly identify the resonant voice from normal during the listening task. We consider that concentration, motivation, and individual skills made the difference among the performances. The acoustic measures showed a statistically significant decrease of irregularity and shimmer and the Hoarseness Diagram demonstrated how the resonant voice moved toward normality for irregularity and noise components. The decrease of the acoustic measures observed in our study raises the hypothesis that the Y-buzz can be useful in our clinical practice to improve regularity and stability of the vocal folds. These acoustic data also may correlate with the laryngeal adjustments discussed in other studies (Orlikoff 1995; Verdolini-Marston et al. 1998). Titze wrote that when the energy conversion process in the glottis is efficient, the vibrations are felt in the head, neck, and chest (Titze 2001; Titze 2004). Titze also studied the wide-narrow configuration of the vocal tract (the inverted megaphone) and found that it may be useful in voice training because it requires less glottis adduction, low amplitude of vibration and low acoustic pressure at the glottis (Titze

2006). According to him, the Y-buzz is an exercise in this category and he supports the notion that the experience of feeling the sound vibration is an essential part of the learning process for economic voice production. We align ourselves with these data and we strongly believe that the Y-buzz may be a good exploration for shaping the vocal tract to help in reaching an enriched and projected sound and for leading the vocal folds to a more regular and safe mode of vibration.

Study 2

Our next project studied the participation of the vocal tract in the production of the Y-buzz, taking into account that an association between voice source and filter is required in producing a resonant voice (Barrichelo-Lindström & Behlau *in press*). Lessac's Y-buzz was perceptually and acoustically investigated, compared to the sustained Portuguese habitual /i/ vowels produced pre- and post-training. The Y-buzz training was offered by the primary investigator to 54 acting students divided in groups (average of 8 subjects per group). It consisted of four sessions of one hour, once a week. The Y-buzz was described to the Brazilian speakers as the vowel /i/ (like in sing), but produced with the inverted megaphone configuration demonstrated by the primary researcher. Each training session was based on Lessac's instructions and experiences and had the sequence of activities defined in order to be the same for all groups (Lessac, 1997). The subjects also received printed information regarding Arthur Lessac's work and the exploration of the Y-buzz. The subjects were encouraged to continuously explore and experience the Y-buzz by themselves. Five voice specialists performed a perceptual analysis, grading how resonant each sample sounded. The acoustic analyzes were developed with Praat 4.4.33. Our results showed that the trained Y-buzz was considered more resonant than the habitual /i/ samples, regardless of gender, and it was described by a reduction of the four formant frequencies. The changes in the formant frequencies suggest a lengthening of the vocal tract, according to what Sundberg and Titze point out: the longer the vocal tract, the lower the formant frequencies (Sundberg 1987; Titze 1994). It is not possible to affirm which articulatory adjustments were responsible for that, but we can suppose, in accordance with Kent and Sundberg, that the vocal tract's length can be influenced by the lowering of the larynx and/or the narrowing of the lip opening (Kent 1993; Sundberg 1987). Linville and Rens also related low formant frequencies to the enlargement of the posterior portion of the vocal tract (Linville & Rens 2001). The change in the formant frequencies contributed to the formant tuning, the ability of the vocal tract to transfer sound and gain more energy, which, in turn, facilitates projection of the voice (Sundberg 1987). The formant tuning was analyzed in our study by looking at the frequency distance between the first formant frequency (F_1) and the fundamental frequency (F_0) for the female subjects and between the first formant frequency (F_1) and the second harmonic frequency (H_2) for the male subject. It is well known that the transference function of the vocal tract is better when two formants or one formant and one partial are close in frequency increasing their respective amplitudes (Sundberg 1987; Titze, 1994). Other studies (Acker 1987; Raphael & Scherer 1987) have found the formant tuning during the Call production, in much the same way as we have found for the Y-buzz. When comparing the productions of the habitual /i/ vowel pre- and post-training, the acoustic data also suggested that the habitual mode of voice production was influenced by the Y-buzz training, significantly in the case of the female group.

Study 3

Since the Y-buzz is described as a tonal guide, our third study aimed to evaluate the impact of this strategy on connected speech (Lessac 1997; Barrichelo-Lindström & Behlau 2007). Before the Y-buzz training, twenty-eight of the same acting students recorded a reading passage in a self-selected habitual pitch and comfortable loudness. After training, they recorded the same passage, this time following the instruction: *"Pay attention to the resonance vibration of the Y-buzz, take a breath and transfer the sensation to your reading."* Both readings were randomly presented to five voice specialists in two sequential listening sessions. In the first one they should indicate the better sample from each pair, for professional purposes, or mark if they sounded equivalent. In the first case, they also should indicate in which aspect (or aspects, should there be more than one) the sample was better. In the second listening test the listeners should only indicate if one reading was more resonant than the other or if they sounded equivalent. The impact of the continuous Y-buzz explorations was better identified when the attention was drawn to the resonance aspect. Still, experienced listeners pointed out improvement also in other vocal aspects such as overall voice quality, articulation, loudness and pitch. We had expected that the resonance would be the improved aspect, but it was interesting to observe the others mentioned, showing that the Y-buzz training can lead to new voice and speech discoveries. Apparently one new adjustment brings others.

Study 4

Our fourth study involved the same acting students and focused on self-evaluations. Fifty subjects accepted the invitation to write down their impressions and the benefits obtained from the training. The answers offered an interesting panorama on the individual impact of the exercises and were not directed in any way. We obtained a rich variety of terms on perceptions (Appendix 1), including resonance improvement, vocal quality stability and less fatigue; and also important, many participants reported a better self-awareness. Among the answers we highlight: the improvement of resonance and the feeling of vibrations mentioned by 17 subjects, of whom 4 affirmed less nasality; more self-awareness pointed out by 16 subjects; the sensation of a more open throat or voice freer defined by 10 subjects; more projection mentioned by 7 subjects; improvement in voice quality or stability affirmed by 7 subjects; diminished sensations of vocal fatigue or pain pointed out by 3 subjects. Some others also mentioned improvement in the articulation, breathing, habitual pitch and its range and the good impact in the singing voice, besides the general appreciation for the training. Some others mentioned the advantage of developing the internal hearing and the ability of the voice to change in a natural and relaxing way. Seven subjects reported the immediate application of the Y-buzz in their careers and the importance of continued explorations. The results show that though the learning ability and the impact of the training varies, the Y-buzz exploration contributes to their vocal lives.

Final Considerations

Direct and indirect positive benefits from the use of the Y-buzz were clear in all studies performed. In spite of the wide range of individual responses, there were not any negative results or sensations after production.

We assume that a longer training period and the association of other practices that belong to Lessac's Tonal NRG would also be worthy studying. Laryngeal analysis as well as videolaryngofluoroscopy could provide important additional information.

Perhaps a longer training period would have been necessary to get setting. The Y-buzz training requires time and continuous exploration. The continuous kinesensic process of experiencing and self-exploration was fundamental. We have observed that not everybody has a well-developed kinesthetic ability, which makes the learning more difficult. Many individuals are locked into their even clearer results and further stabilize the new vocal hearing and could not be "freed from it" easily. We have chosen acting students to participate in our studies because we assumed that previous voice training would help to learn the Y-buzz. This was true for some of them, but not for all.

Besides the acoustic results, an interesting observation was the strict relation between the frequency chosen by the subjects to practice the Y-buzz and the resonant sound they produced. As the subjects found the ideal frequency, the Y-buzz became more evident.

Considering the differences between the languages, we agree with Munro who affirmed that the Y-buzz training is not restricted to English speakers (Munro, 2002).

We strongly believe in the benefits of the Y-buzz, not only for achieving the ring of the voice and speech, but also as an excellent way to become more sensitive to the physical sensations of the voice. This is particularly important for patients, since they are used to hearing the voice problem and making effort to speak. More studies involving subjects with voice complaints are necessary, but our clinical experience, our acoustic data and the literature reinforce the usefulness of the Y-buzz and Lessac's whole NRG training approach.

Coda: a personal note from Viviane Barrichelo-Lindstrom

I first encountered Lessac's work when I did my fellowship in *Care of the Professional Voice* in Philadelphia with Dr. Sataloff and his team in 1999. On a certain day, I had the opportunity to watch a voice coach training the *Call* with a patient and we discussed the Lessac work. So I decided to look for the famous book—*The Use And Training Of The Human Voice: A Practical Approach To Speech And Voice Dynamics*! It wasn't easy and it took me some hours in NY visiting some bookshops. As soon as I started reading it I simply fell in love with the way voice and resonance were described and trained. To feel the voice and not just hear it became my motto. And it made sense, for clinical and training purposes.

Despite not being able to practice the Lessac work with certified teachers I started to explore some strategies by myself, just following the instructions given in the book.

The Y-buzz was the voice exploration first achieved. Fortunately, I had the honor to do some practice with the master Arthur and his team for at least a short period of time, a chance that put me onto the right track and gave me the confidence to continue studying and exploring. As a voice clinician, voice-scientist, voice coach and also a professional voice user, studying and writing about the Lessac work became my duty. Fortunately I found the support of my professor Mara Behlau who joined me in this task. Finally, I'd like to thank you so much, Arthur, for the inspiration!!!

References

Acker, BF. 1987. 'Vocal Tract Adjustments for the Projected Voice.' In *Journal of Voice,* vol. 1, no.1, pp.77-82.

Barrichelo, VMO & Behlau, M. 2007. 'Perceptual Identification and Acoustic Measures of the Resonant Voice Based on Lessac's Y-Buzz—A Preliminary Study With Actors.' In *Journal of Voice*, vol. 21, no.1, pp. 46–53.

Barrichelo-Lindström, V & Behlau, M, 'Resonant Voice in Acting Students: Perceptual and Acoustic Correlates of the Trained Y-Buzz by Lessac.' In *Journal of Voice, in press.*

Barrichelo-Lindström, V & Behlau, M. 2007. 'Resonant Voice in Acting Students: Effects of the Type of Instruction on Perceptual Voice Analysis.' Presented at the *Voice Foundation's 36th Annual Symposium*: Care of the Professional Voice, Philadelphia, Pennsylvania.

Kent, R.D. 1993. 'Vocal Tract Acoustics'. In *Journal of Voice*, vol. 7, no. 2, pp. 97-117.

Lessac, A. 1997. *The Use And Training Of The Human Voice: A Practical Approach To Speech And Voice Dynamics.* California: Mayfield Publishing Company.

Linville, S.E. & Rens, J. 2001. 'Vocal Tract Resonance Analysis of Aging Voice Using Long- Term Average Spectra.' In *Journal of Voice*, vol.15, no. 3, pp. 323-330.

Munro, M. 2002. 'Lessac's Tonal Action in Women's Voices and the "Actors Formant": a comparative study' [doctoral thesis]. Potchefstroom University, South Africa.

Orlikoff, R.F. 1995. 'Vocal stability and vocal tract configuration: an acoustic and electroglottographic investigation.' In *Journal of Voice*, vol. 9, pp.173–181.

Raphael, B.N. & Scherer, R.C. 1987. 'Voice Modifications of Stage Actors: Acoustic Analyses.' In *Journal of Voice,* vol.1, no.1, pp. 83-87.

Sundberg, J. 1987. *The Science of the Singing Voice*. Illinois: Northern Illinois University Press.

Titze, I.R. 1994. *Principles of Voice Production*. New Jersey: Prentice-Hall.

Titze, I.R. 2001, 'Acoustic Interpretation of Resonant Voice.' In *Journal of Voice*, vol. 15, no. 4, pp. 519-528.

Titze, I.R. 2004. 'A Theoretical Study of F0-F1 Interaction with Application to Resonant Speaking and Singing Voice.' In *Journal of Voice,* vol. 18, no.3, pp. 292-298.

Titze, I.R. 2006. 'Voice Training and Therapy with a Semi-occluded Vocal Tract: Rational and Scientific Underpinnings.' In *J Speech Lang Hear Res.*, vol. 49, pp. 448-59.

Verdolini-Marston, K; Druker, DG; Palmer, PM & Samawi, H. 1998. 'Laryngeal adduction in resonant voice.' In *Journal of Voice*, vol.12, pp. 315–327.

Addendum

Translation of the female written feedback regarding the Y-buzz training.

Subjects	
1	My voice is freer and I'm able to speak louder, something that I couldn't do before. The Y-buzz is very interesting and allowed myself to observe my own voice.
2	My voice became less nasal and with vibrations concentrated at the hard palate. I just need to pay attention so I don't forget the inverted megaphone.
3	I think my voice became cleaner. Still, it's easier to pay attention on that during the training.
4	I liked the training a lot. Just one hour per week wasn't enough, but it was worthy! I feel now that I don't use so much my throat to speak.
5	I'm able now to project more my voice; it resonates without harming my throat. I've been practicing the Y-buzz right before going to the stage and this helped a lot.
6	I feel my resonance got better! I liked a lot!
7	*Subject didn't answer.*
8	I liked the training a lot and I feel the difference. My voice was nasal and in high pitch. Nowadays I speak in a more comfortable pitch and my voice is more resonant, less tight.
9	I know I wasn't 100% in training, but I improved. The awareness about the resonance improved. I feel vibrations that were unknown before. The internal space became bigger; my voice is more stable. The breathing also got better.
10	The Y-buzz improved my resonance awareness and made me more sensitive to the internal hearing.
11	My articulation got better!!!
12	*Subject didn't answer.*
13	The training helped to develop the open throat sensation. It's more relaxed (and the sour throat decreased).
14	So interesting the Y-buzz approach. The discovery of a new sonority!
15	I noticed that my speech is more open thanks to the megaphone; it's more resonant and more articulated. I hear my voice softer and resonant, less metallic.
16	I started to feel the vibration of my voice stronger and stronger. My voice was nasal before and with the training I noticed a great improvement.
17	I feel now that my voice is more controlled and has a direction. The training was interesting because the voice change happens in a naturally relaxing way, giving more freedom to the speech.
18	I found easy and difficult days while exploring the Y-buzz.
19	I changed a lot. Now I can project a stronger sound to the audience. I loved the training and I realized that it was great for my career. I'll use my Y-buzz for everything. Thanks!

20	It was great! I feel my voice cleaner and I use the Y-buzz before the play. It was good to develop this awareness.
21	I'm sure the training helped my vocal awareness and it's fundamental to continue it. After the training I don't remember episodes of voice breaks.
22	I'm able to feel the vibration in my face. I don't force the throat; I'm able to let her free.
23	My projection improved and I'm aware to the need of opening more my mouth.
24	I thought the training very interesting. I would like to continue it. Despite the short duration, I noticed some changes, including more perception of my vocal actions.
25	I noticed a big change! Singing in the bathroom, for example…. It seemed that the entire house would hear me!!
26	*Subject didn't answer.*
27	The training was really worthwhile to understand how the resonance happens and this helped me on stage and as a teacher. I know I would have had a better result if I had practiced more at home. But now, working on my resonance, I don't feel my voice tired anymore.
28	Since the training started, I haven't been hoarse or had pain in my throat. I found vibrations in my face and I pay more attention on the words that leave my mouth.
29	The training improved my voice quality. If I pay attention while speaking, I try to bring the resonance to my speech, something that didn't happen before. It's more pleasant to hear my own voice.
30	I developed more awareness and vocal perception, for sure. I also developed more low pitches.
31	I don't feel my voice tired anymore.

Translation of the male written feedback regarding the Y-buzz training

Subjects	
1	The training offered me more vocal awareness.
2	I acquired a vocal awareness that was unknown before.
3	I don't feel discomfort in my throat so often anymore.
4	I've always thought my voice strange – without ring. I started noticing some changes and I guess I can improve if I keep exploring the Y-buzz. The training was short, but enough to inspire everyone to keep on your own search.
5	I've been using the learned strategies in my vocal warming up and I also noticed the impact on my singing voice.
6	I liked it a lot because my voice gained more resonance.
7	Now I feel my voice is more consistent. Automatically, I pay more attention on my voice.
8	The Y-buzz training helps to focus better the voice on stage. I don't think my voice is nasal anymore. I just need to work on the articulation of the sounds.
9	*Subject didn't answer.*
10	I thought it is so nice!!!!
11	I started to observe more myself and pay attention on the use of my voice. The approach was very interesting – easy to understand and practice.
12	I was used to force my throat, but since the Y-buzz training started this has never happened again. I liked the process and it was clear the evolution for everybody.
13	It was very good, but I wish we had more classes. When I started to "find myself", it was over. I realized a different way to listen to myself. I liked to notice the sound passing through my face and to project my voice without forcing the throat. My reference for the Y-buzz is my eyes: it seems that I move the sound with them.
14	I thought the training very interesting for the voice quality and body exploration.
15	I reach lower tones after the Y-buzz training.
16	I thought this training very important, but I considered it too short. I would like it twice a week. It's a nice and focused technical work and this makes a difference for the voice professional. It's a shame that some people realize that too late.
17	It was important to practice the resonance and feel the vibration of my voice. I feel that I can increase the volume when I need.
18	*Subject didn't answer.*
19	I could locate the place where my voice resonates.
20	In one of the weeks of training I practiced more the Y-buzz and then I realized that I should continue in the same pace to get better results.
21	The training helped my speaking and singing voice.
22	I thought great to feel more my speech and voice. Some of the practices are also funny when developed in a group.
23	My resonance got better and I can locate the Y-buzz also in my conversational speech when I prepare the megaphone.

Use of Lessemes in Text-to-Speech Synthesis

Rattima Nitisaroj and Gary A. Marple
Lessac Technologies, Inc., West Newton, MA. USA

Contextualization

For a speech synthesizer to be able to successfully produce natural sounding speech, a considerable part depends on symbolic sound representations of the input text. Over several decades, research and development of text-to-speech synthesis systems have focused on the use of traditional symbolic representations, such as IPA, SAMPA, or ARPAbet, to represent the text to be synthesized. Rather than adopting the traditional symbols, Lessac Technologies, Inc. (LTI) has derived a new set of symbolic units, called Lessemes, from Arthur Lessac's tono-sensory symbols to use in its current text-to-speech system, resulting in more humanlike synthetic speech. This paper demonstrates LTI's Lessac-based symbols, and discusses their several advantages over traditional sound symbols with respect to representations of acoustic properties and text-to-speech synthesis application.

Text-to-Speech Synthesis—Imitating a Human

The human voice simultaneously provides meaning and identity—word pronunciations and phrasings that clarify and enhance the meaning of what is said, and characteristics that identify the speaker. Synthesizing speech to sound like a human reading aloud is difficult. Lessac Technologies, Inc. (LTI) is succeeding in this regard. It has built a working prototype that synthesizes a specific female voice with human sounding pronunciation including changes in pitch, energy and pacing, while relying on plain un-annotated text as the sole input.

The prototype is a computerized system comprising three parts: (1) plain text parsed by a computer as words, sentences, and paragraphs to be spoken or synthesized expressively according to prosodic rules; (2) a recording of a voice actor reading a "human readable" print-out of the parsed text with additional annotated markups indicating how the parsed text is to be spoken; and, (3) a computerized synthesizer searching for acoustic units of speech, many smaller than a phoneme, that are stored as wave files in a database and then properly sequencing them into words, phrases and sentences that are assembled into continuous wave files and "played back" as human speech.

The key to this process lies in the common denominators developed for accurately translating how words, phrases, sentences and paragraphs never explicitly pronounced by the voice actor are to be pronounced according to prosodic rules using small acoustic units from the voice actor's recordings. We call the common denominators Lessemes™ as they begin with Arthur Lessac's tono-sensory symbols that came from his research into speech as a holistic and kinesensic process involving the entire body (Lessac 1997). Using computerized text parsing rules, Lessac's tono-sensory symbols are augmented with prosodic information to become Lessemes. The sequence of Lessemes is used for two separate tasks. First, Lessemes are transformed into annotated text for the voice actor to follow during the recording process. Second, Lessemes constitute the input to the speech synthesizer, which searches for corresponding acoustic units to assemble into synthesized speech.

What is a Lesseme?

Figure 1 below illustrates the two different portrayals of Lessemes that emerge from a computerized parsing of text. The upper portion portrays the graphic representation for the voice actor to read and pronounce, while the lower portion that begins with "Coded Lessemes:" portrays the coded Lesseme stream processed by the computer when synthesizing speech.

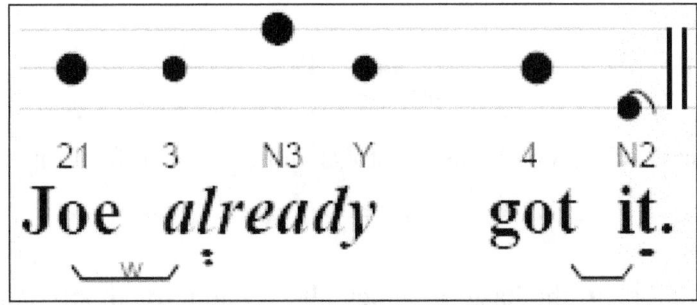

Coded Lessemes: DG 212iHfN cWa_ 32iLfN LcT R N33iHfN D Y2iLfN _ G 42iHfN TcD _ N21iLfW TcS ||

Figure 1. LTI markups

The voice actor markups adopt Arthur Lessac's tono-sensory symbols. Vowel orthographic forms are designated with Lessac's symbols for tonal, structural, and neutral vowels. Consonant orthographic forms are marked with playability information indicating whether the consonant is sustainable (double underlined) or percussive (single underlined), as well as how the consonant is linked to the next sound in connected speech (described in more detail in Section 2.2). On top of the orthographic forms and vowel symbols, LTI markups for the voice actor display additional symbols similar to musical notes. These notes represent the intonation pattern that a person with sufficient voice training can follow. Each syllable corresponds to a note. Higher notes are pronounced with higher pitch. Large notes mean stressed syllables while small notes refer to unstressed syllables. In Figure 1, the last syllable is further specified with an inflection, which reflects a particular shape of pitch movement within the syllable. Inflections can take various shapes, including upglide (✺), downglide (✺), upcircumflex (✺), downcircumflex (✺), and level sustention (●–).

A graphical display such as the upper portion of Figure 1 is used by the voice actor when recording each prompt, whether a word, phrase, sentence, or paragraph. For computer synthesizing, the machine-readable code, shown as "DG 212iHfN cWa _ 32iLfN LcT R N33iHfN D Y2iLfN _ G 42iHfN TcD _ N21iLfW TcS ||" corresponds directly with the graphical display shown above. Lessemes are divided into two classes: vowel and consonant. Each class is explained below and illustrated with an example.

Vowel Lessemes

A vowel Lesseme name consists of four components, as shown in Figure 2.

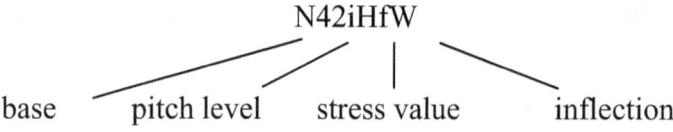

Figure 2. Components of vowel Lesseme

The first component, the base, includes all Lessac's tonal, structural, and neutral vowel notations plus two additional symbols for 'syllabic *n*' in words such as *cotton, garden,* and 'syllabic *l*' in words such as *little, needle*. The pitch level component varies according to the syntactic and semantic importance of the word and lexical stress value. In the current implementation, the greater the syntactic and semantic importance of the word, the higher the pronunciation pitch level. In the future, syntactic or semantic emphasis can be realized by other means such as lower pitch, wider pitch range, amplitude change, duration change, or any combination thereof. Within the word, a primary-stressed syllable is usually associated with the highest pitch level in comparison with secondary-stressed or unstressed syllables. The next component has two values: iH for stressed syllables (large notes in the graphical display), and iL for unstressed syllables (small notes). Finally, the inflection component reflects the pitch movement of the syllable to which the vowel belongs. It can take one of these six values: fU (upglide), fW (downglide), fC (upcircumflex), fD (downcircumflex), fS (level sustention), and fN (no inflection).

Consonant Lessemes

Consonant Lesseme names are composed of two components as shown in Figure 3:

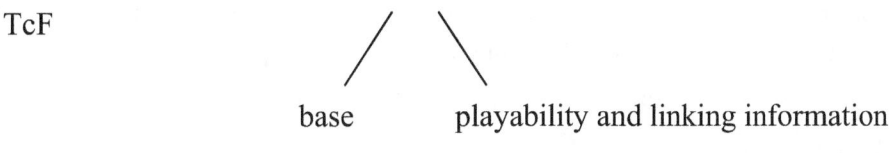

Figure 3. Components of consonant Lesseme

The base can be one of the instruments in the Lessac consonant orchestra. All consonants can be mapped onto the IPA symbols except four symbols to which the IPA symbol set as normally used for transcribing American English speech has no counterpart. They are D°L woodblock click, T°L woodblock click, DZ tambourine, and TS high-hat cymbal. For the playability and linking information, the following values are available:

- cD: direct link (a word-final consonant followed by a word-initial vowel ex. *get it, wash up*)
- cF: percussive sound, play and link (a word-final consonant followed by a word-initial consonant produced at a different point of articulation ex. *get him*)
- cG: sustainable sound, play and link (ex. *wash clean*)
- cP: prepare and link (a word-final consonant followed by a word-initial consonant produced at the same or closely related point of articulation, ex. *get nothing, wash shirts*)

- cS: percussive sound, play (a consonant followed by another consonant with a different point of articulation within the same word ex. *software*)
- cT: sustainable sound, play (ex. *washcloth*)
- cU: prepare (a consonant followed by another consonant with the same or closely related point of articulation within the same word ex. *softness*)
- no tag: natural link (a consonant followed by a vowel within the same word ex. *tall, shall*)

In short, Lessemes can be defined as sound symbols derived from Lessac's tono-sensory symbols plus symbols providing additional guidelines for pronunciation according to the specific prosody required. Note that Lessemes may be altered for use when synthesizing speech from text in other dialects and languages as the Lessac tono-sensory symbols are not restricted to General American English. Kur (2005) and Stern (1983) demonstrated the use of Lessac tono-sensory symbols in several dialects of English, including Standard British, Cockney, New York City, Boston, Southern American, etc. Gert Terny (http://www.voicefactory.be) has taught the Lessac method to Flemish, French, and Dutch speaking actors and singers, and established the European Lessac Center (Terny 2008). In addition, the Lessac work has been introduced to Korean theatre students by Kim (2006).

Lesseme Advantages

This section shows various advantages that Lessemes have over traditional sound symbols with respect to accuracy in representing acoustic properties of sounds and improvement in the unit selection component of a speech synthesis system.

Better Representations of Segments' Acoustic Properties

While traditional symbolic sets, such as IPA (http://www.arts.gla.ac.uk/IPA/ipa.html), SAMPA (http://www.phon.ucl.ac.uk/home/sampa/), or ARPAbet (developed by the Advanced Research Projects Agency), represent segmental properties that are distinctive in speech, Lessemes are abstract representations that capture both segmental and suprasegmental properties of a sound unit in more refined details. To illustrate the point, several samples of a vowel and a consonant are provided in Figure 4 and Figure 5.

Figure 4 includes five waveforms and spectrograms of the vowel N4 extracted from natural speech. This vowel normally corresponds to a schwa sound in other phonetic alphabets and they make at most two distinctions (e.g. ʌ - stressed schwa vs. ə - unstressed schwa in IPA; @ vs. V in SAMPA; and, in ARPAbet, only one representation—AH). In LTI's method there are 36 Lessemes for the N4 vowel. Figure 4 shows five instances of N4 occurring in a phrase medial position, all preceded by the onset nasal M and followed by the coda nasal N in all cases but Example 4c where NG is used (because of data sparseness). We proceed with a series of pair-wise comparisons between Figure 4a and the rest. In the first comparison, 4a vs. 4b, the vowels N42iHfN and N41iHfN can be distinguished by the pitch level component, which is reflected in an overall lower F0 value over the entire vowel as can be observed. In the next comparison, while other components are constant, N42iHfN and N42iLfN display different stress values. Acoustically, the iH value (4a) correlates to longer segment duration and darker formants, and the opposite for the iL value (4c). Then, as mentioned in the previous section, the inflection value corresponds to the pitch movement.

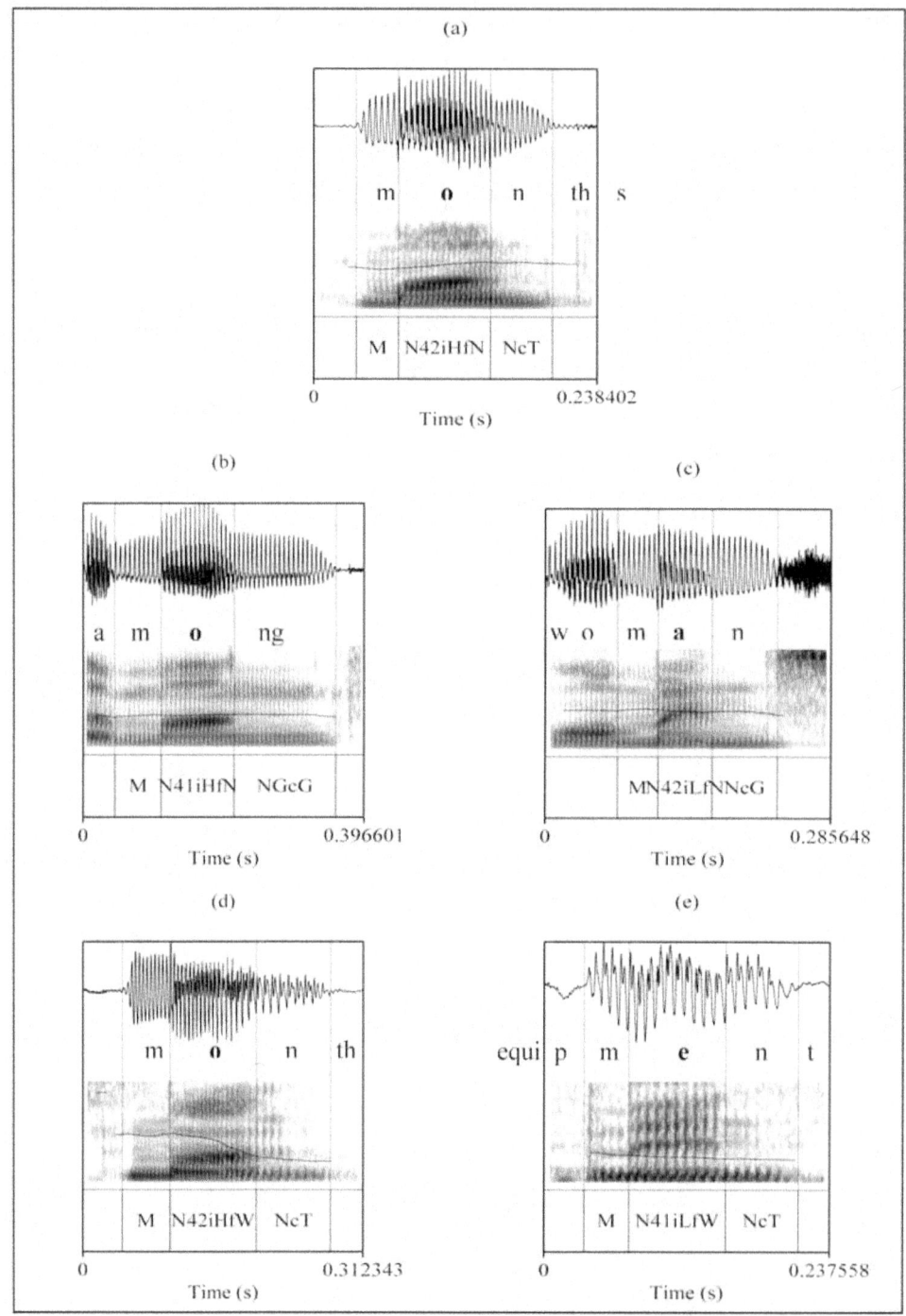

Figure 4. Different acoustic properties of N4

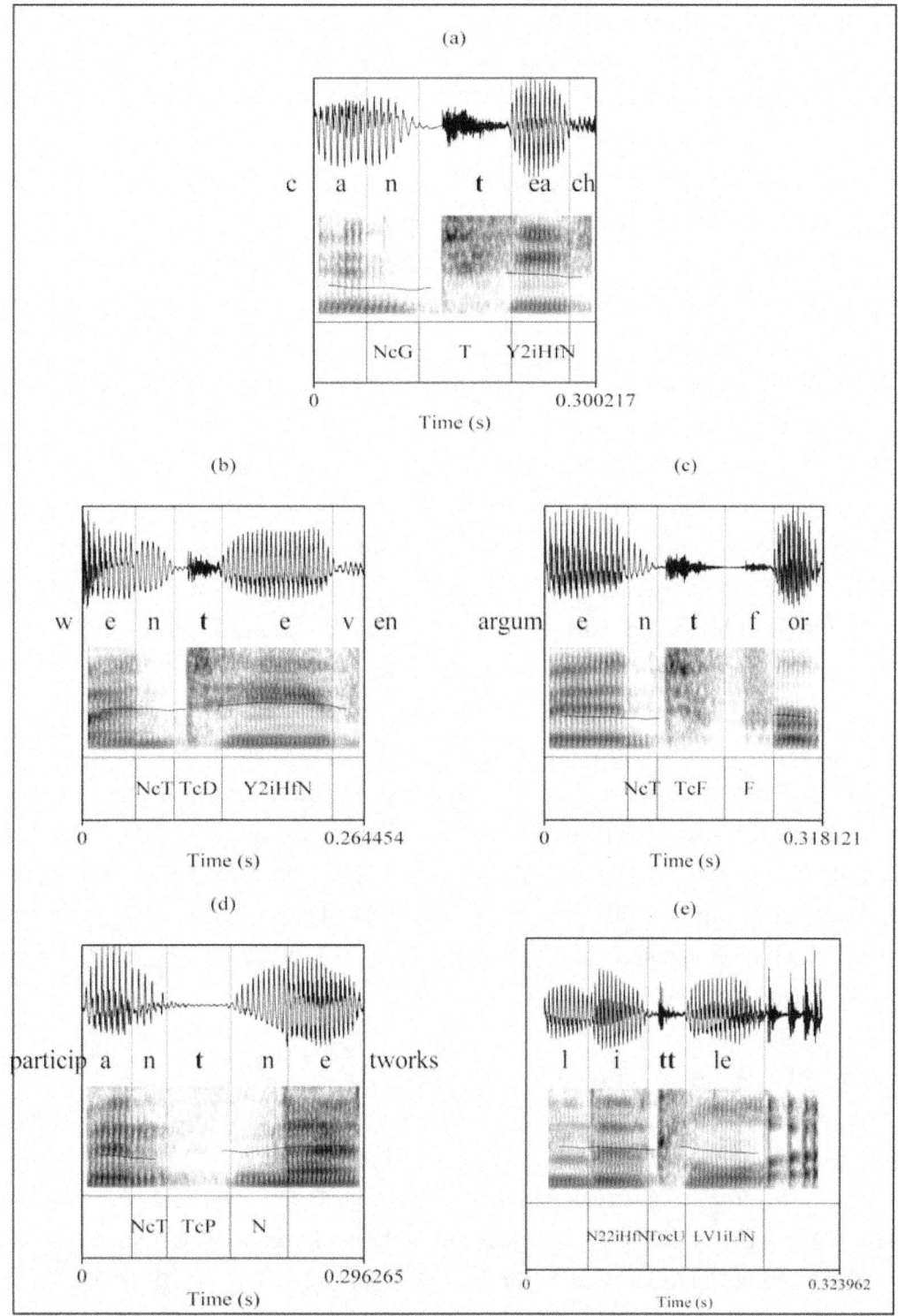

Figure 5. Different acoustic properties of T

With the downglide tag (fW), the vowel in 4d shows a higher degree of pitch movement than that in 4a, which has the no-inflection tag (fN). So far, only one component of the Lessemes under investigation is different in each comparison, namely pitch level, stress value, or inflection type. The last pair-wise comparison, N42iHfN (4a) vs. N41iLfW (4e), illustrates the case where Lessemes are different in all three components. These differences show up in waveforms and spectrograms. The vowel in 4e possesses the observed acoustic properties of those in 4b, 4c, and 4d. Compared to that in 4a, it has lower f0, fainter formants, and downglide pitch pattern.

When using Lessemes, better sound-symbol correspondence can be achieved not only for vowels, but also for consonants. Figure 5 demonstrates the acoustic properties of what other alphabets have only one symbol for. The contexts where these sound instances occur are also provided. Acoustically, the sounds for 't' usually consist of a silent period (representing the closure when the tongue touches the alveolar ridge) followed by a burst (the tongue springs away or releases from the alveolar ridge) and a period of aspiration (the air flows through after the release). Long and strong aspiration takes place when the consonant is in the onset position (5a). When it is followed by a vowel, the aspiration period usually displays the formants of the upcoming vowel (5a/5b vs. 5c). In addition, the consonant shows different characteristics depending on the place of articulation of the following consonant. In 5d, because the upcoming consonant shares the same place of articulation, the consonant under investigation has neither burst nor aspiration that result from the release (compared to 5c where the two consonants are produced at different points and 't' needs to be released before continuing to 'f'). 5e is an example of a voiceless woodblock click. Compared to 5a-c, the burst is stronger, while there is less amount of aspiration.

Benefits of Lessemes for Text-to-Speech Synthesis

The technology of LTI's speech synthesis system is based on Hunt and Black's (1996) idea of unit selection synthesis. For each linguistic type, a number of units, whose acoustic properties vary depending on the context, are stored in the database. At synthesis time, the system tries to select the best unit for each position resulting in a unit sequence that optimally meets the linguistic and acoustic specifications. The selected units are then concatenated to create a fragment, sentence, or paragraph of synthesized speech for the text. This is true even where the particular word, sentence, or paragraph was never recorded by a voice actor and thus does not exist in the recorded database. Most commercial TTS systems nowadays use the unit selection method. Some of the well-known unit selection systems include AT&T (Beutnagel et al. 1999), Nuance (a successor of Breen and Jackson's [1998] Laureate system), and SVOX (Wouters 2007).

To construct a voice database for unit selection, the voice actor records a large number of prompts. After that, the voice recording of the prompts is segmented into small units, each corresponding to the Lesseme as found in the text of the prompts, and appropriately labeled. To a significant extent, success in unit selection synthesis relies on accurate sound to phonetic symbol correspondence. Quality synthesized speech cannot be produced if the symbol does not accurately represent the sound. To achieve sound-symbol correspondence, LTI relies on the unique features of Lessemes to: (1) enhance the accuracy of voice database construction; and, (2) use the precision of Lessemes to identify prosodically important acoustic features relevant to the linguistic context of the text to be synthesized as speech.

Enhanced Accuracy of Voice Database

Figure 6 compares LTI's voice database construction (6a) with that of database approaches used by others (6b). Following the LTI method, the text to-be-recorded is first processed by the text analyzer, which yields the stream of Lessemes and prosodic breaks. The resulting Lessemes and breaks are then transformed into the LTI markups (described in Section 2) for the voice actor to read. The way the voice actor records the prompt is controlled by the markups that include explicit markings of the text segments and intonations. The recordings of the text prompts as pronounced are then segmented and labeled with the same Lessemes and breaks that underlie the markups the voice actor follows. The fact that the same Lessemes are output for the voice actor markups as well as the labeling of the database of recorded prompts guarantees a high degree of correspondence between the symbols representing the sounds to be produced and the sounds as actually recorded by the voice actor. In other systems, as shown in 6b, there is no such guarantee. This is because the voice actor sees only plain text, and the subsequent recordings are labeled with the symbols produced by the text analyzer. Furthermore, other systems use phonetic alphabets without explicit markings as to how segments should be pronounced, which intonation pattern to follow, and where to place a prosodic break. As a result, there is a strong tendency for substantial variation in the way a voice actor pronounces the same text in different prosodic circumstances. This is especially true for intonation levels, co-articulations, and the expressive emphasis of the same words and phrases found in different linguistic contexts. The difficulty with using the other existing methods for pronouncing, identifying, and labeling the recorded sounds is that their lack of precision severely limits their abilities to inform voice actors about changes of pitch, intonation, and articulatory durations required for expressive prosodic speech. This is why speech synthesis of sentences and extended text using existing methods continue to sound robotic and monotonous.

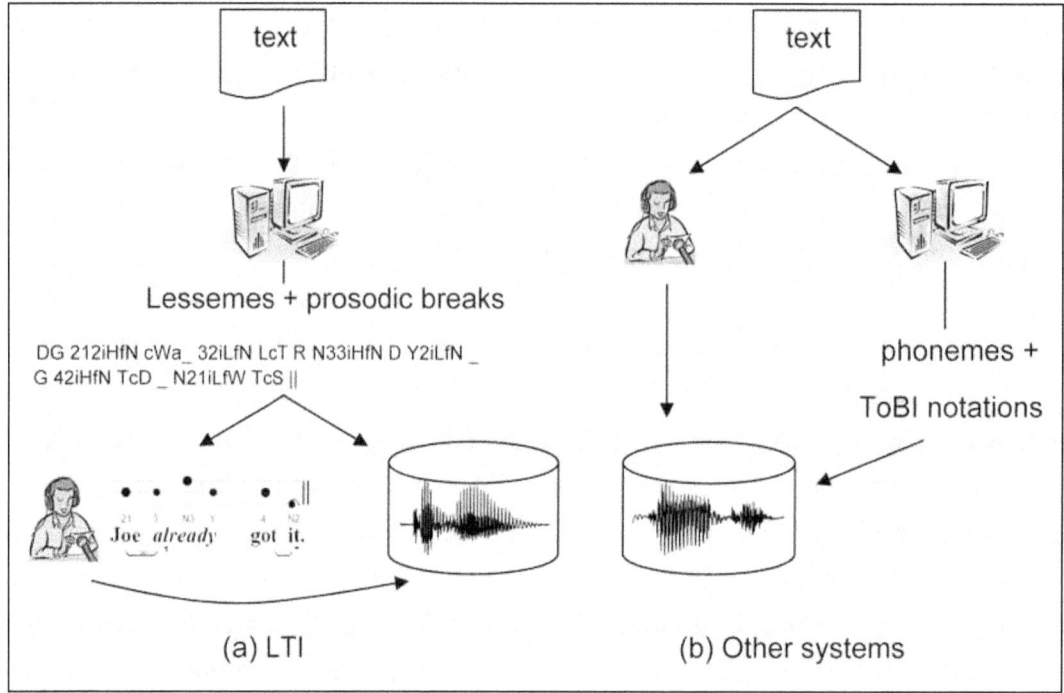

Figure 6. Comparison between LTI's and other systems' voice database construction

Identifying Prosodically Important Features of Recorded Prompts According to the Linguistic Context of Text to be Synthesized as Speech

The other unique characteristic of LTI's text-to-speech synthesis system that significantly contributes to a more natural synthesized speech is the use of Lessemes in their linguistic and prosodic context to locate acoustic candidates to be assembled as synthesized speech. As seen in Section 3.2.1, Lessemes allow a more fine-grained distinction of sounds. Units of the same type share closely similar acoustic characteristics. Compared to a phoneme-based unit selection synthesis system, LTI's Lesseme-based system will identify and select a unit that more accurately possesses the desired segmental and supra-segmental properties. For example, the best onset *t* will be selected from a bin of onset *t*'s, instead of from a bin that mixes all onset and coda *t*'s together. In addition, since prosodic features are encoded in the vowel Lessemes, the LTI system is more specific about the pitch levels and pitch movements of segments than a system that utilizes ToBI (Silverman et al. 1992, Syrdal and Hirschberg 2001, Syrdal and McGory 2000), a relatively impoverished prosodic annotation scheme (some shortcomings of applying ToBI in speech technology are addressed in Mixdorff 2002 and Wightman 2002). LTI's system can select the best vowel Lesseme unit based on the unit's own pitch level and pitch movement in relation to pitch levels and movements of the surrounding syllables.

Concluding Comments

Lessac Technologies Inc. has, by combining Arthur Lessac's tono-sensory symbols and his stress on holistic processes to "feel" sound production within the body with contemporary computer analysis of text plus the examination of the essences of various prosodic styles, succeeded in demonstrating that expressively synthesized speech can be effected directly from the text to be synthesized.

References

Beutnagel, M., Conkie, A., Schroeter, J., Stylianou, Y. and Syrdal, A. 1999. 'The AT&T Next-Gen TTS system.' In *Joint Meeting of ASA, EAA, and DAGA,* Berlin, Germany.

Breen, A. P., and Jackson, P. 1998. 'A phonologically motivated method of selecting non-uniform units.' In *Proceedings of the 1998 International Conference on Spoken Language Processing,* November 30-December 4, Sydney, Australia.

Hunt, A., and Black, A. 1996. 'Unit selection in a concatenative speech synthesis system using a large speech database.' In *Proceedings of the International Conference on Speech and Language Processing 1996,* vol. 1, pp. 373–376.

Kim, S. 2006. 'Introducing Lessac training to freshman theatre students in Korea.' Presented at the 1st Annual Lessac Conference, January 12-15, Denver, CO.

Kur, B. 2005. *Stage dialect studies: A continuation of the Lessac approach to actor voice and speech training.* Published by the author.

Lessac, A. 1996. *The Use and Training of the Human Voice: A Bio-Dynamic Approach to Vocal Life,* Third Edition, Boston: McGraw-Hill Higher Education.

Mixdorff, H. 2002. 'Speech technology, ToBI, and making sense of prosody.' In *Speech Prosody 2002,* April 11-13, Aix-en-Provence, France.

Silverman, K., Beckman, M., Pitrelli, J., Ostendorf, M., Wightman, C., Price, P., Pierrehumbert, J., and Hirschberg, J. 1992. 'TOBI: A standard for labeling English prosody.' In *Proceedings of the 1992 International Conference on Spoken Language Processing,* vol. 2, pp. 867-870.

Stern, D. 1983. *Acting with an accent* [CD series]. Los Angeles: Dialect Accent Specialists.

Syrdal, A., and Hirschberg, J. 2001. 'Automatic ToBI prediction and alignment to speed manual labeling of prosody.' *Speech Communication* 33: 135-151.

Syrdal, A., and McGory, J. 2000. 'Inter-transcriber reliability of ToBI prosodic labeling.' In *Proceedings of the International Conference on Spoken Language Processing,* Beijing, China, 235-238.

Terny, G. 2008. 'Research projects of the European Lessac Center.' Presented at the 3rd Annual Lessac Conference, January 3-5, State College, PA.

Wightman, C. 2002. 'ToBI or not ToBI?' In *Speech Prosody 2002,* April 11-13, Aix-en-Provence, France.

Wouters, J. 2007. 'SVOX participation in Blizzard 2007.' In *BLZ3-2007,* paper 013.

Pedagogical Explorations and Other Applications

Sean Turner

The following writings within this section foster a larger dialogue about the pedagogical implications and possibilities of the Lessac work within and across educational contexts and include perceptions, reflections, and inquiries completed by teachers, students, performers, and researchers. Although aspects of the Lessac work are discussed, the emphasis herein does not appear to be on how to teach Lessac, as much as it is on further inquiry and praxis upon the possibilities for situating Lessac within multiple educational contexts, including acting and voice training, theatre education, health education, arts based inquiry, and educational research.

Pedagogy is generally referred to as either the art or science of teaching, and as such, has significant political, social, and economic implications for those who are being taught. The teaching of voice and body is no different. Who teaches what voice approach has much to do with who learns and in what context. Both of these have significant implications in the real world, including for those who desire to teach the Lessac work, only to find that the school to which they are applying prefers to use another vocal approach; for those who wish to perform for a living, only to find that their voice is not strong enough to get a "call" back at an audition; and for those who wish to integrate Lessac training into another educational context, only to find that there are opposing perceptions and assumptions about how learning should place.

In order for the reader to consider and reflect upon some of the bigger implications situated around notions of teaching and learning, I will highlight some key ideas from Kamberelis and Dimitriadis' (2005) heuristic framework of four chronotopes and discuss how notions of knowledge and language have been viewed differently within the large body of language and education research that has shaped teaching and learning for the past 100 years.
In order for the reader to consider how, if at all, the Lessac work is situated within or outside of these frameworks for knowledge and language, I will briefly highlight some of the significant pedagogical implications that Arthur

Lessac espoused in his early writings. This should allow the reader to draw upon a larger framework in which they are able to discuss and reflect upon threads, disruptions, and tensions between current educational research, some of the pedagogical implications of the Lessac work, and viewpoints of the authors in this section.

Knowledge and language

In today's constantly changing global landscape, the debate over what constitutes acceptable knowledge and language within the process of teaching and learning has become increasingly hostile. This is exemplified by the fact that as measures of accountability have been enacted for many K-12 schools, the stakes for both teachers and students have intensified, leading many to perceive that learning can only be evaluated by how well a student does on a test. While the political rhetoric[1] that is situated around the notion of testing positions those who want national reform versus those who want local control,[2] there are significant philosophical differences about teaching and learning going on, which might have significant consequences for all educators in the future.

In *Approaches to Language and Literacy Research*, Kamberelis and Dimitradis (2005) use a genealogical approach to map out various epistemological and theoretical foundations that have been used in education inquiry, and in the process discuss "what conditions of possibility—ideas, discursive and material practices, social and political forces—[were] in place for [so many] varied forms of inquiry to emerge, develop, and gain legitimacy" (Ibid 2005: 2). Within their overarching discussion, the authors shed light on some of the more complex and contradictory trends in educational research, and offer up what they see as the prevalent chronotopes of inquiry that ground and inform educational policy (Ibid 2005:24).

The word chronotope is not new. Kambrelis and Dimitradis (2005:24) argue that Mikhail Bahktin (1981) borrowed the word from Einstein and "applied it to the study

---

[1] By political rhetoric, I am referring to the United States, and discussion around No Child Left Behind Legislation.
[2] Michelle Rhee and Joel Klein favor hard line reforms, such as national testing, teacher accountability, and charter schools. Linda Darling-Hammonds favors community-based reforms, wherein parents and local school districts shape policy.

of language and literature" in order to shed light on time-space formations. According to these authors, the significance of this is that Bakhtin did not use chronotopes to "link particular times and places with specific cultural events, but to delineate or construct sedimentations of concrete, motivated social situations or figured worlds" (Kamberelis & Dimitriadis 2005:24; Holland, Lachiotte, Skinner, & Cain 1998). As such, I believe that Kambrelis and Dimitriadis' use of chronotopes also allows the readers to delineate and construct a world in which the reader will be able to reflect further on threads, disruptions, and tensions between current educational research, some of the pedagogical implications of the Lessac work, and viewpoints of the authors in this section.

Within the first chronotope, Objectivism and Representation, the correspondence theory of truth is used to frame learning and instruction, whereby knowledge is viewed as a mirror of nature, subjects and objects are separate and non-constitutive, and language is viewed as a neutral vehicle of thought. This is exemplified in Descartes' dualism of mind and body, wherein the notion of dualism posits the "individual human subject as radically separate from the external world and thus able to know this world objectively through the rational separation of subject and object" (Kamberelis & Dimitriadis 2005:29). Furthermore it also resonates in the majority of psychological research used to shape traditional notions of classroom instruction and learning, as advocated in today's educational landscape by E.D. Hirsch (1987), wherein it is assumed that there is one neutral cannon of cultural knowledge that all students should know and which can be attained through cognitive variables.[3]

Within this context it is important to consider that a large amount[4] of today's educational landscape is shaped by the belief that "acts of language" do not embody and accomplish their speakers' and writers' intentions nor do they produce effects on their audiences. "They are unmediated, uninterested, transmissions of fact" (Kamberelis & Dimitraidis 2005:29).

---

[3] Munro (in editorial comment) notes that, according to this paradigm, the cannon can only be demonstrated for these pedagogues in the written form, because the written form demonstrates the cognitive separation from experience. It is as if the conscious and cognitive retranscribing of experience is the only form of presenting knowledge [wherein] the subject "disappears" into the written object.

[4] Objectivism and positivism continue to exercise considerable power within social science research (Kamberelis & Dimitriadis 2005:2).

Within the second chronotope, Reading and Interpretation, the consensus theory of truth is used and philosophical hermeneutics emphasized. Here knowledge is viewed as being socially constructed, subjects and objects are separate, but mutually constitutive, and language, while still viewed as being neutral, is viewed as being constitutive of thought. This is exemplified in the research of Shirley Brice Heath (2004; 1991; 1983), who identifies a real ongoing issue in American education, especially in light of No Child Left Behind (NCLB) legislation, and argues that the sense of being literate goes beyond having literacy skills (disconnected interpretation or production of text) and is actually derived from how individuals are enabled to both feel and create harmony through the use of literate behaviors.

Within this context, it is important to consider that in contrast to beliefs made by researchers within the first chronotope, researchers in this domain believe that "language practices" constitute both individual and community identities, and that language is more than a vehicle to just represent an already existent world, and as such, language becomes the "more powerful means available to human beings for constructing what is real" (Kamberelis & Dimitradis 2005:33-35).

Within the third chronotope, Skepticism, Conscientization and Praxis, neo-marxism and critical social theory emerge. Within this paradigm knowledge is viewed as being socially constructed and inextricably linked to power relations, truth is produced through dialogue within an "ideal situation," subject and objects are separate but mutually constitutive, and language constitutes thought and is a function of existent power relations. This is exemplified in Paulo Friere's (1993) notion of "critical pedagogy," Augusto Boal's (1985) notion of "theatre of the oppressed," Antonio Gramsci's (1971) notion of "cultural hegemony," and Habermas' (1987; 1984) theory of communicative action, all of which embody an imperative for democratic social change.

Within this context, it is important to consider that only through dialogue are critical consciousness and praxis made possible—a space for engagement in dialogue, struggle, and conflict is made and this allows for the transformation of the many worlds of our experiences through loving, imaginative, exploratory, and critical reflection with others.

Within the chronotope of Power/Knowledge and Defamiliarization, postmodern and poststructuralist views emerge—knowledge is an effect of existent power relations, and truth is perceived to be an effect of power/knowledge, subjects and objects are both produced within existent relations of power, and language is a force among other forces that produce the real. This is exemplified in the research of Foucault (1977) that interrogates how power operates concretely through "technologies of the self," and it also resonates in the research of the New Literacies Group who opened up new possibilities for "re-imaging" the human body within instruction and learning (Coiro, Knobel, Lankshear, & Leu 2008).

Within this context, it is important to consider that the roots of understanding language lie in postmodern notions of deconstruction, which never entirely escape inherent dualism of transcendental philosophy or the foundational status of subjective experience, but instead allow for a re-imagining of the subject through foregrounding issues of power and their relation to knowledge (Kamberelis & Dimitradis 2005:51). The significance of this position is that language (thinking, feeling, acting, and being) represents a constant struggle for power and legitimacy and new ways to produce or re-image human subjects.

Pedagogical Implications of Lessac: The Early Years

Early in his career, Arthur Lessac (1942) discussed some of the possible implications of proper voice training in an article that was published in the *New York Times*, and argued that anyone, "including Mayor La Guardia or Sam Jaffe," could have a voice as good as "John Barrymore, Maurice Evans, Paul Robeson, or President Roosevelt if they had proper training" since "all our voices stem from mechanisms that are structurally identical and therefore…can and do function exactly alike and respond to physical training much the same as the body of the prospective athlete."

It was an assumption that resonated with many pedagogical implications for teaching and learning, and, in part, led Arthur to explore new possibilities for how voice training could be situated within and across educational landscapes. This was further exemplified almost 15 years later, when Lessac (1956) wrote a second article for the *New York Times*, in which he questioned the role of the ear within speech training, in particular for those who stuttered, and argued that, by experimenting with bone conduction and the muscular sensations in training, we might find more "trustworthy organs than the ear to use."

While the view "to discard the ear" within voice training would go on to differentiate Lessac from other voice teachers, it is really the assumption that these students could learn through experimenting with bone conduction and the muscular sensations that would serve as the foundation for his training and that separated Lessac from other educational perspectives. For example, Lessac espouses a feeling process, via NRG states, wherein knowledge is not static, but sensed in balance between inner and outer environments. Within this process, Lessac places an emphasis on the modality of learning as being physical,[5] which counters notions that a person can only learn only through thinking and argues that voice, speech, and acting are integrated elements of the organic whole, where the integration of all aspects is created through the discovery of the "feeling" of the physical processes, and awareness of what is happening inside the body.[6] This is exemplified in the following excerpt from his statement of teaching philosophy (1973), wherein Lessac notes the schism between his views and traditional educational thinking:

In general, traditional and educational institutions tend to de-emphasize and even de-value approaches to learning that can best relate to an understanding of our emotions, our bodies and our perceptual and intuitive capabilities.

My teaching is based upon methods by which such instinctive or natural human functioning can be trained to become part of craft, part of creative discipline, part of personal culture and awareness, and when the individual succeeds in personifying his skills, part of art.

---

[5] The term "physical" is taken from Little's (1967) report to the Lessac Institute and Lessac's (1973) personal statement of teaching philosophy and as such. Lessac (1978, preface) says "that at the root of our feeling process is an integral view of the human organism, perceived as naturally capable of instinctive as well as intellectual life within the single body community." The notion of learning being a physical modality is also supported in Lessac assumptions that all our bodies are structurally and organically alike and "capable of organic sensation and perception that leads to kinesthetic understanding and appreciation" (1978, preface). While the term "physical" does not really do justice to some of the Lessac principals now used in the Lessac work, the word does serve a purpose in contrasting Lessac views about the modality of learning to traditional views that learning is controlled primarily in the brain.

[6] Paper presented by Arthur Lessac at 1971 AETA conference. 'Actor Explores Vocal Life on the Stage.' Personal Archives.

In addition to his views about the modality of learning being physical, Arthur Lessac also countered commonly-held[7] notions that the skills of voice and speech should be taught separately and espoused the notion that learning can take place through a continuously creative act. This is supported in his article *A New Definition of Dramatic Training*, wherein Lessac (1969) argued that a theatre training program should include the following: (a) forces should go together, or upon one another, in order to lead to a qualitative effect which is greater than one would expect from a simple combination; (b) vocal life should reflect the natural functioning of the human organism through the integration of a trinity of consciously controllable energies; (c) teachers should integrate both scientific and aesthetic means of self-reflection and evaluation; and (d) every teacher should be a competent and practicing artist.

Although some of these views appear to counter more traditional educational perspectives, and in some cases might sound slightly esoteric, it is important to note that Lessac completed years of scientific analysis upon the mechanisms involved in producing the human voice and distinguished between actions that were instinctive and involuntary and those over which control could be exercised. In the process, he found that there was a relationship between vocal and physical life, vocal life and emotional life, and vocal life and individual personality, and argued, based on these findings, that (a) the use of voice, speech, and body were resources for human creativity and human intelligence, and that (b) "form, function, and language" started with the original concept of esthetics, which is defined as the study and nature of sensation.[8] In addition, it is significant to note that Lessac's views have been supported as being consistent with non-western views of philosophy and humanism,[9] with the school of expressionism,[10] with the Alexander technique and Feldenkrais method,[11] and numerous researchers.[12]

---

[7] During the 1960's.
[8] Taken from statement of teaching philosophy found in personal archives. Date 1973.
[9] Supported by M. Lessac, who in 1972 noted that Arthur Lessac has eastern wisdoms and put them into western understanding of man. Paper found in personal archives.
[10] In Ruth McKenney's (1986) dissertation, she attempts to connect the views of Lessac to Samuel Silas Curry (1847-1921), the school of expression, James Rush (1786-1869), author of *Philosophy of Human Voice*, 1827, Mary Margaret Robb, Rev. Ebenezer Porter of Andover Theological Seminary, Dr. Jonathon Barber of Harvard, and William Russell (First editor of *American Journal of Education*).
[11] Jack Clay (1971) notes similarities between the Alexander Technique and Lessac. Arthur in an interview with me (February 16, 2009) remembered that Moshe Feldenkrais was very curious about his work and that they had some interaction later in his (Feldenkrais') life.
[12] Supported by researchers who either published or completed dissertations on Lessac training.

Pedagogical Implications of Today

The writings within this section clearly highlight and discuss pedagogical implications of Lessac training in various contexts. In terms of arts-based education, Moraitis explores the transformative and restorative value of Lessac voice training as a means of reforming incarcerated youth and sheds light on ways in which Lessac might be situated within a learning context as well as be used by community artists and social activists as a means of transformation and healing. Within her article, Moraitis is able to contextualize her discussion of Lessac around concepts of learning (Cope & Kalantzis 2000), and appears to address issues current in theatre education, applied drama, and the humanizing aspect of theatre (Taylor 2009).

In terms of arts-based inquiry, Robbins (2000) and Tocchetto De Oliveira offer unique learning perspectives within the contexts of acting training and health education. Robbins (2000) details an incredible personal journey wherein she explored Lessac's notion of "familiar event" to relieve stress. Within her article, Robbins (2000) fosters a larger dialogue about the connection between health and Lessac, the difference (effect) of using Lessac training in place of imagery, and new ways in which Lessac training might be used outside of just a theatre context. In particular, Robbins' discussion regarding the use of the familiar event challenges traditional types of problem-solving forces us to consider new possibilities in which we might be able to transform and heal.

Tocchetto De Oliveira uses a humanistic framework to explore ways in which the actor's performance might be transformed through the use of Lessac body energies. In particular, she uses her own experiences as an actor and observations as a researcher to shed light on ways in which body energies might improve acting performance and posits that "Lessac has provided a powerful pedagogical training and strategy to experience the currents of Stanislavski and the dynamics of performance." The significance of this might be in the inquiry itself, as Tocchetto De Oliveira is able to create a space in which the reader is able to reflect, through the eyes of the learner, upon Lessac training.

In terms of theatre education, Campbell and Kur (1987) clearly speak to theatre pedagogues and situate Lessac training within the performance space, including the acting class and the rehearsal process. Within the latter, Kur (1987) discusses new possibilities in which Lessac training allows for the study of stage dialects to go beyond "special skills training" by giving students a process in which they can "self-teach" themselves and integrate the acquisition of the stage dialect into the rehearsal process. In particular, Kur posits that the vocal life of the actor/student can be connected to their emotional life through the development of the physical and psychological apparatus, wherein the actor/student becomes familiar with the sensory difference of each dialect through discovering the different vocal behaviors through which point of view and emotional inner life may be expressed. The significance of this is that Kur's writing fosters a larger discussion about the connection between Lessac training and self-teaching.

In terms of the former, Campbell sheds light on the possibilities in which the connection between text and a character's emotional life might be explored through the use of Lessac within an acting class. In particular, she reflects on the ways in which students learned that they could use Lessac body energies to build upon prior knowledge, go far beyond expected outcomes (boundaries), and intuitively explore vocal energies. Within her reflective inquiry, Campbell develops a space for the reader to reflect upon new possibilities in which teaching and learning might take place through Lessac training, including how student understanding can take place beyond what is already in the "text" or "in the actor" and as part of a transaction between both. This would appear to be significant as this process is supported by many literacy researchers who have noted that meaning does not reside ready-made "in the text" or "in the reader" but happens during the transaction between reader and text, whereby meaning is created by the impact between a material phenomenon and the shared processes of consciousness of those who participate in it,[13] so as to express specifically socially situated identities and activities (Dyson 2004; Halliday 2004; Rosenblatt 2004).

In terms of educational research, Munro and Coetzee (2005) attempt to situate Lessac work within the current discussion of outcomes based education and Munro and Wissing (2007) demonstrate that Lessac training is an effective voice-building tool. In terms of the former, Munro and Coetzee's argument that Lessac training al-

---

[13] Might also point to the field of semiotics and semiology – For example, Kress (2002), Gee (2004), Halliday (1985) and Lemke (2002) also make references to the notion of signifier as a material phenomenon, and the notion of signified as a concept "in" the viewer, and when the one triggers the other, meaning is made (or an act of signification takes place).

lows for a paradigm shift from "teacher-centered transmission of knowledge" to a "learner-centered" approach is significant as it clearly situates Lessac within the larger educational discourse, and in particular within a landscape that paints knowledge as being socially constructed, and language as constituting both the individual and the community (Heath 2004; 1991; 1983).

In terms of the latter, Munro and Wissing (2007) examine the outcomes of Lessac training upon the perceptual evaluation of voice, as both a communicative and performative act, and posit that perceptual notions of voice quality are dependent on acoustical properties, and not necessarily on language specifics. The findings of this study not only support the hypothesis that Lessac training has a direct impact on voice, but they also open up possibilities for Lessac training to be further studied within the fields of education, communication and performance studies.

References

Bahktin, M. 1981. *The dialogic imagination.* Austin: University of Texas Press.

Boal, A. 1985. *Theater of the oppressed.* New York: Theater Communications Group.

Coiro, J., Knobel, M., Lankshear, C., & Leu, D. 2008. *Handbook of research on new literacies.* New York: Lawrence Erlbaum and Associates.

Cope, B. & Kalantzis, M. 2000. *Multiliteracies: Literacy learning and the design of Social futures.* New York: Routledge.

Dyson, A. H. 2000. 'Writing and the sea of voices, oral language in, around, and about writing.' In R. B. Ruddell & N. J. Unrau (Eds) *Theoretical Models and Processes of Reading* (5th Edition), PP 146-160. International Reading Association, Newark, DE.

Halliday, M. A. K. 2004. 'The place of dialogue in children's construction of meaning.' In R. B. Ruddell & N. J. Unrau (Eds) *Theoretical Models and Processes of Reading* (5th Edition), PP 133-145. International Reading Association, Newark, DE.

Freire, P. 1993. *Pedagogy of the oppressed.* New York: Optimum.

Foucault, M. 1977. *Discipline and punish: The birth of the prison.* New York: Vintage Books.

Gramsci, A. 1971. *Selections of the prison notebooks of Antonio Gramsci.* New York: International Publishers.

Habermas, J. 1987. *The theory of communicative action: Lifeworld and system.* Boston: Beacon Press.

Habermas, J. 1984. *The theory of communicative action: Reason and the rationalization of society.* Boston: Beacon Press.

Heath, S. B. 2004. 'The children of Trackton's children.' In R. B. Ruddell & N. J. Unrau (Eds). *Theoretical Models and Processes of Reading* (5th Edition), PP 187-209. International Reading Association, Newark, DE.

Heath, S. B. 1991. 'The sense of being literate: Historical and cross-cultural features.' In R. Barr, M. L., Kamil, P. Mosenthall, & P. David Pearson (Eds.), *Handbook of Reading Research* (Vol II, 3-25). New York: Longman.

Heath, S. B. 1983. *Ways with words.* Cambridge, England: Cambridge University Press.

Hirsch, E. D. 1987, *Cultural literacy.* Boston: Haughton Mifflin.

Holland, D., Lachiotte, W., Skinner, D., & Cain, C. 1998. *Identity and agency in cultural worlds.* Cambridge, MA: Harvard University Press.

Kamberelis. G. and Dimitriadis, G. 2005. *Qualitative inquiry: Approaches to language and literacy research.* New York: Teachers College Press.

Kur, B. 1987. *Stage dialect studies.* College Station, Pennsylvania: Self-Publication.

Lessac, A. 1942. 'On language as spoken from the stage: A voice teacher discusses the speech of theatre, with examples.' *New York Times*. June 28.

Lessac, A. 1956. 'New ways of correcting stuttering.' *New York Times*. April 8.

Lessac, A. 1969. 'A new definition of dramatic training.' In *Quarterly Journal of Speech*. Pp.116-125.

Lessac, A. 1996. *The use and training of the human voice: A bio dynamic approach to vocal life* (3rd Edition). Toronto: Mayfield Publishing Company.

Lessac, A. 1978. *Body wisdom: The use and training of the human body*. Mountain View: Mayfield Publishing Company.

Munro, M., & Coetzee, M-H. 2005. 'The Lessac approach as a pedagogical answer to outcomes based education and training, and whole-brain learning.' *Voice and Speech Review: Shakespeare around the Globe.* Mandy Rees (ed), VASTA, 186- 192.

Munro, M., & Wissing, D. 2007. 'Testing the Use of Lessac's Tonal NRG as a Voice Building Tool for Female Students at a South African University—A Perceptual Study.' *Voice and Speech Review: Shakespeare around the Globe.* Mandy Rees (ed), VASTA, 333-342.

Rosenblatt, L. 2004. 'The transactional theory of reading and writing.' In R. B. Ruddell & N. J. Unrau (Eds) *Theoretical Models and Processes of Reading.* (5th edition). Pp 1363-1398. International Reading Association: Newark: DE.

Taylor, P. 2009. *Theatre behind bars: Can the arts rehabilitate?* Staffordshire, U.K.: Trentham Books.

Unlocking the Voice Inside Rochester Young Offenders: The Impact of Lessac Voice Training Within a Socially Excluded Community.

Katerina M. Moraitis
Course Leader, MA Voice Studies,
The Central School of Speech and Drama, University of London
Year of Certification as a Lessac Voice, Speech and Body Trainer: 2003

Actor training involves the optimal use of the human body: physical, emotional, artistic, intellectual. Voice training in particular makes optimal use of the total human instrument and requires the mastery of breath, speech, non-verbal communication, desiring the improvement of perception and awareness, as well as the projection of emotion and personality....Serious actor training can even lead to the elevation of human behaviour (Lessac 1960:3).

The transformative and restorative value of voice training has widely been recognised in theatrical environments where training focuses on unlocking habitual tensions that impede creative communication and allow actors to alter physical and vocal behaviour. However, can the same process of transformation be adapted to reforming the individual whose behaviour has led to incarceration and social exclusion? Can serious voice and body training lead to the rehabilitation of incarcerated youth and 'elevate' human behaviour, as Lessac states?

Rehabilitation and the Elevation of Human Behaviour

Despite the entrenchment of rehabilitation and restorative action in social and criminal justice policy in the UK, the majority of public opinion sees little benefit to rehabilitation programmes in the prison system and advocates that the function and purpose of prison is not to reform, but rather to punish and protect.

The terms rehabilitation and corrections are widely recognized as nothing but euphemisms believed in by no one with any sense. The value of the prisons is that they keep bad people locked away from the good people. Let them out and, surprise, they are still bad people. Those who want to change do so. Most never will. My primary job as a correctional officer was to keep their hands from around your throat and the throats of your and my loved ones. There are plenty of things that need doing. Wasting time bleeding your heart over bad apples doesn't make the cut (Griff, quoted by Murray 2002:4).

The dominant opinion towards rehabilitation in prison over the last 30 years has been that "nothing works." "Nothing works" was the catch phrase of the now famous sociologist Robert Martinson. Martinson in 1974 deduced that "with few and isolated exceptions the rehabilitative efforts that have been reported so far have had no appreciable effect on recidivism" (Martinson 1974:25).

Nonetheless, in 1979 Martinson reviewed his stance on rehabilitation and concluded that the initial study had been hampered by primitive methodology. In his article for *Hostra Law Review,* he retracted his previous statement, and wrote, "some treatment programs do have an appreciable effect on recidivism....[S]uch startling results are found again and again in our study, for treatment programs as diverse as individual psychotherapy, group counselling, intensive supervision, and what we call individual/help (aid, advice, counselling)" (1979:255).

As a result of these new understandings, he withdrew the contention that "nothing works" and began to believe that effective rehabilitation that has the ability to transform or reform the human being was possible, and one avenue may be through working holistically with individuals. Social behaviour is a function of the whole human organism and action should therefore focus on a variety of options, including building the confidence, changing moral standards and attitudes.

Holistic methods of voice and body training that encourage the rehabilitation of the individual can be found in the progressive biodynamic approaches of American practitioner and researcher, Arthur Lessac. The Lessac approach to voice training relies on the ability of the individual to perceive motion and sensation in the body, as a process of enlightening and informing the self. Murray tends to support and advocate a Lessac style approach advocating that individual responsibility and ownership of the learning allows the individual to make better life choices (Murray, 2008:2). People who make better choices have more chance of being reintegrated into society successfully.

Kalantzis and Cope (2008), in their book, *New Learning*, also encourage holistic educational experiences in order to achieve social change. They indicate that these approaches may have the power to transform behaviour by providing an environment that advocates individual ownership and responsibility. Rejecting the so-called traditional didactic educational experience (didactic education here represents the so-called traditional pedagogy of rote-learning, mass institutionalised education), instead Kalantzis and Cope opt for a more progressive approach to education, known as "Authentic Education": "Authentic is a more useful descriptor for this kind of education....It is authentic in the sense that learning is not merely abstract and formal, as are the 'disciplines' of didactic pedagogy. It works hard to make itself relevant to the lives of learners" (Kalantizis & Cope 2008: 28).

Here education can be viewed as less authoritarian, more student-centred and more tailored towards individual needs, as "it sets out deliberately to transform...and play an active role in changing social conditions [and behaviour]" (Kalantzis & Cope 2008: 18).

Nonetheless, behaviour of individuals is usually portrayed as a shared responsibility between the biological/inheritance of the individual and environmental/social factors. In terms of the nature verses nurture debate there is a continuum of views that describe behaviour as either predominantly resulting from our biological or psychological makeup (nature) at one end of the continuum, or from the influences of our surrounding environment (nurture) at the other end.

Social Behaviour: Nature or Nurture

Sociologists and theorists on deviancy, such as Durkheim, tend to emphasize the nurture end of the debate and hold that external environmental factors may influence behaviour negatively. These factors may include poverty, bad and unsafe housing, sexual and emotional abuse and physical violence, neglect, ineffectual and inconsistent parenting, teenage and single parent families, broken homes, family discord, dyslexia and illiteracy. Young adults may be able to withstand one or two of these negative circumstances but when their lives are shaped by a cluster of them it appears that conscience, empathy with others and the will to be social-minded frequently breakdown (Neustatter 2002: 33).

However, some psychologists suggest that the biological make-up of the individual or the particular temperament of a child may pre-dispose them to behaviour that leads them into trouble: impulsivity, lack of restraint, paranoid learning difficulties, hyper-activity and cognitive impairment, verbal and planning skills (Neustatter 2002: 33). Iain Murray, in his article, "Making Rehabilitation Work: American Experience of Rehabilitating Prisoners," challenges both these polarised views, and instead emphasises individual freedom of choice. He suggests that the individual, regardless of external factors, has the ability to choose the actions that will or will not lead to deviant behaviour: "Offending is, at base, an individual choice....This is not about alleviating an abstract such as 'poverty,' but about helping someone who does not understand or care about the consequences of their actions" (Murray 2008: 8).

The emphasis on external factors rather than individual responsibility (important though it is) tends to leave the individual still relatively disempowered and defenceless against the wider social forces surrounding them. In an attempt to aid and positively reinforce the individual, while social reform is catching up, many social scientists also point to the real need for individuals to take back some control of their destiny. Of course, individuals, by themselves, cannot solve the problems of structural unemployment, family violence, poor education systems etc; nonetheless, they can train themselves to better deal with the society in which they live. David Thomas, Governor, from Lancaster Farms Young Offenders Institution, states that "[T]he young person who walks out the prison gates having learnt to control their anger, their impulsiveness, to like themselves a bit better than they did when they came in and feeling staff valued them enough to help them go out with more skills than they brought in, is less likely to go off and harm someone" (Neustatter 2002:83).

A more realistic explanation of individual behaviour requires a complex mixture of both individual responsibility and environmental/biological influences. Dr Alfred G. Brooks, in the forward to the Lessac text *Body Wisdom: Use and Training of the Human Body* (1978) says the Lessac gestalt training as a rehabilitative measure "is not a system for training the human organism to perform specific functions more effectively, but [for training] the individual to function more appropriately in other environments" (Lessac 1978:ii).

In 2004-05 an opportunity to undertake an investigation using the Lessac voice and body training with socially excluded youth was provided by the Knowledge Transfer Project within the School of Professional and Community Development at The Central School of Speech and Drama, University of London. With the support of the Higher Education Funding Council for England and the London Development Agency, the Knowledge Transfer Project established a prison-based program with Rochester Young Offenders Institution, also known as Rochester Prison, a minimal security penal complex in Kent. The emphasis of the collaboration was to create a training partnership with a community looking to enhance employability. The research enquiry, however, emulating a transformative and authentic educational paradigm, through the Lessac training, sought to move beyond merely improving participants' employment capabilities through vocal technique and therefore to have wider positive psychological and behavioural effects, in essence, to improve social functioning of the individual.

The Socially Excluded

Following the Rochester Prison riot in October 2001 in which an officer was taken hostage and held at knifepoint, and the damning 2003 Board of Visitors report (a panel that acts as an independent watchdog), interest in rehabilitation and reforming possibilities at Rochester Prison had begun to be renewed.

The Institution houses 392 inmates and detains young men from broad ethnic and regional backgrounds, typically from Kent, Sussex and South London. Prisoners are between the ages of seventeen and twenty-one, mostly serving short custodial sentences with minimal incarceration, of less than four years. They present with a diverse range of anti-social behaviour patterns manifest in actions that demonstrate such things as a lack of moral standards, a low development of normal manners, inadequate communication skills, an inadequate perception of self and reality, a shortfall in problem-solving skills, a deficiency of positive thinking, emotions lacking checks and balances, or dependency problems. Newcomers to the system tend to arrive with a defensive energy; however, by their second or third year they often look lost and lonely.

Young offenders meeting for the first time tend not to say very much, avoid direct eye contact and demonstrate depressed and collapsed posture.

The Self-Imprisoned

The group of participants in the intervention consisted of eight willing members, including six young offenders, one trainer from the Central School of Speech and Drama, and a Rochester staff member from the education department, who assisted in the day to day running of the programme. The offenders were a cross-section from the prison population. Meeting each other for the first time they said very little, their voices becoming noticeably less audible and their speech less intelligible. With the upper body slumped, the lower body shifting from foot to foot and back again, the fight or flight response was ever observable and ever present.

The offenders consisted of a garrulous 19-year-old, who spoke so fast and with such little musicality and consonant energy it was hard to make out a word, and after almost three years in prison still carried some of the restless energy of the street. A twitch in his facial musculature and a constant clicking of his fingers indicated his impatience to be released. A Malaysian inmate from north London, fond of affecting an amused indifference to almost everything, evidenced little definition or music in the vowels. Limited space and shape to the oral cavity pointed towards his inability to trust or believe in himself or others. Two young inmates from south London were more quiet and reserved than the others, seemingly unsure about what to expect from the group dynamic. They said very little if nothing at all—both stuck together throughout the sessions and were reluctant to intermingle. There was a distinct lack of tonal NRG in all six participants; however it was most notable in one young offender from Kent, who seemed to have had difficulty accommodating prison life. Other participants included a 20-year-old north London thief, with only two weeks left on a four-year sentence; he had an introverted and suspicious manner and presented with little voice or body NRG. His speech presented with distorted consonants and vowels that made him almost impossible to understand. Lastly, the group was joined by a flirtatious 17-year-old Liverpudlian, with a sardonic wit and charm; he was possibly the most mature of the group and whilst demonstrating an unwillingness to speak, was the most outgoing and confident. His body energy was clearly "Radiant" (as Lessac terms this type of energy), and information from prison staff indicated he suffers with hyperactivity, including paranoid learning difficulties.

Language use in the group was incomprehensible, requiring a certain level of translation. Inmates often spoke in a bizarre, hybrid language of street or prison slang designed to confuse and alienate those from the outside. Nonetheless, one only had to witness the dynamics of daily life in prison to see why voice and body use were so deeply imprisoned by the need to survive. Trust, for example, was not easily acquired; based on inmates' own experience of prison and criminal circles, to trust each other would be wholly irrational and may even lead to life-threatening situations, such as stabbings or grievous bodily harm, which, according to the group, occur frequently at Rochester. When individuals come from abusive and violent backgrounds, trust and respect can, for them, mean very different things:

That's how I got my sentence, my best friend turned out to be a registered police informant…and since I've been away my girlfriend has been with someone else—my brother. So, yeah, I've got a bit of a bad issue with trust. I've been around violence all my life. To me it's normal. Growing up, I seen people getting stabbed or glassed or slashed (Rochester Participant 2005).[1]

When faced with the harsh reality of prison life, it is relatively easy to see how the physical manifestations of anger, protection and mistrust become evident in the musculature of the body and voice. Closed and fixed mandibles, limited flexibility in the face and lips, hunched shoulders and ridged thoracic cavities were observed and seemed ingrained in each participant. Every muscle in the body, it seemed, becomes clamped shut in an effort to protect and survive.

The Liberation of the Self

In order to establish an atmosphere of trust with each individual, it was essential to seek commonality and approval and to build rapport with the group, but most important for the individual participants to place themselves at the centre of the learning experience. An introductory game was established that involved placing cards on the

---

[1] A word needs to be said about the reference to direct quotes from the inmates. I have opted to maintain anonymity and confidentiality in all cases as far as possible to avoid possible repercussions. Furthermore, I have maintained the separation in the body of the text between inmates and offenders, on the one hand, and "participants" (the "correct" word for the type of work that was being done), as the trainers would also be part of the participant group, according to research protocol. When offenders are "individualised," as in the quotation here, I have reverted to "participant."

floor with words capturing behaviours printed on the front, facing up—such as aggressive, loving, and the like. Inmates were asked to identify their own behaviour by standing on the card that best represented them and then move to the card that best represented their own perceptions of their vocal behaviour. Similarities between how voice use and behaviour may be perceived were established, with participants evidencing new understanding of the relationship between behaviour and vocal perception.

Continuing with further awareness of self as a means to liberate the individual, participants were guided to locate and examine musculature involved in posture and breathing. They worked in pairs and moved through Lessac experiments such as upright body posture (bend over series) and pleasure smelling. This entailed imagining there is a flower, pleasant in smell, or a cup of coffee in front of the nose, inhaling deeply, feeling the whole torso fill with the fragrance. Lessac states, "The pleasure and joyful action of smelling a flower's perfume or the pleasurable appreciation of a contented sigh uses the body and effects the muscles differently than when smelling an ugly, foul odor [sic] or sighing out of grief, sadness or anxiety" (Lessac 1960:21).

These explorations enabled inmates to tap into their imagination of a familiar sensation as a tool to unlock the rigidity of the body, particularly the torso, and experience and perceive the sensations of effective breathing. This was a new and exciting adventure for several of the inmates who had little understanding of the power of the breath or its impact on communication. It was the first step in recognising the restorative value of voice training for the individual.

After lunch inmates returned to the wings and their cells, where most slept away the boredom of incarceration. Afternoon sessions, therefore, were fraught with extremely low energy levels and inmates lacked interest in undertaking any activity that required movement or low level physical activity: the excitement of new understandings seemed to disappear. Drained by the unexpected intensity of the first morning the group continued with Lessac experiments in the "creative art of resting"—relaxer-energisers. Relaxation, Lessac states, "requires the entire muscular system: when we relax the voluntary muscles, we clearly exert a direct effect upon the semi-voluntary and involuntary systems of the body" (Lessac 1960:47). The afternoon was spent exploring the energy and relaxation qualities in the body. Using what Lessac terms buoyancy, radiancy and potency NRGs, the group set about discovering that they can perform a physical task, such as a sit-up, so that the action is distributed across the largest number of muscles, eradicating excessive tension and balancing rest and action so the whole body can perform any task required efficiently. The participants welcomed and relished muscle yawn as a force "stronger than brawn" and after exploring the Buddy Body-Yawn Push-ups and Chin-Ups (Lessac 1978:53) became impassioned by the possibilities that the work might unleash for them. At this point the resistance to the work and other members of the group had begun to melt; it was observed that each participant experienced new sensations and new knowledge in the body. There was a noticeable shift towards upright body posture and as the participants moved into 'free-flow', from one wing to the next, there was a more confident individual observed.

Nonetheless, the general level of commitment continued to seem low and, whilst noticing more effective posture in the young offenders, there was a concern about the more vulnerable vocal practice. Voice practice can access the emotional experiencing system vital for the actor in expression, but may expose young offenders to emotional states not wanted or desired in the prison environment.

Nevertheless, day two focused on the development of voice, employing consonant clarity and intelligibility through the Lessac Consonant Orchestra (Lessac 1960:72). The group began with discussion around rap and beat boxing, designed to tap into the creative vocal energy inmates already engage with on a day-to-day level –a familiar muscular event. The group improvised musical instruments while one member of the group stood in the centre and took ownership of conducting the orchestra, indicating with a hand gesture (1, 2 or 3) whether they would improvise the rhythm, the melody or a drone (drumbeat or sustainable consonants only). It was important to begin slowly and allow the group time to develop trust and a sense of ownership and awareness. The idea was to expose and introduce the group to the language and rhythm of Lewis Carroll's *Jabberwocky* and T.S.Eliot's *Rhapsody on a Windy Night.* The participants were informed that these poets were rap artists of their time and that the work of Carroll, in particular, was about how the music of the words informed the meaning of the poem. Their interest was tweaked. Each inmate was given a line of text and asked to use only the consonants that preceded another consonant, exploring it through rhythm, melody and drone.

Carroll and Eliot were chosen due to their imaginative use of consonants within each piece to create music, atmosphere and sense. The prison system, however, is filled with inmates who have never experienced heightened language. Learning disabilities, illiteracy and mental illness all have an impact on the pedagogical choices of the session. The north London thief began to get agitated as text was distributed and he openly admitted in front of the others that he was unable to read. Was he being exposed to the lions? He sheepishly asked "Miss, can you tell me what it says." Surprisingly the others ignored him; there were no jibes that he couldn't read or that he needed help. Self-esteem and status in the prison isn't so reliant on intellectual accomplishment or the ability to read, but rather, it seems, the crime and time. One inmate, for example, brandished a tattoo—a swallow—signifying to other criminals on the outside that he's done time inside; according to him, this elevated him to higher status in criminal circles.

Whilst demonstrating some resistance and reluctance to play with sound, participants were able to engage with consonant NRG once they were given a familiar event, in this case rap music. The familiarity and acceptability of the rap genre alleviated the fear and anxiety that may have been caused by exposure to the new and unknown.

Emotionally and physically drained by the intensity of time behind bars, the group returned in the afternoon on day two to continue with Lessac vocal experiments investigating the "dynamics of structural NRG." These experiments led to Lessac text explorations on *The Lotus Eaters* by Alfred Lord Tennyson, chosen for the open vowels that inhibit the tight jaw and musculature tension that impeded inmates' communication. Using a piece of cork between the teeth at the side of the mouth, each member of the group was asked to reduce the opening of the lip and cheek muscles. Eventually the participants went through a series of explorations, feeling the sensation and perception of the yawn on the zygomatic and orbicularis oris face and lip muscles that were then transferred to *The Lotus Eaters*, through Exploration 1: Lessac Structural Perception Drill (Lessac 1960:169). The inmates performed the poem in small groups in preparation for a presentation to the governor and an audience of peers.

The transformation in vowel clarity and resonant tone was noteworthy and, as the day drew to a close, the course team were overwhelmed by the inmates' achievements. There had been a significant shift in the space potential in the oral cavity and for the first time the group heard the voice coming from an open and released jaw. Considering that the musculatures of the tongue, jaw and face in these young offenders were rarely used, evidence of movement may have been more pronounced and noticeable than that observed in a drama school setting. Nonetheless, a considerable shift was clearly manifest. The impact on social behaviour, whilst not yet evident, would rely on the offender's ability to maintain the new physical experience through awareness and perception. In this sense individual internal feedback guided by positive tutor response was essential in the process. Throughout the project inmates were consistently asked to "feel" the breath, posture and vibration of a vocal or physical action, allowing them to develop sensory awareness of efficient functioning of self.

The group began day three developing tonal NRG, with yawn and forward facial posture, experimenting on various pitches and exploring it in the speaking voice. The inmates attempted a scat (a sung improvisation) with tonal vowels—it was ineffective. The group attempted a call and response exploration using tonal vowels—it too was ineffective. An exploration that exposed the student or demanded an element of trust was often met with a negative response or refusal. This level of rejection was usually accompanied by a mocking comment: "I can't do that exercise, Miss, it's against my religion" (Rochester Participant: 2005). It was hoped that tonal energy would enable a more resonant and confident tone. However, now in day three, the group are evidencing low-level ability to engage with the more exposing tonal NRG—the work on tone therefore was limited and ineffective.

Pedagogical choices made in the classroom usually rely on the intellectual and emotional level of students who participate; however it can be easy to forget that whilst these young offenders are seventeen to twenty-one in age, their intellectual and emotional levels may differ considerably and as such they have difficulty engaging with theoretical and physical concepts for long periods of time and resistance to the work is not uncommon. They presented with emotional instability and low energy levels, leading to feelings of deprivation. However, there is benefit when using voice and text. Cecily Berry, Voice Director for the Royal Shakespeare Company, argues, for example, that

> [t]he feeling of deprivation that is ever present in someone confined like this can charge language in a very special way, and this quite clear enjoyment in

speaking that language aloud confirms my belief....There is power that the human animal gains when he/she can be precise over a feeling or a thought—a sense of their own dignity, their own autonomy—and this sense of power is the right of every citizen....When people realise that words are a tool that everyone can use, it gives both confidence and pleasure (2001: 49).

During her 2005 Key Note speech for the Voice and Speech Trainers Association (VASTA) Conference 2005—"Breaking through the Boundaries: Crossing the Culture Divide"—in Glasgow, Berry reiterated this, and commented that 'the language of Shakespeare is about survival —where words prevail not, violence prevails' (Berry 2005).

Wanting the group to recognise the value and power of language to transform, inmates were encouraged to discuss the value of communication and the power of language. With sudden realisation, one participant stood up and passionately stated, "That's why the defence lawyer at my trial used the word poppycock, I get it, and she wanted me to feel powerless" (Rochester Participant: 2005). It was becoming evident that the inmates were coming to the realisation that voice and communication training could empower the individual to combat the social conditions they faced, such as confrontations with police, welfare, lawyers, as well as family and peers.

For a professional actor, control over the voice is concerned with being a competent practitioner/performer. For the subjects of this program however, voice training was something more vital and important—it was something that could help them deal with some of life's real problems and gave them access to understanding and controlling emotions.

Post course interviews and evaluation deemed the project valuable and significant in the eyes of the participants. Feedback included:

[T]he work I achieved was very beneficial...very enjoyable and a good confidence builder. The part of the course I found most useful was learning about the relaxer-energizers, I've learnt to be more creative and to "feel" what I'm doing, it will be great to take into my interview skills. I could understand how to be listened to (Rochester Participant 2005).

In an interview held several months after the initial sessions, participants were asked to comment on the overall impact of vocal awareness on their day-to-day functioning. The garrulous 19-year-old commenting on his transformation clearly stated that he could "feel the vocal energy" and now had a reference point to transform behaviour and improve his life choices: "Now I know when I mumble what to do about it, and I am much more confident" (Rochester Participant 2005).

The Rochester Conclusions

The following tables show a listing of vocal and behavioural outcomes (data) that were observed during the research and were collected post-program. This data, along with student interviews, student journals (writing), teacher observations and reflections were analyzed and showed three important results from the work. The practice gave participants an emotional control, an empowering of the self, and enabled opportunities to imagine a more productive future livelihood.

TABLE A: VOCAL OUTCOMES

Evidence	Measurement
1. Greater sense of body awareness and confidence in the upright body posture and the effective mechanics of breathing, i.e. an informed awareness of the body.	Teacher observation and reflections.
2. An embodiment of the fundamentals of forward facial yawning, muscle yawning, floating and shaking as body relaxer-energisers.	Teacher observation and Student feedback.
3. Ability to self-evaluate, explore and play with consonants for clarity and meaning in communication.	Teacher assessment and observation.
4. An awareness of; the structural space in the oral cavity, releasing the tongue, jaw and lips, as well as vowel musicality.	Teacher observation and Student feedback.
5. An ability to generally explore text and language.	Teacher assessment and observation.

TABLE B: BEHAVIOURAL OUTCOMES

Evidence	Measurement
1. An embodiment of more refined and appropriate use of manners.	Teacher observation.
2. A more adequate perception of self and reality.	Student feedback and interviews.
3. An ability to self-evaluate, reflect, apply effective problem solving skills.	Student interviews and Teacher assessment.
4. An ability to control and balance emotions more effectively.	Mental Health Assessment and Teacher assessment.
5. An ability to reflect a positive attitude to the future.	Student interviews.
6. Employment of a more confident and empowered vocabulary.	Teacher observation.
7. Demonstrated self-reliance.	Teacher observation.

The positive physiological impact on the emotional balancing system, evident in all six participants, was the first observed result to emerge. The art and technique of vocal practice, once felt and consciously perceived, can become a built-in therapeutic control, resulting in an effective and useful mechanism for managing emotions that arise from an outer environment. A more efficient upright body posture, effective breathing and awareness of vocal clarity, channelled nervous or destructive energy and so that the inmates could better cope with the external forces surrounding their lives.

Participants suffered from at least one of a range of disturbances such as mental illnesses, mental instability as a result of substance addiction, or difficulties in functioning such as hyperactivity and autism, high levels of anxiety, depression, fatigue, and concentration problems. As a result, low self-esteem and a sense of overwhelming hopelessness were common in the group. Work on posture, breathing and body energy as natural therapeutic pain relievers gave participants self-applied techniques and tools to avoid the high levels of loneliness, pain and anxiety brought about by the prison environment.

Whilst recognising that antisocial behaviour is influenced by a number of differing factors, such as illness, culture, attitudes, values and ethics, the second outcome reveals an effective pedagogical practice for empowering the student. This practice places the individual at the centre of the learning experience, giving a sense of self-awareness and responsibility. The absence of awareness, not knowing how to change, leaves the individual disempowered and exposed to the external forces that predispose young offenders to criminal behaviour. Knowledge of self empowers them to implement change and modify behaviour accordingly.

Finally, the third result reveals the inseparable relationship between body, voice and behaviour. Whilst communication methods stem from social and cultural identity and codes of behaviour define our 'right to speak' (Rodenburg 1992:3), the voice and body are the primary means by which we express our inner thoughts and feelings. Our breathing patterns reveal thought processes, tonal energy exposes our delicate emotional states, and the act of speech defines our intellect, status and class. Renowned London voice teacher Michael McCallion believes that.

[v]oice belongs with the deployment of the great emotions, governed by the old brain, right in the centre of the new brain. [The] highly intellectual act of speech, although using the voice, is at a remove from it [the old brain], it is the capacitor of lying. The first gift of language is you can lie (McCallion 1998).

As deceitful an act as it might be, the freedom of choice as to how to manipulate the organs of speech enables the type of speaking that can change lives. The process and intervention offered in this article offers a glimpse of speaking and language tools that can lead to future employment opportunities and improve future livelihood; or it may also lead to a far more skilled and eloquent deviant. The choice is with the individual.

In conclusion, the project aimed to utilise voice training that was based in a holistic approach to deliberately transform and rehabilitate social behaviour, increasing the future livelihood of inmates at Rochester Young Offenders Institution. Its objective was to place the student at the centre of the learning experience, empowering the individual through verbal and non-verbal communication, in order to better deal with the social and environmental influences that may make them susceptible to criminal behaviours.

However, in order to truly transform social interaction and determine the impact of the project in society, it is essential that individual behaviour be tested in various social conditions beyond incarceration over a period of time. Whilst participants benefitted from the project, follow up sessions in a social community outside prison may yet yield results that more accurately reflect the transformative value of holistic voice practices, rather than simply validating current theory. Future projects with Knowledge Transfer at Central School of Speech and Drama, University of London would include young offenders and ex-offenders in a series of sessions during internment and then at liberty.

This project ended on a hopeful and philosophical note. The conclusions suggest that holistic vocal practices, such as the Lessac training, could very well be the key to the health, well-being and re-education and transformation of a community that needs to find and be given a voice.

References

Aitkenhead, D. 2007. *Grendon Prison*, Weekend Guardian, 10.07.07:18-25.

Alexander, F.M. 1932. *The Use of Self*. Kent: Integral Press.

Berry, C. 2001. *Text in Action*. London: Virgin Publishing Ltd.

Berry, C. 2005. "Hearing Voices," Key Note, Voice and Speech Trainers Association (VASTA) Conference 2005—Breaking Through the Boundaries: Crossing the Culture Divide, Glasgow, 10.08.05.

Durkheim, E. 1982. *Rules of Sociological Method*. New York: McMillian Press Ltd.

Eliot, T.S. 1952. 'Rhapsody on a Windy Night.' In *The Complete Poems and Plays*. New York: Harcourt.

Erickson, M.L. 1972. 'Changing Relationship between Official and Self-Reported Measures of Delinquency: An exploratory-predictive study.' In *Journal of Criminal Law and Criminology*. Northwestern University School of Law, Vol. 63, No.3: 63:388.

Jones, F.P. 1976. *Body Awareness in Action: A Study of the Alexander Technique*. New York: Schocken Brooks.

Kalantzis, M. & Cope, B. 2008. *New Learning: Elements of a Science of Education*. Port Melbourne: Cambridge University Press.

Lessac, A. 1960. *The Use and Training of the Human Voice: a biodynamic approach to vocal life. 3rd Ed*, Mountview, California: Mayfield Publishing Company.

Lessac, A. 1978. *Body Wisdom: The Use and Training of the Human Body*. Mountview, California: Lessac Institute Publishing.

McCallion, M. 1998. *Interview discussing the role of the Alexander Technique in contemporary vocal practice,* 17.04.98.

Martinson, R. 1974. 'What Works?—Questions and Answers About Prison Reform.' *The Public Interest,* 35:22-54.

Martinson, R. 1979. 'New Findings, New Views: A Note of Caution Regarding Sentencing Reform,' *Hofstra Law Review,* 7:243-258.

Murray, I. 2008. 'Making Rehabilitation Work: American Experience of Rehabilitating Prisoners', http://ww.civitas.org.uk/pdg/Rehab.pdf (accessed 28.02.09).

Neustatter, A. 2002. *Locked In—Locked Out: The Experience of Young Offenders Out of Society and in Prison.* London: Calouste Gulbenkian Foundation.

Rodenburg, P. 1992. *The Right to Speak.* London: Methuen Drama.

Untermeyer, L (Ed). 1933. 'The Lotus Eaters'.' In *The Albatross Book of Verse, Students' Ed.* London: Collins Publishers.

Untermeyer, L (Ed). 1933. 'Jabberwocky'.' In *The Albatross Book of Verse, Students' Edition.* London: Collins Publishers.

The Ecstatic Birth-Lessac Training and Childbirth Preparation

This essay was originally published in the VASTA Newsletter, Fall 2000, Vol. 14, no. 3. pp 8, 13 and 14. Permission to reprint has been graciously granted by VASTA.

Crystal Robbins

When I began working for Arthur Lessac in September of 1998 I had just completed a decade of active and rewarding work in stage, film and TV both as an actress and director/producer. I'd spent three years traveling the globe, backpacking with my husband and writing about those journeys. I had no idea that my most creatively challenging work lay just ahead. Six weeks into the job with Lessac, I discovered I was pregnant.

I'd already personally witnessed the life joy and wisdom of Arthur Lessac. I'd seen him bound up three flights of stairs with groceries on both arms. I'd seen this 91-year-old man walk with exuberance, rolling on his legs like a dancer in motion. He could racewalk me (and win) and not break a sweat. I asked if he would help me prepare for labor and delivery using his work and we began a 9-month odyssey of experiment and exploration that ultimately may have saved my life.

We started at the beginning, with both body and voice work. I learned how to keep my spine in the c-curve, so very helpful as my belly grew larger and threw my back into a sway. The c-curve eliminated back pain and greatly diminished sciatica problems. In fact, some of the most common complaints of pregnancy were bypassed or very mild indeed as I wandered through the *Body Wisdom* text. I added small ball rolls to my repertoire and was able to do them until my 8th month; and when my middle allowed me to not tuck so compactly, I stayed in the expanded sphere. I found both instrumental in alleviating sciatica pain and so I spent a great deal of time letting the floor gently massage my lower back and buttocks. Cylinder rolls (leg straight, arms stretched overhead) were entirely do-able; and the tiny, atom-to-atom movement, (movement so slight it was nearly undetectable) lent a calming air of meditation as I navigated through an inner wilderness of ease and comfort. As I became increasingly more uncomfortable in my day-to-day life, I found myself turning to the work more and more often. Here I could relieve the stresses on my body and mind. I appreciated the control I could still have though my belly loomed enormous. When my cylinder rolls turned conical, my open rounded arms protected the baby while I lightly rolled over the belly, the floor contact so smooth and minimal it created the barest hint of a tummy rub.

We worked on squats and the process gave my legs such a workout that even at 9 months I could squat in any position at a deliciously slow pace, the buttocks tucked under, the c-curve strongly present to protect the back. Certainly I thought these explorations would be the most beneficial to the physical work required in labor. As the time grew closer, I brought in my Lamaze materials and we played at recreating some of the traditional Lamaze exercises into playful Lessac-friendly goals for childbirth. After all, so many of the prescribed exercises in Lamaze seemed to be anesthetic, (rather than esthetic) and seemed to create tension in order to achieve relaxation.

One Lamaze technique called Progressive Relaxation does just that. The mother is asked to tense each part of the body, one section at a time, then release that tension, exhaling on the release. The idea is to remember the feeling of the tenseness in order to recognize it and then remember the letting go. However, in Lessac Training, we do not emphasize the use of tension to aid in relaxation. So we asked, "how can we achieve this effect without bringing tension into the body? Instead, let's truly minimize tension by not wholly inviting it in." We set about the creative task of exploring with the Lessac Body NRG states (eNeRGy). We threw out the notion of tightening in order to feel something good afterwards and tried to make the whole thing feel good! I did a muscle yawn (Potency NRG) and expanded the body. Remember that great Potent line said on a good, full yawn stretch? "Oh, it feels so GOOOOOD to get up in the morning". Well, I yawned into such a nice, big, long, supple and potent stretch that the muscles became usefully extended and firm (not tight) and I was flooded with energy and fueled with strength. I don't need to mention the need for strength in labor do I? My 22-hour labor was not uncommon. However, my doctor said I would've easily been a candidate for a c-section as the hours grew longer were it not for the fact that my physical strength surprised her.

After the fueling of the Potent Yawn, I mixed some Buoyancy NRG into the game. We've all felt that glorious wafting on a supportive band of water, whether that be in the bathtub, a lake, or the fierce rocking of waves on the Pacific Ocean. By adding the sensation of buoyancy, the muscles loosen on their own and relaxation becomes creative, not prescriptive. The medical terminology of "tighten-release" as Lamaze suggests gives way to "Muscle Yawn—Buoyancy" that in its very nature focuses on something other than pain and innately relaxes the mind, body and spirit. Telling the body to tighten is never as conducive to health as feeling YAWWWWNN. The resulting action may look similar to an observer at first, but it feels entirely different to the person experiencing it. It is healthful, powerful, makes one feel in charge and not at the mercy of pain and contractions. "Pain is simply information," Lessac says. We want to use information, to work with it in the most healthful, even pleasurable way possible. I found Lessac Training doesn't discount or cover up pain, but fully embraces it and assists the body with all its natural and organic ways of dealing with pain.

Many childbirth techniques rely heavily on guided imagery to distract mom into believing that she isn't where she is, with what feels to be the equivalent of a MACK truck between her legs. I found simple imagery to be the least effective in my labor. Instead, when I used a Lessac "familiar event" my body, not just my mind, responded with a fully immersed experience. I wasn't just thinking of a pretty field somewhere. I stooped to smell the flower or swing the golf club and the genuine tactile experiencing of those events organically involved my entire body and *that* became a unifying experience rather than a distraction. A familiar event is an ingrained body-knowledge tool that immediately supported the laboring by creating order out of chaos, and gave a tangible, deep and thorough visualization that developed from within the body.

Lamaze Breathing is one of the most widely used forms of labor assistance. During a contraction, the uterine wall contracts and little oxygen goes to the baby. Deep cleansing breaths help to ensure maximum oxygen while the baby is "hugged" by the uterine walls. During my pregnancy, Arthur took me step by step through his voice text, *The Use & Training of the Human Vice.* I played the consonant orchestra, much to the growing child's delight. She responded to the percussive taps, the lilting strings and most enjoyed the vibrating and resonating Y-buzz and +Y-buzz. I Y-buzzed my days away, calming her when she kicked furiously and I delighted in feeling my entire body as a giant instrument surrounding her in sound. She had her own personal stereo, one that not only gave joy with sound, but one that actually massaged with vibration and tone. I learned to keep my forward facial posture to allow my sound to be more full-toned. I learned to fill the theatre of my head so that my tone was pure and focused. Lessac breath work emphasizes the need to expand the breath reserve of the back and for my breath to be qualitative and not quantitative. Smell that flower; fill the well of the abdomen, ribs and back reserve. But gently, so gently that it is hardly noticeable. Fill with that delicious pervasive, salutary heady smell. Does it feel good? Does it smell good? Is Mom overwhelmed with the sensuous aroma of her flower of choice? That inhalation of glorious smells hugged the baby as the contractions grew. And instead of exhaling on "hee" (short, fast and all-breath with no tone) we added sound.

I have found that by simply working with breath, I get hoarse and tend to hyperventilate…a common problem my Lamaze instructor announced. It seemed logical to create sound, but why moan as Lamaze teaches? Why not create pleasurable full tone? The breath alone felt like a "holding back." If "an open mouth is an open cervix," surely an open and audibly vocal mouth is a healthy, vibratory aid to the opening of the pathway for the baby. If gravity helps the position of Baby, perhaps tone, vibration, and buzzing can also delightfully tremble around Baby and assist the progress along the birth canal. Many moms are vocal anyway in birth, but the tones are out of restriction, tightness and pain. I tried to translate the tones into useful sound. "Think of how you can't open that can of spaghetti sauce," Lessac says, "no matter how hard you try. Now try again, using potency NRG and by saying 'oh it feels so good to get up in the morning.' Not only does it open, but it seems to have used less strength." That's not a moan, that's an ecstatic "call" with a fullness and celebratory glee. Glee in childbirth? Why not? Relaxer-energizers, as Lessac calls them, are all joyful: whistling, dancing, trembling, shaking, smiling and laughing. They all provide tension relief and release natural endorphins in the body.

We certainly sang and made joyful noises in my labor room. The C.D. played our favorite music constantly and as the labor became more intense and my concentration more total, my husband hummed, my labor assistant chimed in and the nurses noticed that between pushes the only thing that completely relaxed my body was to "go to low tones". Before I knew it, the doctor was Y-buzzing along with the rest of them and I was surrounded by a cacophony of sound. Everybody was vibrating gently, the air was filled with that accompanying energy and the baby seemed to recognize that the comfortable buzzing she was so accustomed to was also going on in that strange outside place. Miss Fiona Maeve was born. She didn't cry, she blinked her eyes and stared right at me. Her daddy followed her as the pediatrician checked her over and she stared at him as he hummed to her.

Unbeknownst to me, my lungs began to fill with fluid. Twelve hours later, I found I couldn't breathe easily. My nurse told me I was just nervous about being a mom and tried to give me something to make me sleep. I turned the drugs down and for the next four hours tried to believe her. Soon, I noticed I couldn't breathe at all lying down. I grew more and more unsure of what was happening with my breath. I drew in long slow breaths, worked on expanding gently into the back. When my body suddenly cut short the time I could inhale and would not allow any reserve, I calmly called the nurse for the fifth time and told her to get me oxygen. I smelled the familiar event flower and my short gentle sips of air sustained me while she walked in, still not believing me, and measured the amount of oxygen in my blood. Her face went white. My oxygen level in my blood was very, very low.

Within in a few hours I was transferred to ICU, had x-rays done and an EKG. My lungs indeed had filled with fluid. The stress of labor had affected my heart (apparently weakened by a bout of rheumatic fever as a child—also unknown to me until then). Had I accepted the nurse's explanations and drugs, it is very likely that I would've suffocated from my own fluids. Breathing continued to be difficult and painful for four days and I called upon all my Lessac knowledge to keep calm, to fuel the body with energy and to manage pain. Both my O.B. and the heart doctors commented on my physical strength and commended my body and breath awareness.

Did using Lessac Training save my life? I have no idea. But I sure am glad I took that job.

The Body Energies in the Actor's Performance

Maria Regina Tocchetto de Oliveira
Employed at Chapito, in Lisbon
Freelance actor, director and Theatre educator
Attended Lessac Summer Workshop 2006 in Greencastle

Haven't you experienced it in similar circumstances, when something streamed out of you, some current from your eyes, from the ends of your fingers or out through your pores? What name can we give these invisible currents, which we use to communicate with one another? Some day this phenomenon will be the subject of scientific research. Meantime let us call them rays *(Stanislavski 1990:212)*.

This excerpt from Stanislavski's *An Actor Prepares* shows how, at the beginning of the 20th century, this artist and teacher elaborated on the wordless communion between people and on how understanding this bond could improve the actor's performance. Nowadays, Arthur Lessac along with members of the Lessac Institute offer a concrete approach to the use of vocal and body energies in order to obtain control over, and a better quality of, human performance on stage, or even outside it boundaries.

Arthur Lessac's philosophy is based on a concept of the human being as a totality, on the organic interrelation between the emotional life, the body, and the voice, and on the linkage between perceptive, sensorial and thinking systems. His training (practical and experimental) is founded on the notion of self-knowledge, and not on the assimilation of rules that are contradictory to the natural human actions. This training is experimental inasmuch as it presupposes an investigative attitude. There is no pre-established model to be achieved and it does not require the assimilation of any specific behavioral pattern. The process of discovery is individual and it is continuous. Each person is stimulated to discover her own individual process of adjustment between each new ability and any previously acquired knowledge. From this dynamic equilibrium emerges the improvement of performance.

All the explorations created and used by Lessac[1] are no more than an experiential and profound explorations of our being as we are, meaning the use of our innate capacities and natural proceedings, that he enhances so that they can be explored. Further, through the making conscious of their existence, it is possible to control them and link them to behaviors that depend on our will.

Lessac Training, in accordance with humanist philosophy and psychology that suggests that the human being can transform itself, is based on the perspective that, under normal circumstances, all of us tend to wish for and pursue well-being. In general, behavioral changes can happen at any point of human life, considering that the human being is not a completed and immutable whole, but it is always in interaction with the environment, having energy and emotional exchanges, and perceptions that are always related to the moment. For this reason, another main issue of this approach is the quality of "presence." Lessac avoids quantifying experiences and explorations, thus overcoming the mechanistic understanding of human actions. He does not promote quantitative productivity, but optimum quality, which means the best possible under the present conditions. He values personal commitment during the exploration activities. According to this point of view, being as a whole—integrating body, vocal and emotional lives—means to be sincerely committed to the actions that are being executed, and it resembles the expected and needed actor's Presence on stage.

One of the recurring elements in the Lessac Training is the exploration of vocal and body natural energy states as endless resources to the vital quality and to the esthetic performance.[2] Each body energy is related to a vocal energy (tonal energy, structural energy and consonant energy) but these will not be analyzed in this article.

This article focuses on the four primal body energy stages developed by the Lessac Training up to now: buoyancy, radiancy, potency, and Inter-involvement. My goal is to demonstrate how the exploration of and the control over the body energies, as rec-

---

[1] The training promoted by the Lessac Institute is offered mainly as intensive annual workshops in various academic institutions at the USA (www.lessacinstitute.com).

[2] Lessac prefers using the word *esthetic* rather than *aesthetic*. This is because the word "esthetic" comes from *esthesis,* which is related to the study of sensations, whereas he argues that *aesthetic* has to do with the nature of beauty. See Lessac, Arthur. 1997. *The Use and Training of the Human Voice*. New York: McGraw–Hill. p. 271.

ommended by the Training, can help improve the actor's performance, giving him confidence and stimulating his expressive will.

As an example of this statement, I will describe two experiences. The first one is the exploration I had during the 2006 *Lessac Summer Intensive Workshop*, at DePauw University, in Greencastle, Indiana, from June 18th to July 16th, directed by Deborah Kinghorn, a Lessac Master Teacher and Kathleen Dunn, a member of the Institute's recognized teaching team. The second, in which I also participated, is a research project undertaken at the Federal University of Rio Grande do Sul, named "*A utilização das energias corporais no treino do actor*" *(The use of body energies in the actor's training)* in Brazil guided by Irion Nolasco[3] and Maria Lúcia Raymundo, from 1986 until 1990, in which they intended to spread Lessac's work. It is important to underline that, in this essay, I choose one theme to focus on, namely the energies. However, it must be clear that the work on body energies only makes sense if considered together with all the other elements included in the training.

According to the theoretical and practical basis of the Lessac Training, we acknowledge and explore the operation of various events connected to the body energies in two main functions: the "staying alive" function and expressive function. The first one is at the same time relaxing and vitalizing, it stimulates the body as a whole to be alive, ready to react vigorously to the internal needs and to the outside environment, with a balanced tonus, without contractions or muscular flabbiness. The expressive function is used when we recognize the rhythmical changes, the different relations with space and the various body sensations provided by the three energy states.

Buoyancy is the energy state in which we experience the absence of weight, as if the body was filled up with oxygen and was lighter than air. It feels like an active relaxation, different to that type of relaxation in which we feel the body as heavy and sluggish. The sensation that corresponds to the state of buoyancy is weightlessness, and some of the psycho-physical states that frequently appear to be associated to this sensation are calmness and serenity.

---

[3] Irion Nolasco got in touch with the Lessac Training in the eighties, at a workshop he attended in the USA.

While experiencing buoyancy, we tend to keep a slow-motion rhythm, although it can be developed in high speed. However, the experience of lightness in slow-motion soothes breathing and movement and helps us to understand all the potential of life and internal movement that can be found during this "external steadiness."

The most direct experiences with this energy occur when we are under water. In this situation—for instance, in a bathtub or in a swimming pool—our body naturally experiences the feeling of fluctuation. The balanced breathing, the sensation of fluctuation, the lightness, and fluidity experienced in the water are natural and familiar events, involuntary or semi-voluntary ones that transform themselves into organic instructions when we wish to voluntarily repeat those sensations through sensorial memory without having the water environment of our direct experience.

We can also explore buoyancy as a familiar event through breathing techniques and other procedures. There are many ways to return to the original sensation when we wish to do so. We can do it through an image, a specific rhythm, a position of balance, the memory of a particular odor or even the idea of this energetic state that we can use to instill in us this sensation and vibrate in this energy, changing completely our initial state. The aim is to use the buoyancy energy not only as an act of will, but also as a behavior manifestation that emerges as a familiar event to give support, consistency, weightlessness and a particular type of dynamic to the performance.

Radiancy, another energy state, is characterized by the vibrating excitement of one's body, that can be more sophisticated or subtle, like a smooth and light trembling of one's body or as an electric personification of liveliness and body skills, or even as a state of alertness and anticipation.

Lessac gives various examples of radiancy: due to its characteristics of surprise, excitement, amusement and spontaneity, the radiancy energetic state resembles a child's attitude while playing, with an unlimited energy and liberty, and a balancing of naturally relaxed moments with sudden energy charges.

The precocious kitten with its unpredictable moves and its fascinating, electric eyes – prancing, playing, leaping, turning, rolling, sudden stopping—is all Radiancy energy! The artful, ever-alert body behavior of Charlie Chaplin or Laurel and Hardy in the old silent movies is Radiancy at work! The deer on sudden guard at the first scent of intruders—the great "lighter-than-air" tap dancing of immortal Bill Robinson—the night-watch always loose in order to be always on guard—the track-runner just before the Go signal—the symphony musicians on sudden "nerve-tingly" anticipation of their maestro's first downbeat—all of these images obtain to Radiancy energy (Lessac, 1978: 48).

As the energy liberation of radiancy usually starts at the eyes of small children, one of the explorations used in Training aims to instigate excitement and curiosity of the eyes, looking in various directions and letting this light and funny activity stimulate other parts of the body, like the face, the ears, the mouth, the head; and further, like an electrical current, to let it flow to the fingers, hands, arms, allowing it to fill the whole body, making it a body vibration (sometimes subtle and sometimes explosive), capable of investing in the patterns of a typical Caribbean dance or in the waiting state of the hunter while watching his prey.

The more subtle body vibrato can be used as an important element for the overcoming of the sensation of the dead weight, as opposed to the enjoyment of live weight. As an energizer, the state of radiancy gives life to muscular activity, through expansion and reach, eliminating the feeling of indolence and lack of motivation.

Potency is the energy state that produces the sensation of muscular power. A familiar event for this energy is the extension of the arms and legs with a yawn that revitalizes the body, extending and relaxing its muscles "with a sense of fierce and deep intensity" (*Ibidem:* 52).

In order to be conscious of this natural energy state and to make it an organic instruction, the Training suggests the comparison of the sensation of power as opposed to the tiring sensation of brutal force. The difference resides in the way we breathe. When we are at the peak of our inspiration, our real strength is greater because the body receives a large quantity of oxygen causing the sensation of a high muscular tension. The experience tends to spread, involving a higher area of muscle fibers, avoiding the physical stress caused by holding the breath and by localized effort. Thus, using potency, not only does one feel that one is stronger but one does really have more strength compared with the effort made when one takes the stressful path.

The sensations and some of psycho-physical states linked to potency are extreme strength, unlimited power, intensity and determination. Esthetically it is different from the *legato* reach of buoyancy and from the vivid and vibrating reach of radiancy. With potency the body expands and enlarges in a stable way, caused by the fostering of optimal muscle yawning and effortless body length.

Apart from the healthy and esthetic qualities that the use of these three energies provides to body movement, it is important to highlight their potential in the area of expression. Each of them can contribute different possibilities to enrich body language. This is because each of them has its own way of functioning, its own rhythm and special trends, its own relation between tonus and balance and, in a way, a special relation to different psycho-physical states. Even if the energy states frequently manifest in an associated or interconnected manner, in a laboratory situation each energy may be experienced in isolation, in a free and enhanced manner. In this way different dispositions that relate to the external environment and different behavioral characteristics may emerge. That is why we can pose questions and use these states as stimuli in the search for expression: which theatrical style can be stimulated by the actor's representations that come from rhythm, images, and the balanced dynamics of the different energy states? Which kind of role may be suggested by those energy characteristics? This initiative was one of the focal points of the research conducted at the Rio Grande do Sul University (UFRGS), in Porto Alegre, by Irion Nolasco and Maria Lúcia, when, through the work with students, they were searching for effective ways to help actors to renew and revitalize their performance, avoiding *clichés* and personal conditionings that might have been used to build their characters.

The fourth primal energy state developed by the Lessac Training is the inter-involvement.

> Even the purest technique is poor technique when inner personal involvement is lacking. But to be self-involved with the perception of your own body energy states is not quite the same thing as the sensation of inter-involvement!

Take, for example, the principles of our own work, Body Wisdom. Yes, we can learn to feel the sensations and perceptions of Buoyancy, Radiancy, and Potency and recognize these as part of a network of self-to-self response. But without the overlay of inter-involvement, we can never generate emotionally-charged output from our internal organism to the outer environment. Even in our own work, there will be technicians of Body Wisdom and artists of Body Wisdom. Where the former manipulates the feeling process proficiently but with only one-quarter yield, the artist will orchestrate the different elements of the harmonic overtone sensory system and exploit the psycho-physical instrument to its fullest potential. Inter-Involvement energy is thus a necessary, not merely sufficient, condition for optimal training to Body Wisdom (*Ibidem*: 55).

The *inter-involvement* energy state has to do with the organic communication of our internal environment with the external one. It is the need to relate with our external environment that makes the person synthesize all his internal experience systems while focusing his goals, without being conscious of the use he makes of his energy states or of the other esthetic and expressive elements that improve his performance. The body does not charge itself with energy like in the three other states, but in this case it is the interlacing of the states by the emotional system.

One of the explorations at the 2006 Intensive Workshop was the following improvisation: imagine that a very small child that you love is playing at the edge of an open window on the fourth floor. When you realize the dangerous situation the child is in, you want to take her out of there immediately, but you instinctively know that you can't frighten the child by shouting and working with explosive attitudes because they could cause her to fall. At the same time you realize that you can't lose a second. You should attract her smoothly to you (using buoyancy), while you use the maximum agility to reach her as fast as possible (use of radiancy), and hold her with all your strength to overcome her opposition, but gently and without hurting her in one move pulling her away from danger (use of potency). This is an example of how the four energy states inter-relate and balance each other, with the inter-involvement having the task of synthesizing them. When someone is actually and completely involved in an activity, this state equals "a magnetic force diametrically opposed to sheer brawn" (*Ibidem*: 56).

Inter-involvement could be compared to the involvement of an actor with the given circumstances[4] that define the situation of his character and influence or justify his behavior, or with the way the actor shares his playing with his colleagues and the audience.[5] It can also identify the energy that is present as the actors' background action or as the sense that moves the actor's actions on stage, independently of the play he is in.[6]

The inter-involvement state is related to the attitude of exploration, curiosity and pleasure the actor takes in what he is doing, as well as with the irradiation of his presence on stage, because it integrates in harmony all individual capacities of the actor, in the action and reaction of the play, with the moment the actor is living in.

At the end of the second week in Greencastle, the two teachers, Deb Kinghorn and Kathleen Dunn, gave us an exploration to discover and develop characters playing the energy game. We call this a game—in the sense of children playing, to have fun, not as a competition—as an approach to representation, because this is the sense of the exploring with the energies within the general perspective of the Lessac Training. The attitudes of curiosity, motivation and availability or openness are essential for the exploration and the making conscious of the psycho-physical functioning, as a way to perfect the expressivity and the communication within the external environment. Only through freedom and enthusiasm can one exchange impressions and signs with one's partners, and move toward the unexpected. The game establishes the boundaries of a situation in which we should risk if we want to go further than our present condition, if we want to discover other possibilities of relationships with the world. It is in the action and in letting the other person influence us that we exchange experiences and change our course, motivated by immediate concerns and by planned goals. It is the state of Inter-involvement that finds itself reflected in this attitude while playing the game, testing our acquired skills—in this case, referring to skills that were acquired during the first two weeks of training at the workshop.

---

[4] The term "given circumstances" is directly refered to in Stanislavski's literature. See, for example, *An Actor Prepares* and *Building a Character*.

[5] According to the pedagogy of Philippe Gaulier. See, for example: www.ecolephilippegaulier.com/archives/editorial - visited at 24 September 2007.

[6] About the relation between Lessac and others authors, see, for example, my master's dissertation: Oliveira, Maria Regina Tocchetto de.2008. *The body energies in the actor's work.* Master dissertation presented at the University of Lisbon. pp. 1-103.

In the exploration, we approached one energy state at a time—buoyancy, radiancy, or potency—to discover, inspired by its characteristics, occasional roles, letting ourselves be carried by the transitory impulses that each energy state would suggest. Intuitively, we would play a way of being, looking, walking, wanting, speaking, and establishing contact with the others. The rule established that, while circulating in the room, each character would have a brief contact with each of the other characters, introducing himself, letting this encounter influence him, without losing the original energy matrix. After this phase, we would opt for one of the three possibilities. We would choose one partner and begin to improvise, in couples, a situation of a job interview. With no prior consultation, we would let the game tell us who would play the interviewer and who would be interviewed. At the next step, each couple would play out the situation for the audience, formed by our colleagues and the teachers. As there is no *direct* link between the characteristics of the energies, and character or role for radiancy, buoyancy, or potency, the roles created were all diverse, and, as a job interview suggests, there is a different perspective between the employer and the potential employee and therefore the players' attitudes were always different.

At the moment of the improvisation, the confrontation through words tends to be stronger than the individual planning made beforehand, or the game will not work. That is what scenic presence training prepares us for, in its characteristic "here and now" dynamic. If I were divided between reacting to the influence of the colleague with whom I was relating, by trying, for example, to impose one path whose idea pleased me when I anticipated from my perspective the moment in which we were going to play, than I already had lost the succession of events of our improvisation. Thus, the quality of my presence would be undermined and I would tend to act seemingly mechanistically. But if I wasn't divided by those two ideas, and managed, at the same time, to be influenced by the approach of my colleague but also to influence him, convincing him not by imposition, but by means of a lively negotiation, to embrace my action plan, we would continue to exchange impressions, act and react according to what we felt at the moment, intensifying our presence. The goal of this scenic exploration was to improvise the situation with the partner, maintaining the essence of the character created from one of the energy states.

We were all excited by the experience because it signaled, in the training context, the passage from the explorations of the internal relation to the relation with the external environment. In the specific matter of the use of body energies, we started to understand that there are two distinct moments: the first is the exploration in the "laboratory," where we try to isolate the effect of the particular energy state and fill up the whole body with this energy; the second refers to its use during the performance—that is to say, for all those moments where acts of communication (theatrical, in rehearsal or in improvisation) are "at play"—in which a whole different set of conditions directs and determines its adequate application. This is where the inter-involvement plays its role, or our own ability to intuitively manage a whole set of stimuli of various origins, focusing our attention according to our will. The drama game of the workshop with its characters stimulated us to balance all sorts of information, sensations, impressions, feelings, impulses, and images produced there, in a constant exchange with the partner, the audience and the rules of that improvisation. In a natural way, our consciousness became dynamic, and the feeling, understanding and answering processes turned into only one, as we tended to act organically and instinctively. Thus we chose intuitively and wisely the best way to answer at each moment. Whereas when, in a laboratory situation, we could circumscribe most of the behavioral manifestations of our character within the variations of only one energy state, in the moment we placed the character in a relationship with others the energy flux or flow was completely altered. We kept the energy essence as the base, but varied the qualities of our actions within a much larger spectrum of body energies. In this situation, the qualities expressed by the energy work would be clear to us, not just in terms of its characterizing role that became manifest in the characters, making them more nervous, serene, or authoritarian (for example), but mainly in terms of their role in characterizing or embodying the expressive variations at each moment of the "improvised play" created in the moment of the workshop.

Every situation in life has its own development. From the moment we wake up until the end of our day, we pass through an infinite number of small or big events that come along resonating with a constant change of our state of mind. This also includes a constant energy change, so we can adapt ourselves to the expressive need of the moment. Being inspired by these dynamics to "perform real life" within the dynamics of the drama implies the ability to go through energy, body, mental and emotional changes. That is what I realized watching my colleagues perform and during my own improvisation. All of us, and our couples, varied our energies much further than what we originally planned, because the situation asked for it. Getting to the meeting, introducing ourselves, accommodating, waiting, suspecting, hiding, exposing ourselves, predicting, advancing, backing up, seducing, lying, attacking, giving up, sharing, winning or losing were moments that followed on, one after the other, with the evolution of the situations, always in different ways. It requires flexibility from the players that would not be possible if we didn't do it intuitively, based on a natural wisdom.

What I clearly noticed in the work of every participant of the training course, actors and non-actors, was the function of the energy and the state of Inter-involvement that synergized the energies we worked on in an organic and unforeseen way. I did not see buoyancy, radiancy, and potency characteristics dominate our performance completely. I noticed that there were moments filled with each one of them, but there were other moments in which they were so mixed that it was impossible to name what was the main energy state leading the action. I was surprised to see how all the preparing of that moment resulted in fun and agility for everyone that took part in it. As the energy work helped us to transform nervous energy in radiancy, it turned into the wish to perform better, into a boost for the play, into the complicity with the audience, and into light and free detachment that allowed us to take risks. The awareness of the lesson we had was very recent: energy is a psycho-physical proceeding that flows, disseminates itself, and above all, that changes itself. It is an instinctive way of communication.

We exchange energy with the environment and with other people at all moments, but we just do not necessarily have the awareness of this. This is an issue of huge importance, because playing on stage is not only an intellectual exchange of ideas and goals, but it is also a direct influence of states of mind, feelings and sensations expressed in energy in tune with the general attitude and with all other aspects of the gestural language. The body "speaks" all the time. It communicates even its absence, when we are not focused, and spreads its presence when we wish to show our neutral expression. It is in this scope that we communicate on stage, with larger or lesser intensity and control. It is in this situation that the energy work must be understood, seen as an attitude to be incorporated and not as a technique to avoid the moments of monotony in the performance. Its efficiency depends on the acquired conscience due to the continuous process of self-learning accomplished by us on and off stage. Thus I understood the role of the four body energies: to make the actor flexible for the life that happens on stage and that gives sense to his presence there.

Before this period, learning about body energies while doing the research under guidance of Irion Nolasco and Maria Lúcia Raymundo, I realized how much it is worth for the building of a character and in the integration of body and vocal action. One of the explorations made by the students/actors that participated in the research—and this will be explained here based on my own experience—was founded on choosing and memorizing one monologue from a classical theatre text. For this exploration, I chose the three witches in Shakespeare's *Macbeth*, integrating all their speeches in just one character. After memorizing the text in an automatic way, so we didn't have to stop its flow to remember the next words, we started to explore the text, an activity guided by the directors, with the aim of finding new and provocative ways of expressing it. In order to obtain these new and expressive ways, we had to free the vocal emission from the usual way that we speak, avoiding the normal grammatical pauses and syntax, only stopping the speech when we needed to breathe. We wanted to explore the sounds, as well as finding new meanings to the text references. But the main focus of the exploration was to discover how to integrate the body energies with the vocal action, so that all the expressive variations obtained with the previous body work would infuse themselves into the speech, enriching it with nuances and making it flexible for the performance, as a way to exchange impressions present in the dialogue with other characters in the same internal dialogue. The experience started with the incorporation of one of the three energies in a non-usual way, letting the body assume the reference registered in the memory whilst we did exploratory experiments on the selected energy. As I was pronouncing my speech, the directors selected which body energy changes I should engage with, so that I would be constantly startled, avoiding the choice of personal patterns that would limit the discovery of new ones. By doing this, I aimed to integrate the speech with the energy and rhythmic changes originated by the development of body impulses that were, at the same time, influenced by energy and rhythmic characteristics of the vocal action.

As the energy states are linked to all aspects of our being, the production of sensations, feelings, and meanings arose constantly, together with the unbroken movement and the vocal emission. Instinctively I associated images and ideas that arose at the moment with reminiscences from my emotional and body memory and selected the paths to be followed, influenced by the goals of my will and by the framework of the situation within the exploration.

The use of different perspectives to approach the playing of a character, stimulated by different body energies, helps to explore the character's limits in an organic way, with no need to employ any available stereotypes. The attitude recommended for this exploration is an experiential one, for we don't know what will happen along the way, and the new meanings, whenever they impose themselves as probable and interesting, are always welcome. With this exploration, apart from the evil machinations and the grotesque that are generally seen as the witches' qualities, I discovered characteristics like freedom, submission, power, pleasure, humor and the enormous affective contradictions that are linked to malediction and innocence. The lightness, sensuality, deliverance and self-indulgence that can be encapsulated by the expressive reach of buoyancy allowed, when experienced, to strengthen by opposition the obsessive actions stimulated by fury, that revive the body with its energy for the power of destruction, or for the pragmatic determination of cruelty. The radiancy energy revealed extreme liveliness and a sense of alertness during the games, plays and the completion of the tasks done by the character. Together, the three energies infused the ceremonial works of that witch, putting in relief the lyricism and the esthetic component of her behavior. I refer to the esthetic in the sense Lessac uses, linked more to the harmony of sensations and the resulting expressivity of the player than to the established patterns of beauty. Considering that the focus of the work was the discovery of the vocal expressivity of the character, the guides took us to the next step of the exploration to the transformation of the recently acquired accomplishments into a more moderate speech and gesture.

Lessac establishes different levels of speech according to the communication needs. This vocal experience, applied to the first phase of the application of the four training elements, is considered by him as "extravagant" speech. Formal speech is more moderate and focused, and everyday conversation is more informal. Each one of them can be used in acting, depending on the configuration of the theatre space and its acoustic conditions and of the expressive and aesthetic goals of the project, as well as of the specific moments of the play.

I had to choose from everything that I had experienced through the vocal and body energies in a scattered and uncontrolled way so that in the next improvisation I would act in more moderate and intuitive way, if possible according to the proposed dramatic situation. With this task I could understand that the previous exploration accomplishments were going to be shown in another format. I also understood that the energies originally recalled from broad and extravagant movements would be maintained and indeed would be more intense when I moved to act in a subtle or contained manner.

If we transfer these types of speech to the scope of the drama styles, when one refers to gesture, for example, we can understand that the expression of the body energies does not depend on the form of the gesture, not even on its size, because it can be irradiated from a body externally standing still or through its vocal action.

Another lesson from this experience is related to the development of the trust of internal and intuitive systems, once they respond efficiently while stimulated, generating creative solutions. I have a strong memory of a process that can help me to go beyond the usual patterns in the explorations around sounds, meanings, gestures, and presence. I have come to the conclusion that there is a long way to go to make our presence available to the production of a play, regardless of the presence of a director. The Lessac Training stimulates this continuous learning attitude, based on the exploration of the inherent ability to strengthen the perception the actor has of himself, enriching his performance in balance with the external environment. The next step on this exploration of the *Macbeth* witch would be, in the case where the play was going to be prepared for theatrical performance, to show the director during rehearsals some of the results of these explorations, as a contribution to the play.

The practical understanding that the energies brings about means that the actor can use expressive freedom together with a continuous readjustment and give the proper responses to the external stimuli and to the internal needs. Thus we can have a glimpse—as we have with other interpretation methods—of the possibility of influencing the non-voluntary behavior systems, whose activation and harmony with the voluntary portion of the acting is fundamental to the performance. Using different energies to enrich the actions on stage means also finding a way to bring life-experience to the artistic reality, without creative competitiveness between the two dynamics.

The quality of naturalness in performance is fundamentally dissimilar to daily life spontaneity. Any attempt to emulate the latter directly is likely to result in a degree of banality and falsification in the stage presence of the performer. It is training that increasingly gives form to presence, unleashing its potential power and therefore avoiding any attachment to stereotyped behaviour and individual particularities devoid of artistic value. The Lessac Training proposes a natural and instinctive approach to all such mechanisms, towards the organic and, therefore, to the stage presence of the actor.

At the start of this article I referred to Stanislavski's notion of the "rays" that appear to go from the one person to another in acts of communication. Stanislavski notes that this is an area for scientific research in the future. In my view Lessac has gone a long way towards describing the experience that Stanislavski has identified. Moreover, Lessac has provided a powerful pedagogical training and strategy to experience these "currents" of which Stanislavski speaks. The strength of these experiences and this strategy can be found in the dynamic of performance.

References

Lessac, A. 1978. *Body Wisdom: The Use and Training of the Human Body*. New York: Lessac Research.

Lessac, A. 1997. *The use and training of the human voice*. New York: McGraw-Hill.

Oliveira, M.R.T d. 2008. *The body energies in the actor's work*. Master dissertation presented at the University of Lisbon. pp. 1-103.

Stanislavski, C. 1990. *An Actor Prepares* (1936). London: Methuen.

Sites

www.ecolephilippegaulier.com/archives/editorial - visited at 24 September 2007.

www.lessacinstitute.com - visited at 24 September 2007.

Lessac Energies and Classical Texts

Kathleen Campbell

Professor Communication Studies, Austin College, Sherman
Year of Certification as a Lessac Voice, Speech and Body Trainer: 1996

Lessac Kinesenics is used in actor training to help performers develop flexible and expressive voices and bodies. Training in Lessac Kinesensics, which is highly integrated and holistic, ideally involves full immersion in both the voice and body work. Indeed, the elements of Lessac's work are so tightly connected that it sometimes seems as if one has to teach all of it, or not teach it at all. Working in a theatre program in a small liberal arts college, I am unable to teach all the work in a coordinated series of classes that all of my students will take. I have found, however, that exploration of even a small portion of the work can provide interesting and valuable results, so I routinely introduce parts of the work in various classes. In beginning acting classes, for example, I teach the body energizers of potency, radiancy and buoyancy (Lessac 1981: 34-58) as relaxer-energizers that can be included in a personal warm-up, and explore the potential for shaping character by consciously working with a chosen energy. I also use wafting and waving (Lessac 1981: 42-43) and humming (Lessac 1997: 44) in warm-ups and introduce students to the y-buzz (Lessac 1997:120-136). I reinforce these elements in rehearsals and other classes, but only recently have I explored more extensively the use of Kinesensics. In this paper, I will share the results of a pedagogical experiment using body and vocal energies with students in an acting class unit focusing on classical Greek texts.

I have for some years taught an advanced acting course that focuses on close explorations, physical and vocal, of texts from Shakespeare and contemporary drama. I developed the course to address two areas in which I felt young actors needed work—text analysis and emotional release. I felt strongly that the two were closely related, in part because of my own experience with Lessac text explorations. I have also done a great deal of work with Shakespearean texts emphasizing the connection between the text itself—and by that I mean its technical construction, not just its meaning—and a character's emotional life.

I regretted, however, the relatively narrow focus of the course. In an acting styles course I had taught previously, I had done some interesting work with masks as an approach to Greek texts.[1] I used explorations involving movement, non-verbal sound, and over-sized masks to help students open themselves to the size and intensity required for the classic Greek texts. The work was often exciting, but also very frustrating. Because the students often had little formal voice or movement training to draw on, they rarely reached the potential they might have. After struggling with the styles course through several iterations, I decided that our students were better served by a different kind of course and I developed the course I teach now.

In 2006 a presentation by Kathy Dunn at the annual Lessac conference opened up a new way to utilize kinesensics in the course. Dunn described her work with actors on a production of a Greek play. What was most significant for me was that, working with actors who had not had Lessac training, she was able to introduce and utilize some basic Lessac principles to help the actors achieve greater emotional release. Dunn used music and dance to help explore the body energies as well as using the vocal energies to enliven specific moments in the text. She described introducing the body energies to her actors through what she called "spiritual dancing." She associated each energy with a natural element—buoyancy with wind, radiancy with fire, potency with earth. The actors then chose a moment from the text for each body energy—light inner, open moments, which Dunn called "heart moments" for buoyancy, moments of anticipation or urgency for radiancy, moments of expansive power for potency—and explored them, blindfolded, self to self and then self to other. Carefully chosen music accompanied the explorations. I immediately saw a way that I could use the Lessac work in combination with the mask explorations I had used in the styles course to explore Greek texts within the advanced acting course.

It was not difficult to integrate Dunn's approach into the course. Although we do some traditional text analysis, I try as much as possible, even with the metrical analysis of Shakespearean texts, to explore the texts in right-brained ways. Much of the work we do in the course is grounded in the body. All of the students in the class in the spring of 2006 were familiar with the Lessac body energies from the beginning

---

[1] This work had evolved from an approach used in graduate acting classes at the Dallas Theater Center in the '60s.

acting class. Most of the students also had some familiarity with Lessac voice work. They had learned to use humming, the Y-buzz, and percussive instruments in warm-ups; as preparation for the Greek work, we also did some Call explorations (Lessac 1997:136-148). Thus, while none of the students had taken the voice class, all of them had some experience with Lessac kinesensics on which we could build.

The explorations I developed began by focusing on the body energies, which were combined with music, dance, non-verbal vocalization, and isolation of significant passages from the text. Each student selected a monologue of about two minutes; since speeches in Greek texts are often long, this sometimes meant excerpting or cutting the text. We began our work by creating masks for the characters. Previously I had used oversize papier-mâché masks, which challenge the actor to match their scale with large body movement and strong vocal presence. But these masks take a long time to construct and students sometimes never successfully solve the engineering problems involved in making them wearable. It is difficult for students to move with abandon when they are afraid their masks might fall off. Full-face masks are also best used for silent work, and I wanted the students to explore the texts vocally as well as physically. So this time I chose a simpler mask construction technique that produced lightweight, easy to wear half-masks.[2] I supplied construction paper, poster board, and card stock, along with crayons, markers, paint pins and various kinds of trim—raffia, pipe cleaners, beads, yarn, glitter, etc. After experimenting with designs, the students constructed their masks from whatever they chose from this assortment of materials. The masks were half-masks, but slightly over-sized; rather than creating realistic images, the students tried to capture important qualities of the character in line, rhythm, color, shape, and texture. They were also asked to borrow from our costume storage a long robe in which they could move freely.

With masks and costumes ready, we began the first explorations. We started by reviewing the body energies through explorations using music and hand-held percussive instruments—small drums, rattles of various kinds, pieces of wood that could be struck together. The students explored each energy through dance-like movements,

---

[2] Several books offer good instructions for mask making techniques, including *Maskwork*, by Jennifer Foreman and *The Usborne Book of Masks*; details of both are in the bibliography. Although the latter is intended for use with children, its techniques are suitable for this project.

adding non-verbal sounds as they chose and accompanying themselves with their instruments. I chose music that suggested to me the qualities of the body energies and the natural elements associated with them—wind/buoyancy, fire/radiancy, and earth/potency.[3] Not surprisingly, the buoyancy sounds tended toward open vowels and low gentle calls and humming. Radiancy was often accompanied by hisses and repeated consonant sounds, especially percussives, while potency produced a lot of stronger humming, some Y-buzzes, and stronger Calls. The students were making intuitive connections between the body energies they knew and the vocal energies with which they had little experience.

After these first explorations, we talked about the kind of feelings or communications that might be associated with the body energies—the lightness and openness of the heartfelt communication for buoyancy, the nervous impulses in moments of great urgency for radiancy, the moments of expansive power for potency. The students were asked to identify one significant moment of each kind in their text and to create a movement and sound study built around those three moments; the chosen texts might be an entire sentence, but more often they were a short phrase or even a single word that captured the moment for them. Sometimes the language picked up the imagery of the natural elements—Cassandra's association of Apollo's prophecy with fire, or Io's call to be buried in the earth or, less explicitly, Philoctetes reference to departing ships suggesting images of wind-filled sails. In constructing their studies, they could use movement, any instruments(s) they wished, and non-verbal sound; the only spoken text would be the three lines or phrases they had identified.

We did all of our work for this part of the course in our black box theatre, which gave us a large open space for movement. I kept the lights dim except for a few isolated spots of greater intensity. In this first presentation, and all that followed, the students all donned masks and robes and scattered around the space. Once I started the music I had selected, the students began to move, using their instruments and non-verbal sounds. As they moved, I would signal them by striking two pieces of wood together. On this signal they would pause and I would tap one of them on the shoulder, the signal for that actor to begin

---

[3] Some recordings I have used include selections from *Memento*, by Dead Can Dance, *Tribal Winds*, *Selenography* and *Systems/Layers* by Rachel's, and the soundtrack from the movie *Crash* by Mark Ishan.

his/her study. The other students were encouraged to support the performer by responding with instruments and non-verbal sound. At the end of a performance, the sound of the sticks instructed them to move again. We repeated this until all had done their studies. The format was designed to create something suggestive of a primitive ritual; by making the studies part of a communal event, the students were freer to share and, because they had been moving and making sounds together before their solo performances, were ready to go further into new emotional territory than they might not have been able to do if they had stepped alone from a seat in the audience to an empty stage.

In the class's reflection on these short explorations, we emphasized moments that were particularly effective and those in which the actors seemed to have stretched themselves physically, vocally, or emotionally. We also talked about use of the body and vocal energies and I encouraged them to exploit them further. I also reminded them of the need to use forward facial posture (Lessac 1997:160-61), both for vocal health and clearer communication. I then gave them the next assignment. For this study, they were to build on the "3-moment" study by creating a longer piece that told the character's story (as expressed in the monologue) through movement and non-verbal sound. They could use the words of the text only in a few selected moments (more than the three from the previous exploration but still only isolated words, phrases, or short sentences). These explorations were again done in the empty space with musical accompaniment and using the instruments, with those not performing responding to the performer as described above. After the session, we again talked about particularly strong and affective moments and they encouraged each other to stretch further.

The final assignment in the mask work was to present the complete monologue, using the words, but continuing to use movement, nonverbal sound, and the percussive instruments, and again the listeners were encouraged to respond. Although this version was clearly designed to be more verbal, it was interesting to see the students incorporate their non-verbal work into the monologue, linking lines and phrases with sustained consonant sounds or percussive sequences and, perhaps more importantly, playing consonants, using full structure, and creating clear calls within the lines, without having specific training in these elements. The use of the vocal energies evolved naturally from the body energies, the texts, and the behavior created by the actors and enhanced by the communal nature of the explorations.

After this, the masks were set aside and the monologues were performed again—still using instruments and non-verbal sound and still responding to each other. The idea here was to see if the students could retain the scale, intensity, and daring of the earlier explorations without the mask. This exploration returns them more firmly to the text and to something approaching what might be asked for in a performance. Although scaled down somewhat, the work remained exciting—using voice and body for real communication, but at an emotional intensity far greater than they had achieved previously in the course. The voice and body explorations had helped them release the emotional power of the texts.

The work with the Greek texts was tremendously successful. It was exhausting, but really opened the actors to the possibility of a much fuller range of expression. Using the Lessac body energies enabled the students to begin their work with something with which they were familiar. As they added vocal elements, they discovered that the body could shape the voice with specific movements leading them toward different kinds of vocal expression. They were able to use the vocal energies intuitively, even though they did not have specific training in that part of Lessac's work. They learned they could build on tools they had—body energies, Y-buzz, humming, percussive consonants—to take them far beyond their earlier boundaries.

The Greek work was so successful, in fact, that we decided to see what would happen if we applied some of the same explorations to scenes from modern drama. For their final project in the course, I cast the students in two scenes—one from *A Long Day's Journey into Night*, between Edmond and Jamie, and one from *A Streetcar Named Desire* with Blanch, Stella, and Stanley. I deliberately chose plays that I thought could be played with the emotional intensity of Greek drama. We began with the "3-moment" exploration. Each actor found three moments from the scene—one heart/buoyancy, one urgent radiancy, one for the expanding power of potency—and created a sound/movement study. We used similar music[4] and our instruments again, but they worked without masks. As before, we saw these in a group setting. Even though these studies were somewhat less daring than their Greek studies, they opened the actors to a broader range of expression than they might have normally applied to a modern play. After seeing these performances, I asked

---

[4] The two recordings by Rachel's and the soundtrack of *Crash* were particularly useful for these explorations.

them to create and perform a monologue created by selecting lines from the text that were particularly expressive of their character's emotional journey in the scene. They were asked to think about these as non-realistic speeches, incorporating movement and non-verbal sound into them to help link the moments extracted from the scene. Again, these studies were more restrained than the Greek explorations, but still larger physically and vocally than their previous work with modern texts.

They then took this large physical and vocal work into the scenes. The results, especially with the scene from *Streetcar*, were extraordinary. The students used the body and vocal energies to support characterizations, and emotions were rich and broadly expressed. Among other effects the work created an intense sense of danger in the dinner scene from *Streetcar*. The student actors discovered that even though the language in these scenes seemed closer to their own, the characters' emotions could be as broad and as intense as those of Greek characters.

As I said earlier, all of Lessac's work is so clearly connected that I have been at times hesitant to teach any of it because I could not teach it all. I had introduced small pieces of the work but not fully exploited its potential. What my experience in this course showed was that one can do a lot with a little. This work is so powerful that whatever amount can be worked into a class, a rehearsal, or one's own work can yield valuable results. I find the body energies a particularly effective entry point for the work, and students can benefit from the experience of them almost immediately, whether as warm-up techniques (shaking, wafting and waving, full body yawning), keys to their own habitual rhythms and movements, or part of character development. The surprise to me in this experiment was that intense work with the body energies, combined with other elements, could lead students intuitively to explorations with the vocal energies.

Arthur Lessac's books lay out a wonderful process for teaching kinesensics, and when I teach the voice class, I use the voice text and follow it with little variation. But when using the work in other classes, in rehearsals, in coaching, I have found that I can start almost anywhere, depending on the needs and receptiveness of the people with whom I am working. The work is so tight, so intuitive, that one can enter it at many different places and, with some exploration, find other elements of the work available for experience.

References

Foreman, J. 1999. *Maskwork*. Portsmouth, NH: Heinemann.

Gibson, R. 1994. *The Usborne Book of Masks*. Tulsa, OK: EDC Publishing.

Lessac, A. 1981. *Body Wisdom*. New York: Drama Book Publishers.

Lessac, A. 1997. *The Use and Training of the Human Voice*. 3rd edition. Mountain-view, CA: Mayfield Publishing Company.

O'Neill, E. 1956. *Long Day's Journey into Night*. New Haven: Yale University Press.

Williams, T. 1947. *A Streetcar Named Desire*. In: *Eight Plays*. Garden City, NY: Nelson Doubleday. 91-197.

Lessac Kinesensic Dialect Acquisition
Adapted Excerpts from the Text of STAGE DIALECT STUDIES

Barry Kur

Associate Director and Professor, Pennsylvania State University School of Theatre, University Park, PA, USA

Lessac Master Teacher: 2009

Year of Certification as a Lessac Voice, Speech and Body Trainer: 1977

Introduction

The study of stage dialects can be an integral part of actor voice/speech training. Stage dialect study need not be just a special skills class tacked-on to the end of an actor's curriculum or just an item listed under the heading of "special skills" on an actor's resume.

Rather, the study of stage dialects should provide a continuation of awareness of the actor's vocal instrument, the agility of the actor's vocal instrument, a process through which the actor utilizes the kinesthetic and vibratory awareness of his voice and speech to teach himself the physical changes in the vocal tract required for a stage dialect. In addition, as the actor discovers and becomes familiar with the sensory differences of each dialect he should benefit from discovering the different vocal behavior through which point of view and emotional inner life may be expressed.

The voice training conceived by Professor Arthur Lessac, author of *The Use and Training of the Human Voice* (Lessac 1967; 1997) is the foundation of the stage dialect study I conceived for my textbook, *Stage Dialect Studies* (Kur 1987). The Lessac innovations and text emphasizes a self-teaching mode of training. The key to Lessac training is the perception of physical sensations and the kinesthetic and vibratory recall of these sensations. The concept of the three principal vocal energies, explained under **Points of Reference** in this essay below, provides an immediate, accurate, personal perception of one's voice and speech. It is important to emphasize the fact that in Lessac training, voice skills and speech skills are treated as one discipline, as a total "vocal life."

It is also important to state that Lessac training treats speech and voice as an intrinsic inner activity, not something external or something that should be thrown out of the body. Thus, as Arthur Lessac states, "Vocal life…is part of the same physical and psychological apparatus involved in the perception and control of emotional and other physical behavior," and voice and speech "cannot reasonably be separated from the related energies of feeling, imagery, interpretation, inner expression, and the natural projection of behavior" (Lessac 1967: 180-181). The carry-over of this relationship between vocal life and emotional life to stage dialect study is the key to the avoidance of a "studied" or "cartoon-like" portrayal of a dialect role. If the actor can carry over to stage dialect study the basic voice training approach he has now assimilated as his own perception process, there need not be a separation of self from the role and its dialect. The actor is confident that he can still experience an honest sense of "talking and listening" through stage dialect.

A major benefit to those who have been Lessac trained is that my text utilizes the unique Lessac tono-sensory phonetic transcription.

Points of Reference

There are three majors points of reference to this Lessac based dialect study: (1) The Vocal Energies and A Dialect's Leading Energy, (2) The Lessac Phonetics and (3) A Euphonic-Neutral Standard of Speech.

I. The Three Vocal Energies and A Dialect's Leading Energy

Lessac training emphasizes a self-teaching mode of learning. The actor works with those elements of sound production that he can perceive accurately and recall consistently. These elements are categorized into three energies: structural energy, consonant energy, and tonal energy. Each is described below. Awareness and application of the individual vocal energies produces specific benefits; however, the benefits of the three energies, together or to each other, add up to a "sum greater than its whole." The three vocal energies have a synergistic relationship. When one energy becomes predominant the other two support that "leading" energy. There should never be a sense of fixation, where one energy always leads. There is always a state of balance.

This balanced state is an overall condition to which one will refer in dialect study. (The stage dialect process is explained in more detail in the section of this essay, Stage

Dialects-the Rehearsal Process.) The first step in the study of a specific dialect is the awareness of which vocal energy predominately leads or is modified in such a way as to alter this balanced state.

Structural Energy (Lessac 1997: 160-183): As the name implies, focus is placed on the form, size, shape, and function of the adjustable "sound box"—the oral cavity. Reference will often be made to the physical conditions required to form what is known in Lessac training as a flexible, inverted-megaphone shape. If a dialect's leading energy requires a heightened or limited condition of one's facial posture, the leading energy of that dialect will be structural energy.

Associated with the awareness of the conditions and actions of the facial muscles is the formation of a major group of vowels and diphthongs. The unique Lessac phonetic transcription of those phonemes is utilized in this dialect study. However dialect study often requires that the transcription of diphthongs may be different than those related to one's familiar vocal life.

Tonal Energy (Lessac, 1997: 122-159): "The term tonal energy is to be taken literally and dually. It means the action of the tones—the vibrations of the vocal sound waves transmitted through bone conduction—and it means our action of feeling those vibrations and controlling them through sensory recall" (Lessac 1967: 79).

Tonal energy is the principal method of building the voice. The following section provides a short overview of the basic terminology and perceptions related to tonal energy:

Concentrated Tone: This refers to a very specific sensation of vibrations, particularly strongest or "concentrated" at a point just behind the upper front teeth on the gum ridge and radiating through the hard palate to form what the Lessac work calls a "focal pocket." These focal pockets change in size depending upon pitch. The higher the pitch, the larger the pocket, the lower the pitch the smaller the pocket.

Dilute Tone: The tone quality used in eighty to ninety per cent of conversational speech and fifty to sixty per cent of speech from the stage. These vibrations are felt in the primary bony resonators of the head—the hard palate, the teeth, the nose bone, cheekbones, head bones, sinus cavities, and the nasal cavities—but with a diffused or "diluted" focus. One does not feel the vibrations concentrated on the upper gum ridge but they are forward enough in the oral cavity and head as to avoid a throaty or nasal quality. Dilute tone moves with the tonal energy current but differs from concentrated tone in degree of density or concentration.

If a dialect requires a heightened awareness of the vibratory sensations related to concentrated tone or if the awareness of the sensations is altered to a new location, for example the nasal passages, the leading energy of the dialect will be tonal energy.

Consonant Energy (Lessac 1997: 63-121): Consonant energy is a combination of tactile and vibratory perception and the expression of the individual qualities of the consonants. The basic purpose of consonant energy is intelligibility; however, Lessac's association of these physical sensations with instruments (and sound effects) of the orchestra adds to that purpose musicality, contrast, variety, tempo, and rhythm. If a dialect requires heightened awareness of the consonant instruments, an alteration of the playing of the consonant instruments or an altered use of the articulators (lips, tongue), consonant energy is the leading energy of the dialect.

II. Lessac Phonetics

The Lessac tono-sensory phonetic transcription emphasizes the physical awareness of sounds. It is a broad transcription and yet suitable for the detailed awareness of dialect study when influenced by the physical condition of each dialect's leading energy and predominant pitch/rhythm elements. As each physical sound is always capable of adjustments to duration, tone quality, and pitch, there is a synergistic relationship between the first stages of this dialect study and the stage denoting specific vowel and consonant awareness. A summary of the vowel and diphthong notation is available in both the dialect text and Lessac's text along with the notation for the Lessac consonant orchestral instruments (Lessac 1997: 196-197). All of the Lessac notation utilizes familiar letter and number symbols representing the physical shape or movement required for each sound rather than the auditory recall of the sound.

III. A Euphonic-Neutral Standard Of Speech

Articulating instruction for a stage dialect requires a phonetic point of reference. In each dialect chapter of my text, specific vowel and consonant components are noted as changes from what I call "a euphonic-neutral standard of speech" to the specific phonetic components of the dialect. Students of Lessac Training become aware of the synergistic relationship between voice and speech and that choice of pronunciation is guided by sensations that produce a euphonic quality.

In turn, especially for actors from the United States, a standard of speech evolves which is:

(1) regionally neutral
(2) intelligible and musical
(3) efficient and healthy
(4) generally practiced in their personal vocal life and often professionally required for performance of classical dramatic text.

Below are the components most important for practice of a euphonic-neutral standard of speech. The actor will find some of these phonetic components to be different from those generally heard in colloquial speech of the United States.

a. Distinctive awareness of the following structural energy vowels: #3, as in "all," #4 as in "odd," and #5 as in "drama."
b. Awareness of the #6 vowel when followed by consonants M, N, NG. In this case, the vowel in "have" is the same in the word "hand."
c. Awareness of the #y1 diphthong. This diphthong is often substituted for the single phoneme #1 (when spelled u, ue, eu, ew or ieu) in colloquial speech of the United States after the consonants T, D, N, L and S. It is often utilized for United States productions of Shakespeare and Chekhov but should be a familiar event in one's personal vocal life. This sound is a familiar event after the consonants M as in Music, P as in Pew and B as in Butane. Heightened awareness may be necessary in the following words:
Tune, new, tutor, stupid, Tuesday, neutral, attitude, revolution, dew, duty, introduce, lewd

d. **Awareness of R Between Two Vowels.** This is a major awareness necessary for euphonic-neutral speech. If the R sound is between two vowel sounds, syllabify the word between the first vowel and the R. Now identify the first vowel and give it its full specific vowel identity (without R coloration) and pronounce the second syllable with the R as the initial sound. For example:

	N^3n	
Mary	*Ma*	*ry*
	N^3	
Merry	*Me*	*rry*
	6	
Marry	*Ma*	*rry*
	N^4	
Murray	*Mu*	*rry*
	N^2	
Miracle	*Mi*	*racle*

In the above examples, the first syllable of the first three words is often pronounced with the same sound in colloquial U.S. English. This guide facilitates distinctive pronunciation and improves tone quality.

e. **Awareness of a Diluted R Coloration.** The R trombone before a vowel sound creates a vibrant consonant sound but when final or before another consonant, it has a placement and tone quality that may produce a nasal or throaty tone often referred to as a "hard R." To avoid this "hard-R" coloration, apply good structural and tonal energy to words with the R in the final position or when followed by a consonant, as in the following words:

Poor, peer, pair, pore, cure, surely, lure

Car, farm, are, tarnish

Hurt, irksome, heard, urbane,

Father, singer, doctor, measure

f. **Avoid Neutral²-Neutral³ Substitution.** The substitution of the Neutral ^{2} for the Neutral ^{3} vowel when it is followed by an N or M consonant is a common event for a major geographic portion of the United States. This is not recommended for a euphonic-neutral standard of speech. Maintaining the distinctive awareness of these two vowels will be advantageous for dialect study.

N^2	N^3
pin	pen
din	den
mint	meant
him	hem

N^3
Any, end, engine, again, general, pennies, Dennis, Wednesday, whenever, sensational, embers, membership, empty.

Additional Items

1. Maintain distinctive awareness of final consonants. Below is a sampling of words, each with a distinctive consonant "orchestration."
    ten, tends, tents, tense, tennis, tenths

2. "The" is pronounced with a Y-buzz vowel when it appears before a word that begins with a vowel sound, and pronounced with N^4 when it appears before a word that begins with a consonant sound.

3. WH should have a distinct pronunciation as if spelled HW, rather than a W sound.
    what, when why, overwhelm, whether, whine

4. N^2 rather than Y-buzz is preferred for first unstressed syllables spelled "e" as in enough, "de" as in deny or deserve, "re" as in receive, return.

5. The preferred pronunciation for the article "a" is N^4.

6. Maintain awareness of the medial "T" consonant instrument. Although it may not be in a "playable" position within a word, distinctive awareness of the "T" rather than a " D" enhances intelligibility.
    matter, sentence, water, society, mountain, fertile, rapidity

7. Maintain distinctive awareness of final "D" or final "T" when the next word begins with

   " Y ".did you, could you, can't you, won't you

8. Maintain distinctive awareness of the consonant double drumbeats

PT	*apt*	*wept*	*accept*	*stopped*	*clasped*
KT	*act*	*effect*	*subject*	*fact*	*booked*
KTS	*contracts*	*acts*	*subjects*	*inflicts*	
PTS	*accepts*	*adapts*	*concepts*		
BD	*stabbed*	*robbed*	*bribed*	*rubbed*	
GD	*flogged*	*rigged*	*hugged*	*tugged*	

Stage Dialects—The Rehearsal Process

Through the Lessac Training an actor becomes aware of the synergistic relationship of the three vocal energies. Each specific vocal energy has its own unique dynamics and benefits. Each specific vocal energy also serves to support the other two. Eventually the actor's over-all vocal energy is one of balance. It is this balanced state of the three vocal energies from which one will depart to determine the leading vocal energy of each dialect.

The first step of the study of each dialect is to become familiar with the leading energy of the dialect. The leading energy is determined by what physical conditions or sensations most alters the balanced state of the energies. For example, the leading energy may be " "structural energy" because there is a limitation of size and shape of the oral cavity, or "consonant energy" because the tongue or lips are shaped, placed or directed in an unfamiliar way, or "tonal energy" because the sensation of vibrations is limited to a specific area or range. Because of the synergistic relationship of the vocal energies, the leading energy will probably affect the other two. Within each dialect chapter of my text, a child's poem is utilized to explore the initial effects of the leading energy. This is only the first step of the process and one shouldn't expect to have mastery of the complete stage dialect.

As a result of the leading energy work, some actors may begin to feel a few of the major vowel and/or consonant pronunciations of the specific stage dialect. What is important is the kinesthetic awareness of the dialect's oral cavity shape, resonance feedback and/or unique articulatory movement. When the actor eventually practices with the text's specific vowel and consonant substitution word lists and sentences, carry-over of the leading energy will prevent an overly technical result.

The leading energy gives the actor greater consistency and confidence in performance. It diminishes the concern of having to divide an actor's focus between his objective and the complete list of phonetic changes of a dialect. To borrow from actor terminology, the leading energy is like a "vocal (dialect) through line."

The next step deals with pitch and rhythm. Often a strong pattern of rhythm in a dialect relates to the playing-relishing of specific sounds (especially vowels). A pitch pattern is often related to those sounds that are relished or elongated. The actor should continue to carry over the leading energy conditions to the pitch and rhythm work. (These patterns are described in the text and demonstrated on the compact disc accompanying it.)

Next, the actor becomes familiar with the specific vowel and consonant substitutions of a stage dialect. Some the actor may have experienced previously in the leading energy work and some may be new. Of course, the reference point for this step is the Euphonic-Neutral Standard of Speech.

The substituted sounds are noted like this:

#3............#6

The #3 is the euphonic-neutral pronunciation. The #6 is the substitution required for the stage dialect.

In this case, the vowel in the word "all" would be pronounced with the sound normally used for the vowel of the word "add." If a sound is not listed, it means that the dialect requires no change from the Euphonic-Neutral Standard of Speech pronunciation or no special attention. Some items listed have more detailed instructions or parenthetical notes. Each item listed is followed by a word list and practice sentence(s). It is vital to carry-over the leading energy and pitch/rhythm work to this section. As stated earlier, the carry over of the leading energy and pitch/rhythm elements replaces overly detailed diacritical notation related to duration, pitch or facial muscle activity.

The last step involves application of the specific dialect study to dramatic text. Here is a three-fold process for application work:

I. Tasting

This term means an actor will experience the new action/sensation as if tasting a morsel of food for the first time. Is it a familiar taste? How is it different or similar? Does it have a specific texture? Is it pleasurable?

Read the text, tasting it with the leading energy as a vocal through-line. Taste the text focusing on the specific dialect sounds, rhythm, and pitch. Respond, correct, and make notes, until the action/sensations of the stage dialect become familiar events.

II. Relishing

In each line of the text there are one, two or maybe three sounds that are specifically related to the stage dialect. Read the text aloud confidently playing or "relishing" the dialect sounds of each line. For example in the following text from Oscar Wilde's "The Importance of Being Earnest" the special British sounds or "Britishisms" are under lined:

         #3 n21

Algernon: You have <u>a</u>lways t<u>o</u>ld me it was <u>Ea</u>rnest. I have

 y1   tapped r   5

introd<u>u</u>ced you to ev<u>e</u>ryone as Earnest. You <u>a</u>nswe<u>r</u> to the name of

Earnest. You look as if your name was <u>Ea</u>rnest. You <u>are</u>

  n21   3

the m<u>o</u>st e<u>a</u>rnest-looking p<u>er</u>son I ever s<u>a</u>w in my life.

Or in Arthur Miller's "After the Fall," the "Germanisms" are underlined for Holga's speech:

Holga: It was the middle of the war. I had just come out of a class and there were British leaflets on the sidewalk. And photographs of a concentration camp. And emaciated people. One tended to believe the British. I'd had no idea. Truly. It isn't easy to turn against your country; not in a war. Do Americans turn against America because of Hiroshima? There are reasons always. And I took the leaflet to my godfather—he was still commanding our Intelligence. And I asked if it were true. "Of course," he said, "why does it excite you?" And I said, "You are a swine. You are all swine." I threw my briefcase at him. And he opened it and put some papers in it and asked me to deliver it to a certain address. And I became a courier for the officers who were planning to assassinate Hitler…They were all hanged.

Don't simply accentuate but appreciate the different actions through which personal subtext may be expressed. This relishing step must include previous work in pitch and/or rhythm. Of course, some sounds are relished more than others in order to maintain the sense of the line. However, word stress patterns are sometimes changed when working with a dialect.

The degree of relishing or the playing of specific dialect sounds is an actor's barometer of how strong a dialect is applied to a role. Explore the dramatic text to establish a spectrum of dialect strength. It may help to first establish the extremes of the spectrum and give them names or images.

For example:

Irish

"Blarney"   **"Dublin Streets"**
expansive pitch range, sustained/   limited pitch range, limited
relished vowels, broad characterization   sustained vowels, contemporary

III. Talking and Listening

Here one does their "actor's homework." Out of every actor training class comes a variety of questions to establish objective, actions, activities, and to reinforce a character's positive traits. At this stage, let these be the primary concerns but <u>never</u> drop the dialect! Never speak the words of the role without the dialect!

Through the action/sensations of a dialect the actor expresses his character's thoughts/emotions. Having explored the spectrum of a dialect, the actor is now open and ready to respond with the appropriate degree of dialect needed for a specific role.

Never work in a vacuum. Talk to someone, imaginary or real. The goal is to maintain an honest sense of talking and listening for the given circumstances.

The actor will be performing on a stage in a large space. For the sake of intelligibility or audibility, he may need to modify his dialect speech or voice quality. If a dialect coach is working on the production, he/she will help determine what to modify. If there is no dialect coach, general notes from the director concerning "lost lines" should indicate that modification is necessary.

The dialect instructions that I developed for this textbook came from a self-teaching process. I utilized the "tools" provided by the foundational Lessac kinesensic training. I then developed organized lessons to share with others. Students engaged in the lessons of my textbook have been encouraged to follow the same self-teaching process. For over 25 years, I've been coaching actors for dialect roles and they have appreciated the fact that the instructions have always been based on self-reliant physical recall. I have applied this work to theatre companies of varied training backgrounds and they, too, have adapted well to the process of working with the physical awareness of a dialect. That is the distinctive element of this work and further reinforces the integrity of the Lessac kinesenic training.

References

Kur, B. 2005. *Stage Dialect Studies*. Published by the author.

Lessac, A. 1997. *The Use and Training of the Human Voice.* New York: McGraw-Hill.

---. *1967.* The Use and Training of the Human Voice. *New York: Drama Book Publishers*

The Lessac Approach as a Pedagogical Answer to Outcomes-Based Education and Training, and Whole-Brain Learning

This peer-reviewed article was originally published in the *Voice and Speech Review: Shakespeare around the Globe*. Mandy Rees (ed), VASTA, 2005, 186-192. Permission to reprint has been graciously granted by the Voice and Speech Trainers Association.

Marth Munro & Marie-Heleen Coetzee [1]

After more than ten years of democracy South Africa is still addressing the racial and educational, amongst others, inequalities of the past. In the current dispensation, the government has put structures in place that urge education providers to adopt strategies that will level the educational playing field. The National Qualification Framework (NQF) and South African Qualifications Authority (SAQA) are evidence of this process. The new education and training dispensation resulted in the introduction of the concept of Outcomes-Based Education and Training (referred to as OBET). Under this umbrella concept four divisions of education exist:

- General Education and Training (GET—the first 9 years of formal education),
- Further Education and Training (FET—the last three years of high school, where some form of specialisation will take place),
- Higher Education and Training (HET—the domain of tertiary training institutions), and
- Adult Basic Education and Training (ABET—an attempt to address the massive illiteracy problems amongst adults in South Africa).

The aim of this article is not to examine critically the history of these abovementioned associations or divisions, but rather to focus on how this change in education (specifically the educational strategy or pedagogy) impacts on the work of Voice

---

[1] The authors extend their gratitude to Prof. Allan Munro for the assistance with the structuring of the ideas and academic writing.

Teachers within a Drama department in the Higher Education and Training band (HET) in South Africa.

The principles of OBET:
- Aim to *clarify* progressive, sequential and developmental *outcomes*, whilst
- providing *expanded learning opportunities*, within
- *various modes and methodologies*, with
- clear *criterion based* assessments (Genis, 2001).

In other words, all learning should have clearly defined outcomes that can be assessed using clearly defined criteria.[2] Furthermore, the way that learning to reach these outcomes takes place should follow a sequence of learning moments that follow one another logically, that grow in complexity, that are multidimensional and varied, and that take divergent learning styles and preferences into consideration. These principles are captured within seven critical outcomes, which, according to the South African Department of Education, should be the backbone of any learning opportunity irrespective of the level of education and training as well as field specific content.

These seven critical outcomes state that learners need to be able:

- To identify and solve problems and make decisions using critical and creative thinking;
- To work effectively with others as members of a team, group, organisation and community;
- To organise and manage themselves and their activities responsibly and effectively;
- To collect, analyse, organise and critically evaluate information;
- To communicate effectively using visual, symbolic and/or language skills in various modes;

---

[2] This aspect has created much controversy and debate in the Arts, in our experience. Fundamentally, though, it seems to have been introduced (and insisted upon) so as to attempt to counter potential bias and personal perceptions in the aesthetic field, which may arise from cultural paradigms. In essence this is a good thing (specifically given South Africa's past) but one can understand the difficulties in the endeavour.

- To use science and technology effectively and critically showing responsibility towards the environment and the health of others[3]; and
- To demonstrate an understanding of the world as a set of related systems by recognising that problem-solving contexts do not exist in isolation (http://www.heinemann.co.za/Schools/TeachingTips/OBE2.asp; Olivier: 1998).

The *critical* outcomes are further supported by five *developmental* outcomes, which are:

- To reflect on and explore effective learning strategies;
- To participate as a responsible citizen;
- To be culturally and aesthetically sensitive;
- To explore education and career opportunities, and
- To develop entrepreneurial opportunities (http://www.ru.ac.za/academic/adc/obe_print.htm).

Central to these are the needs of sensitivity to diversity, the pursuit of careers, and civic mindedness. (It is not our aim to pursue these developmental outcomes in the rest of this article.)

Fundamental to all of this is the paradigm shift from the previous "teacher-centred one-directional transmission of knowledge" to (in OBET) a learner-centred approach (van den Berg & de Boer, 2000).

It is important for institutions to position themselves towards this change—not because it is legislation, but to be able better to serve the diversity of the students in the changing profile of Higher Education within the South African learning society (ibid). In the light of the above, a Drama department at a tertiary institution in South

---

[3] Artists have taken some umbrage about this one. Our own feeling is that one should replace "science" with "scholarship" and "technology" with "process." The science debate in South Africa is embedded in a translation problem—the Afrikaans word for "science" is "wetenskap" which shows strong connections and thinking with the German "wissenschaft" which in turn has connections to scholarship, but this last part has got "lost in translation." The technology aspect is somewhat in keeping with one of the author's own institutions (a University of Technology) that is still wrestling with these concepts.

Africa might reflect these critical outcomes in its own specific outcomes (as there are no specific outcomes for the HET band yet) by indicating that it aims to guide the learners to:

- Identify and solve problems within the field of performance studies, and make and implement decisions using critical and creative thinking.
- Work effectively with others as members of an ensemble, group class or buddy system.
- Organise and manage themselves in their class-work, projects and performances, responsibly and effectively.
- Collect, analyse, organise and critically evaluate information about performance and theatre skills.
- Communicate effectively on-stage and off-stage using visual, kinetic, auditory symbolic and/or language skills in various modes.
- Use science (i.e. scholarship) and technology within the performance field effectively and critically showing responsibility towards the performance environment specifically, and generally the environment at large and the health of others.
- Demonstrate an understanding of the performance and theatrical world specifically as a set of related systems by recognising that problem-solving contexts do not exist in isolation and through this in the world at large.

In like manner specific outcomes for Voice and Speech programmes might be developed, which will be pursued below.

In searching for ways to implement these above-mentioned specific outcomes thoroughly by means of deep-structure learning, Herrmann's argument (1995) that optimal learning can only take place when whole-brain modes are applied, supports the OBET notion. Herrmann posits a metaphorical four-quadrant model for whole-brain activity (see Figure 1) and specifically indicates that preferences of knowing may exist for the learners favouring one or more quadrant(s). It is stressed that *preferences* are not *abilities*. One needs to accept that learners in the HET band are capable of all four modes of learning but they might prefer to access only one or two quadrants in their learning strategies.

Figure 1: Herrmann Whole Brain Model (Herrmann, 1995:155).

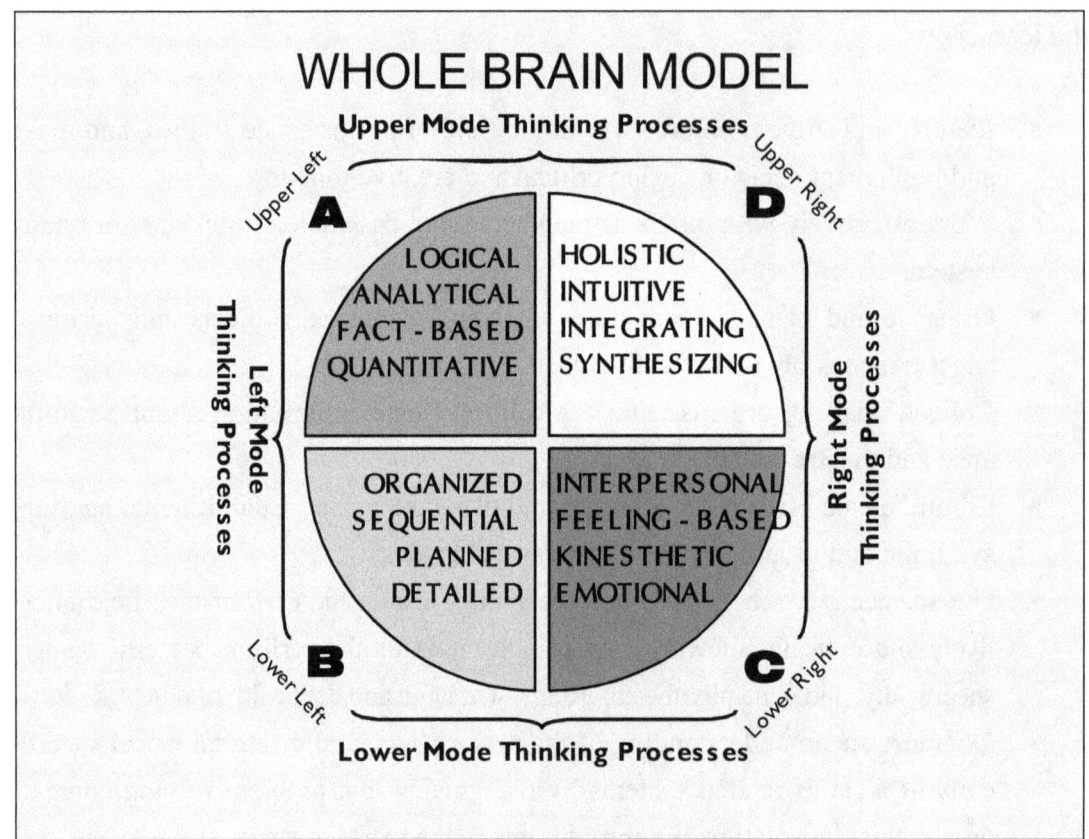

Each quadrant represents specific learning styles and preferences. Each therefore also suggests specific learning strategies that might be most amenable to the particular student's preferences. The task for a teacher, then, is to ascertain the student's preferences, develop teaching strategies that access each quadrant's preferences, and develop strategies to lead students to use the strategies that they might least likely use because of their preference dominance.

More specifically, de Boer, Steyn and du Toit (2001) have demonstrated the interlinking between the Herrmann whole-brain model, and the OBET "critical outcomes" demands. In Table 1 (below) they point out which critical outcomes appeal most urgently to the preferences in specific quadrants.

TABLE 1.

Process necessary to achieve outcomes	Associated Quadrants in the Herrmann model
Critical thinking	A, B, C, & D
Problem solving	A, B, C, & D
Application	B
Appreciation	A, B, C, & D
Analysing	A
Synthesising	D
Evaluation of information	A, B, C, & D
Teamwork	C
Communication	A, B, C, & D
Socialising	C

(de Boer, Steyn and du Toit, 2001: 192)

When looking at Hermann's model it is clear, from the experience of voice teachers in drama departments, that learners from the Arts often prefer to function in quadrant C and D. This notion is supported by unpublished research done by de Boer and Munro A.J, with drama learners at a drama department in HET in 2000. They indicated that in general the drama learners had preferences in three quadrants (B, C, D). This is known as triple dominant profiles (Herrmann, 1995:89). People with these profiles can "iterate freely amongst quadrants" (Ibid) and have the capability of using all four quadrants with equal competence but prefer not to function in the learning modes of the fourth quadrant, which is in this case the metaphorical A quadrant that represents the logical, critical, analytical and factual learning modes (Coetzee, Munro & de Boer, 2004).

Voice teachers in Drama departments in HET in South Africa have to take the following into account when deciding on teaching modes and modalities:

- The learners' ability to learn in all four metaphorical quadrants;
- The learners' preferred modes of learning;

- The notion that deep-structure learning only takes place when all four modes of learning are addressed in the classroom
- The seven critical outcomes.

This culminates in the idea that for integrated learning to take place, the pedagogical approach should entail "Head, Hands and Heart" (Van der Horst and McDonald, 1997:46), which is a catchphrase that refers to Gagné's five learned capabilities: Motor skills, Attitude, Verbal information, Cognitive strategies and Intellectual skills (http://classweb.gmu.edu). In essence the C and D quadrants have to do with the "hands and heart" aspect, whereas the A and B quadrants emphasize the "head" aspect of this metaphor.

In the field of voice for theatre there are several well-known approaches to vocal training. In a broad generalisation it might be claimed that most of them are imbedded in Herrmann's C & D quadrants. In our view and experience one approach specifically can be seen to lend itself very effectively to OBET and to whole-brain learning, namely the Lessac Approach. The purpose of this article is to demonstrate this connectivity. The notion thus is to investigate the suitability of the Lessac Approach as a voice teaching pedagogy in a drama department in South Africa.

The Lessac Approach, as an ongoing evolutionary pedagogy, can be described according to three aspects:

- The epistemological approach to the pedagogy
- The physiological effect of the pedagogy
- The acoustical outcome of the pedagogy.

The epistemological approach of the pedagogy
Epistemologically the Approach is rooted in clusters of fundamental pedagogical principles that foster experiencing and reflecting. These may be subdivided for convenience into the first person subjective, exploratory and experiential mode, and the second/third person reflective and analytical mode. The first person mode has the following cluster of tools:

- Body "esthetics" (or sensory awareness)—anything that promotes sensitivity and induces awareness of sensation (Lessac, 1997:4). It is important to note

that this tool operates for the student at a pre-cognitive level—it is the experiencing that counts;
- Inner harmonic sensing, by which is meant that the results of the sensory awareness are induced to harmonise into a fluid and meaningful dynamic whole (Lessac, 1998). In essence this means that disparate moments of sensory awareness are combined experientially and sensorially;
- Organic instruction which is the acknowledgement of organic flow in the body where the focus will be on the sensorial and the proprioceptive as a self-teaching tool (Tabish, 1995:154);
- The Familiar event refers to something familiar that is recalled to aid in the task at hand (Lessac, 1997:7). Fundamentally, the Familiar Event draws on a set of pedagogical circumstances that led to the production of an optimal sound, pattern or harmonic moment, but it also refers to the sensorial event that can be drawn upon by the student to foster, reinforce and produce the optimal organic event.

All of this leads to an experimental somatosensory "understanding"[4] of the organic process of voice production in the human body (Munro, 2002). This subjective mode primarily utilizes the metaphorical D quadrant of Herrmann's model.

The second/third person objective, observation, reflective mode demonstrates a different cluster of tools, namely,

- Ear training for auditory reflection;
- Visual guidelines of body kinetics (Lessac, 1997).

The fundamental pedagogical principle here is that the student learns to know through hearing and seeing what the optimal voice and the optimal body integration is in others. The critical faculty is non-discursive[5]. Suffice is to say that students are taught to identify and judge, without necessarily having to name or describe. This objective mode primarily

---

[4] It is crucial for the argument to accept that "understanding" is both cognitive, in the sense that the event can be "spoken and written about" (a "cognitive and conscious event" if you will), and demonstrable, in the sense that the "successful outcome" of the event indicates clearly an intrinsic "understanding" in the body.

[5] See "Harrow's Taxonomy of Psychomotor Domain" (http://classweb.gmu.edu/ndabbagh/Resources/IDKB/harrowstax.htm).

utilizes the metaphorical C quadrant of Herrmann's model. Inevitably once this auditory and visual observation has taken place, a verbalisation will follow as a matter of course, and this would access the A and B Quadrants of the Herrmann model.

Methodological ramifications

For the verbalisation of the auditory and the visual/kinetic reflections to occur this specific Approach has developed definite and set terminology and explorations to learn, discuss and evaluate the various elements of voice and speech and are integral to the learning and teaching process. This facilitates instruction and reflection and as such provides a vehicle for an integrated teaching/learning experience, because it allows the learning that has occurred by accessing C and D quadrants to be reinforced and reflected upon by using A and B quadrants.

Fundamentally, the following three aspects, with their concomitant experiential and terminological developments, provide the cornerstone of such instruction and reflection:

- *Consonant NRG* (Lessac, 1997). In line with the holistic orientation of the Approach the Consonant NRG metaphorises the human body as a musical apparatus, and consonants are explored as musical instruments in the classical orchestra. The "playing" of the different consonants is guided by either the sensorial awareness of the vibrations of the voice consonants, or the sensorial awareness of the noise pattern of the voiceless consonants (Munro, 2002:20; Hanson, 1997: 171);
- *Tonal NRG* (Lessac, 1997). In the Tonal NRG the focus is on the sensory awareness of the vocal vibrations on the bony parts of the face (Ibid: 115). Bone conduction within this approach is of utmost importance as a self-guiding tool and is used as a familiar event. Although vocal production happens primarily through the use of an air resonator and bone conduction happens as a secondary effect, Lessac makes the deliberate choice to focus on bone conduction, seeing that the shaping of the air resonator is primarily done by involuntary muscle usage due to the sensory awareness of bone conduction (Munro, 2002:21);
- *Structural NRG*, which focuses on the muscular actions for shaping the oral cavity for clear speech through organic instruction and muscle memory

(Munro, 2002: 32). Lessac posits that the structural NRG refers to the mould, shape and size of the human voice and speech instrument (Lessac, 1997: 60).

These methodological ramifications utilize all 4 metaphorical quadrants of Herrmann's model, which is optimally in keeping with the demands of OBET and therefore facilitates deep-structure learning.

Up to this point we have argued that the Lessac Approach works effectively to foster whole-brain learning. We will now argue that further research flowing from the testing of the efficacy of the Approach lends an added dimension to the pedagogy, and one which allows the accessing and utilisation of the testing processes and procedures to inform reflection in a way that might speak to established outcomes criteria. It must be remembered that although the performance voice is predicated on aesthetics, it also has a large component of healthy and optimal voice usage involved. In essence this reflects on one of the movement principles as postulated by Laban, namely that of the interrelatedness of Function and Expression (Hackney, 1998:45,46).

The Physiological effect of the pedagogy

The physiological effect of the Approach has been well researched and documented by Verdolini and colleagues (1994; 1998; 2001). Accumulatively it can be stated that they posit that the Lessac Approach leads to:

- An intermediate adduction rating of the vocal folds
- Relatively low contact stress between the vocal folds
- A closed quotient proportion that is similar to normal voice
- Whilst it creates a maximum output with sufficient harmonics for projection capabilities (see Munro, 2002).

It is in accessing the ways of coming to these conclusions—in effect replicating the thinking and testing strategies that brought about these conclusions –that is useful for the pedagogy. In essence that which is experienced organically/intuitively and holistically (Quadrants C and D) can now be reflected upon verbally and logically (Quadrant A) and can also be tested in detailed and sequential testing systems (Quadrant B). Although this speaks directly to the critical outcomes that access the need for science and technology, it also encourages an objective and critical engagement with the concepts around performance aesthetics. Indeed, in our opinion it goes some way to addressing potential differences brought about by possible cultural and perspective biases.

The acoustical outcome of the pedagogy

In like manner to the physiological effects of the Lessac Approach, the research into the acoustic properties of voice that flows from the Lessac Approach allows for detailed, more "objective" and cross-cultural analyses. Several scholars have investigated the acoustical outcomes of the Lessac Approach, i.e. Raphael & Scherer (1987), Acker (1987) and Munro. Munro (2002) indicates that the Lessac Approach leads to:

- An increase of F0 energy, which leads to a perception of "loudness";
- A profile change of the LTAS F0-2500 Hz—a possible indication of improved pronunciation;
- An energy increase in the 2500-4500 Hz region which is where literature (especially the studies of Leino) indicates the "actor's formant" appears. This in essence indicates that that which is judged by subjective perception is, in fact, improved projection.

There are two major benefits from this for teaching performer's voice. In the first place an "impartial ear" can be used in the judging process. This means that tools are available for enhancing the accuracy of the reflection process. In this manner the student not only utters the sound but is able to "see" (through the computer, for example) the efficacy of the sound produced. When the student is asked to work with fellow-students and reflect upon their work, then the subjective, experiential and auditory can be supported by a cognitive and discursive system of analysis—all four Quadrants are at play, as it were. Munro (2002) found this a valuable tool when evaluating voice quality within a multi-lingual teaching situation where cultural aesthetic perceptions may differ.

Tangentially, studies (Munro & Groenewald, 2004; Nair, 1999; Repp, 1999) have indicated that, through the use of technology, the voice teacher can determine and programme the unique "vocal profile" built around the unique potential qualities of each learner. More research has to be done on the notion of computer-aided voice training, specifically in relation to the Lessac Approach. It is foreseen that the artist and teacher in the vocal coach, the artist and learner in the student, and the impartial technology may meet in a synergy that demands both intuitive, experiential and kinaesthetic learning and teaching (Quadrants C and D), but also logical, analytical and quantifiable teaching and learning (Quadrants A and B). In this endeavour both teacher and learner are in pursuit of clearly defined outcomes.

Conclusion

The basic Lessac Approach, and specifically the epistemological orientation, is an essential part of the undergraduate training in the drama department at the Tshwane University of Technology, for example. The acoustic outcome is used as means of evaluation and analysis during the undergraduate years. The physiological effect of the Lessac Approach is embedded in the efficient and healthy execution of the explorations provided by the Approach. Should any pathological voice profile exist, a learner will be referred to a therapist where the physiological aspect will be evaluated and treated. The physiological and acoustic synthesis, analysis and evaluation are directly addressed during the final undergraduate year with potential research in graduate studies. As we have argued this supports not only the outcomes of OBET and engages all four quadrants of learning but also ensures deep-structure learning while safeguarding the learner from possible voice damage. Finally, the demands of trying to determine reasonably objective and clearly defined outcomes which are connected to evaluation criteria within the OBET system were enhanced.

Table 2 below indicates the relationship between OBET and whole-brain learning (de Boer, et al., 2001:192, as discussed elsewhere in this paper,) and then proceeds to demonstrate the correlation between these two systems which set the tone for Higher Education in South Africa, and the various aspects of the Lessac Approach as defined earlier in this paper.

TABLE 2:

Process necessary to achieve outcomes	Associated Quadrants in the Herrmann model	Lessac Approach 1=epistemology, 2=physiology, 3=acoustic
Critical thinking	A, B, C, & D	1, 2, 3
Problem solving	A, B, C, & D	1, 2, 3
Application	B	1, 2, 3
Appreciation	A, B, C, & D	1, 2, 3
Analysing	A	1, 2, 3
Synthesising	D	1, 2, 3,
Evaluation of information	A, B, C, & D	1, 2, 3,
Teamwork	C	1 (2, 3)
Communication	A, B, C, & D	1 (2,3)
Socialising	C	1

Within the current South African educational dispensation, the Lessac Approach as voice building pedagogy within a drama department in the HET, potentially answers to the demands of OBET and whole brain learning in order to assure deep-structure learning.

References

Acker, B. 1987. 'Vocal tract adjustments for the projected voice.' In *Journal of Voice*. Vol. 1, No 1:77-82.

De Boer, A-L & Munro A.J. 2000. Unpublished research. Outcomes in possession of the researchers.

De Boer, A-L; Steyn, T & Du Toit, P, H. 2001. 'A whole brain approach to teaching and learning in higher education.' In *South African Journal of Higher Education* Vol. 15, no. 3.

Genis, E. 2001. 'Principles and Practice of Outcomes-Based Education.' Proceedings of the International Conference on Agricultural Education. South Africa: Kruger National Park. 15-17 October 2001.

Coetzee, M-H, Munro, M & De Boer, A-L. 2003. 'Deeper Sites through various Lines: LMS and whole brain learning in body/voice training for performers in the HET band.' Accepted by *SATJ* as peer reviewed article to be printed in 2004 (18).

Hackney, P. 1998. *Making connections: Total body integration through Bartenieff Fundamentals*. Amsterdam: Gordon and Breach Publishers.

Herrmann, N. 1995. *The Creative brain*. North Carolina: The Ned Herrmann Group.

Leino, T. 1993. 'Long-term average spectrum study on speaking voice quality in male actors.' In Proceedings of the Stockholm Music Acoustics Conference, Jul. 28 – Aug. 1, 1993 (Eds: A. Friberg, J. Iwarson & J. Sundberg).

Lessac, A. 1997. 3rd Edition. *The use and training of the human voice: a bio-dynamic approach*. California: Mayfield.

Lessac, A. 1998. 'A short colloquy of how I approach pathological and functional voice in speech disorders through my kinesensic training and research.' In Special interest division 3, *Voice and Voice Disorders Newsletter*, Vol. 8, No. 1. April 1998 (np).

Munro, M. 2002. 'Lessac's tonal action in women's voices and the "actor's formant": a comparative study.' Unpublished PhD dissertation. PU for CHE.

Munro, M. & Groenewald, E. 2004. 'Computer-Aided Voice Training in Higher Education: Participants' Subjective Evaluation.' In *South African Journal of Higher Education* 18(2).

Nair, G. 1999. *Voice—tradition and technology*. New York: Singular Press.

Olivier, C. 1998. *How to educate and train outcomes-based education*. Pretoria: J.L. van Schaik Publishers.

Olivier, C. 2000. *Let's educate, train and learn outcomes-based education*. Clubview: Design Book.

Peterson, K.L., Verdolini-Marston, K., Barkmeier, J.M. & Hoffman, H.T. 1994. 'Comparison of aerodynamic and electroglottographic parameters in evaluating clinically relevant voicing patterns.' In *Ann Otol Rhinol Laryngol* 103: 1994 pp.335-346.

Raphael, B & Scherer, R. 1987. 'Voice modification for stage actors: Acoustic analysis.' In *Journal of Voice*, Vol. 1, No. 1: 183-187.

Repp, S.R. 1999. 'The feasibility of Technology Saturation for Intermediate Students of Applied Voice.' http://music.utsa.edu/tdml/conf-VI/VI-Repp.html.

Tabish, D.R. 1995. 'Kinesthetic engagement technique: Theories and practices for training the actor.' Unpublished dissertation. UMI dissertation services.

Van Den Berg, & De Boer, A-L. 2000. 'Outcomes-based assessment: Challenges for the learning of Criminology.' In: *ACTA Criminologica* 13(2): 107-113.

Van Der Horst, H & Mcdonald, R. 1997. OBE. *Outcomes-based education: a teacher's manual*. Pretoria: Kagiso Publishers.

Verdolini, K. 1998. 'Professional voice corner: Introductory comments.' In Special interest division 3, *Voice and Voice Disorders Newsletter*. Vol. 8, No.1. April 1998 (np).

Verdolini-Marston, K., Drukker, D.G., Palmer, P.M., & Samawi, H. 1998. 'Laryngeal adduction in resonant voice.' In: *Journal of Voice*, Vol. 12, No. 3, pp 315-327.

Verdolini, K. 1999-2002. Personal e-mails. In possession of the researcher.

Norms and Standards for Educators. 2000. Government Gazette no.20844.

NOTICE 1196. 1997. Education White Paper 3. A programme for the transformation of higher education.

http://www.polity.org.za/html/govdocs/white_papers/highed.html … 03/11/2003

http://www.heineman.co.za/Schools/Teaching Tips/OBE2.asp …10/05/2003

http://www.pentech.ac.za/edc/Data/Curriculum/What-is-OBE.pdf …03/11/2003

http://www.classweb.gmu.ndabbagh/Resources/Resources2/gegnetax.htm 9/13/2004

Testing the Use of Lessac's Tonal NRG as a Voice Building Tool for Female Students at a South African University—A Perceptual Study

This peer-reviewed article was originally published in *the Voice and Speech Review: Shakespeare around the Globe*. Mandy Rees (ed), VASTA, 2007, 333-342. Permission to reprint has been graciously granted by the Voice and Speech Trainers Association.

Marth Munro & Daan Wissing

Key words:
Lessac, Voice projection, Perceptual evaluation.

Introduction

The voice of the actor is required to work optimally in the process of performance, and required to repeat vocal tasks on a regular basis. For this to occur, the voice needs to be built and strengthened (Barton & Dal Vera, 1995:79). "Voice-building" might tentatively be defined as developing the voice to deal with the rigors of performance. Laukkanen (1995:11) states that the muscular functions of voice production have to be strengthened and improved in such a way that it will result in an "improved voice and/or phonatory quality." Good voice quality (sustainable over periods of time and repeatable) for theatre specifically may be "defined as a result of an optimal use of the vocal organ in order to establish the maximum possible acoustic output by minimal muscular effort" (Laukkanen, 1995:18), to which will be added the aesthetic dimension, which is culturally bound. To clarify then, voice quality is the component of voice that is not (but may be related to) loudness, duration, or pitch. In scientific research voice quality is measured, among other methods, by determining the acoustic spectrum of a sound. This acoustic spectrum obviously correlates with the muscular function of the vocal apparatus in the moment of voice production.

Lessac (1997: 9) claims that part of his Approach is the building of a good voice. Here he refers specifically to the Tonal NRG part of the work and states that it will enhance audibility (1997: 139; 1967:20). In answers to a questionnaire filled in at the Lessac Swarthmore convention in 1998:[1]

- Respondents all reported that they believe the Lessac Approach to be an effective voice-building tool.
- They agreed that the Tonal NRG enhances projection of both the male and female voice.

The research to be presented here is motivated by the results of that questionnaire, as well as by the desire to determine if the Lessac Tonal NRG approach actually does contribute to students' voice building, and in particular, for female students.

Voice can be analysed in three ways: physiologically, perceptually, and acoustically (Laukkanen, 1995:13; Miller & Schutte, 1999:206). Verdolini and colleagues (Verdolini, Druker et al., 1998; Verdolini-Marston, Burke et al., 1995) did extensive research on the physiological impact of the Tonal NRG of the Lessac Approach. The most important findings from those research projects seem to be that the Lessac Approach leads to low impact stress between the vocal folds and minimum subglottal pressure. The study reported here focused on the perceptual and acoustical analysis of the Tonal NRG as a voice-building tool.

Research Aim

The main aim of this investigation was to evaluate the perceptual and acoustic effects of the Lessac's training approach on the voices of female student actors. This paper will report on the outcome of the *perceptual* evaluation. Perceptual evaluation is very important when evaluating voice. Voice forms the bedrock of most communicative acts in performance events. As such the subjective reaction to voice cannot be omitted from any voice evaluation process. A separate paper (in preparation) will deal with the outcome of the acoustic analyses.

By way of placing the perceptual analysis in context, however, in the sense that perceptual judgment is highly dependent upon the acoustic properties of the sound

---

[1] For more information regarding this questionnaire see Munro, 2002.

heard, an overview of the acoustic characteristics of the "projected voice" is presented. Projection, or more specifically "carrying power," is an acoustic characteristic of the performer's voice (Leino, 1993:209). Sundberg (1988:12) states that this is determined by two factors. The first is the vibratory process of the vocal folds leading to the glottal flow, also known as the voice source, and the second is the shaping of the vocal tract in order to optimally resonate the sound that is produced by the larynx. The vocal tract acts as a filter, or a "frequency selective transmission system" as described by Kent and Read (1992:13).

The fundamental frequency, F0, determines the vocal pitch and is a direct result of the voice source function. There are generally five formants below 5000 Hz that are important for the analysis of the human voice (Leino, 1993:207; Stone et al., 1999:161):

- F1 and F2 primarily determine vowel recognition and quality
- F3 influences vowel characteristics but, linked to F4 and F5, it also influences voice quality
- F4 and F5 are determined by the laryngeal tube that acts as "a separate resonator" to provide the resonance characteristics that lead to a well-projected voice (Sundberg, 1974:842).

When an LTAS (long term average spectrum taken over some time, usually many seconds) of the singing or speaking voice is obtained, it is difficult to pinpoint the various formants because they shift a great deal during the utterance, especially if the utterance contains various vowels. Therefore, references are often made to the intensity clusters around certain frequencies. The frequencies of the actual formant clusters in singing differ between voice types (Stone, Cleveland et al., 1999:161). Titze (1994) mentions that the performer's *speaking* voice differs acoustically from the classical *singing* voice as far as formants are concerned, seeing that no prescribed F0 frequency (pitch) is expected from the professional actor's voice. It is thus necessary to study the professional actor's speaking voice as an independent subject.

Fant (1970) observed earlier that F3 and F4 seemed to be closer in trained than in untrained speaking voices. Leino performed several studies on the quality of the professional actor's speaking voice. It is of importance for this paper to reflect on the results of two of the projects executed by Leino. He reported a "Long-Term Average Spectrum (LTAS) study on speaking voice quality in male actors" (Leino, 1993). Expert listeners perceptually graded the recordings into categories of good, fairly good, rather poor, and poor voice quality. No definition (perceptual or acoustic) for good voice quality was provided. Results indicated that the voices *perceptually* defined as "poor" displayed *acoustically* a clearly steeper spectral slope than the voices defined as "good." Of greater importance, however, was the "most notable" peak near the region of 3500 Hz. The group that was perceptually defined as having "good quality" displayed a higher amplitude than the other voice groups in this frequency cluster.

From this study one can ascertain that what is classified as a good actor's voice is *reflected* in an LTAS analysis with a frequency cluster between 3-4 kHz, with increased amplitude and relatively deep valleys around this phenomenon. In the second study Leino and Kärkkäinen supported the previous study (1995). In this study, the preferred voice quality *perceptually* determined by experts in the fields of theatre and speech, *acoustically* displayed a clearer peak at 3.5 kHz, and an overall spectrum with a less steep slope. It thus seems that the professional actor's voice, when it is perceived to project well and has a sonorous quality (Nawka et al., 1997:422), has as its acoustic characteristics a less steep spectral slope and an enhanced peak in the frequency range between 3 and 4 kHz which seem to be related to F4 and F5 (Leino, 1993:209).

So far most of the findings reflect on the possible relationship between the perceptual and acoustic findings of the male voice. Relatively little is known about the characteristics of the *female* actor's voice. It is generally accepted that it is more difficult to investigate the acoustic properties of the female voice.[2] Leino (PEVOC[3] poster, 2001) reported on research done on the female Finnish voice. A perceptual panel subjectively differentiated between good and poor voice quality. An LTAS analysis of

---

[2] "The woman's pitch has a higher frequency than the man's pitch..." (Mendoza, Valencia, Munoz & Trujillo, 1996). This leads to the harmonics of the female voice being further apart.
[3] Pan European Voice Conference.

these voices indicated that both groups had the tendency to have a peak at 4300 Hz, but that the voices considered as good had a stronger peak (thus a higher amplitude). One can thus ascertain that what an expert panel perceptually defines as a good voice may be reflected in the acoustic profile of the male as well as the female voice, although the acoustic characteristics may somewhat differ.

The project reported on here examined the development of female actors' voice quality, as very little formal research has been done in this specific area. The trajectory of the research followed a procedure of training the female voice using the Lessac Approach and performing a pre-post perceptual panel analysis of voice quality. A pre-post comparative acoustic analysis of the voices was also performed, and will be reported in a subsequent article.

Methods
Experimental design
A one-group before-after design was used in this experiment. Because participants served as their own controls in this type of design, additional participants as a control group were not required.

Participants
Fifteen female students of a voice building class were randomly chosen to serve as the experimental group. Such training is part of the curriculum of an actor-training programme at a tertiary institution in South Africa. Ages ranged between 18 and 23 years. Represented first languages were Afrikaans, 8; English, 2; Tsonga, 1; Tswana, 1; Southern Sotho, 1; Xhosa, 1; Zulu, 1. They all voluntarily agreed to participate in this research having been assured that their identities would be protected. One of the researchers was the responsible teacher for this group. The group had a total of 28 contact hours over a period of 14 weeks.

Training
In the training process the Lessac Approach was used. Initially three-dimensional breathing and optimal body integration were explored, followed by the introduction and exploration of Tonal NRG as defined and described in the Lessac Approach (1997). An organic developmental flow was crucial so as to follow the holistic nature

of the Lessac Approach. The class was thus introduced to the Y-buzz and then proceeded through +Y-buzz to Calls and lastly to Call phrases and limited application.

The medium of instruction in the classes was English. The use of self-developed first language phrases as equivalents to the English modes was encouraged. Students were expected to work in "buddy groups"[4] (20 minutes daily) on the explorations introduced in class, as preparation for the next class.

Recordings

Pre- and post-training recordings were made under controlled circumstances:

- All recordings were made in a sound-treated room at the tertiary institute.
- Recordings were made onto a DAT recorder (Sony ZA5ES Super bit mapping). Rec. level: 5; mode rate of recording: 44.1kHz; Input: analogue microphone.
- Microphone used: Shure SM48. Dynamic LOZ Unidirectional.
- Microphone-to-mouth distance: 40 cm.
- A sound level meter showing SPL (sound pressure level) was used to prevent overloading the DAT recorder. Students were asked not to go lower than 65 dB nor higher than 75 dB. The distance between the sound level meter and the mouth was the dame than the microphone-to-mouth distance, thus 40 cm. It seemed to be easy for the students to stay within these parameters during the pre-training recordings. They struggled to maintain this in the post-training recordings, even going as high as 90 dB. When this occurred, they were asked to repeat the recording within the requested limits.

In the pre-training recording students were asked to do an "uh-uh" sound.[5] This was used to determine the pitch given for the Y-buzz sound in pre- as well as post-training recordings.

---

[4] Buddy groups are used within the Lessac Workshop set-up where two students are responsible for each other and work together during their preparation times between classes. This is an excellent tool, which guides the students towards discussion about the work and provides ear training.

[5] This was borrowed from Timo Leino, a Finnish researcher. He asks the participant to release the head forward and when as relaxed as possible, do an "uh-uh" sound. This sound often has an aspirate quality

The different modes that were named and/or demonstrated were:[6]

1) Y-buzz on the pitch determined for the subject. (The pitch was given using a keyboard.)
2) +Y-buzz
3) Calls
4) English phrases and Call words
5) First language text readings of approximately one minute without the use of words containing an /s/ sound as a high frequency noise pattern.

The instructions given for modes 1-3: "Please do the (different sounds inserted—named and demonstrated) as long and loud as is comfortably possible while staying in the parameters 65-75 dB on the SPL meter." The instructions given for modes 4 and 5 were:[7] "Please read the following (either English Sentences and Call words or first language texts) in a comfortable volume for performers in a speaking voice."

Each mode was recorded three times and the recording that was subjectively perceived by the experimenters as the "best" was selected to be used in this study.

Perceptual evaluation
- The specific perceptual panel for this project was made up of five theatre experts. Three of the five had at least five years of training in performer's voice. The other two work fulltime with students in tertiary institutions, as well as working professionally as directors and performers. They had more than ten years experience each.
- Nine randomly chosen samples from each of the different modes (from three different modes for each subject) were prepared in a listening file[8]. The modes

---

due to the relaxed vocalization. The onset is never glottal. This is a safe way to determine the optimal speaking voice pitch to start the vocal explorations from.

[6] Seeing that the instruction indicates that the utterances were to be done as long as what is comfortably possible, the recordings had different lengths of time reflecting on the participants' levels of competence. The first language text readings were all more or less one minute.

[7] Please note that mode 5 is the first language texts recorded.

[8] Essentially then, pre and post samples from three different modes from each participant were used as tokens to be played to the perception panel. These tokens were played in a random order within each mode. See tables 6 and 7 in the addendum for a graphic presentation of this.

were played from a CD through a PC using a high quality amplifier and stereo speakers: Creative Inspire 2.1 2400[9] in order to maintain good sound quality. There was approximately 3 seconds between each of the 90 utterances (tokens) for the listeners to mark their questionnaire forms.

- An evaluation questionnaire[10] was provided to the panelists with a definition of good voice quality. As indicated above, good voice quality was "defined as a result of an optimal use of the vocal organ in order to establish the maximum possible acoustic output by minimal muscular effort" (Laukkanen, 1995:18). This definition was discussed (and supported by a quote from Lessac himself[11]) with the perceptual panel in order to make sure that they all understood what they were listening for. The questionnaire was set up according to a 5 point rating scale: 1 = very poor, 2 = poor, 3 = average, 4 = good, 5 = very good.

- The 90 (18x5; or 45 pre and 45 post) pre- and post-training tokens were arranged in random order and played to the expert panelists. The randomized samples were again ordered according to the structured teaching progression; thus all randomized y-buzz samples were presented first, followed by all the randomized +Y-buzz samples, etc.

- Cross tabulation tables were used for descriptive statistics. These provided an indication of the preferences of the perception panel should they exist. These tables served as preparation for the inferential statistics.

- For triangulation more than one inferential statistics analysis were performed on the data. 1) Paired t-test: H_o: $\mu_{diff(pre-post)} = 0$; H_A: $\mu_{diff(pre-post)} \neq 0$; $\alpha = 0.01$. H_o accepted when the p-value > α; H_o rejected in favour of H_A when the p-value < α. In this study H_o implies that the scores given to the pre-training recordings and the scores given to the post training recordings were equal (null). Should this be true, it would indicate that there was no change, according to the perceptual panel, in the sound quality of the post-training recordings. But

---

[9] Technical specifications: Satellite: 4.5 watts. 12ms power per channel (2 channels); subwoofer power: 12 watts RMS; Freq. Response 42Hz-20kHz; SNR:>75dB; Dimensions: Satellites (LxWxH) –21.1 cm x 19.2 cm x 19.2 cm.
[10] See addendum.
[11] "When the body produces excellent tones, the voice is not throaty, nasal, or forced; it is produced and resonated effortlessly. It has stentorian, resonant qualities and projection, full pitch range, and rich, warm, colorful timbre" (Lessac, 1997:9).

should H_0 be rejected in favour of H_A, especially if the pre-scores minus the post-scores provide a negative numerical, it would imply that the total of the post scores was higher than the total of the pre-scores. This would indicate that the utterances contained in the post-training recordings improved in voice quality according to the perceptual panel. 2) Chi-square: H_o: 2 variables (phase and score) are independent; H_A: 2 variables (phase and score) are dependent. $\alpha = 0.01$. H_o accepted when the p-value $> \alpha$; H_o rejected in favor of H_A when the p-value $< \alpha$. In this study this H_o means that the scores were randomly attributed to the phases (pre- and post- training recordings) and that there is no correlation between the scores given to the voice quality and whether it is a pre- or post-recording. H_A in this case means that the pre-recordings have lower scores attributed to them and the post-recordings have higher scores attributed to them. This would indicate that the training had a positive influence over the voice quality as perceived by the perception panel.

Data analysis and processing of the perceptual evaluation

The evaluation scores of the perception group were statistically processed through the use of SAS[12] (Statistical Analysis Software package, version 8). A paired t-test for independence was done to compare pre-score means with post-score means for all the sound modes combined. For this paired t-test, null hypothesis testing was done where the mean difference equals zero (H_o: $\mu_{diff(pre-post)} = 0$), against the alternative where the mean does not equal zero (H_A: $\mu_{diff(pre-post)} \neq 0$).

The paired t-test for all the sound modes combined had the null hypothesis (H_o) as:

There is no statistically significant difference between the pre- and post-training recordings (referred to as phase in the t-test) of Test Group S (H_o: $\mu_{diff(pre-post)} = 0$) as indicated by the scores allocated by the perception panelists;

and the alternative hypothesis (H_A) as:

---

[12] Credit to the Department of Statistical Support of the (then) Pretoria Technikon for assistance and guidance in this matter.

There is a statistically significant difference between the pre- and post-training recordings (phase) of Test Group S (H_A: $\mu_{diff(pre-post)} \neq 0$) as indicated by the scores allocated by the perception panelists. For this study to indicate that the training did affect the voice quality positively, the post-training recordings' scores have to be higher than those of the pre-training recordings.

Frequency procedures were carried out and cross-tabulation tables were made for the different variables of all the different sound modes. These procedures and tables provide a descriptive profile of the weighting of the scores in relation to the pre- and post-training recordings as phase.

For the sake of triangulation, chi-square tests were done on appropriate cross tabulations, but due to expected cell frequencies being less than 5, regroupings were done. Sound modes 1, 2 and 3 (being Y-buzz, +Y-buzz, and Calls) were grouped as "Lessac Tonal explorations," whilst sound modes 4 and 5 (being English Phrases and Call words as well as first language texts) were grouped as "applications," seeing that these modes represent the carry-over of the explorations into functional speech. In the H_o (null hypothesis) of the Chi-square test, the two variables (phase and score in this study) were independent. The question to determine was whether this H_o is accepted or rejected for the alternative where the two variables are dependent.

The chi-square test for the Lessac explorations as well as for the applications had the null hypothesis (H_o) as:

The scores (ratings 1-5) were assigned/attributed to the utterances of the pre- and post-training recordings (phase) of Test Group S at random, without any statistically significant relations between the ratings and the 2 phases (being pre- and post-recordings). This will be indicated as the p-value being > 0.01;

and the alternative hypothesis (H_A) as:

The scores (ratings 1-5) were assigned/attributed to the utterances of the pre- and post-training recordings (phase) of Test Group S according to a statistically relevant relationship between the ratings and the 2 phases (pre- and post-recordings). For this *study to indicate an improvement of voice quality, the ratings allocated to the post-training recordings have to be higher than the ratings allocated for the pre-training recordings. This will be indicated as the p-value being < than 0.01.*

The different language groups were sometimes too small, and as such could not be used to provide any statistically significant indication. Descriptive statistical analyses were conducted for the different first language groups.

Results
Perceptual evaluation results

As mentioned above, a t-test for independence[13] was done for all the sound modes combined. The rule used was that H_o (H_o: μ_{diff} =0) will be rejected if the p-value < α (alpha) with alpha =0.01. It was decided on alpha as 1% to make the Type 1 error small.[14] The results of this study lead to the rejection of the null-hypothesis (H_o) in favor of the alternative where the mean difference was significantly different from zero (H_A: $\mu_{diff} \neq 0$) seeing that the p-value was shown as <.0001 (see Table 1). Since the mean differences were negative,[15] it indicates that the pre-scores were significantly less than the post-scores (μ_{diff}< 0). The perceptual evaluators, in general, thus preferred the voice quality of the post-recordings of the Test Group.

TABLE 1: T TEST FOR INDEPENDENCE, TEST GROUP S.

		Analysis Variable: DIFF				
N	Mean	Std Dev	Minimum	Maximum	t Value	Pr> /t/
225	-1.2755	1.2191	-4.0000	2.0000	-15.69	<.0001

The cross tabulation tables for *all* the different sound modes (Y-buzz, +Y-buzz, Calls, English Phrases, and Call words, as well as first language text readings) indicated a clear difference between the pre- and post-training recordings where the post-

---

[13] Paired data.
[14] Alpha (α) = P(Type 1 error); Alpha = P(reject H_0 when H_0 true).
[15] For example observe the mean in Table 1.

recordings[16] were reflective of the preferred voice quality. In Table 2 the cross tabulation table of the Y-buzz of the Test Group[17] is provided as an example.

TABLE 2: TEST GROUP S, Y-BUZZ: TABLE OF PHASE BY SCORE.

	Score					
Phase	1	2	3	4	5	Total
Pre	16	12	12	3	2	45
Post	1	8	11	19	6	45
Total	17	20	23	22	8	90

Table 2 indicates that the perceptual evaluators rated the Y-buzz modes of the pre-training recording primarily as very poor—score 1 (16/45 divided by 100 = 35.56%), poor—score 2 (26.67%), and average—score 3 (26.67%). The weighting of the post-training recording perceptual evaluation leans strongly towards average—score 3 (24.44%), good—score 4 (42.22%), and very good—score 5 (13.33%). This pattern is basically followed in all four of the other sound mode groups[18] with the score weighting moving from being centered on scores 1 and 2 to scores 4 and 5.[19]

As mentioned under "Data analysis and processing of the perceptual evaluation," chi-square tests were done on appropriate cross tabulations. For chi-square the H_o is that the two variables (phase and score) are independent. This was tested against the alternative (H_A), which indicates the two variables are dependent. Regrouping had to be done due to expected cell frequencies being less than five. Sound modes 1, 2, and 3 (Y-buzz, +Y-buzz, and Calls) were grouped as Lessac Tonal explorations, whilst sound modes 4 and 5 (English Phrases and Call words as well as first language texts)

---

[16] In the cross tabulation tables the pre-training recording is indicated as Pre and the post-training recording as Post.
[17] In frequency of score per phase.
[18] The +Y-buzz, Calls, English phrases and Call words as well as first language texts all reflected the same pattern and are available upon request.
[19] As previously mentioned, the cross tabulation tables are descriptive statistics and don't have a null-hypothesis. This profile thus does not feed directly into the acceptance or rejection of an H_O, but, seeing that these tables are used in preparation for the chi-square test, it is already obvious that a positive relationship exists between score and phase, seeing that the weighting of the scores for the post-recordings is higher than the weighting of the scores for the pre-recordings.

were grouped as applications. The score possibilities were also combined so that scores 1 and 2 on the perception panel questionnaire were in the chi-square test regrouped as score 1; score 3 on the perception panel questionnaire remained 3 in the chi-square test and scores 4 and 5 on the perception panel questionnaire were regrouped as score 5 in the chi-square tests.

For the chi-square, the H_o (null hypothesis) states that the two variables (phase and score in this study) are independent. This would be accepted should the p-value be > α, and rejected should the p-value be < α. Alpha (α) was set to 0.01^{20} in order to make the type 1 error very small. The alternative (H_A) is that the two variables (phase and score) are dependent. Should the null hypothesis be rejected, it would thus be an indication that a relationship existed between the rating received by the perception panel and the phase (pre- or post-training recording). This relationship is positive or negative depending on the outcome of the cross tabulation and the chi-square test.

Table 3a provides the cross tabulation (of phase by score) in preparation for the chi-square test. Table 3b provides the chi-square test results of the Lessac explorations—sound modes 1, 2, and 3.[21]

---

[20] Please note that the numerical contributed to Alpha is only applicable for the perceptual evaluation. Should the p-value be < α in this case, it would be statistically very significant.

[21] Y-buzz, +Y-buzz and Calls.

TABLE 3A: CROSS TABULATION IN PREPARATION FOR CHI-SQUARE OF THE LESSAC EXPLORATIONS.

Frequency Expected Percent Row Pct Col Pct	Table of phase by nscore			
		nscore		
	phase	1	3	5	Total
	Pre	85 50.5 31.48 62.96 84.16	37 39.5 13.70 27.41 46.84	13 45 4.81 9.63 14.44	135 50.00
	Post	16 50.5 5.93 11.85 15.84	42 39.5 15.56 31.11 53.16	77 45 28.52 57.04 85.56	135 50.00
	Total	101 37.41	79 29.26	90 33.33	270 100.00

TABLE 3B: THE CHI-SQUARE RESULTS OF THE LESSAC EXPLORATIONS

Statistic	DF	Value	Prob
Chi-Square	2	92.9662	<.0001

Table 4a provides the cross tabulation (of phase by score) in preparation for the chi-square test. Table 4b provides the chi-square test results of the applications—sound modes 4 and 5.[22]

TABLE 4A. CROSS TABULATION IN PREPARATION FOR CHI-SQUARE OF THE APPLICATIONS

Frequency Expected Percent Row Pct Col Pct	Table of phase by nscore				
	phase	nscore			Total
		1	3	5	
	Pre	52 29.5 28.89 57.78 88.14	26 29 14.44 28.89 44.83	12 31.5 6.67 13.33 19.05	90 50.00
	Post	7 29.5 3.89 7.78 11.86	32 29 17.78 35.56 55.17	51 31.5 28.33 56.67 80.95	90 50.00
	Total	59 32.78	58 32.22	63 35.00	180 100.00

---

[22] English Phrases and Call words and First language texts.

TABLE 4B. THE CHI-SQUARE RESULTS OF THE APPLICATIONS.

Statistic	DF	Value	Prob
Chi-Square	2	59.0856	<.0001

The tables indicate a preference for the post-training recordings. The Lessac explorations pre-training recordings only have 9.63% of their total amount for scores allocated as score 5, but the post-training recordings have 57% of their total scores allocated to score 5. Similarly, the application modes only have 13.33% of the scores being 5 for the pre-training recordings but 56.67% of the scores being 5 in the post-training recordings. Since the p-value for both the Lessac explorations (Y-buzz, +Y-buzz and Calls—see Figure 3b) and the applications (English Phrases and Calls words and first language—see Figure 4b) is less than .0001, the p-value of both these cases is smaller than α (α=0.01). The null hypothesis[23] is therefore rejected. It is therefore evident that phase does affect score. The perception panelists rated the post-recordings in both cases (explorations and applications) significantly higher than the pre-recordings, indicating that the post-training recordings contained the preferred sounds and improved voice quality.

Cross tabulation tables were made for the scores of the three pre-training recordings, as well as three post-training recordings for each participant in Test Group S that were played to the perception panel. Table 5 depicts this cross tabulation for one of the participants (called AA in the table), selected at random.

TABLE 5: CROSS TABULATION TABLE:
GROUP S, PARTICIPANT AA, ALL SOUND MODES.

Phase	Score 1	Score 2	Score 3	Score 4	Score 5	Row Totals
Pre	1	11	2	1	0	15
Post	0	0	3	11	1	15
Total	1	11	5	12	1	30

---

[23] The null hypothesis is that the two variables are independent.

Seeing that this table is typical, it functions as an example to indicate that *each* participant's voice has, according to the perception panel, improved during the training process, as the post-training recordings ratings centre around the higher scores.

Although an indication of the profiles of the perception panelists has been provided before, it will contribute to the effectiveness of this study to reflect on their reliability as a group. Statistical analysis on the inter-reliability of the perception panel was done according to the information gathered. All the perception panelists (raters) separately indicated a significant improvement in the post-training recordings versus the pre-training recordings, with the results of the paired t-tests done for each rater indicating a p-value of $<.0001$. It is thus clear that the H_o ($\mu_{diff} = 0$) was rejected in favour of the HA ($\mu_{diff} \neq 0$) with $\mu_{diff} < 0$ by each rater.

Conclusion

Perceptually it is strongly suggested from this study that the Tonal NRG of the Lessac Approach significantly contributes to voice quality improvement (and therefore to voice building) of female students at the South African University where the study was performed. There are strong indications that this improvement is not language specific. Further research needs to include the use of larger test groups as well as the inclusion of more language groups. It may also be of interest to use test groups taught by other independent Lessac Teachers.

References

Acker, B. 1987. 'Vocal Tract Adjustments for the Projected Voice.' In *Journal of Voice* Vol. 1, No 1:77-82.

Bartholomew, W.T. 1934. 'A Physical Definition Of Good Voice Quality.' In *Journal of the Acoustical Society of America.* Vol. 6, pp. 25-33.

Barrichello, O; Heuer, R.I; Dean, C.M & Sataloff, R.T. 2001. 'Comparison of singer's formant, speaker's ring, and LTA spectrum among classical singers and untrained normal speakers.' In *Journal of Voice.* Vol.15. No 3. pp. 344-350.

Barton, R. & Dal Vera, R. 1995. *Voice: Onstage and off.* Fort Worth: Harcourt Brace College Publishers.

Dmitriev, L & Kiselev, A. 1979. 'Relationship between the formant structure of different voice types of singing voices and the dimensions of supraglottic cavities. In *Folia Phoniatrica.* 31:238-241.

Fant, G. 1970. *Acoustic theory of speech production.* Paris, France: Mouton.

Gauffin, J & Sundberg, J. 1989. 'Spectral correlates of glottal voice source waveform characteristics. In *Journal of Speech and Hearing Research.* Vol. 32, 556-565, September 1989.

Kent, R.D. & Read, C. 1992. *The Acoustic analysis of speech.* San Diego: Singular Press.

Laukkanen, A-M. 1995. *On speaking voice exercises.* Academic dissertation. ACTA Universitatis Tamperensis. Ser. A vol. 445. Tampere: University of Tampere.

Leino, T. 1993. 'Long-term average spectrum study on speaking voice quality in male actors.' In *Proceedings of the Stockholm Music Acoustics Conference*, Jul.28 - Aug.1, 1993 (Eds: A. Friberg, J.Iwarsson, E.Jansson & J. Sundberg).

Leino, T. & Kärkkäinen, P. 1995. 'On the effects of vocal training on the speaking voice quality of male student actors.' In *Proceedings of the XIIIth International Congress of Phonetic Sciences.* Stockholm, Sweden, 13 - 19 Aug. 1995. (Eds: K. Elenius & P. Branderud).

Leino, T. 2001. 'Voice quality of Finnish female actors.' Poster presented at PEVOC, Stockholm 2001.

Lessac, A. 1967. 2nd edition. *The Use and training of the human voice.* New York: Drama Book Publishers.

Lessac, A. 1997a. 3rd Edition. *The Use and training of the human voice: a bio-dynamic approach to vocal life.* California: Mayfield.

Mendoza, E., Valencia, N., Munoz, J., & Trujillo, H. 1996. 'Differences in voice quality between men and women: use of the long-term average spectrum (LTAS)." In *Journal of Voice.* Vol. 10. No. 1. pp. 59-66 (1996).

Miller, D, & Schutte, H. 1999. 'The Use of the spectrum analysis in the voice studio.' In *Voice-tradition and Technology.* Nair, G. pp. 211-226.

Munro, M. 2002. 'Lessac's tonal action in women's voices and the "actor's formant": a comparative study.' Unpublished PhD. Dissertation, North West University (formerly PU for CHE).

Munro, M., Leino, T., Wissing, D. 1996. 'Lessac's y-buzz as a pedagogical tool in the teaching of the projection of an actor's voice.' In *South African Journal of Linguistics.* Suppl.34, Dec. 1996. pp. 25-36.

Nair, G. 1999. *Voice Tradition and Technology.* New York: Singular Press.

Nawka, T., Anders, L.C., Cebulla, M., Zurakowski, D. 1997. 'The Speaker's formant in male voices.' In *Journal of Voice.* Vol 11. No. 4, pp. 422-428. 1997.

Raphael, B. & Scherer, R. 1987. 'Voice modification for stage actors: Acoustic analysis.' In *Journal of Voice*, Vol. 1, No. 183-87.

Rietveld, Amc, & Van Heuven, 1997. V. *Algemene fonetiek.* Bussum: Coutinho.

Stone, R.E. (Ed); Cleveland, T.F & Sundberg, J. 1999. 'Formant frequencies in country singers' speech and singing.' In *Journal of Voice.* Vol. 13. No. 2, pp. 161-167.

Sundberg, J. & Gauffin, J. 1978. 'Waveform and spectrum of the glottal voice source. In *Speech Transmission Laboratory*, Quarterly status and progress report, 2-3/1978, 35-50. Stockholm: Royal Institute of Technology.

Sundberg, J. 1974. 'Articulatory interpretation of the "singing formant"'. In: *JASA*. Vol. 55, No. 4. April 1974.

Sundberg, J. 1987. *The Science of the Singing Voice.* Dekalb: Northern Illinois Univ. Press.

Sundberg, J. 1988. 'Vocal tract resonance in singing.' In *The NATS Journal* March/April 1988:11-31.

Titze, I. 1994. *Principles on Voice Production.* New Jersey: Prentice Hall.

Vennard, W. 1967. *The Mechanism and Technique.* New York: Carl Fischer.

Verdolini-Marston, K., Burke, M.K., Lessac, A., Glaze, L. & Caldwell, E. 1995. 'A Preliminary study on two methods of treatment for laryngeal nodes.' In *Journal of Voice.* Vol. 9: 74-85.

Verdolini, K., Druker, D.G., Palmer, P.M. & Samawi, H. 1998. 'Laryngeal adduction in resonant voice.' In *Journal of Voice.* Vol. 12, No. 3, pp 315-327.

Addendum:

Perceptual evaluation sheet of Pre- and Post recordings.

Good voice quality may be "defined as a result of an optimal use of the vocal organ in order to establish the maximum possible acoustic output by minimal muscular effort" (Laukkanen, 1995:18).

"When the body produces excellent tones, the voice is not throaty, nasal, or forced; it is produced and resonated effortlessly. It has stentorian, resonant qualities and projection, full pitch range, and rich, warm, colorful timbre" (Lessac, 1997:9).

Please evaluate the voice samples as either:

- Very poor
- Poor
- Average
- Good
- Very Good

1) Y-BUZZ:

Sample number	Very poor	Poor	Average	Good	Very good
1					
2					
3					
4					
5					
6					
7					
8					
9					
10					
11					
12					
13					
14					
15					
16					
17					
18					

The same type of grid was used for all the other modes: +Y-buzz; Calls; Sentences and Mother tongue. In total 5 separate grids were used, one for each mode.

TABLE 6: EXAMPLE OF RANDOMIZED SELECTION PROCESS OF PRE AND POST SAMPLES OF EACH MODE TO BE PLAYED AS TOKENS TO THE PERCEPTION PANEL.

Participant	M1	M2	M3	M4	M5
1	x		x		x
2	x	x		x	
3			x	x	x
4	x		x		x
5	x	x		x	
6		x	x		x
7	x	x		x	
8		x	x		x
9	x			x	x
10		x	x		x
11	x	x		x	
12		x		x	x
13	x		x	x	
14		x	x		x
15	x		x	x	

M=mode. M1 will thus indicate y-buzz; M2 +Y-Buzz and so forth.

TABLE 7: AN EXAMPLE OF THE RANDOMIZED ORDER OF THE TOKENS PLAYED TO THE PERCEPTION PANEL

Token	Mode 1: Y-buzz
1	Participant 1 pre
2	Participant 15 post
3	Participant 2 post
4	Participant 4 pre
5	Participant 1 post
6	Participant 4 post
7	Participant 7 pre
8	Participant 15 post
9	Participant 7 post
10	Participant 2 pre

An Oral History[1] of Lessac Summer Workshop Intensives[2] 1966-1978

Year	Location	Faculty
1965	New York City (Two Weeks)	Arthur Lessac, Sue Ann Park, James S. Kennedy, Dick Pyatt, Bobby Troka, Michael Lessac.
1967	New York City	Arthur Lessac.
1969	SUNY Binghamton	Arthur Lessac, Sue Ann Park.
1969	Ohio University	Arthur Lessac, Robert Hobbs.
1970	SMU	Arthur Lessac, Sue Ann Park, Jack Clay.
1970	SUNY Binghamton	Arthur Lessac, Sue Ann Park, Michael Lessac.
1971	Trinity University[3]	Arthur Lessac, Sue Ann Park, Jack Jones, Vincent Park, Randy Moore, Steve Mackenroth.
1972	SUNY Binghamton	Arthur Lessac, Sue Ann Park, Randy Roman, Steve Mackenroth, Libby Roman, Dick Cuyler.
1973	SUNY Binghamton[4]	Arthur Lessac, Dick Cuyler, Jeffrey Preiser.[5]

---

[1] Although some of the intensives identified were documented within Arthur Lessac's personal archives, the majority of this document was developed from the recollections of Lessac Master Teachers. Some reports found in Arthur Lessac's archives suggest more workshops took place during the 1965-1972 period, but this was difficult to confirm.

[2] Intensive Workshops starting in 1967 were approximately six weeks. Currently they are approximately four weeks.

[3] According to Arthur the workshop took place at Trinity University. Dick Cuyler remembers it being at SUNY Binghamton.

1974	SUNY Binghamton	Arthur Lessac, Sue Ann Park, Libby Roman, Dick Cuyler.
1975	SUNY Binghamton	Arthur Lessac, Jack Jones (one week), Libby Roman, Dick Cuyler, Jeffrey Preiser.
1977	SUNY Binghamton	Arthur Lessac, Sue Ann Park, Libby Roman, Dick Cuyler.
1978	SUNY Binghamton	Arthur Lessac, Libby Roman, Dick Cuyler.

---

[4] Dick Cuyler and Arthur Lessac both remember this workshop taking place at SUNY Fredonia, but Deb Kinghorn (a student at Fredonia) says she does not recall that, and that she was involved in the summer theatre program at the time.

[5] One Master Teacher thought it was "possible" that Jeffrey Preiser was on the faculty but couldn't confirm.

An Oral History of Lessac Summer Workshop Intensives 1979-1999

1979	SUNY Fredonia	Arthur Lessac, Sue Ann Park, Libby Roman, Dick Cuyler.
1980	University of Minnesota at Duluth	Arthur Lessac, Sue Ann Park, Libby Roman, Dick Cuyler.
1981	University of Minnesota at Duluth	Arthur Lessac, Sue Ann Park, Libby Roman, Dick Cuyler.
1982	University of Minnesota Duluth	Arthur Lessac, Sue Ann Park, Libby Roman, Dick Cuyler, Sandra Cuyler.
1984	University of Minnesota Duluth	Arthur Lessac, Sue Ann Park, Dick Cuyler.
1986[1]	Texas Women's University	Arthur Lessac
1987	University of Colorado at Boulder	Arthur Lessac, Sue Ann Park, Libby Roman, Dick Cuyler, Saundra Cuyler.
1988	University of Colorado at Boulder	Arthur Lessac, Sue Ann Park, Libby Roman, Dick Cuyler, Saundra Cuyler.
1989	California State Fullerton	Arthur Lessac, Sue Ann Park.
1990	Central College (Iowa)	Arthur Lessac, Sue Ann Park, Libby Roman, Dick Cuyler, Saundra Cuyler.
1991	Central College (Iowa)	Arthur Lessac, Sue Ann Park, Libby Roman, Dick Cuyler, Saundra Cuyler.

---

[1] 1986 workshop was abbreviated. No documentation on length.

1993[2]	Pomona College	Arthur Lessac, Sue Ann Park, Libby Roman, Kathleen Dunn.
1995	Mary Baldwin College	Arthur Lessac, Sue Ann Park, Kathleen Dunn. Nancy Krebs.
1996	Ball State University	Arthur Lessac, Sue Ann Park, Kathleen Dunn, Nancy Krebs, Mary Thomas.

---

[2] Some teachers remembered multiple intensives taking place at Pomona during 1991-1993 while others noted that only one took place at Pomona College during this time.

An Oral History of Lessac Summer Workshop Intensives 1999-2009

1999	SUNY Fredonia	Arthur Lessac, Sue Ann Park, Nancy Krebs, Yanci Bukovec.
2000[1]	Mercersburg Academy	Arthur Lessac, Sue Ann Park, Kathleen Dunn.
2001	University of New Hampshire	Sue Ann Park, Nancy Krebs, Deborah Kinghorn.
2002	Mercersburg Academy	Sue Ann Park, Nancy Krebs, Kathleen Dunn, Kate Ingram.
2003	Mercersburg Academy	Arthur Lessac (Intro), Sue Ann Park, Nancy Krebs, Deborah Kinghorn.
2004[2][3]	DePauw Univeristy	Arthur Lessac (Intro), Sue Ann Park, Deborah Kinghorn, Barry Kur.
2005[4]	University of Florida	Arthur Lessac (Intro), Sue Ann Park, Deborah Kinghorn, Yanci Bukovec, Diane Gaary.
2006[5]	DePauw University	Deborah Kinghorn, Kathleen Dunn.
2007	DePauw University	Arthur Lessac (One Week), Nancy Krebs, Deborah Kinghorn,

[1] 2000 is last year Arthur Lessac teaches full time.
[2] In 2004, Deb Kinghorn takes on role of workshop coordinator.
[3] In 2004, *Lessac for You,* (Laurie Mufson/Crystal Robbins) and a one-week *Introductory* workshop (Nancy Krebs) are introduced.
[4] In 2005, a one-week *Teacher Training* workshop is developed and approved by the institute (Nancy Krebs/Barry Kur).
[5] In 2006, Sue Ann Park is appointed role of Director of Training, and oversees teaching at all summer workshops.

| 2008[6] | DePauw University | Nancy Krebs, Deborah Kinghorn. |
| 2009[7] | DePauw University | Nancy Krebs, Deborah Kinghorn, Kathleen Dunn. |

---

[6] In 2008, *Dialects* workshop was approved (Barry Kur).
[7] Additional workshops in 2009 include a one week *Teacher Training* (DePauw), one week *Introductory* and *Dialects* workshops (Mary Washington),

Citation Map

EDITORS' NOTE: The following references have been gleaned from extensive *burrowing in Arthur Lessac's archives and the like. Some of the references are incomplete but the editorial team has made every effort to find the missing information, without success. The team has decided to include the material here in the best form that they could, for those scholars who might have access to the information, or who might wish to pursue the references. While the works cited are inclusive of works either identified or referenced by the contributors within this compilation, archives of Arthur Lessac that were made available to the editors, and on-line research engine searches completed by the editors, and concern either Arthur Lessac or Lessac Kinesensics, they are not inclusive of every piece of literature that references Arthur Lessac or Lessac Kinesensics, or which has critiqued his work. The decision was taken to present as much cross-referencing to the material as was possible. It is our feeling that "echoes" sometimes find unforeseen resonances.*

Acker, B. 1987. Vocal Tract Adjustments for the Projected Voice. *Journal of Voice.* 1(1)77-82.

Barrichelo, V.M.O & Behlau, M. 2007. Perceptual identification and acoustic measures of the resonant voice based on "Lessac's Y-Buzz" - a preliminary study with actors. *Journal of Voice.* 21(1):46-53.

Barrichelo-Lindström, V., Behlau, M. 2007. Resonant Voice in Acting Students: Effects of the Type of Instruction on Perceptual Voice Analysis. Presented at the *Voice Foundation's 36th Annual Symposium: Care of the Professional Voice*, 2007, Philadelphia, Pennsylvania.

Barrichelo, V., Cukier-Blaj, S & Behlau, M. 2007. Contribuição do Treinamento da Emissão Y-Buzz de Lessac - Estudo de Caso. *Anais do II Encontro do Departamento de Voz da Sociedade Brasileira de Fonoaudiologia.* São Paulo, SP, Brasil.

Barrichelo, V & Behlau, M. M. 2007. Resonant Voice in Acting Students: Perceptual and Acoustic Correlates of the Trained Y-Buzz by Lessac. *Anais do II Composium*

Internacional da IALP (International Association of Logopedics and Phoniatrics). São Paulo, SP, Brasil.

Barrichelo, V & Behlau, M. 2006. Voz Ressonte em Atores: Efeito Imediato da Emissão Y-Buzz de Lessac na Fala Encadeada. *Anais do XIV Congresso Brasileiro de Fonoaudiologia*, Salvador, BA, Brasil.

Barrichelo, V & Behlau, M. 2005. Identificação Auditiva e Análise Acústica da Emissão Ressoante "Y-Buzz" de Lessac comparada à emissão habitual – Estudo Preliminar com Atores. *Anais do XVIII Congresso Brasileiro de Fonoaudiologia,* Santos, SP, Brasil.

Berkely, N. 1973. The crowded Lessac-60-1: A speech program to beat the odds.

Berry, D.A., VerdolinI, K., Montequin, D.W., Hess, M.M., Chang, R.W., Titze, I.R. 2001. A Quantitative Output-Cost Ratio in Voice Production. *Journal of Speech, Language and Hearing Research*. Febr. 2001. Vol. 44. pp 29-37.

Bristow, D. 2006. Going beyond Theatre Appreciation: Making the Introduction to Theatre Course Pertinent to non-majors. Paper presented at the *International Conference on the Arts in Society.* Scotland: Edinburgh.

Burke, K. 2006. Help for Monticello's Guides. VASTA Newsletter. 2(1).

Carroll, L.M.2000. Application of Singing Techniques for the Treatment of Dysphonia. *Otolaryngologic Clinics of North America*. Vol. 33. Issue 5, pp1003-1015.

Chabora, P. D. 1995. A Descriptive Study of the Application of Research in Neurophysiology to Self-use Training for Actors. Unpublished dissertation. UMI Dissertation Services.

Clay, J. 1972. Self-Use in Actor Training, *The Drama Review*, March 1972.

Clay, J. 1968. Speech for the performer: Arthur Lessac's Revolution. *Educational Theatre Journal*.

Connell, M. P. 1988. A comparison of the voice training techniques of Arthur Lessac and Kristen Linklater. (Dissertation)

Day, S. 1975. An experiment in applying the Lessac principals in human voice and body training to remedial reading. A thesis paper submitted to Department of Theatre. SUNY Binghamton.

Hampton, M & Acker, B. (eds.). 1997. The Vocal Vision: Views on Voice. New York: Applause.

Hanson, A.M. 1997. *An analysis of the Physiological Assumptions in Vocal Instructional Systems for actors.* Unpublished PhD. Dissertation. University of Kansas. UMI Number: 9827481.

Hardie, Y. 2001. An Outcomes-Based Approach for the Optimal Development of the Adolescent Voice. *The Voice and Speech Review, The Voice in Violence*: 186-200.

Hardie, Y. 1999. The Emerging Voice and Outcomes-Based Education: Voice Building at Secondary Level (Grades 8-12". M.Tech in the Drama Department, Pretoria Technikon. Studyleader: M. Munro.

Kimbourgh, A.M. 2002. The Sounds of Meaning: Theories of Voice in Twentieth Century Thought and Performance. Unpublished PhD dissertation. Louisiana State University
(http://etd.lsu.edu/docs/available/etd-0405102-074904/unrestricted/Kimbrough_dis.pdf).

Krebs, N. 2002. Reflection on the Lessac Summer Intensive Workshop 2002. *VASTA Newsletter,* 16(2):3.

Kur, B. 1987. Stage Dialect studies: a continuation of the Lessac approach to actor voice and speech training. Self-publication.

Kur, B. 2005. Stage Dialect studies: a continuation of the Lessac approach to actor voice and speech training. 2nd Ed. Self-publication.

Kur, B. 1999. Lessac Institute Teacher Certification Procedure. *VASTA Newsletter*, 13(2):10. Spring/Summer.

Lemmer, K. 2007. Accent/Dialect Coaching for a Multilingual Student Cast - A Case Study. *Voice and Speech Review, Voice and Gender*: 120-127.

Lessac, A. 2000. Lessac Kinesensics: A Short Treatise of some of its Vocal Life aspects. In: *Standard Speech and other Contemporary Issues in Professional Voice and Speech Training*. Dal Vera, R (ed). New York: Applause: 91-192.

Lessac, A. 1998. A Short Colloquy of How I Approach Pathological and Functional Voice and Speech Disorders through my Kinesensic Training and Research. In: *Special Interest Division 3, Voice and Voice Disorders Newsletter*, 8(1)April 1998 (np.).

Lessac, A. 1997. From Beyond Wilderness to Body Wisdom, Vocal Life and Healthfu Functioning: A Joyous Struggle for our Discipline's Future. In: The Vocal Vision: Views on Voice. Hampton, M & Acker, B. (eds.). New York: Applause: pp 13-24.

Lessac, A. 1997. The Use and Training of the Human Voice: A Bio-Dynamic Approach to Vocal Life. Mountain View: Mayfield Publishing.

Lessac, A. 1981; 1978. *The* Use and Training of the Human Body. New York:

Lessac, A. 1971. The Actor explores - Vocal life on the stage. Paper presented at *AETA (Chicago)*. Personal Archives.

Lessac, A. 1970. The Use and Care of the Adolescent Voice. Paper presented at *AETA*. Personal Archives.

Lessac, A. 1969. Voice Training for Actors. *Players Magazine*.

Lessac, A. 1969. A new definition of dramatic training, *Quarterly Journal of Speech*, 1969, 2.

Lessac, A. 1967. *The* Use and Training of the Human Voice: A Practical Approach to Speech and Voice Dynamics. DBS Publications (New York, NY).

Lessac, A. 1967. A single approach and a euphonic standard in voice and speech training. Paper published by *Emerson College*.

Lessac, A. 1965. Speech for the actor: An Eclectic Colloquy. Paper presented at *AETA*. Personal archives.

Lessac, A. 1962. Your Personal Management – You can Learn To Relax: *Supervisory Management.* American Management Association.

Lessac, A. 1960. The Use and Training of the Human Voice. Self-Publication.

Lessac, A. 1956. New Ways of Correcting Stuttering. *New York Times*, April 08, 1956.

Lessac, A. 1954. How you can Cut, Cultivate Foreign Accents. *Sunday News,* NYC, October 24, 1954.

Lessac, A. 1947 What dreadful voices you women have. August 6, 1947. *New York Post.*

Lessac, A. 1942. On the language as spoken from the stage. June 28, 1942. *New York Times.*

Maes, K. 2003. Applying Theories of Learning Styles and Modalities to the Challenges of Coaching. In: *The Voice and Speech Review, Film, Broadcast & e-Media Coaching*:77-79.

Maes, K. 2007. Examining the Use of Lessac Exploration in Shakespearean Text. *The Voice and Speech Review, Voice and Gender*:263-272.

Markowitz, S. & Lessac, A. 1954. What do you know about Jewish religion, history, ethics, and culture.

Marx, D. 1999. Teaching Voice at the Secondary Level – Is it possible? *VASTA Newsletter*. 13(1):1,3. Winter.

Master, S, De Biase, B, Chiari, B & Laukkanen, A-M. 2008. Acoustic and Perceptual Analyses of Brazilian Male Actors' and Non-Actors' Voices: Long-term Average Spectrum and the "Actor's Formant". *Journal of Voice*. 22(2):146-154.

McAllister-Viel, T. 2007. Casting Perceptions: The Performance of Gender as a Career Strategy. In: *The Voice and Speech Review, Voice and Gender*: 279-223

McKenney, R. 1986. The Contribution of Arthur Lessac to American Voice and Speech Pedagogy. Dissertation prospectus submitted to the faculty of the College of Arts and Sciences, University of Missouri-Columbia: March, 1986.

Melton, J. 1999. Common Denominators – Speaking and Singing. *VASTA Newsletter*. 13(1):11, Winter.

Mulholland, M. 1984. *Speech Training for Actors in the Twentieth Century America: change and continuity.* Unpublished PhD disseration: University Microfilms International

Munro, M. & Wissing, D. 2007. Testing the Use of Lessac's Tonal NRG as a Voice Building Tool for Female Students at a South African University – A Perceptual Study. *Voice and Speech Review, Voice and Gender*: 333-342.

Munro, M. & Coetzee, M-H. 2005. The Lessac Approach as a Pedagogical Answer to Outcomes-Based Education and Training, and Whole-Brain Learning. *Voice and Speech Review: Shakespeare Around the Globe and other contemporary issues in professional voice and speech training*: 186 -191.

Munro, M. & Coetzee, M-H. 2004. Lessac Approach as answer to outcomes-based education and training and whole-brain learning. *Lessac Newsletter*. Lessac Training & Research Institute, Inc. May 2004 Volume 1, Issue 2.

Munro, M. 2002. Lessac's Tonal action in Women's voices and the "Actor's Formant": A Comparative Study. Unpublished PhD Dissertation. PU for CHE, South Africa. Studyleaders: D. Wissing (SA), K. Verdolini (USA), A-M Laukkanen (Finland).

Munro, M. 2001. Towards demystifying Voice-Building in the new Millennium. *South African Theatre Journal*. 15: 107-118.

Munro, M & Laukkannen, A-M. 2001. On The Effects Of Lessac Method On Female Voices: Preliminary observations. Poster presented at PEVOC, Stockholm, 2001.

Munro, M. & Wissing, D. 1999. Teaching Voice in a Multi-Lingual Set-up: Some ideas for the Future. *VASTA Newsletter*, 13(2): 1, Spring/Summer.

Munro, M. Leino, T., Wissing, D. 1997. Lessac's Y-Buzz as a Pedagogical Tool in the Teaching of the Projection of an Actor's Voice. *S.Afr. Tydskrif. Taalk.* Suppl. 34: 25-36. 1997.

Munro, M. 1993. 'n Inleiding tot stemproduksie in die teater: Die Wetenskap van projeksie. Unpublished MA Thesis, PU fro CHE, South Africa. Studyleader: P.J. Schutte.

Munro, M. 1999. The Lessac Institute gets ready for the new Millennium. *VASTA Newsletter*. 13(2):10, Spring/Summer.

Nix, J.P, Simpson, C, B. 2007. Semi-occluded vocal tract postures and their application in the singing voice studio. J. Acoust. Soc. Am. Volume 121, Issue 5, pp. 3087-3087 (May 2007).

Park, S. 1997. Voice as a Source of Creativity f Acting Training, Rehearsal, and Performance. In: The Vocal Vision: Views on Voice. Hampton, M & Acker, B. (eds.). New York: Applause. Pp 107-119.

Park, S. 1996. "The voice as a major source of creativity". Paper. Personal Archives.

Park, S. 1995 "Lessac Voice and Body Energies as Acting Training". Paper. Personal Archives.

Peterson KL, Verdolini-Marston K, Barkmeier JM, Hoffman HT. 'Comparison of aerodynamic and electroglouographic parameters in evaluating clinically relevant voicing patterns.' Ann Otol Rhino Laryngol 1994;103:335-46.

Raphael, B. 1997. A Consumer's Guide to Voice and Speech Training. In: *Vocal Vision: Views on Voice.* Hampton, M & Acker, B. (eds.). New York: Applause Books. pp 203-214.

Raphael, B. 2001. Stage Violence: Greater than the sum of the parts. In: *The Voice and Speech Review, The Voice in Violence*: 22-29

RaphaeL, B. 2005. A Voice for Owen Meany. In: *The Voice and Speech Review, Shakespeare Around the Globe*:167-169

Raphael, B. & Scherer, R. 1987. Voice modification for stage actors: Acoustic analysis. *Journal of Voice*, 1:183-187.

Readerson, J. 1973. An analysis by comparison of portions of the Lessac system of voice and speech with principals of singing pedagogy. (Dissertation).

Robbins, C. 2001. Lessac's Last Summer. VASTA Newsletter. 15(1):1, Winter.

Robbins, C. 2002. Why Buzz? Putting Lessac's Y-buzz to work. *VASTA Newsletter.* 16(1):6.

Robbins, C. 2007. Training the Trainers – A Review of the leading programs for training voice trainers: The Lessac Voice, Speech & Body Work. In: *The Voice and Speech Review, Voice and Gender*:59-60

Romanov, P. 1994. Training Opportunities for Voice Professionals: Lessac Workshop. VASTA Newsletter. 8(1):6-7, Winter

Runk Mennen, D. 1998. Arthur Lessac: 1998 ATHE. *VASTA Newsletter.* 12(3):7, Fall
Smith, C., Finnegan, E., Karnell, M. 2005. Resonant Voice: Spectral and Nasoendoscopic Analysis. *Journal of Voice.* Iowa City, Iowa Resonant Voice Therapy.

Sonnerberg, L. 2005. A therapeutic approach for improved vocal performance in individuals in teaching occupations. Unpublished MA Thesis. University of North Carolina: Greensboro

Spivey, N. 2008. Music theater singing…let's talk. Part 1: on the relationship between speech and singing. *Journal of Singing.* Mrch/Apr 2008 (http://findarticles.com/p/articles/mi_6726/is_4_64/ai_n28503952/).

Stern, D. 1979. Understanding voice quality by understanding voice function. *Theatre News*. May 1979.

Tabish, D. R. 1995. Kinesthetic Engagement Technique: Theories and Practices for Training the Actor. Unpublished dissertation. UMI Dissertation services.

Tobolski, E. 2003. Coaching the Television Journalist. In: *The Voice and Speech Review, The Voice in Violence*:126-129

Truce, G. 1971. Kinesensics education: The effect on long-distance running. Dissertation submitted to SUNY at Binghamton.

Utterback, A.S. 1997. Broadcaster Stress: A Chronic Problem. *VASTA Newsletter*. 11(3):4.

Verdolini, K. 1998. Professional Voice Corner: Introductory Comments. In: *Special Interest Division 3, Voice and Voice Disorders Newsletter*. 8(1) April 1998 (np.).

Verdolini, K. 1997. Principles of skill acquisition: Implication for Voice Training. In: *The Vocal Vision: Views on Voice*. Hampton, M & Acker, B. (eds.). New York: Applause. Pp 65-80

Verdolini K. 'Voice therapy and its effectiveness: overview of newsletter and special challenges in formal research.' *American Speech-Language-Hearing Special Interest Divisions Newsletter: Voice and Voice disorders.* 1993;3:1-4.

...arston K. Burke MD, Lessac A, Glaze L, Caldwell E. 1995. 'A preliminary ... two methods of treatment for laryngeal nodules.' *Journal of Voice* Vol. 9 pp. 74-

Verdolini K, Druker DG, Palmer PM, Samawi H. 1998. Laryngeal Adduction in Resonant Voice. *Journal of Voice. Vol.12, No. 3, pp 315-327.*

White, K. 1973. The Lessac system of vocal exploration: an approach to Arthur Kopits' *Chamber Music* through creative improvisation.

White, J. 1976. Notable Names in the American Theatre.

Wren, C. 1999. The Complete Lessac. *American Theatre,* 6(1): 40

www.ingramcontent.com/pod-product-compliance
Lightning Source LLC
Chambersburg PA
CBHW060456010526
44118CB00018B/2436